# The Great Ideas

1473　COPERNICUS　1543

# The
# Great Ideas
# Today

# 1973

Helen Hemingway Benton, *Publisher*

*Encyclopædia Britannica, Inc.*

Chicago • London • Toronto • Geneva • Sydney • Tokyo • Manila • Johannesburg • Seoul

# The Great Ideas Today 1973

"The Silent Slain" by Archibald MacLeish is reprinted by permission
of Houghton Mifflin Company.

*In Defense of Socrates* by Xenophon is reprinted by permission of
the publishers and The Loeb Classical Library. E. C. Marchant,
translator. Xenophon, *Memorabilia*. Cambridge, Mass.:
Harvard University Press.

"The Second Coming" by William Butler Yeats is reprinted with
permission of Macmillan Publishing Co., Inc., from *Collected Poems*
by William Butler Yeats, copyright 1924 by The Macmillan Company,
renewed 1952 by Bertha Georgie Yeats; and with permission of
A. P. Watt & Son.

Printed in the U.S.A. Library of Congress Catalogue Number: 61-65561
International Standard Book Number: 0-85229-286-4

*Distributed to the trade by* Praeger Publishers, Inc., New York, Washington

# Contents

## A NOTE ON REFERENCE STYLE

In the following pages, passages in *Great Books of the Western World* are referred to by the initials '*GBWW*,' followed by volume, page number, and page section. Thus, '*GBWW*, Vol. 39, p. 210b' refers to page 210 in Adam Smith's *The Wealth of Nations*, which is Volume 39 in *Great Books of the Western World*. The small letter 'b' indicates the page section. In books printed in single column, 'a' and 'b' refer to the upper and lower halves of the page. In books printed in double column, 'a' and 'b' refer to the upper and lower halves of the left column, 'c' and 'd' to the upper and lower halves of the right column. For example, 'Vol. 53, p. 210b' refers to the lower half of page 210, since Volume 53, James's *Principles of Psychology*, is printed in single column. On the other hand, 'Vol. 7, p. 210b' refers to the lower left quarter of the page, since Volume 7, Plato's *Dialogues*, is printed in double column.

*Gateway to the Great Books* is referred to by the initials '*GGB*,' followed by volume and page number. Thus, '*GGB*, Vol. 10, pp. 39-57' refers to pages 39 through 57 of Volume 10 of *Gateway to the Great Books*, which is James's essay, "The Will to Believe."

*The Great Ideas Today* is referred to by the initials '*GIT*,' followed by the year and page number. Thus '*GIT* 1968, p. 510' refers to page 510 of the 1968 edition of *The Great Ideas Today*.

## PART ONE

# The Hero and the Heroic Ideal

# A Symposium

# Introduction

Each year for a number of years the editors of *The Great Ideas Today* have presented a symposium in which eminent persons undertake to discuss an idea that is of current interest. Each time this has been done, four or five such persons have been invited to contribute to the discussion. Usually they have been persons of very different backgrounds, with extremely divergent views of the subject at hand, whose comments have reflected these disparities, sometimes to good effect and sometimes not. The editors have therefore thought it proper to bring a measure of unity to the proceedings by adding a sort of coda or appendix in which they recall the ways in which the idea being considered is treated in the great books, and what the tradition with respect to it is.

This year the editors have reversed their usual procedure. In arranging a symposium on the hero and the heroic ideal, they have not begun by inviting comments on the subject, nor have they gone on to add the customary discussion of relevant material from the great books at the end. Instead, they have prepared a summary of this material at the outset, and have submitted it to the contributors for their use, as background, in preparing their comments. For this reason, the summary—or editorial essay, as perhaps it should be called—has been made considerably longer than usual. Based upon a draft submitted by our consulting editor, Otto Bird, the essay undertakes to review the great books tradition concerning the hero and the heroic ideal in an effort to suggest just what tradition it is that we are talking about when we use those terms, which we hope other readers will understand in the same way. The assumption in preparing such a review was that the contributors, having it before them, would not feel obliged to cover the same ground themselves (except where they thought that our report was inadequate or mistaken), and would thus be free to concentrate upon contemporary aspects of the subject. On that same assumption, it was felt that their comments could be shorter than the comments have been in previous years, with the result that it has been possible to include a somewhat greater number of contributors than we have had in the past: there are six this year, rather than four or five.

That there was and is some reason to consider the idea of heroism and the figure of the hero as they may appear in, or may be absent from, the contemporary world will seem obvious to some readers of *The Great Ideas Today*, perhaps not obvious at all to others. Among the latter are likely to be those who will not have thought that there is anything timely to say about human characteristics that they regard as permanent. And in deference to these readers, it may be acknowledged that there is a conventional regard for heroes and heroism nowadays—at least as they are discussed by the media or in popular literature, or in everyone's casual conversation—which is probably as strong as it ever was, and which implies that we are dealing with a fixed and familiar aspect of human affairs.

Nevertheless, it is from a sense of the opposite—a sense that the hero and the heroic ideal are no longer evident or even conceivable in the world as we know it, or are no longer evident or conceivable as they used to be—that the editors have proposed the subject for consideration. How such a sense could have developed may be easy enough to understand for anyone who regards the low estate of various roles—the military, for one—that the hero has traditionally seemed able to fill, either within society or outside it. Further recognition may come after reading the editorial summary with which the symposium begins. This summary is not organized in historical terms and does not attempt more than to suggest the current status of the idea of heroism—that is left to the contributors—but it records what may be thought of as a decline, or at any rate a profound change (perhaps several profound changes), in the force of the idea and in the extent of its acceptance since ancient times. Of course that is itself a well-worked theme. One has only to compare the *Odyssey* with James Joyce's *Ulysses* to see how great the difference is, and how well at least one modern writer has understood it. Still a further grasp of the matter may be derived from other contemporary witnesses who have remarked the fact that heroism does not fare—does not, indeed, regard itself—in the modern world as it once did. Thus Mr. Norman Mailer observed recently that the astronauts, who performed prodigies of skill and strength and even intelligence in getting to the moon, were all the same disappointing as heroes—did not seem to wish to be heroes, and if they had wished, did not seem to know how. The same thing was noted many years ago with respect to Charles A. Lindbergh, who was hopelessly incompetent in the heroic role that a frenzied public, inspired by his solitary flight across the Atlantic, attempted to force upon him. And examples of this sort could be multiplied indefinitely.

With such considerations in mind, the editors of *The Great Ideas Today* have solicited comments from a variety of contributors, asking them to regard the occasion as one on which they should "address themselves to the question whether the idea of the hero is any longer viable in the modern world, and if they think it is viable . . . to suggest what form it can credibly take." It seemed wise to allow each contributor to put this question to himself in particular terms if he liked. If he felt especially qualified to consider whether the hero can exist in the army of today, given the complex, remote, highly technical character of its mission, he was free to do that. If he were competent to suggest whether heroes can be imagined among the leaders of contemporary nation states, except as creatures of propaganda, he could do that instead. If he wished to confine himself to deciding whether there can be heroes in commercialized sports, he could also do that. Those who could sensibly discuss the lack of heroes in contemporary fiction, poetry, and drama, were not required to speak of other human enterprises. On the other hand, those who wished to consider whether heroism is possible at all in our psychoanalytical age, given what we know or think we know about subconscious motivations, were free to discuss human endeavors generally.

While not all of those who responded to our invitation accepted the assignment on quite these terms, and while, even if they had, they could not have dealt with every aspect of the subject, the symposium covers a considerable range. On the one hand is the defense of heroism offered by S. L. A. Marshall, brigadier general, USA (retired), who speaks as a dedicated soldier. At perhaps the opposite extreme is the sharp criticism of the heroic ideal provided by Ron Dorfman, editor of the *Chicago Journalism Review*, who writes as a journalist who must contend with the pretenses and deceptions of men in public life. Alternatively, we have the philosophical and even theological implications of the heroic life considered by Josef Pieper, the author of *Leisure, the Basis of Culture,* and other works; and, as distinct from that, we have a discussion of the ways in which heroes are currently portrayed in films by Joy Gould Boyum, the film critic of the *Wall Street Journal,* who specializes in the study of this form of popular art. And whereas Professor Sidney Hook undertakes to suggest the heroic possibilities of contemporary power figures on the world stage, Chaim Potok, the novelist, reflects upon the common stuff out of which all men, and thus even heroes, are made.

In the opinion of the editors, these several discussions of heroism and the heroic ideal are better differentiated than has been the case with symposiums in the past, and yet there is at the same time, if not quite a unity, at least a measure of common understanding that seems to run through them all—the result, as we like to think, of the fact that each contributor had our editorial summary before him to start with. However this may be, we hope that readers of this year's *Great Ideas Today,* who themselves should begin by reading the summary before going on to what the contributors have to say, will find their comments more than usually interesting, and that the symposium as a whole will seem both fresh and substantial in its consideration of the subject.

# The Hero and the Heroic Ideal in Great Books of the Western World

For readers of *Great Books of the Western World,* the obvious place to begin in undertaking a study of the hero and of heroism is with the *Syntopicon.* As is indicated there in the "Inventory of Terms," the main consideration of this subject is to be found in the chapters on History, Honor, and Life and Death, under the following topics:

> History 4a (4).   The role of the individual in history: the great man, hero, or leader
> Honor 5.   Honor, fame, and the heroic
> > 5a. Honor as a motivation of heroism
> > 5b. Hero-worship: the exaltation of leaders
> > 5c. The occasions of heroism in war and peace
> > 5d. The estimation of the role of the hero in history
>
> Life and Death 8c.   The contemplation and fear of death: the attitude of the hero, the philosopher, the martyr

Subsidiary treatments of the subject can also be found under:

> Courage 5.   The motivations of courage: fame or honor, happiness, love, duty, religious faith
> Honor 3a.   The reaction of the community to its good or great men
> Love 3d.   The heroism of friendship and sacrifices of love
> Temperance 6a.   Asceticism: heroic temperance
> War and Peace 8.   The desirability of war: its moral and political benefits

This survey of the places where discussions of heroism can be located in our set of books serves at once to indicate something of the range and scope of the idea. The chapters into which the treatment of it falls identify the great ideas with which it is most closely associated, the company it keeps.

## Definition

In some of these discussions, the word *hero* is practically synonymous with that of great man or leader, as in History 4*a* (4). Heroism is then considered to be identical with the greatness of men in general, and with human achievement in any course of action or kind of work. Such is the sense in which Carlyle, for example, used the term, when in 1840 he began a famous series of lectures by declaring:

> *We have undertaken to discourse here for a little on Great Men, their manner of appearance in our world's business, how they have shaped themselves in the world's history, what ideas men formed of them, what work they did;—on Heroes, namely, and on their reception and performance; what I call Hero-worship and the Heroic in human affairs.*[1]

In this sense of the term, we have to deal, as Carlyle went on to say, with "a large topic; indeed, an illimitable one; wide as Universal History itself." And in fact the hero and heroism are found associated with the idea of history not only in the discussions listed under History 4*a* (4) but also in those under Honor 3*a* and 5*b*, the last of which uses Carlyle's own expression, "hero-worship."

In other places the consideration of heroism is stricter than this. The term is used to denote a form of human greatness that is thought to be essentially distinct from other forms, though it may have something in common with them. Such a use occurs, for example, in Life 8*c*, where in connection with the attitude that one may have toward death the hero is distinguished from the philosopher and the martyr. The hero in this narrower sense of the term is commonly identified with military greatness, with valor, prowess, and extraordinary achievement in war. Some writers limit the subject still further and suggest that only a certain kind of military greatness is truly heroic. Thus La Bruyère, the seventeenth-century French moralist, says:

> *It seems that the hero has only one profession—that of arms—whereas the great man can belong to any—to that of the robe, the sword, the cabinet, or the court. . . . In war the distinction between the hero and the great man is a fine one: Both need all the military virtues. Nevertheless, it appears that the former is young, enterprising, of great valor, steadfast in perils, intrepid; whereas the latter excels in great sense, vast foresight, great capacity, and long experience. Perhaps, Alexander was only a hero, whereas Caesar was a great man.*[2]

However he is defined, the warrior-hero is not only discussed both by the authors in our set of books and by others outside it; he appears also by example, often as a figure of invention, in many works. He is most familiar, perhaps, in the stories of Homer, particularly the *Iliad*. Virgil, too, depicts him, as in much later times do Chaucer, Shakespeare, and Cervantes. Of course military heroes are also historical figures in the writings of Herodotus, Thucydides, and Plutarch, among older authors, and among more recent ones, in Tolstoy.

Few of these authors—indeed, perhaps only Homer, and to a lesser extent Plutarch and Tolstoy—concern themselves with the hero who, as one might say, is nothing *but* a warrior. The battles fought by Aeneas are important to Virgil only insofar as they are necessary to the business of founding Rome. Shakespeare in his historical plays is concerned with kingship, of which warfare is only a part. Cervantes, himself a soldier, gives us in Dox Quixote a man who cares about combat only because he is a knight, or would like to be one. Even Tolstoy's preoccupation with Napoleon in *War and Peace* is less with the warrior than with the world conquerer. And Plutarch does not confine himself to military figures any more than he does to morally good ones in rendering his *Lives* of the noble Greeks and Romans; his requirement is simply that the subjects of whom he writes be those who, as the *Syntopicon* chapter on Honor states, "were acknowledged to be great men, leaders, figures of eminent proportions, engaged in momentous exploits."[3]

Poetry, in the sense of the term that includes all imaginative literature as well as the great myths, depicts still other heroic types. Chief among them, perhaps, are the heroes of tragedy, who are discussed by the authors listed in the *Syntopicon* at Poetry 4*b*. Of such heroes the earliest is really Achilles in the *Iliad,* though by *tragic hero* is usually meant a figure of the sort that appears in the Greek dramas of a later time (not to speak of the plays of Shakespeare, the French classical drama, or a work such as *Samson Agonistes),* and who is discussed as a type by Aristotle in the *Poetics.*

There are heroes, too, of comedy, who as a kind are more difficult to define (the portion of the *Poetics* in which Aristotle presumably did so is not extant), and who, insofar as they constitute the antithesis of their tragic counterparts, are in some conventional respects not heroic at all. Homer may be said to be the original poet also of this kind of hero, who appears first as Odysseus in the *Odyssey*—which is not to say, of course, that he is a clown, or that the *Odyssey* is a funny book. A later Greek instance of a deeply comic character is the Socrates who dominates the *Dialogues* of Plato (himself originally a dramatist, according to some accounts). Still later examples of the type are the narrator (as distinct from the author) of the *Divine Comedy,* the Gargantua of Rabelais, Falstaff, Don Quixote, Lemuel Gulliver, Tom Jones, and Don Juan.

Earlier than either of these types of hero is the hero of myth, such as Hercules, Perseus, or Theseus, who achieved his status by virtue of great deeds that he performed, or who was held to have brought benefactions to mankind. On the other hand, of mostly subsequent formulation is the anti-hero (as he has come to be called) who explicitly defies either God or man—among the great examples is Faust, and likewise Melville's Ahab—though precedents for this heroic type are perhaps to be discerned in both the Prometheus of mythology and the Satan of *Paradise Lost,* as well as in the Robin Hood of legend, and may include all those tempters and corrupters of mankind (Fielding's *Jonathan Wild* is another example) whom Dr. Johnson once called the "splendidly wicked."[4]

Religion, like poetry and history, has also provided a fully formed conception of the hero and the heroic life. Particularly has this been so, as the *Syntopicon* chapter on Honor points out, since the days of medieval Christianity, when the practice of heroic virtue was regarded as a form of sanctity that was considered to be manifest in the lives of those martyrs, virgins, confessors, doctors, and others who through grace received the superhuman strength that was acknowledged in conferring sainthood upon them. It became settled Christian doctrine, as Sainte-Beuve in more recent times has pointed out, that "the soul arrives . . . at a certain fixed and invincible state, a state which is genuinely heroic, and from out of which the greatest deeds which it ever performs are executed."[5] Less settled, perhaps, but not without support has been the idea that there can be something heroic not only in great deeds but in great patience. So at least we seem to hear the old, blind Milton say in the famous sonnet where, contemplating his inability to do more than he can do in the service of his God, he reminds himself that

> God doth not need
> *Either man's work or his own gifts, who best*
> *Bear his milde yoak, they serve him best, his State*
> *Is Kingly. Thousands at his bidding speed*
> *And post o're Land and Ocean without rest:*
> *They also serve who only stand and waite.*[6]

Finally, there seems to be at least one further distinct heroic type in the tradition of which we are speaking—the hero of intellectual pursuits, the man of genius, whose eminence is not in worldly affairs, nor in godly ones, but in the life of the mind. The paradigm of this type is perhaps the Socrates of the Platonic dialogues, and more particularly the philosopher described in the *Republic,* who Plato seems to have hoped might replace the poetic conception of the warrior-hero that dominated the Athenian education of his time. But the tradition offers many figures in real life who have had something of the same quality. One of these is Saint Augustine, who in the *Confessions* tells us how he rejected the pagan learning he had taken years to master for the sake of the Christian doctrine that alone could satisfy his mind. There is Dante (the poet), who in his *Comedy* likens his genius to a little ship that sails along easily enough until it comes to the task of depicting paradise, when he notes that "the water which I take was never crossed."[7] There is Milton, expressing similar concern at the beginning of *Paradise Lost,* where he sets out to sing of "things unattempted yet in Prose or Rhime."[8] There is Gibbon, a century later, recalling the resolve with which, musing "among the ruins of the Capitol,"[9] he undertook to tell the long story of Rome's decline and fall. There is Marx, still later, struggling in exile to write *Das Kapital;* there is Freud, analyzing himself as the condition of analyzing others; there are the two Curies, unswerving in the researches that led to the discovery of radium. Not all of these figures, perhaps not any of them, would have regarded themselves as among those "men of great genius" of whom Schopenhauer speaks, who "stand in all ages like isolated heroes" against the multitude.[10] But such phrases reflect only a particular attitude, in a particular idiom, toward a kind of human greatness that nevertheless appears in essence to be rightly named.

## Characteristics

The qualities that distinguish the hero from other men vary somewhat according to the kind of heroism that is being considered, but certain characteristics are constant. First among these is some form of strength or skill. The hero is typically capable of feats that are beyond the ability of ordinary men. Compared with them he can throw the spear farther, pull the stronger bow, run the faster race. Sometimes such abilities are of prodigious or fantastic extent, as with Hercules, or in American legend with Paul Bunyan, the logger, and Mike Fink, the riverboatman (of whom it was said that he could dive deeper, swim farther, and come up drier than any man alive). At other times heroic capacity is of a quite different order, belonging rather to the mind than to the body. It is then a strength of spirit, a defiance of soul. Milton's Satan seems to embody this in *Paradise Lost:*

> *What though the field be lost?*
> *All is not lost; the unconquerable Will,*
> *And study of revenge, immortal hate,*
> *And courage never to submit or yield:*
> *And what is else not to be overcome?*[11]

Whatever his moral condition, the hero cannot be himself without his power. Where that is diminished, or is seen as insufficient to support heroic reputation, the reputation withers. So Shakespeare's Cassius thinks, hearing the public shout for Caesar, and reflecting that the object of its adoration is really a fearful and short-winded fellow. To be sure, the power that is lost may be recovered:

> Samson *hath quit himself*
> *Like* Samson, *and heroicly hath finish'd*
> *A life Heroic. . . .*[12]

*"It seems that the hero has only one profession—that of arms. . . . it appears that [he] is young, enterprising, of great valor, steadfast in perils, intrepid."* (Left) Achilles; (above) American soldiers

But it is more usual that the hero is always what he is, not only at times, and certainly not just on some single, fortuitous occasion. There must be more than accident or impulse in the contest between any hero and his adversary, his task, his fate. "The characteristic of heroism is its persistency," Emerson says.[13] Tennyson's Ulysses, old though he is, is still not sated in his quest for experience as he embarks on one last voyage.

Along with strength or durability goes the characteristic heroic virtue of courage. Except in one instance, which we will discuss in a moment, some form of this is everywhere acknowledged to be indispensable to the heroic role, whatever else that role entails. As the *Syntopicon* chapter on Courage states, "The heroes of history and poetry may be cruel, violent, self-seeking, ruthless, intemperate, and unjust, but they are never cowards":

> *They do not falter or give way. They do not despair in the face of almost hopeless odds. They have the strength and stamina to achieve whatever they set their minds and wills to do. They would not be heroes if they were not men of courage.*[14]

Some writers indicate that it is courage that gives heroic stature not merely to those who accomplish great things but to all those serious and thoughtful persons who, contemplating the harsh uncertainties of human existence, are nevertheless able to endure it. "When a dreadful object is presented," William James writes,

> *or when life as a whole turns up its dark abysses to our view, then the worthless ones among us lose their hold on the situation altogether. . . . But the heroic mind does differently . . . it can face them if necessary, without for that losing its hold upon the rest of life. The world thus finds in the heroic man its worthy match and mate. . . . He can stand this Universe.*[15]

Other, special forms of courage have been thought in certain instances to make heroes of the scholar, the scientist, and the saint. One such special kind of courage was that which the Greeks recognized in the heroes of tragedy, and to which they gave the name *ate*. By this they meant the high bravery, amounting to a sort of inspired madness, that enabled such heroes to plunge into the sea of difficulties that surrounded them and force their fate to reveal itself, though the cost of doing so was death or ruin. Some analogue to this quality, often thought to indicate the intercession of the gods, may be found in most other forms of heroism as well.

The excepted instance, mentioned earlier, in which not courage but prudence seems to be the characteristic heroic virtue is found among the heroes of comedy, who are therefore by some authors considered to be misnamed, and are disallowed as a variety of the heroic ideal. And it is true that even the great comic prototypes—Odysseus, for instance, or Socrates, or Don Quixote—appear unheroic alongside the tragic or epic or romantic heroes with whom they invite comparison. That is how they are supposed to appear. But apart from anything else that may be said about them, it may be argued that in their various destitute, impoverished, or absurd fashions, they actually possess courage of a very rich and complex kind, and it has been suggested, notably by Socrates in the *Symposium,* that other forms of heroism cannot finally be understood except by those who understand the comic form of it.

We commonly know the hero also by one further characteristic. That is his apartness, even his isolation, from other human company, if not as well from every abstract context—home, history, and laws both human and divine—in which other men move and have their being. There is something elect in the heroic role that makes each instance of it unique. The great warriors of the *Iliad* battle in what may be regarded as armies only up to a point. Beyond that, each man carries the fight, or is forced to carry it, wholly on his own. On the other hand, when a monument was erected to the Spartans who died at Thermopylae, instructing whoever came upon it to tell their countrymen that they had given their lives in obedience to their country's laws, heroic status was thereby rejected by them, or in their behalf. It is fundamental to the great tragic dramas— *Oedipus at Colonus,* for instance, or *King Lear*—that they explore the farthest implications of what it means to be naked, wretched, and alone. Even the heroes of comedy, who cannot be themselves unless they are in human company, are as a rule rejected, ridiculed, or otherwise despised, at least through some part of their careers. And in the case of the Romantic hero, the rejection is not so much endured as it is actively sought. Such a hero does not suffer isolation, he asserts it.

A question arises as to whether this isolation of the hero can or should be complete. It seems to be so among the heroes of the *Iliad,* given as they are to furthering their individual reputations, though the individuality of Achilles, say, for which all things—friends, honor, and ultimately life itself—are sacrificed, is something much greater than a mere private ego. Since the time of Virgil, however, a less extreme conception of heroic isolation has offered itself, if it has not always prevailed. It is of the essence of the hero of the *Aeneid* that he pursues an end which is not personal to himself—in the interest of which, indeed, he sublimates his own judgment and feelings. As founder of the race that in time will rule the earth, Aeneas acts in obedience to the expressed will of Jove, and while this sometimes puts him in conflict with other men and sets him always at some distance from them, it secures him against the kind of abandonment that occurs when fate itself turns hostile or seems indifferent, as it does with the heroes of epic tragedy. The result seems at first to be a loss of stature. By comparison with those heroes, Aeneas is a protected and somehow insufficient figure in whom we shall always be disappointed until we realize that it was Virgil's purpose to redefine the heroic role. From his Roman point of view the heroes of the epic tradition, especially the Achaeans of the *Iliad,* were of an obsolete type, willful and wantonly destructive, who could no longer be accepted as models in a world dedicated to peace under the rule of law.[16]

A further and related question about heroic isolation is whether it can be extended into the historical order of things without becoming either a part of that order, and thereby no longer isolated, or opposed to it, and thus something merely futile. Carlyle, for one, denied that this must happen. He insisted that throughout the course of history the dominating force in historic events had been and would continue to be the words and acts of great men. But Hegel considers such men to be great only insofar as they sense some historical process, identify themselves with the wave of the future, and conform to the irresistible march of worldly events. They are "world-historical individuals," he says, whom we may like to think of as heroic, but who are really only puppets, creatures of historical forces that come about as the result of innumerable acts by countless human beings.[17] These opposed views of Carlyle and Hegel would appear not to be reconcilable. But a compromise of sorts between them seems to be achieved by William James when he affirms that

> *the relation of the visible environment to the great man is in the main exactly what it is to the "variation" in the Darwinian philosophy. It chiefly adopts or rejects, preserves or destroys, in short selects him. And whenever it adopts and preserves the great man, it becomes modified by his influence in an entirely original and peculiar way. He acts as a ferment, and changes its constitution, just as the advent of a new zoological species changes the faunal and floral equilibrium of the region in which it appears.*[18]

## Motivation

The heroes of the Trojan War are what they are, Homer indicates in the *Iliad,* by virtue of the ideal to which they hold, and which they endeavor to realize by their acts. It is an ideal of preeminence. Whatever the differences among them—and each of the important figures in the poem is rendered memorably distinct—they are all alike in that by training, aspiration, and continual exertion they strive to be the best. We are told that Achilles, who is called "chief of heroes," was brought up by his father, Peleus, "to be ever the best and to excel all others."[19] Precisely the same words are used by the Trojan, Glaukos, to describe what his own father wished of him. Such claims of supremacy can be demonstrated only by putting them to the test. Hence the great battle scenes of the poem are among other things the testings of the various heroes—the proofs, as it were, of their merit. In fact, it is customary to identify certain parts of the poem by these trials, which are known variously as the *aristeia* of Diomedes (Book 5), of Agamemnon (Book 11), of Menelaus (Book 17), and—longest of all—the *aristeia* of Achilles (Books 19–22).

This word is derived from the adjective *aristos,* which means "best," and that in turn comes from the noun *areté,* which for Homer means something like "excellence," and which has been said to embody as well as any single word can the heroic ideal of the *Iliad. Areté* was later used by Aristotle to mean excellence of a moral and intellectual kind, or virtue, and in this sense it can, as for Aristotle it does, mean virtue in general. In the *Iliad,* however, it is something that only warriors have, the virtue that is peculiar to them, the thing that *makes* them "best." We could embrace much of what it means, though not all, if we translated it as "valor."

A similar evolution seems to have overtaken the Latin word that has the same meaning. Plutarch relates that among the early Romans, who were as remote from him as Homer was from Aristotle,

*"The hero is typically capable of feats that are beyond the ability of ordinary men. Compared with them he can throw the spear farther, pull the stronger bow, run the faster race."* (Left) The "Discobolus" (discus thrower), Roman copy of a bronze by Myron, ca. 450 B.C.; (below) Mark Spitz after the 1972 Olympic Games

> *that kind of worth was most esteemed which displayed itself in military achievements; one evidence of which we find in the Latin word for virtue, which is properly equivalent to manly courage. As if valour and all virtue had been the same thing, they [the early Romans] used as the common term the name of the particular excellence.*[20]

It is consistent with this, as Plutarch means to indicate, that the word *virtue* includes the Latin word *vir,* or "man," and that the root meaning of *virtue* is therefore "manliness."

What presumably underlies the old equation of manliness with military distinction is the fact that among men it is chiefly the warrior who undergoes the ultimate trial, which is the threat of death, as a matter of deliberate confrontation. We must say chiefly here, rather than only, because of course the hunter of savage beasts does the same thing, or once did (and was then regarded as heroic), as does the person who commits ritual suicide (in a different tradition), and perhaps certain others. But at any rate the acceptance of mortal danger is fundamental to the profession of arms and is the basis of claims such as Don Quixote makes when he argues that no other profession, not even that of clergy or the law, stands so high. Indeed, a readiness to die is by itself sufficient to raise a man above his fellows, in the opinion of some writers, whatever kind of man he is, and providing only that he act with some cause. "No matter what a man's frailties may otherwise be," William James has said in discussing what he called "life's supreme mystery,"

> *if he be willing to risk death, and still more if he suffer it heroically, in the service he has chosen, the fact consecrates him forever. Inferior to ourselves in this or that way, if yet we cling to life and he is able to "fling it away like a flower," as caring nothing for it, we account him in the deepest way our born superior.*[21]

The heroes of the *Iliad,* who are depicted by Homer as facing death with grim awareness and understanding, would appear to be the signal instance of what James has in mind. Yet they are none of them careless of life in the way his statement implies they should be. As Achilles says, when death after all has overtaken him and his spirit has gone to Hades, "rather would I live on ground as the hireling of another, with a landless man who had no livelihood, than bear sway among all the dead that be departed."[22] The meanest life is better in his view that the highest place among those who have ceased to live at all.

Nor does any of the heroes forget that death as such is no distinction, is only what all men, heroic and otherwise, must suffer. Again it is Achilles who says, with bitterness,

> *We are all held in a single honour,*
> *the brave with the weaklings.*

> *A man dies still if he has done nothing,*
> *as one who has done much.*[23]

What makes the heroes different from ordinary men is their determination to force the issue, to place their lives in danger which they could, if they chose, avoid. They do this in part knowing it is expected of them, because their position demands it. The honors and perquisites accorded to them in this world, withheld from lesser men, are given to them in recognition of their willingness to leave it. But the willingness itself comes from their perception of the fact that they are doomed to die in any case. As mortal men, hatefully limited by their condition, they feel that they can exist beyond their alloted time only in the sense, and to the extent, that they are remembered by those who come after them. It is in the effort to gain such remembrance, the nearest men can come to being like the deathless gods, that the heroes put their lives in the balance, striving to do great deeds. If an easier way were open to them, they would take it—so Sarpedon the Trojan at one point frankly admits:

> *Man, supposing you and I, escaping this battle, would be able to live on forever, ageless, immortal, so neither would I myself go on fighting in the foremost nor would I urge you into the fighting where men win glory. But now, seeing that the spirits of death stand close about us in their thousands, no man can turn aside nor escape them, let us go on and win glory for ourselves, or leave it to others.*[24]

There is no easier way. Unable to avoid death, the heroes can only hope to transcend it.

James's essential point seems borne out, however, by the Greek dramas of a later age. The prospect of death, or at least of destruction, enters into the lives of the heroes of all the great tragedies. It is not, perhaps, so clearly visible to them as the likely consequence of their acts as it is for the heroes of Homer. Nor do the protagonists of the tragedies see themselves as endeavoring in the same way to overcome it. Oedipus, who as portrayed by Sophocles seemed to Aristotle the best representative of the type, is not a warrior but a king, with problems that may perhaps be described as political or moral, but are at any rate not military. The same is true of Orestes in the trilogy by Aeschylus. Yet the question of life and death, of survival or annihilation, is there for both figures to confront, and it is their willingness to do so that gives them—that for the Greek audience certainly gave them—their heroic stature. It was fitting that this audience, which in other terms comprised the citizenry of Athens, should be seen subsequently as the hero of a tragedy of real life, its long struggle with Sparta, and that its fate should have been recorded with dramatic insight by one of its own number, the historian Thucydides, in *The Peloponnesian War*.

Death or the threat of death is faced, too, by the Virgillian hero. But whereas the Homeric warrior confronts it in hope of the glory he may win, and the protagonists of the tragedies to the end that they may, for at least one brief instant, be masters of their fate, the hero of the *Aeneid* risks his life in the furtherance of the mission he has been elected to perform. This election is security against the dangers and difficulties through which he must pass. We realize that Aeneas cannot really die, in the ordinary sense, any more than he can fail in what he undertakes to do; either result would violate Jove's plan, which for the reader of Virgil's poem has become history. At the same time, it is clear that in another sense Virgil does have a kind of death in mind, and that he depicts Aeneas as having with much pain and sense of loss to undergo it. This is the death of his former self, belonging to the heroic age that is past, which must be supressed insofar as its feelings are in conflict with the high public duty to which he has been called. Among these feelings is love for Dido, the queen of Carthage to whose land Aeneas comes in his wanderings, and with whom he would remain if he could. "Not self-impelled steer I for Italy," he tells her when the time comes for him to leave.[25] Yet leave he must, the lover in him denied, his personal wishes opposed, for the sake of the great city whose progenitor he has been chosen to be. The Latin word for Rome is *Roma,* which is *amor,* the Latin word for love, spelled backwards.

There is much in the poem to indicate that Virgil means to set forth an idea of heroism that is not only different from the Homeric one but anti-

Just as history has recorded the great deeds of heroes, so too the artist has invented figures of heroic stature. Some are the heroes of comedy and tragedy, embodying the ideal or circumstance of heroism. (Opposite) Cervantes's Don Quixote drawn by Gustave Doré and Charlie Chaplin's "Little Tramp." (Right) Shakespeare's Hamlet painted by Delacroix and (below) Arthur Miller's Willie Loman

thetical to it. Both the *Iliad* and the *Odyssey,* dissimilar as they are, deal with ways in which the hero loses or remains or recovers himself, in peace no less than in war. The *Aeneid* shows him in the same situations as *relinquishing* himself, not in the manner of one who is defeated or withdrawn from human concerns but for the sake of a higher identity that he comes to accept—the identity of a participant in a great world task. No such identity is available to the Homeric hero, in whose universe there is nothing between the individual man and the Olympian gods, and whose heroism consists precisely in his efforts to close the gap. This means, since he cannot bring the gods down to his level, that he must try and raise himself to theirs—must endeavor to enlarge himself beyond his mortal limits. In the Virgillian universe, however, the gods have descended part way, in the sense that they have revealed their purpose, and the Virgillian hero has to rise only to the intermediate level which is the realization of that purpose in human terms. To accomplish this is in its own right a heroic undertaking, since much must be risked for it, and much rejected. But at least it does not require the utter abandonment of the mortal condition, which in Homeric terms is the price of glory. And although it does not confer true immortality either, which is what glory in the root sense of the word means, what it does give is the honor of having served the living god upon the earth, so that his work, if not his worker, may survive.

It is easy to see in this Virgillian conception a prefiguration of Christianity, and particularly, in heroic terms, of the Christian knight. Even the language that Virgil uses reinforces our sense of connection between the two. Where Homer speaks of Achilles as "wrathful" or "swift-footed," and of Odysseus as "of many councils," or just "wily," the standard Virgillian epithet for Aeneas, in Latin, is *pius.* This cannot be translated properly as "pious," though it sounds much the same, since it does not for Virgil have the specifically religious connotation of that term. Nor can the Latin noun from which it comes, which is *pietas,* be translated as "piety," for the same reason. Nevertheless, and although Virgil never defines either word explicitly, it is clear from the context of his poem that by *pietas* he means the virtue Cicero had in mind when he spoke of "that through which one conscientiously renders duty and reverence to kin, country, and friends." [26] We are on firm ground, therefore, if we interpret *pius* as meaning "dutiful and reverent," or perhaps "obedient," and if we understand Aeneas to be possessed of the qualities those terms describe. And it is but a step—a very great step, to be sure, but one that Rome itself eventually took—if we add the religious, specifically Christian, meaning that *reverence* and *obedience* later acquired, and find that we have arrived at, though we have by no means altogether encompassed, the Christian, knightly, medieval idea of the hero.

Although there is an extensive literature on this kind of hero in the medieval romances, particularly the stories that deal with King Arthur and the Knights of the Round Table, and although something about his general character may be learned, for example, from Chaucer's story of the Knight in *The Canterbury Tales,* the richest and best account of him is by Cervantes, who professed not to believe in him, and who wrote *Don Quixote,* as he said, so that those foolish persons who did believe in him would realize how incredible he was. We do not know how seriously Cervantes meant this, or if he ceased to mean it as he wrote the book. All we know is that his intention, if it was real, somehow backfired, that the absurd and gallant figure of the Don turned out to be strangely convincing, so that he is the only knight that ever was, as one reader has said, in whom we *can* believe, and that his adventures, which were ostensibly set down to destroy chivalry, have preserved it in the world's imagination ever since.

The Christian pretensions (as Cervantes allows us to believe they are) of knights are described by Don Quixote early in his story, when he compares what he calls his "profession" of arms with that of priests and other churchmen. "My meaning is," he says,

> that churchmen in peace and quiet pray to Heaven for the welfare of the world, but we soldiers and knights carry into effect what they pray for, defending it with the might of our arms and the edge of our swords, not under shelter but in the open air, a target for the intolerable rays of the sun in summer and the piercing frosts of winter. Thus are we God's ministers on earth and the arms in which his justice is done therein.[27]

But it is part of Cervantes's own meaning that Don Quixote does not perceive all that he is saying here—does not acknowledge the conflict between the welfare of the world that churchmen pray for and what may be accomplished by force of arms, overlooks the pride in his assumption that he is the agent of divine justice. It is true, he understands very well what he says later on, when he explains to his listeners that in his knightly adventures he is limited by his Christian responsibility, which gives his acts their true significance:

> In what we do we must not overpass the bounds which the Christian religion we profess has assigned to us. We have to slay pride in giants, envy by generosity and nobleness of heart, anger by calmness of demeanor and equanimity, gluttony and sloth by the spareness of our diet and the length of our vigils, lust and lewdness by the loyalty we preserve to those whom we have made the mistresses of our thoughts, indolence by traversing the world in all directions seeking opportunities of making ourselves, besides Christians, famous knights.[28]

Yet it is one thing to understand this and another to be able to live up to it, and one of the things *Don Quixote* is about is the fact that being a knight, or trying to be one, can become a self-serving enterprise. The Don

*". . . the hero of intellectual pursuits, the man of genius, whose eminence is not in worldly affairs, nor in godly ones, but in the life of the mind."* (Above) Marie Curie; (opposite) "The Death of Socrates" by Jacques Louis David

himself seems to take note of this when he asserts that the rewards of knightly exploits "are, were, and will be, the work of fame that mortals desire as a reward and a portion of the immortality their famous deeds deserve." He then corrects himself, as it were, by observing that Christian knights "look more to that future glory that is everlasting . . . than to the vanity of the fame that is to be acquired in this present transitory life." But this leaves him open to the question Sancho Panza asks, which is whether in that case the two of them had not better join a religious order and "set about becoming saints . . . [in order to] obtain more quickly the fair fame we are striving after." In answer, Don Quixote, trying to defend the heroic life he has chosen, can come up only with the perilous doctrine that chivalry too is "a religion, there are sainted knights in glory." [29]

What is evident in these various works, taken together, is a sort of progression or enlargement of heroic motivation. This is derived at first from a sense of the person. At a later time, it arises from an idea of country or the State. Still later it is found in religious zeal. We have seen that there is a fundamental conflict between the first and second stages of the progression, and we can infer a still greater conflict between the first and the third. For, as the glorification of the person in Homeric terms is incompatible with the glorification of the state that Virgil celebrated, so it is even more profoundly opposed to the glorification of God that is proper to Christianity. It is not surprising that such conflicts show themselves in the internal struggles of the hero, who has greater difficulty meeting the requirements of these successive allegiances as they become more abstract and otherworldly. That the Homeric warriors value women, who indeed provide their heroic occasions, is not regarded as inconsistent with their status. Aeneas, on the other hand, suffers a kind of fall, from which he must recover, in his infatuation with Dido. And the Christian knight, or at least the knight-errant, though he always serves an idealized mistress, as Don Quixote says, nevertheless can and sometimes does become the lover of a real one, with an irretrievable loss of purity. Of all the knights of the Round Table, only Gawain was worthy of the Holy Grail.

It is not surprising either that, as the third of the motivations, which is the glorification of God, is an ultimate one, the progression of which we are speaking should seem to reach an end with it. And it is true that after the decline of Christian chivalry any fresh conception of heroic purpose, as being in the service of a new doctrine or idea, is hard to find. Only with modern times, perhaps, and the idea of Revolution, does such a thing appear. Of course there have been reaffirmations at different historical periods of the idea of the national hero, who is a descendent of Aeneas, as there have been revivals of the heroic ideal in individual terms. The latter reappears notably during the romantic era of the last century, and to some extent in more recent times, when it is discerned, for example, in the figure of the artist. It may be doubted, however, whether the modern heroic ideal, if any such can be said to exist, is a person of any kind, so much as an abstraction or a collectivity. The true hero of the present seems to be a country, a people, or a movement—even history itself, as Hegel would appear to have believed. Or perhaps the person in whom we find it is the person of Everyman. Freud, who was convinced that "the secret of heroism," its psychological root, was not so much the desire to win immortality as the inability of the unconscious to recognize or admit death, argues that the heroic act arises from the conviction every man unconsciously has that he cannot really die, that he is somehow immortal. "The rational explanation for heroism," Freud writes,

> is that it consists in the decision that the personal life cannot be so precious as certain abstract general ideals. But more frequent, in my view, is that instinctive and impulsive heroism which knows no such motivation, and flouts danger in the spirit of Anzengruber's Hans the Road-Mender: "Nothing can happen to me." [30]

## Criticism

While there does not seem to have been any period of history in the tradition of which we are speaking that has utterly lacked heroic ideals, neither has there been any age in which these ideals were immune to criticism or above disbelief. This has sometimes been expressed, as we have seen, by those who seek to establish a different conception of the hero from one that happens to prevail. More often it has been articulated by authors who dislike or are skeptical of heroism in any form. Such an attitude is found in Euripides, of whom Aristotle remarked that, as compared with Sophocles, he depicted men not as they ought to be but as they are, and who seldom missed an opportunity in his plays to attack heroic pretensions. Typical is a passage from *Medea:*

> *Great people's tempers are terrible, always*
> *Having their own way, seldom checked,*
> *Dangerous they shift from mood to mood.*
> *How much better to have been accustomed*
> *To live on equal terms with one's neighbors.*
> *I would like to be safe and grow old in a*
> *Humble way. What is moderate sounds best,*
> *Also in practice is best for everyone.*
> *Greatness brings no profit to people.*
> *God indeed, when in anger, brings*
> *Greater ruin to great men's houses.*[31]

Similar words are used later by Montaigne when he asserts that he prefers Socrates to Alexander, since he feels he "can easily conceive Socrates in the place of Alexander, but Alexander in that of Socrates, [he] cannot." All that Alexander can accomplish, he says, is contained in the command, "Subdue the world," whereas Socrates acts according to the maxim, " 'Carry on human life comformably with its natural condition'; a much more general, weighty, and legitimate science than the other."[32] On the other hand, Cervantes is more severe (or seems to be; again, we never know just how serious he is) with his own hero, Don Quixote, whose goings-on are characterized as not only futile and destructive but insane, the result of reading too many chivalric romances. And Pope simply takes it for granted, in the *Essay on Man,* that heroism is in general the product of derangement or perversity:

> *Heroes are much the same, the point's agreed,*
> *From Macedonia's madman to the Swede;*
> *The whole strange purpose of their lives, to find*
> *Or make, an enemy of all mankind.*[33]

Some authors—Cervantes, of course, is one—provide their own commentary on the heroic ideal they present. The greatest critic of the Homeric warrior, notwithstanding Virgil, is Homer himself—if we can assume, as tradition has it, that the man who wrote the *Iliad* also wrote the *Odyssey.* For the latter tells us how it is that, in making his way home, one of those who fought at Troy, Odysseus, unlearns his warrior role, and of how this is in a profound moral sense the price of his safe return. Just

what sort of figure he becomes in the process is something that only his complete story is sufficient, perhaps, to explain. The heroic ideal that emerges from the *Odyssey,* if ideal it can be said to be, is much more difficult to define than its counterpart in the *Iliad.* This is partly because it reflects the distinction Aristotle made between tragedy and comedy when he said that the former was simple and disastrous, while the latter was complicated and moral. It is also because we perceive the *Odyssey*'s heroic type only in its embodiment, which is Odysseus himself, of whom the single conclusive thing there is to say is that—wanderer, pretender, and liar that he is—there is nothing fixed or final to be said. It is clear, however, that he is something different from the Achaean warriors, his former comrades, of whom he hears along the way of his return, since they have already become the stuff of which songs are sung and stories are told before he reaches home. Infinitely artful, he uses all his skills on that long journey to preserve his life and extend his experience—as distinct from Achilles, who had been intensely alive, and who elected by the manner of his dying to turn himself into a work of art. The course Odysseus takes leads him, too, toward immortality—not, however, through a death that is gloriously met but by a resourcefulness that keeps off any death at all.

26

"We have undertaken to discourse here for a little on Great Men, . . . how they have shaped themselves in the world's history, what ideas men formed of them, what work they did." (Opposite-left) Moses by Michelangelo; (opposite-right) Joan of Arc by Ingres; (above-left) Winston Churchill, 1940; (above-right) a painting of young Mao

Achilles is the prince of the fallen, but Odysseus is the king of survivors.

To say that Homer, in depicting such a figure, is a critic of the tale he —or someone—told in the *Iliad* is not to imply that he had come to disapprove of that earlier production (as we must assume it was), or of its central hero, but only that he understood the different nature of his later task. For the point of view that makes the *Odyssey* possible is inherently critical of the passion that creates the *Iliad*, which it has time to see around, and which in its wide perspective looks rash and ruinous. Odysseus may and does love the memory of those with whom he fought at Troy, as he is proud of the glory they achieved, but he knows he can no longer afford to be what they were, that he must reconstitute himself if he is to recover his place in the common world of men, in the normal order of things. The heroism of the *Odyssey* excludes the heroism of the *Iliad*, as peace displaces war.

A similar kind of understanding produces another hero with some of the same qualities in the Socrates of the Platonic dialogues. There is general agreement that this figure is in part Plato's invention, though a real Socrates did exist, did teach in the manner Plato describes, and was tried and executed for the crimes that are discussed with such devastating irony in the *Apology*. What Plato brought to the account of him, among other things, was a purpose that in the nature of the case his career could not have acquired on its own, though the real Socrates may have intended that it should. For his death more or less coincided with the final defeat of Athens in its decisive war with Sparta. He was thus unable to complete or perhaps even consciously to begin the project that Plato, his most brilliant student, undertook on his behalf, which was an inquiry into the causes of that catastrophe. The *Dialogues* can be read as steps in such an inquiry. Plato seems to have decided to write them because he saw, as perhaps the real Socrates also saw, that what had happened to their city was not so much that it had lost a war as that in the process it had somehow lost its soul. The *Dialogues* explore the implications of this tragedy, which raise questions about the nature of men and things and the origin of the world, but which lead at the end to the task of reconstituting the laws. Plato, the guiding spirit of the inquiry, having, so to say, taken the city on a lengthy speculative journey, at last brings it home to contemplate its civil condition.

It is appropriate not only to his ultimate situation but to the special nature of his heroic role that in the last discussion he has with his followers, just before he dies, Socrates is concerned with life and death and the immortality of the soul. The followers, despairing in the fact that they are about to lose him, seek reassurance that in doing so they will not lose the life of the mind as well. "I would ask you to be thinking of the truth and not of Socrates," he tells them. In thus addressing himself to their doubt and grief he is likened to "a general rallying his defeated and broken army," determined to restore their faith in the power of rational discourse to survive his impending death.[34] It was his last accomplishment to make this event seem less important than the speculative enterprise that had brought it about, and that seemed finally to require it.

Christian writers, at least until the time in the tenth and eleventh centuries when chivalry brings about an uneasy union of Christian and heroic ideals, are also critical of the heroic tradition, which they perceive only as a pagan thing. Augustine even regarded it as vicious, since it seemed to him grounded in the sin of pride. If great Rome, the seat of Christian faith, had been built by men who nevertheless adhered to such a tradition, what could be discerned in the fact but the providence of God, who had chosen that method of building his empire upon earth? Heroic ambition, though sinful in Augustine's eyes, was yet capable of great undertakings, for which reason, he wrote, God could be supposed to have instilled it in

> *such men as, for the sake of honour and praise, and glory, consulted*
> *well for their country, in whose glory they sought their own, and*
> *whose safety they did not hesitate to prefer to their own, sup-*
> *pressing the desire of wealth and many other vices for this one vice,*
> *namely, the love of praise.*[35]

Of course Augustine could not accept the higher mission of Aeneas that Virgil had conceived to justify the founding of Rome and assert her destiny. Though cast in verse that Augustine never ceased to love, that conception was in his view merely an expression of civic vanity accorded the false sanction of a pagan god.

Dante seems more tolerant than Augustine does of some of the ancient heroes, to whom in the *Divine Comedy* he grants a place in limbo. Yet he cites others, such as Capaneus the blasphemer, who defied the gods before the gates of Thebes, in illustration of grave sins. Odysseus, in particular, who was known only by tradition in medieval times, occupies a place far down in Hell among the evil counselors. He is there as the symbol he had become for Dante's age (a very different age of course from Tennyson's, which took a very different view) of those who look not heavenward for their salvation but to the world and worldly things for the satisfaction of their vain and idle curiosity, and who persuade other men, their followers, to do the same thing.

It is rather the analogue of heroism which consists of martyrdom that is honored by Dante, as it is by Christian tradition generally. And what we might otherwise think of as heroic courage in Dante himself, the voyager who makes his way through the terror of Hell, the trial of Purgatory, and the vision of Paradise—what would seem to be courage, too, later on in the story of *The Pilgrim's Progress*—is really not that in Christian terms but something very much greater. It is the work of the specifically Christian virtues of faith, hope, and charity, which are required of those who take salvation's path. Nor can those who follow that path be regarded as heroic in this tradition. For they are thought of as distinguished less by the effort they have made than by the grace they have received, without which the effort would come to nought.

Even where among later authors an idea of heroism survives the restraints, amounting almost to suppression, that Christianity places upon it, there is apt to be criticism of what are considered its extremes. Shakespeare's plays imply as much in some of their characterizations. Hotspur in *Henry IV, Part I* is clearly an instance of a distempered heroic spirit, as is Falstaff, though his distemper is of the opposite kind. On the other hand, Prince Hal, who in the same play appears worse than either of these figures, shows himself to be their better upon his father's death—

> *The breath no sooner left his father's body,*
> *But that his wildness, mortified in him,*
> *Seem'd to die too; yea, at that very moment*

Whatever form the idea of the hero takes and however the idea may change, people reach out to touch their heroes. They will have their heroes

> *Consideration, like an angel, came*
> *And whipp'd the offending Adam out of him,*
> *Leaving his body as a paradise,*
> *To envelope and contain celestial spirits.*[36]

—when he proceeds to become, as Henry V, what we are given to understand is the ideal hero-king. But Shakespeare seems to have recognized the poetic limitations of this type, if not the political ones, in his later plays. When in those plays he drew imperfect men, he did not pretend that they were heroes—as, at the same time, in contemplating perfect ones, he ceased to pretend that they were real:

> CLEOPATRA: *I dream'd there was an Emperor Antony.*
> *O, such another sleep, that I might see*
> *But such another man!*
> DOLABELLA:                *If it might please ye—*
> CLEOPATRA: *His face was as the heavens; and therein stuck*
> *A sun and moon, which kept their course, and lighted*
> *The little O, the earth.*
> DOLABELLA:              *Most sovereign creature—*
> CLEOPATRA: *His legs bestrid the ocean; his rear'd arm*
> *Crested the world; his voice was propertied*
> *As all the tuned spheres, and that to friends;*
> *But when he meant to quail and shake the orb,*
> *He was as rattling thunder. For his bounty,*
> *There was no winter in't; an autumn 'twas*
> *That grew the more by reaping. His delights*
> *Were dolphin-like; they show'd his back above*
> *The element they lived in. In his livery*
> *Walk'd crowns and crownets; realms and islands were*
> *As plates dropp'd from his pocket.*
> DOLABELLA:              *Cleopatra!*
> CLEOPATRA: *Think you there was, or might be, such a man*
> *As this I dream'd of?*
> DOLABELLA:       *Gentle madam, no.*[37]

The idea that heroism is larger than life, and that it is therefore contrary to nature, is what Dr. Johnson also seems to have had in mind when he said that "Shakespeare has no heroes; his scenes are occupied only by men who act and speak as the reader thinks that he should himself have spoken or acted on the same occasion: Even where the agency is supernatural the dialogue is level with life." In this Shakespeare is superior to other dramatists, Johnson wrote, who "can only gain attention by hyperbolical or aggravated characters, by fabulous and unexampled excellence or depravity, as the writers of barbaric romances invigorated the reader by a giant and a dwarf."[38]

For Hegel, however, as for other writers of the romantic age, the hero, far from being contrary to nature, can exist only *in* "a state of nature." But of course by *nature* Hegel does not mean what Dr. Johnson meant, which was more or less what we would mean by the term *human nature;* Hegel means what might be called the primal order of things, or in Hegelian terminology, "a state of affairs where mere force prevails and against which the Idea establishes a right of Heroes." It was Hegel's theory that the hero serves the evolution of ethics—the Idea of Right—in the world, where he is of use to the Idea, at a time when brute strength would otherwise prevail, in organizing human life. But such a use lasts only until the Idea has brought about the creation of the State, which for Hegel is not civil society but rather its constitutional form and sanction. When this occurs, Hegel says, "there can no longer be any heroes," since the "uncivilized conditions" that make it right for such figures to found cities, establish institutions, and maintain order, no longer exist.[39]

This assertion of a kind of subordinate moral right in heroic action recalls Hegel's belief that heroes, or at least great men, are the creatures of something larger than themselves—specifically, of "historical forces" that it is their heroic distinction to perceive and seem to lead. Hegel's views on that subject are discussed in the *Syntopicon* chapter on History. Such a belief leaves little to the hero, of course, except an extraordinary capacity for insight. And even that is denied by Tolstoy, whose favorite figure in *War and Peace,* General Kutúzov, does not pretend to know what will happen, still less how to make it happen, in Russia's struggle with Napoleon, and whose strength derives precisely from his lack of any illusion that he does. No other attitude, Tolstoy feels, is really consistent with history. "We need only penetrate," he writes,

> to the essence of any historic event—which lies in the activity of the general mass of men who take part in it—to be convinced that the will of the historic hero does not control the actions of the mass but is itself continually controlled.[40]

It follows from this, Tolstoy adds, that once we have disabused ourselves of false notions of historical causality, "not only shall we have no need to see exceptional ability and genius in Napoleon and Alexander, but we shall be unable to consider them to be anything but like other men."[41] Tolstoy is thus in sharp disagreement, as Hegel is also, with ancient historians such as Thucydides, who regarded Pericles as the controlling figure in the fate of Athens, or Plutarch, for whom the history of civilization could be told in terms of the *Lives* of the noble Greeks and Romans.

The idea that the hero is at bottom like other men is exhaustively explored, too, in the plays of Bernard Shaw, who as a comic artist made it his business to puncture heroic pretensions. "There's no such thing as a real hero," says the character of Napoleon in *The Man of Destiny.*[42] Raina, in *Arms and the Man,* implies the same thing when she remembers that at her last meeting with her heroic lover, Sergius, "it came into my head just as he was holding me in his arms and looking into my eyes, that perhaps we only had our heroic ideas because we are so fond of reading Byron and Pushkin."[43] And in their various ways Shaw's greatest people —Caesar, John Tanner, Andrew Undershaft, Saint Joan, and so forth—all stand corrective of the heroic ideal in its romantic form.

Corrective, it is important to note, rather than destructive. For Shaw develops a heroic conception of his own in the man—or woman— of reason and good sense who reveals the vanities and vital lies by which most men attempt to live. This is the figure that dominates so many of his plays—that is to be found, perhaps, in all of them. Sometimes the figure is merely a critic, uninvolved, content to point out what other men do not see. At other times he seems to foreshadow the Superman, capable of changing the world, of whom Shaw liked to talk. Always he is possessed of supreme self-confidence. "What is the secret of your power?" the Lady of *The Man of Destiny* asks Napoleon:

> *Only that you believe in yourself. You can fight and conquer for yourself and for nobody else. You are not afraid of your own destiny.*[44]

Even Shaw's Joan, of whom it must rather be said that she does nothing for herself, least of all fight and conquer, and who believes not in any destiny of her own but only in what her voices direct her to do, has this confidence, this high courage, this immense personal force. As she has something also of the wit, the brilliance, and the intellectual passion of her creator, whose dramatic projection she partly is.

In more recent times a far more radical challenge to the traditional idea of the hero, or at least to some of its familiar forms, has of course appeared in the conception of the antihero, who takes many forms of his own. An interesting account of this peculiarly modern figure is offered by Maurice Merleau-Ponty, who maintains that he is distinct from such prototypes as Lucifer or Prometheus in being marked by an experience of confusion and failure that is an inescapable part of the modern condition. A more extended philosophical justification of him is to be found in the writings of Jean-Paul Sartre, who sees him, at least in the form of the intellectual, which is the form Sartre cares about, as doomed to failure from his very lucidity. By this Sartre means that because such a hero is necessarily conscious of himself, he is unable to lose himself in any commitment he makes to action. That is his tragedy, Sartre argues. Forced nevertheless to act by his moral sense, in doing so he merely reinforces his private ego. The more intensely he gives himself to others, the more completely he is alone. Fulfilled at last by his very inability to fulfill himself, he is finally made aware of his "impossible condition" when he suffers the realization that he cannot even suffer, that he must endure the ultimate anguish of not being able to feel pain.[45]

But these recent discussions of the heroic role, implying as they do a critique and a rejection of previous formulations, are as yet imperfectly absorbed—are perhaps not possible to absorb at all—into the long tradition that we have been considering. And whatever may ultimately be made of them, they have not so far been as influential, nor are they as widely known, as certain personifications of the type they undertake to define that appear in the work of still other contemporary writers—Samuel Beckett, for instance, and Albert Camus. Particularly has Camus, with his celebrated essay *The Myth of Sisyphus* and still more with his brief novel *The Stranger,* seemed to create the hero of his time. It is a long way from Achilles to Meursault or Sisyphus—too long, it may be argued, for any connecting line to stretch. But it may also say something about the strength of the heroic tradition we have discussed that at least in Camus's own view the doomed and lonely figures he conceived, unheroic as they may seem, represent no denial of heroic possibility but its contemporary affirmation.[46]

---

[1] *On Heroes, Hero-Worship, and the Heroic in History* (London: Oxford University Press [World's Classics], 1946), p. 1.

[2] *Les Caractères,* "Du mérite personnel."

[3] *GBWW,* Vol. 2, p. 731.

[4] *The Rambler,* no. 4.

[5] Quoted in William James, *The Varieties of Religious Experience* (London: Longmans, Green & Co., 1908), p. 260.

[6] Sonnet XVI; *GBWW,* Vol. 32, pp. 66–67.

[7] *GBWW,* Vol. 21, p. 107.

[8] *GBWW,* Vol. 32, p. 93.

[9] *The Decline and Fall of the Roman Empire; GBWW,* Vol. 41, p. 598.

[10] "On Reputation," from *The Art of Literature,* in *Complete Essays of Schopenhauer* (New York: Willey Book Co., 1942), bk. 4, p. 87.

[11] Bk. 1, lines 105–9; *GBWW,* Vol. 32, p. 95.

[12] Milton, *Samson Agonistes,* lines 1709–11; *GBWW,* Vol. 32, p. 377.

[13] "Heroism," in *Essays, First Series.*

[14] *GBWW,* Vol. 2, p. 252.

[15] *The Principles of Psychology; GBWW,* Vol. 53, p. 826.

[16] Virgil seems to have felt, however, that a world without heroes, though better in that respect than any previous world, would in every other way be a diminished thing. For if the heroic age, which he thought of as the age of the Greeks, had been self-destructive, it had also been brilliant. That Rome would have no such brilliance in its own right, but would be distinguished only for the stern arts of war and peace, is the melancholy purport of a famous passage of the *Aeneid* (6. 847–53; *GBWW,* Vol. 13, pp. 233–34) in which the Greek and Roman achievements are looked forward to prophetically and compared:

> *Others the breathing brass shall softlier mould,*
> *I doubt not, draw the lineaments of life*
> *From marble, at the bar plead better, trace*
> *With rod the courses of the sky, or tell*
> *The rise of stars: remember, Roman, thou,*
> *To rule the nations as their master: these*
> *Thine arts shall be, to engraft the law of peace,*
> *Forbear the conquered, and war down the proud.*

17 See the discussion in the *Syntopicon* chapter on History, *GBWW*, Vol. 2, p. 717.

18 "Great Men and Their Environment"; *GGB*, Vol. 7, p. 177.

19 *Iliad* 11. 784. Cf. *GBWW*, Vol. 4, p. 80.

20 *Lives*, "Coriolanus"; *GBWW*, Vol. 14, p. 175.

21 *The Varieties of Religious Experience*, p. 364.

22 *Odyssey* 11. 488–91. Cf. *GBWW*, Vol. 4, p. 247.

23 *Iliad* 9. 318–19; trans. Richmond Lattimore (Chicago: University of Chicago Press, Phoenix Books, 1961), p. 206. Cf. *GBWW*, Vol. 4, p. 60.

24 Ibid., 12. 322–28; Lattimore, pp. 266–67. Cf. *GBWW*, Vol. 4, p. 85.

25 *Aeneid* 4. 364; *GBWW*, Vol. 13, p. 177.

26 *Rhetoricae Libri Duo, sine de Inventione Rhetorica* 2. 53. There is a discussion of the same term in Aquinas, *Summa* 2–2, Q. 101.

27 *Don Quixote*, pt. 1, chap. 13; *GBWW*, Vol. 29, p. 33.

28 Ibid., pt. 2, chap. 8; *GBWW*, Vol. 29, p. 227.

29 Ibid., pt. 2, chap. 8; *GBWW*, Vol. 29, p. 228.

30 *Thoughts on War and Death; GBWW*, Vol. 54, pp. 761d, 765.

31 Lines 119–30. Cf. *GBWW*, Vol. 5, p. 213.

32 *Essays*, bk. 3, chap. 3; *GBWW*, Vol. 25, p. 391.

33 Epistle IV, lines 219–22. Cf. Henry Fielding, *Jonathan Wild* (London: J. M. Dent & Sons, 1964), p. 176, "Greatness consists in power, pride, insolence, and doing mischief to mankind."

34 *Phaedo; GBWW*, Vol. 7, p. 236.

35 *The City of God*, bk. 5, chap. 13; *GBWW*, Vol. 18, p. 219.

36 *King Henry V*, act 1, sc. 1; *GBWW*, Vol. 26, p. 533.

37 *Antony and Cleopatra*, act. 5, sc. 2; *GBWW*, Vol. 27, p. 347.

38 *Preface to Shakespeare; GGB*, Vol. 5, p. 319.

39 *The Philosophy of Right*, "Additions" 58, Par. 93; *GBWW*, Vol. 46, p. 125.

40 *GBWW*, Vol. 51, p. 563.

41 Ibid., p. 647.

42 *GGB*, Vol. 4, p. 317.

43 Act 1; *Selected Plays of Bernard Shaw* (New York: Dodd, Mead & Co., 1948), 3:127.

44 *GGB*, Vol. 4, p. 318.

45 Cf. Victor Brombert, "Sartre: The Intellectual as 'Impossible' Hero," in Victor Brombert, ed., *The Hero in Literature* (Greenwich, Conn.: Fawcett Publications, 1969), pp. 239–65.

46 Cf. Conor Cruise O'Brien, *Albert Camus of Europe and Africa*, in Modern Masters, ed. Frank Kermode (New York: Viking Press, 1970), pp. 31–34.

# We Must Have Heroes

## S. L. A. Marshall

Born in Catskill, New York, in 1900, Brigadier General S. L. A. Marshall
began his military career early, becoming at eighteen the youngest American
officer in World War I, when he fought with the AEF in France. After the war
he became a newspaperman, working for various papers, notably the *Detroit
News,* for which he was a military critic and editorial writer from 1927 to
1961, and which he served also as a correspondent in Latin America (1927–
35) and Spain (1936–37). In 1942 he reentered military service as special
consultant to Secretary of War Stimson, and was subsequently chief of orientation for the army before joining the newly formed Army Historical Division
in 1943. As army historian he covered campaigns in both the Pacific and
Europe, and at the end of the war was historian of the Armies of Occupation.
He reentered military service in 1948 to prepare army staff studies for NATO,
and later served as operations analyst for the Eighth Army in Korea. After
further assignments in the Middle East and Africa he returned to the United
States, where at his retirement in 1960 he was deputy chief of information
for the army. Awarded numerous military and academic honors, among
them a presidential citation, he is the author of some twenty-seven books
and many technical articles, as well as of frequent reviews and comments on
military affairs in newspapers and periodicals. General Marshall lives in
Birmingham, Michigan.

An overextended, hand-to-hand experience with the making of heroes does not necessarily qualify one to dilate on the question: The Hero Image, indispensable or outmoded? But it does harden a view, and may narrow it. Having worked overlong the field where more legitimate heroes are made than any place else, I am not concerned about contemporary doubts that cause the question to be raised. The hero image will not be retired short of Utopia, which is some distance off.

I am convinced of this principally because I know there is nothing to replace that image. I see no prospect of an increase in man's humanity to man, should the time arrive when acts of supreme courage are no longer revered by society. Were life on this planet to degenerate until great risks for the good of others seemed no longer worth running, we would have a surrender to selfishness that would ultimately result in passive submission to tyranny.

So, reversing the usual order of things in a trial court, I start with my conclusion, then call to the stand my star witness, the late Justice Oliver Wendell Holmes. More and more as he aged, the Great Liberal loved to dwell upon the lessons he had learned under ordeal by fire. Some term this tendency a weakness in old soldiers.

Risking being called a militarist, Holmes spoke of war virtually as a therapy. At the Harvard commencement of 1895 he said: "Some teacher of the kind we all need. In this snug, over-safe corner of the world we need it, that we may realize that our comfortable routine is no eternal necessity of things, but merely a little space of calm in the midst of the tempestuous untamed streaming of the world, and in order that we may be ready for danger."

Then he moved to the essential point: "High and dangerous action teaches us to believe as right beyond dispute things for which our doubting minds are slow to find words of proof. Out of heroism grows faith in the worth of heroism."[1]

Other writers have gone even beyond this, of course. John Ruskin, artist and lover of peace, extolled war as the crucible for the proving of character. "The great justification of this game is that it truly, when well played, determines *who is the best man*—who is the highest bred, the most self-denying, the most fearless, the coolest of nerve, the swiftest of eye and hand. You cannot test these qualities wholly unless there is a clear possibility of the struggle's ending in death." [2]

That I call a little extreme, however. Monk Watson, a World War I hero, had been a New York gangster. The boldest flamethrower operator in the Pacific in World War II had been a derelict until battle reclaimed him. What I know from firsthand experience is that battle stress is felt less by some men, just as there are others who feel less pain from wounds. They are the fortunate, not the most heroic.

My thoughts are Holmesian. I agreed with these commencement words when I first read them. That was after my first go in battle. Many years and more battles later my beliefs are unchanged.

Unless courage is itself to be discouraged as no longer the chief virtue when coupled with honor, the need to raise up the hero image will not be less in the unforeseeable future than it was in those distant ages when mythology flowered that mortals might be inspired by examples of immortal courage.

In his will to endure, man has not measurably grown since his beginnings, though today his hunger for some little success that will lift him above the crowd must be greater than ever before. Lacking courage, he cannot make it. Denied a star to guide him, he must stumble in the dark. Were there no heroes, it would be necessary to invent some. And indeed, it is done every day by the media, as if they feel compelled to gratify some natural longing in mankind.

The Vietnam War being unpopular, its heroisms were largely ignored, though that was a phase, of passing significance only. The urge to honor the heroic did not diminish; there was merely a temporary shifting of standards. The vacuum being there, the synthetic hero, the lone adventurer, the minor nobleman, and even the small bureaucrat who purloined papers in the name of peacemaking were given more than due homage by press and public. Not to be placed in that category is the epic deed of the young British Columbian who recently married the girl he rescued when she was attacked by a grizzly. Although he might have held back from the encounter without being shamed as a coward, he fought off the bear with an eight-inch hunting knife. So doing, he lost one ear, one eye, and the whole of his scalp, besides breaking a wrist. But he won the Royal Humane Society's Stanhope Gold Medal, the Carnegie Medal for heroism, and—still more important—the girl. [3] What human does not feel pride in kinship with such a man? It would be the same heart that felt no shame on reading the mournful story of the young woman in New York who was torturously murdered while dozens of neighbors watched, making not one move to help her lest they get involved.

Finally, however, the pent-up emotions caused by public confusions over Vietnam created its own ironic aftermath. The popular hunger for military heroics did not die; it was simply dormant. The same people who had stayed indifferent to the valorous acts of men in the fighting line made heroes en masse of the returned American POWs. It was a transfer of adulation without precedent in all military history.

True heroism essentially is a selfless act with a degree of ultimate risk. By definition, this excludes the athlete and the sportsman, the race driver, alpinist, poloist, and others who voluntarily risk life and limb when they participate, for thrill, fame, or fortune, taking the same gamble as the steeplejack and test pilot take to earn a living.

Risk-taking is not in itself heroic. The only way to avoid risk is to curl up and die. Moreover, we are where and what we are only because, through the centuries, some individuals have accepted nigh incalculable risk. I cannot conceive of civilization's making any advance without that spirit being present.

Paradoxically, however, the person who satisfies some urge to take risks, whether in the hope for glory or the easing of self-doubt, contributes directly to making a hero image. So does the adored professional athlete or the actor who, playing the hero role, is more likely to become lionized than is his real life prototype. Though it sounds like a contradiction, the authentic hero, the synthetic hero, and the stage hero have much in common. That is as elementary as is the fact that there would be no heroes if there were no one to sing them. An act may be intrinsically heroic yet not make a hero. He who perishes out of sight trying to save his friend has made a wasted sacrifice. By the same token, an act may be unheroic and still a hero may come of it. Recognition and acclamation are the essentials in image-making.

"Show me a hero," wrote F. Scott Fitzgerald, "and I will write you a tragedy."[4] He might more accurately and sensibly have said: "Show me a hero and I will still be from Missouri."

A few examples should illuminate these points. Start with Major Rowan. At the suggestion of his son, Elbert Hubbard elected Rowan as the no. 1 hero of the 1898 war with Spain, not for what he did but for how he set about it, a theme on which Hubbard so rhapsodized that the tale lives on to this day. What gripped Hubbard was that when President McKinley handed Rowan a message to be delivered to Garcia, Rowan went on his way without asking one question. That was not heroism. Rowan merely responded to an order in the manner prescribed for an officer, and being no fool, he did not seek to draw from his commander in chief answers that are only to be found at operating levels.[5]

In the small battle of Pork Chop Hill, Korea, April 1953, a shrunken garrison under 2d Lt. Joe Clemons beat off attacks by Chinese Communists for three days. The losses in dead and wounded were two-thirds of the defending force, whose heroism was monumental. The U.S. press missed it wholly. Being the only writer present during the battle, I wrote a book about the defense. The book was a commercial failure until Gregory Peck used two of its chapters as the scenario for a war movie still celebrated for its realism. Thus Pork Chop came to be bracketed with such famous stands by Americans as Bunker Hill, the Alamo, and Bastogne. Then who made the heroism of Pork Chop Hill legendary? Not Joe Clemons, nor this writer, but Gregory Peck.[6]

Recently, the front pages of metropolitan dailies and the voices of John Chancellor and Walter Cronkite acclaimed the heroism of Roberto Clemente. The great outfielder of the Pirates was always good sports copy. In death he was practically canonized by senior editors, and the Baseball Writers' Association set aside the rules and voted him into the Cooperstown Hall of Fame at once. Had he been killed in a car crash while on holiday or had an unknown Puerto Rican met death trying to help Nicaraguan earthquake victims, the event would have been little noted. But because Clemente was on a mercy mission when his plane failed, the diamond hero became superhero.

War has been my school and combat my major course. My experience with situations under fire spanned fifty years, extending from Soissons in July 1918 to the Delta, Vietnam, in June 1968. In that time I cited thirteen men for the Medal of Honor, of which number eleven were pinned with it. The count of soldiers I put up for the Distinguished Service Cross, the Silver Star, and lesser valor awards runs well into the hundreds.

Many of these men I came to know well. Remembering them, I am only amused when I hear it said that the hero type is thus-and-so. The novelist, the playwright, or possibly the psychiatrist might wish us to think this way. But as is said of good horses, legitimate combat heroes come in all shapes and sizes.

On the other hand, it may be said with some accuracy and fairness that individuals bent on winning regard as heroic figures have certain characteristics in common. The foremost is a drive for recognition, how this is gained being a lesser consideration. I think first of Douglas MacArthur and George S. Patton, Jr. Their early papers and much else make their aim quite clear. If there was anything the early Patton cared more about than proofs of his male fortitude, which he discussed in letters to his wife and her father, it was the decorations for which he pressed in official correspondence.[7] MacArthur at Veracruz cited himself for the Medal of Honor, narrating an action that no one else had witnessed. In Pershing's AEF, where he won several DSCs, it was invariably when he was the senior officer present.[8] To most serving officers, the winning of baubles in those circumstances is beneath dignity.

Patton had something that MacArthur lacked: an almost hypnotic sway over the military crowd. Tens of thousands of men believed they were lucky to be in his army rather than some other. Whether he was as superior as all that is irrelevant. His achievement was the quintessence of generalship. If the men believed it, they must have tried harder, and some died making the extra effort. To them he was indeed the heroic figure.

Ernest Hemingway was the literary counterpart of these men. More astonishing than his great courage and his penchant for risk-seeking was his parading of these qualities, his vainglory.[9] He wore his heart on his sleeve, or more accurately, he wore his complex. In bold company he would go out of his way to impress with his boldness, which was plain boring. Yet in spite of this, his friends loved him. To the end, he was still the adolescent, holding high for the camera a woodchuck, shot dead center.[10]

When we dwell on classical heroism, that of antiquity and mythology, the temptation is to get away from the nature of heroism itself—the exceptional readiness of the singular individual to dare greatly for the sake of someone else because no one else steps forward. Regarding that sort of man, I would have to say that since the time when our ancestors descended from the trees there has been no doing without him. He is identified in the Bible long before the birth of Christ. He had to be present during the Dark Ages, active in the Hundred Years' War and the Thirty Years' War. Things do not finally work together for good; mankind is not saved by some law in nature or because faith works miracles. So I speak of the uncommon courage of common men.

In April 1957, Walter Reed Army Institute of Research conducted a three-day symposium on preventive and social psychiatry. Present at the meeting were psychiatrists serving the armed forces. One speaker was Dr. James S. Tyhurst, the brilliant Canadian who had devoted a quarter century to studying the phenomena of natural disaster in the hemisphere —ravaging floods, holocausts, the explosion from which chain reaction shattered a community.

When Tyhurst spoke on that subject, I sat as critic on his lecture as he did later on mine, which was titled Combat Leadership. Perplexing him more than all else was the nature and motive of the faceless leader. In every great emergency he had analyzed, where constituted authority could not cope with the problem owing to its magnitude or to human frailty, there came out of the crowd four or five persons who took charge and organized the recovery amid danger. Their duty done, once the crisis had passed, these persons returned to the crowd and did not again figure in the forefront of activity. Their disappearance baffled him.[11]

Responding, I said that I saw no mystery. My experience with combat leadership ran parallel. At the breaking point in every company fight covered by my field notebooks (there are more than eight hundred), the situation was saved by the heroic action of two to five individuals previously inconspicuous and unmarked for promotion or citation. If they survived, and if the company was similarly endangered some days later, they again came to the fore. They could continue being repeaters until they died.

But they did not aspire to leadership or seek the role of hero. Out of an instinctive reflex, they moved in and took over because other men had failed, and they were equal to the task. Fear of death was not to them a deterrent, and a medal was not an esteemed prize. The very select company here described included a high count of reservation Indians, Mexicans, and European-born immigrants. They were not antisocial recluses or withdrawn individuals. They enjoyed military comradeship. None was an illiterate, most were in the middle I.Q. range, and only one could be properly described as a scholar.

What might have happened in the situations that Dr. Tyhurst and I described to the meeting had these individuals not been present is beyond speculation. The only reasonable assumption is that the stress would have been prolonged, the cost in life would probably have been higher, the social distress, disorder, and final damage would have been greater.

There is no profit in inquiring if any of these leaders who emerged was inspired by a hero image, though I learned at Pork Chop Hill that fifty-two of the seventy-three prime movers, decorated as such, felt that way about their fathers. What counts is that each in his own way became a hero to others. They were adored by the people closest to them. These people were heartened by their example and rallied around to find greater resources of strength within themselves. Such is the impact of the hero image at point-blank range.

What line of reasoning then may justify its devaluation?

I am well aware of the stentorian outcry against war. Far from being anything new in this world, it is more ancient than the Sphinx or Nineveh and Tyre. If I believed war could be exorcized by indignant noisemaking, I would join the clamor.

What may be new and in some degree different about the present round of discussion is the vehemence of the assertion that the ideals that make it possible for armed forces to hold fast when life is at stake are to be discounted herewith and hereafter. For these are the same ideals that make possible a congenial living together, which is peace. Hence when I regard some of the people who preach against war nowadays, I am reminded of a descriptive passage from Edmund Burke:

"The slightest severity of justice made their flesh creep. The very idea that war existed in the world disturbed their repose. Military glory was no more, with them, than a splendid infamy. Hardly would they hear of self-defence, which they reduced within such bounds, as to leave it no defence at all." [12]

Unthinking pacifism is no more courageous or heroic than is outright militarism. The patience to carry on, holding the head high, is the prerequisite to progress. As C. F. Smith said: "You can pursue the ideal of peace, that is, until there's nothing left but apathy—and then, on the rebound of appeasement, have nothing left but war."[13]

To say that we should have learned better may be to imply that someday we can and will learn not to fight. Fair enough. But not knowing how much time is allowed us for learning, we need heroes no less and hero images the more.

---

[1] *The Mind and Faith of Justice Holmes,* ed. Max Lerner (New York: Modern Library, 1954), pp. 18, 23.

[2] *The Crown of Wild Olive* in *The Works of John Ruskin,* eds. E. T. Cook and Alexander Wedderburn (London: George Allen, 1905), p. 470.

[3] The Associated Press file, Dec. 15, 1972.

[4] *The Crack-Up* (New York: New Directions, 1945).

[5] *A Message to Garcia* (East Aurora, N.Y.: The Roycrofters, 1917).

[6] *Pork Chop Hill* (New York: Wm. Morrow & Co., 1956).

[7] Martin Blumenson, *The Patton Papers, 1885–1940* (Boston: Houghton Mifflin Co., 1972).

[8] D. C. James, *The Years of MacArthur* (Boston: Houghton Mifflin Co., 1970).

[9] *Why Man Takes Chances,* ed. S. Z. Klausner (Garden City, N.Y.: Doubleday & Co., Anchor Books, 1968).

[10] M. H. Sanford, *At the Hemingways: A Family Portrait* (Boston: Little, Brown & Co., Atlantic Monthly Press, 1962).

[11] *Symposium on Preventive and Social Psychiatry* (Washington, D.C.: U.S. Government Printing Office, 1958).

[12] *A Letter to a Noble Lord,* ed. Albert H. Smyth (Boston: Ginn & Co., The Athæneum Press, 1898), p. 41.

[13] T. V. Smith, *Live without Fear* (New York: Signet Key, 1958), p. 18.

# No More Heroes

Ron Dorfman

Ron Dorfman is editor of the *Chicago Journalism Review* and president of the Association of Working Press.

A native of Philadelphia, Mr. Dorfman was graduated in 1963 from the University of Chicago, where he was active in movements for civil rights and university reform, and was an editor of the quarterly *New University Thought,* a progenitor of much of the New Left political thinking of the 1960s. Upon graduation, he became editor of the *Mine-Mill Union,* the organ of the International Union of Mine, Mill and Smelter Workers, in Denver, Colorado. Returning to Chicago the following year, he became a reporter and deskman for the City News Bureau of Chicago and in 1966 joined the staff of *Chicago's American* (now *Chicago Today*). Mr. Dorfman was a professional journalism fellow at Stanford University in 1968 and again returned to Chicago to cover the Democratic National Convention, after which he participated in the founding of the *Chicago Journalism Review.* He lectures widely on journalism before professional and lay audiences and is considered a leader and spokesman of the movement for institutional democracy in news organizations. He has served as a consultant to many media organizations and groups dealing with the media.

Society requires for its internal stability—that is to say, for the preservation of its hierarchical arrangements and the myths that shore them up—a continuing supply of external menaces and the motivation to cope with them. Hence it fights wars, and in fighting wars it creates heroes —or it used to. The system thrives only as it is celebrated, and that requires minstrels willing to compose songs of glory. Without music, the myth fails. When Homer is David Halberstam, Agamemnon becomes General Westmoreland—not a hero, but a bureaucrat. Plato knew what he was doing when he excluded from the *Republic* any poet who told human truths about the gods.

I hold that a free society has neither room for nor need of heroism, because the heroic ideal is rooted in a soil of moral and ideological absolutism, and flowers in an atmosphere of xenophobic ignorance and cruelty. Of course, this is not how acts committed in its name are justified. As John of Salisbury once wrote:

> But what is the office of the duly ordained soldiery? . . . The high praises of God are in their throat, and two-edged swords are in their hands to execute punishment on the nations and rebuke upon the peoples, and to bind their kings in chains and their nobles in links of iron. But to what end? To the end that they may serve madness, vanity, avarice, or their own private self-will? By no means. Rather to the end that they may execute the judgment that is committed to them to execute; wherein each follows not his own will but the deliberate decision of God, the angels, and men, in accordance with equity and the public utility. . . . For soldiers that do these things are "saints," and are the more loyal to their prince in proportion as they more zealously keep the faith of God; and they advance the more successfully the honor of their own valor as they seek the more faithfully in all things the glory of their God.[1]

God, it may be presumed, conveys his decisions to the bishop's office (no madness, vanity, or avarice there!), which in turn relays them to the prince for implementation. It is but a short step to the Crusades.

In his novel *Grendel,* which is based upon the medieval tale of *Beowulf,* John Gardner places a character called the Shaper, who turns up one night in the meadhall of King Hrothgar. The Shaper, who is blind, carries a harp, on which he begins to play:

> As if all by itself, then, the harp made a curious run of sounds, almost words, and then a moment later, arresting as a voice from a hollow tree, the harper began to chant:
>> Lo, we have heard the honor of the Speardanes,
>> nation-kings, in days now gone,
>> how those battle-lords brought themselves glory. . . .
>
> He knew his art. He was king of the Shapers, harpstring scratchers (oakmoss-bearded, inspired by winds). . . . He would sing the glory of Hrothgar's line and gild his wisdom and stir up his men to more daring deeds, for a price.[2]

The monster Grendel knows the history of the world, knows the Shaper's tale is a lie. But who among the thanes can resist the thought of himself being someday sung of in such a manner? And so the hero Unferth seeks out Grendel in his cave beyond the lake of the fire snakes, where at last, exhausted from his pursuit, he collapses on the floor before the creature by whose hand he expects, quite mistakenly, to die.

> "It will be sung year on year and age on age that Unferth went down through the burning lake—" he paused to pant "—and gave his life in battle with the world-rim monster." He let his cheek fall to the floor and lay panting for a long time. . . .
>
> "Go ahead, scoff," he said, petulant. "Except in the life of a hero, the whole world's meaningless. The hero sees values beyond what's possible. That's the nature of a hero. It kills him, of course, ultimately. But it makes the whole struggle of humanity worthwhile."
>
> [Grendel] nodded in the darkness. "And breaks up the boredom," [he] said.[3]

Unferth's speech may be read as a morbid parody of our most recent, and perhaps our last, hero. "Great crises produce great men," John Kennedy wrote as a young man—and proceeded, when he had the power, to produce the crises that would, in the management of them, lend credence to his and the nation's determination to "pay any price, bear any burden" in defending the ramparts of liberty.

The American press played the Shaper to Kennedy's Hrothgar. The president's very language rang with echoes of an epic age, great rolling periods expressing the loftiest motives and the grandest designs. Kennedy wanted to "go forward," wherever that was: the journalists, who enjoyed under Kennedy a proximity to power previously unknown in Washington, thought it would be a good direction, after the aimlessness of the Eisenhower years.

Henry Fairlie, in *The Kennedy Promise: The Politics of Expectation*, expresses bewilderment at the journalists who allowed—indeed, who encouraged—the president and his courtiers to use them as heralds and troubadours. There was Benjamin Bradlee, now executive editor of the *Washington Post*, who fell "flat on his face before this one politician, and before no other," Fairlie says,[4] and "even as careful a reporter as Hugh Sidey"

> . . . *could write of "an awesome presence in that Oval Chamber which was then quiet, cool, sunlit," just as he said of the televised press conferences that they showed "the worried face of a young man with an amusing accent trying desperately to do a job which anybody could tell you was impossible, beyond the bounds of human capacity." It will appear to be beyond the bounds of human capacity only if one expects of politics, not the modest arrangements which are their proper concern, but a superhuman achievement, an inhuman fulfilment.*[5]

Those were the heroic terms on which Kennedy—with the help of the press—defined his task. But it is one thing for a hero to go out with lance and shield and risk his own life for honor, or even the lives of a few vassal heroes who play the same game. It is quite another matter when the hero is armed with atom bombs. They are dangerous men, these heroes, for one never knows what voices they hear, or how "the deliberate decision of God" will be made known to them. It may be that in the modern world the voice of the people is the voice of God, but it is also the case that, for all practical purposes between quadrennial Novembers, the people speak only through their elected leaders.

It is important that our journalists note well and long remember the lessons of the decade that is just past. True, President Nixon clearly and explicitly desires the press to return to its previous role as celebrant of the civil order and protector of the official mythology. But the press has tasted of forbidden fruit.

It has reported from an enemy capital in wartime (Harrison Salisbury, of the *New York Times*, in Hanoi). It has revealed the government's own inner doubts and ambiguities about the war even while that same government publicly preached a bellicose patriotism and sent fifty thousand young men to their deaths (the Pentagon Papers). It has helped to force one president into retirement, and to make politically necessary the withdrawal from Vietnam that another president claims as his own inspiration.

That is heady stuff for an institution that a decade ago sang of Camelot and the new frontiers of freedom. One can only hope that our journalists will continue to live in sinful curiosity, that they will have done with the inflated rhetoric of heroes and the choplogic of the notion that because men *can* be stirred to battle for ideals, they *ought* to be so stirred at every opportunity.

As this is written, the word *hero* appears with increasing frequency in the popular press. It is used to describe the returning prisoners of war. But the term is strangely applied to these men except as it may serve to acknowledge the ordeal of their imprisonment. For almost all of them are field-grade officers who as highly trained professionals, skilled in the operation of complex technical systems, were remote from their antagonists until shot down on bombing runs, and never fought on the naked terms that heroism, as traditionally understood, would seem to require. On the other hand, those who did fight on such terms—the grunts, as they were called, who slogged their way through the jungles of Vietnam under conditions of constant danger and hardship—have returned to another sort of welcome from their countrymen, who regard them with indifference if not outright hostility. It would thus appear that the POWs are heroes not so much because of anything they did as from the fact that many people have an emotional investment in them, and because the government thinks it has a stake in preserving the myth of war's nobility.

Whatever sympathy one may feel for the POWs, was there not a disquieting contrivance in their carefully staged return, wrapped in the flag and a public relations cocoon, their "freely elected" spokesmen (always the senior officer aboard the flight) repeating a litany of thanksgiving to God, country, and commander in chief, their subsequent statements indicating their belief that the press's reporting from Hanoi prolonged their captivity by boosting the enemy's morale?

United Press International has ceased to use the word *enemy* in reference to those with whom the United States is at war. UPI Editor H. L. Stevenson has explained that "the dispatches of an international news agency go to news media in many countries that are uninvolved . . . and 'enemy' would clearly be objectionable to them." He might have added that it is also objectionable to many in this country who opposed its involvement in Vietnam. If "objective journalism" means anything, it means being able to transcend nationalistic visions, through an attitude that is not unpatriotic but nonpatriotic. The journalist's job is to provide information, not inspiration, which will come if it must from the people's own experience of their institutions and leaders.

---

1 *Policraticus,* in *Medieval Reader,* ed. James Bruce Ross and Mary Martin McLaughlin (New York: Viking Press, 1949), p. 90.

2 *Grendel* (New York: Alfred A. Knopf, 1971), pp. 41–42.

3 Ibid., pp. 87–89.

4 *The Kennedy Promise: The Politics of Expectation* (Garden City, N.Y.: Doubleday & Co., 1973), p. 218.

5 Ibid., p. 220.

# Heroism and Fortitude

Josef Pieper

Josef Pieper, who is among the most respected and widely read philosophers
of the present day, was born near Münster, Germany, in 1904. He studied
philosophy, jurisprudence, and sociology at the University of Münster and
also at Berlin. In the course of his career he has at various times worked as
an assistant at a sociological research institute and has been a free-lance
writer. Since 1946 he has been on the faculty of the University of Münster,
where at present he is professor of philosophical anthropology. He has spent
considerable time in the United States, having served as visiting professor
at Notre Dame (1950) and Stanford (1956 and 1962), and has taught also in
India and Japan. In 1967 he was appointed centennial professor at the
University of Toronto, Canada, and in 1968 he received the Aquinas Medal
of the Philosophers' Congress held in New Orleans.

Of Professor Pieper's voluminous writings, a number are available in
English, among them *The Four Cardinal Virtues: Prudence, Justice, Fortitude,
Temperance* (1965); an essay on Plato's *Phaedrus* called *Enthusiasm and
Divine Madness* (1964); *A Guide to Thomas Aquinas* (1962); and, what is
perhaps his best-known work, *Leisure, the Basis of Culture* (1963). These
and other books by Professor Pieper have to date been translated into twelve
languages and have sold more than a million copies.

# I

Can the "hero" be conceived as the principal figure of a great modern novel or a drama? Is "heroism" to be found in the real life of contemporary society? The first of these questions might be answered immediately with a spontaneous "no." Obviously the age of the heroic epic is a thing of the past. Yet we observe that the popular literature of our time abounds in heroes of adventure, is full of hero worship. Even in works produced under totalitarian regimes, glorification of the worker-hero is as evident as the "cult of personality" that supports the political leader. At the same time, we should recall that some of the great poetic works of the past, which we may have regarded as fundamentally simple in their portrayal of the heroic type, are actually sophisticated and multi-faceted in this respect—as Schiller, for one, acknowledged when he observed, in connection with the *Iliad,* that after all it is Patroclus who lies buried and Thersites who returns. And those who in my opinion are the finest modern writers remain greatly interested in heroism, even where they appear, like Virgil, Calderón, and Cervantes before them, to reject it. Perhaps the modern difference is only that we realize a little better than past ages seem to have done how hidden, how endangered, how close to caricature true heroism is, and how easily it can be misconstrued.

# II

The second question, whether heroism is to be found at the present time in real life, requires us to suppose that we know what "true" heroism is. And if we conceive of this mainly or exclusively as exceptional ability, developed through extraordinary effort in any sphere—football, boxing, scientific experimentation, or landing on the moon—or, similarly, if we demand of the "hero" exceptional success, the brilliant fortune of the general, the surgeon, and the politician that captures the popular imagination, then we are saying that the hero is nowadays as much alive as he ever was—for heroism in this sense is not less evident in the contemporary world than it was in previous epochs. But what if we conceive it otherwise? What if we recognize and accept the fact that the essence of true heroism is the virtue of fortitude—that it is through this virtue, indeed, that the "hero" differs from the average man? Because if we do this, we shall have to acknowledge that fortitude cannot be described except through a multitude of ostensibly (or perhaps seemingly) contradictory characteristics. And if we concede that this is so, we shall understand better than we are otherwise likely to do how it is that the image of the hero in the great works of world literature (which is based to a large extent upon the idea of fortitude), far from being as simple as our notion of the "true" hero of real life, is instead bewilderingly ambiguous.

Fortitude is one of the four cardinal virtues; the others are prudence, justice, and temperance. For more than two thousand years these virtues have been looked upon, in the tradition of Western thought, as a kind of four-color spectrum in which the concept of the "good" person fans out. In the formulation of this spectrum, all the original forces of the Occident—the Greeks and the Romans, Judaism and Christianity—participated. This explains why the concepts of "prudence," "justice," and "temperance" are also complex for us, and even contradictory in their elements, quite as much as "fortitude" is, which came into being in the same manner.

### III

The concept of fortitude will be misunderstood if the world-view that underlies it is not clearly comprehended. The German author Bertolt Brecht says: "When I hear that a ship needs heroes for sailors, I ask whether the ship is not too old or moldering away." In his opinion there is something rotten about a state that forces the average man always to be brave. "The world—an abode for heroes: where do we come in then?!" A similar idea appears (as Brecht would not have suspected) fifteen hundred years earlier in the writings of Saint Augustine. Fortitude, Augustine says in *The City of God*,* is a testimony to the existence of evil —by which he means that fortitude is necessary because, in the world, evil is powerful, is even at times a superior force. In view of this, to be brave can be taken to mean that something must be risked whenever the obviously weak offers resistance to evil. And nobody who wishes to be a good human being, and who is unwilling to commit an injustice, can avoid this risk.

Christianity has always been convinced that something really is, as Brecht remarks, rotten in the world. This is not, of course, the same thing as saying that the world is absurd—an existentialist thesis which may seem even more terrible, though curiously enough it causes contemporary man few difficulties. No, here it is stated: the world, along with existence itself, has lost the primordial order; but, like existence, it still remains capable of good and is directed toward it. At the same time, the good is not realized by itself, but requires for that end the effort of an individual who is willing to struggle and if necessary to sacrifice on its behalf. It is simply a liberalistic illusion to believe that one can be consistently just, for example, without having to risk something for it. That is why fortitude is necessary. What is risked, if the occasion arises, may be something less than life itself. It may instead be a question of immediate well-being, of daily tranquillity, possessions, honor, or face-saving. On the other hand, what is required may be the surrender of life, or more exactly, the acceptance of death at another's hands. The martyr is the ultimate symbol of fortitude.

In these terms, of course, fortitude is both a virtue fundamentally required of everyone and the essence of "heroism." And if that is so, then "heroism" is viable in every age, today no less than in the time of Homer or in that of the *Song of the Nibelungs*. But it is not for this reason a quality that is easily identifiable, and it obviously cannot be represented adequately in the unproblematic, radiant figure of the "hero."

## IV

Fortitude is not an absolute ideal, nor is it even foremost among the cardinal virtues. Its realization is linked to several requirements. A brief adage of Saint Ambrose states: "Fortitude must not trust itself." It matters little that we "live *dangerously*," according to Nietzsche's maxim, but rather that we lead a "good" life. For this the virtue of prudence is the first necessity. That is to say, we must be able to recognize the elements of life as they really are and to translate this recognition into resolution and action. Otherwise, because the fearful is encountered as a stark reality in the world, we may be fearless in a manner that should not be confused with true fortitude—as, for example, when we make a false evaluation of danger, or when we are reckless from an inability to love anything or anyone ("Fear is fleeing love," says Saint Augustine). Sigmund Freud's assertion that most heroism stems from an instinctive conviction that "Nothing can happen to *me*" is true in a sense that possibly he did not perceive—the deep sense in which it is seen that for one who loves good, death cannot be entirely evil (as Socrates, along with Saint Paul, realized and affirmed).

Another requirement of true fortitude is justice. The fortitude of a criminal is a misconception; there are no criminal heroes. Our generation is aware that the fruits of fortitude can be corrupted by injustice, chiefly by the injustice of political power. We have come to know firsthand the truth of the old adage: "The praise of fortitude is contingent upon justice." When I used this in the second year of National Socialist tyranny (1934) as the motto of my short book, *On the Meaning of Fortitude*, my friends immediately recognized its dangerous implications; and these were probably noticed as well by others who were less kindly disposed toward me.

---

* *GBWW*, Vol. 18, pp. 129–618.

## V

It has been said that the hero is a figure whose proper element is war. And it is precisely on this point that the complexity of the relationship between heroism and fortitude comes to the fore most dramatically. On the one hand, there may be agreement that fortitude presupposes the conflict of hostile forces; it manifests itself in combat, though *combat* does not necessarily mean *war*. Even where it does mean war, it does not necessarily mean enthusiastic war. There is a statement by Thomas Aquinas, as there is one by Aristotle, to the effect that perhaps the better soldiers are those who are less brave. Here the word *perhaps* is to be underlined, for it is bravery and aggressiveness that distinguish the born soldier. But that is something different. The surrender of one's life, which can be demanded of a soldier in the just defense of the community, can scarcely be expected without the moral virtue of fortitude.

On the other hand, we are more apt to perceive and honor the hero in the figure of conqueror than in one who merely suffers. And since fortitude means precisely to endure "wounds" incurred on behalf of justice (from loss of reputation or well-being to imprisonment or bodily harm), we are really looking, when we contemplate someone who has manifested this virtue, at the antithesis of the "conqueror." Such a person does not vanquish, he sacrifices. In the ultimate test of fortitude, which is martyrdom, there is absolutely nothing of the victorious, though this characteristic is essential to our more usual conception of the hero as conqueror. Nor is there any supposition that fortitude or heroism will be spoken of in true cases of martyrdom. If such things are discussed, it is almost a sure sign that no instance of genuine fortitude has occurred. When it comes to a pornographic novel, which may be hailed as "daring" or "bold," the author in reality risks nothing. Far more courage and perhaps genuine fortitude is required to call such a product repugnant, or to say in public that purity is a fundamental element of human dignity. Talk of the "martyr" always occurs *post festum*. In the act of fortitude itself, such a person does not appear to be a martyr but is rather the accused, the prisoner, the crank, or the lone wolf, abandoned and ridiculed; above all, he proves himself to be a mute. Perhaps doubt even penetrates his own heart, so that fortitude itself may be in question, leaving him to speculate whether he is really *der Dumme* (the "dumb" one) in the end.

Thus fortitude is, according to its very nature, *not* the virtue of the stronger but instead that of the seemingly vanquished. Accordingly, it can almost be said that we are dealing with a falsehood in the prevailing notion of the "hero," which veils and perverts the essential qualities of genuine fortitude. It should be remembered that in the eyes of the ancients the decisive criterion for fortitude consisted primarily in steadfastness and not in attacking.

To be sure, the coin must be turned over again so that its reverse side is displayed. The reverse side is that this mortal steadfastness of the martyr has always been *understood* as a victory and celebrated as such, not only from the Christian standpoint but also from that of Plato's Socrates. "We conquer while we are being slain," wrote Tertullian. Who was ultimately the victor: the boasting commandant of Auschwitz or the Polish Franciscan father Maximilian Kolbe, who, in order to save a fellow man, went into the starvation bunker and perished miserably there? In spite of everything the martyr is truly a "hero," and so is every unimposing or unknown individual who risks his life for the sake of truth and good, whether in the pointedly dramatic act of martyrdom or in lifelong devotion—in acquiescence to the absolute will of God at the cost of one's own worldly comfort. The great Santa Teresa of Ávila writes in her autobiography that an imperfect human being needs greater fortitude to travel the path of perfection than to take martyrdom upon himself in a brief moment. Perhaps this statement, based upon life experience, renders a little more plausible the term *heroic* virtue, which is the signum of a hallowed life in the Christian tradition.

## VI

From time immemorial, heroism has been looked upon as inseparable from honor and glory; the hero is, by the same token, always the celebrated, the one distinguished by universal acclaim. It is not customary to reduce this stature even if he seeks self-recognition and accomplishes his deeds for that reason. Strangely enough, the great teachers of Christianity have regarded the virtue of fortitude in much the same way, designating as one of its fundamental elements *magnanimitas,* which seeks high honor above all else and makes itself worthy of such. Is this in keeping with the conception of that virtue, the highest act of which is supposed to be martyrdom before the triumphant force of evil? It is consistent with that conception under *one* condition, namely, that one is capable of realizing the idea of *gloria,* which the ancients defined as *clara cum laude notitia* and by which they meant the state of "becoming acknowledged publicly," the attainment of recognition through God himself. This also means the infallibly true sanction by the Sovereign of the world who, in the presence of the whole of creation, at once declares and effectuates that it is "glorious" to be what one is.

I fear that whoever, for whatever reason, is incapable of accepting this dimension of reality—the life beyond death—will have to be on his guard against the danger of being fascinated by a pseudo-hero borne on the acclaim of the entire world. From the time of John at Patmos to that of Wladimir Solowjew, Christendom has held a certain idea about the end of the world. This idea implies that in the final age we must be prepared for a figure who, though the ultimate personification of evil, will be a hero of a bewitching splendor hitherto unknown to all of mankind: the Antichrist. His almost irresistible allure and universal fame will overshadow all other false heroes of history, while his global tyranny will force true fortitude into the most merciless of trials. It will further render totally unrecognizable this fortitude, the essence of all genuine heroism— the virtue of martyrs.

*     *     *     *     *

I cannot see why this conception of heroism, both the true and the false, should lose even an iota of viability in the present age or in the future.

# Heroes in Black and White

Joy Gould Boyum

Joy Gould Boyum is professor of English education at New York University. Born in New York City in 1934, she graduated from Barnard College in 1955 (with a year at the University of Michigan and a summer at Harvard) and took her M.A. (1957) and her Ph.D. (1962) from New York University. Her chief professional interest is teacher education, and her current course offerings include one intended primarily for teachers of secondary schools in which she undertakes to contrast films and the literary sources from which they are drawn. Besides a weekly column "On Film" for the *Wall Street Journal,* she has published articles on film, literature, and television for professional journals, and she contributed the article on motion pictures for the 1973 *World Book Year Book*. She is coauthor, with Adrienne Scott, of a text, *Film as Film: Critical Responses to Film Art* (1971). Married in 1960 to Asmund Boyum, she has two children, David and Ingrid.

To say that it is no longer possible to believe in the great man, the man distinguished by his special excellence—in, that is, the traditional hero of literature, legend, and history—may be only to admit, somewhat regretfully, to our cultural age. Heroes, we can suppose, are the stuff that youth is made of, and the passing of youth is painful to contemplate, perhaps especially so in our time. It is not surprising that we are unhappy at the thought, if the thought is one we happen to have, that as a society we have grown up, are now skeptical of ideals, and certainly of the heroic ideal, in the manner of those who have reached their middle years.

Of course, a peculiar set of historical circumstances has hastened what seems to have been an aging process over the course of the century in which we live. Within thirty years of each other two devastating wars have occurred, producing disillusionment and a crisis in values. Particularly has this been so with respect to the heroes, statesmen as well as soldiers, whose reputations were created by those conflicts and then were forgotten or brought down. Many of the great names of the first World War had become pathetic or villainous, so far as they were remembered at all, when the second one began, and in the interval since that one ended grave doubts have been expressed as to the integrity and even the competence of many of its own leaders—doubts that have made it hard to look on any of the contemporary forms of human greatness without distrust.

On top of this has come the exponential growth in this century of science and technology. The paradox of such growth is that while it seems to affirm the largest dreams of human achievement, at the same time it has worked to reduce human stature. Earlier, the comprehensive structure of biology had brought man down from something created in the image of God to a place among the animals. Then physics and astronomy reduced him to a speck in the vastness of the universe. Still later, instructed in psychology, he came to doubt his moral being. Now, caught as he is in the great web of the electronic media, his freedom seems impossible, a distrust of himself and all his institutions almost imperative. For our technology has succeeded in democratizing *angst,* once the special privilege of artists and thinkers. Television, film, and radio, processing the cultural materials of the past and present, making palatable for mass consumption great art and great ideas, have informed the self-satisfied *homme moyen* of what the *élite* had thought it alone was able to perceive: that the human condition is absurd, that man is alienated and miserable. Popularizing contemporary philosophy and literature, the mass media have made "hope" and "meaning" seem naïve terms; domesticating war they have made "courage" and "glory" seem incredible fictions; peddling statesmen, and marketing politics, they have made "honor" and "dignity" into sick jokes. And if the greatness of man has come to seem an illusion, how can there be great men? In our time the star system seems finished, both in the movies and in real life.

It may seem frivolous to mention the movies in connection with "the great ideas today," but movies can in fact tell us a good deal about the status of ideas in our culture. For even in their economic decline, movies remain both our most popular art form and our most telling social barometer. We are, after all, the media's children, and movies depend for their life on their sensitivity to our values and attitudes. Looking for immediate returns on their very large investments, needing popularity and committed to what is topical, they will rarely risk exploring truly innovative ideas. Movies tend, instead, to adopt attitudes in the public mind that have already been put to the test of acceptability. Movies will, of course, widen the audience for whatever viewpoint they express, which they emphasize and perhaps even clarify, but it is the proven idea they are after, just as much as they seek the proven property.

Thus, in the period of the two great wars, and in the century's youth and Hollywood's own, the movies overwhelmed us with heroic men and heroic actions. And the range of the special skills dramatized for us was extraordinary. On a single Saturday afternoon, we could see one man test his valor and strength in a struggle with a crocodile while another proved his superior mettle merely through ratiocination. The following week we might encounter the mighty modern warrior, outnumbered but steadfast on his lonely Pacific isle, and featured with him the man of faith whose wisdom and patience brought straying humans back to the straight and narrow. But our most pervasive fictional heroes at that time were our American knights errant, lone and courageous creatures righting wrongs in crowded metropolises and in wide open spaces: the private eye and the gunfighter. If today the hero no longer persists in these particular guises, that is sign enough, for a good many of us, that the heroic ideal has vanished.

True, we seem unable to let go of it completely. If that had happened, films would simply ignore the traditional hero—as some of them do anyway, having gone the way of modern literature, often by borrowing from it. Such films of the late sixties and early seventies as *M\*A\*S\*H, Carnal Knowledge,* and *A Clockwork Orange* offer us that by now familiar anti-heroic type, the victim, in his various guises: the schlemiel, the delinquent, the disaffiliate, the self-destroyer. But for the most part, and in those genres most deeply committed in the past to the portrayal of heroic action, the traditional hero has remained with us—if only to the end of being unmasked. This is indeed the chief intent of westerns in the new style, sometimes (and not insignificantly) called "adult." These films take a representative figure, quite frequently a historical hero who has often been pictured in films (Wyatt Earp, for instance, or Doc Holliday, or General Custer), and then pierce through his myth to what purports to be reality. Once in this real world, we find the formerly heroic figure's motivations to be impure, his skill ordinary, his morality ambiguous. But we do not debunk with unalloyed delight. Such realism is somehow deeply unwelcome, as John Huston, for one, has recognized with his current film, *The Life and Times of Judge Roy Bean.* "West of the Pecos, there was no law, no order," a title reads at the outset of this comic tall tale. "Maybe that isn't the way it was, but the way it should have been." In putting it that way, we are affirming our lost dreams, lamenting our lost youth, in which heroes had a place.

Our attitude reveals itself in many recent works, among them Sam Peckinpah's much revered *The Wild Bunch,* a 1969 release that can serve us well as an example of the new-style western and of its ambiguous view of the hero. From one angle of vision, we can say the film has no heroes, only protagonists—specifically, a gang of outlaws. And they are not outlaws of any familiar breed: not rebels against their fate or badmen who will either reform or give up their lives with generosity to pay for past sins. They lack moral necessity of any kind, just as they lack relevance. The time is 1913, and while these men ride on horseback, other men are driving automobiles. Most significantly, they are all middle-aged, aware of their mortality and their lack of purpose. They are weathered and weary Sisyphuses, tied to a boulder of violence. And partly because there is no moral center anywhere in their world, neither in the bounty hunters who pursue them, nor in the Mexican rebels who hire them, nor in the townspeople slaughtered by their crossfire (the film has begun with a sequence where we see a group of children take delight in watching ants devour a scorpion), our sympathies go out to them. We bemoan with them the passing of time that has drained their energy and carried away opportunities for heroic action. At one point in the film the gang's leader (a very paunchy William Holden, whom we remember in the youthful image of a very golden boy) cannot quite make it up on his horse, and our bones ache with his.

Perhaps even more direct in its exposure of the heroic ideal and its simultaneous romantic yearnings is another western released in 1969, George Roy Hill's highly successful *Butch Cassidy and the Sundance Kid.* Again, the setting is the turn of the century; again, the protagonists are outlaws of dubious morality; again, they are out-of-date; and again, they engage our sympathies largely because of their obsolescence. But this time the protagonists are younger men in fact and very much younger in fantasy. They play, and charmingly, on bicycles, in their bedrooms, and of course at the game of banditry. But it is the harmful fun of men who won't put away childish things, and because these two are no more skillful and no more brave than other men, they are bound sooner or later to be losers. And they know it, too, being self-conscious to the point where they recognize their own value as emblems of roguish youth. One day they enter a movie theater, and we watch with them a film within a film where facsimiles of themselves are shown upon the screen. *There* is the heroic myth in all its glorious danger; here in the audience is safe, mundane reality. With *Butch Cassidy and the Sundance Kid* we find ourselves in the ironic mode, where ideals and heroic actions generally have little place.

This is the mode, of course, of James Bond, who in our politicized, international age is appropriately the private eye *cum* secret agent, saving the entire Western world rather than mere damsels in distress, and who in his enormous popularity tells us all we need to know about current attitudes toward this variety of hero. A conscious ironist, Bond never really demands that we suspend our disbelief before his astounding feats and larger-than-life adversaries. Instead, he presents himself to us as a mock hero, a superhuman blend of the exquisite taste and stunning intelligence of a Sherlock Holmes with the supercharged sexiness and raw physical toughness of a Sam Spade. But Bond's creators are aware that we are unwilling skeptics and provide him with sufficient glamor so that he is never completely comic, with sufficient danger so that his actions are never totally trivial. With Bond, in other words, we enjoy the pleasures of the double vision. We can have our hero, and dismiss him, too.

Such contradictory impulses pervade our attitudes toward the hero. Still, there seem to be some among us who hold more tenaciously than others to faith in the heroic ideal: the implied audiences for that new genre, the black movie, and especially its subgenres, the black western and the black crime melodrama. Although such representative films as *The Legend of Nigger Charley* and *Shaft* are marked by a tongue-in-cheek quality, they do present us with unambiguously heroic types, men superior to other men in their physical prowess and often in their moral fiber as well. Their scales tipped on the side of belief in this figure, these films have only such irony as can be directed at the hero's environment, not the kind that points at the hero himself. His world may be undependable, his opponents may invite our laughter, he may have a sidekick for comic relief, but the hero in his superstrength is reminiscent of the heroes of our youth.

And yet the black hero is different, too, from the heroic type of which he reminds us. As a black gunfighter, Nigger Charley has a more clearly defined social identity than, say, the Lone Ranger, and a less patronizing attitude toward the people he serves. The old-style hero of a thousand westerns was a man who stood outside society, a man without class or rank. Perhaps this was American democracy's way of embodying the aristocratic spirit that lay in the European background of the heroic tradition. In any case, the hero of the old western was never one with those he served. The black hero, on the contrary, stands strongly rooted in a particular milieu, where he has been brutally victimized before rising to heroic stature. His daring deeds thus inevitably affect his own well-being and not merely (as in the case of the Lone Ranger) the fortunes of those he rescues. Nigger Charley is at the outset of his story a slave, driven to rebellion and superhuman feats by the cruel mistreatment of his white owners. Here, as in most black films, evil is situated in white society, goodness in black. In these modern morality plays, hero and villain have exchanged color imagery—and with what seems an ever growing consistency. Where private eye John Shaft in his first screen appearance fought black villains from his Greenwich Village base, in his subsequent appearance (in *Shaft's Big Score*), he was situated in Harlem and brought white hoodlums down to defeat.*

Whatever else one can say about these black films—that they are really exploitative, since they are made, by and large, by whites, or that they are therapeutic for the angry audiences who attend them—their huge box-office returns make clear that they are striking a responsive chord among the black population and that here the heroic ideal has a viability it lacks in the mainstream. Of course, to see the heroic ideal as still vivid within black films is, in a sense, to see these films as other than "adult" and to risk the offense of reviving the stereotype of the black man as child. But it is a risk one must take, since black culture is, in fact, in America much younger than white. It is only now that blacks have begun to assume mastery over their lives; it is only now that they have been able to work toward a positive self-identity; and it is only now that the media have begun to address them. In this process, blacks cannot afford the luxury (if that is what it is) of existential despair, of distrust in possibility, of a dismissal of hope. They must assert the vigorous optimism of the youthful imagination—even at the expense of realism and complexity. They need an instant imagery of inspirational powerful figures. In other words, they cannot yet relinquish the hero and the heroic ideal.

---

* This same racial antagonism emerges from those black films that would seem to be reviving still another heroic type traditional to American movies: the gangster hero. In *Super Fly*, for example, the central character is a cocaine pusher who sells his wares to whites. *The Godfather* notwithstanding, such a belief in the gangster hero does not seem to be reasserting itself elsewhere. In any case, *The Godfather*, with its painstaking recreation of the forties and its emphasis on time past, seems once again an exercise in nostalgia rather than a reaffirmation of an ideal. Moreover, the implication is that Don Vito's heirs will in the present generation be absorbed by mainstream society and will become indistinct from other organization men. They will then have lost the absolute requisite for heroism: individuality.

# The Hero as a World Figure

Sidney Hook

Sidney Hook was born in 1902 in New York City. He attended the city's public schools and took his degree at the College of the City of New York, where he studied under Morris R. Cohen. In 1926 he received his master's degree and in 1927 his doctorate in philosophy from Columbia University, working chiefly with John Dewey and F. J. E. Woodbridge. Afterward he joined the philosophy faculty at New York University, where he became a full professor in 1939 (he is now professor emeritus) and where he was subsequently head of the philosophy department. He was also for many years on the faculty of the New School for Social Research in New York. He is the author of *The Metaphysics of Pragmatism* (1927), *From Hegel to Marx* (1936), *John Dewey: An Intellectual Portrait* (1939), *The Hero in History* (1943), and *Education for Modern Man* (1946), among other works. The recipient of numerous academic awards and honors, he has been president of the American Philosophical Association (Eastern Division, 1959–60) and has been elected to the American Academy of Arts and Sciences and the American Academy of Education. Recently appointed by the White House to the Council of the National Endowment for the Humanities, Professor Hook is currently a senior research fellow at the Hoover Institution on War, Revolution and Peace, Stanford, California.

Judging by the popular mood, we are living in an age of the anti-heroic. This reflects a growing disenchantment with leading figures in the political life of the nation, past and present. It has also been fed by certain currents in the climate of intellectual opinion. Skepticism and moral relativism in judgments about the past have combined with an emerging moral absolutism regarding the present to diminish the stature of heroes.

In addition, the diffusion of psychoanalytical approaches in historical studies has led to a sophisticated debunking of the proclaimed ideals and motives of the great men of the past. It has become fashionable to disregard the "good reasons" offered in explanation of human behavior in a quest for the "real reasons" behind them. These invariably turn out to be more self-regarding and less flattering to the principals in historical actions of importance. Once reasons are dismissed as "rationalizations," scholars spend little time in seeking and weighing the *grounds* of human conduct. They focus on laying bare the *causes* or springs of human action, psychological or biological, that make all men akin. In the vocabulary of these reductive sciences there is no room for terms like *great* or *small,* some would even say for terms like *sane* or *insane.* It is not surprising, therefore, that the dimensions of the giants of the past, once the mists of legend are dissipated, dwindle in the ever lengthening historical perspective from which we survey them.

At the same time, vehement political moralists without a sense of historical perspective have also contributed to the decay not only of hero-worship but of belief in heroes. I refer here to the harsh judgment of self-righteous absolutists for whom the founding fathers and philosopher-statesmen of the American republic are primarily "racist slaveholders," and who regard the compassionate Lincoln as an opportunist and hypocrite because of his views on slavery. The heroes of the counterculture and the so-called New Left, especially on American campuses, are more likely to be drawn from third world countries than from their own. And they are invoked not because of the existence of any exemplary attributes and personality traits for which a convincing case can be made but as symbols of resistance to oppression. In the judgment of this counterculture the national temple has been emptied of its altars. Only the Hall of Fame remains—and to be famous is obviously not the same as to be heroic.

Perhaps of greater influence in bringing about the current acceptance of a "demythology" of the heroic in history is the increasing mechanization and computerization of industrial society. Despite the clamor for participatory democracy, and notwithstanding the genuine growth in forms of shared power, there is widespread testimony to a pervasive cultural and political malaise. Complaints abound on all levels of a sense of frustration in shaping the patterns of personal life, and especially of social life. As the power of man collectively to control things becomes more manifest, the more numerous seem the confessions of a mood of personal helplessness before massive anonymous forces whose presence dwarfs the individual's role. Indignant or acquiescent, he stands overwhelmed by the happenings that engulf him. Just as no individual created the Industrial Revolution and no individual, however powerful politically, could have prevented it, so seemingly no one person in our time can initiate or abort the successive technological revolutions that accelerate the dizzying pace of social change.

Nonetheless, there is an instructive paradox in the judgments of the estranged and helpless. Eloquent in their lamentations on the passing of effective human initiatives, at the same time they are aware and alarmed that in our world of baffling complexity the decisions of a few strategically situated men may destroy civilized society. Ours is the age in which the sudden death of cultures at the hands of men rather than nature is possible. The command of Richard Nixon or Leonid Brezhnev to trigger nuclear weapons could produce the holocaust of holocausts. Deplore it as one will, the fact remains that we still live in a world in which the acts or failures to act of some individuals can have more momentous consequences than was the case with any heroic figure of the past. If a nuclear Pearl Harbor were genuinely threatened by a first strike from an enemy power and averted by a response that still left the free world viable, the president responsible for the decision would be more fervently acclaimed than President Kennedy was at the time of the Cuban missile crisis or than Woodrow Wilson was when he first reached Europe at the close of the first World War with the unsullied Fourteen Points. In the absence of effective world government holding a monopoly of all weapons, the existence of hostile nuclear powers creates a condition in which no matter how executive power is curbed or shared, the decision of one person might determine the destiny of mankind. This is an unprecedented situation in human history.

There are other less awesome and dramatic contexts in which the activity or leadership of one man or woman may be responsible for profound changes. One thinks of the work of Ralph Nader, still unfinished, who has succeeded in focusing the attention of the country on the needs and rights of the consumer to a degree not hitherto achieved. Or the public lobby organized by John Gardner. Prosaic these undertakings may be, but they have a revolutionary potential. Despite the widespread complaint about the powerlessness of the individual, it is risky to discount with finality what individuals can succeed in doing in advance of their effort. To be sure, in most of the situations in which individuals like Nader and Gardner have succeeded in initiating great changes, one may predict that sooner or later someone else would have appeared on the scene and played a similar role. But one cannot reasonably make such a prediction in the fateful case where a national leader is confronted by a threat that requires a quick decision between the alternatives of surrender or war. For what follows on either choice—and even if none is made—may be irreversible.

The demythologizing of the hero is facilitated by a recurrent tendency to conceive of the hero in moral terms. The result is that it appears almost a contradiction in terms to think of the hero as wicked or cruel. Yet almost every great figure in history from Alexander to Napoleon, from Pericles to Bismarck and Churchill, has been regarded by some historian or defeated opponent, or from some variant cultural perspective, as morally monstrous. At the time of the Cuban missile crisis, Bertrand Russell characterized President Kennedy as "the most wicked man in history," worse than Hitler and Stalin, for risking war with the Soviet Union. And this despite the fact that Russell himself previously had urged that atomic war be unleashed against the Soviet Union if it refused to accept the Baruch-Acheson-Lilienthal proposals to internationalize all sources of atomic power.

Moral judgments are indeed relevant to any adequate historical narrative. But whether such judgments are positive or negative has no bearing on an analysis of the actual consequences of the work and life of historical figures. Morally, one man's hero is another man's villain. It is not likely that in the eyes of the defeated Southern Confederates Lincoln had the same heroic stature as he did in the eyes of many Northern Unionists. This does not affect the assessment of the actual consequences of the Emancipation Proclamation, of dubious constitutional validity at the time, on the outcome of the war.

Since history is written by the survivors, it is safe to say that it will be their moral judgments that determine who is acclaimed as a hero and who is not. But the question "If this particular man or woman had not been on the scene or had not done such and such, would the ensuing history have been substantially different from what actually occurred?" is not one that depends for a warranted answer on how we grade the historical actor morally. If the question is answerable in principle—and sometimes we do not know enough to answer it at all—the answer is of the same order as answers to questions like these: What would have probably happened to X if his car had not been stopped by the guardrail when it skidded on the icy mountain pass? If Columbus's ships had foundered, would the New World have been discovered anyhow? If Oswald, Kennedy's assassin, had missed, would Johnson have been president of the United States?

Unless the concept of the hero is interpreted at least for historical purposes in an ethically neutral way, we shall never escape confusing ambiguities in usage. Ambiguities in the conception of the hero enrich folklore and literature, and it would make one an unimaginative pedant to insist upon precision and consistency in such contexts. For the understanding of history, however, some semantic clarification and economy are required if agreement is to be reached, especially on what is true or false in causal attributions to historical agents.

There is no one moral or even psychological trait that is uniformly present in the conceptions of historical greatness or heroism in legend, folklore, or literature, classic or popular. If the hero is conceived as possessing exemplary courage, we people the historical stage with too many characters. And we would shrink back in horror from some who would emerge into the light. No one can deny that the terrorists of the Palestinian Black September group displayed great courage and daring in performing their frightful deeds at the Munich Olympiad. But who except some fanatical Arab groups would regard them, no less refer to them, as heroes? Or shall we conceive of the hero as one who has withstood prolonged suffering or who has a vocation for martyrdom? Once more we shall find heroes multiplied beyond necessity, and some of them rejected by latter-day Nietzscheans. The hero is not necessarily a victor. Preeminence of any kind, even in defeat, may be a sufficient condition for achieving heroic status among some national or religious or ideological group. But because of the plurality and conflicts among such groups, there are no universal heroes.

Whatever moral or psychological assessment is made of the personalities of Alexander, Caesar, Paul (who brought Christianity to the Gentile world), Mohammed, Constantine, Luther, Henry VIII, Cromwell, Peter of Russia, Catherine II, Napoleon, Lincoln, Wilson (who kept the United States out of the first World War and then brought her in), Lenin, Stalin, Hitler, and Churchill, there is one clear sense in which they are among the great men and women of history. What makes them great? The fact that if they had not lived when they did or acted as they did, the history of their countries and the history of the world, to the extent that the histories are intertwined, would have been profoundly different. This does not entail an acceptance of the Carlylean view, because other large factors enter into historical outcomes. But it is incompatible with the theological determinism of Augustine and Tolstoy, with the organic determinism of Hegel and Spengler, and with most varieties of Marxism.

The basic and oft-repeated objection to this approach to the heroic in history is that it assumes it is possible to give intelligible and confirmable answers to "if" questions or to hypotheticals contrary to fact. If we bear in mind that the operative word is *possible,* the assumption is correct. It is often possible, but rarely easy. If causal relations between events were logical relations, as they are in the Hegelian world view, or if the web of human affairs was of such spectacular complexity that isolable causal chains could not be discerned, then answers could not possibly be made one way or the other. But the world is not so constituted.

In an alliterative aside in one of his stories, Herman Melville warns the reader, "But the might-have-been is but a boggy ground to build on." Granted. The admission, however, is not fatal. For unless we can discourse validly about the would-have-beens and might-have-beens, we cannot rightfully claim to understand the whys or the causes of anything that happens in human life. Human behavior on the streets, in the home, in the courts, in the commercial marts would be completely unintelligible. The logical analysis both of hypotheticals which are contrary to fact, as of their speculative causes, may be difficult. Nonetheless, common sense and common practice—indeed, human survival—depend upon our awareness of such things. We stake our lives on them every moment of the day. "You might have been (or would have been) hurt if you had not stepped out of the path of the speeding car" is an expression that no sane man would disregard as meaningless or as not worth his consideration.

Does any informed person seriously believe that it makes no difference to the pattern of events who stands at the levers of power in our world? Whatever one may believe about the past, today, because of the destructive potentials of military technology, it would border on the frivolous to affirm such a proposition. Even so, if we stopped here our analysis would be incomplete. Grant that who stands where would make a great difference. By itself this would make some individuals *eventful* but not necessarily *event-making*. By recognizing the distinction between the eventful and the event-making man we can do justice to some of the elements associated with traditional conceptions of the heroic.

The eventful man is one who affects history in virtue primarily of the position he occupies. Confronted by a fateful alternative, he may reach a world-shaping decision, but the alternative that presents itself to him is not of his own making. The ideal type of the eventful man would be Harry Truman faced with the question whether to drop the atomic bomb or risk millions of casualties on both sides storming the beaches of Japan. The event-making man is one who by extraordinary traits of character or intelligence or some other facet of personality has largely shaped the alternatives between which he must choose, alternatives that but for him would probably not have emerged. The role of Lenin in the Russian October Revolution is a paradigm case. An event-making man may also be someone who by virtue of the strength of personality or preeminent talents reverses the direction of social change against great odds, and overcomes the heavy inertia of institutions and mores. Peter the Great or Mustafa Kemal would be instances in point.

Elsewhere I have elaborated this distinction (*The Hero in History: A Study in Limitation and Possibility*. New York: John Day, 1943), and have characterized the eventful man in terms of the legendary figure of the little Dutch boy whose finger in the dike saved the town. He was a hero by happenstance; almost any little Dutch boy could have plugged the hole. It is in this special sense that one can say that some men have greatness thrust upon them. No man is born great. But the event-making man is one who acquires greatness. If we expand the connotation of the heroic to include the demonic, the event-making man comes closest to the more poetic and picturesque classic views of the hero.

The heroes of our time, because of the cumulative consequences of the scientific-technological revolutions, and because of the extension of the democratic political process, are more likely to be eventful men and women than event-making ones. In the days of political absolutism there were greater areas for creative maneuvers, like those available to Henry VIII, who played a major role in redetermining the religious and cultural destiny of England, than in the decade of Edward VIII. Even if the latter had possessed the forceful personality of the former, he would have been elbowed off the throne.

Those who contend that the direction of historical and social change is so completely determined by economic forces that there are no momentous alternatives of development must of necessity deny the presence of eventful men in history. On this view, any man in any place of strategic command would have acted like any other. In fact, the very significance of the notion of strategic command becomes problematic. We have seen, however, that this is incompatible with the recognition that in our historical epoch, the decision a commander in chief of a nuclear power may have to make within hours, or even less, may literally make all the difference in the world.

The moral of this analysis is that the anti-heroic mood of our age may result in mediocre leadership just at a time when we need at the helm of affairs men of great intelligence, compassion, imagination, and moral courage—individuals who will not panic in crises, who can see the human being in the enemy and therefore realize that not all things are permissible. At the same time they should know that mere survival cannot be an absolute end in itself save at the cost of all the moral goods and values that make life worth living.

The great and unsolved problem of all democracies is to develop an enlightened leadership through mechanisms of popular control which, unfortunately, lend themselves to manipulation by the unenlightened. One may argue that the character of presidential leadership in the United States since the administration of Woodrow Wilson is a not altogether unplausible argument for the wisdom of the Greek system of election by lot. But inasmuch as the latter was a disastrous failure, it is obviously not good enough. The remedy for unenlightened leadership in a democracy is not less democracy, as totalitarians from Plato to Santayana have taught, but a more enlightened citizenship, the never ending task of enlightened education.

69

# Heroes for an Ordinary World

Chaim Potok

Chaim Potok was born in New York City in 1929. He graduated from Yeshiva
University and the Jewish Theological Seminary of America, was ordained
as a rabbi, and earned his Ph.D. in philosophy from the University of Penn-
sylvania. He entered the U.S. Army as a chaplain and was in Korea sixteen
months with a frontline medical battalion and a combat engineer battalion.
In 1967 he published the first of three novels he has written to date, called
*The Chosen,* which dealt with imagined possibilities of his orthodox background and upbringing, and which received the Edward Lewis Wallant Memo-
rial Award. A second novel, *The Promise,* published in 1969, drew upon the
same materials, and was given the Athenaeum award. His most recent novel,
*My Name Is Asher Lev,* was published in 1972. The author also of various
articles and a number of short stories, he has been editor of the Jewish Publication Society since 1965. He is married, with three children, and lives in
Philadelphia.

When a system of values becomes so charged with vitality that people are willing to live by it and die for it, heroic figures are born. Heroes are the inevitable concomitant of a system of value and thought that has been embraced by an aggregate of men. An idea gone public produces heroes as dividends.

Heroes and the thought system in which they are embedded stand in a complementary relationship to one another: the former is the action aspect of the latter. Values and ideas that do not give rise to heroes remain abstract exercises of the mind; heroes not embedded in a system of values and ideas resemble the vacuous inhabitants of comic strips.

Heroes are often the result of man's need to salve his battered conscience. An adopted value system that is more mouthed than lived is fruitful in the production of heroic figures. Such figures help bridge the fetid gap between gritty reality and professed ideals. The Trojan War was probably an ugly trade war, but it has come down to us as a heroic response to an ungallant abduction.

In the childhood of human culture, heroes answered man's psychological need for security, his political and social needs for leadership, and his moral need to strive for perfection in thought and deed. Above all, they answered man's fundamental need to comprehend and come to terms with the world around him. Such heroes were mythic gods, demigods, extraordinary sacred mortals, or historic or fictive ordinary mortals caught up in extraordinary situations.

Now we have demythologized the sacred literature of the past with our new skills at reading and comprehending ancient texts; we have deromanticized the great personalities of the past with our new understanding of the dark motives underlying human behavior; we have leveled the world views of the past with our acquired knowledge of parallel and primitive societies; we have deflated distant heroes and epochs with our new historiographic methodologies. Those who have not yet lost the heroes of their youth are able to live on in the childhood era of civilization. Those who have lost their heroes to the new knowledge look back upon the wreckage and feel not a little bereaved.

Let us see which heroes are alive and which are dead.

There are three kinds of heroes, each dwelling in the different worlds of communication men have used when contemplating or talking to one another about the world around them. There are the heroes of myths, of sagas, and of folktales.

Myths are dim visions of reality—crude constructs or models—perceived by prescientific and prephilosophical man as being the true and fixed nature of things underlying the ever changing world that surrounded him. The heroes of myths are gods, demigods, and other supernatural beings. Myths are ritualized public models that claim to impart truths grounded in knowledge or intuitive awareness about the origin and nature of the universe and man. They are the precursors of science, philosophy, and theology.

Sagas are accounts of true past events—a long journey, a protracted battle, a great victory—that have fixed themselves upon the imagination of an aggregate of men. The heroes of ancient sagas are kings, warriors, and the like, figures who have lived in the arena of history. At the heart of each saga is truth, though the repeated telling almost always results in embellishment. This embellishment is often the outcome of a greater inclination on man's part for the ought than the is. A victory that was costly, a conquest that was bestial, a migration that was long and anguishing— these are distorted in the retelling as the popular imagination mutes the is with the ought. Sagas, then, are a kind of popular history—public models that purport to make objective statements regarding real people and events. They are the precursors of modern historiography.

Folktales are born of the storytelling nature of man. They make no assertions of truth. "We all tell a story with additions," wrote Aristotle, "in the belief that we are doing our hearers a pleasure."* The heroes of folktales may be anyone or anything—the gods and demigods of ancient myths, historical figures, creatures of the imagination. The teller of the tale may draw from anywhere—myth, saga, his imagination, the tales of others—to relate his own tale. Folktales are instruments of communication through the imagination. They have come down to us from prehistoric times, are prevalent in epic poetry, and are the precursors of the short story and the novel. It cannot be said of them that they are true or false, for they are not statements of fact; they belong to the "art of framing lies in the right way," as Aristotle put it in his discussion of Homer and epic poetry.† They can only be good or bad stories, dull or fascinating, credible or incredible, beautiful or ugly, passionate or cold. The criteria by which they are evaluated are subjective, emotive, aesthetic.

Over the centuries, the statements of mythology have had to yield to the testings of science. The result has been a loss of faith in mythological constructs that is in direct proportion to the increase of human knowledge and sophistication. It is fairly safe to say that as far as Western man is concerned the enterprise of mythmaking is at an end. The heroic inhabitants of the ancient myths are dead now, along with the world that gave them life.

The heroes of sagas and subsequent history have had to undergo investigation by historians whose task it has been to separate the ought from the is. Many an assumed major figure in history has suffered reduction, and many a minor figure has enjoyed elevation. As a result, some of us tend to look carefully at the leading figures of our contemporary world before we accept them as extraordinary; too many turn out to be the product of the image makers.

We adopted heroes easily once—political leaders, sports figures, actors, scientists, writers; their faces adorned the walls of the rooms in which we grew up. But we have grown older and are more cautious now; we have been disappointed too often. I am not referring to motivations but to accomplishments. We know of the ugly darknesses that motivate all men. If we were to use that against man, then all human achievement should be reduced to insignificance—and that is absurd. The darkness is a given, as is our biology. Psychoanalysts evaluate motivations; historians evaluate accomplishments. And in the realm of historical truth there can be real heroes only after the fact.

The area of the folktale is considerably more complex than that of myth and saga, for we are dealing here not with statements of fact but with forms and tastes. Nevertheless, it is impossible to deny that attitudes regarding the nature of the hero in literature have undergone radical change since Aristotle wrote the well-known thirteenth chapter of the *Poetics.*

"We assume that, for the finest form of Tragedy," wrote Aristotle, "the Plot . . . must imitate actions arousing fear and pity." The tragic hero must be "the intermediate kind of personage, a man not preeminently virtuous and just, whose misfortune, however, is brought upon him not by vice, and depravity but by some error of judgement, of the number of those in the enjoyment of great reputation and prosperity; e.g. Oedipus, Thyestes, and the men of note of similar families."‡

The nature of the hero is made even clearer in the second chapter of the *Poetics:* "Comedy . . . [makes] its personages worse, and the other [tragedy] better, than the men of the present day."§ And in chapter fifteen, during a detailed account of the nature of characters in tragedy, Aristotle wrote: "As Tragedy is an imitation of personages better than the ordinary man, we in our way should follow the example of good portrait-painters, who reproduce the distinctive features of a man, and at the same time, without losing the likeness, make him handsomer than he is. The poet in like manner, in portraying men quick or slow to anger, or with similar infirmities of character, must know how to present them as such, and at

---

\* *On Poetics; GBWW,* Vol. 9, p. 696.

† Ibid.

‡ Ibid., p. 687.

§ Ibid., p. 682.

the same time as good men, as Agathon and Homer have represented Achilles.''*

For Aristotle, the quality of courage—the most significant attribute we accord the term *hero* today—is a necessary but insufficient characteristic of the heroic. A hero is in all ways, not merely in acts of courage, in war, in conflict, but in all ways, superior to the ordinary mortal. He is of noble stature, a favorite of the gods. He walks with the gods and consorts with them. Still, despite his status as an idealized human, he shares in our basic feelings and emotions. And so we feel pity for him when we witness his fall from eminence, and we experience the fear that a similar tragedy might one day overtake us. The disaster that shatters the life of the hero is not caused by an evil act on his part but by some error or weakness, a minor or major flaw in his character. This flaw has been variously understood in Aristotle: an error of judgment resulting from haste or carelessness; an error due to unavoidable ignorance; a defect of character resulting from human frailty or moral weakness but not from purposeful malevolence.

Thus there are two fundamental aspects to the tragic hero in antiquity: eminence and flaw.

The serious novel has been at war with this notion of the hero throughout most of its history. Trimalchio's feast in the *Satyricon* is the opening shot in the war. With few exceptions, the great novels have been host to the ordinary world and the day-to-day conduct of life. Their concern has been with the gritty flatness of human existence. It is in such surroundings that their heroes, if they can be called heroes, have been placed. In its dense depiction of environmental detail, in its often merciless account of the seamy soil upon which the Aristotelian hero once stood so cleanly, the novel raised the level of importance of that soil and mocked the lofty eminence of that hero.

Further, the novel moved the flaw from its locus within the hero to a place outside him. Dublin; London; Hannibal, Missouri; German bourgeois society; the slums of New York and Chicago; the small towns of midwestern America—these are the locations of the flaws in most of the great novels in Western literature.

More than any other art form—with the possible exception of montage—the novel has served to reflect the breakup of the old order of things, often at the cost of committing the fallacy of imitation. Witnessing the onset of modernism, the novel has recorded events through the prism of private imaginations and has drawn for us a new model of reality. The result is a picture of things so utterly at variance with the world of the ancients that their sort of hero is no longer conceivable as an artistic possibility. The way we see the world today enables us to accept without much squeamishness the very ordinary position assumed by Leopold Bloom when Joyce brings him before us for the first time. It is intriguing to conjecture about the kind of reaction that brief scene of squatting would have elicited from Aristotle. The novel may and often does depict heroes of courage, stamina, brilliance, valor—as does the drama—but not one of those heroes can be an Oedipus. Bloom is the ultimate hero of today; his is a kind of nobility of the ordinary. The value system of the Greeks is gone; thus one of the action aspects of that value system—the tragic hero—is gone now too. The ordinary is king and hero today. And the ordinary, in all its mundane and splintered grittiness, gives every indication of being with us for a very long time to come.

Yet, having said that, I must add that those same tragic heroes still speak to me in the dimension of the mortal. I am unable to relate to their idealized status and nature, but their pain and passion are sharply felt by me. Pain and passion, after all, are quite ordinary human experiences.

I came to literature not through the heroes of Greek drama but through the people of the Hebrew Bible. Cain and Abel, Noah, Abraham, Isaac, Jacob, Joseph and his brothers, Moses and Aaron, Joshua, David, Solomon, and the others—those were my early heroes, all of them mortals with smoldering passions, jealousies, many of them experiencing moments of grandeur as well as pitiful lowliness and defeat. Rabbinic literature embellished the biblical accounts, but none of those embellishments yields an Oedipus. The depiction of King Saul is the closest historical or fictive approximation in the literature of the ancient Hebrews to the flawed tragic hero of the Greeks; yet Saul bears no significant resemblance to Oedipus. To the world of the Hebrew Bible and the Talmud, an Oedipus was an impossibility in form and thought; that was simply not the way the ancient Israelites and the rabbis took their stance in the world. Biblical heroes were not detached and sublime members of a ruling class; they came from the people, they interacted with the people; there was always for me a picture of a leader in relationship to the felt presence of the mass, never a leader alone, noble, a special favorite of the divine, working out his own private destiny. Even when we were told that God had chosen one man over others, there was never a sense that he was "better than ordinary men" in the way that Aristotle had understood those words. As a matter of fact, there is often a great deal of back talk in the Bible on the part of those chosen for leadership; few of them seem eager to take on the job.

Above all, there was always for me a sense of the real when I read about those people—a feeling that the Bible did not conceal from me the truth about the less pleasant side of man. Cain is a murderer, Noah is a drunk, Lot's daughters commit an act of incest, Abraham yields to the jealousies of Sarah, Jacob steals a birthright and a blessing, Moses, David, Solomon— all of them struggling, erring, groping about in attempts to come to terms

---

* Ibid., p. 689.

with their passions, their fears, their loves, their faith, and their tenuous lives. Beyond it all, and at the same time deep within it, reaching down to the very lowest levels of existence, was a presence—the only real hero, as it were, in the Hebrew Bible—which was not the brutally indifferent presence of the gods of Sumeria and Akkadia, or the barbarous orgiastic presence of the Thracian Dionysus, or the coolly charming and manipulative presence of the Homeric gods but a passionate and caring presence, a Being who was like a father with a child he deeply loves and to whom all those struggling humans were reaching out.

Those were the heroes that formed the action aspect of my early pictures of reality. Later, when Cain and Abel and Noah and others could no longer be historical figures for me, they still seemed all too human even in their fictive state; they remained vividly alive as heroes in a literature sacred to my people—sacred because it mirrored the commitment of my people to man and God and history; it was a record of a thousand years of my people's vision of the world.

I was in my early teens when I began to read the great novels of Western literature. I remember marveling at the honesty of those novels and at the same time feeling puzzled by the cynicism and rage of some of their heroes —or anti-heroes—at the world around them, at what they took to be its sham, its hypocrisy, its stagnation, its sordid games and masks. And I was even more puzzled by what I took to be the surprise of some of those heroes when they first encountered the true nature of the world. Hadn't their creators read the books of Samuel and Kings, the Prophets, the book of Job? Later, when I read the literature of ancient Greece, I wondered if the Greek heroes had somehow combined with the heroes of the Puritan ethic to produce a heightened, idealized, rigid picture of reality. Had this resulted in hurt and rage when those novelists had first come up against the hard and simple truth that the world was really ordinary, a place of sweat and odors, where people loved and hated and hurt one another and suffered and stumbled about and tried to carve for themselves moments of joy and meaning out of the darkness?

I was spared that particular kind of rage and never put it into my created heroes when I began to write about my own world—my ordinary world, where study and faith and a coming-to-terms with other cultures were the quite normal enterprises of life, had been the daily preoccupation of my people for at least two thousand years, and where a certain binocular vision of reality fused all activity into a meaningful unity. The heroes of my writing are the action aspect of that vision of things; they are the ordinary people of my own private and precious world.

That is what we all do when we choose or create heroes: we tell one another how we see the world and what we take to be the most important things in our lives. Through our heroes we announce to one another who and what we truly are.

## PART TWO

# Review
# of the
# Arts and Sciences

# The Widening Gyre: Philosophy in the Twentieth Century

W. T. Jones

Born in Natchez, Mississippi, in 1910, W. T. Jones was educated at Swarth-more, from which he graduated in 1931; at Oxford University, where he was a Rhodes Scholar (1931–34); and at Princeton, from which he received a doctorate in philosophy in 1937. In 1938 he joined the faculty of Pomona College, Claremont, California, where he became a professor in 1950, and which he has recently left to become professor of philosophy at the California Institute of Technology (he was elected a trustee of Pomona upon his departure). During the Second World War he served in the naval reserves and subsequently taught social and political philosophy at the U.S. Naval War College (1953–54). He is the author of *Morality and Freedom in Kant* (1941), *Masters of Political Thought* (1947), *Approaches to Ethics* (1962), *The Romantic Syndrome* (1962), and other works, as well as of a highly useful and very readable *History of Western Philosophy* (4 volumes, 1952). Professor Jones lives in Claremont.

*Turning and turning in the widening gyre*
*The falcon cannot hear the falconer;*
*Things fall apart; the center cannot hold;*
*Mere anarchy is loosed upon the world. . . .*
                    —W. B. Yeats, *The Second Coming*

## The Kantian paradigm

At the turn of the century the leading philosophers were Bradley and Bosanquet in Britain, Bergson in France, and James and Royce in this country. Were they to return to Oxford and Harvard and the Sorbonne today they would encounter few familiar signposts: not only the topics that engage philosophers but even the ways of "doing" philosophy have changed so much that they would feel lost indeed.

Has there then been a revolution in philosophy in the twentieth century? Many philosophers would say that there has been, but if we think of earlier debates—those that divided Plato from the Sophists, the Thomists from the Scotists, the Aristotelians from the Cartesians—we may suspect that this contemporary estimate of the contemporary scene is an exaggeration. In every period, for contemporaries, it is the disagreements, rather than the agreements, that command attention. But gradually, as the time passes, the similarities, not the differences, come into focus. Since there is no reason to think that the twentieth century is exempt from such perspectival foreshortening, later generations, looking back on us from a distance, will probably decide that twentieth-century philosophy is less revolutionary than twentieth-century philosophers now judge it to be.

Indeed, all the disagreements, from major engagements to minor skirmishes, have been conducted within, around, or over what may be called the Kantian paradigm. When Kant's *Critique of Pure Reason* was published in 1781, the dominant philosophical school was a form of metaphysical and epistemological dualism. According to this way of thinking, there are two sorts of entities in the universe: minds and material objects. A mind knows objects (and other minds) by means of mental states (variously called "ideas," "representations," "impressions," "phantasms") that are caused by these objects and that resemble them. Despite differences on many points, the Lockeians and the Cartesians agreed that the mind is directly acquainted only with its own states, that is, its ideas are its only means of access to the outside world.

The difficulty with this view, as Hume pointed out, is that if the mind knows only its own states, its own states are all that it knows. Suppose that there exist a number of photographs claiming to be likenesses of Richard Nixon, but that Nixon himself, immured in the White House, has been seen by no man. In these circumstances, it is obviously impossible to say that any of the photographs is the likeness of Nixon it claims to be. Similarly, if we have access only to ideas, we can compare ideas with each other but never with the external reality they claim to represent. Indeed, we can never know that an external world, or that other minds than ours, exist. Hume did not argue that only Hume exists. On the contrary, he believed in the existence of other minds and of an external world. But these beliefs, which he shared with all men, he held to be incapable of proof. So far from being supported by evidence, they are merely the expressions of "a blind and powerful instinct of nature." It is not reason or logic, but only "custom," that is "the great guide of human life."

It was at this point, where the whole post-Renaissance philosophy threatened to collapse in solipsism and skepticism, that Kant came on the scene. Since Hume had demonstrated the breakdown of the hypothesis that truth consists in the mind's being in agreement with objects, Kant proposed to try the opposite hypothesis that truth consists in the agreement of objects with minds. That is, he proposed to abandon the old view that the mind passively records what is "out there" and to try instead the hypothesis that it selects and structures what is out there. This in turn required him to suppose that the mind contains selecting and organizing principles and that it is possible to learn what those principles are. If we can ascertain this, as Kant believed he could, it follows that an absolutely certain knowledge of nature can be had—not an absolutely certain knowledge of particular facts but of the basic structure of nature as far as we can experience it. For the basic structure of nature so considered is a product of the mind's activity, not something independent of that activity.*

It follows that particular causal laws such as "all bodies gravitate" or "friction causes heat" are only probable, because they depend on empirical observation—that is, they are arrived at a posteriori. But the basic law that every event has a cause, on which the whole procedure of physics rests, is a priori, i.e., certain, because the human mind structures its experience in a cause-effect way. Within the range of that structure it can be sure of its ground. And while the extent of its assured knowledge may seem limited in scope, yet Kant believed that the mind's organizing and synthesizing activities were sufficient to justify and warrant the fundamental principles of Newtonian physics, above all the principle of the uniformity of nature, as to which Hume had maintained that our belief rests on mere blind instinct rather than on logic or evidence.

Kant described his hypothesis about the knower and his relation to the objects of his knowledge as a Copernican revolution. Just as Copernicus had shifted the frame of reference from the earth to the sun, so Kant shifted the frame of reference from objects to the mind. What Copernicus brought about admittedly was an enormous shift in perspective, with momentous consequences; in calling his own hypothesis "Copernican,"

Kant was claiming that it was an equally revolutionary shift in perspective. In this estimate he was correct, but, paradoxically, his hypothesis had an almost directly opposite effect. Whereas Copernicus's astronomical hypothesis had demoted the earth (and with it man) from the center to the periphery, Kant's epistemological hypothesis brought man, the knower, back to the center.

Most pre-Kantian philosophers had conceived the mind as a receptor of impressions from outside. In Locke's phrase, it was a *tabula rasa*, a blank tablet, until experience wrote upon it. They granted, of course, that the mind could combine in various ways (e.g., in accordance with the "laws" of association) the materials it received from the outside world, but they held that in its essential nature the mind was passive. The Kantian revolution transformed all this. The mind was no longer a Cartesian substance contemplating other Cartesian substances from a distance. It was not a "thing" at all but an activity, a number of "transcendental syntheses." And from this epistemological change there followed a profound metaphysical change: The so-called objective world (the objects of the mind's experience, not the world of things-in-themselves) is a construct, a product of the synthesizing activity of mind working upon and organizing the materials of sense (what Kant called the "sensuous manifold"). For this reason, views of the Kantian type are sometimes called constructivist theories.

From the beginning, reactions to the constructivism that Kant introduced were varied, but always strong. For some, it was a liberating thing. In *The Prelude,* for instance, Wordsworth emphasizes the active, synthesizing power of the mind in true Kantian fashion. When "the infant Babe" stretches out his hand toward a flower, he does not experience merely the physical flower out there; "already love . . . hath beautified that flower" for him. He has synthesized his response to his mother's loving, protective care into the material object. The babe is already "creator and receiver both," and what is true of the babe is even truer of the poet.[1] Thus, by assigning a positive function to what Coleridge called "the primary Imagination," the Kantian revolution allowed the poet to exalt his role. No longer merely a pleasing imitator of nature, he is a creative god, albeit only a minor one, in his own right.

---

*As a rough analogy, think of the relation between a camera, the film it contains, and the objects photographed by it. The film does not record indiscriminately what is "out there," for mediating between the film and the object is a system of lenses with varying focal lengths. If we know what focal length has been chosen by the photographer, we can make a number of a priori (i.e., absolutely certain) judgments about what has been photographed. Suppose that the stop has been set at $f/4$ and that the distance has been set at nine feet. Though we cannot say, prior to seeing the developed film, what object has been photographed, we *can* say that whatever was nearer than nine feet and further than twelve feet will be out of focus. We know this, prior to seeing the developed film, (1) because the camera is a selecting and organizing medium between the film and the object photographed and (2) because we know the principles by which this selection and organization occur.

For others, Kantianism had a profoundly disturbing effect. Nietzsche quotes a letter of Heinrich von Kleist's:

> *Not long ago I became acquainted with Kant's philosophy; and now I must tell you of a thought in it, inasmuch as I cannot fear that it will upset you as profoundly and painfully as me. We cannot decide whether that which we call truth is really truth or whether it merely appears that way to us. If the latter is right, then the truth we gather here comes to nothing after our death; and every aspiration to acquire a possession which will follow us even into the grave is futile. . . . My only, my highest aim has sunk, and I have none left.*[2]

These very different responses to Kantianism, representing very different temperaments, can be traced through the whole subsequent history of philosophy. For those who experienced a strong metaphysical urge, "despair of truth," as Nietzsche wrote, was a likely response. "As soon as Kant would begin to exert a popular influence, we should find it reflected in the form of a gnawing and crumbling skepticism and relativism."[3] For such philosophers the main question was "How can objectivity be saved?" Saving objectivity obviously depended on being able to keep at a minimum the role mind plays in constructing the world-of-experience. But the course of nineteenth-century philosophy demonstrated that, once the camel of constructivism got its nose within the philosophical tent, it was very hard to prevent the rest of the animal from following.

Hegel was the first to expand the constructivist role of mind. Whereas Kant had conceived his twelve categories as timeless features of all of mind's activities everywhere, Hegel argued that mind has a history. It passes through a sequence of stages, to each of which there corresponds a particular form, or level, of experience. It is true that Hegel believed that these levels of experience succeed each other according to a standard pattern such that each later level of experience includes all the earlier levels, while transcending them. Thus there was still, according to Hegel, something a priori about human experience, namely the sequential pattern of development that the history of culture reveals. The next step was precisely to attack this remnant of apriority.

According to Marx, the various worlds of experience, so far from revealing a pattern of spiritual development, reflect, and so are relative to, changing modes of economic production and exchange. Nietzsche was even more relativistic: "We invent the largest part of the thing experienced," he wrote. "We are much greater artists than we know." That is, what each of us experiences (our world) is not merely a function of the social class of which we are members; it is a function of personal interests, and hence varies from individual to individual. "Most of the conscious thinking of a philosopher is secretly guided by his instincts and forced along certain lines. . . . every great philosophy up to now has been . . . a type of involuntary and unaware memoirs." Science, Nietzsche thought, is no better off than philosophy: "Physics, too, is only an interpretation of the universe, an arrangement of it (to suit us, if I may be so bold!), rather than a clarification."[4]

Meanwhile, and independently of this process of relativizing the categories, other philosophers pointed out that if things-in-themselves are unknowable, there can be no evidence that they exist. F. H. Bradley expressed a commonly held opinion in his gibe at Herbert Spencer's unknowable:

> I do not wish to be irreverent, but Mr. Spencer's attitude towards his Unknowable strikes me as a pleasantry, the point of which lies in its unconsciousness. It seems a proposal to take something for God simply and solely because we do not know what the devil it can be.[5]

Bradley replaced the Unknowable with "Absolute," but since this Absolute was supposed to transcend all finite (i.e., human) experience, it is not easy to see in what way it was an improvement on unknown things-in-themselves. Do we, for instance, have a "positive idea" of the Absolute? Bradley was obliged to admit that

> fully to realize the existence of the Absolute is for finite beings impossible. In order thus to know we should have to be, and then we should not exist. This result is certain, and all attempts to avoid it are illusory.[6]

He did indeed claim that we can nonetheless "gain some idea of its main features"—it is all-inclusive; it is one; it is a system—but he confessed that this idea, though "true as far as it goes," inevitably remains "abstract and incomplete." This was the best Bradley could do, and it was not enough to satisfy what we may call the falcon's metaphysical urge, that is, his urge to find a center about which to orient his flight.

Bradley's *Appearance and Reality* was published in 1893. Thus by the end of the century the Kantian strategy of substituting a human center for the old external and objective center was increasingly perceived by philosophers as a failure. What Kant had thought of as a single, firm center around which the falcon could orient his flight, because it was rooted in the universal and necessary characteristics of the human mind, had become a plurality of individual centers—and so no true center.

## The revival of realism: G. E. Moore

At the turn of the century a vigorous counterattack was launched. It was based on a theory of the nature of consciousness advocated by Brentano and Meinong, which appealed because it made possible a radical departure from the whole idealistic, constructivist paradigm. The most influential of this group of publications—at least in English-speaking countries—was G. E. Moore's "The Refutation of Idealism" (1903).

The heart of Moore's refutation was his account of the structure of human experience. Instead of being a product, experience is the simple juxtaposition of two radically different sorts of elements: the object of experience (what is experienced) and the act, or activity, of experiencing this object. Anybody, Moore maintained, who attends carefully to very simple experiences—such as the difference between an experience of a blue sense-datum and an experience of a green sense-datum—will see that these two elements, and only these two elements, are involved. They are also the elements, and the only elements, involved in more complex perceptions and in cognition, though in such cases the presence of these elements, and the distinction between them, is less obvious and can, therefore, be overlooked by a careless observer.

> *We all know that the sensation of blue differs from that of green. But it is plain that if both are* sensations *they also have some point in common. What is it that they have in common? . . . The element that is common to them all . . . is consciousness. . . . The sensation of blue includes in its analysis, besides blue, both a unique element "awareness" and a unique relation of this element to blue. . . . Introspection [enables] me to decide that . . . I am aware of blue, and by this I mean, that my awareness has to blue . . . the simple and unique relation the existence of which alone justifies us in distinguishing knowledge of a thing from the thing known, indeed in distinguishing mind from matter.*[7]

There is no problem, Moore thought, about the nature of the element blue as it occurs in the experience: blue is just blue, no more or less, one item among the millions of items in the universe, but the item of which we happen, at this moment, to be aware. But what about consciousness, the other element in experience? The difficulty is that consciousness is "transparent."

> *The moment we try to fix our attention upon consciousness and to see what, distinctly, it is, it seems to vanish. . . . When we try to introspect the sensation of blue, all we can see is the blue: the other element is as if it were diaphanous. Yet it can be distinguished if we look attentively enough.*[8]

And now, supposing we have looked attentively, what does consciousness contribute to experience? Moore's answer is that it contributes absolutely nothing; it does not alter blue in any way. It merely selects blue—this particular item from amongst the millions of other items in the universe —and holds it before the mind.

*Whenever I have a mere sensation or idea, the fact is that I am then aware of something which is equally and in the same sense* not *an inseparable aspect of my experience. . . . There is, therefore, no question of how we are to "get outside the circle of our own ideas and sensations." Merely to have a sensation is already to* be *outside that circle. It is to know something which is as truly and really* not *a part of* my *experience, as anything which I can ever know.*[9]

This, then, was Moore's mode of escape from the solipsism and skepticism in which, as Hume had shown, Cartesianism ended, and it wholly bypassed the Kantian revolution. Hume had pointed out that if what we know are only our own ideas, then we can never "get out of the circle of our own ideas." Whereas Kant's strategy for escaping from this dilemma had been to suggest that some of our ideas are a priori organizing elements in experience, rather than images of the world outside our experience, Moore's was to maintain that in an act of awareness there is no intermediary idea at all. Consciousness in its essential nature is consciousness *of*. When we are conscious of blue, we are not contemplating some mental image that is somehow supposed to resemble blue; we are contemplating blue.

The universe, of course, contains not only items like blue and green; it contains in fact

*an immense variety of different kinds of entities. For instance: My mind, any particular thought or perception of mine, the quality which distinguishes an act of volition from a mere act of perception, the Battle of Waterloo, the process of baking, the year 1908, the moon, the number 2, the distance between London and Paris, the relation of similarity—all of these are contents of the Universe, all of them are or were contained in it.*[10]

These items divide into two main classes—items that are "mental" (or "psychical") and items that are not. Some of the items that are not mental are physical objects; some are not. But all of these items have the characteristic of being, in their nature, independent of minds. They exist (they are what they are) even if they are not for any consciousness at all. What is more, this objective and public world which is thus revealed to view is just the world that common sense believes in. Finally, that all this is true Moore held to be obvious to anyone who takes the trouble to look carefully at his experience.

It would be difficult to exaggerate the effect of this analysis on those, like Russell, who had been disturbed by the subjectivism of idealism:

*G. E. Moore . . . took the lead in rebellion, and I followed, with a sense of emancipation. . . . With a sense of escaping from prison, we allowed ourselves to think that grass is green, that the sun and stars would exist if no one was aware of them [and that] mathe-matics could be* quite *true, and not merely a stage in dialectic.*[11]

It was not long, however, before both Moore and Russell began to see grave difficulties with the new position. How, for instance, are sense-data related to physical objects? When, for instance, I see a dime and a quarter lying on the ground in front of me, I am (they thought) obviously not directly aware of the whole of either coin—I don't see the other side of either, still less the inside of either. Further, if the coins are a little way off, I am directly aware of two elliptical sense-data (though the coins themselves are round) and, if the dime happens to be nearer than the quarter, the sense-datum associated with the dime may be larger than the sense-datum associated with the quarter.

Moore saw that one way of dealing with this problem would be to define a physical object (e.g., the coin) as the whole set of sense-data that all possible observers would experience under all possible conditions of observation. Then the obscure and puzzling relation of "being a property of" would be replaced by the straightforward and readily understood relation of "being a member of a class": the elliptical sense-datum would be simply one element among others in the well-ordered set of sense-data which together constituted the coin. This, as we shall see, is the type of solution for which Russell opted, but since Moore's main aim was to "vindicate" common sense against speculative philosophy, and since he believed that common sense holds material objects to be more than mere collections of sense-data, he could not take this way out. As he wrote, "on this view, though we shall still be allowed to say that the coins *existed* before I saw them, are *circular* etc., all these expressions, if they are to be true, will have to be understood in a Pickwickian sense."[12]

What, then, is the alternative for a realist? In the end, Moore said, he inclined to a position "roughly identical . . . with Locke's view," that some, at least, of the sense-data "resemble" the physical objects which are their "source." But, as Moore recognized, this seems indistinguishable from just that representative theory of perception which Moore's own original formulations were designed to avoid: "How can I ever come to know that these sensibles have a 'source' at all? And how do I know that these 'sources' are circular?" Moore confessed that he did not know how to answer these questions. If, along with our experience of sensibles, there were an "immediate awareness" that the sources exist and are circular, the problem would of course be solved. But *is* there such an immediate awareness? The most Moore felt he could say was that there is no con-clusive evidence that there is not.[13]

This is not the only difficulty in which realism was involved: When a color-blind man looks at a traffic signal, where are the gray sense-data that he sees? If they are objective, as Moore's theory must hold them to be, they must be somewhere in physical space. Are they in the same region of space as the red and green sense-data that the man with normal vision sees? How can this be? And what about the silvery circular sense-datum that we see when we look at the moon? Where is it? Out there, where the moon itself is, 250,000 miles away?

Still another nest of problems emerged in connection with developments of modern physics. For physics the coin was neither the solid material object that common sense believes it to be nor yet the collection of sense-data that, as we have seen, one philosophical theory held it to be. On the contrary, for physics, it seemed, the coin was mostly empty space, occupied here and there by electrical charges. Thus arose what Sir Arthur Eddington called "the two-tables problem": What is the relation between the table of physics and the table of common sense? If the former is real, must not the latter be an illusion? This was one of the questions to which Russell addressed himself.

## Russell

Temperamentally, Moore and Russell differed markedly; it is hardly surprising, therefore, that, despite their agreement on the basic "realistic" thesis, their philosophical theories developed in very different directions. Moore, as we have seen, took his stand on common sense—so much so that he declared that neither the world nor the sciences had ever suggested to him "any philosophical problems. What has suggested philosophical problems to me is things which other philosophers have said about the world or the sciences."[14] He used what he called "analysis" to vindicate common sense by showing that the problems about which philosophers typically worry are the results of muddle and confusion.

Russell, in contrast, "came to philosophy through . . . the wish to find some reason to believe in the truth of mathematics."[15] The difference is fundamental. His introduction to Euclid, when he was eleven, was a "great event," though he was—characteristically—disappointed to discover that the axioms "had to be accepted without proof." What "delighted" him chiefly in mathematics was "the restfulness of mathematical certainty."[16] The animating drive of Russell's philosophy was, in fact, a "quest for certainty" as strong as Descartes's—the quest for a much more certain certainty than those deliverances of common sense that satisfied Moore. But whereas Descartes could assume both the certainty of mathematics and also its applicability to the real world, the intervening period of idealism complicated the situation for Russell. He saw that if idealism were correct, mathematics was but a stage in the Hegelian dialectic and so was contradicted and superseded by successively higher stages. Russell was attracted to the realistic distinction between consciousness and its objects not because it seemed to validate common sense but because it seemed to validate mathematics, by revealing a set of entities, wholly independent of the mind and its synthesizing activities, that are simply there, before the mathematician's mind when he is thinking mathematically.

What else, in addition to the universals contemplated in mathematics, is included in the inventory of the universe? Russell's view evolved over time. Indeed, according to his critics, "evolved" is too generous; his views, they say, changed about as frequently as Picasso's styles in painting. But throughout all these changes he clung to (1) the distinction which, like Moore, he drew between those objects about whose existence we are absolutely certain because we are directly aware of them, and those which we know about, or believe in, by inference, and (2) the desire, in the interest of simplicity and certainty, to reduce as much as possible the numbers of inferred entities. Initially, Russell allowed that the universe also contains, in addition to universals, sense-data, minds, and physical objects. Later, he decided that physical objects could be eliminated, and still later that acts of consciousness—and with them the minds in which these acts were thought to occur—could also go:

> If there is a subject, it can have a relation to the patch of colour, namely, the sort of relation which we might call awareness. . . . The subject, however, appears to be a logical fiction, like mathematical points and instants. It is introduced, not because observation reveals it, but because it is linguistically convenient and apparently demanded by grammar. . . . The functions that [nominal entities of this kind] appear to perform can always be performed by classes or series or other logical constructions, consisting of less dubious entities. If we are to avoid a perfectly gratuitous assumption, we must dispense with the subject as one of the actual ingredients of the world.[17]

These conclusions, so far from the common sense of Moore, reflect the main drive of Russell's philosophy: to find an absolutely secure basis for the world that science describes and that we experience in ordinary perception. The data of direct awareness are, he thought, such a basis; since we are not directly aware either of minds or of physical objects— since these are, at best, only inferred entities—he looked for ways to eliminate them from the inventory of real constituents of the universe.

He did not want, of course, to write them off as "mere appearance"— that would mean admitting that physics and psychology were not about the real world. The way to deal with minds and physical objects was to show that they are logical (or grammatical) fictions. Because the grammar and vocabulary of ordinary language are, as Russell thought, very muddled, having grown in a higgledy-piggledy manner, we do not realize that they are fictions, but suppose them all—such nouns as *man* and such descriptive phrases as "the author of *Waverley*"—to denote entities in the real world. By means of what he called "logical construction" Russell held it is possible to replace such nouns and phrases by other terms that *do* denote real entities. Russell's "logical construction" is very different from the constructivism of idealism, which was, of course, anathema to him. What Russell meant is better suggested by such terms as *reduction* or *symbolic substitution*.

Russell first developed this method, whatever it be called, in connection with a problem concerning judgments about nonexistent objects. What is the judgment "Round squares do not exist" about? It is easy, in such a judgment as "Lions roar," to say what the judgment is about: it is about lions and what is asserted is that lions roar. But "Round squares do not exist" cannot be handled in this way, for round squares do not exist and, what is more, the judgment explicitly says that they do not. Hence, if we suppose that there must be round squares in order for there to be an object judged about (just as lions must exist to be the objects judged about), we contradict ourselves. It was from Meinong that Moore and Russell adopted their basic realist premise that in every act of consciousness (and this of course includes acts of judging) there is an object that is independent of, and distinct from, the act. Meinong himself was a sufficiently determined realist to say that there must be an object judged about even in judgments of nonexistence, and he sought to escape from the dilemma just outlined by arguing that while round squares do not exist, they nevertheless subsist. Since it did not take Moore and Russell long to become extremely suspicious of subsistence, if realism was to be saved another analysis of judgments of nonexistence had to be found, which would eliminate the apparent need to suppose that such judgments have nonexistent, but subsistent, objects.

Consider, then, such a phrase as "the author of *Waverley*." It is a mistake, Russell said, to suppose that "the author of *Waverley*" denotes some objectively real entity included in the inventory of items in the universe. "The author of *Waverley*" does not denote what "Scott" denotes, because if it did, "The author of *Waverley* was Scott" would be a tautology, and it is not a tautology because it could be false. The fact is, Russell maintained, that "the author of *Waverley*" does not *denote* anything. What, then, do sentences containing this phrase, such as "The author of *Waverley* was Scott," mean? Well, "The author of *Waverley* was Scott" means that "one and only one man wrote *Waverley*, and he was Scott."

Note that when we get *clear* as to what it means to say that the author of *Waverley* was Scott, the phrase "the author of *Waverley*" has been eliminated from the sentence: we mean just what we meant when we said, "The author of *Waverley* was Scott," but we have now said what we mean in such an unambiguous way that nobody can fall into the error of supposing that the universe contains an entity named "the author of *Waverley*." Russell deals with judgments of nonexistence in an exactly parallel way: "round square," for instance, is a descriptive phrase that does not any more denote an existent object than does the descriptive phrase "the author of *Waverley*." A correct analysis of "Round squares do not exist" eliminates this phrase from the sentence, just as a correct analysis of "The author of *Waverley* was Scott" eliminates that phrase from that sentence.[18]

To return from logic to ontology, words like *matter, physical object, electron, molecule,* Russell held, are also to be treated as descriptive phrases, that is, as terms which do not name anything, and which therefore can be eliminated, rather than as the names of entities of whose existence we are less than certain since their existence depends on the correctness of inferences from what we directly experience. It will be seen how much, even from very early in his career, Russell was concerned with language, not however with rehabilitating common sense language but with constructing a new, pure language in which certainty is achievable, because the terms in this language denote only entities about whose existence there can be no doubt.

What are these entities? Russell's answer was that the ultimate constituents of the universe are not physical objects (tables, chairs, the sun, the moon) but

> a multitude of entities which . . . I shall call "particulars." . . . The particulars are to be conceived, not on the analogy of bricks in a building, but rather on the analogy of notes in a symphony. The ultimate constituents of a symphony (apart from relations) are the notes, each of which lasts only for a very short time. We may collect together all the notes played by one instrument: these may be regarded as the analogues of the successive particulars which common sense would regard as successive states of one "thing." But the "thing" ought to be regarded as no more "real" or "substantial" than, for example, the role of the trombone.[19]

Since each note, in this analogy, corresponds to a sense-datum that some observer has directly experienced, a physical object (e.g., the moon) is not a single, persistent entity located 250,000 miles away from us; the moon is a vast assemblage of sense-data of many different shapes, sizes, and colors, the assemblage that all possible observers have experienced and will yet experience of the moon. Each observer's sense-data fall into a pattern, or "perspective," like the pattern of notes that constitute the role of the trombone. My sense-data of the moon are within my private three-dimensional spatial perspective, and every other observer's are within *his* private perspective, all of these private spaces fitting into the public space of the real world.[20]

This analysis applies also to the problem as to where, on the realistic thesis, illusions and hallucinations are, e.g., to Moore's worry about where the gray sense-data experienced by the color-blind man are located. Russell's answer was that they lie in the private three-dimensional space of the color-blind man, but that this space (along with the private three-dimensional spaces of men with normal vision) fits into public space. Russell's solution is, as Moore would say, "Pickwickian." Whether a Pickwickian solution is thought to be satisfactory is perhaps a matter of temperament, but it is important to see that Russell's solution, however Pickwickian, is also only programmatic. He did not actually carry through a "logical construction," or "elimination," of matter, still less of mind. He merely sketched out the lines along which such a construction might possibly be worked out. If the program could be carried through to completion, the falcon would be firmly reoriented in a real world—certainly not the commonsensical world of Moore, and admittedly a neutral, value-free world which the falcon might not much enjoy—but still a real world.

But *can* Russell's program be completed? That is the question, and Russell himself could not answer it. He had wanted, with Descartes, to vindicate the claims of physics; in the end, he confessed that he believed in the world of physics "without good grounds."

## Logical positivism

Russell's program of logical construction (or reduction) was launched in the years just before World War I. A similarly ambitious but much more radical program was launched by a group of thinkers in Vienna in the years following that war. These thinkers, who initially called themselves the Vienna Circle and later, as the group expanded, became known as logical positivists, differed much among themselves, but for the purposes of this sketch it will be more useful to concentrate, so far as possible, on the beliefs and attitudes which they shared. In the first place, they were all passionately antimetaphysical. In this respect they differed from Moore and Russell, both of whom had aimed at ascertaining the true nature of reality. The positivists, in contrast, held that realism, as much as idealism, is nonsense. The positivist, they held, does not contradict metaphysicians, but merely says, "I don't understand you. What you say asserts nothing at all!"[21]

The second point on which all positivists agreed was that it is only in the sciences—and especially in physics—that we have anything that can properly be called *knowledge*. If we want—and who does not?—to increase the amount of reliable information available to us, we should therefore extend the use of scientific method in all domains and by its means test every assertion, eliminating any that do not measure up. Why is it that science yields reliable information? It is because all assertions made in the sciences are warranted by experiment and controlled observation. For instance, when the existence of an ether pervading space was questioned, physicists designed an experiment that would settle the issue.

They reasoned that if the ether were present and if a beam of light were first transmitted across and then along the direction of the flow of ether, there would be a discernible difference in the times of transmission. Since no difference was in fact observed, they concluded that the ether does not exist. The term *ether* should therefore be eliminated from the vocabulary of science as a meaningless word.

Generalizing from what they thus took to be the essential feature of scientific method, the positivists formulated what came to be called the Verifiability Principle. This asserted that the method of verifying a proposition is the meaning of that proposition. Since it follows that propositions for which no means of verification exist are literally meaningless, the positivists saw that they had in their hands an instrument that would totally destroy metaphysics, once and for all. To the earliest positivists the Verifiability Principle seemed "the justified unassailable nucleus" of their whole position, and all the positivists adopted the principle in one form or another. It proved anything but unassailable, however, as we shall shortly see.

There is a third point on which all positivists agreed. This was the importance of "modern" logic and the analysis it made possible. Here, of course, they learned much from Russell. The aim of logical analysis, according to the positivists, is to clarify the statements that are made in the sciences, in order to reveal their true cognitive content. We have seen that, though "The author of *Waverley* was Scott" is true, unwary readers —even the literary historian who makes the assertion—may attribute a false cognitive content to it until its precise cognitive content has been exposed by analysis. The positivists recognized that scientists could go astray in a similar way. Without a logical analysis there was a danger that physicists themselves—let alone philosophers and laymen—might misread such a true statement as "Electrons exist" and attribute a metaphysical content to it.

Underlying logical analysis as Russell and the positivists practiced it was the conviction that, when language has been correctly analyzed, it will be isomorphic with the world; the linguistic relational structures that are exposed by means of analysis exactly mirror the relational structures that characterize the world. As Russell wrote in his introduction to Wittgenstein's *Tractatus,* "There must . . . be something in common between the structure of the sentence and the structure of the fact."[22]

The *Tractatus* was intended to display the isomorphism that, as Wittgenstein and Russell believed, must exist between the basic structure of sentences and the basic structure of facts. Wittgenstein had been impressed by an account of a trial arising out of an automobile accident, in which the lawyers used dolls and miniature cars to represent the real people and automobiles involved in the accident.[23] It seemed to Wittgenstein that propositions must represent the world in the same way. "We picture facts to ourselves," he wrote, and the picture "must have something in common with what it depicts."[24] What it has in common is "its pictorial form."[25] Because the doll used in the trial occupied the same place in the miniature car that the man occupied in the real car, it represents the accident truly. "A picture agrees with reality or fails to agree; it is correct or incorrect, true or false."[26] Just as it is in virtue of pictorial form that pictures are either true or false, so it is in virtue of logical form that propositions are true or false.

What, then, is the basic logical form of propositions? Since "every statement about complexes can be resolved into a statement about their constituents,"[27] eventually analysis must terminate on simple, unanalyzable elements: "It is obvious that the analysis of propositions must bring us to elementary propositions which consist of names in immediate combination."[28] Each such name is a "primitive sign," since it is incapable of further "dissection." Accordingly, "the meanings of primitive signs" must be "explained by means of elucidations," since further analysis is impossible. "Elucidations are propositions that contain the primitive signs."[29] Since the names that occur in elucidations "are like points," the function of elucidations is to draw our attention to those simple, atomic facts pointed to by the names the elucidations contain.[30]

The *Tractatus* was a work on logic, not on ontology. Hence Wittgenstein thought it sufficient to show what follows from the nature of logic about the sort of basic structure the world must have. For instance, "The world divides into facts,"[31] and each of these facts is completely independent of every other. And again, "Each item can be the case or not the case while everything else remains the same."[32] Since the positivists, in contrast, were interested in logic chiefly as a preliminary for, and a clarification of, science, they had to go beyond the *Tractatus* and formulate a program for ascertaining in detail what the basic structure actually is. Accordingly, they proposed, first, to reduce all complex scientific statements to elementary statements, and second, to provide elucidations for these elementary statements. But what, exactly, is the nature of an elucidation? According to Russell, an elucidation was the report of the occurrence of a sense-datum, but sense-data seemed too subjective to the positivists, and, after a good deal of backing and filling, most of them decided that elucidations were what they called "protocol sentences."

A protocol sentence records an observation—either a simple observation or, as in the following example proposed by Otto Neurath, one of the early positivists, an observation of an observation—

> *Otto's protocol at 3:17 o'clock:* [*At 3:16 o'clock Otto said to himself: (at 3:15 o'clock there was a table in the room perceived by Otto)*].[33]

Analysis begins from a sentence in the "system language" in which

93

scientific assertions are formulated—say, the sentence, "The ether does not exist." From this one deduces a sentence in the protocol language—say the sentence, "If the ether does not exist, then no time difference is observed by Michelson and Morley." One then compares this sentence with the actual protocols of Michelson and Morley. Michelson: "No time difference observed." Morley: "No time difference observed." Accordingly, the sentence in the system language, "The ether does not exist," *means* "No time difference observed." That is, it means the protocol sentences that verify it.

Applying this method of analysis to sentences about God (the atheist's assertion that he does not exist, as well as the theist's that he exists), about the Absolute, about ultimate reality, it was easy to *show* that, since they are unverifiable, they are meaningless. Equally so are all normative sentences, for instance, those about the good and the beautiful. Some of the positivists were content simply to write off all sentences containing normative predicates as pseudostatements, but others allowed them a kind of use after all. Thus, "Capital punishment is wrong" tells us nothing whatever about the world, but it permits the speaker to express his disapproval of capital punishment, and it may persuade listeners to disapprove of capital punishment also. Carnap was even willing to allow a kind of use for metaphysical statements: "They serve for the *expression of the general attitude of a person towards life . . .* his emotional and volitional reaction to the environment, to society, to the tasks to which he devotes himself, to the misfortunes that befall him." Metaphysics is a kind of poetry, but since it lacks the expressive power of poetry, metaphysics is "inadequate."[34]

Thus, the positivists proposed to put the falcon at ease by assuring him that what he thought were real problems are only pseudoproblems. They believed they could relieve his metaphysical itch by eliminating all meaningless words from his vocabulary and by clarifying all the meaningful words in it. When their program was fully carried out, the falcon would find himself living in a world in which all the questions he could ask would be answerable by a unified science in terms of protocol sentences in the language of physicalism. This point of view was effectively stated by Wittgenstein near the end of the *Tractatus:*

> *Doubt can exist only where a question exists, a question only where an answer exists, and an answer only where something* can *be said. . . . The solution of the problem of life is seen in the vanishing of the problem.*[35]

Wittgenstein was eventually to find that a different therapy was needed, but even before he realized this, the positivist program had collapsed, for the Verifiability Principle, which had looked so straightforward, proved to involve one puzzle after another.

For instance, are the sentences in the protocol language incorrigible?

The positivists first assumed, and subsequently hoped to show, that they are. Thus, for "Otto" in the protocol sentence quoted above, it is possible to substitute "the body at such-and-such a place," and for the report of perceiving a table, it is possible to substitute a description of some movement by the body in question. For instance, the body might be instructed, whenever it perceives a table, to push a button or a lever, instead of reporting that it perceived one. But even this radical behaviorism did not save the incorrigibility of protocol sentences, according to Neurath:

> There is no way of taking conclusively established pure protocol sentences as the starting point of the sciences. . . . *We are like sailors who must rebuild their ship on the open sea, never able to dismantle it in dry-dock and to reconstruct it there out of the best materials. . . . Vague linguistic conglomerations always remain in one way or another as components of the ship. If vagueness is diminished at one point, it may well be increased at another.*[36]

But if it be allowed that protocol sentences are corrigible, then they require verification, and to admit that they require verification is to become involved in an infinite regress. System sentences are to be verified by other protocol sentences, which are to be verified by other protocol sentences, and these in their turn by still others. No process of verification can ever be completed.

To put this differently: the positivist program had assumed that the whole structure of science could be firmly based on a set of incorrigible protocol sentences, like a ladder resting securely on the ground. It now looked as if the sciences were a floating spiral, open at both ends.

> *In unified science we try to construct a non-contradictory system of protocol sentences and non-protocol sentences. . . . When a new sentence is presented to us we compare it with the system at our disposal, and determine whether or not it conflicts with that system. If the sentence does conflict with the system, we may discard it as useless (or false). . . . One may, on the other hand,* accept *the sentence and so change the system that it remains consistent even after the adjunction of the new sentence. The sentence would then be called "true."*[37]

Readers of this passage were astonished to find a positivist reverting to the idealist theory that the truth of a proposition depends on the degree of its coherence in a system.

As another example of the difficulties the Verifiability Principle encountered, consider the question, "What is the status of the Verifiability Principle itself?" On the positivist view, all meaningful sentences are either analytic (i.e., tautologies) or are verifiable by empirical means. Clearly, the principle is not analytic. Is it, then, an empirical generalization and, if so, how can it be verified? A. J. Ayer, whose *Language, Truth, and Logic* had been an early and influential exposition of positivism, finally came around to saying:

> *The Vienna Circle tended to ignore this difficulty: but it seems to me fairly clear that what they were in fact doing was to adopt the verification principle as a convention. . . . It became prescriptive with the suggestion that . . . only statements which were capable of being either true or false should be regarded as literally meaningful.*[38]

But if the Verifiability Principle is only a recommendation, or suggestion, that the terms *meaningful* and *meaningless* be used in a certain way, then the whole positivistic program as it had been originally conceived has really been abandoned. There is no longer one ideal language, whose structure is revealed by logical analysis and which, when revealed, exactly mirrors the world. Rather, there are now a variety of languages, none of which is isomorphic with the world, and all of which can be recommended on different grounds.

This radical change in point of view was also implicit in a distinction Carnap came to draw between what he called internal and external questions regarding language. Carnap pointed out that

> *we must distinguish two kinds of questions of existence: first, questions of the existence of certain entities . . .* within the [linguistic] framework; *we call them* internal questions; *and second, questions concerning the existence or reality* of the system of entities as a whole, *called* external questions.[39]

The scientific system provides rules for answering internal questions, so that, once we have accepted this system, we can decide whether King Arthur existed, whether unicorns and centaurs are real or imaginary, and whether there is a piece of white paper on my desk now. But these are all questions that are internal to the "thing language," and

> *To accept the thing world means nothing more than to accept a certain form of language. . . . The thing language . . . works indeed with a high degree of efficiency for most purposes of everyday life. . . . However, it would be wrong to describe this situation by saying: "The fact of the efficiency of the thing language is confirming evidence for the reality of the thing world"; we should rather say instead: "This fact makes it advisable to accept the thing language." . . . Let us be . . . tolerant in permitting linguistic forms.*[40]

We have now traced, from its start at the beginning of the century, one more or less continuously developing line of philosophical thought. It had begun as a revolt against idealism, but by midcentury, it had almost completely reversed itself and was, in many respects, more idealistic than realistic. Though it had not returned to the idealist doctrine of the relativity of experience to categories or conceptual forms, it had now affirmed a not very different version of relativism—the relativity of "the world" to language. Since thought and language are intimately related, the shift of attention from the former to the latter is less significant than might appear. What is chiefly significant is that once more the attempt had been abandoned to establish an objective reality independent of man. In a word, we have witnessed a return to a linguistic version of the Kantian paradigm.

What other philosophical developments occurred during this half-century? Three must be mentioned even in a sketch like this: the philosophy of organism, instrumentalism, and phenomenology-existentialism.

## Whitehead

The philosophy of organism was philosophy in the grand manner—philosophy on the same scale as Hegel's and therefore an anachronism in the twentieth century. But in contrast to Hegel it was conceived in the realistic spirit that had animated Moore and Russell and the other opponents of idealism. Of course, Moore's interest in common sense beliefs left him indifferent to Whitehead's vast speculative synthesis, but it may be said that Whitehead attempted to do what Russell would have liked to do, had Russell not set himself so high a standard for certainty. Whitehead's deepest conviction was that "the ultimate natures of things lie together in a harmony which excludes mere arbitrariness."[41] He was a rationalist in the sense that he held this harmony to be *intelligible* to the human mind. The function of philosophy is to "seek the form in the facts," to make explicit the pattern that is otherwise only implicitly present in the social system and so only "ignorantly entertained." But because "we are finite beings," grasp of the pattern "in its totality . . . is denied us."[42] Because philosophy is an "attempt to express the infinity of the universe in terms of the limitations of language,"[43] every formulation of the pattern will itself sooner or later descend into the "inactive commonplace." Hence the work of philosophy is never finished.

These sentences show that Whitehead's view of language was diametrically opposed to the view of Russell, the positivists, and the tractarian Wittgenstein that the business of philosophy is to construct an ideal language that is isomorphic with the facts into which the world divides. Because he saw philosophy as "akin to poetry" and to mysticism, rather than to logic,[44] Whitehead could afford to be speculative, as Russell could not.

Whitehead also shared the interest of almost all twentieth-century philosophers in science. But he modeled his theory less on what he took to be the implications of scientific method (as with the positivists) than on what he took to be the discoveries of physics in this century. He thought that the science of the eighteenth and nineteenth centuries had had a deleterious impact on man's view of himself and of the world he lived in. It had, he thought, "bifurcated" nature. On the one side was man, with his hopes and fears, his thoughts and emotions. On the other side was nature, but nature, according to nineteenth-century physics, "is a dull affair, soundless, scentless, colourless; merely the hurrying of material, endlessly, meaninglessly."[45] Such a physics, Whitehead believed, was responsible for Eddington's two-tables problem, and the trouble, he thought, was that most men had concluded that science requires them to admit that the table of perception is not real, but only a subjective product of the interaction between light waves, optic nerve, and cortex. On this view, "the poets are entirely mistaken"; it is we, not the nightingale, to whom Keats should have addressed his Ode. But Whitehead held the poets to have been correct in believing that nature carries with it "a message of tremendous significance" and that it "cannot be divorced from its aesthetic values." Or from its moral implication. For the occurrence of every event is fully determined by the occurrence of antecedent events, according to the theories of nineteenth-century physics, and is therefore in principle predictable. But if the molecules blindly run, as nineteenth-century physics proclaimed they do, then, Whitehead pointed out, since "the human body is a collection of molecules . . . the human body blindly runs," and free will and moral responsibility are "swept away."[46]

It was thus the poetic, moral, and humanistic view of man and the universe that Whitehead wanted to rehabilitate, and he thought that recent developments in science—especially relativity theory and quantum physics—provided a way of doing so. He believed that the basic concepts of the "new" physics could be generalized to form a "categoreal" scheme providing a unified, instead of a bifurcated, account of the world. This scheme, which involved a "category of the ultimate," eight "categories of existence," twenty-seven "categories of explanation," and nine "categoreal obligations," is much too complex and difficult for a short summary, but perhaps it will be possible at least to suggest how the bifurcation of nature was to be healed.

The ultimate constituents of the universe, according to the scheme, are neither Russell's "particulars" nor material things nor egos: they are events, and each event is the "grasping into unity," or "prehending," of other events. It is easy to understand the notion of "prehending into unity" at the human level—to perceive a castle across the valley or a planet in the sky is to prehend these objects and myself into the unity of a single experience. But Whitehead held that an electron is equally a center of prehensive activity; to limit the activity of prehending to the human level of conscious perception and cognition would be to abandon realism and lapse into the idealism that Whitehead wanted to avoid. Thus the castle and the planet are prehending (feeling) me whilst I am perceiving them. What are the castle and the planet and I save three of the endless variety of standpoints from which, and into which, they, and I, are prehended, or felt? Every event in the universe is prehending every other of the "simultaneous events throughout the rest of the universe." What makes each event unique is that each feels all other events from a particular standpoint, or in a particular "perspective."

Further, a prehending center is not merely a passive contemplator of all the other manifold "aspects of nature" from its particular point of view. Each center is a life, a process having a beginning and ending in a consummation: this, again, is as true of an electron as of a human life, and for the same reason. Each involves a principle of selection and exclusion; each is "a unit of emergent value." Hence, whereas nineteenth-century physics had regarded the physical world as inert matter, fundamentally different from man, quantum physics (at least in Whitehead's view) requires us to think of nature as involving processes that, even at the most elementary level, are not different in kind from human cognition and volition.

Thus Whitehead offered the falcon what, presumably, it longed for—a world whose nature was such that the falcon could feel at home in it. Why, then, did the philosophy of organism not "take on"? One answer, surely, is that it was too difficult to be readily understood. But that is not the whole answer. Another reason is that in the 1920s and 1930s, when Whitehead was developing his theory, positivism was at the height of its influence, and not merely among philosophers. Whitehead wrote as if the Verifiability Principle had never been heard of; at a time when philosophers were contracting their horizons and concentrating on "piecemeal, detailed and verifiable results," he indulged in speculation on a large scale. But perhaps the most fundamental reason is that he really did not appreciate the depths of the falcon's distress. Whitehead, who had been born in 1861, was a civilized, cultivated English gentleman. If he experienced those "deep disquietudes" that are the center of Wittgenstein's later writings and the main preoccupation of the protagonists of Sartre's novels, he did not show it in his writings. Because his theory did not meet the mood of the times, it missed what was to become the wave of the future.

## Dewey and instrumentalism

The philosophy of organism was virtually the work of one man. In contrast, instrumentalism had its origins in the work of James and Peirce, and was carried forward by many writers, during the first half of the century. Nonetheless, Dewey was so clearly its preeminent figure that it is fair to concentrate our attention on his views. Like almost all philosophers, of whatever school, Dewey was impressed by the sciences, but whereas Whitehead had focused on science as giving us clues to the ontological pattern hidden behind the flux of change, and the positivists had focused on science as a procedure for eliminating nonsense and advancing knowledge, Dewey focused on science as an instrument for improving men's "traffic with nature" and so making their lives "freer and more secure."

The fact that Dewey's emphasis was on results, rather than—as was the case with most of his contemporaries—on truth, is fundamental for understanding instrumentalism. "The two limits of every unit of thinking," he wrote,

> *are a perplexed, troubled or confused situation at the beginning and a cleared-up, unified, resolved situation at the close. . . . In between [are] states of thinking.*[47]

That is, thinking starts only when something blocks an ongoing activity (a man out for a walk in the country comes to a stream too wide to be jumped); thinking ends when action can be resumed (the man recalls having seen a log a short way back, fetches the log, finds that it is indeed long enough to bridge the stream, and so continues his walk). Thinking, in this case, has produced "a situation that is clear, coherent, settled, harmonious." Of course the situation will not *stay* coherent and harmonious. New problems are bound to arise—that is what life is. But we can hope, by reflective self-criticism, to learn how to improve our problem-solving techniques and so solve our problems more efficiently. "Improving our problem-solving techniques" is advancing from common sense, rule-of-thumb, trial-and-error methods to scientific methods (quantification, controlled experimentation, etc.); "learning how by reflective self-criticism to improve" is logic. That is, the norms in terms of which various human activities are assessed and evaluated are not abstract, ideal rules imposed from outside as infallible judges; rather, they arise from critical reflection on these activities and what they accomplish. Logic, in a word, is a human activity and, like all other human activities, it reflects human needs, and it changes in response to changes in them.

Thus Dewey's conception of logic differed radically from Russell's. The Russellians thought Dewey psychologized logic; he thought they etherealized it. They held logic to be the analysis of propositions, an analysis that terminates in logical simples. "A proposition has one and only one complete analysis," Wittgenstein wrote.[48] For Dewey, in contrast, so far from there being only one complete analysis, it made more sense to talk about "logics" than about "logic." Since logic is but the reflective criticism of actual problem-solving techniques, there are as many logics as there are different kinds of problems that need solving. There is, for instance, a logic of historical studies, which is the critical assessment, by historians, of their own methods of interpreting documents, and this logic is quite different from the logic of physics. And, so far from logic being terminating in logical simples, there are no such simples; or rather, there are simples, of course, but they are merely the end products of a particularly abstract and rarified activity, the activity of logical analysis. They have no superior ontological status.

> *Realism argues that we [must] admit that something eulogistically termed Reality . . . is but a complex made up of fixed, mutually independent simples. . . . For instrumentalism, however, the alleged . . . results of abstraction and analysis are perfectly real; but they are real, like everything else, where they are real. . . . But there is no reason for supposing that they exist elsewhere in the same manner.*[49]

When, for instance, do we experience a blue sense-datum? Typically, when it is the stain by which we recognize a cellular structure. But recognition of a cellular structure is part of one of those "units of thinking" that are intermediate between a confused and a cleared-up situation. Sense-data, in a word, "are not objects but means, instrumentalities, of knowledge: things by which we know rather than things known." The realist has erected sense-data into the ultimate constituents of the universe only because he "ignores the contextual situation. . . . [His sense-data] exist only within the procedure." [50]

So too for the protocol sentences of the positivists. Since the aim of the positivists was to put science on a secure basis, they were naturally disturbed when their protocol sentences proved to be corrigible. But Dewey, for his part, took it for granted that sentences in the protocol language, as well as sentences in the system language (to use, for the moment, the language of the positivists), are corrigible. Nothing can be absolutely secure, not even science. But science is secure enough if, by its means, we manage continuously to improve our ongoing traffic with nature and with other men.

Thus our metaphor of a spiral open at both ends, in contrast to a ladder resting firmly on the ground, would have been congenial to Dewey. If challenged by the realists to characterize the nature of this spiral, Dewey would not have evaded them by adopting the positivists' line, "To ask about the nature of Reality is a meaningless question"; he would have answered, "It is experience." And what is experience? It is not a passing show at which we are merely spectators. We are primarily agents, doers, not observers, and the concepts by which we organize experience are not more than instruments that we revise or discard if they prove to be ineffective tools in our traffic with nature.

Experience is thus anything but the object of consciousness-of. Consciousness, for Dewey, is not a transparent element that *contains* experience; it occurs *within* experience, and just at those points where problems arise that impede action. Hence consciousness "is only a very small and shifting portion of experience." [51]

And, just as we find consciousness in experience and facts in experience, so also we find values in experience. "Experience actually presents esthetic and moral traits." Such traits are as real as are "the traits found by physical inquiry." They all stand "on precisely the same level" ontologically speaking, in that all are found in experience. Indeed, in a way, values are prior: "Things are objects to be treated, used, acted upon and with, enjoyed and endured, even more than things to be known. They are things *had* before they are things cognized." [52]

Thus Dewey rejected both the old metaphysical notion of a realm of transcendent values and also the positivist claim that sentences about values are noncognitive. Such sentences may of course be expressive and persuasive, but they are also as factual as are statements about any other facts. Just as a fact is an element in our experience that has—so far—survived criticism, so a value is an enjoying that has proved to be—so far—a satisfaction. Some philosophers have argued that in order to escape subjectivism and to be able to draw a real "distinction between likings and that which is worth liking, between the desired and the desirable, between the is and the ought," it is necessary to be armed with an absolutely valid criterion. This is not the case. Whenever we weigh the claim of some liking by the test of experience, we make a viable distinction between "genuine, valid goods" and "counterfeit goods."

But to make use of the test of experience is simply to apply science (conceived as the method of intelligent inquiry) to questions about values, which have too long been the preserve of theology and other dogmatisms.

> *What the method of intelligence . . . will accomplish, if once it be tried, is for the result of trial to determine. . . . To claim that intelligence is a better method than its alternatives, authority, imitation, caprice and ignorance, prejudice and passion, is hardly an excessive claim.*[53]

Dewey was, as these lines show, both an optimist and a democrat. He believed in democracy because it is

> *the best means so far found, for realizing ends that lie in the wide domain of human relationships and the development of human personality. . . .*
>
> *The foundation of democracy is faith in the capacities of human nature; faith in human intelligence and in the power of pooled and coöperative experience. It is not belief that these things are*

*complete but that if given a show they will grow and be able to generate progressively the knowledge and wisdom needed to guide collective action.*[54]

To many people today this faith in the efficacy of "pooled intelligence" will sound naïve. Not everybody any longer shares Dewey's confidence that the problems created by technology can by technology be solved. And what about the alienation and dissociation of sensibility that so many people feel today? Here again Dewey's diagnosis may seem superficial. He thought there is nothing new in these anxieties. Indeed, since they stem from man's relative inability to control his environment, they were much more characteristic of primitive than of twentieth-century man. But wherever and whenever, for whatever reason, man has "distrusted himself," he has sought "to get beyond and above himself." This pathetic quest for certainty, this desire to escape from contingency, not only explains belief in gods; it also explains the philosopher's belief in a transcendent reality that is "universal, fixed and immutable," and also his insistence on absolute truths, absolute values, absolutely reliable sense-data, or an ideal language that is isomorphic with the world.

Moderate anxiety is of course reasonable—after all, the world is an uncertain place—and it is also socially useful. In contrast to dogmatic assurance, it is a spur to improving our instruments of control. But extreme anxiety is unreasonable, since it ignores the empirical evidence that intelligent inquiry does indeed pay off.

Of course, the acceptability of this account depends on the falcon's being contented to live in the relativistic and uncertain world that Dewey allows him. It depends, that is, on anxiety's not being existential, on its not being rooted in the divisiveness of consciousness or in the fact that we have been "thrown" into an indifferent and absurd universe. Dewey himself would have thought that belief in the absurdity of man's existence is neurotic; existentialist critics can reply that Dewey was insensitive to man's deepest needs and blind to his real nature. Who is correct? We can only say that, for the present at least, the culture as a whole seems to have moved away from Dewey's view of man.

## Phenomenology-existentialism

Like realism, the phenomenological movement started at the turn of the century, from Brentano's and Meinong's assertion that consciousness is directional, or intentional, in nature. Unlike realism, which had a relatively short life, the phenomenological movement is still very vigorous and has spread from Germany, where it was launched, to the rest of the continent and to the United States. In this sketch we shall concentrate mainly on Husserl, the "father" of phenomenology, but we shall also note some representative subsequent developments at the hands of Heidegger and Sartre.

Though Husserl's starting point was the same as Russell's and Moore's, phenomenology developed in a very different way. First, as regards consciousness itself: From the fact that consciousness is always consciousness-of and that there is no mediating idea between the mind and its object, the realists concluded that consciousness can be ignored; with their interest in validating science, they concentrated on the object, which the new intentional view of consciousness had shown to be uncontaminated, as they maintained, by mind and its "constructions." And their contention was later reinforced by a behaviorism which, starting with James, sanctioned by Russell, and supported by the positivists' Verifiability Principle, held that sentences containing assertions about inner states can be eliminated and replaced by sentences about bodily states.

For Husserl this was an appalling mistake. In his view, if one attends carefully, one discovers that, so far from being directly aware only of sense-data, one is directly aware of an immense variety of entities and acts. Husserl maintained that the realists—and all previous philosophers —wholly overlooked this vast realm because observation of it requires the cultivation of a special attitude which he called "phenomenological reduction."

Second, unlike most of the philosophers we have considered, Husserl was utterly opposed to recent developments in science—indeed, to the whole development of science since Galileo. Scientific method, which Dewey admired because of its practical achievements, Husserl condemned because he regarded it as based on a series of false assumptions. Einstein's theories, for instance, are about an "idealized and naïvely objectivized nature." He "does nothing to reformulate the space and time in which our actual life takes place." [55] And what is bad enough in the natural sciences is still worse in psychology. Aping physics and chemistry, it tries to be as external and as quantified as if its object were nature, not man. In a word, it studies behavior, not "the proper essence of spirit."

Some of what Husserl says about science could have been written by Whitehead, who was as critical as Husserl of the metaphysical assumptions that led scientists to bifurcate nature, or, in Husserl's terminology, to ignore "the environing world of life." But Husserl would have had no use for the philosophy of organism. It was, from his point of view, as "relativistic" as all earlier philosophies had been. Just as realism of the Russellian type had presented us with only a limited view of reality— one relative to its assumption about the atomicity of the world and to the way it draws the distinction between direct acquaintance and inferential knowledge, so Whiteheadian realism presents us with a different but equally limited view of reality—one relative to Whitehead's assumptions about the interconnectedness of all things.

Whereas such considerations led Whitehead to conclude that completely objective knowledge, even in science, is impossible, Husserl simply decided that we must free ourselves from all presuppositions and so achieve, not merely one more view of reality, but a face-to-face confrontation with reality itself in all its purity. A science based on such a presuppositionless confrontation with reality itself would be apodictically certain, and such a science must somehow be possible, since (according to Husserl's reasoning) to deny its possibility is to fall into contradiction. For consider: Do the relativists, who argue that there is no absolutely valid knowledge, claim that their arguments are valid? They must do so, but then they are asserting what they deny. They are maintaining that they have an absolutely valid knowledge that there is no absolutely valid knowledge.

It is easy to see how Dewey would have replied to this line of reasoning. He would have pointed out that an objectively valid science is not at all necessary to render our traffic with nature freer and more secure. For that we need only a progressively improving science. We would need an absolutely objective science only if it were reasonable to hope to render our traffic with nature absolutely free and absolutely secure. But what do *absolutely free* and *absolutely secure* mean? Such terms, Dewey would have said, merely reflect the insecurity and instability of those like Husserl who resort to them.

A quest for certainty was indeed the ruling passion of Husserl's life. In 1906, for instance, he entered in his diary, "I have been through enough torments from lack of clarity and from doubt that wavers back and forth. . . . I must win clarity, else I cannot live; I cannot bear life unless I can believe that I shall achieve it."[56] Thus Husserl shared Russell's animating drive, but whereas Russell sadly confessed that most of what he believed he believed "without grounds," Husserl concluded not only that an absolutely objective science must, logically, be possible but that it was actually within his grasp. He held that what transcendentally reduced observation accomplishes is precisely the stripping away of all presuppositions. This stripping away, progressively, of presuppositions brings one into the presence of reality itself, and a science starting from such a presuppositionless confrontation with reality will indeed be objectively valid.

But what is transcendentally reduced observation? And what is the nature of that absolutely pure reality encountered in it? To begin with, Husserl contrasted the stance, or attitude, that he desires us to adopt with what he called "the natural standpoint." In this standpoint

> *I am aware of a world, spread out in space endlessly, and in time becoming and become, without end. . . . [Moreover,] this world is not there for me as a mere world of facts and affairs, but, with the same immediacy, as a world of values, a world of goods, a practical*

> world . . . *with value-characters such as beautiful or ugly, agreeable*
> *or disagreeable, pleasant or unpleasant. . . . To know* [*this world*]
> *more trustworthily, more perfectly than the naïve lore of experi-*
> *ence is able to do . . . is the goal of the* sciences of the natural stand-
> point.[57]

It would be hard to find a better description of what Dewey called
"experience" or of what Moore thought of as the world of common
sense. But whereas they saw no reason for shifting out of the natural
standpoint—indeed, they saw every reason for remaining in it—Husserl's
whole philosophy depends on making such a shift.

> Instead now of remaining at this standpoint, we propose to alter
> it radically . . . we set it as it were "out of action," *we* "disconnect
> it," "bracket it." *It still remains there like the bracketed in the*
> *bracket, like the disconnected outside the connexional system.*[58]

Bracketing, at least as far as this passage goes, thus amounts to suspending judgment—neither believing nor disbelieving. Now it is obvious
that if I succeed in suspending my belief in everything that can possibly
be suspended, then whatever survives suspension is indubitable and
hence apodictically certain.

> What can remain over when the whole world is bracketed? . . .
> Consciousness in itself has a being of its own which in its
> absolute uniqueness of nature remains unaffected by the phe-
> nomenological disconnexion. *It therefore remains over as a "phe-*
> *nomenological residuum," as a region of Being which is in*
> *principle unique, and can become in fact the field of a new science*
> *—the science of Phenomenology.*[59]

"Residuum" is an unfortunate term; it is not true that a part of the
content of experience is lost in the course of bracketing and that a part
remains. No content is lost; everything remains. Yet, as a result of
bracketing, everything is different.

> *Let us suppose that we are looking with pleasure in a garden at a*
> *blossoming apple-tree, at the fresh young green of the lawn, and*
> *so forth. . . . Between . . . the real man or the real perception on*
> *the one hand, and the real apple-tree on the other, there subsist*
> *real relations. . . . Let us now pass over to the phenomenological*
> *standpoint. The transcendent world enters its "bracket." . . .*
> *Together with the whole physical and psychical world the real*
> *subsistence of the objective relation between perception and per-*
> *ceived is suspended; and yet a relation between perception and*
> *perceived (as likewise between the pleasure and that which pleases)*
> *is obviously left over, a relation which in its essential nature*
> *comes before us in "pure immanence."* [60]

That is to say, when I "bracket" the apple tree, I merely suspend my belief in its independent existence as an object. I continue to experience myself experiencing (and taking pleasure in) its fresh green color, and I can now concentrate my attention on this relationship between my experiencing and that which I experience—a relationship that I was likely to ignore as long as I was in the natural standpoint and busily reflecting on what I could do with the tree: when the apples would be ripe, how much they would bring in the market, and so on.

As a result of bracketing, my attitude has become wholly disinterested; I observe that which I never before observed, the essential nature of "pure" consciousness. In this transcendentally reduced observation I encounter a multitude of mental acts—perceivings, thinkings, imaginings, dreamings, and the like—and a multitude of different objects intended by these diverse acts. Suppose, for instance, that I bracket the experience that in the natural standpoint we call looking at a die. What do I find?

> *I see in pure reflection that "this" die is given continuously as an objective unity in a multiform and changeable multiplicity of manners of appearing, which belong determinately to it. These, in their temporal flow, . . . flow away in the unity of a synthesis, such that in them "one and the same" . . . identical die appears, now in "near appearances," now in "far appearances." . . . Thus the near-thing, as "the same," appears now from this "side," now from that; and the "visual perspectives" change. . . . Always we find the feature in question as a unity belonging to a passing flow of "multiplicities."* [61]

This account of what we actually experience when we look at a die can be compared with Moore's account of what we see when we look at two coins. Husserl's account is surely far more reliable; Moore's is colored by an unconscious presupposition about the superior ontological status of atomistic, encapsulated sense-data, each itself and not another thing. But Husserl's better reporting of his viewing of the die as it actually occurs hardly requires a phenomenological reduction. Dewey, for instance, or Whitehead could have given, and indeed did give, similar descriptions of sense perception, without the aid of bracketing.

Husserl's next move was to report his observation of "essences" in transcendentally reduced experience. What is an essence? It is that about an object that makes it this sort of object rather than another sort of object—that about a die that makes it a die and not an apple tree, that about an apple tree that makes it an apple tree and not a die. It was fortunate for Husserl that he was able to observe essences, because he did not want to have to allow that we are directly aware merely of appearances of an object; to admit this would have involved him in all the puzzles that plagued realism. What, for instance, is the relation between an appearance of a die and the die that is presumably its cause?

One of the great virtues of phenomenology, in Husserl's view, was that transcendentally reduced experience "consists in the self-appearance, the self-exhibiting, the self-giving" of objects themselves. That is, in transcendentally reduced experience we do not have to infer the existence of a die that is not directly present from data that are directly present; we directly intuit the essence of the die (as it appears).

So much, by way of brief summary, for intentional objects, i.e., the objective pole of pure consciousness. But we not only observe the die (or the apple tree); we also observe ourselves examining the die and enjoying the apple tree. And what is more, just as we observe, not the appearance of the apple tree, but the apple tree as it appears, so we observe, not the appearances of our enjoying, but our enjoying as it appears. Similarly, of course, for all the other mental (intentional) acts— perceiving, thinking, dreaming, imagining, and the rest. The essence of these acts is self-evidently present to us in transcendentally reduced experience, just as the essence of the die, the essence of the apple tree, and the essence of physical objects generally are also directly present to us.

These directly present, and therefore self-evident, intentional acts and intentional objects were to be the basis for the "objectively valid science" that was Husserl's goal. But unfortunately this science remained as programmatic as the very different program of the positivists. Instead, Husserl's energy was distracted into the Pandora's box of metaphysical and epistemological problems which he thought his phenomenological method had forever eliminated.

The method he devised was supposed at one stroke to settle all the disputes that had ravaged post-Cartesian philosophy. All parties to these disputes started from the common presupposition that there is a basic distinction between the mental and the physical. One ended up by saying that everything is mental (the idealists); the other by saying that everything is physical (behaviorists, materialists, naturalists). Husserl claimed to have shown that the distinction which resulted in all of these irreconcilable theories, so far from being basic, is wholly unwarranted: transcendental reduction reveals that we are not dealing with independently existing minds nor with independently existing objects; we are dealing, instead, with the subjective and objective poles of pure consciousness.

In a way, this was Dewey's position—that minds and objects are occurrences within experience, but for Dewey they are "emergents" there, not revealed there in all their essential purity, and of course Dewey was quite ready to accept the constructivist, and so relativist, implications of this account. Since Husserl was not, his solution was, even within his own philosophical development, in unstable equilibrium. This instability results from a deep conflict at the heart of Husserl's thought between phenomenology as a method of describing experience accurately and phenomenology as a quest for certainty.

Phenomenology as description has had a salutary effect on the social sciences. By calling attention to "experiential variables," it has counterbalanced a tendency in psychology to think exclusively in terms of experimental variables and a stimulus-reflex model; by emphasizing "social reality" as it is perceived and actually lived by people, it has corrected a tendency in sociology to concentrate exclusively on overt, "observable" interactions.

But description, however accurate, can never establish the certainty of what is described. It can, indeed, express *feelings* of certainty, and these feelings can be explored and described in detail. But description never makes it certain that these apparent certainties are what they claim to be. This might not disturb psychologists or sociologists, especially those with instrumentalist leanings, but it was a fatal limitation for a philosopher, like Husserl, who was in search of an objectively valid science. Hence Husserl came increasingly to incline toward a Kantian type of solution to the problem of a priori knowledge: the findings of phenomenological description were to be guaranteed by the activities of a transcendental ego. But where Kant had held that this ego and its categorical syntheses are *behind* experience, Husserl held that they are *in* experience. And whereas Kant had only to present logical arguments that justify our inferring the existence of these syntheses, Husserl's phenomenological method, which he never thought of abandoning, required him to *find* the synthesizing operations of the transcendental ego in experience. Since these operations did not appear in transcendentally reduced observation as he had previously practiced it, more and more rigorous bracketing, a more and more narrow focusing on "pure" consciousness, became necessary.

Though Husserl thought this would bring to light the "hidden achievements" of the ego, few of even the most devout phenomenologists were prepared to go along with him. To them, the whole line of reasoning seemed too idealistic. From Husserl's point of view, the fact that the transcendental ego's activities were supposedly revealed in experience saved him from the nineteenth-century version of idealism. But from the point of view of his phenomenologist critics, the transcendental ego ruined everything. Husserl wrote about its activities as "constituting" the experiental world; they saw little difference between constituting and constructing. Thus phenomenology, like its great rival, positivism—both of which had been launched as efforts to break out of the Kantian paradigm—threatened to collapse back into it.

Moreover, to many phenomenologists Husserl's version of phenomenology was too intellectualistic. For Husserl, man was chiefly an observer, a spectator, of reality, and this bias naturally colored his account of the subjective pole of pure consciousness. The phenomenologists who resisted the development of his thought in that respect shared Dewey's emphasis on man as a doer, not merely knower, but since they did not share Dewey's optimism and practicality, their conception of man as a doer differed radically from his. These phenomenologists perceived man as an alien, cast into an indifferent universe where he is forced to act and to choose, rather than as a social being competent to solve the social problems he confronts.

Thus the phenomenological movement underwent a dual development. First, there was an attempt to found an ontology on the basis of phenomenological description; second, there was a shift from the conception of the self as knower to an existential interpretation of consciousness, in which the self is regarded as a moral and social agent, living, acting, and suffering in the world. Since most phenomenologists shared these ontological and existential concerns, the two developments were closely related. In this connection we will briefly consider the theories of Heidegger and Sartre.

As regards the return to ontology, it is noteworthy that Heidegger's chief work, *Being and Time,* opens with a quotation from Plato:

> *For manifestly you have long been aware of what you mean when you use the expression* "being." *We, however, who used to think we understood it, have now become perplexed.*

Heidegger then asks:

> *Do we in our time have an answer to the question of what we really mean by the word* "being"? *Not at all. . . . Our aim in the following treatise is to work out the question of the meaning of* Being *and to do so concretely.*[62]

This, Heidegger thought, required a wholly new approach. The entire development of philosophy since Descartes was obviously a blind alley. Descartes's introduction of the fatal distinction between knower and known had led Kant to abandon Being (which Kant had called "things-in-themselves") and to concentrate on the phenomenal world. From that time on, Heidegger argued, philosophy had wallowed in subjectivism, and though the so-called realists claimed to tell us about the real world, they had not the slightest idea what Being is—they were merely interested in establishing the objectivity of the physical world in order to vindicate the claims of physics.

The Aristotelian-Scholastic tradition, for its part, Heidegger regarded as little better than the post-Cartesian philosophy. It is true that this tradition at least gave a preeminent place to metaphysics, the science of Being, but Heidegger held that the philosophers who represented this tradition concentrated their attention on the various species and genera of being, not on Being itself; it seemed to him that so far as these philosophers thought at all about Being as such, they took it to be only the highest genus, the most universal of concepts.

*Metaphysics thinks about beings as beings. Wherever the question is asked what beings are, beings as such are in sight. Metaphysical representation owes this sight to the light of Being. The light itself, i.e., that which such thinking experiences as light, does not come within the range of metaphysical thinking; for metaphysics always represents beings only as beings . . . the light itself is considered sufficiently illuminated as soon as we recognize that we look through it whenever we look at beings.*[63]

In another metaphor Heidegger proposed that if the sciences are the branches of a tree of which the roots are metaphysics, then Being is the ground, the soil, in which these roots grow. Just as the root "sends all nourishment and strength" into the tree and ignores the ground in which it lives and on which it depends, so metaphysics "remains concerned with beings and does not devote itself to Being as Being."[64] And just as the light (alternatively, in the other metaphor, the nourishing soil) is always there, waiting to be looked *at,* instead of being looked *with,* so Being is always present to us, waiting for us to feel its presence in our lives. Thus, as Plato said, we all know what we mean by Being. "We always conduct our activities in an understanding of Being";[65] we have simply forgotten where—and above all, how—to look.

Since our oblivion to the absence of the "involvement of Being in human nature" has "determined the entire modern age," since it has left us forsaken and "more and more exclusively [abandoned] to beings," Heidegger conceived it to be his mission to "go back into the ground of metaphysics." "If our thinking should succeed, . . . it might well help to bring about a change in human nature."[66] But how do we, who "used to understand Being," come to understand it once again? The answer is that it is possible to reach Being only through beings, and above all through the being of human beings, for, after all, man is the being who cares about Being.

It is easy to see why, given this approach, Husserlian phenomenology would initially appeal to the young Heidegger—it claimed to undercut Cartesian dualism and so to eliminate both idealism and realism, and in transcendentally reduced experience it claimed to put us in direct contact with the true reality that, in our ordinary experience, we completely overlook.

Again, Husserl seemed to Heidegger correct in emphasizing that the clue to an understanding of Being is human experience. But Husserl seemed mistaken in concentrating on "pure consciousness"—not only because to emphasize consciousness led him down the road to idealism but also because "purity" overlooks man's existential and moral involvement in the world. Hence, instead of characterizing "that sphere of being in which man stands as man" by Husserl's term "consciousness," Heidegger dramatized his difference from Husserl by characterizing it as

"Dasein" (presence). This is not, he says, "simply a matter of using different words." What is at stake is "to get men to think about the involvement of Being in human nature," and by thinking of this involvement, to come to understand the nature of Being itself.[67]

But what is there about the mode of man's existential involvement in the world that provides a key to Being? In the first place, to say that man is existentially involved in the world is to say that he lives in a world not of merely neutral objects but of things that are "ready-to-hand." And this is true not merely of the things he deliberately constructs for his use but of natural objects. "The wood is a forest of timber, the mountain a quarry of rock; the river is water-power, the wind is wind 'in the sails.' "[68] So far, Heidegger is merely repeating what Husserl had said about the "environing world of life" in contrast to that "idealized and naïve" world that physics and behavioristic psychology presuppose. But for Heidegger the fact that our environing life world is "ready-to-hand" is relatively unimportant. Far more important, this environing life world is one into which we have been "thrown" and in which therefore we are strangers.

Our experience of the world as alien and of ourselves as thrown into it generates an anxiety from which we seek to escape. "In the face of its thrownness Dasein flees to the relief which comes with the supposed freedom of the they-self."[69] In less-Heideggerian language, instead of living an authentic life in which we courageously confront the ineradicable loneliness, facticity, and alienation of human existence, we retreat into an inauthentic social existence whose daily round is determined by what "they" (other people) expect of us. But there is one fact about human existence which nobody can elude—death.

> *Dasein cannot outstrip the possibility of death. Death is the possibility of the absolute impossibility of Dasein. . . . As such, death is something* distinctively *impending. . . . Thrownness into death reveals itself to Dasein in a more primordial and impressive manner in that state-of-mind which we have called "anxiety." . . . Anxiety in the face of death must not be confused with fear in the face of one's demise. This anxiety is not an accidental or random mood of "weakness" in some individual; but, as a basic state-of-mind of Dasein, it amounts to the disclosedness of the fact that Dasein exists as thrown Being towards its end.*[70]

What this seems to mean, to revert again to non-Heideggerian language, is that our knowledge that we are inevitably to die and that the being of human beings is therefore "impossible" makes us aware that, by contrast, it is precisely the character of the Being of Being that it *cannot* die.

However this may be, it is clear that, at the time *Being and Time* appeared, Heidegger believed that it would be possible, using as clues such insights as these about human existence, to give a formal account of Being. But the second part of *Being and Time* was first postponed and then cancelled, as he came to feel that anything like a formal, philosophical exposition of Being is impossible. Poets, he thought, were better than philosophers at revealing Being, but in the end he concluded that even they must fail.

"Language," he wrote, is "the house of Being," and since there are many languages, Being has many houses. "If man by virtue of his language dwells within the claim and call of Being, then we Europeans presumably dwell in an entirely different house than Eastasian man. . . . And so, a dialogue from house to house remains nearly impossible."[71] Indeed, it is not merely a matter of communication—it is not merely impossible for participants in the dialogue to say *to each other* what Being is; one cannot *say* what Being is; one can only hint. And the best hint, it turns out, is silence.

> *The course of such a dialogue would have to have a character all its own, with more silence than talk. Above all, silence about silence.*[72]

Thus, by the phenomenological route we seem to have reached the conclusion already reached by the positivistic route: that the ideal of a language isomorphic with reality is an illusion. And not only this. The pursuit of sheer immediacy has led Heidegger a long way beyond Husserl's bracketing of pure "consciousness" to a community of mutual silence.

While Heidegger was thus converting Husserl's "rigorous science" into something hardly distinguishable from mysticism, Sartre was subjecting it to a different pattern of pressures, especially, perhaps, the pressure of atheism. What is a world without God? What is man's role in such a world?

In attempting to answer these questions Sartre started from Husserl's central thesis that reality consists in consciousness-of, but he launched a frontal attack on the transcendental ego. It seemed to him that Husserl had mistakenly introduced it because, with Kant, he supposed that a synthesizing activity is necessary to make mine all those consciousnesses-of that I experience as mine. Now it is true that ordinarily I am at an "unreflected level" where I am conscious only of the object and unaware of being conscious of it, and this of course is why Husserl supposed that a special unifying consciousness is necessary. But since, as Sartre pointed out, I can at any moment move from the unreflected to the "reflective level," where I am conscious of being conscious of the object, it is evident that every consciousness of an object is *also* a consciousness of self. Hence Husserl's transcendental ego is unnecessary; it has no raison d'être.

Getting rid of the transcendental ego not only eliminated idealism and reestablished the possibility of ontology; it also eliminated the notion of a self that, being somehow the source of our psychic life, is both responsible for what we do and also a limitation on our human freedom. At the subjective pole there is now only pure spontaneity. "Genuine spontaneity must be perfectly clear: it *is* what it produces and can be nothing else."[73] There are thus no limitations, either psychological or ontological, on what I may become.

> *This monstrous spontaneity is at the origin of numerous psychasthenic ailments. Consciousness is frightened by its own spontaneity. . . . This is clearly seen in an example from Janet. A young bride was in terror, when her husband left her alone, of sitting at the window and summoning the passers-by like a prostitute. Nothing in her education, in her past, nor in her character could serve as an explanation of such a fear. . . . She found herself monstrously free.*[74]

If freedom leads to anxiety and despair that may require psychiatric treatment, it is also a challenge and an opportunity. Most of us flee from freedom and live the roles provided for us by our family, our education, and the social class to which we belong. We never know despair; we never have any real moral problem, for the answers to our questions are provided by society. But we are hardly men. "Human life begins," as Orestes says in Sartre's play *The Flies*, "on the other side of despair."

But man is not only free; he is conscious. We have to ask then, "What sort of being is consciousness-being?" It is, says Sartre, "for-itself." To understand its nature we must contrast it with being-in-itself, the sort of being an oak tree or an ashtray has. The in-itself is "massive," "solid," "glued to itself"; it is "undivided singleness." It simply is what it is. In contrast, the for-itself "is what it is not and is not what it is." By this characteristically enigmatic phrase Sartre calls attention to the fact that men, unlike oak trees and ashtrays, can imagine possibilities that are not —for instance, a homosexual can imagine being a heterosexual; a waiter can imagine being a capitalist. Further, a homosexual is not just a homosexual; a waiter is not just a waiter. Each has other roles, and is aware, when acting out any particular role, of the other roles in his repertory of roles. This awareness cannot but affect the homosexual's or the waiter's playing of his role as homosexual or waiter. Hence man is almost always *acting*, rather than living. He is in "bad faith."

That man's mode of life is not one of undivided singleness like that of the ashtray, that men can imagine alternatives, consider possibilities, and critically reflect on what they are doing, no philosopher would deny. "The unexamined life," Socrates declared, "is not worth living," * and many philosophers have prized consciousness precisely because (as they would say) it enriches life with additional dimensions. Not so Sartre. The characters in his novels detest consciousness and the distancing, or mediation, it introduces into experience. So in *The Reprieve* Daniel, a homosexual, asks,

> *Why can't I be what I am*, be *a pederast, villain, coward, a loath-*
> *some object that doesn't even manage to exist? . . . Just* to be. *In*
> *the dark, at random! To be homosexual just as the oak is oak. To*
> *extinguish myself. Extinguish the inner eye.*[75]

But he cannot; he is doomed to the divided, for-itself mode of being.
Thus consciousness, like the recognition of freedom, is a source of
despair.

There is still another source of despair. Man is a questioner who
demands final, absolutely complete and definitive answers. Only a God
who knows all could give such answers. Therefore, man yearns to be God.
But alas!—not only is man not God; God does not, and cannot, exist.
This is easily proved. The concept of God is the concept of being wholly
in-itself-for-itself. But being wholly for-itself is entire consciousness and
being wholly in-itself is absolute unconsciousness. It follows that the concept of God—of a being that is both entirely conscious and absolutely
unconscious—is a logical contradiction. Nevertheless, man, poor pathetic
man, passionately longs to be God—that is, he longs to encompass a contradiction that cannot exist. Since this hope is absurd, man is doomed to
disappointment. He is in fact "a useless passion."[76]

Poor falcon!

## Philosophical Investigations and beyond

Having now reached midcentury by another route, we must consider
Wittgenstein's bombshell and some of the fallout from it. The *Tractatus*,
which had appeared in 1921, had been a major influence on the
positivists, as we have seen. Thereafter Wittgenstein published nothing,
but it was known that his views had undergone a transformation and
various versions of his new theory had circulated without his permission.
In 1953, two years after his death, *Philosophical Investigations* appeared,
probably the most influential philosophical work of this century.

*Philosophical Investigations* begins with a devastating critique of the
picture theory of language—the theory which, as we have seen, had been
a central feature of the *Tractatus*. If Wittgenstein had been led to adopt
the picture theory by an account he had read of a trial in which miniature cars represented the cars in an automobile accident, he is said to
have suddenly come to see the inadequacy of the picture theory when an
Italian friend made a typical Neapolitan gesture and asked, "What does
*that* picture?"

The *Investigations* does not maintain simply that the picture theory
presented in the *Tractatus* is mistaken; if that were the difficulty, the

---

\* *GBWW*, Vol. 7, p. 210.

remedy might be to provide another, better focused picture. No; the *Investigations* maintains that the picture of language as a picture is a lens through which we have been looking at the world, but without realizing that there is this lens between our eyes and reality. In other words (though Wittgenstein does not say so), the *Investigations* uncovered an unconscious presupposition of exactly the kind that Husserl believed could be uncovered only by bracketing. And the picture theory did not only distort the view set forth in *Tractatus*; it also distorted the views of Russell and of the positivists. As Wittgenstein noted, in the *Tractatus* he had written, "The general form of propositions is: This is how things are." And now he commented:

> *That is the kind of proposition that one repeats to oneself count-less times. One thinks that one is tracing the outline of the thing's nature over and over again, and one is merely tracing round the frame through which we look at it.*[77]

Pictures, it might be said, hold us captive.

The picture, in this case, is of course the picture of language as a picture. This picture is not *wholly* false. If the question be asked whether the description of language as a picture is "appropriate," the answer is,

> *Yes, it is appropriate, but only for this narrowly circumscribed region, not for the whole of what you were claiming to describe.*
> *It is as if someone were to say: "A game consists in moving objects about on a surface according to certain rules . . ."—and we replied: You seem to be thinking of board games, but there are others. You can make your definition correct by expressly restrict-ing it to those games.*[78]

Similarly, as regards language. Anyone who reviews the immense variety of ways in which people actually use language—

> *Giving orders, and obeying them—*
> *Reporting an event—*
> *Speculating about an event—*
> *Making up a story; and reading it—*
> *Play-acting—*
> *Singing catches—*
> *Guessing riddles—*
> *Asking, thanking, cursing, greeting, praying—*[79]

will see not only that the picture theory does not cover the whole range and variety of usages but that no description, no theory, can do so. Suppose someone were to reply that it is a general description of language to say that every word signifies something. But what, Wittgenstein asks, does such a general description amount to?

> *Think of the tools in a tool-box: there is a hammer, pliers, a*
> *saw, a screw-driver, a rule, a glue-pot, glue, nails and screws.—*
> *The functions of words are as diverse as the functions of these*
> *objects. (And in both cases there are similarities.) . . .*
>
> *When we say: "Every word in language signifies something" we*
> *have so far said* nothing whatever; *unless we have explained*
> *exactly* what *distinction we wish to make. . . .*
>
> *Imagine someone's saying: "All tools serve to modify something.*
> *Thus the hammer modifies the position of the nail, the saw the*
> *shape of the board, and so on."—And what is modified by the rule,*
> *the glue-pot, the nails?—"Our knowledge of a thing's length, the*
> *temperature of the glue, and the solidity of the box."—Would*
> *anything be gained by this assimilation of expressions?*[80]

This passage is a good example of Wittgenstein's new technique of philosophizing that was to have so great an influence on the next generation of philosophers. He did not *argue;* he produced counterexamples to any generalization that might be put forward. He said in effect, "Yes; your generalization covers such-and-such cases, but it does not cover such-and-such other cases. The reason you have not realized that you have overgeneralized is that the cases covered by your generalization seem to you especially important. But to someone else, in a different context, other cases will seem equally, or more, important."

The passage shows something else. The overgeneralizer has not only overgeneralized; he makes the generalization look plausible only by stretching language artificially, often to the point of absurdity. ("Our knowledge of a thing's length is modified by the rule.") Wittgenstein held that stretching language in this way in the interest of achieving generality was typical of philosophy as it had been practiced in the past. This was why, as Moore had complained, philosophy departed so far from common sense. Wittgenstein's aim was to dissolve traditional philosophical problems by showing that these problems arise only when, in the interest of some special philosophical demand, such as the demand for generality, language is stretched artificially. Everybody knows what language is, just as everybody knows what a tool is. There is no puzzle about language (or about tools) until philosophers, assuming that language (and tools) must have a "nature," look for that nature and cannot find it.

Alternatively, and in a characteristic metaphor, philosophical problems arise when language loses traction, when the wheels spin without taking hold. The problems disappear as soon as language is put back into traction. Language is in traction when it is a part of some goal-directed social activity, an activity whose end is furthered by the language the participants in this activity use in communicating with one another. Suppose a man is building with building stones and that he has an assistant whose job is to bring him the stones as he needs them. "For this purpose they use a language consisting of the words 'block,' 'pillar,' 'slab,' 'beam'. . . . Conceive this as a complete primitive language."[81]

In order to emphasize that language is instrumental to some goal-directed activity, Wittgenstein called the whole enterprise into which language and action are "interwoven," a "language game." Since language is instrumental to a goal-directed activity, language is effective (is "good" language) if it furthers that activity. This is why a language consisting only of the words *block, pillar, slab,* and *beam* can be a complete language; it is complete if, by calling out these words from time to time, the builder gets the materials he needs. It follows that there are as many different languages as there are "games," i.e., different kinds of goal-directed activities. (This is why there is no "essence," or "nature," of language to be found by philosophical analysis.) Hence Wittgenstein's injunction: look, not to the meaning, but to the use: Don't look for the meaning, for there is no one meaning that is *the* meaning. Look, instead, at the way the word is actually being used in the language game that is under discussion; that use is its meaning in *this* game.

For millenia, philosophers have argued over the "status" of universals —is the universal "game," for instance, *ante rem, in re,* or *post rem?* Instead of adding to this sterile debate, as it seemed to him, Wittgenstein proposed to dissolve the whole problem: the only reason anybody could have for believing in the existence of universals at all is his desire for certainty, his desire to have a rule that makes it absolutely certain whether any particular object is, or is not, a member of a class—for instance, the class of games. But Wittgenstein held that such rules have no use except to satisfy this special need.

> I can *give the concept "number"* [or *"horse," or "cow," or "game"*] *rigid limits, . . . but I can also use it so that the extension of the concept is* not *closed by a frontier. . . .*
> *"But then"* [asks the worried traditional philosopher] *"the use of the word is unregulated, the 'game' we play with it is unregulated."—It is not everywhere circumscribed by rules; but no more are there any rules for how high one throws the ball in tennis, or how hard; yet tennis is a game for all that and has rules too.*[82]

A definition of *game,* a rule for deciding whether a particular activity is, or is not, a game, is like a signpost. A satisfactory signpost is one that guides travelers along their way; if too many travelers misread a signpost and lose their way, it can be made less ambiguous. But no signpost can be designed that is absolutely unambiguous, that could never be misread by anybody under any circumstances. Similarly, for the definition of *game:* this can be revised as needed, but it cannot be, and it need not be, decisive for all possible cases. It is, therefore, theoretically possible always to doubt whether some particular activity is, *for sure,* a game. But is such doubt reasonable? We are not in doubt merely *because it is possible for us to imagine a doubt. I can easily imagine someone always doubting before he opened his front door whether an abyss did not yawn behind it, and making sure about it before he went through the door (and he might on some occasion prove to be right)—but that does not make me doubt in the same case.*[83]

If this sounds familiar, it should: Dewey had said it all earlier. Wittgenstein—at least the Wittgenstein of the *Investigations*—shared Dewey's belief, first, that concepts are instruments and, second, that nobody would fail to see that this is the case whose view was not distorted by an almost neurotic quest for certainty. If one looks at the world without this distorting lens, what one sees is not universals but merely "family resemblances." Consider, for example, some of the activities we call "games."

*I mean board-games, card-games, ball-games, Olympic games, and so on. What is common to them all?—Don't say: "There* must *be something common, or they would not be called 'games'"—but look and see whether there is anything common to all. . . . Don't think, but look!—Look for example at board-games, with their multifarious relationships. Now pass to card-games; here you find many correspondences with the first group, but many common features drop out, and others appear. . . . Look at the parts played by skill and luck; and at the difference between skill in chess and skill in tennis. . . .*

*And the result of this examination is: we see a complicated network of similarities overlapping and criss-crossing. . . .*

*I can think of no better expression to characterize these similarities than "family resemblances"; for the various resemblances between members of a family: build, features, colour of eyes, gait, temperament, etc. etc. overlap and criss-cross in the same way.*[84]

Family resemblances, then, are what we see when we actually look. So much for all those essences and other verities that Husserl supposed to be disclosed in transcendentally reduced observation.

And what applies to *essence* and to *universal* applies to all those other words that are the special favorites of philosophers—*knowledge, being, object, I, proposition, name.* Each of these has generated seemingly insoluble puzzles because philosophers have never asked themselves the simple question "Is the word ever actually used in this way in the language game which is its original home?" The answer, of course, is that it is not. "What *we* do," in contrast, "is to bring words back from their metaphysical to their everyday use." [85]

As an example of "what *we* do," consider the word *analysis.* Analysis decomposes a complex into its simple constituents. But

> *What are the simple constituent parts of a chair?—The bits of wood of which it is made? Or the molecules, or the atoms? ... We use the word "composite" (and therefore the word "simple") in an enormous number of different and differently related ways.*[86]

Thus an answer to the question "What are the simples that analysis yields?" depends on the circumstances. Given a specification of the circumstances, language is in traction when questions about analysis are asked. But *philosophical* talk about an analysis that yields "ultimate simples" or "logical atoms" is spinning; it is out of traction because no circumstances are, or can be, specified.

As to "ideal language": of course the mathematical calculi of the logicians are useful for special purposes, but to call them "ideal"

> *is liable to mislead, for it sounds as if these languages were better, more perfect, than our everyday language; and as if it took the logician to shew people at last what a proper sentence looked like.*[87]

What Wittgenstein said about the subject-to-revision character of definitions and signposts applies equally to logic. Where did logicians get the idea that "there can't be any vagueness in logic"? The "crystalline purity" that they believe they *find* in logic is actually a requirement that slipped in unnoticed at the start of their investigation, a requirement that is but the reflection of the logician's quest for certainty.

In this attack on what he called the "subliming" of logic, Wittgenstein again sounds like Dewey; he is also like Dewey in wanting to reform philosophy. But their emphases are different. Dewey wanted to reform philosophy in order to improve our traffic with nature; Wittgenstein wanted to reform philosophy in order to free us from "the bewitchment of our intelligence by language." But there is another and deeper difference. Wittgenstein thought that our intelligence has been bewitched by language because we suffer from "deep disquietudes"—among them, the passion to say the unsayable. In a way this was what the positivists had maintained: To hold that metaphysics is nonsense is a way of holding that metaphysicians have been trying to say the unsayable. But what a different way of saying this Wittgenstein's way of saying it is!

The positivists' way of saying it reflects their lack of interest in—some would want to say "insensitivity to"—the unsayable, a lack of interest (insensitivity) that Dewey shared. In contrast, Wittgenstein's way of saying it shows that he shared this passion. In this respect, he reminds us—to our surprise—of Heidegger. But he wanted to *cure* people of this passion, not, as with Heidegger, to render them open to "the claim and call of Being."

Wittgenstein's notion of philosophy as therapy—at the opposite pole from the old notion of philosophy as the most general of the sciences—

caught the attention of John Wisdom, who developed it further. The positivists were correct, Wisdom thinks, in comparing metaphysics with poetry, but this is not—as they thought—to derogate it. When a poet writes that "the red rose is a falcon and the white rose is a dove," he is certainly using language in an odd way, for red roses are red roses and white roses are white roses. But the "verbal impropriety" of this kind of talk is "not without a purpose." [88] Its purpose is to reveal "what is known and hidden"—in this case, a similarity between doves and white roses, and between falcons and red roses, that we might otherwise overlook. So, too, for philosophical talk to the effect, for instance, that "time is unreal" or that "everything is determined." What aspects of our lives and of the world does the oddity of philosophical talk forcefully bring to our attention? This talk, however abstract and arid it may sound, has in it "echoes from the heart." [89] In this respect philosophy is like psychoanalysis. The metaphysician, like the psychiatrist,

> *seeks to bring into the light those models from the past which for good and evil so powerfully influence our lives in the present, so powerfully distort reality and so powerfully illuminate it. . . . In the labyrinth of metaphysics are the same whispers as one hears when climbing Kafka's staircases to the tribunal which is always one floor further up.* [90]

Though we try to hurry away from such whispers or to drown them in chatter, we would do better to return and "force the accusers to speak up. . . . We can hardly do this by ourselves. But there are those who will go with us and, however terrifying the way, not desert us."

It was not, however, this aspect of *Philosophical Investigations* that attracted most philosophers. Those who had participated in the positivists' program for eliminating metaphysics but who had been disappointed by the failure of the Verifiability Principle to do the job assigned it naturally welcomed Wittgenstein's linguistic method of dissolving philosophical problems. Those who had been influenced by Moore's defense of ordinary beliefs were impressed by Wittgenstein's advocacy of ordinary language. Thus it came about that refinement and extended application of the method of analysis inaugurated in *Philosophical Investigations* became the chief occupation of almost all philosophers who did not belong to the phenomenological-existentialist camp.

One notable exception is Wilfrid Sellars, who has continued the realistic tradition, but in a very sophisticated form. "The aim of philosophy," Sellars declares,

> *is to understand how things in the broadest possible sense of the term hang together in the broadest possible sense of the term. . . . To achieve success in philosophy would be, to use a contemporary term of phrase, to "know one's way around" with respect to . . .*

> *such radically different items as "cabbages and kings," numbers*
> *and duties, possibilities and finger snaps, aesthetic experiences and*
> *death.*[91]

Since all of these items fall within the scope of one or another of the special sciences, philosophy differs from science only in its greater generality. It is in fact only "the 'eye on the whole' which distinguishes . . . the philosopher from the persistently reflective specialist."[92]

It is impossible here to discuss the details of the synoptic view at which Sellars believes philosophy must aim. For us, the points to note are, first, that he believes it possible to obtain a view of the world that is true of the world, not merely relative to some conceptual scheme or other, and, second, that he holds this true view to be the view that quantum physics is gradually disclosing.

More representative of contemporary philosophizing is the work of J. L. Austin and Gilbert Ryle. Austin's critique of sense-data theories is a good example of the so-called "ordinary-language" philosophy in action, especially if it be contrasted with Dewey's approach. Where Dewey invited our attention to experience (When do we, as a matter of fact, actually experience sense-data?), Austin invited our attention to the way in which Englishmen actually use such words as *illusion* and *delusion*.

It will be recalled that to Moore and Russell it seemed absolutely unquestionable that there is a distinction between what is directly perceived and what is not directly perceived but only inferred. Austin undermined this distinction, which was the starting point for all versions of realism, by simply listing the circumstances in which people distinguish between directly perceiving something and indirectly perceiving something. What are these circumstances? Well, we "contrast the man who saw [a] procession directly with the man who saw it *through a periscope;* or we might contrast the place from which you can watch the door directly with the place from which you can see it only *in the mirror.*"[93] Examination of usage shows that we talk about perceiving something indirectly when there is "some kink in direction"—when we are "not looking straight at the object in question." That is all there is to the distinction: philosophical use of it to maintain that we don't directly perceive a coin, but only a sense-datum, when we are looking straight at the coin from a few feet away is "not only false but simply absurd."[94]

If Austin attacked philosophical usage of individual terms, Ryle concentrates on whole clusters of such terms, undertaking to show that philosophical problems arise because terms belonging to different "categories" are mistakenly grouped together. But his approach is still linguistic, and the underlying assumption is that ordinary usage is the criterion for evaluating philosophical usage. As Austin wrote, "One can't abuse ordinary language without paying for it."[95]

*The Concept of Mind* is a good example of Ryle's method. He begins by pointing out that this book "does not give new information about minds. We possess already a wealth of information about minds," information furnished not by philosophers but by scientists. Instead, the book is intended "to rectify the logical geography of the knowledge which we already possess." [96] Rectifying the logical geography means learning which concepts "correlate" with one another and which do not.

To put this differently and more formally, every proposition has certain "logical powers," meaning that it is "related to other propositions in various discoverable ways." [97] Ascertaining the logical powers of a concept—say, the concept of "existence"—is like ascertaining the boundaries of a right of way across a field: just as the boundaries of the right of way indicate where one is permitted to walk and where one is forbidden to walk, so a concept's logical powers indicate which of the sentences in which this concept occurs are meaningful and which are nonsensical. Thus we can say (1) There exists a cathedral in Oxford; (2) There exists a three-engined bomber; (3) There exists a square number between 9 and 25. Anyone who didn't understand, at least "by wont," that "existence" in these three sentences has very different logical powers might find himself saying, "The square of 4 is older than the square root of 5," which is nonsense. And it is nonsense because the concept of existence (1) correlates with, and the concept of existence (3) does not correlate with, such concepts as the concept of "aging," the concept of "younger than," and the concept of "coming into being at a particular point of time."

In such a case as this the difference in logical powers is obvious, and indeed people do know "by wont" the logical powers of most of the concepts they use. Thus they can "appraise [another man's] performances, assess his progress, understand his words and actions, discern his motives and see his jokes." [98] Unfortunately, for three hundred years we have been trying to "coordinate" all this genuine knowledge about the mind and how it works by means of a set of abstract ideas, inherited from Descartes, whose "logical cross-bearings" have never been determined. Concepts like "intellect," "emotion," and "will" have been mistakenly correlated with the concept of "substance," or "thing," a concept that has a very different set of logical powers, thus producing muddles as bad as the muddle that would be created by trying to correlate the existence of square numbers with aging.

It is important to Ryle that, though we may lack explicit knowledge of "the rules governing the logical behavior of propositions," [99] we nevertheless know their use "by wont." This means that philosophical criticism does not operate in terms of an ideal standard of the kind Wittgenstein attacked. Instead, it only uncovers the correlations implicit in ordinary, everyday languages. Philosophers in the past have confused themselves and ordinary people by failing to determine the correlations that actually obtain among the concepts we all use all the time; it is up to philosophy in the future to undo the damage.

Since the new philosophy does this by exposing the absurdities to which mistaken correlations lead, it may seem destructive. But the *reductio ad absurdum* arguments that it uses against muddled "galaxies of abstract ideas" are "neither more nor less nihilist than are threshing operations."[100] When the chaff has been eliminated, the grain remains.

Meanwhile, in the very heart of ordinary-language territory a revival of metaphysics has occurred. The initiator of this development is P. F. Strawson, who does what he calls "descriptive metaphysics," in contrast to "revisionary metaphysics." Whereas revisionary metaphysics is concerned to produce a better structure of our thought (and therefore shares a certain similarity of aims with positivism and ideal-language theory, which are concerned to produce a better structure of our language), "descriptive metaphysics is content to describe the actual structure of our thought."[101]

Thus descriptive metaphysics conforms to Wittgenstein's injunction: "We must do away with all *explanation,* and description alone must take its place."[102] But it differs from ordinary ordinary-language philosophy in that, though it too starts from "the actual use of words," it does not stop there. The structure that the descriptive metaphysician seeks "does not readily display itself on the surface of language, but lies submerged." It is obvious that Strawson would be dissatisfied with the analytical techniques of Wittgenstein and Austin, for they deliberately stay at the surface of actual usage. But it might be thought that he would find the approach of Ryle more satisfactory. The trouble is, however, that Ryle's "galaxies" of abstract ideas are so near the surface that they change through time. Strawson's whole procedure presupposes that "there is a massive central core of human thinking . . . [of] categories and concepts which, in their most fundamental character, change not at all."[103]

Here again, then, philosophy has returned to the Kantian paradigm, and not to the later, relativizing versions of idealism but to something very close to Kant's contention that there is an a priori structure in which all minds everywhere share. Thus Strawson has duplicated the Kantian move of offering the falcon a human, instead of an objective, center about which to orient his flight. The ordinary-language philosophers provide such a center, too, but in a less obvious way. In their analyses ordinary language has become in effect a kind of supreme court of final appeal. Or, to revert to a metaphor we have used before, for them ordinary language is a firm basis on which the ladder of thought and action can securely rest.

But with philosophy thus coming round again almost full circle, we are bound to ask ourselves whether the proposed center is likely to remain fixed. Will the shift from a nonlinguistic to a linguistic formulation be enough to prevent history from repeating itself? How secure a basis will ordinary language prove to be?

It would seem that, for most ordinary-language philosophers, ordinary language is their own language, the language of upper-class Englishmen (and Americans). Most linguistic analysts also operate as if this ordinary language is static and unchanging. It is true that Austin and Ryle both recognize that, as Ryle says, "new theory-shaping ideas are struck out from time to time . . . by men of genius" and that, as a result, the logical powers of these new "crucial ideas" have to be determined and coordinated with the old.[104] Thus—in their view but in Strawson's terminology—philosophy cannot be merely descriptive; it has to be revisionist, if only because "men of genius" are constantly changing Strawson's unchanging core.

Though Austin and Ryle recognize, as it were officially, that language changes, change is not in the focus of attention for them or for most ordinary-language philosophers. Their practice is better represented by Austin's observation that "the ordinary 'concepts' employed by English speakers . . . have evolved over a long time: that is, they . . . have faced the test of practical experience, of continual hard use, better than their vanished rivals."[105] Hence Strawson's warning against "tampering"— usages that have won out in an evolutionary struggle for survival have a fitness that philosophers are seldom able to improve on. "Tampering . . . is not so easy as is often supposed [and] is not justified or needed so often as is often supposed."[106]

But what do poets and other men of genius do but "tamper" with the language? It is no accident that linguistic analysts usually ignore poetry when they are looking for examples of usage, for to emphasize the cognitively meaningful "oddity" of poetry and philosophy, as Wisdom does, is to call attention to the fact that language is an open spiral, not a firm floor.

Nor is it just a matter of the openness of even the most ordinary of ordinary English; we have also to consider the implications of Wittgenstein's deep remark that "to imagine a language means to imagine a form of life." That is, since language expresses and articulates the beliefs that underlie some social group's way of living, different social groups have different languages. Wittgenstein was perhaps thinking chiefly of differences in such everyday practices as buying apples, weighing cheese, or calling for slabs, but this view of the relation between a language and a form of life also applies, if it applies at all, to the relation between (say) the Hopi language and the Hopi form of life. Agreements about the nature of time, about values, about the structure of the world can be reached within a particular form of life, but not across forms of life. "What has to be accepted, the given, is—so one could say—*forms of life*."[107] We are back once more to Heidegger's many houses, with Europeans and East Asians—not to mention Hopis—dwelling in entirely different houses.

But is this relativistic conclusion correct? About this, as about so much else, there is no agreement. Linguists such as Chomsky and anthropologists such as Levi-Strauss, who believe that there is a universal "deep structure," support Strawson's thesis—if there are as many houses as there are languages, it is nonetheless true that all of these houses have a common architectural plan.

Surprisingly, few philosophers have seriously considered this question, but Quine is one who has, and he has reached the opposite conclusion. Suppose, he says, that an anthropologist or a linguist observes that a native uses the word *gavagai* whenever he (the observer) would use the word *rabbit,* and never uses *gavagai* when the observer would not use the word *rabbit.* Can the observer conclude that *rabbit* and *gavagai* have the same meaning? No; it is true that the two words are "stimulus-synonymous," but it is impossible to devise any test by which the observer could ascertain whether the native *means* by *gavagai* just what the observer means by *rabbit.* What the observer means by *rabbit* is the whole rabbit.

> *Who knows but what the objects to which [*"gavagai"*] applies are not rabbits after all, but mere stages, or brief temporal segments, of rabbits. . . . Or perhaps the objects to which "gavagai" applies are all and sundry undetached parts of rabbits. . . . When from the sameness of stimulus meanings of "Gavagai" and "Rabbit" the linguist leaps to the conclusion that a gavagai is a whole enduring rabbit, he is just taking for granted that the native is enough like us to have a brief general term for rabbits and no brief general term for rabbit stages or parts.*[108]

The fact is that every term, even the simplest, is "theory-laden," and there is no way to tell whether *rabbit* and *gavagai* are laden by the same theory or by different theories, for any evidence by which one might seek to determine this is itself theory-laden. We can never free ourselves from all theories and face the facts themselves in their purity. "We can never do better than occupy the standpoint of some theory or other, the best we can muster at the time." [109]

Wittgenstein had declared that he wanted to help the fly escape from the fly bottle. That is, he wanted to help man free himself from the "bewitchment" of language. He wrote as if he thought that the way to escape from the fly bottle is to get back to ordinary language, and, as we have seen, many linguistic philosophers have assumed that there exists such an easy way out. But it now looks as if this may itself be a linguistic illusion. Though the fly may escape from this or that fly bottle, he only lands in another: perhaps there is no common ground, no common world, outside all fly bottles.

Thus there is no agreement even on the question of whether agreement is in principle possible or in principle impossible. Here it seems fair to characterize twentieth-century philosophy as a widening gyre.

1 W. Wordsworth, *The Prelude,* bk. 2, lines 233, ff.

2 Quoted by Nietzsche in *Schopenhauer as Educator,* in *Existentialism from Dostoevsky to Sartre,* trans. and ed. W. Kaufmann (New York: Meridian Books, 1956), p. 103.

3 Ibid., p. 102.

4 F. Nietzsche, *Beyond Good and Evil,* trans. M. Cowan (Chicago: Henry Regnery Co., 1955), pp. 101, 3, 6, 15.

5 F. H. Bradley, *Appearance and Reality* (Oxford: Oxford University Press, Clarendon Press, 1930), p. 111, note 1.

6 Ibid., p. 140.

7 G. E. Moore, "The Refutation of Idealism," in *Philosophical Studies* (Patterson, N.J.: Littlefield, Adams & Co., 1959), pp. 17, 24–26.

8 Ibid., pp. 20, 25.

9 Ibid., p. 27.

10 G. E. Moore, "The Subject-matter of Psychology," in *Proceedings of the Aristotelian Society* (London: Williams and Norgate, 1910), 10:36.

11 B. Russell, "My Mental Development" in *The Philosophy of Bertrand Russell,* ed. P. A. Schilpp (Evanston, Ill.: Library of Living Philosophers, 1946), p. 12.

12 G. E. Moore, "The Status of Sense-Data," in *Philosophical Studies,* p. 190.

13 Ibid., pp. 195–96.

14 G. E. Moore, "An Autobiography" in *The Philosophy of G. E. Moore,* 2d ed., ed. P. A. Schilpp (New York: Tudor Publishing Co., Library of Living Philosophers, 1952), p. 14.

15 B. Russell, "Logical Atomism," in *Contemporary British Philosophy,* ed. J. H. Muirhead (New York: The Macmillan Co., 1924), p. 359.

16 B. Russell, "My Mental Development," in Schilpp, p. 7.

17 B. Russell, *The Analysis of Mind* (London: George Allen & Unwin, 1921), pp. 141–42.

18 B. Russell, "Knowledge by Acquaintance and Knowledge by Description," in *Mysticism and Logic* (London: Penguin Books, Pelican Books, 1953), pp. 212–14.

19 B. Russell, "The Ultimate Constituents of Matter," in *Mysticism and Logic,* pp. 124–25.

20 Ibid., p. 133.

21 M. Schlick, "Positivism and Realism," in *Logical Positivism,* ed. A. J. Ayer (Glencoe, Ill.: The Free Press, 1959), p. 107.

22 B. Russell, "Introduction," in *Tractatus Logico-Philosophicus,* by L. Wittgenstein (London: Routledge & Kegan Paul, 1961), p. x.

23 G. H. von Wright, "Biographical Sketch," in *Ludwig Wittgenstein: A Memoir,* by Norman Malcolm (London: Oxford University Press, 1958), pp. 7–8.

24 L. Wittgenstein, *Tractatus,* sec. 2.1, 2.16.

25 Ibid., sec. 2.17.

26 Ibid., sec. 2.21.

27 Ibid., sec. 2.0201.

28 Ibid., sec. 4.221.

29 Ibid., sec. 3.26, 3.263.

30 Ibid., sec. 3.144.

31 Ibid., sec. 1.2.

32 Ibid., sec. 1.21.

33 O. Neurath, "Protocol Sentences," in *Logical Positivism,* p. 202.

34 R. Carnap, "The Elimination of Metaphysics through Logical Analysis of Language," in *Logical Positivism,* pp. 78–79.

35 L. Wittgenstein, *Tractatus,* sec. 6.51, 6.521.

36 O. Neurath, *Logical Positivism,* p. 201.

37 Ibid., p. 203.

38 A. J. Ayer, "Editor's Introduction," in *Logical Positivism,* p. 15.

39 R. Carnap, "Empiricism, Semantics, and Ontology," in *Meaning and Necessity,* 2d ed., enl. (Chicago: University of Chicago Press, Phoenix Books, 1958), p. 206.

40 Ibid., pp. 208, 221.

41 A. N. Whitehead, *Science and the Modern World* (New York: The Macmillan Co., 1925), p. 27.

42 A. N. Whitehead, *Modes of Thought* (New York: The Macmillan Co., Capricorn Books, 1938), p. 58.

43 A. N. Whitehead, *Essays in Science and Philosophy* (New York: Philosophical Library, 1948), p. 15.

44 A. N. Whitehead, *Modes of Thought*, p. 237.

45 A. N. Whitehead, *Science and the Modern World*, p. 80.

46 Ibid., pp. 127, 113–14.

47 J. Dewey, *How We Think* (Boston: D. C. Heath & Co., 1933), p. 107.

48 L. Wittgenstein, *Tractatus*, sec. 3.25.

49 J. Dewey, *Essays in Experimental Logic* (New York: Dover Publications, 1953), pp. 37–38.

50 Ibid., pp. 39, 41, 43.

51 Ibid., p. 6.

52 J. Dewey, *Experience and Nature* (Chicago: Open Court Publishing Co., 1929), pp. 96, 21.

53 Ibid., p. 437.

54 J. Dewey, "Democracy and Educational Administration," in *Intelligence in the Modern World*, ed. J. Ratner (New York: Random House, The Modern Library, 1939), pp. 400–402.

55 E. Husserl, "Philosophy and the Crisis of European Man," in *Phenomenology and the Crisis of Philosophy*, trans. Q. Lauer (New York: Harper & Row, Harper Torchbooks, 1965), p. 186.

56 Quoted in H. Spiegelberg, *The Phenomenological Movement*, 2d ed. (The Hague: Martinus Nijhoff, 1965), 1:82.

57 E. Husserl, *Ideas: A General Introduction to Pure Phenomenology*, trans. W. R. Boyce Gibson (New York: The Macmillan Co., 1931), sec. 27, 30.

58 Ibid., sec. 31.

59 Ibid., sec. 33.

60 Ibid., sec. 88.

61 E. Husserl, *Cartesian Meditations*, trans. D. Cairns (The Hague: Martinus Nijhoff, 1960), pp. 39–40.

62 M. Heidegger, *Being and Time*, trans. J. Macquarrie and E. Robinson (London: SCM Press, 1962), p. 19.

63 M. Heidegger, "The Way Back into the Ground of Metaphysics," in *Existentialism from Dostoevsky to Sartre*, p. 207.

64 Ibid., p. 208.

65 M. Heidegger, *Being and Time*, p. 25.

66 M. Heidegger, "The Way Back . . . ," pp. 211, 209.

67 Ibid., p. 213.

68 M. Heidegger, *Being and Time*, p. 100.

69 Ibid., p. 321.

70 Ibid., pp. 294–95.

71 M. Heidegger, "A Dialogue on Language," in *On the Way to Language*, trans. P. D. Hertz (New York: Harper & Row, 1971), p. 5.

72 Ibid., p. 52.

73 J.-P. Sartre, *The Transcendence of the Ego*, trans. F. Williams and R. Kirkpatrick (New York: Farrar, Straus & Giroux, Noonday Press, 1957), p. 79.

74 Ibid., pp. 99–100.

75 J.-P. Sartre, *The Reprieve*, trans. E. Sutton (New York: Bantam Books, 1968), p. 101.

76 J.-P. Sartre, *Being and Nothingness*, trans. H. Barnes (New York: Philosophical Library, 1956), p. 615.

77 L. Wittgenstein, *Philosophical Investigations*, trans. G. E. M. Anscombe (New York: The Macmillan Co., 1953), sec. 114.

78 Ibid., sec. 3.

79 Ibid., sec. 23. (Some of Wittgenstein's examples have been omitted.)

80 Ibid., sec. 11–14.

81 Ibid., sec. 2.

[82] Ibid., sec. 68.

[83] Ibid., sec. 84.

[84] Ibid., sec. 66–67.

[85] Ibid., sec. 116.

[86] Ibid., sec. 47.

[87] Ibid., sec. 81.

[88] J. Wisdom, "Philosophy, Anxiety and Novelty," in *Philosophy and Psycho-Analysis* (Oxford: Basil Blackwell, 1953), p. 112.

[89] J. Wisdom, "Philosophy and Psycho-Analysis," in *Philosophy and Psycho-Analysis,* p. 181.

[90] J. Wisdom, "Philosophy, Metaphysics and Psycho-Analysis," in *Philosophy and Psycho-Analysis,* pp. 276, 282.

[91] W. Sellars, "Philosophy and the Scientific Image of Man," in *Frontiers of Science and Philosophy,* ed. R. G. Colodny (Pittsburgh: University of Pittsburgh Press, 1962), p. 37.

[92] Ibid., p. 39.

[93] J. L. Austin, *Sense and Sensibilia,* ed. G. J. Warnock (New York: Oxford University Press, 1964), p. 15.

[94] Ibid., p. 19.

[95] Ibid., p. 15.

[96] G. Ryle, *The Concept of Mind* (New York: Barnes and Noble, 1971), p. 7.

[97] G. Ryle, *Philosophical Arguments: An Inaugural Lecture* (Oxford: Clarendon Press, 1945), p. 7.

[98] Ibid., p. 7.

[99] Ibid., p. 8.

[100] Ibid., p. 6.

[101] P. F. Strawson, *Individuals* (Garden City, N.Y.: Doubleday & Co., Anchor Books, 1963), p. xiii.

[102] L. Wittgenstein, *Philosophical Investigations,* sec. 109.

[103] P. F. Strawson, *Individuals,* p. xiv.

[104] G. Ryle, *Philosophical Arguments,* p. 20.

[105] J. L. Austin, "Three Ways of Spilling Ink," reprinted in *Approaches to Ethics,* 2d ed., ed. W. T. Jones, F. Sontag, M. O. Beckner, and R. J. Fogelin (New York: McGraw-Hill Book Co., 1969), p. 654.

[106] J. L. Austin, *Sense and Sensibilia,* p. 63.

[107] L. Wittgenstein, *Philosophical Investigations,* p. 226.

[108] W. van O. Quine, *Word and Object* (Cambridge, Mass.: M.I.T. Press, 1960), pp. 51–52.

[109] Ibid., p. 22.

## NOTE TO THE READER

The history of the issues raised by Professor Jones's review of twentieth-century philosophy can easily be traced in *GBWW*. Hume's analysis of causation, which prompted, in part, the revolutionary philosophy of Kant, is contained in Section VII, Parts I and II, of his *Enquiry Concerning Human Understanding,* which appears in Volume 35; while all of Kant's major works, of which the most pertinent is the *Critique of Pure Reason,* are contained in Volume 42. The idealism of Hegel, against which Moore and Russell rebelled, is implicit in his *Philosophy of History,* for which see Volume 46.

Relevant discussions of the questions raised by Professor Jones may be found in the *Syntopicon.* In Chapter 66, on PHILOSOPHY, see Topics 1 and 1*b,* which treat the scope of philosophy and its relation to mathematics. See also, in the same chapter, Topic 3*a,* which deals with the foundations of philosophy in experience and common sense, and Topic 3*d,* on the methodological reformation of philosophy. In Chapter 45, on LANGUAGE, see Topic 1*a* on the role of language in thought, Topic 2*a* on the hypothesis of one natural language for all men, and Topic 5*b* on meaningless and absurd speech.

# The Anatomy of Justice in Taxation

## Walter J. Blum and Harry Kalven, Jr.

Walter J. Blum and Harry Kalven, Jr., both of whom attended the University of Chicago Law School, have been members of the faculty of the school since 1946 and have often collaborated with each other. The collaboration has produced two books—*The Uneasy Case for Progressive Taxation* (1953) and *Public Law Perspectives on a Private Law Problem: Auto Compensation Plans* (1965)—as well as a number of articles for law journals. The book on taxation, which has become a standard work in its field, was an attempt to explore the community sense of justice as it relates to the tax burden, and drew upon a study, admittedly tentative and incomplete, of popular attitudes toward progressive taxation. These attitudes are assumed, and are now and again explicitly referred to, in the essay that follows.

Professor Blum, who specializes in corporation finance and other subjects as well as taxation, is a member of the American Law Institute and was a consultant to its Federal Estate and Gift Tax Project, 1960–67. Professor Kalven is an authority on both constitutional law and the law of torts. He is the author of *The Negro and the First Amendment* (1965) and *The American Jury* (with Hans Zeisel, 1966).

This is an essay on tax justice addressed to the citizen generalist. The subject, which must have been of concern as far back as the time when taxes were first introduced in human affairs, is a difficult one. In any modern society the principles for judging tax justice will necessarily be applied to a tax system that is formidably complex and inaccessible. There is, however, a level of judgment that the citizen can bring to bear on these matters without first having mastered technical details. Our effort will be to map the main issues of tax justice rather than to argue their merits.

It is not as easy as it once may have been to isolate tax justice from other issues of fiscal policy. The raising of taxes was long regarded as belonging in a compartment of its own. Taxes were generally thought of as the indispensable method of financing government; what the government did with the tax money afterward was not seen as relevant to assessing the justice of how it was raised. But in recent years at least four factors have served to soften this stark image of taxation. These are (1) the increasing share of the national income that is spent through government, (2) the wider range of functions performed by government, including making of welfare or transfer payments, (3) the deliberate use of taxation as one form of government intervention to accomplish social objectives, and (4) the greater awareness we now have of the possibilities of controlling deliberately the value of money—of bringing about inflation or deflation. Although concerns about taxation are increasingly linked to these other aspects of fiscal operations, it is still profitable to pursue certain issues of policy as distinctively attached to the concept of tax justice.

## I  Locating taxation

To locate ourselves analytically, it may help to begin by juxtaposing taxation and charity. On the surface, the decisive difference is that tax contributions are exacted by legal compulsion, while charitable contributions are not. But the similarities nevertheless are arresting. Like tax moneys, funds for charity are devoted to nonprivate, community purposes. Where the habit and practice of charity are strong, as in certain religious communities, the compulsion to give may be formidable. Even more striking, there are explicit standards or canons of "proper" giving. It is reported that in early history, subjection to taxation was sometimes deemed inappropriate for aristocrats and seen as a badge of inferiority: the aristocrat was allowed, and expected, to make his contributions voluntarily. Common speech, too, offers its insight. With reference to charity, we talk about the quality of the individual donors—they are magnanimous, niggardly, and so on; with reference to taxation, we talk about the quality of the law —it is just or unjust.

If the element of coercion makes it easy to distinguish taxation from charity, the same element makes it awkward to distinguish the coercion of taxation from confiscation. It is a fundamental principle of our society, enshrined in constitutions, that private property cannot be taken for public purposes by the state without just compensation; yet these same constitutions explicitly confer the power to tax. The similarity is obvious: there is a taking by the state without compensation in both cases. But the difference is more troublesome to isolate than one would expect. It appears to reside essentially in the difference between taking money and taking specific property. What is surprising is that this difference becomes so value laden; taxation is at least a neutral word, while confiscation is pejorative in the extreme. Perhaps the answer is that the taking of specific property by the state is more intrusive than the creation of obligations to be satisfied in money; perhaps it is implausible that specific property is being taken to pay for the operations of government; perhaps it is suspected that the taking of property will be not systematic or disciplined by principle. But these clues may on occasion fail to keep taxation and confiscation clearly apart. Taxes can be set so high that the taxpayer is forced to dispose of specific property or simply turn it over to government in order to satisfy his tax obligation. This perception is at the core of the notion of confiscatory taxation. Indeed, revolutionary regimes have sometimes used the format of 100 percent taxation as the very vehicle of confiscation.

As we can distinguish taxation from charitable donations and public confiscation, so we can distinguish it from the purchase of services from government. The postal system furnishes, or did until recently, an example sufficient for our purposes. The classic postal service provided a model that appeared to have avoided all issues of tax justice. Supplying mail delivery throughout the country was widely thought to be an essential governmental function. The postal system like other government services could have been wholly financed out of general tax revenues, as in part it was whenever the receipts did not cover all operating expenses. What was underwritten was a government activity that provided pervasive benefits throughout the society, since everyone benefited to some degree by the availability of a postal network. But in the main this network was financed by selling the service directly to users; stamps stood in the place of taxes.

The public did not think of buying stamps as paying a tax but merely as buying a service; if they were led to see the charge as a form of taxation, they found it perfectly fair, at least so long as postal revenues equaled postal costs.

On a closer look one could, however, detect elements of tax justice. Had receipts *exceeded* postal costs while the government kept a monopoly on the service, the excess would have been a tax. Such an excess would put in issue the justice of raising taxes from postal users as a group. Moreover, postal surplus or deficit apart, to the extent that rates for various classes of services were not set strictly according to costs, one could not escape issues of justice among classes of users, again mirroring issues of justice among taxpayers.

The example of selling essential government services invites the question of how far the same strategy could be used to replace taxes. Could the government, to take an obvious example, sell police protection the way it sold mail delivery? No modern state seems ever to have experimented with the possibility, and for more than one sufficient reason. There would be administrative difficulties in estimating what to charge various groups; there would be the inescapable free-rider problem once a large number had elected to buy protection; there would be the awkwardness of requiring the very poor to pay for protection or go without it; and there would be the spillover effects in the larger community if any sector refused to buy police protection or were unable to do so. Some taxes, rather than user charges, are apparently necessary if government is to function.

It was once argued on the basis of so-called benefit theory that if we could not literally employ voluntary charges for government service, we should do the next best thing. The proposal was to apportion taxes on the basis of estimates of total benefits received from government. But benefit theory turned out to share most of the difficulties of relying directly on user charges, especially the embarrassment of fixing the proper charge on the poor. And upon serious scrutiny, most government services conferred benefits in too diffuse a fashion to permit the formulation of a tax schedule based upon them.

There nevertheless remains vitality to the related position that, whenever possible, particular government services should be financed by selling them to the users, thus minimizing any issues of tax justice. Financing such services via taxation, it is urged, must necessarily yield a less fair way of allocating that burden. Some have carried this theme a step further and argued that any service that could be financed by a user charge thereby proves itself not to be a government service, strictly speaking; it should either be ceded to the private sphere or turned over to a "self-sustaining" public corporation, which is indeed the intended fate today of the postal service.

The point is that while we all agree that taxes are the price we pay for government and its services, there is in the end an intractable difficulty in using this insight as a guide in allocating much of the tax burden.


Thus far the analogies have run from other familiar concepts to taxation in order to underscore certain characteristics of taxation. We turn now and analogize from taxation to other institutions in modern life, citing three instances: the military draft, land-use zoning, and inflation.

There is no doubt that, especially in peacetime, the government could *hire* an army. If it did, it would pay the total cost, presumably out of general tax revenues. By drafting its soldiers and paying them without regard to market price, the government meets the total cost of the venture only partly out of general revenue, but partly also by underpaying the soldiers drafted. This gap in payment, since it is the result of compulsion, can be reasonably viewed as a tax on the soldiers. We have then a tax that falls only on a part of the population, and a part that, for tax purposes, has been most arbitrarily selected. One can perhaps perceive the unfairness of the draft without utilizing the idiom of taxation, but the perception is sharply clarified by translating it into tax terms. No one would explicitly set up a tax to fall only on a part of the population that, from a tax perspective, had been so arbitrarily chosen.

Much the same analysis holds for zoning. The government action in zoning for land use, however beneficial overall, will operate to prevent some property holders from utilizing their property as they wish. The right to use the property in some of the outlawed ways might have made it more valuable on the market. The difference in value of the property, prior to zoning and after zoning, amounts to a public taking of some value from the owner. Here too, as in the case of the draft, the gap in values resulting from the government action can, with added insight, be described as a tax, a tax that again falls on an arbitrarily selected fraction of the population. One might be led from viewing this as a tax to the question of whether there are not some circumstances under which owners prejudiced by zoning restrictions, justified by the general good of the community, should be compensated for the loss of value.

Whenever government deliberately pursues a policy of inflation on behalf of some objective such as stimulating the economy, we can again detect what is in effect a tax at work. The burden imposed by inflation is obscured by the fact that a rise in price levels is accompanied by a rise in incomes, so that there appears to be a rough setoff, higher prices against higher incomes. There are, however, many in the society for whom there will be no compensating offset. These include annuitants, bondholders, bank depositors, owners of life insurance, and so forth. The gap for such persons is between the old and the new purchasing power of their fixed income. Here again it is reasonable to talk of the gap as a tax levied on a fraction of the population, selected by an altogether arbitrary criterion.

One more point is needed to locate ourselves analytically: taxation, and therefore tax justice, presupposes a system of private wealth. For the government to take in taxes an amount of money from a citizen implies that the citizen had a claim to the money beforehand. Clearly there are some communities in which the very idea of taxation is alien. Consider a monastic group in which the "income" of the members consists of that which is furnished them by the authorities. If a need for more revenue arises for the community, it may be met by giving each member somewhat less initially than he would otherwise have had, rather than by taking back or taxing back something that has already been given. Taxation thus posits a distinctive property relationship between taxpayer and government. If nothing is as certain as death and taxes, nevertheless it seems extreme to regard the government as having a continuing inchoate property interest in the income and wealth of its citizens. For most of us, each payment of taxes is a fresh event and a new taking, even when it occurs in the form of payroll or salary deductions. Tax justice frames the issue as one of fairness in taking something from you rather than as fairness in not allocating to you that something in the first place. These two kinds of fairness need not be mirror images of each other.

## II Vertical equity

Since the essence of taxation lies in coercive takings by government, there is always the question of how the act of taxing has affected the distribution of property or income among citizens. The relative shares of the citizens in property or income may have been altered when the situation before the tax is compared with the situation after the tax. Lurking among these rudimentary relationships lies perhaps the central question of tax justice.

Any tax can be characterized in one of three ways. First, there is the tax that is regressive. Here the distribution of property or income, whatever it was before the tax, is made *less equal* by operation of the tax. The obvious illustration is a tax to be levied only on the poor and not on the more wealthy. But regressive taxes may also include taxes that are equal in dollar amount as between the poor and the more wealthy. A universal head tax, of a given amount, would necessarily reduce the after-tax shares of the poor as compared with the after-tax shares of the more wealthy.

The second type is the tax that is progressive. Here the distribution of property or income, whatever it was before the tax, is made *more equal* by operation of the tax. A tax on income or wealth in which the rates are graduated upward would necessarily reduce, after taxation, the shares of the more wealthy as compared to the shares of the less wealthy.

The third type of tax is that which is neither regressive nor progressive. It may be designated "neutral" or "proportionate"; it would leave the relative shares of property and income *unchanged* before and after taxes.

While these types are readily differentiated as models, it may prove more difficult to characterize taxes in the real world. A particular tax, such as an excise tax on amusements, cannot be classified in this scheme unless we know something about the distribution of tastes for amusements. Moreover, the regressive or progressive impact of one tax may be offset by the progressive or regressive impact of another—as, for example, in a combination of a sales tax and an income tax. Further, the tax may nominally fall on one person but actually be borne by someone else. These complexities in the incidence of total tax systems pose genuine problems and are today subject to elaborate empirical study, but they lie outside this essay. Our discussion can proceed on three simplifying assumptions: first, that any composite of taxes may be viewed as a coordinated single levy; second, that the incidence of the *composite* of taxes is known; and third, that we can ignore the possibility that the composite may not operate with the same impact throughout the total range of property and income in the society—in some parts of the range it may be progressive, while in others it may be proportionate or even regressive.

Which of these three models best satisfies the requirements of tax justice is a question of fundamental importance. Since any tax must conform to one of them, with effects that are either regressive, progressive, or neutral, we must determine the effects we should prefer. And in the effort to do this, we find our task simplified by the fact that there is a wide consensus that a regressive tax, unless justified by achievements apart from its distributional effects, has effects that are flatly unjust. The grounds of this damning judgment are evident: there is, to say the least, enough inequality in the society to make any attempt to increase it perverse.

But, having rejected regressive taxation out of hand, can we with equal confidence choose between a progressive system and a neutral one—i.e., one that is proportionate? At first blush, the choice might seem fairly clear. We risk the injection of no new injustices by choosing a neutral system. Since taxation, unlike most other laws, can achieve its objective—of raising revenue—by a neutral route, it would seem compatible with justice that it do so. And yet the most interesting chapter in the history of tax justice deals with why the case for neutrality turns out to be so much less forceful than it initially appears.

One obstacle that confronts this aspiration toward tax neutrality will be readily acknowledged, once it is pointed out. It arises from the brute fact that there is poverty in the society or, more precisely, that there is a level of income or resources that falls below an acceptable standard of living. Under these circumstances a fully neutral tax just does not work. It simply exacerbates the social problem the poor present, and requires that the money taken from them in taxes be returned as welfare or some other kind of transfer payment.

Any discussion of economic equality across the society must take into account this question of putting a floor under inequality. Taxation involves setting a cutoff point. A tax system with exemptions for the poor provides a relatively congenial context in which society can face up to the fact that some government intervention on behalf of the poor because they are poor is necessary, and as a corollary, it provides a context for making a judgment of who we see as the poor.

This inevitable compromise of the neutrality principle turns out to be pervasive and complex, and the point is worth pausing for. It might be thought that we could give the exemption only to those below the cutoff point and not in any way affect those above that line. There would be no exemption for those taxpayers with incomes above the line; they would pay the full rate on their total income. But the effort to simplify matters this way precipitates an unacceptable injustice. To illustrate, assume an exemption of $5,000 and a flat rate of 25 percent. A man with an income, say, of $4,000 or $4,500 or $5,000 will pay nothing in taxes; but a man with a slightly larger income, say, of $5,100 or $5,500 or $6,000 will end up literally worse off after taxes than if he initially had had an income under $5,000. Indeed, the system will find itself using a marginal rate of tax on that additional $100, $500, or $1,000 that is over 100 percent. To avoid the injustice of this "notch" rate effect, tax systems have almost invariably elected to give the exemption to everybody, including those who are comfortably above the cutoff point. This move eliminates the injustice, but yields an unexpected set of consequences for those above the exemption level.

As income above the exemption line increases, the percentage of that income subject to the flat tax increases; the result is that the *effective* rates of tax on the total income, including the exempt income, also increase. Assume again a $5,000 exemption and a flat 25 percent tax. A man with a $9,000 income will pay the 25 percent tax on $4,000—a tax of $1,000, which is 11 percent of his total income; whereas a man with an income of $29,000 will pay the 25 percent tax on $24,000—a tax of $6,000, which is about 21 percent of his total income. The higher the income the closer the effective rate of tax will come to the flat rate of 25 percent, though it will never exceed the flat rate. The approach to the level of the flat rate that results as we advance through higher levels of income constitutes a progression. But as the progression leads in this case to a diminishing gap between the effective rate of tax and the flat rate, it is technically called degression. We can increase the range of degressive effect in such a scheme by increasing the flat rate, or by increasing the exemption level, or by doing both.

This is not a technical point; it is one that lies close to the heart of any concern with distributive tax justice. The logic of degression leads inexorably to *some* redistribution of incomes among those above the exemption level. The important question then becomes: does this logic imply that the tax system can or should be used to effect a *greater* redistribution of incomes among those above the exemption level?

The answer is that it neither improves nor worsens the case for doing this by, for example, graduating tax rates upward above the exemption. There are significant differences between degression, on the one hand, and other progression patterns that rest on graduated rates. Degression has two built-in limitations: the effective rates, however progressive, can never exceed the flat rate; and more important, the *marginal* rate on any added dollar of income for taxpayers above the exemption level will always be the same because it will always be at the flat rate. To revert to our example, the man with the $9,000 income and the man with the $29,000 income will both pay the same twenty-five cents on the last dollar of their income.

There are possibly important political differences between degressive and graduated tax systems, also. The judgment that results in degression is a purely mathematical one based on revenue needs. It entails only a determination of the level of the flat tax rate and where to set the exemption, and does not in any way require a judgment as to how much redistribution it is desirable to impose upon those whose incomes are above the exemption level. Further, in a degressive system the position of the wealthy is anchored to that of other taxpayers in the society; the only way under a degression pattern to raise the marginal rate on the income of the wealthy is to raise it across the board for all taxpayers above the exemption level.

The fact that degression involves a progression of effective rates above the exemption level does not require us to alter any convictions we may happen to have as to the desirability of redistribution above the exemption level. One can readily reconcile the distributional effects of degression with acceptance of the existing distribution of incomes above the exemption level. The way to do this is to ignore that part of income that is exempted, and to take into account for purposes of comparison only the disparity among "surplus" incomes. So viewed, the degressive tax does not affect the relative shares of surplus income before and after taxes. To illustrate once more with the $9,000 man and the $29,000 man, each will retain after tax the same share—75 percent—of their respective *surplus* incomes; that is, one will be left with $3,000 and the other with $18,000. Perhaps the essential feature of *graduated* tax rates now emerges: *they* operate and are intended to operate to effect redistribution among "surplus" incomes.

But if we accept that degression neither adds to nor subtracts from the case for progression via graduated rates, are we left with only a trivial question of policy to decide? Has the central issue of tax justice been reduced to a technical choice between progression via degression and progression via graduated rates? It should be clear that the answer is no. The much more fundamental question that is raised by juxtaposing these two rate patterns is whether society should concern itself with redistribution only insofar as it is necessary to deal with poverty, or whether it should extend its concern to inequalities of "surplus" income. For it can deal with poverty simply by means of the exemption that a degressive system entails. And on the other hand, if it has overcome poverty—which is to say, if it has raised the level of income to a point where everyone has a "surplus"—it must decide whether there is any justification for redistributing further.

Unfortunately, as soon as we put the question in these terms, we discover that we have lost our topic. To pass a judgment on whether a given schedule of graduated rates achieves "tax justice" from a redistributive perspective, we must resort to criteria that lie altogether outside the province of taxation. The rate schedule will be adjudged fair insofar as it moves in the direction of what one regards as a just distribution of the goods of society; and, conversely, it will be adjudged unfair insofar as it moves away from the just distribution. What is at stake, and all that is at stake, is the central and formidable question of distributive justice in the society. If we can reach a wide consensus on this underlying issue—a consensus that has always been most unlikely—the judgment of the justice of the tax rate schedule follows as a by-product. And more important, in the absence of consensus on the underlying issue of distributive justice, we are not equipped to make any judgment at all about the justice of the tax rates from this vantage point. To echo a famous aphorism, we are at sea without a rudder in selecting among possible patterns of graduated rates.

Seeing the distributive justice issue through tax schedules does not reduce the perennial perplexities that attend any serious discussion of equality and inequality among men. What can equality of men mean in light of their manifest inequalities? How important is *economic* inequality among the various manifestations of inequality? How does one take into account the inequalities of inheritance, both economic and cultural? Are there significant functional aspects of inequality—especially those that induce to work or investment? And if there are, how do we choose between increases in productivity and decreases in inequality? To what extent can we correct for the malfunctioning of the market as a distributor of economic shares—the skewing due to monopoly, fraud, and uneven information? Is there a sufficient relationship between that which the society perceives as praiseworthy and that which the market rewards? Is the focus to be on rewarding individual achievement—if indeed one can isolate that in complex human affairs—or on meeting common needs? Would we be more or less aware of unpleasant inequalities in other areas of life if there were greater economic equality? What is the relationship between economic inequality and the viability of political democracy?

These questions, along with others they suggest, are important and worthy, and are directly relevant to deciding how much progression is desirable in the tax system. But, we repeat, there is nothing in the study of taxation itself that contributes to the discussion—except perhaps to pro-

139

vide a more congenial, less abrasive context in which to confront issues of distributive justice. All the perceptions that inform this core judgment of tax justice turn out to transcend taxation.

That such emphasis should be put on redistribution may seem surprising to many persons today. To prior generations, certainly, it would have seemed a strange basis from which to argue tax rates. Neither in England nor in America was progressive taxation introduced as a reform aimed at redistribution. Its justifications were sought on very different grounds. Indeed, the effort to find some other rationale for going beyond a proportionate tax to graduated tax rates marks one of the most curious episodes in modern intellectual history.

The effort seems to have been dominated by a desire to stay within the principle that taxation should be neutral. Argument took the form of efforts to show why graduated rates *were* neutral in an ultimate sense. Some ingenuity was required to sustain such contentions. Consider an income tax. If the burdens imposed on taxpayers are compared in dollars taken, the neutrality principle would demand that the tax be proportionate to income. The man with ten times the income should pay ten times the tax, but no more. Since a graduated schedule of rates by definition proposed to take more than ten times the tax, its justification required that the true comparison between taxpayers be in other than dollar terms.

One approach was to compare taxpayers in terms of benefits received from government. The argument was that since the rich get more from government than the less wealthy, they should pay more in taxes. But this fell far short of what was needed as a justification for progression. Over and beyond the problems already noted in tracing the particular benefits received from government by individuals, there was a more decisive difficulty. Even if it is granted that the rich do receive greater benefits, to justify progression it is necessary to establish that the benefits increase more rapidly or steeply than does the income, that the man with ten times the income has received more than ten times the benefits from government. Once this requirement is acknowledged, the effort to justify progression by benefit must fail; it can be sustained only by fiat.

Vulnerable as the benefit argument was, it is further impeached when examined today in the light of contemporary income maintenance and welfare arrangements. Insofar as redistributive objectives are being pursued by government, the poor arguably emerge as the chief beneficiaries.

Another approach was to compare taxpayers not in terms of dollars taken or benefits conferred but in terms of the sacrifices imposed. While this sacrifice approach had a much more elaborate and elegant history, involving some of the great names in moral philosophy and political economy, the flaws that finally impeached it as a justification turned out to be strikingly similar to those undermining argument from benefit theory.

Sacrifice analysis stemmed from the general thesis of the utilitarians that problems of government policy should be worked out through a calculus of pleasures and pains. This seemed an especially promising notion with respect to taxation, which was conventionally viewed as the imposition of burdens. Neutrality in taxation readily was translated into pursuit of equality of sacrifice among different taxpayers. The key insight, amply corroborated by everyday experience, was that goods—a third auto or a second house, for example—had declining utility to the individual user. If this was true of particular goods, presumably it was true also of money, the most versatile and attractive "good" of all. Neutrality of sacrifice seemed to call for taking more in taxes from the rich than from the less rich. The larger tax on the rich was thought to impose no greater sacrifice on them in utility units than the lesser tax imposed on the poor. This same line of analysis seems always to justify taxing the rich not merely more, but progressively more, calling for tax rates graduated upward. When neutrality is to be measured in terms of sacrifice, only such graduated rates can be genuinely neutral.

The fascination of sacrifice theory is that all efforts, and there were many, to refine and buttress this plausible intuition have served only to impeach it. An early unsettling ambiguity was whether the sacrifice that was called for was an equal sacrifice. People with different total amounts of income must have different total amounts of "utility units." Assume that one man's income totals 100 such units and another man's income totals 10. To take 5 units from each obviously imposes a heavier burden on the man with only 10 units. Thus, if neutrality is the goal, it would seem that proportionate, not equal, sacrifice is called for. And, proportionate sacrifice seemed to lead directly to a justification of progressive (i.e., graduated) taxation; assuming *any* decline in the utility curve for money, only graduated rates would appear to accomplish the objective of proportionate sacrifice.

Framed this way, the problem moved into the realm of mathematics and involved making a complex comparison of two curves—the first, a curve describing the rates of tax, and the second, a utility curve for money. But once the mathematicians are called in and the intuitive comparison is made more precise, a surprising difficulty emerges. To yield progressive rates of tax, even under proportionate sacrifice, the utility curve for money has to decline very sharply. Whatever the common sense of the notion that money has *some* declining utility, it can hardly be invoked to support the far more exacting notion that the order of the decline is very steep.

A new idea was then put forward that appeared to preserve the intuition as to utility without requiring so exact an understanding of the money curve. The mistake, it was argued, had been to treat proportionate sacrifice among individual taxpayers as the goal; the proper goal, rather, was to minimize the total sacrifice of all taxpayers in the society. Pursuit of minimum sacrifice for the society as a whole called for taking in taxes only the least "painful" dollars. Any degree of declining utility, however gentle the slope of the curve, would dictate taking additional money from the more wealthy before the state took *any* money from the less wealthy. Rigorous pursuit of such a formula obviously would result in steeply progressive tax rates. And only a little less obviously, it would result in the progressive equalizing of incomes after tax, since, so long as A still had one dollar more than B, it would produce less sacrifice to take that dollar from A rather than to tax B.

This route to progression in taxation is astonishing. Its logic would dictate 100 percent marginal rates and the successive leveling of incomes after tax. Indeed, any schedule of graduated rates would come in through the back door, so to speak. Such a schedule would reflect the need to temper the otherwise 100 percent rates out of regard for economic incentives. More remarkable still, this argument arrives at progression from an egalitarian premise of the oddest sort—the concern is not with distributive injustice but rather with the objective of maximizing total utility in the society by holding to a minimum the sacrifices imposed by taxation. Such a rationale is altogether remote from any popular view of the matter.

The radical sweep of the conclusion dictated by the minimum sacrifice approach—however mild the slope of the money utility curve—served to call into doubt the key premise that money really had declining utility. And on further thought it became evident that this premise was most difficult to maintain. The utter versatility of money for consumption purposes sets it apart from any particular goods; with additional increments of money, one does not have to resort to buying a third car or a second house, but might elect to acquire a first yacht (to select an offensive example). Moreover, the declining utility notion rested on analogies drawn entirely from the consumption of goods. But money to be useful does not have to be spent; it can be saved or invested. Who could say that the new enjoyment found in savings or investment is not to be counted in the utility of money?

Nor is this the only difficulty with the intuition that money has declining utility. To be useful to the argument at hand, the utility curve must be assumed to be the same for each taxpayer, and this requires that his subjective response to money be somehow independent of his individual tastes and character. Once critical scrutiny of the intuition is stimulated, one cannot help but note how wide the variations among individual lifestyles really are; and one becomes introspectively aware of how much one's own attitudes toward money have varied over a lifetime.

Today, partly because utilitarianism has gone out of fashion and partly because of these specific difficulties with its application to taxation, there is virtually no talk of sacrifice theory. The intuition about the declining utility of money has not been put to rest, however. The old arguments are continued at the popular level in a slightly new guise. Taxes, we are repeatedly told, should be progressive because they should be based on "ability to pay." The content of the new term is seldom defined, but a greater ability to pay taxes must imply an ability to pay them more effortlessly, with less of a burden. This in turn leads directly back to the notion of paying them with less sacrifice.

There have been ingenious efforts to avoid such an equation of an ability to pay with the idea of diminished sacrifice. It has been urged that "money makes money," so that it becomes progressively easier for the more wealthy to obtain their income; sacrifice is to be measured by the effort involved in obtaining income rather than the loss of enjoyment because it is taxed away. Even if there were grounds for believing that it is easier to earn the nth dollar than the first dollar, which we seriously doubt, this rationale for progression suffers from precisely the same defects that bedevil all sacrifice theory: the inability to measure such a capacity with any accuracy, and the sheer implausibility that the curve, this time keyed to ease of making money, would be steep enough to yield a progressive tax.

Another line of thought has proceeded from the notion that milk is more worthy socially than champagne. The argument is that money to be taken from the more wealthy in taxes would otherwise be spent in less worthy ways than money to be taken in taxes from the less wealthy. This approach may avoid some difficulties of sacrifice theory, but it does so at the price of ignoring the role of savings and investment, and of resting its case on sumptuary judgments, which are always dubious in a free society. And in any case, it compares the wrong things. The distance between milk and champagne, on which the rhetorical force depends, is the distance between incomes below the exemption or poverty level and incomes above. What is needed, again, is not an argument to support exemptions but to support graduated rates of those incomes above the exemption level.

The elaborate efforts to find a rationale for progression on grounds other than its redistributive effects include arguments derived from certain economics theories that flourished in the recent past. Both distributive justice and sacrifice perceptions were put to one side, and justification was sought in support for mass purchasing power. It was contended that a progressive tax would deflect money from the group that would have saved it to the group that would spend it. The economic underpinnings of this line of analysis have almost disappeared. The interesting thing for present purposes is that, far from leading to tax justice, it leads away. For if the analysis is applied consistently, it must call for the deliberate use of *regressive* taxes whenever it is thought that the society is spending too much and saving too little.

The precise details of all this convoluted intellectual controversy are not important except perhaps to the specialist. What is important is the persistent effort to lower the visibility of the redistributive function of graduated tax rates. For at least a century, the overwhelming majority of

143

those who found a progressive tax system attractive always did so on grounds other than its redistributive impact. Only recently has a willingness, and a desire, to confront the redistributive question begun to appear. Behind this curious history one detects the ambivalence of democratic society over distributive justice in general, taxation apart. To put the matter perhaps too simply, the impulse to do something to mitigate existing economic inequalities is inhibited by anxiety at the prospect of candid public discussion and direct confrontation. Progressive taxation offers a statesmanlike formula. It makes it possible to adjust inequalities without talking too explicitly. The public discussion of social justice can be carried out in the less colorful vocabulary of tax rates and tax bases.

If it is diplomatic to tie strategies of distributive justice to taxation, it is also quite peculiar to do so. The potential for redistribution obviously depends on how much taxes will take out of the private sector of the economy. When the government is collecting only a modest total in taxes, as was the case at the time the income tax was enacted in 1913, the distributive leverage provided via the tax system will necessarily be small; and as the tax total rises, as it did for example during World War II, the redistributive potentialities rise with it. As an egalitarian strategy, taxation is dependent on judgments about the revenue level that may be unrelated to any redistributive goal.

In any event, whenever serious change in the level of revenue is proposed either upward or downward, it serves to reopen the issue of how progressive the system should be. Consider a proposal to reduce taxes dramatically. There would inevitably arise a sharp question as to how the reduction should be distributed. If all taxpayers are given the same percentage of reduction in their tax burdens, the ratios of income after tax will not be disturbed, and the revised tax schedules will be pursuing the same redistributive patterns as before. But the dollar amounts of tax reduction given to the wealthy will be appreciably greater than the dollar amounts afforded the less wealthy. This is certain to lead to clamor that it is unfair and that it is surely the less wealthy who are more deserving of the tax relief. Much the same reactions will be invoked in the converse case of a sudden need for significantly higher tax revenues. The point has been taken far enough to disclose how fragile any consensus on the distributive aspects of taxation must in the end be.

## III  Horizontal equity

While it is a widely held popular notion that the rich escape paying a fair share of the tax burden, the idea that taxation can be used as a vehicle for redistributive equity has been of interest largely to experts and intellectuals. The ordinary citizen's sense of injustice is more likely to be stirred by other issues, those of *horizontal* equity. These group about the simple perception that people who are in similar circumstances ought to bear a similar tax burden; it is unfair if they do not. The redistributive effects of taxation, staying with the metaphor, can be said to raise issues of *vertical* equity. They appear to be a matter of tax justice only if one has in mind standards of distributive justice.

It is easy to see why the vertical equity problem does not preoccupy the ordinary citizen. It is always difficult for him to assess his own total tax burden, let alone that of others, given the multiplicity of taxes, the shifting of incidence, and the ambiguity as to precisely which payments are taxes. He is, moreover, likely to be most interested in comparing himself to people he thinks of as his economic peers. But a perception of vertical equity requires comparison over a wide range of economic levels. And the very idea of graduated tax rates, and vertical equity, is imbedded in the mathematics of ratios, which are inaccessible to many. In contrast, the ordinary citizen should find more congenial the comparisons involved in judgments of horizontal equity. It is, after all, the cardinal idea of justice that like cases be treated in like manner and unlike cases in unlike manner. The idea is so basic it has the quality of a self-evident axiom; it need not and cannot be argued; it is the aspiration of all law throughout history. Any deviations from like treatment always involve an insistence that the cases are not like in some relevant way. The very idea of a rule of law lies in the commitment to delineate which are the like cases.

Anything seen as a horizontal inequity in the tax system is readily accepted as the peculiar business of the tax system alone. In the most narrow and literal sense, it is a matter of tax justice; the inequity can always be removed simply by changing the tax system. Issues of vertical inequity do not arise from the tax system, and while they can be ameliorated through it, their perception and resolution necessarily involve matters more basic than taxes. The comparisons invited by consideration of horizontal equity are always finite. They always can be framed as one-to-one comparisons, and to make them, information outside the tax law does not seem to be needed.

In the case of vertical equity, the choice of principle itself was historically the subject of deep controversy, and the discussion of the topic consisted of a discussion of competing rationales for proportional or progressive taxation. In the case of horizontal equity, however, the choice of principle is perfectly clear and inarguable. All that remains for discussion is the application of the principle to a particular instance and the question of whether the cases are or are not similar. But this is a matter that hardly lends itself to general discussion, and it would seem there is nothing further to be said on it at a general level.

A nagging question of some generality nevertheless remains. Why do controversies over horizontal inequities in the tax system so firmly persist?

Why, in a democratic regime at least, does not the tax system, through public debate and criticism, work itself pure of these defects?

One reason is that through technical errors or oversights in drafting, or through failure to anticipate certain consequences, arbitrary distinctions from time to time creep into the tax laws. Although virtually no one will defend them, they tend to persist because of general inertia, and because they are too insignificant to have any political resonance. These are matters that normally must wait upon a broad technical revision of the tax law.

Perhaps another reason is that in some instances efforts to eliminate horizontal inequities will themselves result in fresh injustices. A ready example may be drawn from the real property tax. Even if it is agreed that property A is overvalued for tax purposes and overtaxed as compared to property B, and this discrepancy has continued for many years, the correction may present a stubborn problem where property A has changed hands in the market while the discrimination existed. Market prices for land reflect the relative tax burdens on the land; hence, assuming that properties A and B are otherwise comparable, the price of the overtaxed property A will reflect its extra tax burden, and be lower. If now the tax assessment on property A is corrected and brought in line, the result will be to increase the market value of the property and in this respect confer a windfall on its current owner. There is no way of correcting the injustice to the real victim, the seller of property A.

Then there will be occasions on which the question whether we should give greater recognition to the similarities or the differences between cases remains somehow intrinsically controversial. Law is never simply taxonomic. For example, when it comes to the comparison of earned to unearned income, which is a matter of perennial debate in connection with the income tax, the question whether these two kinds of income present like cases translates into the question of whether they should be taxed in the same way. They are both alike and different in obvious respects. Any effort to resolve the question of whether they should be taxed according to their similarity or according to their difference must soon implicate a wide range of deep value judgments.

Another intrinsically controversial instance is afforded by the problem of selecting the tax unit for a progressive income tax. In the search for like cases, is comparison of taxpayers to be made on the basis of individuals, the marital unit, the immediate family, or the de facto sociological household? There are of course numerous similarities and differences among these various households. Since the tax is on persons and not on things, the system must choose at the outset whether and how to group the persons, and the choice will have tax dollar consequences. Under graduated rates, distribution of the tax burden will be very different depending on whether a husband and wife are seen as two wholly distinct taxpayers each with his income, or as a single unit with one aggregate income, or as two taxpayers each having half the family income. In making a determination of this matter, one might want to take into account social policies, such as encouraging marriage or conceivably discouraging communal living. But even if the legislature were wholly indifferent as to these specific policies, it would still have the problem of selecting the tax unit. The unit remains a structural feature of the system, generating controversy that cannot be eliminated.

But by far the most striking source of persisting controversy over horizontal equity comes from what might be called *deliberate departures* from the canon that like cases be treated in like manner. These departures are dictated largely by policies that lie outside taxation itself, and that reflect the use of taxation as a tactic for promoting particular social or political or economic goals. Take the income tax portions of the Internal Revenue Code. If the statute were judged on its face, one would be hard put to defend the equity of the longstanding preferential treatment associated with such features as the exemption of interest received from state and municipal bonds, deductions for accelerated depreciation or amortization, high depletion deductions for oil and gas, deductions for charitable contributions, credit against taxes for investment, low tax rates on income from export operations, deductions for certain state and local taxes, and the reduced tax rates on income in the form of capital gains. In each of these instances, the argument for the preferential treatment appeals to objectives that are not explicit in the statute, such as stimulating oil exploration, encouraging philanthropy, increasing the formation of capital, and stimulating the formation of capital goods.

Today, departures from horizontal equity furnish much of the fuel for public debate over the fairness of the tax system. They present a complex case for appraisal in terms of justice because the statute is not, of course, to be judged on its face. Those not persuaded to the wisdom of the specific policy being fostered through the tax system will perceive the discrimination simply as the arbitrary favoring of one group of taxpayers over others. Those persuaded of the merits of the specific policy will see the differences in treatment as having a sensible purpose. For the unpersuaded, the difference in treatment poses a question of tax injustice, but for the persuaded it is not, it should be pointed out, an instance of tax justice so much as an instance of overriding public policy. The persuaded are willing that on these occasions considerations of horizontal justice be subordinated to other ends of the society.

But even some of those persuaded of the specific policy may see the deliberate difference in the treatment as an injustice. Taxation almost never is the only effective way to implement the specific policy. When it is not, we confront the generic policy issue of whether to use the tax system for extrinsic purposes. Those who feel that it is in general a mistake to resort to taxation as a tactic of influencing behavior may well continue to feel that way even though they favor the specific policy being advanced.

Accordingly, they will find the tax discrimination unjustified and arbitrary and hence see it as a tax injustice.

We meet here what is today, among students of taxation, one of the most actively debated issues, especially as it applies to the income tax. An emerging view is that whatever the differential treatment has caused the government to surrender in taxes by not collecting more than it does in taxes from the favored group is equivalent to a direct expenditure by government. If the government elects to "forego" a given number of dollars in revenue to encourage, for example, those engaged in oil exploration, it is said that this is very like an expenditure of that number of dollars in support of oil ventures. The policy issue so framed is whether the "subsidy" should be given through the "tax expenditure" or in one of the other possible ways.

The metaphor of tax expenditure, although helpful and dramatic, is hard to confine. It can be quickly extended by adopting the premise that as there is virtually nothing government *could* not tax, anything it *does* not tax is a tax expenditure. The consequence is that the society is inundated with tax expenditures. To take an extreme illustration: the federal government could have, but has not, added a consumption tax to the income tax; to conclude that this restraint represents an "expenditure" on behalf of consumption does not advance analysis.

But vulnerable or not, the metaphor of tax expenditure does serve to capture and to isolate some key issues in using the tax system for extrinsic policy purposes. There are important differences between a literal expenditure and a tax expenditure. The tax expenditure will necessarily be hidden and may to some extent escape notice; the amount will be uncertain and will fluctuate with other changes, such as in tax rates. Because the item is not budgeted as an expenditure, it will not come up for periodic review and will tend to slip into a more or less permanent expenditure. Usually it will be difficult to know just who is receiving the subsidy. Taken together, these characteristics mean that use of tax expenditures will always involve some degree of political irresponsibility; it will blunt or deflect confrontation over the merits of the specific policy, its duration, its magnitude, and the assessment of how well the tax incentive is achieving the avowed purpose.

When the tax utilized to finance extrinsic policies is one with graduated rates, a whole new series of problems arises, intimately related to the concern with tax justice. Tax expenditures, under graduated rates, generate a number of secondary and often unwanted consequences. Any preferential treatment in the form of a "bargain" rate, or an exclusion, or a deduction will save more in tax dollars for those in a higher than for those in a lower marginal rate bracket. The inducement to take advantage of the preferential treatment thus increases directly as income reaches the higher tax brackets. Moreover, the ability to take such advantage will

148

depend in considerable part on mobility of the taxpayer's economic position: not everyone is equally ready to invest funds in oil exploration. As more tax expenditure features are introduced into the tax structure, the law becomes more complicated and less accessible, and the possibilities of combining specific preferential treatments create a greater potential for tax savings. Over time, the wealthier, who have the most to gain from tailoring their economic behavior, will recruit and utilize a cadre of professionals who are expert in realizing that potential.

Evaluating deliberate departures from horizontal equity thus requires a complex calculus. The one-to-one comparison involved in testing whether like cases are being treated alike becomes heavily overlaid with additional factors. Something simpler and more personal may be required to trigger the sense of tax injustice in the ordinary citizen. That something frequently appears associated with the slightly tainted complaint that, while the tax system is manipulable, the ordinary citizen does not have an equal opportunity to take advantage of it. We would hazard the unflattering guess that such a citizen would be far less vigorous in his complaints about tax avoidance possibilities if only he had an equal chance to utilize them.

In the end, departures from horizontal equity impede the effort to achieve vertical equity, and conversely, the more intense the pursuit of vertical equity—meaning the greater the progressivity of the tax—the higher the "stakes" become for departures from horizontal equity. The result of the complicated adjustments and distinctions of the tax statute may well be that some of the very wealthy pay a smaller percentage of their income in taxes, and even a smaller number of dollars, than the less wealthy. It is when this happens that a sense of grievance arises. The vast majority of taxpayers can hardly avoid a simple and blunt comparison with themselves, testing the justice of the tax system. What sparks indignation is not, ironically, that the horizontal equities have been violated but that there has been a gross departure from expectations as to vertical equity. There is then a popular outcry about "loopholes."

## IV   Administrative inequities

Discussions of horizontal and vertical equity—the anatomy of justice in taxation—deal with substantive provisions of the tax statute. They miss, however, an important component of the popular sense of tax injustice— those grievances that arise from procedural aspects or, better, from the law in action.

There are the sheer and obvious irritations with bureaucracy. One could array types of taxes on an axis measuring degrees of contact between citizen and government official. It would be a fair guess that the less sensitive the tax to considerations of equity, the better it would score. A flat all-inclusive sales tax, necessarily regressive, would entail on the side of the consumer-taxpayer no contact with, and no irritation over, government bureaucracy. Taxes, such as the income tax, based on personal situations rather than on things or transactions, invite the greatest complications for the ordinary citizen. The more sensitive a personal tax becomes to considerations of vertical or horizontal equity, the more complex and irritating its administration.

One can isolate various other sources of irritation with taxation in operation, again using the income tax as the example. Since it is self-assessing—a great and undervalued decency—this tax requires the taxpayer to answer to government annually a formidable questionnaire about his financial affairs, and imposes on him a considerable burden of record keeping. The complexity can be so great that the taxpayer may well feel that his taxes are based on answers to questions he does not understand. If, nevertheless, he goes it alone, he risks making mistakes in calculating his taxes; if he seeks assistance from government officials, he risks not only frustration with bureaucracy but also getting biased answers; and if he employs a private intermediary—a lawyer, an accountant, or one of the burgeoning commercial return preparers—he may well be irritated by the social costs.

Now that the income tax has become a mass tax, there are also the difficulties with enforcement and policing. As a practical matter, only a fraction of all self-assessed tax returns can be scrutinized for content each year. This fact is apt to evoke suspicions on the part of taxpayers. If one happens to be selected for direct scrutiny, he may feel he was unfairly singled out. The very process of scrutiny may appear deeply intrusive to him and unfairly to impeach his integrity. Should he become aware of how small a percentage of returns are actually audited each year, he may feel that the system permits the dishonesty of other taxpayers to flourish. His confidence that errors will be detected and tax cheaters will be caught is unlikely to be sturdy. Everyone can understand that uneven enforcement of the tax system is a clear departure from the canon that like cases be treated alike.

The enforcement problems of the income tax go beyond the familiar perplexities of discretion and the rule of law. Under self-assessment, the income tax emerges as an honor system, but because of the enormous stakes involved, it is an honor system only within limits. It dare not take the taxpayer altogether at his word as to how much he owes in taxes, and it cannot, and perhaps dare not, question all taxpayers with equal persistence and intensity about their affairs.

When the format of a tax does not utilize the honor system but relies upon the findings of government officials, as for example with valuations for real or personal property taxes, the focus of grievance shifts. There is so large a component of discretion in the valuation of real property that the tax levy is always vulnerable to the charge that like cases are in fact not being treated alike. In the case of personal property, the valuation process is not only discretionary but inescapably intrusive. Indeed, in some communities enforcement of the personal property tax became so patently partial and uneven that it was finally decided to abandon the tax altogether. The self-assessment feature of the income tax may not be merely a matter of style; a government-assessed tax on income would be surely so deep an invasion of privacy as to be intolerable.

Another set of grievances arises not because of what is taking place on the tax side of the government ledger but because of what is happening on the expenditure side. This raises tax justice questions in the limited sense that the grievance affects the paying of taxes.

Reactions in the United States to the Vietnam War suggest the possibilities of using the tax system as a vehicle for protesting a particular variety of government activity and expenditure. Thoreau's classic gesture, after all, was a refusal to pay taxes. Some of the grumbling over property taxes these days undoubtedly stems from dissatisfaction with the high level of expenditures on education. But the concern need not be so sharply focused on particular expenditures: it may reflect merely a diffuse complaint that taxes are unjustly high because government is so inefficient and wasteful. The complaint may go beyond this and take us back to redistributive considerations. To the extent that government expenditures represent welfare measures and transfer payments to the poor, antagonism to the level of taxes can be read as antagonism to excesses in the pursuit of redistribution. This reaction can spread to all taxes whatever their form or the pattern of rate structure.

## V  The political dimension

In a democracy, taxes are ultimately set by operation of majority rule. Does this circumstance have a bearing on issues of tax justice? Some have urged that it provides a reason for not pursuing vertical equity through taxation. The principle of majority vote, it is argued, cannot be trusted with setting graduated rates under a system of private property and universal suffrage. Graduated rates necessarily afford the less wealthy, who will be the more numerous, the opportunity to vote taxes they will not have to bear themselves onto the minority of more wealthy. The conclusion—dictated, it should be noted, by concern for political responsibility, and not by argument from justice—is that tax rates should never be graduated upward. An argument for proportionate taxation is thus reached via the political route.

Despite the elegance of the argument, the arresting fact is that the predicted outcome seems never to have occurred in our society. Somehow, given a substantial middle class, the majoritarian principle has proved sturdy and flexible enough to handle the voting of taxes in a not altogether irresponsible fashion.

It has been also argued that, at least in matters of taxation, there can be too much clarity and coherence for the democratic process. Serious political frictions would appear if we somehow reached the millenium with a single comprehensive income tax as the only exercise of the taxing power. Under such a coherent scheme, the perception and awareness of the issues of tax justice would be greatly enhanced, but the ease of reaching a political concensus on taxes would be impaired. There may be unsuspected political strengths in what appear to be weaknesses, complexities, and confusions in the current system.

This contention seems at best weak. Although it may have some special bite in the context of taxation, it is nothing more than an application of a very general and very debatable thesis asserting a benign role for confusion and ambiguity in keeping democracy viable.

Finally, there are those who would short-circuit all the considerations we have been wrestling with in this essay and insist that the only content to the term *tax justice* is that the tax burdens have been voted by the majority. In this view, the exclusive criterion of tax justice is the procedural one that the electorate and its representatives are functioning according to procedural and constitutional proprieties. Just as many issues of taste should be left to the economic marketplace, so it is argued that these value issues should be left to the political marketplace. A just tax is seen as the exact analogue of a just price.

This in one sense is undeniably true. Departures from political proprieties in setting taxes, as the experience of the American Revolution reminds us, provide the most fundamental instances of tax injustice. But put thus bluntly, the contention that what is just is simply what is correctly done misses the function of normative discussions in taxation. The crystallizing of political strengths through the voting process presupposes that public discussion of policy has taken place. In any such discussion of tax policy, the consideration of tax justice will necessarily be salient, and at the very least will provide the rhetoric that all sides are obligated to employ.

NOTE TO THE READER

The questions raised by Professors Kalven and Blum are dealt with, directly or indirectly, by many of the authors in *GBWW*. In the *Syntopicon*, see Chapter 31, GOVERNMENT, Topic 4, and Chapter 99, WEALTH, Topic 9*e* (2), for writings on taxation in general. See also Chapter 42, JUSTICE, Topic 5, which lists writings on the relation between justice and equality (and inequality), and Topic 8*a,* where writings concerned with the just distribution of economic goods are noted. Chapter 76, QUANTITY, lists writings on the relation between equality and proportion (Topic 1*b*).

In *GGB,* see the essay "Of Taxes" by David Hume in Vol. 7, pp. 85–88.

# A Fresh Look at Copernicus

Owen Gingerich

Owen Gingerich, an astrophysicist at the Smithsonian Astrophysical Ob-
servatory, also serves as a professor in two different departments at Harvard
University—those of Astronomy and of the History of Science.

Professor Gingerich's research interests range from the recomputation of
an ancient Babylonian mathematical table to the interpretation of the solar
ultraviolet spectrum. He is coauthor of two successive standard models for
the solar atmosphere, the first to take into account rocket and satellite
observations of the sun.

Professor Gingerich is currently president of the International Astronomical
Union's Commission on the History of Astronomy. He also serves as chairman
of the editorial board for that organization's proposed multivolume General
History of Astronomy. He has been a member of the Kepler Committee of
the International Union of the History and Philosophy of Science (the 400th
anniversary of Kepler's birth was celebrated in 1971), and he has played an
active role in the Copernicus Commission of that union, having organized the
astronomical portion of the Copernicus celebration to be held at Torun,
Poland, later this year.

Besides numerous technical articles and reviews, Professor Gingerich
has written popular accounts of astronomy in several encyclopedias and in
journals such as *Scientific American,* the *Atlantic Monthly,* and *American
Scientist.* He has also translated Kepler's *Astronomia Nova.*

One of the most remarkable artifacts of the scientific renaissance of the sixteenth century is the original autograph copy of Copernicus's great work, *De revolutionibus* ("Concerning the Revolutions"). Bound in an old parchment manuscript and lovingly preserved in a gray chamois pouch, the priceless handwritten document rests in the Jagiellonian University Library in Krakow. That it remains intact after centuries of wandering through central Europe is little short of miraculous. When a book was printed in the sixteenth century, its manuscript generally lost its value and was usually recycled into bookbindings or into new paper. Because it escaped this fate, Copernicus's work survives in a sense that is almost unique among sixteenth-century writings.

Beyond the manuscript, precious little remains that can be associated with the great astronomer personally. Two dozen books known to have been owned or studied by him were carried off to Sweden in 1626, and are there to this day. In Ferrara is preserved the diploma for his doctoral degree in canon law. On a cloister wall in Olsztyn (Poland), traces of a sundial thought to be from Copernicus's hand may still be seen. One of his instruments survived long enough to be collected, admired, and criticized by the great Danish observer Tycho Brahe, but now it too has vanished. Even the grave of the astronomer, in the Frombork Cathedral where he lived and worked, is unmarked.

The venerable Copernican manuscript, which expressed revolutionary views on the place of the sun and the earth in the universe, is thus the only substantial memento of that illustrious Renaissance man. But to the historian of science, the manuscript is far more than a sentimental reminder of one of the greatest astronomers of all time. It is an invaluable source of clues as to how, when, and why Copernicus reached his epoch-making conclusion that the sun, not the earth, was the fixed center of our planetary system.

In this quincentenary year of Copernicus's birth, the nature of his scientific achievement appears at least superficially clear: "He stopped the sun and moved the earth." To us the idea seems simple enough, even though we know that it marks the divide between our modern conception of the universe, with its vast spaces and far-flung galaxies, and the world view in 1473, with its compact, neatly nested crystalline spheres.

But upon further reflection, we find ourselves asking two puzzling

155

questions: *If the heliocentric idea is really so simple and necessary, why was it so long in coming?* Did it really require a man of genius to find it? If so, what kind of trail led to the conception of a sun-centered system of planets? *And if the heliocentric cosmology is so obvious, why was it first ignored and then resisted?* To answer these questions is the central challenge faced by Copernican scholars today. For an indication of how the challenge can be met, we shall turn first to the manuscript and its publication history.

Even a casual examination of the manuscript reveals the painstaking care with which Copernicus drafted his work. The constellation tables are neatly lettered in red and black, and precise diagrams are drawn in niches specially made in the text. Indeed, the carefully crafted pages convey the impression that Copernicus intended the manuscript itself as the final product of his labors—an elegant contribution to the library shelf, not a volume to be marked and cut by a printer.

The book might not have been printed until decades or even centuries after his death except for the enthusiasm of a brilliant young German astronomer named Georg Joachim Rheticus. Exactly how Rheticus, who was professor of mathematics at Wittenberg, heard about Copernicus's work is still a mystery. As early as 1514, a quarter of a century before, Copernicus had circulated a manuscript précis of his theory to a few friends, and perhaps Rheticus came across a copy of this *Commentariolus,* or "little commentary."

In any event, Rheticus decided that only a personal visit to the source would satisfy his curiosity about the new heliocentric cosmology. Copernicus himself described his home in Frauenburg (now Frombork), where he served as canon in the cathedral, as "this most remote corner of the earth." Thus, only after a long journey did the twenty-five-year-old Rheticus arrive, in May 1539, at the door of the sixty-six-year-old master. The visit, intended for a few weeks, stretched into months and years—a fact all the more remarkable when we note that Rheticus was a Lutheran from the central bastion of the Reformation, while his cordial host was a staunch Catholic in Catholic territory.

Rheticus did not come to Polish Prussia empty-handed. He brought with him four volumes, the latest in scientific publishing, each handsomely bound in stamped pigskin. Included were Greek texts of Euclid and Ptolemy, as well as three books published by Johannes Petreius, the leading printer of Nuremberg. By the time Rheticus returned to Wittenberg in September 1541, he had persuaded Copernicus to send along a copy of his work, destined for Petreius's printing office.

The original manuscript, which stayed behind with Copernicus, reveals some of the last-minute changes made for the publication. The original Book One, containing Copernicus's cosmological assumptions, was merged with the original Book Two, which provided a short manual of trigonometry, complete with tables. As a result, an interesting passage about ancient precursors of the heliocentric view was removed and reworked into a new preface and dedication to Pope Paul III. In the process, the name of Aristarchus, who is sometimes called "the Copernicus of antiquity," was eliminated, perhaps inadvertently.

As a further consequence, the beautiful preface found in the manuscript was not printed in the early editions (although happily it is found, translated somewhat differently, in *GBWW*, Vol. 16, pp. 510–11). Indeed, this preface gives us a rich insight into Copernicus's reverent and aesthetic view of nature:

> *Among the many and varied literary and artistic studies upon which human ingenuity is nourished, I think that above all the things most beautiful and worthy of knowledge should be embraced and pursued with the greatest devotion. . . . For what could be more beautiful than the heavens, which contain all beautiful things? Even their very names declare this: Caelum [heavens], naming something artistically carved; and Mundus [world] meaning purity and elegance. . . .*
>
> *For who, after studying the things that he sees established in the optimum order and directed by divine ruling, would not, through diligent contemplation and through a certain familiarity with them, be awakened to that which is best and would not wonder at the Creator of all things, in Whom is all happiness and every good? For the divine Psalmist surely did not say gratuitously that he took pleasure in the workings of God and rejoiced in the works of His hands, unless by means of these things as by some sort of vehicle we are transported to the contemplation of the highest Good.[1]*

Back in Wittenberg, Rheticus extracted the trigonometrical manual from Book One and had it printed in 1542 as a thin mathematics text for the students at the university. At the same time the complete manuscript with its six books full of astronomical diagrams and tables went to Nuremburg for printing. Petreius published about a dozen works each year, some religious or historical, but with an increasing number of scientific titles. For Copernicus's book, he engaged the services of Andreas Osiander, a theologian who had previously helped him edit Lutheran materials. How much editorial work Osiander did on the *Revolutions* we do not know, except that he added—anonymously—a very influential introduction at the very beginning of the book.

Osiander designed his introduction to disarm critics who might have been offended by the heliocentric hypothesis of the book. This he did almost too successfully. Writing "To the Reader, concerning the Hypotheses in this work," he said,

> *Since the novelty of the hypotheses of this work has already been widely reported, I have no doubt that some learned men have taken*

*serious offense because the book declares that the earth moves, and that the sun is at rest in the center of the universe; these men undoubtedly believe that the liberal arts, established long ago upon a correct basis, should not be thrown into confusion. But if they are willing to examine the matter closely, they will find that the author of this work has done nothing blameworthy. For it is the duty of an astronomer to compose the history of the celestial motions through careful and skillful observation. Then turning to the causes of these motions or hypotheses about them, he must conceive and devise, since he cannot in any way attain to the true causes, such hypotheses as, being assumed, enable the motions to be calculated correctly from the principles of geometry, for the future as well as for the past. The present author has performed both these duties excellently. For these hypotheses need not be true nor even probable; if they provide a calculus consistent with the observations, that alone is sufficient. . . . The philosopher will perhaps rather seek the semblance of the truth. But neither [the astronomer nor the philosopher] will understand or state anything certain, unless it has been divinely revealed to him. . . . So far as hypotheses are concerned, let no one expect anything certain from astronomy, which cannot furnish it, lest he accept as the truth ideas conceived for another purpose, and depart from this study a greater fool than when he entered it. Farewell.*[2]

To the twentieth-century physicist or astronomer, for whom model-building seems the order of the day, Osiander's introduction strikes a remarkably modern chord. And to the sixteenth-century natural philosopher, the introduction stated ideas so reasonable that most of them must have assumed that Copernicus himself approved and accepted them.

But Rheticus, for one, did not approve of the new introduction to Copernicus's original text. In at least two presentation copies from him, still extant, the introduction has been struck out with a red crayon. He sent two other copies to Bishop Tiedemann Giese, who had been an intimate friend of Copernicus until the astronomer's death in 1543. Giese, outraged by the added introduction, wrote an irate protest to the Nuremberg City Council. After hearing Petreius's angry rebuttal, the council informed Giese that the printer would not be required to produce a corrected edition.

There the matter stood throughout the rest of the sixteenth century. Then, in 1609, Kepler placed on the back of the title page of his *Astronomia Nova* an indignant notice revealing Osiander as "the author of this fiction." "It is a most absurd fiction, I admit, that the phenomena of nature can be demonstrated by false causes," wrote Kepler. "But this fiction is not in Copernicus. . . . As evidence, I offer this work." [3]

Kepler's bold claim was accomplished by another extraordinary paragraph. Petrus Ramus (1515–72), professor of philosophy and rhetoric in Paris, had offered his chair to anyone who could produce an "astronomy without hypotheses," and Kepler declared that he would have claimed this reward if Ramus had still been alive. Clearly, Kepler and his predecessors used the word *hypothesis* in a sense different from our modern usage. In fact, to astronomers of the sixteenth century, "hypotheses" were the arbitrary geometrical devices used to explain astronomical appearances—in the quaint phrase handed down from antiquity, "to save the phenomena." We must examine how Copernicus used these hypothesized devices before we can understand the reception of his greatest hypothesis, the heliocentric cosmology. First, however, we must turn to the medieval background.

## The dual tradition of geocentric cosmology

In a remarkable essay on the heavens in his book *The Discarded Image,* C. S. Lewis urges his readers to take a nocturnal walk under the stars, trying to view the sky in terms of the medieval cosmology. From the solidly fixed, central earth, we must look not *out* but *up*. To gaze out "on the night sky with modern eyes is like looking out over a sea that fades away into the mist." But to gaze up at "the towering medieval universe," with its concentric "spheres" or "heavens," is like looking up at a great building. "The 'space' of modern astronomy may arouse terror or bewilderment," Lewis writes, but "the spheres of the old present us with an object in which the mind can rest, overwhelming in its greatness, but satisfying in its harmony."

"Nothing," Lewis continues, "is more deeply impressed on the cosmic imaginings of a modern than the idea that the heavenly bodies move in a pitch-black and dead-cold vacuity. It was not so in the Medieval Model. . . . For their system is in one sense more heliocentric than ours. The sun illuminates the whole universe. . . . Night is merely the conical shadow cast by our Earth. . . . Since the Sun moves and the Earth is stationary, we must picture this long, black finger perpetually revolving like the hand of a clock; that is why Milton* calls it 'the circling canopie of Night's extended shade' *(Paradise Lost,* III, 556)." [4]

Just as this vast (but finite) space is not dark, so neither is it silent. As Lorenzo whispers to Jessica in Shakespeare's *The Merchant of Venice,*

> *Look how the floor of heaven*
> *Is thick inlaid with patines of bright gold:*
> *There's not the smallest orb which thou behold'st*
> *But in his motion like an angel sings.†*

---

* *GBWW,* Vol. 32, p. 147.
† Act 5, sc. 1; *GBWW,* Vol. 26, p. 431.

Thus, in our medieval, starry stroll we must conceive ourselves looking up at a world brilliantly illuminated and resonant with harmony.

A magnificent woodcut in the *Nuremberg Chronicle* of 1493, the most splendidly illustrated book printed in the fifteenth century, furnishes a graphic illustration of the medieval universe (*see* page opposite). Four spheres, made up of the four terrestrial elements posited by Aristotle—earth, water, air, and fire—rest in the middle of the universe. Surrounding them are the transparent, crystalline spheres of the planets, the firmament, and the *primum mobile* or first moving sphere. Above all sits God Enthroned, the Heavenly Father with his angelic hosts. The scheme was in the main the one that Aristotle had given, but where the ancient philosopher stopped, Christian theologians took over, adding the beatific domains so well described in Dante's *Paradiso*.

Although the concentrically nested spheres offered a celestial architecture philosophically satisfying to most men, a mathematical genius such as the Alexandrian astronomer Ptolemy (fl. A.D. 135) could aspire to still greater understanding of the heavens. His *Almagest* begins with an epigram:

> *I know that I am mortal by nature, and ephemeral; but when I trace at my pleasure the windings to and fro of the heavenly bodies I no longer touch earth with my feet: I stand in the presence of Zeus himself and take my fill of ambrosia, food of the gods.*[5]

Astronomers of Aristotle's time had attempted to trace the wanderings to and fro of the planets within the framework of multiple concentric spheres, but it remained for Ptolemy to describe a predictive scheme that really worked. For the moon, Mercury, Venus, Mars, Jupiter, and Saturn, he adopted an epicyclic mechanism: that is, a smaller circle or epicycle riding upon a larger deferent circle. The deferent circles corresponded only approximately to the ethereal spheres of Aristotle, for each was eccentrically centered with respect to the earth. Finally, the motion of the epicycle was not uniform along the deferent itself; instead, Ptolemy invoked yet another mechanism, the so-called equant, a pivot of uniform angular motion lying elsewhere inside the deferent. Later critics, including Copernicus, objected that the equant destroyed the aesthetic principle of uniform circular motions, but for predicting planetary positions, Ptolemy's invention of the equant was a sheer stroke of genius.

Within the *Almagest* Ptolemy gives little hint that he allotted any reality to his epicycles and deferents. Indeed, because he discusses alternative arrangements for the solar mechanism, he creates the impression that his scheme is a mathematical model with no claim for the actual existence of the epicyclic wheels in the heavens. Later astronomers recognized this even more clearly when they noticed that according to Ptolemy's lunar model, the moon at its maximum should be twice as big as its smallest apparent size, a prediction plainly contradicted by nature.

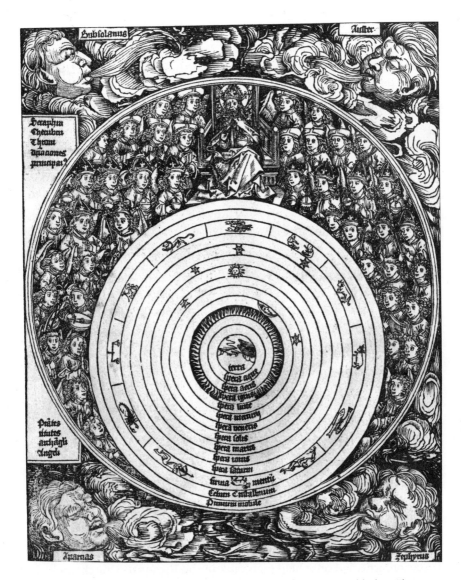

The *Chronicle,* written by Hartmann Schedel, is a history of the world since the Creation, containing many fine woodcuts. This particular one may have been the work of Michael Wolgemuth, the teacher of Dürer

The difference between Aristotle's qualitative picture of the heavenly spheres and Ptolemy's involved but quantitative circles troubled both the Islamic and the Latin astronomers of the Middle Ages. The *Almagest's* circles could have been more easily dismissed as mere geometrical models had it not been for another, presumably later and more mature work by Ptolemy, the *Planetary Hypotheses,* which showed how his entire scheme fit together if proper spaces were allowed for the movement of each epicycle. With the individual planetary mechanisms assembled in this way, Ptolemy could determine the distance to each planet; and because these results agreed with previously accepted distances for the moon and sun, the scheme gained a certain aura of reality.

Thus, the medieval conception of the universe was not nearly so monolithic as our nocturnal stroll would suppose. In fact, astronomical thought in the Middle Ages hung suspended between two world systems—urged toward the concentric spheres by respect for the opinions of Aristotle, yet drawn to the mechanisms of Ptolemy by a desire for a natural science in conformity with experience. The existence of competing cosmologies not only invited the interpretation that *neither* described "reality" but also opened the way to further model-building.

## The renaissance of astronomy

By the early fifteenth century, shortly before Copernicus was born, the technical details of Ptolemy's work were at best imperfectly understood. With the rise of universities and the revival of classical learning came the desire to restore astronomy to its former technical sophistication. At midcentury, two profoundly important events provided the impetus for such a restoration: the invention of printing with movable type, and the fall of Constantinople to the Turks in 1453.

Among those astronomers who proceeded to exploit the resulting possibilities, the most successful were Georg Peurbach and his student Johann Müller, known as Regiomontanus. Stimulated by a visit from Cardinal Bessarion, who had once held high rank in the Byzantine church, and who had hoped himself to make a new translation of the *Almagest* directly from the Greek, Regiomontanus resolved to learn Greek and to collect or copy the Greek scientific manuscripts that had been carried away from besieged Constantinople and were now available in the West. In 1471 Regiomontanus settled in Nuremberg, where he founded his own printing office in order to disseminate the fruits of his scholarly labors. (Even many years later his manuscript heritage provided an important source of material for Johannes Petreius, the printer of Copernicus's work.)

Among the items published by Regiomontanus was Peurbach's *New Theory of the Planets,* the first book in Western Europe to expound Ptolemy's epicyclic theory, indeed the first newly written treatise on

Page from a so-called volvel manuscript of the late fifteenth century, derived from Peurbach's work, in which the diagrams were constructed as demonstration (not scale) models, operable by hand, to indicate the motion of the heavenly bodies. The motion shown in this case is that of a planet in an epicycle (small white circle) that moves on the deferent (large white band), which could be revolved by pushing the tab marked *orbis defferens epic[iclu]m*. The planet itself is the black dot at the edge of the epicycle, which could be revolved by means of the tab marked *epiciclus*. What were called crystalline lunulas, represented in the diagram by the black background, could also be revolved, as could the *primum mobile* containing the signs of the zodiac

astronomy ever to be printed. Peurbach had discovered how to reconcile schematically the Aristotelian system of concentric spheres and Ptolemy's eccentric deferents: by embedding the Ptolemaic circles and epicycles within additional crystalline lunulas (the black zones on art above), the inner and outer boundaries became concentric circles, capable of nesting one within another.

Peurbach's scheme might have resolved the tension between the two great geocentric cosmologies, the Aristotelian and the Ptolemaic, but apparently it did not. Perhaps it served only to make astronomers more aware of the philosophical incompatibilities between the two systems. Copernicus, when he first sketched out and defended his own heliocentric system, described the astronomy that had hitherto prevailed in terms of opposed conceptions, neither of which he could regard as satisfactory, though each seemed defective for a different reason:

163

*Callippus and Eudoxus, who endeavored to solve the problem by the use of concentric spheres, were unable to account for all the planetary movements; they had to explain not merely the apparent revolutions of the planets but also the fact that these bodies appear to us sometimes to mount higher in the heavens, sometimes to descend; and this fact is incompatible with the principle of concentricity. Therefore it seemed better to employ eccentrics and epicycles, a system which most scholars finally accepted.*

*Yet the planetary theories of Ptolemy and most other astronomers, although consistent with the numerical data, seemed likewise to present no small difficulty. For these theories were not adequate unless certain equants were also conceived; it then appeared that a planet moved with uniform velocity neither on its deferent nor about the center of its epicycle. Hence a system of this sort seemed neither sufficiently absolute nor sufficiently pleasing to the mind.[6]*

## Copernicus as a cosmologist

We have now prepared the stage for the entrance of Copernicus—a stage sparsely set with philosophical props and almost devoid of astronomical trappings. That philosophical considerations nevertheless entered into his work was indicated by Copernicus in the preface and dedication to his *Revolutions:*

*Then in setting up the solar and lunar movements and those of the other five wandering stars, [mathematicians] do not employ the same principles, assumptions, or demonstrations for the revolutions and apparent movements. For some make use of homocentric circles only, others of eccentric circles and epicycles, by means of which however they do not fully attain what they seek. For although those who have put their trust in homocentric circles have shown that various different movements can be composed of such circles, nevertheless they have not been able to establish anything for certain that would fully correspond to the phenomena. But even if those who have thought up eccentric circles seem to have been able for the most part to compute the apparent movements numerically by those means, they have in the meanwhile admitted a great deal which seems to contradict the first principles of regularity of movement. . . . Accordingly, when I had meditated upon this lack of certitude in the traditional mathematics concerning the composition of movements of the spheres of the world, I began to be annoyed that the philosophers, who in other respects had made a very careful scrutiny of the least details of the world, had dis-*

*covered no sure scheme for the movements of the machinery of the world, which has been built for us by the Best and Most Orderly Workman of all.*[7]

What Copernicus actually accomplished was far from what is described in many secondary sources today. According to these popularizations, Copernicus found an astronomy burdened with epicycle upon epicycle, a fiendish complexity tottering upon the brink of collapse. In a clean sweep, he replaced this geocentric nightmare with the true and simpler heliocentric system, thereby producing an accurate astronomy in far better agreement with the phenomena.

This grossly distorted version is wrong on three counts. First, the story of epicycles-on-epicycles, though widely repeated, is a myth without foundation. Before Peurbach and Regiomontanus, accurate observations were so rare and the understanding of Ptolemy so insecure that any substantial embroidering of the simple epicyclic scheme was out of the question. Second, Copernicus's work did not, in fact, produce a marked increase in the accuracy of planetary predictions. By basing his astronomy primarily on the time-honored observations of Ptolemy, he necessarily found almost identical parameters to characterize the orbits, and thus the improvements in his results were not immediately obvious.

Third, because the choice of coordinates is a relative matter, the wanderings to and fro of the planets could be as accurately explained by a geocentric as by a heliocentric system. Thus, when Copernicus complains that "in the first place, mathematicians are so uncertain about the motion of the sun and moon that they cannot establish and observe a constant length even for the tropical year,"* he expresses his general dissatisfaction with the state of astronomy, but surely not a cogent reason for switching cosmologies.

Indeed, the change to a sun-centered world view is so little demanded by sense impressions of the phenomena that Galileo was later to exclaim, "I cannot admire enough those astronomers who, *in spite of their senses,* accepted the Copernican theory."

Yet there is a kernel of truth in the popular accounts. In some profound philosophical sense, the heliocentric system *is* simpler, purer, more beautiful—even, perhaps, more "true."

How, when, and why Copernicus decided to adopt it is still a puzzle. Certainly his life seems to have been a preparation for the studies that made such a decision possible. Born in Torun in 1473, he was orphaned at eleven and adopted by an influential uncle who became bishop of Warmia, and who eventually arranged for him to have a financially secure, lifetime position as one of the sixteen canons at the Frombork Cathedral. At the Krakow university, Copernicus pursued astronomy

---

* Cf. *GBWW,* Vol. 16, p. 507.

with a passion uncharacteristic of an undergraduate; immersed in a thriving Renaissance environment, he may even have heard of Aristarchus or of the paean to the sun written by the learned Italian Platonist Marsilio Ficino. In 1496 he traveled to Bologna for graduate study in canon law. Surely there, if not already in Krakow, he listened to accounts of the exploration of the New World—discoveries destined to make Ptolemy's highly regarded geography obsolete.

No doubt it was in Italy that Copernicus added a printed copy of Regiomontanus's *Epitome of Ptolemy's Almagest* to his small but growing library. The importance of this volume, printed in 1496, can scarcely be underestimated in analyzing the development of Copernicus's astronomy. The *Epitome* not only gave a perceptive and accurate abridgment of Ptolemy's work but also included data from the Islamic astronomers. Furthermore, it discussed alternate strategies for arranging the details of the planetary mechanisms. If Copernicus had been a student only fifty years earlier, he would have had access neither to printed materials nor to a clear account of Ptolemy's *Almagest*.

Perhaps, when Copernicus pondered the arrangements of deferent, eccentric, equant, and epicycle, he systematically worked his way to the alternative configuration with the sun in the center. He must have noticed that with a fixed sun near the center of the earth's orbit, the other planets fell into a particularly pleasing arrangement, with the fastest-moving Mercury nearest the sun and the slowest-moving Saturn in the outermost position. The earth, with a 365-day revolution, fell neatly between the 225-day period of Venus and the 687-day cycle of Mars. Copernicus describes this in his *Revolutions,* going on to say:

> At rest, however, in the middle of everything is the sun. For in this most beautiful temple, who would place this lamp in another or better position than that from which it can light up the whole thing at the same time? . . . Thus indeed, as though seated on a royal throne, the sun governs the family of planets revolving around it. . . .
>
> In this arrangement, therefore, we discover a marvelous symmetry of the universe, and an established harmonious linkage between the motion of the spheres and their size, such as can be found in no other way.[8]

Copernicus extends his glowing description of the new astronomy by noting how a heliocentric system explained the various sizes of retrograde motions in a natural and rational manner. "Yet none of these phenomena appears in the fixed stars," he continues. "This proves their immense height, which makes even the sphere of the annual motion, or its reflection, vanish from before our eyes. . . . So vast, without any question, is this divine handiwork of the most excellent Almighty."

(Top) The manuscript of Copernicus's *De revolutionibus orbium coelestium* (1543) in the Jagiellonian University Library, Krakow. The manuscript, consisting of 428 pages (214 leaves), is open to folio 9–10, on which appears the famous diagram showing the sun, not the earth, at the center of the universe—or as we would now more narrowly say, of our planetary system. On page 10 (the right hand page), in the second line from the top, occur the words that made the modern world: *In medio vero omnium resident Sol* ("In the center of all rests the sun"). See *GBWW,* Vol. 16, p. 526.

(Bottom) Detail of the diagram on page 9 of Copernicus's manuscript, above. *Merc,* or Mercury, was placed in the seventh circle counting in from the fixed stars, hence the number 7, and its interval by the approximate figures that Copernicus used is *XXC dierum,* or eighty days. Actually the interval is eighty-eight days, as indicated at *GBWW,* Vol. 16, p. 526. The words *noni mestris* ("nine months") indicate the period of Venus, the sixth planet, whose period is actually seven and a half months

## Copernicus as a model-builder

The early 1500s were a time of immense and rapid change in man's intellectual outlook. The information explosion, brought about by the invention of printing, disseminated news of the age of exploration, and, soon, of the Protestant Reformation. We might well imagine that the world was also ready to accept a new cosmology. But such a supposition, made from a twentieth-century vantage point, seems false.

Sometime before 1514, Copernicus had caught the first glimpses of a sun-centered astronomy, for we know that by then he had distributed a few manuscript copies of his *Little Commentary*. In this essay he criticized the theory of concentric spheres and Ptolemy's equant, then outlined the assumptions of his alternative heliocentric cosmology, and finally elaborated briefly on the configurations of circles required for each planet in order to eliminate the equant. For all practical purposes, this *Little Commentary* was completely ignored—neither rebuttals nor acclaim appear in the contemporary literature—and it was so totally forgotten that not until the nineteenth century was the manuscript rediscovered and printed.

Even after the printing of Copernicus's *Revolutions,* the heliocentric cosmology was still largely ignored. In the half century after its publication, only a few authors addressed themselves to the new cosmology in any substantive fashion: Thomas Digges, who in 1576 translated part of Copernicus's book under the title *A Perfit Description of the Caelestiall Orbes;* Giordano Bruno, who in 1584 espoused a garbled version of Copernican ideas, only to abandon them later in favor of Tycho's geocentric theory; the Jesuit Christopher Clavius, who in 1581 rejected the Copernican system in favor of Ptolemy; Tycho Brahe, who in 1588 spurned it in favor of his own geocentric theory; and Johannes Kepler, who in 1596 endorsed heliocentrism as the true road to a cosmic physics.

During these same years, however, Copernicus held an impressive reputation as a mathematician and even as the "new Ptolemy." That Copernicus was frequently quoted as an authority (even when the sun-centered cosmology went unmentioned) attests the skill and technique of the *Revolutions* as a treatise on astronomy. Although heliocentric assumptions color the entire text, only the first dozen leaves stress the cosmology. Indeed, these were the most accessible parts of the volume, and they probably had a fairly wide readership. But it was the remaining 360 pages, constituting the bulk of the book, that made it the most impressive astronomical work of the century, quite apart from the novel arrangement of the cosmos that it proposed.

For the most part the *Revolutions* was a very technical work, in which Copernicus wrestled with the details of lunar and planetary motions. He carefully reviewed the observations reported by Ptolemy, and then considered contemporary observations, almost always his own. By so doing he discovered a small variation since antiquity in the orientation of the planetary orbits. Another complex problem arose from the so-called motion of the eighth sphere—the slow precessional changes in star positions when measured with respect to the equinoctial point. This had been treated by Ptolemy, who had assigned a very inaccurate value to the rate of precession. When the Islamic astronomers noticed this discrepancy, they added a secondary correction called trepidation. By 1500, even the rate of trepidation had proved faulty, and Copernicus spent much effort trying to establish more secure constants for this phenomenon. A third challenge, which he set for himself, was the elimination of Ptolemy's philosophically unsatisfactory equant. This he managed to replace by including an additional small circle—for Mars, Jupiter, and Saturn, this circle became an epicyclet.

Astronomers interested in technical improvements found much to admire in Copernicus's treatise. Consider in this context the case of Erasmus Reinhold. A colleague of Rheticus, Reinhold was professor of higher mathematics (that is, geometry and astronomy) at Wittenberg and the cleverest mathematical astronomer in the generation following Copernicus. When the *Revolutions* was published, Reinhold promptly obtained a copy for study and annotation. On its title page he wrote a short phrase epitomizing his impression of the book: *"The Axiom of Astronomy: Celestial motions are uniform and circular, or are composed of uniform and circular parts."* Not the heliocentric cosmology but Copernicus's replacement of the equant by a small epicyclet won Reinhold's praise! Reinhold then worked out the "handy tables" for predicting planetary positions, carefully preserving the technical discoveries of the *Revolutions*, but concealing its cosmology.

What helped greatly to prevent Copernicus's technical astronomy from being thrown out along with his "absurd" theory was Osiander's unsigned introduction picturing the astronomer as a model-builder, not as a seeker for reality. Certainly Reinhold accepted and appreciated Copernicus's work as model-building par excellence, and in his teaching at Wittenberg he helped to establish a strong tradition that regards all astronomical structures as hypothetical.

But did Copernicus himself view that heliocentric system as a model, or did he believe it to be a description of the heavens as they really are? To what extent did he fill the role of astronomer as model-maker? With these questions our essay has come full circle, back to that remarkable artifact, the autograph manuscript of the *Revolutions*.

The 214 leaves of the manuscript provide an invaluable archaeological treasure. The various kinds of paper act like strata, enabling scholars to detect different stages in the development of the work. Thus the figure of a serpent, impressed as a watermark, identifies the oldest leaves. Pages marked with a hand and a crown form the next layer, and these are inter-mixed with yet a later stage watermarked with an elaborate letter *P*. Finally, in the years just before his death, the aged astronomer added a few new pages impressed with the watermark of a hand and a four-petaled flower.

The paper, as well as the dates of observations within the text, suggests that Copernicus wrote out the manuscript primarily between 1515 and 1530. The intermixing of the various kinds of paper shows him engaged in a continual process of revision. Particularly interesting in this context is the crossed-out and much reworked section on Venus. Here the mechan-ism chosen to replace the equant is an eccentric orbit carried on a tiny eccentric circle, rather than the epicyclet on an eccentric orbit used for the superior planets. But what is interesting is that Copernicus explicitly mentions the alternative possibility. Surely here is an unambiguous case of modeling—Copernicus could hardly have claimed that one case was more real than the other.

The Copernican theory of planetary latitudes, described in the sixth book of the *Revolutions,* furnishes another situation where the mechan-ism is clearly a mathematical construction with no claim to reality. If the orbits postulated to account for the longitudes (the angular motion around the sun) represented the real trajectories of the planets in space, then the same orbits should have yielded the latitudes (the deviation out of the earth's orbital plane). However, Copernicus, like Ptolemy before him, chose independent procedures in his sections on latitudes.

Yet another example can be found if we examine the earlier account of the heliocentric system given by Copernicus in his *Little Commentary.* There he replaced the equant not by a single epicyclet but by a pair of small circles, essentially an epicyclet-on-an-epicyclet. Once again, the alternative schemes reveal the arbitrary nature of the devices and show Copernicus as a builder of geometrical models.

The foregoing distinction between Copernicus as a cosmologist and as a model-maker makes it possible to understand several otherwise puzzling features of the Copernican revolution, and suggests the answer to our basic queries concerning the formulation and reception of the helio-centric theory. We can see, in the prototype example of Erasmus Rein-hold, how Copernicus was esteemed in the sixteenth century for the technical 97 percent of the *Revolutions,* the part almost unstudied today. In contrast, we honor Copernicus in the twentieth century for the cos-mological 3 percent of his book. Yet without the 97 percent, the 3 percent with its remarkable defense of the heliocentric system might have perished forever.

Was Copernicus a cosmologist who believed in the reality of his sys-tem? Or was he primarily a highly proficient model-builder working with-in the mainstream of the astronomy of his day? Because of the ambiguity within the *Revolutions,* and because of the scarcity of less formal manuscript materials, commentators in subsequent centuries have seen their own views mirrored in Copernicus. The traditionalists of the sixteenth century could see him as one of their own, as a first-rate model-builder. But Kepler and Galileo, who looked at Nature with new eyes, proclaimed him as a comrade in the search for the underlying reality of the world. Even today the ambiguity remains, and whether we classify Copernicus as the last of the old geometrical astronomers or as the first of the new astronomical physicists depends on the relative weight that we give to the different parts of his great opus.

We began by asking *If the heliocentric idea is really so simple and necessary, why was it so long in coming?* In that form the question is of course loaded; to the sixteenth-century astronomer the idea was neither simple nor necessary. The views of Christopher Clavius, an intellectual leader among the Jesuits in Rome, were characteristic of the times, and particularly interesting because he called Copernicus "that most excellent geometer who, in our time, has put astronomy on its feet again and who will, in recognition thereof, be celebrated and admired by all posterity as Ptolemy's equal." In his *Commentary on the Sphere of Sacrobosco* he wrote:

> *That Copernicus should have succeeded in saving the phenomena in a different way is not at all surprising. The motions of the eccentrics and epicycles taught him the times, the magnitudes, and the quality of appearances, future as well as past. Since he was exceedingly ingenious, he was able to conjure up a new method, in his opinion more convenient, of saving the appearances. . . . All that can be concluded from Copernicus' assumption is that it is not absolutely certain that the eccentrics and epicycles are arranged as Ptolemy thought, since a large number of phenomena can be defended by a different method. . . .*
>
> *If the Copernican assumption implied nothing false or absurd, one might, so long as it were a question of preserving the phenomena, be in doubt whether it is better to adhere to the opinion of Ptolemy or to that of Copernicus. But the Copernican theory contains many absurd or erroneous assertions; it assumes that the earth is not at the center of the firmament; that it moves with a triple motion—a thing I find inconceivable, since, according to the philosophers, a single simple body has by rights a simple motion; [it further assumes] that the sun is at the center of the world and that it is bereft of any motion—all these things clash with the commonly accepted doctrine of philosophers and astronomers. Moreover, . . . these assertions seem to contradict what Holy Scripture in many places teaches us. This is why it seems to us that Ptolemy's opinion should be given preference over the opinion of Copernicus.*[9]

In a similar vein Tycho Brahe commented:

> *This innovation expertly and completely circumvents all that is superfluous or discordant in the system of Ptolemy. On no point does it offend the principles of mathematics. Yet it ascribes to the earth, that hulking, lazy body, unfit for motion, a motion as quick as that of the ethereal torches, and a triple motion at that. By this it stands refuted, not only in the name of the principles of physics, but also in the name of the authority of Holy Scripture.*[10]

We must, therefore, rephrase our question to ask *When and why was the heliocentric system generally seen as simple and necessary?* This acceptance came about in the 1600s, almost a century after the publication of the *Revolutions*. Two men played the leading roles in changing the prevailing opinions: Johannes Kepler, who found that the aesthetic arrangement of the Copernican system led to a coherent mathematical description of the motions, and Galileo Galilei, whose telescopic observations helped convince people that the Copernican system was not so absurd after all.

Kepler's own account of becoming a Copernican appears in the preface to his *Mysterium Cosmographicum* ("Cosmographic Secret") of 1596:

> *When I was studying under the distinguished Michael Mästlin at Tübingen six years ago, seeing the many inconveniences of the commonly accepted theory of the universe, I became so delighted with Copernicus, whom Mästlin often mentioned in his lectures, that I often defended his opinions in the students' debates about physics. I have by degrees—partly out of hearing Mästlin, partly by myself—collected all the advantages that Copernicus has over Ptolemy. At last in the year 1595 in Graz when I had an intermission in my lectures, I pondered on this subject with the whole energy of my mind. And there were three things above all for which I sought the causes as to why it was this way and not another—the number, the dimensions, and the motions of the orbs.*[11]

After describing several false attempts, Kepler continued:

> *Almost the whole summer was lost with this agonizing labor. At last on a quite trifling occasion I came nearer the truth. I believe Divine Providence intervened so that by chance I found what I could never obtain by my own efforts. I believe this all the more because I have constantly prayed to God that I might succeed if what Copernicus had said was true.*

What Kepler found was that the spacing of the planets could be closely approximated by an appropriately arranged nesting of the five regular

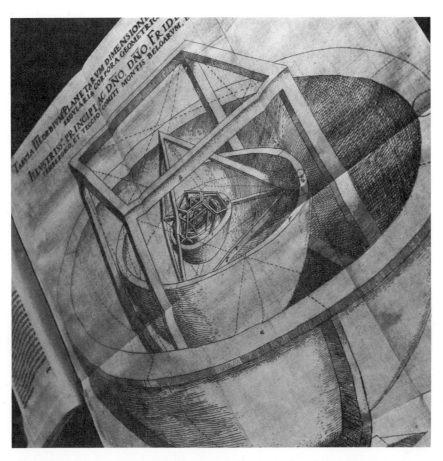

Diagram from Kepler's *Mysterium Cosmographicum,* or "Cosmographic Secret," of 1596. Kepler's discussion of planetary spacing in terms of five regular solids is given in his *Epitome of Copernican Astronomy* (1618–21), *GBWW*, Vol. 16, pp. 860–72, especially 864 ff.

polyhedra between spheres for the six planets of the Copernican system.

Fantastic as these polyhedra may appear today, we must remember the revolutionary context in which they were proposed. Kepler's *Cosmographic Secret* was essentially the first unabashedly Copernican treatise since the *Revolutions.* But whereas a heliocentric cosmology was almost incidental to that work, as we have seen, without such a cosmology the entire rationale of Kepler's book would have collapsed. Even Kepler's inquiry into the basic causes of the number and motions was enough to constitute a novel break with the medieval tradition, which considered the "naturalness" of the universe sufficient reason for such phenomena. To Kepler the theologian-cosmologist, nothing was more reasonable than to search for the architectonic principles of creation.

But Kepler demanded also to know how God the architect had set the universe in motion. He recognized that although in Copernicus's system the sun was near the center, it played no physical role. Kepler argued that the sun's centrality was essential, for the sun itself must provide the driving force to keep the planets in motion.

Kepler knew that the more distant a planet was from the sun, the longer its period; indeed, this was one of the most important regularities of the heliocentric system, already noted by Copernicus in the *Revolutions:*

> *In this arrangement, therefore, we discover a marvelous symmetry of the universe, and an established harmonious linkage between the motion of the spheres and their size, such as can be found in no other way.*

Kepler's first attempt to establish this linkage mathematically, in his *Cosmographic Secret,* can hardly be considered successful; but, driven by his continuing attempts to search out the celestial harmonics, he eventually found his celebrated law relating planetary distances and periods. This relationship, which could be found only in a Copernican system, became an important input to the Newtonian synthesis.

Kepler continually attempted to reason from physical causes, in spite of the admonition of Mästlin, "I think that one should leave physical causes out, and should explain astronomical matters only according to the astronomical method with the aid of astronomical, not physical, causes and hypotheses." Kepler was convinced that the physics would lead him to the true planetary orbits. In his *Epitome of Copernican Astronomy* he wrote:

> *Astronomy can easily do without the useless furniture of fictitious circles and spheres. But of the true figures in which the paths of the planets are arranged, there is such an absence of imagination that we are impoverishing Astronomy. The major task and work of the true astronomer is to demonstrate from observations what figures the planetary orbits possess; and to devise such hypotheses, or physical principles, as can be used to demonstrate the figures that are in accord with the deductions made from observations. Therefore, when once the figure of the planetary orbit has been established, then will come the second and more popular exercise of the astronomer: to formulate, and to give the rules of, an astronomical calculus in accordance with this true figure.*[12]

For Kepler there was a crucial physical difference between a geocentric and a heliocentric universe; only in the latter case would the sun provide a central driving power for the planetary system. Hence Kepler believed firmly in the reality of the Copernican system, and in the form of the orbits as well. Armed with this conviction, Kepler saw that the same orbit must yield latitudes as well as longitudes; this provided a fundamental tool for his attack on the problem of Mars, an important link in the chain that led to the discovery of Mars's elliptical orbit. Thus, for Kepler's work, belief in the heliocentric system really mattered, and made a crucial difference in his approach to the subject. Kepler's audacious claim that he had created an astronomy without hypotheses was made in this context.

Galileo, unlike Kepler, was not particularly interested in the details of celestial mechanics. But the impact of his telescopic observations, where he saw that the moon was earthlike and that around Jupiter revolved four satellites, a miniature Copernican system, convinced him as to the reality of the heliocentric cosmology. Galileo appealed to observations for a physical confirmation of the Copernican hypotheses. "We shall concentrate on confirming them and establishing them by means of the appearances," he wrote.

Convinced of the physical reality of the sun-centered system, both Galileo and Kepler addressed themselves to possible apparent contradictions with the Bible. Writing to the Grand Duchess Christina about interpretation of scripture and the *Revolutions*, Galileo said:

> *When printed, the book was accepted by the holy Church and it has been read and studied by everyone without the faintest hint of any objection ever being conceived against its doctrines. Yet now that manifest experiences and necessary proofs have shown them to be well grounded, persons exist who would strip the author of his reward without so much as looking at his book, and at the shame of having him pronounced a heretic. . . . [Copernicus] did not ignore the Bible, but he knew very well that if his doctrine were proved, then it could not contradict the Scriptures when they were rightly understood.*
>
> *. . . I think that in discussions of physical problems we ought to begin not from the authority of scriptural passages, but from sense-experiences and necessary demonstrations; for the holy Bible and the phenomena of nature proceed alike from the divine Word, the former as the dictate of the Holy Ghost and the latter as the observant executrix of God's commands. It is necessary for the Bible, in order to be accommodated to the understanding of every man, to speak many things which appear to differ from the absolute truth so far as the bare meaning of the words is concerned. But Nature, on the other hand, is inexorable and immutable; she never transgresses the laws imposed upon her, or cares a whit whether her abstruse reasons and methods of operation are understandable to men.*[13]

Elsewhere, Galileo wrote even more strongly:

> *The quickest and surest way to show that the position of Copernicus is not contrary to Scripture is, as I see it, to show by a thousand proofs that this proposition is true and that the contrary position cannot be maintained at all. Consequently, since two truths cannot contradict each other, the position recognized as true necessarily agrees with Holy Scripture.*[14]

In the introduction to his *New Astronomy* Kepler wrote:

> *But the Sacred Scriptures, speaking to men in an everyday manner on ordinary matters (not intended for instruction), used expressions granted by all so as to be understood. . . . Is it any wonder then, if the Scripture speaks according to man's comprehension, that at such times truth differs from the conceptions of mankind?* [15]

The answer to our second question—*Why was the heliocentric cosmology first ignored and then resisted?*—now begins to appear. As long as no reality was ascribed to the new astronomy, it provided a working scheme, beautiful if unbelievable. The attitude of the mid-sixteenth-century Dutch astronomer Gemma Frisius is particularly remarkable in this regard. In a letter published by a contemporary ephemeris maker, Gemma pointed out that the Copernican heliocentric hypothesis gave a better understanding of planetary distances and certain features of retrograde motion. Gemma added, however, that those who objected to the ephemerides because of the underlying Copernican hypothesis understood neither causes nor the use of hypotheses. "For these are not posited by the authors as if this must exist this way and no other." He further remarks:

> *Nay, even if someone wished to refer to the sky those motions that Copernicus assigns to the earth, he could do so and according to the very canons of calculation. However, it did not please that most learned and prudent man, on account of his invincible intellect, to invert the entire order of his hypotheses, and so he was content to have posited those that sufficed for the true discovery of the "phenomena."* [16]

What an astonishing statement! Copernicus is simultaneously praised and criticized for being satisfied with a hypothesis that could truly explain the celestial phenomena. With Kepler and Galileo there could be no such ambiguity. Kepler with his "physical causes" and Galileo with his "thousand proofs" changed the face of science.

As long as opinions like Gemma's held sway, heliocentrism could be safely ignored. But when Galileo and Kepler began to argue that it was absurd to suppose that phenomena of nature could be demonstrated from false hypotheses, a revolution was clearly under way. And when they began to suggest new interpretations of Scripture, active resistance grew within the Catholic church. In many ways the papal reaction to Galileo must be viewed in the broader context of the Counter-Reformation, when the church was resisting the possibility of the personal and "nonofficial" interpretations of the Scriptures that lay at the foundation of the Protestant Reformation. The trial of Galileo then appears as a vindictive response to one who was rocking the boat of official policy in what the Catholic church necessarily viewed as a critical time.

Nevertheless, a central issue of the Copernican revolution was the nature of scientific hypotheses and their claim to truth. The Inquisition did not ban Copernicus's *Revolutions;* it merely amended it in a dozen places. A characteristic change was the rewriting of the title of chapter 11 in Book One. The original title read "A Demonstration of the Three-fold Motion of the Earth"; this was altered to "The Hypothesis of the Threefold Motion of the Earth and Its Demonstration."

In the twentieth century both the rise of quantum mechanics and Einstein's relativity have shaken scientists' faith in the unique truth of any particular theory. Einstein himself wrote, "The sense-experiences are the given subject-matter. But the theory that shall interpret them is man-made. It is the result of an extremely laborious process of adaptation: hypothetical, never completely final, always subject to question and doubt." [17] Much of modern science is viewed as model-building, in many ways akin to the geometrical devices of the sixteenth century.

Regardless of Copernicus's own philosophical views, which have been as repainted by later generations as Leonardo's *Last Supper,* his work has nevertheless provided the foundation for a science radically different both in content and approach from the astronomy he studied in fifteenth-century Krakow. The model-building of modern science is based on the continuing interaction of theory and observation, and tempered by a frank appreciation of the finite lifetime of acceptable models. Contemporary scientists would agree that false hypotheses and models will eventually prove their inadequacy under the unending scrutiny of experimentation and observation.

Kepler and Galileo have taught us the necessity of the perpetual interplay between the data and its interpretation, but it was Copernicus who by his work showed us how fragile time-honored scientific conceptions can be. Perhaps inadvertantly, he taught us to anticipate continuing scientific revolutions as our understanding of the universe progresses. A visionary who sought a purer and more satisfying view of the universe, he became an unwitting revolutionary and founding father of our modern science.

1 *GBWW*, Vol. 16, pp. 510–11; Polish Academy of Science, Nicholas Copernicus, *Complete Works, The Manuscript of Nicholas Copernicus' "On the Revolutions" Facsimile* (London, Warsaw, Cracow, 1972), fol. 1–2.

2 Edward Rosen, trans., *Three Copernican Treatises* (New York: Columbia University Press, 1939), pp. 24–25. Cf. *GBWW*, Vol. 16, pp. 505–6.

3 Johannes Kepler, *Astronomia Nova* (Heidelberg, 1609).

4 C. S. Lewis, *The Discarded Image* (Cambridge: Cambridge University Press, 1964), pp. 111–12.

5 B. L. van der Waerden, trans., in *Scientific Change,* ed. A. C. Crombie (London: Heinemann Educational Books, 1962), p. 58.

6 N. Copernicus, *Commentariolus*, trans. Edward Rosen, *Three Copernican Treatises,* p. 57.

7 *GBWW*, Vol. 16, pp. 507–8.

8 *GBWW*, Vol. 16, pp. 526–28. This passage and the following one (ibid., p. 529) are quoted here in a new translation by Edward Rosen in Polish Academy of Science, Nicholas Copernicus, *Complete Works,* Vol. 2 (London, Warsaw, Cracow, 1973).

9 Christopher Clavius, *In Sphaeram Ioannis de Sacro Bosco commentarius* (Rome, 1581), pp. 436–37, 193; trans. Edmund Dolan and Chaninah Maschler in Pierre Duhem, *To Save the Phenomena* (Chicago: University of Chicago Press, 1969), pp. 94–95.

10 Tycho Brahe, *De mundi aetherei recentioribus phaenomenis* (Uraniborg, 1588), pt. 2, p. 95; trans. in *To Save the Phenomena,* p. 96.

11 Johannes Kepler, *Mysterium Cosmographicum* (Tübingen, 1596), p. 6; trans. Owen Gingerich in the forthcoming article "Kepler" in *Dictionary of Scientific Biography,* vol. 7, ed. C. C. Gillespie (New York: Charles Scribner's Sons, 1973).

12 Cf. *GBWW*, Vol. 16, p. 964.

13 Galileo Galilei, "Letter to the Grand Duchess Christina" (1615), trans. Stillman Drake in *Discoveries and Opinions of Galileo* (Garden City, N.Y.: Doubleday & Co., Anchor Books, 1957), pp. 178–82.

14 Letter of Galileo to an unknown recipient, trans. in *To Save the Phenomena,* p. 109.

15 Johannes Kepler, *Astronomia Nova,* Introduction (Heidelberg, 1609); paraphrased from a seventeenth-century translation by Thomas Salusbury.

16 Letter of Gemma Frisius printed in Johannes Stadius, *Ephemerides novae* (Cologne, 1556); translated in a forthcoming article by Owen Gingerich, "The Role of Erasmus Reinhold and the Prutenic Tables in the Dissemination of the Copernican Theory" in *Studia Copernicana VI* (Wroclaw, 1973).

17 Albert Einstein, *Ideas and Opinions,* trans. Sonja Bargmann (New York: Crown Publishers, 1954), pp. 323–24.

NOTE TO THE READER

Readers who wish to pursue the matters discussed by Professor Gingerich should read the *Syntopicon* chapters on Astronomy (5) and Hypothesis (36). In particular, see the references listed under Topic 2*b* of Astronomy, which deal with the use of hypotheses in the heliocentric and geocentric theories of the universe; also Topic 5, in which astronomy and cosmology are considered; Topic 8*c*, which treats of celestial motion; and Topic 13, which covers the history of astronomy. In the chapter on Hypothesis, see especially the readings under Topic 4*b*, which have to do with the idea of saving the appearances, and Topic 4*c*, in which consistency, simplicity, and beauty are considered as standards of hypothetical construction. See also Chapter 83, Science, particularly Topic 4*c*, dealing with the role of cause in science, and of explanation and description as aims of scientific inquiry; and see also Topic 4*e*, where the certitude and probability and the finality and tentativeness of scientific conclusions are discussed.

## PART THREE

# The Review of a Great Book

# The Canterbury Tales

## Mark Van Doren

This discussion of Chaucer's *Canterbury Tales,* which constitutes the first
of what the editors of *The Great Ideas Today* intend as a series of contemporary readings by eminent persons of works included in *Great Books of
the Western World,* was the last extended piece of prose undertaken by Mark
Van Doren, who finished it shortly before his death on December 10, 1972.
Readers of *The Great Ideas Today* will recall Mr. Van Doren as a contributor
to the volumes published in 1961 and 1969; in the latter, at the request of the
editors, he offered a list of books which he thought might survive as great
works of the twentieth century in literature—a selection difficult to make,
he said, and one that, as he did not say, only an experienced and accomplished reader could with any credibility have made at all. In asking Mr. Van
Doren to commence this series, the editors gave him his choice among a
number of titles, from which he selected *The Canterbury Tales.* The sadness
with which we record his subsequent death is tempered for us, so far as
possible, by the fact that he lived to complete the task, and by our belief that
the result is a fresh and perceptive study, at once lucid and loving, of one of
the great poems of the world.

Geoffrey Chaucer, who wrote *The Canterbury Tales* in England at the end of the fourteenth century, was then and is now one of the most lovable poets in the world, and this in spite of the fact that the substance of his tales is bitter quite as often as it is sweet, and in spite of the further fact that his language, his English, has grown difficult with time. To hear his verse as he expected it to be heard—as he himself read it in the English court, for he wrote before the invention of printing—requires now a student's knowledge of Middle English, a language that is ours and yet not ours, for many things about it both look and sound strange. Even then, however, the words that Chaucer so cunningly put together, no matter how imperfectly we say them to ourselves, caress us as we read, make love to our hearts and minds, and find their way into our memories where they manage to remain. But even if we have to read him in modernized form we still can be convinced that the charm his contemporaries praised him for is real. He is so good a poet, so great a poet, that he survives translation; and his substance is so rich and rare—so familiar too, as coming from the most companionable of poets—that he is never truly alien to us.

He was born a few years after 1340 and lived in London until 1400, when he died famous as the author of *The Canterbury Tales,* of *Troilus and Criseyde,** and of other works that need not concern us here, though many of them are beautiful too, and *Troilus and Criseyde,* the longest of his poems, is sometimes called his masterpiece. Of Chaucer's life nothing whatever is known that throws any light upon his poetry. He moved through the London of his day as anonymously as Shakespeare did two centuries later—as anonymously, that is, in his capacity as genius. The

---

* *Troilus and Cressida; GBWW,* Vol. 22, pp. 1–155.

only records of him are of the offices he held and of the public work he did. He was a soldier, an ambassador of minor rank, a traveler on the Continent with special commissions to perform; and latterly he was such things as comptroller of the customs and subsidy of wools for the port of London, justice of the peace for Kent, and clerk of the king's works for royal properties in or near London. About his wife, Philippa, nothing much is known beyond her name and, though he may have had a daughter and a son, it is not certain that this was so. For years he enjoyed the favor of John of Gaunt, and he was never out of favor with any of the three kings he served: Edward III, Richard II, and Henry IV.

All of which adds up to so little that the modesty with which he introduces himself in *The Canterbury Tales*—he is there, even if only as a figure of fiction—has led us all to assume that he was mild of manner, quiet of voice, and unimposing in his person, though none of these assumptions is warranted by any evidence. The only thing of which we have a right to be sure is that he was born old—born, that is to say, always to be wise beyond his years, and always to be possessed of the comic genius that comes with wisdom of the ripest, finest sort, the wisdom that sees far and remembers everything, and is so intimate with feeling as to be full of it after all.

His English has been a problem for readers of him ever since the century that followed upon his death. Edmund Spenser in 1596 could hail Chaucer as a "well of English undefyled," but Spenser was a lover of the antique both in language and in thought, and even then he lamented the ravages that "wicked Time" had inflicted upon the fair body of Chaucer's poems, which he feared were already "quite devourd and brought to nought." It is a fear that anyone at any time may feel in the face of evidence that obsolescence is working to obliterate precious things, literary or not—morals, for example, and good manners.

Dryden in 1700 found the language of Chaucer so unfamiliar in its forms that he thought it necessary to modernize certain of *The Canterbury Tales* for inclusion in his *Fables*. By this time even the memory of how Chaucer's English was pronounced had been lost, so that Dryden could say that his verse was no longer harmonious, though "they who lived with him, and some time after him, thought it musical," a judgment which Dryden only partially accepted, granting that

> *there is the rude sweetness of a Scotch tune in it, which is natural and pleasing, though not perfect. 'Tis true, I cannot go so far as he who published the last edition of him; for he would make us believe the fault is in our ears, and that there were really ten syllables in a verse where we find but nine: but this opinion is not worth confuting; 'tis so gross and obvious an error, that common sense . . . must convince the reader that equality of numbers . . . was either not known, or not always practised, in Chaucer's age.*

*. . . We can only say, that he lived in the infancy of our poetry, and that nothing is brought to perfection at the first.*

Whereas we now know that Chaucer was one of the most musical of poets, and a master of English verse. What Dryden did not believe was that the letter *e,* now mute at the end of many words and elsewhere too, was sounded in Chaucer's time, so that *longe,* for example, like *bookes* and *goode,* to take three instances quite at random, had two syllables instead of one, at least in positions where the *e* was not elided. And this makes all the difference. It creates what Matthew Arnold called "Chaucer's divine liquidness of diction, his divine fluidity of movement," virtues of which Arnold found it "difficult to speak temperately," so entranced he was with the lovely sound of Chaucer's lines. The sweetness of Chaucer's verse, in other words, was not rude but real. Dryden, whose praise of Chaucer laid the foundation for his reputation as we know it, was wrong about him only in this one respect, and we cannot hold it against him in view of the fact that he went ahead anyway to discover the great poet whom his own generosity still helps us to appreciate.

Meanwhile, let us remember that the music of Chaucer's verse is something like the music of Mozart—high and fine, and yet so powerful that it never breaks: a golden wire that stretches between heaven and earth, sounding incessantly its own note, its own idea. We shall have no occasion to meet him as a lyric poet, but he is superb in that role—indeed, in his "Balade" from *The Legend of Good Women,* supreme:

> *Hyd, Absolon, thy gilte tresses clere;*
> *Ester, ley thou thy meknesse al adoun;*
> *Hyd, Jonathas, al thy frendly manere;*
> *Penelope and Marcia Catoun,*
> *Mak of youre wyfhood no comparisoun*
> *Hyde ye youre beautes, Ysoude and Eleyne;*
> *Alceste is here, that al that may desteyne.*
>
> *Thy faire body, lat it not appere,*
> *Lavyne: and thou, Lucresse of Rome toun,*
> *And Polyxene, that boughte love so dere,*
> *Ek Cleopatre, with al thy passioun,*
> *Hide ye youre trouth in love and your renoun;*
> *And thou, Tysbe, that hast for love swich peyne:*
> *Alceste is here, that al may desteyne.*
>
> *Herro, Dido, Laodomya, all in-fere,*
> *Ek Phillis, hangyne for thy Demophoun,*
> *And Canace, espied by thy chere,*
> *Ysiphile, betrayed with Jasoun*

> *Mak of youre trouthe in love no bost ne soun;*
> *Nor Ypermystre or Adriane, ne pleyne:*
> *Alceste is here, that al that may disteyne.**

Nothing is said here except that Alcestis bedims all other good women with whom she may be compared. Nothing except just *that,* and it is everything, as the sound of the words keeps on saying, as the movement of the lines, so urgent, so exigent, keeps pressing us to believe and feel. *Rome* has two syllables, surely, and *espied* and *betrayed* both have three. The long *i* is pronounced *ee,* and the long *a* is like the *a* in *father.* Still more could be said about the difference between Chaucer's voice and ours, but let it suffice to suggest that the reader is free to find what music he will in this imperishable song. The music is there, waiting for him to realize its triumphant, almost tearful perfection.

But our subject is story, not style, and so we come at last to *The Canterbury Tales,* which Chaucer himself came to last, for he died writing them, or perhaps only arranging and ordering them, some of them from manuscripts of an earlier day. Perhaps the work was finished after all; perhaps Chaucer wanted it to strike us as incomplete, which on the whole it does. The effect might have been intentional; he hated prolixity except when it served his comic purpose, and he was too sensible a man to suppose that completeness itself is a virtue; for him, indeed, there could be an art of incompleteness, a trick of leaving things undone that would only bore us if they *were* done. In any event, and however he regarded them, the tales were his crowning achievement, and the one for which he will always be best known. *Troilus and Criseyde* had been matchless in its kind, and it continues to be admired by all who read it to its profoundly moving end. *The Canterbury Tales,* however, are more than admired; they are loved as folklore is loved, they live on with a certain casual air that seems to say they may pass for anonymous for all the author cares. They give us the impression of having been easy to write. A false impression, doubtless, but the fact that we have it is somehow connected with the truth.

Chaucer was one of those happy authors who discover before they die what they always should have been doing. Cervantes, who in *Don Quixote* made the same discovery, had previously been a competent student of the conventions, and as such had written romances that we might find admirable if we ever read them. The vein he opened with *Don Quixote,* however, was bright with his own life's blood, and the result was one of the immortal books—real and romantic both, as life itself is. So Chaucer, serving his apprenticeship as the author of dream poems, abstractions, and al-

---

* Glossary: *Hyd,* hide; *gilte,* golden; *clere,* clear, bright, splendid; *desteyne,* bedim; *Ek,* also; *swich,* such; *peyne,* toil, distress; *in-fere,* together; *espied,* disclosed; *chere,* appearance; *bost,* boast; *soun,* sound, boast; *pleyne,* complain, lament.

legories such as the age can be said to have demanded, did fine work which yet now counts for little, or relatively little, alongside the plain surface of *The Canterbury Tales,* the familiar look and feel of their images and figures, the casual, conversational tone they take with us their readers, the amateur effect they manage to provide without appearing to have striven for it. Not that the years of preparation were wasted, either for Chaucer or for Cervantes. Plainness and lifelikeness come late, not early, as simplicity does. And both Chaucer and Cervantes brought with them to their final work a certain courtliness, a cushion of "gentilesse," to use Chaucer's own term, which kept the realism of their masterpieces from being too brutal and flat, as realism in shallower imaginations may all too easily be.

*The Canterbury Tales* were easy to write, then, in the special sense that they were not written against the grain. Nevertheless, they were work, and if Chaucer was glad to do it, and did it with all of his old energy, we should not fail to recognize how busy the man's mind was as he proceeded, how actively it ranged over an immense territory that lay open for exploration. Chaucer was among other things a great reader; it is clear that he loved books, just as it is clear that he delighted in telling us about them, as if they were good friends he was proud to say he knew. He read, one can imagine, incessantly—until, he suggests in one of his autobiographical poems, he was "dumb" and "dazed"—and he seemed to remember every word on every page. In order to write *The Canterbury Tales* he had to find plots for them, to translate or adapt these plots, and then to conceal the signs of his having done so, for the tales must seem to be his own, as of course in the last analysis they are. But he had to find them somewhere first; they had to be in books, as Shakespeare's plots did also; neither poet was ready to write until he had before him the substance of his action, and people bearing names—historical, fictitious, dramatic, it mattered not which—who acted out the parts, and even spoke some of the lines, though Chaucer was to give them better lines, the lines that we ourselves remember.

The last thing he expected to be praised for was the thing we sometimes call originality, meaning by the word a cleverness in making up stories out of nothing. For him there had to be something, and it had better be something old, that more than one mind had handled, though if only one had, and it was Boccaccio's, so much the better, for in Boccaccio he recognized a master whom it was a pleasure to rewrite, making as free as he liked with the materials being borrowed—the original materials, which now are his because he made them his, and in doing so managed to be original in the richest sense of the word. But the author he used did not have to be as famous or as great as Boccaccio; he could be anybody, and sometimes he has been hard for the scholars to dig out of the record; but there he almost invariably is. Most of Chaucer's *Tales,* that is to say, have their sources, and in due course these will be mentioned.

Chaucer's hunger for stories was something he shared with the writers of his time; they all were cormorants, diving and devouring discernible creatures in the human sea. In this respect they were like writers at any time: like the Greek poets who ransacked myth and legend for the stuff of their tragedies, like the Elizabethan playwrights who plundered both ancient and modern literature for plots, like the makers of movie and television scripts who proceed in the same fashion, searching in every known corner for stories to retell. Perhaps the medieval poets had one special advantage: the diversity of their field, the range of it, the color, the richness of texture. Chaucer at any rate made the most of this advantage. His mind was naturally skeptical; he never seemed to know just what he should believe; but his skepticism was of that delightful sort which permitted him to believe everything—not nothing, but everything, on the chance that it might be true. Such skepticism—such loving skepticism—is what underlies, we must suppose, the account of the fairies that occurs in the first twenty-five lines of *The Wife of Bath's Tale.* Chaucer was at home in mythology; in the lore of chivalry; in popular folklore; in the legends of Arthur and his knights; in the literature of astronomy, astrology, and alchemy; in the lives of the saints and the degrees of power among the clergy; in the biographies of heroes; in the fineries of privilege and rank—for the English court in his time was the most luxurious in Europe; in the arts of costume and display; in the involutions of allegory as all contemporary poetry practiced it; in the spectacles of injustice, real or alleged, of which the time was full—injustice, without which fiction cannot flourish; in the backyard domain of the *fabliaux,* those dirty stories that everybody seems to have relished; in the deep wells of proverb and allusion that sent up buckets of wisdom and dishes of wit whenever anybody plumbed them.

The England of Chaucer's century had only four million people in it, and half of those died in the plagues that came again and again, but who feels this while reading *The Canterbury Tales*? Their world is densely populated, and every possible idea seems to exist in it. It is the world of the Middle Ages, which was so far from ignorant that it could invent the university and build the cathedrals we never cease to wonder at. It was sophisticated to the hilt; it thought of itself as old, not young, as corrupt, not innocent, as luxurious, not barren, as rich, not poor, though plenty of people were poor as plenty of people still are. It was this world that Chaucer knew so well—knew at first hand, but also knew from books, whose pages he once said were as delicious to his taste as the breath of a May morning; and who does not remember how Chaucer, like all of his countrymen for that matter, adored the darling month of May that took so long to come?

It was this world that he played upon in his *Canterbury Tales* like an instrument with strings, like an organ with many pipes. It was this world that he knew so well he often refused to describe it, for he thought his readers knew it too; he is constantly dismissing details as of no importance in comparison with his main theme, and he does so as if he were not aware that he is using a rhetorical figure familiar to everybody in his audience; but he knows they know he is aware, and he smiles a certain secret smile that we associate with his very name. Not so secret either, perhaps. "There is a sort of penumbra of playfulness round everything he ever said or sang," says G. K. Chesterton, who is one of his best critics, "a halo of humor" that we never miss if we read him well. At the same time there is the music in him of hidden tears, a piercing music that never lets us forget the power of his pity, the seriousness of his soul as he contemplates reality.

The reality of his times was terrible, and he could never have doubted that it was. The Black Death, the Hundred Years' War, the peasant rebellions that burned sections of London and beheaded archbishops, the ghastly executions, the beggars in the streets, the famines in the fields—Chaucer may not speak of these things, but he could not have been indifferent to them, and if nothing else his silence may be taken as meaning much; it has been remarked that throughout his part of the Hundred Years' War he never wrote one patriotic line; and if he was neither a Lollard nor a Wycliffite—that is to say, a social and theological liberal—at least his Plowman in *The Prologue* to the tales is given an almost ideal character, as distinguished from the contempt with which it was fashionable to treat the lower orders.

## The Prologue

*The Prologue* is justly one of the most famous poems in English. It sets the company of pilgrims in motion toward Canterbury, on an April morning as they leave the Tabard Inn on horseback with Harry Bailey, their host, directing the order in which they shall ride, and in which they shall tell the tales—two for each of them on the way, and two others for each of them coming back—that are Chaucer's principal business; he too is of the company, and will take his turn with most of the others. Not all of the twenty-nine will have tales to tell, and the riders for that matter never return to London, for the action stops at Canterbury; one hundred and sixteen stories would have been a staggering number in any case, and surely Chaucer never intended that there should be so many—told, incidently to a music of hooves and bridles and jingling ornaments, and with the company strung out so far along the road that no one voice could have reached every ear. Chaucer, to tell the truth, does not let us think of things like this as he starts to describe his pilgrims and goes on with such spirit that his people come alive before us and remain long after in our minds; he has the supreme gift that every storyteller would have if he only could, the gift of being able to bring the reader in and make him feel that he is there.

The pilgrimage was to the shrine of Saint Thomas à Becket, who was murdered at the altar in the cathedral of Canterbury in 1170, and who had become a figure of holiness for countless of the faithful who still journeyed there in Chaucer's century. The motive for such a journey varied with the persons who took it: some were devout, some were merely on a vacation, and for some it might have been hard to assign any motive at all; but all who went did have a common purpose which it was not necessary to discuss, so that with Chaucer's pilgrims there was no talk of anything but what passed through their minds as they rode more or less harmoniously along. "The time chosen," wrote William Blake of the painting he made of the pilgrims and advertised in a catalogue in 1809,

> *is early morning, before sunrise, when the jolly company are just quitting the Tabarde Inn. . . . The Landscape is an eastward view of the country . . . as it may be supposed to have appeared in Chaucer's time. . . . The characters of Chaucer's Pilgrims are the characters which compose all ages and nations: as one age falls, another rises, different to mortal sight, but to immortals only the same; for we see the same characters repeated again and again, in animals, vegetables, minerals, and in men; nothing new occurs in identical existence; Accident ever varies, Substance can never suffer change nor decay.*

"The Canterbury Pilgrims," engraving by William Blake, 1810; in the British Museum

This is a rather grand way of saying that Chaucer's pilgrims are presented to us both as typical and as individual—a necessary ingredient in any narrative that hopes to be memorable. The secret of fiction, if there is only one, consists in the author's firm understanding that any person is at least three things simultaneously: a member of the human race, a member of a group within the race—a class, a type, a profession, a sex, a youth, an elder, a nondescript—and simply himself. How well Chaucer understood this was noted by Dryden in the preface to his *Fables*:

> *He must have been a man of a most wonderful comprehensive nature, because, as it has been truly observed of him, he has taken into the compass of his* Canterbury Tales *the various manners and humours (as we now call them) of the whole English nation in his age. Not a single character has escaped him. All his pilgrims are severally distinguished from each other; and not only in their inclinations, but in their very physiognomies and persons. . . . The matter and manner of their tales, and of their telling, are so suited to their different educations, humours, and callings, that each of them would be improper in any other mouth. Even the grave and serious characters are distinguished by their several sorts of gravity: their discourses are such as belong to their age, their calling, and their breeding; such as are becoming of them, and of them only. Some of his persons are vicious, and some virtuous; some are unlearn'd, or (as Chaucer calls them) lewd, and some are learn'd. Even the ribaldry of the low characters is different: the Reeve, the Miller, and the Cook, are several men, and distinguished from each other as much as the mincing Lady-Prioress and the broad-speaking gaptoothed Wife of Bath. But enough of this; there is such a variety of game springing up before me that I am distracted in my choice, and know not which to follow. 'Tis sufficient to say, according to the proverb, that* here is God's plenty. *We have our forefathers and great-granddames all before us, as they were in Chaucer's days: their general characters are still remaining in mankind, and even in England, though they are called by other names than those of Monks and Friars, and Canons, and Lady Abbesses, and Nuns; for mankind is ever the same, and nothing lost out of Nature, though everything is altered.*

Better things than that have never been said about Chaucer; with those words he was welcomed into the circle of the great. Even Matthew Arnold, who in 1880 denied that Chaucer *was* one of "the great classics," was forced by Dryden's eloquence to agree with him as far as he went. "Chaucer's power of fascination," said Arnold,

> *is enduring; his poetical importance does not need the assistance of the historic estimate; it is real. He is a genuine source of joy and*

*strength, which is flowing still for us and will flow always. He will be read, as time goes on, far more generally than he is read now. His language is a cause of difficulty for us; but so also, and I think in quite as great a degree, is the language of Burns. In Chaucer's case, as in that of Burns, it is a difficulty to be unhesitatingly accepted and overcome.*

*If we ask ourselves wherein consists the immense superiority of Chaucer's poetry over the romance-poetry—why it is that in passing from this to Chaucer we suddenly feel ourselves to be in another world, we shall find that his superiority is both in the substance of his poetry and in the style of his poetry. His superiority in substance is given by his large, free, simple, clear yet kindly view of human life—so unlike the total want, in the romance-poets, of all intelligent command of it. Chaucer has not their helplessness; he has gained the power to survey the world from a central, a truly human point of view. We have only to call to mind the Prologue to* The Canterbury Tales. *The right comment upon it is Dryden's. . . . It is by a large, free, sound representation of things that poetry, this high criticism of life, has truth of substance; and Chaucer's poetry has truth of substance.**

*The Prologue* is more than a series of portraits; there is so much life in the manner of its painting that it may be taken as the first unit of a narrative: the first chapter of a novel or the first scene of a play, it scarcely matters which. The opening lines can remind us now of the miracle that spring once was anywhere in the temperate zone; it is still a miracle, but it has become a muted one, what with our heated houses, our plowed and salted highways, our conveyances which themselves are heated so that many of us seldom have the sense of really being out of doors. In Chaucer's time, as for that matter in Shakespeare's and in Dryden's, and on for nearly two centuries after that, winter was an ordeal from which mankind emerged in April and May with song and thanksgiving for gentle winds and the voices of returning birds; life was literally beginning again. So Chaucer's pilgrims gaily begin their trip, and the host manages, at least at first, to maintain pleasant relations among them all. Harry Bailey, who as it happens tells no tale, is far from being the least important of the pilgrims. He has a lively sense of who his people are and of how they ought to be addressed. The entire work would be weaker without him.

So would it be without the clergy who are so numerous among the troupe. It takes a certain effort of the imagination to recall that England was once a Catholic country, with priests and monks, with friars and canons, with abbeys and cathedrals everywhere at hand. It has been Protestant so long that one can be startled by realizing that it was Catholic for even

---

\* *The Study of Poetry; GGB,* Vol. 5, pp. 29–30.

longer. So too with the professions and the trades, and the relations between husbands and wives. Everything was different, as Dryden says, yet
everything was the same. All of which means that Chaucer had the richest
of opportunities before him: the opportunity of dealing with both eternity
and time, with both the representative and the unique in human behavior. Not that he needs to be understood as ever saying such a thing to
himself; he was more modest than that. But he did, we can be sure, feel
somewhat free at last to talk his own language and think his own thought,
to feel as Geoffrey Chaucer felt, and say so in the liveliest language he
could command.

The whole of *The Canterbury Tales* is a story that could be summarized without retelling the tales themselves; the links between the tales,
the conversations, the quarrels, the compliments, the oaths, the asides are
actually so interesting that some commentators have advocated the radical
procedure of ignoring the tales and concentrating on their framework.
But it is simply not true, as Chesterton asserts, that the tales are inferior
in interest to their tellers. The tales are still the thing, as the following
pages hope to show.

## The Knight's Tale

The evening before the pilgrims set forth, their host, the big man with the
merry voice and the protuberant eyes, got their assent to a plan he had
for their comfort and amusement on the way. He proposed that each of
them tell two tales going and two returning, and they voted their agreement. Now in the morning, at the first watering place where they stop to
refresh the throats of their horses, he suggests that they draw cuts to see
which of them shall tell the first tale.

> *And, to make short the matter, as it was,*
> *Whether by chance or whatsoever cause,*
> *The truth is, that the cut fell to the knight.*

Chaucer is doubtless hinting here that the host made sure the Knight
would be first. For knights were still first in everything, despite the decay
of chivalry which many men deplored, and the host might have been uncomfortable with any different result. At any rate the Knight, being the
perfect gentleman described in *The Prologue,* the worthy man who loves
truth and honor, freedom and courtesy, beyond all other things, is willing
to keep his promise of the night before, and so with the briefest of pre-
ambles begins the tale of Palamon and Arcita.

It is a proper tale for him to tell, since the very stuff of it is love and
honor, and the style of it has the dignity and splendor that we soon learn
to associate with Chaucer's own knight, a most excellent man who also

possesses a sense of humor. The story given him to tell had probably been written by Chaucer several years before under the title "Palamon and Arcite," though if this is true nothing is known of any changes made in it now. It had been taken from Boccaccio's epic poem *Il Teseida,* which Chaucer translated so freely that only a few hundred of its lines are traceable to the original; the rest is adaptation, or else it is Chaucer's own. He also made use of the Roman poets Statius and Ovid, of the philosopher Boethius, and of the *Roman de la Rose,* which for

every fourteenth-century poet was a gold mine of materials. Dryden modernized Chaucer's reworking of these sources in his *Fables,* where it occupies first place.

The story of Palamon and Arcita as Chaucer's knight tells it is grave and painful, with an unhappy ending for one of its heroes which only philosophy can render endurable—the philosophy, that is to say, of Boethius, a sixth-century Roman scholar and Christian martyr who wrote his *Consolation of Philosophy* in prison while awaiting execution at the order of the emperor Theodoric. It is a stoic philosophy, counseling men to accept whatever fate offers them no matter how unjust it may seem. Boethius was widely read in the Middle Ages, and Chaucer turned to his doctrine in many of his own works. In *The Knight's Tale* its chief exponent is Thesëus, duke of Athens, who is called upon to preside over the destinies of two Theban knights, cousins by birth, whom he has taken captive and now at the beginning of the tale holds in prison without ransom till they die. Year after year they suffer confinement in a tower that overlooks the garden where Emily, sister of Hippolyta the wife of Thesëus, sometimes walks; and one day Palamon, seeing her there, falls in love with her beauty; but so does Arcita, even more deeply if that is possible, and hence a rivalry springs up between the noble cousins, a rivalry that will have the most tragic consequences.

Both knights are made free of the tower, Arcita by exile and Palamon by escape, but both are unhappier away from the vision of Emily than they were before. By chance they encounter each other in a grove and renew their rivalry to the point of deciding upon a duel, for which they duly arm themselves and come at last to blows, fighting, says Chaucer, up to their ankles in blood. It chances that Thesëus, walking nearby with Hippolyta and Emily, arrives upon the scene and commands them to meet in more formal fashion on a day he will appoint. The day of the tournament dawns; each cousin with the hundred knights he has been supplied with as seconds prays to his chosen deity—Palamon to Venus and Arcita to Mars—and the contest begins.

It is won by Arcita, whom Thesëus judges to be the victor; but Arcita, riding in triumph and looking up at Emily, soon he thinks to be his bride because he has won her in fair fight, is thrown from his horse when the horse shies, and is injured so terribly that he has no chance of living. His death, and the ceremonial burning of his body, Chaucer treats with a fine eloquence such as he can always summon when he cares to, just as he gives Palamon and Arcita, when they are praying to their deities, the full benefit of a rhetoric he has studied to make magnificent if the occasion demands magnificence. The sage and serious Thesëus, through whom we hear the voice of Boethius speaking as if no centuries intervened, may remind us of the Theseus who was duke of Athens in Shakespeare's *A Midsummer-Night's Dream,** and who in that play also had Hippolyta to wife.

All the while, however, what has been called the elvish disposition of Chaucer is delightfully in evidence—rarely, to be sure, yet unmistakably. Chaucer could never contemplate extravagance of thought or feeling without wincing and grinning a little. So here, where much of the action borders upon the preposterous, and where what Arnold called romance-poetry might be at home, Chaucer refuses to suppress his own intelligence, and lets us know this, as it were, between the lines. His two heroes are breathless in adoration of Emily, but Chaucer can say:

> . *Her yellow hair was braided in one tress*
> *Behind her back, a full yard long, I guess.*

And he can wake her on the morning of the tournament that will decide her future with a line that has become famous wherever Chaucer is known:

> *Up rose the sun and up rose Emily.*

If that is not irreverent, two lines about the death of Arcita surely are:

> *His spirit changed hous, and wente ther,*
> *As I cam never, I can nat tellen wher.†*

Yet not so surely either, for the sequel is a description of Arcita's burial pyre that is authentically Homeric in its full-throated grandeur. And the mingling of sorrow and joy in the wedding of Palamon and Emily is ordered by a poet who wholly understands such things.

---

* *GBWW,* Vol. 26, pp. 352–75.
† Cf. *GBWW,* Vol. 22, p. 206.

## The Miller's Tale

It used to be considered a grotesque accident, an editorial blunder, that *The Knight's Tale,* so stately and superb, is followed in the manuscripts by a tale so different from it, so grossly and shockingly different, as to jolt the reader into an amazed attention. The Miller, who in *The Prologue* has been called "a stout churl," chunky and broad, with a red beard as wide as a spade, with a wart on his nose from which rose a tuft of hairs as red as the bristles of a sow's ears, with huge black

nostrils and a mouth like a furnace door, with a habit of ribald speech, and with a bagpipe in his possession which he has blown to bring the party out of town—this fellow, hearing the host ask the Monk for a tale to follow that of the Knight, puts in drunkenly, for he is pale with liquor and sits unsteadily on his horse, that he wants to be next; he has a good lively tale, he says, of a carpenter who had a wife, and a clerk made a fool of him; at which the Reeve, himself a carpenter, calls out that the Miller must shut up, for wives should not be traduced; but the Miller, unstoppable, proceeds to tell his tale of two young men in the town of Oxford who become rivals for the pretty young wife of a wealthy old carpenter.

In other words, here is the situation in *The Knight's Tale* all over again on another level, and doubtless a lower one, though as the tale continues we forget about levels and thoroughly enjoy a brilliant and beautiful *fabliau*—meaning, a dirty story and a funny one, such as medieval courts loved to laugh at between romances of courtly love, themselves also concerned with adultery, but high-toned adultery, and the language was elevated. Not so in the *fabliaux,* of which *The Miller's Tale* is one of the best-known examples. It is rank with reality, and candid in every word, and funny in the heartless way of stories that have no other end than laughter in view. Perhaps we should feel pity for the witless old carpenter here who is made a cuckold without even knowing he is, but pity is alien to farce, and this is farce at its finest.

The two rivals for the favors of his wife are Nicholas, a poor but clever clerk, or scholar as he is sometimes called, and Absalom, a parish clerk who is something of a dandy, though for all the beauty of his curly golden hair and his somewhat mincing ways he has no chance against Nicholas because Nicholas lives in the carpenter's house, and because he has already handled Alison, the young wife, in such a bold, surprising way that when the time comes she will be all his for the asking. She has a body as slim and small as a weasel's, wears bright clothes, and is lickerish of eye.

195

She sings like a swallow, dances like a kid, and is as skittish as a colt. In other words she is irresistible, and neither young man can wait for the moment he has imagined. The moment will give him less pleasure than he plans, but that is a part of the joke on everybody that this hilarious story was framed to tell. Only Alison escapes without humiliation or pain. The three men bring their troubles on themselves, in a double plot which deserves all the praise it has been given for the ingenuity of its contrivance.

For there are two *fabliaux* here, joined so neatly that one word— "Water!"—can signal the climax for both. At the same instant that the carpenter, aloft in his tub which he has tied to the ceiling in anticipation of a latter-day Noah's flood, hears Nicholas crying for relief of his backside, which Absalom has burned in revenge for Alison's insulting kiss, he cuts the rope that holds him there and falls and breaks his arm; nor can he get any sympathy from those who listen to his explanation of what he has been doing, for he sounds as crazy as Nicholas says he is—Nicholas, who has persuaded him to take refuge in the tub so that Alison might be enjoyed without interruption; but Absalom does interrupt them twice.

Any summary of the action tends to be longer than the tale itself. Chaucer, who sometimes loved to be long, here chose to be short, and the result is one of his masterpieces. Indeed, it is one of *the* masterpieces, for very few tales have ever been told with such spirit or with such aptness and beauty of detail. Furthermore, the Miller's telling of it gives *him* a satisfaction that he must have thirsted for as he listened to all the fancy business of Palamon and Arcita and Emily—all that talk of love without anybody doing anything about it, all that yearning and mooning and philosophizing to what end? So the Miller must have wondered, boozily, while the Knight held everyone else's attention but after a while lost his. This would have been why he was so insistent upon being second: he would show life as it really is, he would make them all sit up and listen. No courtly love now; back to the barnyard be it.

## The Reeve's Tale

Probably the Miller does not know that the Reeve has at one time learned the carpenter's trade—he is now steward of an estate in Norfolk, hence his title—and therefore might be offended by a tale told at the expense of another carpenter, and an old one too. Not that the Reeve is ancient, but *The Prologue* has described him as lean and long-legged and saturnine of countenance, which perhaps is the reason that he always rides hindmost of the troupe and has little to say at any time. Now he refuses to laugh with the rest of the company at the tale the Miller has told, and even breaks into speech about millers in general as men given to ribaldry and abusive talk. It is therefore natural that the host should ask him for a

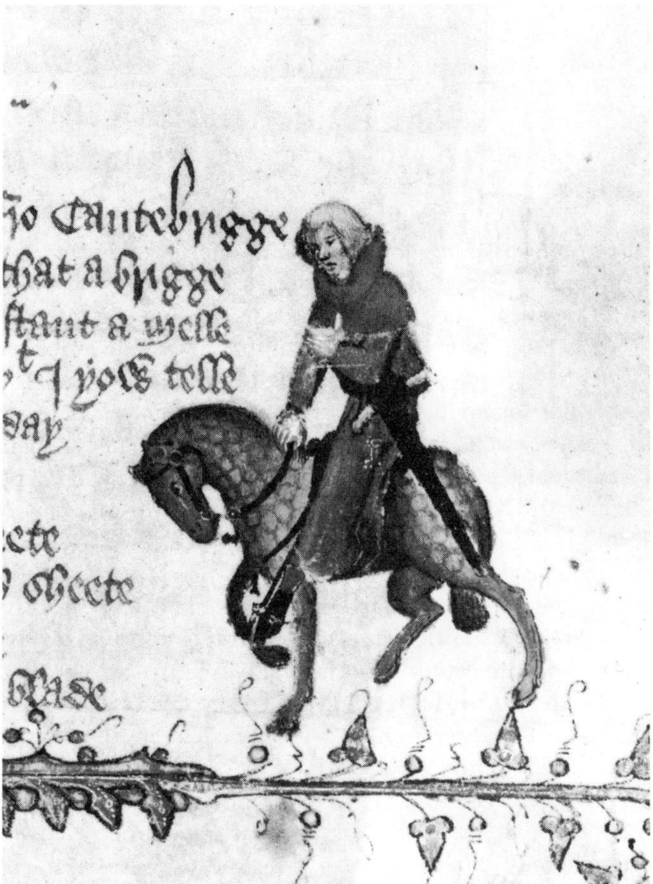

tale, suspecting him of knowing one about a miller; and sure enough he does, and instantly complies, remarking before he begins:

> *This drunken miller has related here*
> *How was beguiled and fooled a carpenter—*
> *Perchance in scorn of me, for I am one.*
> *So, by your leave, I'll him requite anon;*
> *All in his own boor's language will I speak.*
> *I only pray to God his neck may break.*

His neck, that is to say, rather than merely his arm. The morale of the expedition would seem already to have suffered damage. More damage is to come, but more good feeling too; the unity of the group will never be destroyed.

*The Reeve's Tale* is another *fabliau,* and a bitterer one as befits the character of the teller; he admits to being an old man who has put love behind him yet recollects the language of it, so that now he can relate how a miller was once repaid for his dishonesty to two students of Cambridge by their making free with his wife and daughter in his own bedroom. It is not known in what form Chaucer read either this *fabliau* or that of the Miller; such stories circulated widely, and everybody knew them; they survive today in many places, often to the private delight of scholars. At any rate Chaucer did know these two, along with two others still to be considered; and it is clear that he enjoyed them, just as it is clear that he knew how to make us do so.

*The Reeve's Tale* is not merry like the Miller's, but it gets to its point with a like celerity. This miller of Trumpington is not only a snob but a thief, and there is a connection between the two faults: he cheats customers of their grain so that he can become richer and rise high enough in the world to marry his daughter well; the fact that her mother, the miller's wife, is herself the daughter of the village parson, and therefore illegitimate, seems not to trouble him. The two students he has robbed of some of their corn have little more than revenge in mind when they climb in bed with the wife and daughter, just as the Reeve when he tells his tale may have uppermost in his mind the desire to get even with the Miller. Yet there is one touch near the end that renders the whole more human than farce by definition is permitted to be. It is the dialogue between the daughter and Alain the student when he prepares to leave her:

> *Alain grew weary in the grey dawning,*
> *For he had laboured hard through all the night;*
> *And said: "Farewell, now, Maudy, sweet delight!*
> *The day is come, I may no longer bide;*
> *But evermore, whether I walk or ride,*
> *I am your own clerk, so may I have weal."*
> *"Now, sweetheart," said she, "go and fare you well!*

*But ere you go, there's one thing I must tell.*
*When you go walking homeward past the mill,*
*Right at the entrance, just the door behind,*
*You shall a loaf of half a bushel find*
*That was baked up of your own flour, a deal*
*Of which I helped my father for to steal.*
*And, darling, may God save you now and keep!"*
*And with that word she almost had to weep.*

That is poetry, and that is Chaucer almost at his best. The daughter is presumably less marriageable now, but she has so lost her heart to Alain that her father and his affairs have ceased to be of consequence to her. Her father may think she has lost everything, but she has the memory of this night.

## The Cook's Tale

A third *fabliau* follows, but in so unfinished a state that Chaucer can be supposed to have decided that two were enough, at least just here; though there are other possible reasons why *The Cook's Tale* is merely a fragment. It is a lively beginning, and we shall always wonder about the middle and the end. The irresponsible apprentice, Perkin, gives promise of being a rogue whose fortunes we might be more than willing to follow, though the pilgrim who presents him to us is far from attractive; nobody forgets the running sore on his shin.

## The Tale of the Man of Law

In the prologue to his tale the Man of Law complains that a poet named Chaucer has got ahead of him and written most of the stories he might have told, so that he is reduced to telling one in prose—though he then proceeds in verse, and elaborate verse at that, since he uses a seven-line stanza. Our Chaucer, who of course has written the rather condescending words spoken of himself by the Man of Law, is dismissed as a vulgar versifier although a crafty rhymester; he enjoyed such sly pleasantries at his own expense, but in this case he may have had some practical or professional reason for listing numerous works of his own, including the *Legend of Good Women*. The Man of Law gives him credit for only one thing: he never has told stories of incestuous loves, as for example between father and daughter. This has a bearing on the Man of Law's own avoidance of that theme as he writes the life of Constance. Not that Constance has ever been involved in such a relationship, but heroines like her, and there were many of them in the literature of the Middle Ages, sometimes were so cursed. The type as such was an innocent, long-suffering woman falsely accused of hideous deeds and persecuted by her stepmother, her mother-in-law, her father, or someone else close to her, until after long and painful trials she rejoined her family and witnessed the punishment of her enemies. Chaucer took his plot from Nicholas Trivet's prose *Chronicle,* a French work of the early fourteenth century, and perhaps also from the *Confessio Amantis,* a long poem by his contemporary, John Gower.

The story can be recounted briefly. Constance, daughter of the emperor of Rome, goes to marry the sultan of Syria, but at her wedding feast sees all of the guests massacred by order of the sultan's mother because the sultan has become a Christian. As the only survivor she is placed in a ship and sent to sea, where she wanders for years before landing in England on the shores of Northumberland; she eventually marries King Alla—after being cleared of the charge of murdering Dame Hermengild, her savior and dearest friend—and has a male child by him; but the king's mother, who hates her because she is a Christian, intercepts letters between her and Alla and substitutes forgeries that order her banishment by boat; once more she is put to sea, this time with her young son, and it is five years before she reaches Rome again and through a series of miraculous meetings is reunited not only with Alla but with her father, the emperor.

None of this sounds probable, but Chaucer never raises the question, and so the vessel of his verse moves musically on and takes us willingly with it. The terse, tart language of the *fabliaux* is not heard here; his chronicle of Constance returns us to the style that we shall encounter many a time hereafter, especially in *The Clerk's Tale,* where it is even more magical than it is in these stanzas that all but hypnotize us as we read. Yet it does not tire, nor at his best is Chaucer ever tiresome, no matter how long his subject, no matter how strange to us it is. His mind is eternally fresh; he himself seems never to tire; eagerly, confidently, he continues to explore his theme, which it never occurs to him that we shall be less delighted by than he is. There is no more precious gift than this. Shakespeare has it, Cervantes has it, Homer has it, but few others.

Constance herself might be thought to be tiresome after, say, Alison of *The Miller's Tale,* she is so perfect in resignation, so uncomplaining under persecution that continues for years. Yet she is anything but dull, she is never inane; and this is partly because she does not contemplate her own virtue, which indeed she does not seem to know she has, but also because the poet who gives her to us loves her as comic geniuses always love their characters, without sentiment or self-deception. There is no surface comedy in *The Man of Law's Tale,* only an intelligence that never abdicates, a sense of proportion that leaves the outline clear and keen, that keeps the essence of Constance—her patience—steadily before us.

How are we to believe that she could drift on the sea in an open boat for three years, and then again for five? Once more it is pertinent to say that Chaucer does not prompt us to ask the question. To ask it would be to doubt her perfection, and that has already been established. Her perfection is itself a work of art, a sculpture, a strain of music that carries on and on like a single note played forever on some unearthly violin. It is powerful, it is moving, as the fidelity of Shakespeare's later heroines is— Imogen, Hermione, Marina, Miranda—because it is conceived with purity and executed with passion. The final reward for the reader is the eloquence with which Constance after long silence can cry out, as here when she sets sail with her child in the belief that Alla's letter of banishment is genuine. She is addressing the Virgin—"O thou bright Maid, Mary"—in full recognition that there is no comparison between Mary's woe and her own, and yet she calls as one distressed mother to another:

> *"Thou sawest them slay Thy Son before Thine eyes;*
> *And yet lives now my little child, I say!*
> *O Lady bright, to Whom affliction cries,*
> *Thou glory of womanhood, O Thou fair May,*
> *Haven of refuge, bright star of the day,*
> *Pity my child, Who of Thy gentleness*
> *Hast pity on mankind in all distress!*
>
> *"O little child, alas! What is your guilt,*
> *Who never wrought the smallest sin? Ah me,*
> *Why will your too hard father have you killed?*
> *Have mercy, O dear constable!" cried she,*
> *"And let my little child bide, safe from sea;*
> *And if you dare not save him, lest they blame,*
> *Then kiss him once in his dear father's name!"*

## The Tale of the Wife of Bath

Then, however, comes a different kind of woman altogether: in the flesh, as we have seen her in the general *Prologue* to all the tales; in direct address, as we hear her now in her own prologue; and finally in her tale, which is briefer than her prologue because her prologue is about herself, and nothing interests her more than the person, the absolutely astonishing person, she knows very well she is.

The general *Prologue* is known for few things better than for its portrait of her—a housewife from near Bath, somewhat hard of hearing, with teeth set wide apart (a sign of amorousness, she thinks), with a bold, red face and doubtless a vigorous voice; wearing scarlet hose and sharp spurs, around her ample hips an extra skirt, and on her head, which is well swathed with a wimple, a hat "as broad as is a buckler or a targe" (a shield). On Sundays she wears a towering headdress that weighs all of ten pounds, and she will never let any other woman get ahead of her with an offering at church: a sign, some have said, of sinful pride. She has known

many men, both as a girl and later as a wife, for she has been married five times. She has also made numerous pilgrimages: to Italy, to France, to Spain, to Germany, and three times to Jerusalem. She is a great cloth-maker; she laughs a lot as she talks; and she knows everything there is to know about love.

We learn this much from Chaucer in 32 lines, and from the 828 lines of her own prologue we naturally learn volumes more, almost forgetting that Chaucer wrote this too, so close it brings us to the speaker. The Wife of Bath is one of those creations that really are creations, for we cannot see how they are put together, nor can we imagine them as ever having been made merely with words. Here at any rate she is, sitting easily on her nag, dominating the company while she tells them things they wouldn't have supposed anyone could say. She is as far from Constance as any woman could be: she is rank, she is gross, she is willing to call things by their commonest names, she is frank, she is cynical, she is wonderful to see and hear. Her first three husbands were old and rich, and she does not hesitate to say that she wore them out in bed. As for that activity, she refuses to believe that God frowns upon it; otherwise, why did He supply us with organs of generation? It has been the very center of her life, the thing she lived for and the thing she now treasures in her memory.

> *But Lord Christ! When I do remember me*
> *Upon my youth and on my jollity,*
> *It tickles me about my heart's deep root.*
> *To this day does my heart sing in salute*
> *That I have had my world in my own time.*

Her fourth husband, a reveller, was unfaithful to his vows; he kept a paramour. The Wife got even for this by studying all sorts of ways to make him jealous; she took no lover, but she made him think she did, and that was all she wanted; she got him to frying in his own grease.

Well, he died, and then there was Jenkin, once a student at Oxford and still no more than half her age: twenty years against her forty. She married him for love, not money, and was foolish enough to make over all her land to him. They were insatiable lovers, but he developed the unfortunate habit of reading aloud to her books that denounced and defamed all women, from Eve on down. He kept this up until one day she grabbed the book from which he was reading and tore three pages out of it. He retaliated by striking her on the head and knocking her down—the cause of her deafness, she believes—but then he knelt to ask her forgiveness, and in due course she had the upper hand of him; sovereignty, not to speak of house and land, was henceforth hers, not his. The solution was therefore perfect:

> *After that day we never had debate.*

The only trouble was, Jenkin died too, and now the Wife does not deny that she would be willing to wed a sixth husband if one appeared.

The tale she tells, after a passage of words between the Summoner and the Friar—each has at least one story in mind that will discredit the other's profession, but the host will have none of that now, he is all impatience to hear the Wife's tale—contains a theme consistent with the burden of her prologue. It is the theme of sovereignty in love and marriage, and she has no doubt as to which of the sexes deserves to possess that prize. Her tale has its origin in a body of story, amounting almost to a literature in itself, about a "loathly lady" who turns out to be beautiful after all. Chaucer sets it in King Arthur's time, and assigns to one of King Arthur's knights the traditional role of the man who discovers what it is that women most desire.

The knight in question has ravished a maid and is condemned to death for the crime, but at the last moment, at the request of the queen, is given a year of grace in which to find out what it is that women want more than any other thing. He sets out hopefully, but has no luck until he meets with a hideous old hag who promises him, if he will do whatever she asks of him, to supply him with an answer that will save his life. She whispers it in his ear; they go to court together; he repeats the answer:

> *"Women desire to have the sovereignty*
> *As well upon their husband as their love,*
> *And to have mastery their man above."*

No listener denying this, the knight is saved, only to be told now what it is that the hag has in mind for him to do. It is to marry her. Disgusted, he refuses; then, reminded of his vow, he consents, but once in bed with her cannot bear to kiss her as she desires; won by arguments to the effect that beauty is more than skin deep, he finally gives in to her, only to realize that he holds in his arms a damsel supremely fair; and they live happily ever after. The moral is clearly to the Wife of Bath's liking, and no more is said upon the subject.

Dryden's modernization of this tale in his *Fables* begins with a spirit and a grace that he maintains throughout. Perhaps this is the place to show what Chaucer could become in his skillful hands, in his melodious voice. Few translations have ever been more successful than these opening lines of the Wife's tale, amplified to be sure, but nevertheless bewitching in their way:

In days of old, when Arthur fill'd the throne,
Whose acts and fame to foreign lands were blown,
The king of elfs and little fairy queen
Gambol'd on heaths, and danc'd on ev'ry green;
And where the jolly troop had led the round,
The grass unbidden rose, and mark'd the ground:
Nor darkling did they dance; the silver light
Of Phoebe serv'd to guide their steps aright,
And, with their tripping pleas'd, prolong'd the night.
Her beams they follow'd, where at full she play'd,
Nor longer than she shed her horns they stay'd,
From thence with airy flight to foreign lands convey'd.
Above the rest our Britain held they dear;
More solemnly they kept their sabbaths here,
And made more spacious rings, and revel'd half the year.
   I speak of ancient times, for now the swain
Returning late may pass the woods in vain,
And never hope to see the nightly train;
In vain the dairy now with mints is dress'd,
The dairymaid expects no fairy guest,
To skim the bowls, and after pay the feast.
She sighs, and shakes her empty shoes in vain,
No silver penny to reward her pain:
For priests with pray'rs, and other godly gear,
Have made the merry goblins disappear;
And where they play'd their merry pranks before,
Have sprinkled holy water on the floor;
And friars that thro' the wealthy regions run,
Thick as the motes that twinkle in the sun,
Resort to farmers rich, and bless their halls,
And exorcise the beds, and cross the walls:
This makes the fairy choirs forsake the place,
When once 'tis hallow'd with the rites of grace.
But in the walks where wicked elves have been,
The learning of the parish now is seen,
The midnight parson, posting o'er the green,
With gown tuck'd up, to wakes, for Sunday next
With humming ale encouraging his text;
Nor wants the holy leer to country girl betwixt.
From fiends and imps he sets the village free,
There haunts not any incubus but he.
The maids and women need no danger fear
To walk by night, and sanctity so near:
For by some haycock, or some shady thorn,
He bids his beads both evensong and morn.

## The Friar's Tale and the Summoner's Tale

The Friar and the Summoner, both of whom have been sharply drawn in the general *Prologue* as rogues—and even that is a mild term for them, for Chaucer has spared no effort to make them thoroughly loathsome, the Friar as a cynical travesty upon the original image of the friar, the Summoner as a sneak, an informer, and a pimp, with a hideous complexion in the bargain—now tell their tales, each at the expense of the other, the Friar making it clear that the summoner of his tale is indistinguishable from the devil, and the Summoner bringing the friar of his tale to an ignominious and humiliating defeat. Both tales are unsavory, so that our escape from them into the world of *The Clerk's Tale* is a profound and blessed relief.

## The Clerk's Tale

The Clerk of Oxford, who in the general *Prologue* has been said to be as lean as his horse, a sober and scholarly young man not yet provided with a benefice (a living within the Church), more content with his twenty books bound in black and red than he would be with rich robes and gaiety, supposing those things to be available, hopeful only for an opportunity to keep on learning and to teach his Aristotle—this model person, notable for the few words he speaks, and those  always sensible, is suddenly asked by the host for a "merry" tale. With great courtesy he declines, explaining that he prefers to entertain the audience, if it will be kind enough to listen, with a tale he learned in Padua, from a learned clerk named Francis Petrarch. He would have added, had he known it, that Petrarch had learned it from Boccaccio, for it is in his *Decameron*. Chaucer's text follows the Latin of Petrarch and the French of an anonymous prose translation of Petrarch—follows them faithfully, except for alterations and additions which make *The Clerk's Tale* one of the most beautiful poems in the world, and one of the most moving. Even the prose of Petrarch is moving—so much so that once a friend to whom its author showed it broke down in tears and had to have the rest of it read aloud to him.

There is a strange power in the story, no matter how it is told, that suggests a folklore, fairy-tale origin, and presumes in Walter the husband and Griselda the wife a supernatural dimension. Both of them are so difficult to believe that they *must* be true, according to the logic that rules the world of popular story; both are monsters perhaps, yet how wonderful it would be if all people existed with their intensity, and acted with their undivided purpose, their unrelenting purity of conviction.

The Wife of Bath, listening as the Clerk recites the tale, undoubtedly says to herself that he is somehow commenting upon the thesis she had developed both in her prologue and in her tale—the thesis that women should be sovereign—and there can scarcely be a question that the Clerk does so intend, and Chaucer for him; if there is a Marriage Group within *The Canterbury Tales,* as much of the criticism maintains, then here we are at the heart of it: the Clerk is presenting a sovereign husband for the Wife to consider, and if the Wife is thinking that she had never contemplated *this* much sovereignty in even the most powerful imaginable woman, then that is the kind of drama that Chaucer may have hoped to develop in the interstices of his work, in the spaces between his tales.

And the tale is told in stanzas like those of *The Man of Law's Tale* and of *Troilus and Criseyde*—that is to say, in stanzas that weep with a sense of their own beauty, that break their own hearts even before they break yours. Again it is true that Chaucer writes without evident humor, though the comic genius he cannot help being proves its presence by the startling reality of these preposterous events: the marriage of Walter, marquis of Saluzzo, to the penniless girl, Griselda, and the series of tests he subsequently makes of her patience and obedience—the taking of her children from her, the having her suppose that they are killed, the announcement after twelve years that she is to be put away in favor of another wife, her submission to this even to the point of returning to the palace as a servant in rags who will wait on her successor, the arrival of the new child-wife with her brother, and the disclosure to Griselda that they are her own children, who all the while have been safe in Bologna.

Many readers have found the sadness unbearable, or else the madness of Walter, if it is madness, unforgivable. Why should a man need so much proof of something that needs no proof? For the sweetness of Griselda is there all the time for us to feel as if we ourselves were the beneficiaries of it; it is created in the very music of the stanzas that describe her, and that tell how she was taken from the house of her old father, Janicula, directly to the palace and established in a luxury that she would never have demanded had she been given ten thousand wishes.

Strangely enough, the sympathy of Chaucer for his heroine—the pity so eloquent, in spite of its never being directly expressed, that it pierces our sides with a like pity—is communicated to us through an intensification of Walter's cruelty, and of the pressures that consequently bear down upon Griselda, rather than upon any effort to relieve the picture of her suffering. It is almost as if Chaucer himself wanted to hurt her more. Whereas he is preparing for the recognition and reconciliation scene that is comparable with any similar scene in Shakespeare's last plays, which is all that needs to be said in praise of it.

> *O young, O dear, O tender children mine*

That one line, spoken by Griselda before she swoons with joy, in the only outburst she permits herself throughout her lengthy trial, is ample evidence of the strength and the sweetness that had grown in Chaucer himself through every moment of his career.

## The Merchant's Tale

But so had the strength and the bitterness, testimony to which we turn a single page and find in the savage tale of January and May, the old man and the young wife he never should have married, any more than the old carpenter in *The Miller's Tale* should have married Alison. The depth of Chaucer shows finally in his variety, and impresses us nowhere so much as in the juxtaposition of tales as different from each other as these two. Both have roots in the past of human story, countless analogues to them having been discovered by scholars in the literature of many countries. In the case of *The Merchant's Tale* the root runs back and down to tales of adultery in a fruit tree, usually on the part of a young wife and her young lover, though the special emphasis here on the unloveliness of the old husband is not a necessary ingredient of the fiction. Chaucer's interest was chiefly, it would seem, in January, the meagerness of whose spirit matches the ugliness of his beard and body. He deserves whatever punishment May inflicts upon him for his total inadequacy as a mate. His cynicism precedes hers, and presumably causes it.

And the reader can wonder just what prompted the Merchant, as soon as the Clerk finished his tale, to speak up about his own wife of no more than two months, who is so little like Griselda that it isn't funny. Is she anything like May? Probably not, for she is a shrew, and cruel, yet something drives the Merchant with his forked beard and his Flemish beaver hat to tell this tale which nothing except its cleverness redeems.

## The Squire's Tale

And no sooner is that done than the host, who has nothing good to say about his own wife, calls upon the Squire to tell a tale of love, possibly in the hope that the handsome young bachelor, son of that fine gentleman the Knight, will turn the tide of melancholy and bitterness that has flooded in without anyone's particularly desiring it. The Squire, an active youth of twenty or so, a warrior who also likes to play the flute and dance, and who is as fresh as the month of May even though love keeps him awake

all night, who wears dashing clothes and sits well on his horse, obliges with a tale that does indeed brighten the sky: a romantic tale with magic in it. It has never actually suffered by being incomplete, for it breaks off without warning at the beginning of the third part; if anything it benefits by this, sparkling all the more brilliantly as it resembles a diamond that accident has divided. Spenser was moved to continue the tale in his *Faerie Queene,* and Milton, musing in "Il Penseroso" upon the power of old stories to beautify imagination's world, immortalized it in seven lines:

> *Or call up him that left half told*
> *The story of Cambuscan bold,*
> *Of Camball, and of Algarsife,*
> *And who had Canace to wife,*
> *That owned the virtuous ring and glass,*
> *And of the wondrous horse of brass*
> *On which the Tartar king did ride.**

The tale itself is so charming that we can wonder why Chaucer was content to abandon it—unless, to be sure, death cut it off with much else that is missing from the entire work, or unless the poet tired of it, or unless he preferred the truncated form we have. The scene is the court of Cambinskan, a Tartar king whose name may be a corruption of Genghis Khan. It is related that Cambinskan (or Cambuscan, as Milton spelled it) had three children by his queen, Elpheta: two sons, Algarsyf and Cambalo, and a daughter, Canace. Into his palace one day, while a feast was going on, there rode a strange knight astride a steed of brass, holding in his hand a mirror of glass, wearing on his thumb a golden ring, and dangling at his side a naked sword. He explained to Cambinskan that the king of Araby and Ind had sent these gifts by him, and he recited their several virtues: the steed of brass could bear the Tartar king anywhere in the universe he desired to go and could then, at the twisting of a pin, bring him back and set him down unharmed; the mirror could reflect any adversity or treachery that was about to be, and thus forewarn the person who gazed into it; the ring, worn on Canace's thumb, for it was sent specifically to her, could make her understand the language of any bird beneath the heaven; the sword, capable of cutting through the thickest armor, could both kill and cure, for if laid flat against a wound it would heal the wound.

This is familiar stuff of romance—we at once remember the Green Knight who invaded King Arthur's court and astonished all the warriors and ladies there; and indeed every detail of the story is more or less commonplace in tales of the mysterious East. So also with the remarkable things that Canace, wearing the magic ring, hears a peregrine falcon saying in a dead tree far overhead, weeping as she speaks and tearing at her

---

* Cf. *GBWW*, Vol. 32, p. 23.

flesh with her own beak until there is danger of her falling from her perch and dying. What she discloses is that her falcon lover has left her for a kite flying elsewhere in the sky; so now she is "love-lorn without remedy," and does not know what to do except hurt herself as she continues doing. Shortly after this the fragment ends, having contributed to the spectrum of the tales a brilliant patch of color and sound.

## The Franklin's Tale

The Franklin, having listened to the Squire, laments aloud the looseness of his own son's life, wasted as it is on dice and other such follies; he is nothing like this excellent young Squire, who though handsome and gay is still courteous and modest, and in no sense a wastrel. The host, impatient for the moment with talk about courtesy, a virtue which perhaps is often overpraised in his opinion, brusquely bids the Franklin get on with his tale without more ado, and the Franklin does so. A franklin was a freeholder or country gentleman, and this specimen of the class represents it at its best; he is, according to the general *Prologue*, white-bearded and ruddy-faced; he loves food and drink, being "Epicurus' very son": he is noted for his hospitality and for the generosity of his table, which is always set; he is fond of partridges; he has a fishpond full of bream and pike; and he requires of his cook that highly seasoned sauces be always available; he has been a sheriff, and he presides at county sessions.

The tale Chaucer gives him to tell is once again from Boccaccio: not this time from the *Decameron,* though it is there too, but from *Il Filocolo.* It is clear that Boccaccio was Chaucer's favorite source for plots, and no wonder, for Boccaccio was an extraordinarily fertile and fascinating storyteller. In this case he was supplemented for Chaucer by Geoffrey of Monmouth's *History of the Kings of England* and a Breton lay which has not been identified, though it is the only source the Franklin says he knows. If there is a Marriage Group among the tales, this can be considered the maturest member of it, though not necessarily the most moving one: that would be either the tale of Griselda or *The Wife of Bath's Tale,* and the first of those would certainly be preferred by most readers. The controversy about whether husband or wife should have the sovereignty in marriage is settled and dismissed as soon as Arviragus and Dorigen decide on matrimony. He volunteers the promise

> *That never in his life, by day or night,*
> *Would he assume a right of mastery*
> *Against her will, nor show her jealousy,*
> *But would obey and do her will in all*
> *As any lover of his lady shall;*
> *Save that the name and show of sovereignty,*
> *Those would he have, lest he shame his degree.*

In another kind of story Arviragus would prove unable to keep his promise; with the best will in the world he would sooner or later become possessive and jealous. But this is not that kind of story, and so not only Arviragus maintains his nobility of mind but Dorigen also never wavers from the position she outlines in an answering speech:

> *She thanked him, and with a great humbleness*
> *She said: "Since, sir, of your own nobleness*
> *You proffer me to have so loose a rein*
> *Would God there never come between us twain,*
> *For any guilt of mine, a war or strife.*
> *Sir, I will be your humble, faithful wife,*
> *Take this as truth till heart break in my breast."*
> *Thus were they both in quiet and in rest.*

So for a year or more their lives pass smoothly and blissfully; then Arviragus, being a knight, crosses the Channel from Brittany where they live to serve awhile at King Arthur's court; and Dorigen misses him so dreadfully that she does nothing but grieve in solitude and brood among other things over the terrible black rocks that line the cliffs of her native peninsula, hating them for their hardness and blackness, and fearing them for the damage they may do to the vessel that will bring Arviragus home. Her friends eventually prevail upon her to be social again, and once at a dance she is told by a squire named Aurelius, a man she has been aware of for two years but has not especially noticed, that he is sick with love for her and will doubtless die unless she gives him herself in the time-honored manner of courtly lovers.

Because she is unable to return his devotion, her only response is playful: she will accept him as her lover provided he causes the black rocks along the coast to disappear. She assumes that this will leave her safe, but Aurelius has a brother who knows a magician in Orleans; the magician is consulted, and for a thousand pounds he offers to remove the rocks. He does so by deep devices and optical illusions which Chaucer does not claim to comprehend, and the rocks do cease to be there. Dorigen, confronted with this fact, is desperate to the point of planning suicide when Arviragus returns from England and she cannot refrain from telling him what has happened. He at once decides that she must carry out her part of the bargain, since truthfulness is the better part of love; and she endeavors to do so, only to be told by Aurelius that the nobility of Arviragus is such that

> *I would myself far rather suffer woe*
> *Than break apart the love between you two.*

So now the only question is how Aurelius shall pay the magician his thousand pounds. He takes half the sum in earnest of the remainder he will get by begging if necessary; but now it is the magician's turn to be magnanimous; he cancels the debt, and the tale is ended. Presumably the rocks reappear, for the magician has not undertaken to remove them for longer than a week. And the Franklin has only one thing to add:

> *Masters, this question would I ask you now:*
> *Which was most generous, do you think, and how?*

The question is not answered by anyone, nor is it a very interesting question, since the virtues of these persons have a certain synthetic quality and therefore are not of the stuff great fiction is made of. In Chaucer's best tales the people are free of Chaucer; they do not take their places in a pattern, a symmetry, that he has arranged; they are free because they are truly created, and the good in them is seldom a thing that they intend, nor is the evil a thing that they either acknowledge or enjoy. *The Franklin's Tale* is expertly told, and it is justly admired, but it has neither tears nor laughter in it, none of the unpremeditated passion, none of the unrehearsed intensity that can make the strongest of us helpless all at once.

## The Physician's Tale

The Doctor of Physic, whose portrait in the general *Prologue* is singularly dull, manages to make the tale he takes from Livy's *History of Rome* and from the *Roman de la Rose,* the tale of Appius and Virginius, quite as unimpressive as he himself is. It is at least a grisly fable—Virginius beheads his beautiful young daughter, Virginia, to save her from the corrupt judge, Appius, who has suborned witnesses to swear that the girl is actually his own daughter—but the force of it is lessened by the determination of Virginius to tell Virginia what he is going to do. She pleads for a little time to lament her death as Jephthah's daughter did in the Book of Judges, but Virginius proceeds to strike off her head and carry it by the hair to Appius in court. The conclusion is just enough: Appius, seized by a crowd sympathetic to Virginius, is thrust into a cell where he kills himself, and the false witnesses are hanged.

The story as it stands is probably too short; at any rate it is barren of the interest it ought to have. The host is excited by it and cries out in wrath against so vile a judge as Appius, but he is not listened to. Then, as if he needed relief from pain, he calls upon the Pardoner to tell "some pleasant tale or jest." The other pilgrims say no, for then the Pardoner will be ribald. They would rather have from him "some moral thing." Which he agrees to supply, but first he must think and drink.

## The Pardoner's Tale

His tale is both a sermon and a story, the two of them embedded in a confession so outrageous that the pilgrims who listen—and all of them must be supposed to listen, for the speaker has an eloquence from which no one can turn away, even for all the rottenness in it—are silent until the end, when the furious host, moved to obscenity by what he has heard, is so insulting to the Pardoner that no more is spoken by him that day. The whole episode, in the light of the Pardoner's portrait in the general *Prologue,* where Chaucer tells us that he has long, stringy yellow hair, a voice that bleats like a goat, shiny eyes like those of a rabbit, and a perfectly smooth face—no possibility of a beard

("I think he was a gelding or a mare"), though he can sing merrily and loud and talk forever until stopped—is one of the richest things in any literature, one of the most astonishing and memorable. The spectacle of this rogue haranguing a company of strangers with proofs of his own viciousness—he begins by saying he is vicious and rejoices in it—has no parallel in fiction. He is a mountebank, a hypocrite, a liar, and a thief—he hints once that he is also a lecher, though we can doubt that—and he carries a wallet full of religious relics that he offers for sale along with spurious pardons said to come direct from Rome. And just to make sure that all of his talents are appreciated, he preaches a sermon, a specimen sermon, on his favorite text: *Radix malorum est cupiditas,* which we know best in English as "The love of money is the root of all evil."

He preaches against other things than avarice—drunkenness, gambling, gluttony, lust—but avarice is the sin he bears down on. Why? Because he thereby satisfies his own greed for money: the more people he convinces that they should give away their money, the more he gets. He is quite frank about this, and sometimes funny in his frankness, though most of the time he is merely shocking. We never hear what the religious pilgrims think of his exhibition—the Prioress, the Parson in particular—but we do observe at least one reaction to what he has said when at the close we observe that the Knight, gentleman that he is, hushes the host as the host curses the Pardoner, and insists that they kiss each other before they go on, which then they do. There is no better Christian in the company than he who told the tale of Palamon and Arcita.

It is *The Pardoner's Tale,* however, that gives the episode its ultimate distinction. It has been said that no better short story exists, and this could very well be true. What it accomplishes it accomplishes with a celerity that takes the breath. The plague has come to Flanders, and among the wretched people still alive are three young men in a tavern, carousing there as if there were no woe in the world.

> *And as they sat they heard a small bell clink*
> *Before a corpse being carried to his grave.*

Upon asking who has died they learn that he was sitting and drinking in this very place last night when a stranger called Death came by with a spear and clove his heart in two. This stranger Death has been busy everywhere of late; in one village nearby no living souls are left. The three roisterers drunkenly declare war on Death and go forth to find him. They meet an old man near the village whose inhabitants are dead and ask him why he is all wrapped up except for his face. The ancient says it is because he can find no man who will "give his youth in barter for my age," and so he must keep his old age until God chooses to relieve him of it.

> *"Not even Death, alas! my life will take;*
> *Thus restless I my wretched way must make,*
> *And on the ground, which is my mother's gate,*
> *I knock with my staff early, aye, and late,*
> *And cry: 'O my dear mother, let me in!*
> *Lo, how I'm wasted, flesh and blood and skin!*
> *Alas! When shall my bones come to their rest?' "*

The roisterers rudely insist that he tell them where Death is, and he at last does so. Death is up this crooked road, at the foot of an oak tree. They run there, and find not Death but eight bushels of gold florins, which to be sure will be Death to them, but at the moment they do not know this.

They gloat over their treasure for a while; then one of them, realizing that they will attract too much notice if they carry it away now, calls for a drawing of straws to determine which one of them shall go into town for bread and wine to sustain them all until dark. The youngest of them, sent by lot, is no sooner on his way than one of his elders proposes to the other that they murder him on his return so that each of them will have a half instead of a third of the shining treasure. The young one, alone in town, conceives meanwhile a plan whereby he can come into possession of all the treasure. He buys poison, telling the merchant it is for rats, and on the way back to his companions with the bread and wine, puts enough of the poison into two of the bottles to dispose of his friends for good. The three of them are soon victims of that stranger Death whom they had vowed to eliminate.

The tale has a power which defies analysis, especially as Chaucer tells it; for of course he is only retelling it. The old man whose face we never really see, Death whom we only hear about, and the plague that rages even while we read—all three of these, to name no other thing in this country where everything is terrible, take on an almost otherworldly force that is only in part explained by the circumstance that the tale in its outline is one of the most widely distributed narratives ever known. The telling here is by a master, and the sign of his mastery is a terror we feel without being able to assign a cause for it. The irony in the three murders, yes, and the presence of the plague, of course; but some darkness that overhangs this world and renders every inhabitant of it hoarse—that is the element of mystery, the contribution of genius, which we can only recognize before going on.

## The Shipman's Tale

The Shipman, represented in the general *Prologue* as a prosperous sea captain who at times can be a bit of a pirate, making the masters of vessels he captures walk the plank, has not too nice a conscience to keep him from telling with relish a *fabliau* tale, known also to Boccaccio in the *Decameron,* of a merchant's wife who cashes in on her sexual charm, to the tune of a hundred marks, first with a monk who makes free with women whenever he pleases, and second with her own husband, elaborately deceived by both churchman and spouse, with no one caring because no money is actually lost. It is a tale of cleverness, cleverly told, and nothing more. The monk in it is like the Monk who goes among the pilgrims: an "outrider," a buyer of supplies for his monastery, a man whose religious function is practical, not spiritual, a lover of hunting, of expensive clothes, of fine horses, of rich food—his specialty is roast swan—and of soft boots; he is bald as glass and his bulging eyes gleam like fire beneath a pot. Perhaps the Shipman thinks all monks are like this one, or may as well be for all he cares.

## The Prioress's Tale

The portrait of the Prioress in the general *Prologue* is probably the most famous portrait in that famous gallery. She is smiling, modest, and quiet; she is known as Madam Eglantine, and the French she speaks is not of Paris but of an English nunnery; her table manners are exquisite, and in general her deportment is courtly; sensitive to the pain of others, she will weep if she sees a mouse caught in a trap; she keeps little dogs whom she feeds roasted meat, mild, and fine white bread; she has blue eyes, a small mouth, and a fair, broad forehead; she wears coral beads for ornament, and a gold brooch on which is written *Amor vincit omnia,* "Love conquers all."

This delicate lady tells without hesitation a tale she may have known by heart, and tells it in Chaucerian stanzas that have the quality with which the tale of Constance and the tale of Griselda have already made our ears familiar. The accent of her speech is childlike, perhaps, in its extreme simplicity, but this seems to go with her character as we know it, and possibly excuses a certain obtuseness in her view of the material her

narrative treats. For her tale is of a murder supposedly committed in some Asian city by Jews, and the details of the murder are not nice; neither are the details of the murderers' punishment later on—their bodies are drawn by wild horses and then hanged. But first the crime itself: it is a ritual murder by Jews who cannot bear to hear a seven-year-old Christian choir-boy singing the *Alma redemptoris* antiphon as he walks along the street. They waylay him, cut his throat, and dispose of his body in a privy. How-ever, he refuses to die, or at any rate to stop singing; his voice is heard, he is looked for and found, and even as he is being buried he continues with the miraculous help of the Virgin to sing his song in praise of her.

All this is far from agreeable to contemplate, but the Prioress does not shudder as she proceeds. She seems to take for granted that the myth of the ritual murder is verifiable history, though it is not. And while it might be asking too much of her that she be a critical historian of popular be-liefs, yet we remember her daintiness at table and her little dogs of which she is so fond, and we conclude, as perhaps Chaucer did, that the love she celebrated on her brooch was a limited thing. Of course she had never seen a Jew, since Jews had been expelled from England in 1290 and were not readmitted until the seventeenth century, so that Shakespeare never saw one either. In the reign of Richard I, late in the twelfth century, all the Jews of York had either killed themselves and their families or had been massacred by the citizens of York in the royal castle. It is a terrible story, and we do not know what Chaucer thought about it, or of course what the Prioress did. It does appear, however, that Chaucer, whose por-trait of the Prioress is gently satirical, may be suggesting that a lady who takes such tender care of her pet animals—in violation, too, of the rules of her Order—might have winced a little more at the spectacle she spreads before us here. Not that her tale is undeserving of its reputation. It is beautifully told, and Matthew Arnold selected one of its lines,

> *O martir, souded to virginitee*

as being by itself "enough to show the charm of Chaucer's verse."* It is perhaps an untranslatable line, but that does not greatly matter. The im-portant thing is how the story moves, is the power of the mother's agony to pierce us once again and the steadfastness of the child that refuses to be silent until he has no further reason not to. And all the while, music as of a mass is sounding.

## Chaucer's Tale of Sir Thopas

We may have forgotten that Chaucer himself is one of the pilgrims, so seldom has he mentioned himself. Then suddenly, after the Prioress is

---

* *The Study of Poetry; GGB,* Vol. 5, p. 30.

finished, and after a period of sober silence has passed in contemplation of the miracle she celebrated, the host, ready as always for a change of tone and pace, glances over at Chaucer and says: "What man are you?"

> *"You look as if you tried to find a hare,*
> *For always on the ground I see you stare.*
> *Come near me then, and look up merrily.*
> *Now make way, sirs, and let this man have place;*
>
> . . . . . . . . . . . . . . . . .
>
> *Why, he seems absent, by his countenance,*
> *And gossips with no one for dalliance.*
> *Since other folk have spoken, it's your turn;*
> *Tell us a mirthful tale, and that anon."*

Chaucer replies that he has no tale, only a long rhyme he learned long ago; and the host says, "That is good."

But the host doesn't find it very good, for after Chaucer has recited thirty-one stanzas and begun another, he breaks in abruptly, beseeching Chaucer to be done with doggerel, for that is what he thinks of Sir Thopas. He is right; the tale is doggerel; but he does not appreciate it as a parody of many a popular romance that was no sillier than it is. It describes a Flemish knight who dresses himself, goes forth on a grey stallion, is challenged by a giant, and returns to prepare himself for mortal combat —which we never behold because it is then that the host interrupts him. The poem is a piece of literary satire, and very amusing of its kind; but the host is not literary, and neither are the pilgrims, judging by the fact that none of them protests and asks for more. Sir Thopas is a homespun knight who has never seen the inside of a real castle; nor has his poet, who can write:

> *They brought him, first, the sweet, sweet wine,*
> *And mead within a maselyn,*
>   *And royal spicery*
> *Of gingerbread that was full fine,*
> *Cumin and licorice, I opine,*
>   *And sugar so dainty.*

And what does he draw over his white skin, what garments of finest linen, clean and sheer?

> *His breeches and a shirt.*

## Chaucer's Tale of Melibeus

Why not, says the host, a tale in prose that wouldn't waste your time and ours, as this rhyme has? Preferably one with doctrine in it, "good and plain." Chaucer with alacrity says that he does have "a moral tale, right virtuous," with many proverbs in it for good measure. And so we get his excellent version of the tale of the rich man Melibeus and his wife, Prudence, which an Italian judge had written in Latin in the thirteenth century and a Dominican friar had freely translated into French in Chaucer's own century. Chaucer is more faithful to the French text he translates than the friar was to the work of the judge, but even then it is plain how fine a craftsman in prose he was. As for the doctrine, it is unimpeachably wise. Melibeus, injured by three old enemies who in his absence enter his house and beat his wife and grievously wound his daughter, Sophie, does not know how to retaliate; but his wife does—with forgiveness. After long argument he gives in to Prudence, and all parties live in peace thereafter.

## The Monk's Tale

The host, after exclaiming that his wife is no such woman as Prudence was, for she is violent and vindictive, turns suddenly to the Monk, tells him to be of good cheer, and remarks that he does not look like a man of religion, a denizen of cloisters. He does not look like a celibate person, and he probably isn't one, the host hints, or at any rate he shouldn't be; he should be a "hen-hopper," and fill the world with his husky, healthy kind. All the vitality of the world seems to have settled in monks, says the host; laymen are feckless and feeble.

Nothing is said about the way the Monk takes all this—the host himself says he isn't serious. And it does appear to be true that the Monk is a conspicuously burly, vital character. Yet all he says is that he intends to keep his promise by telling not one tale but several: of persons who have "stood in great prosperity" but then have fallen into misery and ended their lives wretchedly. In other words, the "falls of princes" will be his theme, as it was the theme of Boccaccio in his *Falls of Illustrious Men* and of other writers whose conception of tragedy, the conception current in medieval times, was that it was nothing but reversal and disaster. The Monk goes on then to rehearse the melancholy fortunes of seventeen persons, from Lucifer to Ugolino, who went from high to low and became legendary in the process.

## The Nun's Priest's Tale

"Hold!" cries the Knight. "Good sir, no more of this." Enough of heaviness; now let there be light and life again. The host, agreeing, demands from the nun's priest a tale that will make all their hearts glad; and the priest says he will try.

All readers of Chaucer know that he succeeded, *The Nun's Priest's Tale* is often said to be the high point of all the tales, and certainly it gladdens the heart. Chaucer, for whom it was probably a late work, was never in better form, never in more perfect possession of the comic genius that was his most precious gift. He was never lighter in his touch, never happier in the play of his mind. His scene is a barnyard, but it might just as easily be the world, with a handsome cock and seven hens playing parts that could also be the parts of a human husband and seven wives, so indistinguishable are the species here, and so profound the vanity of Chanticleer. So profound also the practicality of Pertelote his favorite hen, the female who takes no stock in dreams, and who has no sympathy for any male, even her wedded one, if he gives way to fear. But on the fine morning when the story opens, Chanticleer has had in fact a very terrible dream, and it distresses him that Pertelote is not impressed by it. He has dreamed that a strange beast, like a dog yet not a dog, appeared in the barnyard—only appeared there, but that is enough to terrify the cock. Was it a fox? Neither of them says so, but we can suppose they think it.

Pertelote doesn't even believe the beast was there. It was only a dream, an illusion, caused no doubt by vapors, bad secretions, and perhaps plain bile. The cure is a laxative; Chanticleer in her opinion needs to be cleaned out. Which outrages him, for he believes in the efficacy of dreams as foretellers of things to come, and to convince her of this he tells her a hair-raising tale of a murdered man who told his friend in a dream where his body would be the next morning: at the gate of the city, in a dung cart. So it was, and the murderers were hanged. He tells other tales, and he reminds her of Daniel, of Joseph, of Croesus who dreamed that he would hang and did, of Pharoah's butler and baker, of Andromache who dreamed of Hector's death which happened the next day.

None of this seems to carry weight with his pretty wife, who is in fact so pretty that he ceases to care about anything except feathering her, which he does twenty times before prime; and is so happy in consequence that he carelessly falls victim to the flattery of a fox (the one he has dreamed of, naturally) that praises his singing, which the fox says is quite the equal of his father's. Will Chanticleer sing for the fox, closing his eyes as his father did and rising on tiptoe and stretching his neck for the maximum result? Chanticleer does all this, only to be grabbed by the neck and carried away—with all the inhabitants of the barnyard shrieking and whooping in pursuit. It looks bad for Chanticleer, but he thinks of something that saves him. He says to the fox, who now has reached the edge of the woods, that this would be the moment to pause and shout triumphant insults to his pursuers. The fox opens his mouth to do so; Chanticleer flies into a tree; and the tale is done.

The action in it is minor in terms of the space it occupies; most of the tale is talk—digression, if one pleases, but Chaucer is never so happy as when he is digressing, or never so charming. It is his intellect at play, and since his intellect was fine and tireless he is never tedious when he indulges it. On the contrary, he is most alive then, as we his readers are then most alert. "Sir," cries the host when the priest has finished, "for your tale, may blessings on you fall!"

## The Second Nun's Tale

Chaucer prefaces this life of Saint Cecilia with a statement in four stanzas of his reason for writing it. He has written it, or rather translated it, to save himself from idleness. It is hard to believe that he was ever idle, or even tempted to be, but confessions to that effect were conventional in the poetry of his time; and so for that matter were saints' lives, of which medieval readers seem never to have tired. Chaucer used the famous *Golden Legend* as his source, and other narratives too; he was seldom content with one original when others were available; he loved to rummage among books for material to reshape. His Saint Cecilia, written in his favorite stanza, tells of a martyrdom in Rome of the third century: Cecilia prefers death by beheading to the sin of sacrifice to the pagan gods. The beheading is botched, so that she suffers long enough to know and even to rejoice that she suffers. A bloody tale it is, encompassing not only Cecilia's death but that of her husband, a Roman whom she has converted, and two other men as well. In later centuries Cecilia became the patron saint of music, celebrated in annual odes; but that was after Chaucer's time.

## The Canon's Yeoman's Tale

As the tales approach their end, Chaucer grows more and more interested in the dramatic interludes—if dramatic is the word—that usher the speakers in and out. At this point the most elaborate of them all takes place. At Boughton-under-Blean the company is overtaken by a man in black and his yeoman, or servant, both of whom ride sweaty horses because they have hastened to come where they now are. The man himself, a cleric of some sort, cuts a poor figure in his shabby clothes, and the yeoman is even less impressive. The host, wondering who they are and why they are so excited, learns first from the canon—for that is what his garments show him to be—and then from the yeoman that the two of them have of late been desperate for diversion, and seeing the pilgrims on the road have spurred their horses to catch up. The yeoman, however, goes further than that. Something moves him all at once to blurt out the truth about his master. His master is an alchemist, which is to say, a charlatan, a fraud, and the yeoman is now so disgusted with his performances that he has decided to desert him for good. The canon, listening to this, endeavors to hush his betrayer, but then, the yeoman persisting in his course, mounts his horse and flees away "for very grief and shame."

The tale the yeoman now tells is of the career he has shared with a man who may once have believed that he could convert baser metals into gold but who has latterly been reduced to swindling the credulous and the greedy with mock demonstrations of his skill. Even at that he makes a poor living, and it could still be that alchemy for him is a true science, though the yeoman doubts it, and so do we. The canon himself, of course, is already out of sight for good, so we shall never learn the truth from him. Chaucer, whose interest in the pseudosciences of astrology and alchemy, both popular in his age, was always lively and healthily skeptical, had studied them enough so that in the present case he documents his tale with an immense amount of lore collected by him from numerous sources. His curiosity, never at rest, was seldom busier than it is here.

## The Manciple's Tale

The Manciple, by virtue of his office a buyer of supplies for a college, a monastery, one of the inns of court, or some other such institution, precedes the telling of his tale by teasing the Cook because he is drunk, but upon being reprimanded by the host for this, although the host has been doing precisely the same thing, makes amends by giving the Cook still more wine to drink before he begins his tale of Phoebus and his white crow. It seems that Phoebus Apollo once chose to dwell on earth as a mortal man, and to marry a mortal woman with whom he was very much in love. His being a deity in disguise did not provide him with the wisdom to comprehend that no wife ever should be watched lest she be unfaithful. If she is by nature faithful, Chaucer explains, she needs no watching; and if she is by nature false, then no amount of watching will work—she will deceive you whether or no. Apollo's wife, being by nature false, was entertaining a lover one day as the white crow of the house looked on. When Apollo returned home, the crow informed upon his mistress; whereupon Apollo shot her dead with an arrow; but then, reasoning that the crow's being an informer was worse than her being an adulteress had been, he plucked out all the crow's white feathers, replaced them with black ones, and deprived him of his gifts of speech and song, so that he became what all crows after him in the world have been.

## The Parson's Tale

The sun is now low in the sky, and the day's end is near. The host, aware of this perhaps because of a touch of chill in the air, a presentiment of shadow, looks over at the Parson and asks him for something jolly—"a fable now, by Cock's dear bones." But the Parson, whom the general *Prologue* has represented as perfect in his calling—sober, responsible, faithful, self-sacrificing, generous, kind, a true shepherd of his flock, in every part of him so good that nobody has ever forgotten this portrait of him, nobody has ever ceased to be moved merely by the recollection of its musical sweet tone, its reverent eloquence—the Parson declines the invitation. If the company, he says, wishes to hear something in which "the moral virtues will appear,"

> *"But if you wish the truth made plain and straight,*
> *A pleasant tale in prose I will relate*
> *To weave our feast together at the end.*
> *May Jesus, of His grace, the wit me send*
> *To show you, as we journey this last stage,*
> *The way of that most perfect pilgrimage*
> *To heavenly Jerusalem on high."*

The host, accepting the gentle rebuke, replies:

> *"Say what you wish, and we will gladly hear."*

And adds for only the Parson to hear:

> *"But pray make haste, the sun will soon be down;*
>
> . . . . . . . . . . . . . . . . . .
> *And to do well God send to you His grace!"*

The reader is advised to pay particularly close attention to all of the words the Parson has just spoken. For all we know he is willing to agree that stories may contain much truth, though ever since Plato there have been those who doubted that they contain enough, or even any at all; but for the Parson it is better to make the truth "plain and straight," without any admixture of make-believe. So, while he hopes his tale will strike its hearers as a pleasant one, he will tell it in prose; and he will endeavor through it to gather up whatever threads have been left hanging by those who preceded him—whatever meanings, whatever morals, have been left unstated. He will weave all these together at the end of a pilgrimage that he would like his companions to consider as a rehearsal for the perfect one they will sooner or later be making, not to Canterbury, not to any earthly town, but to heaven itself, to "Jerusalem on high."

What follows is not a tale at all, is not a narrative in any sense with which we now are familiar, though if the silence of the pilgrims is any indication of the view they take of its content, it could well be that to the last of them they are interested and respectful. The Miller, the Wife of Bath (yes, that old rip), the Reeve, the lusty Squire, the Monk with his bulging eyes, the wanton Friar, the well-fed Franklin, the delicate Prioress, the loathsome Summoner, and the impossible Pardoner, to name only a few of the listeners, would appear to have been as receptive an audience as the Clerk, the Knight, and the Plowman who had told no tale but who knew how to live in peace and perfect charity, and who loved God most of all but next loved his neighbor even as himself.

Are we to suppose that Chaucer is only pretending that none of this motley crew on horseback protested against the sermon they were offered in place of the jolly fable the host had begun by asking for? At least we hear no protest, and so must assume that the skill of the Parson's rhetoric, the beauty of his poem in prose, the suspense he manages to build up as he discusses penitence and describes the seven deadly sins, and discourses upon contrition and confession, adds up to a masterpiece in its own right, a triumph of language and thought that moves under its own power and establishes its own harmony with the mood Chaucer has chosen to create at the close of his *Canterbury Tales* and indeed of his entire career as a poet and storyteller.

No greater mistake could be made than to suppose that he was merely stuffing into the manuscript at this point a pious nothing that he himself did not take seriously. He was unmistakably serious—as serious as the Parson himself—and we do him no service by denying it. *The Parson's Tale* is sometimes dismissed as dull, but in fact it is exciting. It has a wonderful eloquence which is Chaucer's as well as St. Raymund of Pennaforte's, and as well as that of Guilieumus Peraldus, for Chaucer was putting into English the Latin and the French of those two worthies. *The Canterbury Tales* have been called unfinished; it would be better, as some critics have suggested, to call them incomplete, which manifestly they are in many places; but surely this is the finish that Chaucer was aiming at.

As he looked back over the world of his tales and the people in them, what did he see? His eyes were not our eyes, and so we cannot be certain of what they saw, or at any rate of how they assessed it. The stately Thesëus and the two noble kinsmen Palamon and Arcita; the beautiful lady they both loved and fought to possess; the carpenter's young wife Alison whom two less noble youths found equally attractive; the miller's wife and

daughter whom the Cambridge students made merry with at night; Constance and Griselda whose patience under suffering was almost supernatural and yet we believe it in each case and are powerfully moved; hideous old January and his girl-wife May; Arviragus and Dorigen, those paragons of wedded faith; the three roisterers who almost at the same moment encountered Death; Chanticleer and Pertelote and the fox who was not so canny after all—what do these persons mean, severally or collectively? Do *The Canterbury Tales* have a moral—a single moral—that is plain and straight?

The question is actually embarrassing, so alien it is to the habits and minds most readers, perhaps all readers, have today. And so we tend to dodge it, saying it is not being asked of us. Of whom then *is* it being asked? Of Chaucer, that companionable man with the sophisticated intelligence, the skeptical temper, who makes us so much at home with him as he tells of things both near and far, both ugly and beautiful, both tender and cruel? Is Chaucer probing his own conscience, is he trying to decide whether or not it was well that he wrote what he did write when other things had been possible? And above all, is he asking himself what final difference his stories make? Do they have anything you could call a character? Are they unified in their force, or are they meaninglessly various, are they experiments rather than solutions? Are they, in a word, so many acts of vanity of which in his prime Chaucer might have been proud but for which in these last days of his life, when the sun is low in the sky and will never for him be high again, he should be contrite?

His answer has disturbed and distressed such of his readers as cannot believe he was serious when, rather suddenly they suppose, he added to *The Parson's Tale* an Envoy, a retraction. For in this last utterance he apologizes to Our Lord Jesus Christ because he has written the masterpieces for which posterity adores him. Not just some of the masterpieces but all of them, which he goes ahead and lists, including the Book of Troilus and "The Tales of Canterbury, those that tend toward sin," and certain further writings by him which have not survived save in this mention of their names. Only his pious works, "the translation of Boethius's *de Consolatione,* and other books of legends of saints, and homilies, and of morality and devotion," are recorded here in gratitude, as worthy and not requiring forgiveness.

How is such a statement to be taken? Shall we believe Chaucer, and if we do, what shall we understand him to be saying? That all was vanity, that nothing in these pages means enough? Or shall we regard it as a perfunctory gesture, enjoined by a priest who had charge of him in his last helpless moments? This has been alleged by certain of his readers who allow that he could be serious but doubt that in his right mind he could ever have been as serious as the Envoy on the face of it bids us believe he was. On the other hand, the Envoy does not have the sound of something a man is being forced to say. It seems to be Chaucer's own voice that we hear. And if it is, why on earth is he renouncing his life's work? What should we make of this?

Perhaps we should make of it what we make of Don Quixote's saying to the Bachelor Sampson, when Sampson tries to arouse him from thoughts of death by speaking of new adventures he might undertake: "No more of that, I beseech you. . . . Pray, gentlemen, let us be serious. There's no trifling at a time like this; I must take care of my soul."* Or if such a precedent proves nothing, since Don Quixote may have been mad—was all but universally said to be mad by those who met him, though others who knew him well could doubt that he was—then there are other cases, such as Tolstoy's, who repudiated *Anna Karenina, War and Peace,* and all the rest of his fiction except the tales for children and peasants. Or if Tolstoy proves nothing either, since in his last years he too was strange to say the least, there is Shakespeare, who retired from the stage at forty-eight though he had just written *The Tempest*† and still had four more years to live: four years during which he made no provision for the printing of his plays.

What we should make of such occurrences is the acknowledgement that to any poet as to any man may come a moment when it seems necessary to take into account something greater than any work he happens to have done. And if we acknowledge this, we may be able to perceive how it is—how in so many striking cases it has been—that those whose work is of the highest order, far from being anxious to secure its place, are in the end least concerned about such matters, because they are most capable of seeing beyond them and most interested in coming to terms with what they see. Chaucer himself indicates as much when he tells us in the last sentence we have from him that his renunciation is "so that I may be one of those, at the day of doom, that shall be saved." We must believe he means this, as we must believe that in meaning it he is not diminished but enhanced. For it is only the greatest artists who know how to mean such things. Only those who had everything are willing to be left with nothing in the end. Nothing, that is, except their souls—except their souls, as Hamlet might have said.

---

* Cf. *GBWW,* Vol. 29, p. 427.
† *GBWW,* Vol. 27, pp. 524–48.

BIBLIOGRAPHY

The best edition of Chaucer in one volume is *The Works of Geoffrey Chaucer,* edited by F. N. ROBINSON. 1933. 2d ed. Boston: Houghton Mifflin Co., 1957.

*Chaucer's Poetry: An Anthology for the Modern Reader,* selected and edited by E. T. DONALDSON, is a copious selection with excellent commentaries on all the poems. The text is slightly modernized. New York: Ronald Press Co., 1958.

For scholars, but for readers too, a work of endless interest is *The Text of the Canterbury Tales: Studied on the Basis of all Known Manuscripts,* by JOHN M. MANLY and EDITH RICKERT. 8 vols. 1940. Chicago: University of Chicago Press. This is the nearest that anyone may now come to seeing how *The Canterbury Tales* looked on the page before the invention of printing. The 83 surviving manuscripts, many of them incomplete, are thoroughly described, dated, analyzed, collated, and compared.

A highly readable prose translation of *The Canterbury Tales* is by R. M. LUMIANSKY. New York: Simon & Schuster, 1948.

For anyone interested in the sources of Chaucer's tales, the indispensable work is *Sources and Analogues of Chaucer's Canterbury Tales,* by many hands but collected and edited by W. F. BRYAN and GERMAINE DEMPSTER. 1941. Reprint ed. New York: Humanities Press, 1958.

Of the numerous collections of commentaries on Chaucer, two are especially rewarding:

> *Chaucer Criticism,* vol. 1, *The Canterbury Tales,* edited by RICHARD J. SCHOECK and JEROME TAYLOR. Notre Dame, Ind.: University of Notre Dame Press, 1960.

> *Discussions of the Canterbury Tales,* edited by CHARLES A. OWEN, JR. Boston: D. C. Heath & Co., 1961.

Of the many critical works by individual authors on Chaucer and *The Canterbury Tales,* these are especially recommended:

> *Medieval English Literature,* by W. P. KER. 1912. Rev. ed. London and New York: Oxford University Press, 1969. The final chapter is on Chaucer, but the entire work is illuminating and wise.

> *The Poetry of Chaucer,* by ROBERT KILBURN ROOT. 1900. Rev. ed. Gloucester, Mass.: Peter Smith, 1957.

> *Chaucer and His Poetry,* by GEORGE LYMAN KITTREDGE. Originally published 1915. Cambridge, Mass.: Harvard University Press, 1970.

> *Some New Light on Chaucer,* by JOHN MATTHEWS MANLY. 1926. Reprint. Gloucester, Mass.: Peter Smith, 1959.

> *The Poet Chaucer,* by NEVILL COGHILL. 1949. 2d ed. New York: Oxford University Press, 1967.

> *Chaucer,* by G. K. CHESTERTON. Originally published 1932. New York: Greenwood Press, 1969. The best of them all, because the most like Chaucer.

On Chaucer's times:

> *The Fourteenth Century: 1307–1399.* The Oxford History of England, vol. 5. By MAY McKISACK. New York: Oxford University Press, 1959.

> *Chaucer and His England,* by G. G. COULTON. 1908. 8th ed. London: Methuen & Co., 1963.

> *Chaucer's World.* Compiled by EDITH RICKERT. Edited by CLAIR C. OLSON and MARTIN M. CROW. New York: Columbia University Press, 1948.

> *Geoffrey Chaucer of England,* by MARCHETTE CHUTE. New York: E. P. Dutton & Co., 1946.

*Illustration note:* The eleven portraits of the Canterbury Pilgrims accompanying this article are from the Ellesmere Manuscript (ca. 1410) of Chaucer's *Canterbury Tales.* This exceptional manuscript (EL 26c 9), now in the Henry E. Huntington Library, San Marino, California, is distinguished by the complete set of illustrations portraying each of the twenty-three Canterbury storytellers. These paintings and the decorated margins are considered the handsomest example of Middle English manuscript illumination. The style of the work suggests that perhaps three or four different artists produced the portraits, yet each portrait closely reflects Chaucer's description in *The Prologue.* Of particular interest is the portrait of Chaucer, which appears on page 225 of this article.

NOTE TO THE READER

*The Canterbury Tales* is, as its name indicates, a collection of stories; but it is also a poem, or perhaps a collection of poems, which in Chaucer's time meant the same thing. Thus, the reader will find most of the relevant material in the great books cited and discussed in Chapter 69 of the *Syntopicon,* which is concerned with poetry. See especially Topic 4*b,* which deals with tragedy and comedy; Topic 5*a,* which considers the aims of poets (among them Chaucer) to instruct as well as delight; Topics 7*a,* 7*b,* and 7*c,* in which the poetic elements of narrative, plot, and diction are separately considered (there are a number of citations to Chaucer himself in connection with the last of these); and Topic 8*b,* where rules as to poetic language and standards of style are taken up, with numerous references to *The Canterbury Tales.*

Volume 5 of *GGB* contains discussions of poetry and poets by various writers, among them Dr. Johnson, Schiller, Shelley, Arnold, Whitman, and T. S. Eliot. Arnold's comments on Chaucer may be found in his essay "The Study of Poetry," which appears in this volume.

# A Special Feature

# The Idea of Freedom
## Part Two

# The Idea of Freedom — Part Two

Charles Van Doren, Associate Director,
Institute for Philosophical Research

## Introduction

We present this year the second installment, consisting of Chapters III and IV, of *The Idea of Freedom,* an abridgment of a much longer work with the same title written by Mortimer J. Adler and published in two volumes (1958, 1961). These volumes, which draw upon research done by the Institute of Philosophical Research, of which Dr. Adler is director, comprise some 1,500 exhaustively annotated pages—not too many for serious students of the subject but more than most other persons are likely to want to read. For this reason, and because the two volumes have for some time been out of print (a new printing will appear shortly), it has seemed that a useful purpose could be served if the material they contain were made available in shortened form. That is what Charles Van Doren, associate director of the Institute, has undertaken to do. The resulting abridgment is itself of considerable length, for the subject is a complex one, and many formulations of it exist to be summarized. We have therefore published it in two parts, of which the first part, consisting of Chapters I and II, appeared in last year's issue of *The Great Ideas Today.* For subscribers who do not own that volume, it should be pointed out that Chapter IV of the abridgment, which appears this year, briefly recalls and distinguishes all the kinds of freedom that were discussed earlier.

The outline of Part One, published last year, was as follows:

Chapter I. The Freedom of Being Able to Do as One Wishes
1. The circumstantial freedom of self-realization
2. Individual liberty in relation to law
3. Political liberty
4. Liberty and license: the attack on self-realization freedom

232

Chapter II. The Freedom of Being Able to Will as One Ought

Part Two, which appears now, consists also of two chapters:

Chapter III. The Freedom of Being Able to Determine What One Shall Do or Become

The first of these two chapters has to do with what is popularly though inaccurately known as "free will." This is defined generally as the freedom of being able to determine what one shall do or become. Section 9 considers the sense in which this kind of freedom is natural to man. Sections 10, 10a, 10b, 11, and 12 treat issues that arise from attempts to assert or deny this kind of freedom, or that are raised by such attempts, whether those issues have been truly joined or not. Chapter IV discusses the conclusions to which the study of freedom as a whole leads. Section 13 explains why there are three basic freedoms—no more, and no less. Section 14 takes up the general understanding of freedom and pursues the generic meaning that all the kinds of freedom have in common. Section 15 considers the relation between law, freedom, and responsibility—basic terms in any discussion of the subject. And Section 16 sets forth a number of concluding observations.

In offering this long study of freedom to the readers of *The Great Ideas Today,* the editors feel they are providing something that is not only instructive in itself (it is fair to say that no consideration of freedom can proceed very far without noting the distinctions and confronting the issues that the study sets forth) but that is indicative of the uses to which both the *Syntopicon* and *GBWW* can be put. Anyone who has done some reading in this set of books, and who has made himself familiar with the *Syntopicon,* must have wondered what the result might be if all the references listed under any one of the 102 great ideas were followed out —must have been interested to think what grasp of the idea he would have if this were done. *The Idea of Freedom,* as originally published, constitutes as good an indication of this as we are ever likely to have, and even in its shortened form it suggests how such an investigation would proceed. For freedom is the subject of Chapter 47 of the *Syntopicon* (where it is called Liberty), and there the references will be found on which *The Idea of Freedom* is partly based. It is based on still other references as well, of course, since it surveys a much wider literature than *GBWW*—indeed, there is no considerable work on the subject of freedom, ancient or modern, that it does not comprehend. But at its core, as at the core of the study of any of the great ideas, are the great books, which may therefore be seen here, in respect of at least this one idea, revealed to their full extent.

# The Idea of Freedom — Part Two

## Chapter III. The Freedom of Being Able to Determine What One Shall Do or Become

### 9. The natural freedom of self-determination

The form of freedom we have named the natural freedom of self-determination, which will be the main subject of this chapter, was not of much interest to pagan antiquity. Freedom, of course, in some of its meanings, was the subject of much discussion by the Greek and Roman writers—philosophers, historians, poets, and playwrights. But the forms of freedom treated by them were, for the most part, the forms that we have named: first, the circumstantial freedom of self-realization—the freedom of being able to do as one wishes without being hindered by external constraints (we discussed this freedom in Part I, Chapter 1); and, second, the acquired freedom of self-perfection—the freedom of being able to will as one ought according to standards derived from the universal laws of reason, nature, or God (we examined this freedom in Part I, Chapter 2). The problem of the freedom of the will—the best known and most widely argued problem in the discussion of the form of freedom we will consider in this chapter—was simply not a problem for the ancients.

It became a problem with the advent of Christianity, and the reason is not far to seek. According to the Christian story of the Fall of Man, Adam brought sin into the world by disobeying the explicit injunction of God against tasting the forbidden fruit—and God knew that Adam would disobey. There, of course, is the problem. If God's foreknowledge of Adam's disobedience meant that Adam was somehow forced to disobey, then it would certainly not be fair, by anyone's lights, to blame Adam for what he did. And it would be even more unfair to blame us, Adam's descendants, for what Adam did—as the Christian doctrine of the Fall does blame us in asserting that Adam's original sin had to be atoned for by the suffering of Jesus Christ, and requires baptism as a condition for salvation.

The ancients, having little or no interest in the Christian concept of sin, and not being disposed to accept the story of Adam's fall from grace together with its fateful consequences for his descendants, did not concern themselves much with the freedom of the will. But Christian philosophers and theologians, almost from the very beginning, had to be concerned with it. The doctrine of sin, punishment, and redemption is absolutely basic to Christian beliefs. But is there sin without responsibility? And is there responsibility if human beings—ourselves, as well as Adam before us—are not free?

Admittedly, the argument from responsibility (we shall treat it almost *passim* throughout this chapter) is a rather backhanded one. From an absolute point of view, the argument is not a very good one for the existence of a freedom that some writers—the determinists, so-called—think does not exist. True, we often refer to the concept of responsibility in everyday affairs; we say, for example, that the responsibility of a criminal for his crimes is mitigated if he was not free to act otherwise. Indeed, there is a whole branch of law that is concerned with such mitigations and, as it were, justifications. Still, the argument from responsibility is not the only one, nor even the best one, for the existence of another form of freedom, different from any we have discussed so far. Before turning to those arguments, however, we shall try to describe this form of freedom. We shall do so, as before, by explaining the meaning of the terms we have used to name it.

### *The meaning of* natural

We have called this freedom the natural freedom of self-determination. *Natural* is one of three terms—the others being *circumstantial* and *acquired*—that signify the ways in which freedom is possessed by human beings. Circumstantial freedom, as we saw in Chapter 1, is conferred upon men by circumstances, and is removed by circumstances. All human beings possess it at one time or another and to a greater or lesser degree; but all, too, can be deprived of it, and are so deprived from time to time and to some extent. Acquired freedom, as we saw in Part I, Chapter 2, is possessed not by all but only by good or virtuous men and women—those who have fought to restrain and contain impulses within themselves that are by some called evil, by others primitive, by others unconscious, and who thereby attain to an ability to will as they ought in conformity with the dictates of the highest standards of human conduct. While this freedom is not possessed by all, it is a freedom of which those who possess it cannot be deprived by circumstances. One may not have it; but if one does, he will never lose it, unless he betrays himself.

*Natural* is the third in this trio of terms signifying ways in which freedom can be possessed. As with the other terms, our task is to give *natural* a meaning that is both neutral and common to all the differences of opinion among the relevant authors—Saint Augustine, Boethius, Saint Thomas Aquinas, Martin Luther, John Calvin, Descartes, John Locke, Leibniz, Bishop Berkeley, Jean Jacques Rousseau, Immanuel Kant, Hegel, William James, Henri Bergson, John Dewey, Alfred North Whitehead, Jacques Maritain, and Jean-Paul Sartre.*

We think it is possible to give the word *natural*, as applied to freedom, a meaning that expresses the understanding of this mode of possession by all the authors who affirm a freedom thus possessed. We can state it in the following terms, which we think remain neutral with respect to all the philosophical differences among these authors.

A freedom that is natural is one that is (1) inherent in all men, (2) regardless of the circumstances under which they live, and (3) without regard to any state of mind or character that they may or may not acquire in the course of their lives.

There is no trouble with the second and third of these points. They assert that, whatever else it means to say that freedom is natural, such freedom can be possessed under unfavorable as well as favorable circumstances, and by good and bad men alike. But there is considerably more difficulty with the first point. Does the phrase "inherent in all men" express a common understanding of the natural among these authors?

To begin with, let us consider two authors who represent contrary views that appear to affect our use of the word *natural* as an identifying term: Rousseau and Sartre.

On the one hand, Rousseau maintains that "the specific difference between the man and the brute [is] the human quality of free agency." [1] The expression "specific difference" carries the connotation that man has an essence or nature that is essentially or specifically different from that of brutes. Other authors, such as Aristotle, Aquinas, Descartes, or Maritain, may differ with Rousseau about whether it is rationality or freedom (in the sense of "free agency") that essentially differentiates man from brute. But they agree with him in holding (1) that man has a definable essence or specific nature, (2) that among terrestrial beings only men have free agency, and (3) that all men do have it in virtue of their being human.

On the other hand, Sartre maintains that "human freedom precedes essence in man and makes it possible; the essence of the human being is suspended in his freedom." [2] In Sartre's view it makes a great difference whether one posits the essence of man first and then derives from it man's freedom, or posits man's freedom first, which then makes it possible for each human being to determine his own essence for himself. If man had

---

* This list of authors suggests the difficulty, and complexity, that is involved in finding a neutral, common meaning for the term. The difficulty is compounded by the fact that many of these writers actually use the term *natural*, in *apparently* quite different senses.

an essence or, as Sartre says, "a fixed and given human nature," the determinations it would impose would also limit or even abolish his freedom. But, "if existence really does precede essence . . .. there is no determinism, . . . man is freedom." [3]

Freedom, according to Sartre, is thus not a property that belongs to the essence of the human being. At the same time, however, he emphasizes that "with man the relation of existence to essence is not comparable to what it is for the things of the world." [4] In other words, man is the only being in whom existence precedes essence and, therefore, man alone has a being that is identical with being-free. And since, in the case of man, being-free is identical with being-human, all men have freedom in virtue of their being human.

Our first problem, then, is this. Can the word *natural* be given a neutral meaning for authors who, like Sartre (Kant, Hegel, and John Dewey present similar difficulties), either do not hold or explicitly reject the theory of natures or essences? We think so, in the way in which we have suggested a resolution of the problem posed by Sartre, who may actually reject the theory of essences, but who nevertheless maintains that men alone are free and are free insofar as they are men, whether or not freedom or some other quality constitutes their nature or essence.

Natural freedom, in short, for these and other authors whom they represent, is a freedom that (1) all men possess and (2) only men possess. But there is a second group of authors who pose a quite different problem by affirming that men are not alone in possessing freedom. The philosopher Paul Weiss, for example, holds that "every[thing] has [its] own kind of native freedom which [it] did nothing to achieve." [5] Whitehead and the theologian Paul Tillich appear to agree, although Tillich qualifies his agreement by attributing to man a special sense of freedom. "Freedom," he says, ". . . can be applied to sub-human nature only by way of analogy." [6] Bergson is another who finds freedom inherent in other things than man, and he is joined in this view by the anthropologist Teilhard de Chardin, who, following a long tradition in French thought that bears the name of *panpsychism*, feels that all things—even inanimate beings—have a kind of consciousness, and thereby a kind of freedom.

Thus, whether the freedom that other things exhibit differs in degree from human freedom, as Bergson and Whitehead maintain, or whether, as Weiss and Tillich maintain, it also differs from human freedom in kind, it is regarded by these authors as a freedom "natural" to man only in the sense that whoever is a man possesses it, and not in the sense that men alone possess it. It is a freedom that all men possess, regardless of their circumstances and their individual attainments.

The views we have just examined require us to restrict the meaning of the word *natural* to a single positive point: namely, that a freedom that is natural is one that all human beings possess. But while this meaning catches what is commonly understood by *natural* in spite of all the philosophical differences we have considered, the word *all* by itself fails to identify natural, in contradistinction to circumstantial, and to acquired, freedom. All men may possess circumstantial freedom, at least at some moments in their lives if not always, and in certain connections if not in others. So, too, it is at least possible for all men to possess acquired freedom, even if in fact they do not all actually come to possess it in any significant degree in the course of their lives.

The point that a natural freedom is one that all men possess must, therefore, be made more precise by the following additional point. The ability in which this freedom consists is one that men *always* possess and one that they possess under any circumstances. They actually possess it at all times, no matter how they change or develop in the course of their lives.

To say that men have this freedom is to say precisely this: that whoever is a man, and simply in virtue of being a man, is always and actually in possession of an ability to determine for himself what he wishes to do or to become. He may not always be able to do as he wishes because of unfavorable circumstances. He may not actually be able to live as he ought, because he has failed to acquire the requisite virtue or wisdom. But neither of these obstacles can prevent him from always having an ability with which he is naturally endowed; nor can either remove that ability or transform it from an actuality into a mere possibility.

It should be noted that we did not say that whoever is a man is at every moment actually free. We cannot say that because authors differ on the point whether men are actually free simply through having an ability with which they are naturally endowed or only when they exercise it. Those who hold that human beings are actually free only when they exercise their natural ability to determine for themselves what they wish to do or to become maintain that men are not always actually free in this sense. For example, an infant could not be said to make actual use of the freedom in question; nor could an adult during hours of sleep or when, for any reason, he is non compos mentis.

Nevertheless, these authors, like those with whom they differ on this last point, attribute to every human being an ability that is always actually his by natural endowment. Since having an ability is the condition sine qua non of exercising it, natural freedom remains distinct from circumstantial and acquired freedom; for, in the cases of these other freedoms, every man does not always actually have the circumstantial ability to do as he wishes or the acquired ability to live as he ought.

That is why those who are concerned with circumstantial freedom are concerned with doing something about the circumstances under which men live. They are interested in all the social, political, economic, or other changes in the environment, both natural and social, by which men can be affected in their actual possession of the ability to do as they wish. Similarly, those who are concerned with acquired freedom are concerned with all the changes that can be effected in men themselves by which they may come actually to possess an ability to live as they ought.

In sharp contrast, no one who is concerned with natural freedom is concerned with any changes whatsoever, either in the human environment or in human beings themselves; for no change can affect a person's actual possession throughout life of his ability to exercise this freedom, even if he does not always exercise it.

This confirms our final formulation of the meaning of *natural* as we apply it to freedom to signify one of the ways in which it is thought to be possessed. Regardless of how else they differ, the authors who affirm a freedom we identify as natural conceive that freedom to be (1) one that all men possess, insofar as (2) they always actually have the inherent ability in which it consists. Circumstances may affect the ways in which people exercise this ability, and so may the mental and moral traits they acquire or fail to acquire, but neither circumstances nor acquirements of any sort can confer this freedom upon human beings or deprive them of it.

### *The meaning of* self-determination

The language used by typical proponents of natural freedom might seem to make the further identification of such freedom a relatively easy task. They speak of "free will," "free decision," "freedom of choice," and "*liberum arbitrium*" or its literal English equivalent, "free judgment." But such common phrases fail to identify this freedom satisfactorily, as we have already observed. More than that, they seriously complicate our present task, which is to complete the identification of a freedom that has already been partially identified as natural.

We completed the identification of circumstantial and of acquired freedom by describing a *mode of self*—such as self-realization or self-perfection—that identified a freedom that was already partially identified by reference to a *mode of possession*. So, here, our problem is to say what mode of self further identifies a freedom that is naturally possessed. Before we can attack this problem, however, we must deal with the difficulties raised by such phrases as *free will* and *free choice*. The following considerations will make clear why these phrases cannot be used to identify natural freedom.

(1) Some upholders of natural freedom ascribe such freedom to man's very being, his personality or self as a whole, not to one of his faculties; or they attribute it to his intelligence, his reason, his mind or consciousness, not to his will. They take pains explicitly to deny that man's will is free, or they find no use for the word *will* in enumerating the factors that play a significant part in man's inner life or outward behavior. In some cases they question the reality of the will as that is conceived by authors who do use the word for one of man's basic faculties or powers. Thus the term *free will* does not have the neutrality required for our purposes.

(2) The word *choice* or a synonym of it, such as *decision* or *selection,* is used by typical proponents of natural freedom who deny that this freedom depends on favorable circumstances. But it is also used by some self-realization authors who hold that favorable circumstances are indispensable to freedom. A man is free, they claim, only when the circumstances under which he acts are such that he could have acted otherwise, had he wished to. Given such ambiguity of the word *choice* in the literature on freedom, the word scarcely serves to identify a freedom that some authors who employ it affirm and others deny. While we will have to use it in treating natural freedom, we will try to do so only in contexts that enable us to identify what is meant without ambiguity.

(3) Among authors who speak of free will, some have in mind the will's freedom from sin, injustice, or the passions. In their view a free will is possessed only by the man who has acquired the virtue that enables him to hold his desires in check, or by the man who has been saved from sin by God's grace, whereby he acquires the power to will as he ought. This use of the phrase *free will* clearly shows that what is being considered is not a freedom all men naturally possess but is rather that acquired freedom of self-perfection that only good men enjoy. Thus we see that the term *free will,* in addition to being objectionable to some of the authors who affirm a natural freedom that involves choice, is also ambiguous, for it is used with reference to an acquired as well as to a natural freedom by authors who affirm both. And it has the further ambiguity of being used, like *choice,* by authors who reject natural freedom entirely.

We must, therefore, find some term other than these to identify the freedom that a large group of authors attributes to anyone who is a man. The identifying designation must not only be wholly unobjectionable, in the sense of being without prejudice to the theory of any author in this group;* it must also be capable of conveying unambiguously a meaning that is distinctive of natural freedom. We propose to use *self-determination* for this purpose.

We think it has the requisite neutrality. While *self-determination* is not used by all the writers in this group, it is used by many of them. And it is used by them exclusively in connection with natural freedom and in a sense that contrasts sharply with the meaning of self-realization and self-perfection.

The power of self-determination is related by many authors to the freedom of self-perfection and to that of self-realization. A preliminary clarification of the meaning of self-determination may therefore be achieved by an effort to contrast this freedom with the other two.

Two texts, one from Aquinas and the other from John Dewey, will

---

* Besides those previously mentioned, the names of Aristotle, Epicurus and Lucretius, Pascal, Montesquieu, Edmund Burke, George Santayana, and Yves Simon should be added to the authors in this group.

help to make clear the distinction that is maintained by many authors between self-determination, on the one hand, and self-realization, on the other. Aquinas says:

> *In a man's activity two elements are to be found: (1) the choice of a course of action; and this is always in a man's power; and (2) the carrying out or execution of the course of action; and this is not always within a man's power. . . . Thus a man is not said to be free in his actions, but free in his choice.*[7]

According to Dewey, "Freedom does not consist in keeping up uninterrupted and unimpeded external activity."[8] In his view the absence of external impediments to action is only the negative side of freedom,

> *to be prized only as a means to [the positive] freedom which is power: power to frame purposes . . . power to select and order means to carry chosen ends into operation.*[9]

At the same time, Dewey insists that "this external and physical side of activity cannot be separated from [its] internal side . . . freedom of thought, desire, and purpose."[10] This raises for him "the essential problem of freedom . . . the problem of the relation of choice and unimpeded effective action to each other."[11] While the solution Dewey offers emphasizes "an intrinsic connection between choice as freedom and power of action as freedom," it also acknowledges that each of the two factors can be present by itself, and can contribute something to a man's freedom in spite of the absence of the other.

The significant point in the foregoing is that a man's determining what he is going to do precedes his doing of it, and therefore the freedom of decision can be examined quite apart from whether circumstances permit or prevent the carrying out of the decision. All of the authors here hold that the freedom that they think resides in making decisions remains the same in its character as freedom, whether or not the individual is circumstantially able to translate his decision into overt actions. With such freedom the individual, in their view, always has the ability to change himself by the decisions or plans he makes, even if, unable to put them into practice, he cannot affect anything else in the world.

In this respect, self-determination is sharply contrasted with self-realization.

In self-realization, that which I realize is some desire or wish of mine, and this is accomplished by the occurrence of whatever action it calls for. Such action I call "my own" precisely because it executes my own desire and is not, therefore, a movement I have been forced to make by someone or something other than myself. In self-determination, as contrasted with self-realization, that which I determine is myself alone; and this change in what I am is accomplished by whatever decisions or plans I make concerning what I shall do or shall become.

But what entitles me to call such decisions or plans "my own"? It is not enough that nothing outside of me compelled me to make them. They may still have been formed by processes occurring within me over which I exercise no control. In that case, emerging irresistibly out of my past, they would have been *in* and *for* me, but not *by* me. According to authors who attribute a freedom of self-determination to man, that freedom lies in his power to determine himself by decisions or plans he has himself determined by his control or mastery over the process by which they are formed.

So much for the difference between self-determination and self-realization. Let us turn now to the difference between self-determination and self-perfection. Authors who affirm both regard the first as an initial freedom, the good use of which issues in the second as a terminal freedom. Augustine's definition of virtue as the proper employment of our freedom refers to the use a virtuous man makes of his power to choose between good and evil. Through exercising his natural freedom in this way he acquires with virtue the freedom of being able to will as he ought. "It is . . . to reach this freedom of autonomy, this terminus of freedom," says Jacques Maritain, "that man is given freedom of choice." [12]

The same point is sometimes made in a different way. The freedom of self-perfection, it is said, presupposes the freedom of self-determination, for without the latter a man is not morally responsible for willing as he ought or failing to do so. Unless he has inherently the power to will as he wishes, that is, unless he can freely choose what he wills, his willing as he ought is as compulsory as the coerced movements of his body.

For most self-perfection authors there is no freedom in a man's obeying the moral law or doing his duty unless he does so willingly. They maintain that the obligations imposed by the moral law impose a moral necessity on him, which must be compatible with the possibility of disobedience as well as obedience on his part. They contrast the inviolable laws of nature, which, as statements of natural necessity, describe how things always or for the most part do behave ("what goes up must come down"), with moral rules, which, being violable, prescribe how free or self-determining agents ought to behave ("thou shalt not covet thy neighbor's wife"). The view they commonly hold is summarized by Immanuel Kant's assertion that *ought* implies *can* and *need not*.

There is, of course, a sense in which—as authors such as Aquinas, Descartes, and Maritain acknowledge—a man's external actions can be called free when, like the uncoerced and unconstrained movements of animals, they are voluntary without being chosen. But no author who affirms the freedoms of self-determination and self-perfection acknowledges any sense in which a man can be called free in living as he ought unless he does so willingly, that is, by choice or his own decision. It is not enough to be able to conform one's plan of life to moral rules or ethical ideals; one must also be able to make plans for one's own life, and the power of doing so must include the ability to make plans that do not conform as well as plans that do.

A more important difference is still to be mentioned. All authors who affirm both a freedom of self-determination and a freedom of self-realization think that the freedom that resides in making decisions remains the same in its character as freedom whether or not the individual is circumstantially able to translate his decisions into overt actions. Not so with authors who affirm both a freedom of self-determination and a freedom of self-perfection. Typically, they think that when a man is not able to will as he ought, his lack of the freedom of self-perfection alters the character of his freedom of self-determination. It becomes a defective freedom, circumscribed in scope and beset by a certain impotence. In the language of the Christian theologians, only the man of virtue, to whom grace has restored the full use of his natural powers, possesses the power of self-determination in all its pristine amplitude. In the language of other writers, only the man who, through wisdom or virtue, has acquired mastery of his own passions can attain the maximum freedom that the power of self-determination affords.

According to Augustine, "there is always within us a free will, but it is not always good." [13] According to Aquinas, "without grace free choice is incapable of the kind of good which is above human nature"—the good to which "man is led . . . by charity, which unites man's heart to God." However, Aquinas continues,

> *the kind of good which is proportioned to human nature . . . man can accomplish by his free choice. Augustine accordingly says that man can cultivate fields, build houses, and do a number of other things by his free choice without actual grace.*[14]

The free will remains a power, in short, whereby man can choose to will this or that, but while he remains in bondage to sin no choice he makes is of itself a good choice in the sense of being moved by the love of God and so ordered to the right end.

Other writers, such as Descartes, who do not distinguish between an initial freedom of self-determination and a terminal freedom of self-perfection, nevertheless hold that man achieves the highest degree of freedom in choice when he exercises his power of self-determination to choose that which attracts him most. "In order that I should be free," Descartes maintains,

> *it is not necessary that I should be indifferent as to the choice of one or the other of two contraries; but contrariwise the more I lean*

*to the one—whether I recognise clearly that the reasons of the good and true are to be found in it, or whether God so disposes my inward thought—the more freely do I choose and embrace it. And undoubtedly both divine grace and natural knowledge, far from diminishing my liberty, rather increase it and strengthen it.*[15]

Let us now try to get at this difference between self-determination and self-perfection in still another way. We have seen, in regard to the freedom of self-perfection, that the man who is able to will or live as he ought is one whose intentions or plan of life express his higher or better self.* When that part of his makeup dominates his lower nature, or is at least not thwarted by a kind of inner coercion or constraint that arises from forces within himself, what he ought to will becomes identical with what he himself (that is, his true or better self) desires to will. The law, duty, or ideal he conforms to no longer imposes an obligation that is antithetical to his freedom, for what it requires of him he is able to do willingly. Not compelled by another from without or within, what he wills springs from himself alone, and in that spontaneity he has his freedom. The moral law exerts compulsion or restraint only upon the alien forces within him, which represent the *other* opposed to his *true self*.

Now with regard to the freedom of self-determination, we have said that the decisions or plans a man makes are his own only if they are made *by* him, not just *in* him or *for* him. Even if nothing outside compelled him to make them, they are not initiated by him if their formation and adoption resulted from processes beyond his control. In order for his decisions or plans to be an instance of self-determination, they must be determined by himself, and by nothing other than himself.

But what is this *self* that is the principle of freedom, and what is the *other* that prevents self-determination? It is here that comparing self-perfection and self-determination affords us some insight into the latter.

In the case of self-perfection we found it necessary to acknowledge the division of the human being into a higher and a lower self, in order to perceive the self that is the principle of his freedom. When what a man wills issues from his true or ideal self, he is free because it stems from *him* and not from *the other*—not from the alien forces he harbors within him.

In the case of self-determination we find it necessary to distinguish the self that is at any moment of a man's life the active and creative source of his future from the passive self that is at any moment the deposit of the past he has already lived, or something evoked in him by forces working on him. The passive self thus, in a sense, represents the other— the things to which he reacts, the formations deposited by the past. When it determines his plans or decisions, it does so as the instrument of some-

---

* *See* Chapter 2, Section 1.

thing other than his present, active self. The active or creative self alone holds man's power of self-determination. The plans or decisions he makes through its agency are his own in a way that makes his adoption of them free.

\*     \*     \*     \*     \*

We have learned two things about the power of self-determination by isolating it from self-realization and self-perfection and by contrasting it with them.

The first is that the individual who exercises his power of self-determination *changes his self* by whatever decisions or plans he makes concerning what he shall do or shall become. That which is determined by freely made plans or decisions is the individual's own self. A changed self, in other words, is what is effected by the self-determining act.

What is presupposed here is that the self is determinable in a number of possible ways—that at the present moment its future holds the possibility of its becoming this or that. The plan adopted or the decision made, which is the self-determining act, determines that which is determinable in the self by causing it to become this rather than that.

The second thing we have learned concerns the self-determining act as a cause productive of such effects. Plans adopted or decisions made may determine the self in one way or another; but if a plan or decision, as a self-determining act, is not also self-determined, then it is not freely adopted or made in a sense that entitles the individual to call that plan or decision his own.

What must be excluded here are plans or decisions that result wholly from processes over which the individual does not exercise control. A plan or decision is self-determined as well as self-determining only if it does not emerge irresistibly out of the individual's past, or is not formed in him and for him by influences impinging on him at any moment. A plan or decision is made by the individual only if, at the moment it is adopted, its adoption is caused by the individual's active self, or by an active power that he possesses.

As we have seen, the word *active* in this statement means that the self-determining act is an independent and initiating cause, that is, a cause that, at the moment of producing this effect rather than that one, is not caused to do so by other causes antecedent to itself or other causes concurrent with it. Such other causes may be present and, taken all together, may be represented in what we have called the individual's passive self—the self that has been formed by the past life of the individual or is even at this moment being formed by influences currently impinging upon him.

According to authors who affirm man's inherent power of self-determination, the self-determining act is self-determined and so free, rather than other-determined and so unfree, only if all these other causes, whatever their influence, do not determine the individual to make this rather than that decision or adopt this rather than that plan. The particular decision or plan that, as an effect, creatively changes the self is actively caused by virtue of the power it has to cause a particular effect without being *caused* to cause that particular effect. Hence, in calling the free decision or freely adopted plan an act of self-determination, these authors are asserting three things: (1) that it is creatively self-determining in effect; (2) that it is actively self-determined as caused; and (3) that these two things are inseparably connected.*

## 10.  Issues concerning the freedom of self-determination: the shape of the controversy

In Chapter 1, Section 2 of Part I, we reviewed the arguments against the existence of the kind of freedom we have called the circumstantial freedom of self-realization on the part of authors who affirm the kind of freedom we have called the acquired freedom of self-perfection; and in Chapter 2, Section 4 of the same part we discussed the counterattack by the self-realization authors against the self-perfection position. In effect, what is involved in those disputes are questions about the existence of one or the other of these two forms of freedom, as well as about how they should be conceived. But those disputes and arguments are relatively simple as compared with the controversy about the natural freedom of self-determination, which will be treated in the remainder of this chapter.

Three things distinguish this subject from all others in the general controversy about freedom: first, the large number of authors who dispute the existence of natural self-determination or question its genuineness as a kind of freedom; second, the extent to which the literature affords evidence of actual debates or at least direct interchanges between authors who take explicit cognizance of each other's views and respond to each other's arguments; and, third, the fact that the differences of opinion are such that we must formulate at least four distinct issues, not just one, in this part of the controversy.

---

* The analysis of the discussion in the literature of freedom of the various modes of causality involved in this formulation of self-determination is actually a good deal more complicated than the formulation may suggest. There are many fine points, having to do with the theory of causation, with the intrinsic unpredictability of the free act as an element in the meaning of self-determination, with causal initiative or independence as an element in that meaning, and with creativity through choice as still another element in that meaning. Some of these fine points are adumbrated below, in our treatment of the issues about self-determination that arise in the literature of the subject. But for a more extensive treatment of the points, in themselves rather than in the context of the issues, the interested reader should refer to *The Idea of Freedom*, Vol. 1, chaps. 21–25, pp. 423–583.

What is traditionally called "the problem of free will" concerns questions about the existence or genuineness of natural self-determination as a kind of freedom. In the extensive literature on freedom, these are the questions that loom largest and that have received the greatest attention, especially in the last three hundred years. The number of authors who deny natural self-determination, either on existential or on conceptual grounds or on both, matches, if it does not exceed, the number of those who affirm this freedom. In almost every case, that denial is explicit. The writers who take a negative stand do so plainly, taking cognizance of the subject in question and addressing themselves to the disputed questions about it. In addition, they usually give us some indication of their reasons and often advance fairly elaborate arguments.

In neither of the issues concerning the freedoms of circumstantial self-realization or acquired self-perfection do we find instances of direct confrontation on the part of writers whom we have construed as joining issue. In a few instances, it is true, some of the authors on the negative side mention by name adherents of the position they oppose. But in no instance do these writers respond directly to the attack or engage in any interchange with their opponents. It is only in regard to natural self-determination that we can report a number of actual disputes in the form of written interchanges between writers who take opposite sides of one or another of the issues in the general controversy about this freedom. To name only the most prominent instances of this sort, there are the Hobbes-Bramhall dispute in the seventeenth century, the Priestley-Price dispute in the eighteenth century, the interchange in the nineteenth century between Mansel and Mill occasioned by Mill's critique of Sir William Hamilton's views, and several disputes of greater or lesser fame in recent years.*

We will treat the four issues in the controversy about natural self-determination in the remainder of this chapter. The first two issues will be discussed in this section. A third issue, concerning the theological dimension of the problem, will be treated in Section 11. And Section 12 will deal with a possible conceptual issue about the relation of chance, responsibility, and freedom.

### Summary of topical agreement

Before embarking on this task, let us attempt to summarize what we have learned about the understanding of self-determination that is shared by authors who affirm man's possession of such freedom. They consider it, as we have already suggested, to be "a freedom that is possessed by all human beings, in virtue of a power inherent in human nature, whereby a man

---

* The reader who is especially interested in the above mentioned disputes, as well as others in this controversy, for their own sake, should refer to *The Idea of Freedom*, Vol. 2, chaps. 8–10, pp. 223–463.

is able to change his own character creatively by deciding what he shall do or shall become."

It should be emphasized that "being able to change one's own character creatively by deciding for one's self what one shall do or shall become" expresses the topical agreement about self-determination only when at least two of the following three points are affirmed:

> (1) that the decision is *intrinsically unpredictable,*
> that is, given perfect knowledge of all relevant causes, the decision cannot be foreseen or predicted with certitude;
> (2) that the decision is *not necessitated,*
> that is, the decision is always one of a number of alternate possible decisions any one of which it was simultaneously within the power of the self to cause, no matter what other antecedent or concurrent factors exercise a causal influence on the making of the decision;
> (3) that the decision flows from the *causal initiative of the self,*
> that is, on the plane of natural or finite causes, the self is the uncaused cause of the decision it makes.

These three points, as we will see, generate three distinct existential issues about man's natural freedom of self-determination. Writers who deny (3) that there are any uncaused causes on the plane of natural or finite causes deny, in consequence, the existence of a freedom the conception of which posits such causes. Writers who deny (2) that an effect can be caused in a manner that does not necessitate it deny, in consequence, the existence of a freedom the conception of which attributes to the self the power of causing but not necessitating the decisions it makes. The existence of self-determination is also denied by writers who claim (1) that God's omniscience excludes a freedom the conception of which involves the intrinsic unpredictability of decisions that are the product of man's power of self-determination.

As we have already pointed out, if a conception of freedom presupposes certain things, and if the existence of these is questioned, then an existential issue is raised about the freedom itself.

For example, in the case of the acquired freedom of self-perfection, we saw that, on the one hand, those who affirm such freedom presuppose the existence of a number of things, while, on the other hand, those who deny the validity of these presuppositions (that is, those who deny the existence of the things presupposed) consequently deny that the conception that involves these things has any reality corresponding to it. The root of the disagreement about the reality of the freedom of self-perfection is thus a disagreement about something else, such as the existence of moral obligations binding on all men. The existence of such universally binding obligations being presupposed by the conception of a freedom of self-perfection, those who take opposite sides on the question of the reality of such freedom do so in virtue of taking opposite sides about the existence of that which is presupposed. The complex question that covers both points may be phrased as follows: "Is there any reality corresponding to a conception of freedom, such as that of self-perfection, that presupposes the existence of moral obligations binding on all men?"

Of the three existential issues about self-determination, the two principal ones—which will be dealt with in this section—take the same form as the existential issue about self-perfection to which we have just referred. In the first of these, the presupposition being questioned is causal initiative; in the second, it is causal indeterminacy. The third existential issue, which involves intrinsic unpredictability, takes a somewhat different form and will be dealt with in Section 11 of this chapter.

## 10a.  The existential issue concerning causal initiative

The question at issue can be formulated in a number of ways: If the existence of a freedom of self-determination for man depends upon his having causal initiative, does man really have such freedom? Or, if the conception of a freedom of self-determination involves causal initiative, and if the existence of such a freedom depends upon the existence of causal initiative on man's part, does such freedom exist? Or, is there any reality corresponding to a conception of freedom, such as that of self-determination, that presupposes the existence of causal initiative on man's part?

Of these the last, which is not hypothetical, may be preferred for that reason. It clearly focuses the issue on the validity of the existential presupposition—causal initiative. Writers who are in topical agreement about the meaning of this presupposition but disagree about its validity also disagree about the existence of a freedom of self-determination in human life. They come into disagreement in the following manner.

Taking the affirmative side of the issue are authors who hold conceptions of self-determination that involve causal initiative on man's part. They acknowledge that their affirmation of self-determination presupposes the existence of causal initiative. But they assert the validity of this presupposition, and, therefore, they assert the reality of man's power of self-determination, as they conceive it.

Taking the negative side of this issue are authors who address themselves to conceptions of self-determination that involve causal initiative on man's part. They recognize that the existence of self-determination as thus conceived presupposes the existence of causal initiative. But they deny the validity of this presupposition, and, therefore, they deny the reality of man's power of self-determination, as conceived by most of its adherents.

Among the authors who take the affirmative side of this issue are Bishop Bramhall, Joseph Price, Henry Mansel, and William James; while the negative side is supported by, among others, Thomas Hobbes,

David Hume, Joseph Priestley, Jonathan Edwards, John Stuart Mill, and
T. H. Huxley.*

Since the issue is raised, in the first place, by the denial of causal initiative, it is appropriate to begin by considering the arguments advanced
on the negative side. These fall into two main types, one more general
than the other. The more general attack appeals to the universal principle
of causation and argues that there can be no exception to it in the sphere
of human action; that is, in human action, as in all other natural
phenomena, there can be no effect without a cause and no cause that is
not also the effect of some prior cause. The less general attack, based on
a causal analysis of volition itself, argues that a man's character and his
motives cause the decisions he makes, and that these causes are themselves
all effects of other causes, which were operative in the past or are now
operative in the present.

To these attacks the defenders of causal initiative respond by calling
attention to their reasons for thinking that both fail. It is important to
observe that the reasons given are, for the most part, to be found in the
theories of man's freedom of self-determination that they propound, quite
apart from any exigency to defend causal initiative against such attacks.
They are not, in other words, invented ad hoc. Rather it is as if the
defenders of self-determination were saying to their opponents: "If you
will examine the things we have said to explain and support our assertion
of causal initiative, you will see why we think your arguments fail. To
make them effective, you must deal with the grounds on which our
assertion rests, not just with the assertion itself."

Many of the authors on the negative side of the issue do attack the
grounds on which certain defenders of self-determination claim to rest
their case. They, too, can be interpreted as saying to their opponents:
"We have not overlooked the things you posit as the basis for your
assertion of causal initiative; but our position remains the same, for we
deny the reality of what you posit, and so we continue to deny the causal
initiative that you think can thus be supported or defended."

Those who base their denial of causal initiative on the principle of
causation regard this principle as stating a universal truth to which there
is no exception. In their view, the exponents of causal initiative appear to
claim that, in human behavior, the self or the will acts in a way that
would constitute an exception to the universality of the causal principle.
Hence, they argue, that claim cannot be sustained.

Their arguments are of two kinds, according to the manner in which
the principle of causation is formulated.

---

* Much more extensive lists of authors on the two sides will be found in *The Idea of
Freedom,* Vol. 2, pp. 257–58.

One formulation of it is that nothing moves itself to action; that is, everything that acts does so only as a result of being acted upon by something else. But the exponents of causal initiative claim that the self or the will moves itself to action, that is, that it acts without being acted upon. Since this claim violates the principle, it must be false.

The other formulation of the principle is that there is no effect without a cause, and no cause that is not itself the effect of some antecedent cause. The chain of causes has no first link. Nothing happens without a cause of its happening or coming to be. But the exponents of causal initiative claim that man's volitions constitute a break in the chain of causes, positing here either an uncaused cause or a cause that is not the effect of any antecedent cause. Since this claim violates the principle, it must be false.

The formulations are alike in several respects but differ in one significant respect. The first seems to admit that the stream of causes involves substantive beings (that is, enduring entities or continuing existences, such as a man, his self, or his will) that both act and are acted upon; it simply denies that any such beings act without being acted upon. The second seems to recognize no continuing existences, but only events or occurrences, and puts volitions into the stream of events, regarding them as effects of prior events and as causes of subsequent ones.

The second way of formulating the principle of causation is best exemplified by Hobbes, and is found in most of the writers who follow him, or who are influenced by him. The first way of formulating the principle is an earlier one and is no longer much used. However, in responding to these arguments based on the universal principle of causation, formulated in either way, the defenders of causal initiative adopt, for the most part, that view of the causal nexus that involves enduring beings or their powers.

A few examples of the negative view will suggest what the position is. In *The Questions Concerning Liberty, Necessity, and Chance, Clearly Stated and Debated between Dr. Bramhall, Bishop of Derry, and Thomas Hobbes of Malmesbury,* Hobbes declares it to be a universal principle of change that "nothing taketh beginning from itself, but from the action of some other immediate agent without itself." This, he says, applies to the action of the will as to everything else: like everything else, the will is "caused by other things whereof it disposeth not." [16] Furthermore, Hobbes points out, it is not only impossible to imagine anything happening, or beginning to be, without a cause, but even if we could imagine a happening without a cause, we could not answer the question why it should occur at one time rather than another.[17]

Jonathan Edwards argues in the same vein against the Arminians, whose doctrine he interprets as maintaining that "the faculty or power of will, or the soul in the use of that power, determines its own volitions; and that it does it without any act going before the act determined." [18]

He insists, however, that "if the particular act or exertion of will, which comes into existence, be anything properly determined at all, then it has some cause of its existing . . . which cause is distinct from the effect, and prior to it." [19] Hence, he concludes, that cause cannot be "the will exercising a sovereign power over itself, to determine, cause and excite volitions in itself." [20]

The scientist T. H. Huxley puts the argument in somewhat more familiar terms. "We are conscious automata," he asserts,

> *endowed with free will in the only intelligible sense of that much-abused term—inasmuch as in many respects we are able to do as we like—but none the less parts of the great series of causes and effects which, in unbroken continuity, composes that which is, and has been, and shall be—the sum of existence.* [21]

Finally, the form in which Hume states the argument can be summarized as follows. Necessity (that is, the necessitation of the effect by the cause), according to Hume, is by definition an essential aspect of causation. But liberty (that is, a free choice between alternative decisions or volitions) is, again by definition, incompatible with necessity. Consequently, it is also incompatible with causation. Liberty, in his view, is thus reduced to causelessness which, he maintains, "is the very same thing with chance." But, "as chance is commonly thought to imply a contradiction, and is at least directly contrary to experience, there are always the same arguments against liberty or free-will." [22]

Now what are the answers to these attacks on the existence of self-determination?

To Hobbes's remark that "nothing taketh beginning from itself, but from the action of some other immediate agent without itself," Bishop Bramhall responds by making two distinctions.

(1) If Hobbes is talking about the will as a faculty or power of the human soul, then Bramhall thinks he would be right to say that the will does not take its "beginning from itself, but from God, who created and infused the soul into man and endowed it with its power." If, however, in distinction from the will as a faculty, Hobbes used the word *will* to refer to the act of willing, then Bramhall thinks it is also right to say that "it takes not beginning from itself, but from the faculty or from the power of willing." [23]

(2) Bramhall then distinguishes between two possible meanings for "taking a beginning." One is "a beginning of being"; the other, "a beginning of working and acting." If Hobbes means the first, then, according to Bramhall, he is quite right to say that nothing—at least nothing on earth—has the beginning of its being or existence from itself. But if Hobbes means the second, then Bramhall thinks he is wrong, since the question then concerns the act of willing, not the faculty or power of the will; for since one and the same thing can be both mover and moved in

different respects, the active power of the will can be assigned as the cause of particular acts on the part of the will.[24]

Finally, Bramhall takes up the question that Hobbes had propounded for him: "How can a man imagine anything to begin without a cause, or if it should begin without a cause, why it should begin at this time rather than at that time?" Agreeing with Hobbes that nothing can begin *to be* without a cause, Bramhall nevertheless reiterates that the will can "*begin to act* of itself without any other cause." And, he continues, since the will is a free cause, in virtue of having the power to cause its own acts, it also has the power to choose the time when it will act, in contrast to a determined cause, which is not only determined to act by extrinsic causes but is also determined by them *when* to act.[25]

The English philosopher Joseph Rickaby outlined the response to the attacks of such writers as Hobbes, Hume, and Mill in a book called *Free Will and Four English Philosophers,* published in 1906. The response is worth reporting because it has been followed by other defenders of the freedom of self-determination. The trouble with Hobbes, Hume, and Mill, together with others such as Huxley, Rickaby charges, is that they ignore the difference between the types of causes that operate in the spheres of material and mental phenomena. "As men blinded by physics to everything above the physical and material order," Rickaby writes, "they ignore a vital difference between beings *conscious of the ego* and beings totally *unconscious,* between *persons* in fact and *things*." [26] Excluding all causes except those of the physical type, they make, in Rickaby's view, the simple error of converting the statement that volitions are not caused in this way into the statement that volitions are uncaused. Speaking specifically of Mill, Rickaby has this to say:

> *I reject, equally with Mill, "the hypothesis of spontaneousness."*
> *. . . That is to say, I do not believe an act of the will to come out*
> *of nothing, a causeless phenomenon. I hold that the person who*
> *wills causes his own volition, under certain motives as conditions.*
> *To Mill the person is nobody; that is why he would call a free*
> *act "spontaneous," meaning that it has no cause.*

It *is* caused, Rickaby insists, but not "in Mill's sense of the term," nor can the same kind of explanation be found for volitions "as for physical events." [27]

One point that is implicit in this criticism of Mill, Rickaby makes explicit in his criticisms of Hobbes and Hume. Not only do these writers ignore the difference between physical and mental causes but, in his view, they also misconceive the nature of causes, physical as well as mental. They reduce causes and effects to antecedent and consequent events in the sequence of phenomena, excluding substantial existences, whether persons or things. But, according to Rickaby, changes take place in enduring substances, and are caused by the action of other substances on them, as in the case of the motions of inert things, or by the subject of the change itself, as in the case of the free actions of persons. In the latter case, the principle of causation, correctly understood, is not violated by the statement that nothing outside the will of a voluntary agent—no antecedent event or extrinsic thing—is the cause of volitions.[28]

As we pointed out above, the arguments advanced on the negative side of the issue about causal initiative fall into two main types, one more general than the other. We have just considered the more general type of attack.\* It rests its denial of causal initiative on the universal principle of causation, arguing that, in human behavior as in everything else, there is no cause that is not itself an effect. We turn now to the less general type of attack. It focuses more narrowly on the psychological process of volition; and from the account it gives of how human volitions are actually caused, it argues against any causal initiative on man's part.

The argument runs as follows. A man's motives, purposes, or desires are the proximate, efficient causes of his volitions. But these in turn spring from his character in its reaction to present circumstances. How a man is motivated to act in any particular situation is causally determined by how his character reacts to the alternatives afforded him; and, should conflicting motives arise, the one most consistent with his character will predominate and determine what he wills to do. His character is itself the product of causes that go back to his inherited traits and dispositions and to the shaping influences upon them of the circumstances of his life. The motive that causes the volition of this moment is merely the last link in the chain of causes that stretches back into the individual's past. Unable to interrupt that chain of causes at any point or to act against his character, such as it is at the moment, the individual has no causal initiative, that is, he has no power to cause a volition in a way that makes a causal break with his past.

This argument against causal initiative is presented in its most typical form by Joseph Priestley in his dispute with Dr. Price, in the eighteenth century. It is in this form that it is most frequently repeated by other writers.

According to Priestley, a man's volitions are caused by his state of mind and the view he takes of things. The latter, says Priestley, "is generally called the motive." "In no case whatever," he contends, "can the mind be determined to action, i.e., to a volition without something that may as well be called a motive as be expressed in any other manner. . . . For, exclusive of what necessarily comes under the description either of motive, or state of mind, the mind itself can no more be the cause of its

---

\* The discussion of this attack, and of the answers to it, could be much more complex, and is so in *The Idea of Freedom*, Vol. 2, pp. 258–87.

own determination, than the beam of a balance can be the cause of its own inclination." [29] Elsewhere, Priestley speaks of "the previous disposition of the mind," together with the individual's present "view of the objects" that elicit his action, as being the two factors that causally determine his volitions.[30] Summing both factors up under the term *motives,* he concludes that "motives [are] the proper causes of volitions and actions. . . . All volitions and actions are preceded by corresponding motives." [31]

In replying to Priestley, Dr. Price offers typical counterarguments on this question. He insists that motives are only "the *occasions* of our putting ourselves into motion." In his view, nothing could be "more absurd than to say that our inclinations act upon us, and compel us, that our desires and fears put us into motion, or produce our volitions, i.e., are agents." It is ourselves who are agents, through the active self-moving power that we have to be the cause (that is, the efficient cause) of our own volitions.[32]

In somewhat different terms, William James also denies that motives or reasons are by themselves the causes of voluntary actions. Rather it is the effort of attention, which James identifies with willpower, that makes one motive prevail over another. "The essential achievement of the will," he says, "is to *attend* to a difficult object and hold it fast before the mind." [33] By holding "some one ideal object, or part of an object, a little longer or a little more intensely before the mind," we give what James calls "our voluntary fiat" to one "amongst the alternatives which present themselves as *genuine possibles*," and make that one effective.[34] Hence, the cause of the voluntary act is not the predominating object or motive but the energy of the will, that is, its power to attend to some object or motive and make it predominate. It is this energy or willpower that James regards as a cause that is not an effect.[35]

## 10b. The existential issue concerning causal indeterminacy

The issue to be treated here closely resembles the one that was just treated. Both issues turn on a question about causation, or, more strictly, a question about the character and operation of causes in the sphere of human behavior.

Though both issues turn on questions of causation, there is a significant difference between the questions in the two cases. This can be indicated in the following manner.

Let the effect with which we are concerned in both cases be represented by a particular act, which we will call "volition A." Let us consider the self or the will as the cause of the act that is volition A. The issue about causal initiative is then raised by the question whether, in causing volition A, the self or will is itself uncaused. In contrast, the issue about causal indeterminacy is raised by the question whether, given the very same conditions under which it caused volition A, the self or will could have caused other effects, let us say, volition B, volition C, and so forth.

In the one case, the question is about the power of a cause to produce a single effect without being caused to do so; in the other case, the question is about the power of a cause to produce any one of two or more effects under identical conditions. In both cases, we are confronted by the relation between a cause and an effect; but in the one case, we ask about other *causes*—that is, whether or not the cause is itself caused and in the other, we ask about other *effects*—whether or not this particular effect is the only one that could have been produced by the cause under the given conditions.

The writers who deny causal indeterminacy say in effect that, given the conditions under which volition A is caused, no other volition could have been produced by the self or will. The very opposite is said by the writers who affirm causal indeterminacy; and they in effect go on to say that it is precisely because the self or will can, under identical conditions, produce either volition A or volition B that they attribute to it the power of free choice. The issue about causal indeterminacy can, therefore, be briefly stated in the question: "Does man have the power of free choice in the sense just indicated?"

A large number of authors may be found on each side of the issue. Of particular interest to us here are, on the affirmative side of the issue (holding that man does have free choice in the sense indicated):

|                |                |
| -------------- | -------------- |
| AQUINAS        | MARITAIN       |
| BERGSON        | PRICE          |
| KANT           | SIMON          |

Of particular interest on the negative side are:

|                |                |
| -------------- | -------------- |
| HOBBES         | PRIESTLEY      |
| HUME           | SCHOPENHAUER   |
| J. S. MILL     | SPINOZA*       |
| NIETZSCHE      |                |

In the view of those whose theories of causation lead them to deny that man has a power of free choice, the causal indeterminacy required for free choice is self-contradictory and, therefore, impossible. In their view, to cause is to determine; that which is caused is causally determined; and, consequently, it is impossible for something to cause without determining an effect, or for something to be an effect without being causally determined.

Many of the writers who hold this view also regard the relation of cause and effect as a necessary connection. That which is caused is also

---

* More extensive lists of authors on the two sides will be found in *The Idea of Freedom,* Vol. 2, pp. 335–36.

necessitated in the sense that, given the efficacious operation of the cause, the effect cannot fail to occur, nor can anything other than this one effect occur as a result of the cause's efficacious operation. To say that a cause necessitates its effect is to say that it produces, results in, or leads to one and only one effect.

Furthermore, those who regard the relation of cause and effect as a necessary connection also identify determinacy with necessity. In their view, to cause an effect, to necessitate it, and to determine it are all one. Being a necessary connection, the causal connection is also a determinate relation, that is, a relation of one cause, or one set of causal factors, to one effect. "Causal necessity" and "causal determinacy" are thus synonymous.

To those who hold the foregoing theory of causation, the name *necessitarians* was once applied; more recently, with equal appropriateness, they have been called *determinists*. Their opponents, in turn, have been called *indeterminists* and *libertarians,* usually without any differentiation in the connotation of the names.

The situation is actually somewhat more complicated than these names suggest. For the purposes of this summary of the discussion of the issue, we will use three names—*determinist, libertarian,* and *causal indeterminist*—as labels for upholders of positions that are distinguishable in the discussion. The positions are as follows:

I. The position of the determinist, who takes the negative side in this dispute concerning the existence of a freedom of self-determination that involves causal indeterminacy.

   A. Nothing happens by chance; which is to say, nothing is causally undetermined. If anything is undetermined, it is not caused; if it is caused, it is not undetermined.

   *Note:* Some determinists admit that an effect may be produced by a composition of independent causes, but they do not regard this as indeterminacy or contingency.

   B. Whatever happens is caused and, as causally determined, is necessitated; the cause-effect relation is determinately a one-one relation; that is, given one and the same cause, or set of composite causes, one and the same effect always results or follows.

II. The position of the libertarian, who takes the affirmative in this dispute.

   A. Nothing happens by chance, in the sense of *chance* indicated in I. A, above.

   B. Not everything that is caused is causally determined or necessitated. The same cause does not always have the same effect (for some causes are superabundant).

   1. Some things are causally determined or necessitated, in the sense of causal determination or causal necessity indicated in I. B, above.

2. But there are also instances of causation that involve causal indeterminacy in the sense that the cause-effect relation is indeterminate; that is, it is a one-many relation such that, given one and the same cause, or set of causes, any one of a number of alternative effects may result or follow.

III. The position of the causal indeterminist, who takes the affirmative side in this dispute.

A. Nothing happens by chance, in the sense of *chance* indicated in I. A, above.

B. Nothing that is caused is causally determined or necessitated, as the determinist asserts in I. B, above. No cause-effect relation is determinately a one-one relation.

C. Causal indeterminacy is universal; that is, in every instance in which a given cause or set of causes is efficaciously operative, it is able to produce any one of a number of alternative effects.

The foregoing summary omits any reference to the position of the extreme indeterminist who asserts that some things happen by chance (in the sense of a total absence of causes). Since the libertarian and the causal indeterminist agree with the determinist in rejecting this extreme position, it is not really relevant to the dispute, even though some determinists interpret the causal indeterminacy upheld by their opponents as being the same as the indeterminacy of chance.*

The arguments against causal indeterminacy, which claim that it is inconsistent with the principle of causation, all employ the same fundamental premise. The premise asserts the identity of being caused with being causally determined and causally necessitated. When the premise is combined with the assertion that whatever happens is caused, the conclusion follows that nothing can be causally indeterminate.

This fundamental premise is expressed in three slightly different ways. (1) It is said that a sufficient cause, by virtue of its being a sufficient cause, cannot fail to produce its effect. (2) It is said that it is in the very nature of a cause, when operative, to necessitate its effect. (3) It is said that, given the same cause, or set of causes, the same effect always follows. The first expression is found in the works of Hobbes, who writes:

> *I hold that to be a sufficient cause, to which nothing is wanting that is needful to the producing of the effect. The same is also a necessary cause: for if it be possible that sufficient cause shall not bring forth the effect, then there wanted somewhat which was needful to the producing of it; and so the cause was not sufficient.*

---

* For an examination of this charge, *see* Section 12, below.

> *But if it be impossible that a sufficient cause should not produce the effect, then is a sufficient cause a necessary cause; for that is said to produce an effect necessarily, that cannot but produce it. Hence it is manifest, that whatsoever is produced . . . hath had a sufficient cause to produce it, or else it had not been. And therefore, also voluntary actions are necessitated.*[36]

For Spinoza, as for Hobbes, the attribution of contingency to things is an expression of our ignorance, not of anything real in the order of nature. "A thing can in no respect be called contingent," he writes, "save in relation to the imperfection of our knowledge." [37] In reality, everything that exists or happens is conditioned by causes, proximate or ultimate, and whatever is caused is thereby necessitated. Only the infinite substance of God is unconditioned or uncaused, but even God exists from and acts by the necessity of his own nature. This applies to the will as it does to everything else: the will is a necessary cause, not a free cause, both in the case of God and in the case of man. However, Spinoza does distinguish between the "free necessity" with which God acts (that is, the necessity of his own nature) and the "constrained necessity" with which all other things act (that is, their necessitation by extrinsic causes).[38]

For Hume, also, necessitation is inseparable from causation. "According to my definitions," he says, "necessity makes an essential part of causation; and consequently liberty, by removing necessity, removes also causes, and is the very same thing with chance." [39] Whether the actions are those of matter or mind, they are links in a chain of necessary causes and effects. In neither case does anything happen except as it is necessarily determined to happen by its causes.

If, according to Hume, the doctrine of liberty (that is, of the freedom of the will) involves the will's exemption from necessity in its acts of choice, then such liberty is as nonexistent as chance. He writes:

> *It is universally allowed that nothing exists without a cause of its existence, and that chance, when strictly examined, is a mere negative word, and means not any real power which has anywhere a being in nature. But it is pretended that some causes are necessary, some not necessary. Here then is the advantage of definitions. Let anyone* define *a cause, without comprehending, as a part of the definition, a* necessary connexion *with its effect; and let him show distinctly the origin of the idea expressed by the definition; and I shall readily give up the whole controversy.*

However, Hume continues, "if the definition above mentioned be admitted, liberty, when opposed to necessity, not to constraint, is the same thing with chance; which is universally allowed to have no existence." [40]

That the same causes always produce the same effects is a corollary of the proposition that the relation between causes and effects is a necessary connection. Once we recognize, says Joseph Priestley, that "throughout all nature, the same consequences . . . result from the same circumstances," we realize that "no event could be otherwise than as it has been, is, or is to be." [41] He goes on to argue that, given the same circumstances and the same state of mind, a man would always, voluntarily, make the same choice and come to the same determination. Arthur Schopenhauer makes the same point, in asserting that

> *every man, being what he is and placed in the circumstances which for the moment obtain, but which on their part also arise by strict necessity, can absolutely never do anything else than just what at that moment he does do. Accordingly, the whole course of a man's life, in all its incidents great and small, is as necessarily predetermined as the course of a clock.* [42]

And John Stuart Mill makes the same point, too, in his discussion of Sir William Hamilton's discourses on the freedom of the will. "When we think of ourselves," Mill says,

> *hypothetically as having acted otherwise than we did, we always suppose a difference in the antecedents: we picture ourselves as having known something that we did not know, or not knowing something that we did know; which is a difference in the external inducements; or as having desired something, or disliked something, more or less than we did; which is a difference in the internal inducements.* [43]

Finally, we may mention Nietzsche, whose argument against causal indeterminacy is somewhat different from those we have already considered. It is different because Nietzsche denies causal necessity or causal determinism, rejecting what he calls "the mechanical interpretation of the world," based on the notions of cause and effect, as misleading.[44] But although he is thus opposed to what he calls the "non-free will" doctrine of causal determinism, he is equally opposed to what he calls "the crass stupidity of the celebrated conception of 'free will.' " [45] His reason for rejecting the indeterminacy of free choice—that is, for denying that anything could have ever acted otherwise than it did—lies in his view that everything is absolutely necessitated, not by its causes, but by its own nature.

"There are no laws," Nietzsche declares; "every power draws its last consequence at every moment. Things are calculable precisely owing to the fact that there is no possibility of their being otherwise than they are." [46] Elsewhere he writes:

> *The fact that something always happens thus or thus, is interpreted . . . as if a creature always acted thus or thus as the result of obedience to a law or a law-giver: whereas apart from the "law"*

261

> *it would be free to act differently. But precisely that inability to act otherwise might originate in the creature itself, it might be that it did not act thus or thus in response to a law, but simply because it was so constituted. It would mean simply: that something cannot also be something else; that it cannot be first this, and then something quite different; thus it is neither free nor the reverse, but merely thus or thus.*[47]

Though it is based on a necessity that is rooted in the nature of things rather than in the relation of cause and effect, Nietzsche's argument against the indeterminacy of free choice has an obvious affinity with the arguments that are based on the affirmation of causal necessity.

Let us turn now to the other side of the issue. As we have already pointed out, the exponents of causal indeterminacy uphold the principle of causation as universally true. Like their adversaries, they also deny that anything happens without a cause. But unlike their adversaries, they deny that every effect is causally determined or necessitated in the sense that, given the operation of the cause, the effect could not have been otherwise. Their arguments for causal indeterminacy are therefore based on theories of causation that differ in certain fundamental respects from the principle of causation as that is understood by their opponents. But they also differ among themselves with regard to the theory of causation.

Some of the exponents of causal indeterminacy affirm that it exists either exclusively or preeminently in human acts of choice, affirming also that causal necessity exists in nature. Other exponents of causal indeterminacy affirm that it obtains in every relation of cause and effect, denying that causal necessity exists anywhere in nature. Accordingly, there are two main types of arguments for causal indeterminacy. These include not only reasons for rejecting the position of the causal determinist but also, at least in some cases, replies to the arguments advanced by the determinists.

For example, replying to an argument similar to that of Hobbes, as outlined above—although of course advanced some five centuries earlier —Aquinas denies that a sufficient cause always necessitates its effect. He does not say that sufficient causes never operate with necessity but only that "not every cause brings its effect about by necessity, even though it is a sufficient cause." [48] In other words, it is possible for a cause to be sufficient for the production of its effect, and yet fail under certain circumstances to produce that effect.

The conditions he has in mind are those in which some impediment occurs to interfere with the operation of the cause in question; as, for instance, when sunlight, oxygen, soil nutriment, and so forth, the set of causes sufficient for plant growth, are present and operative on a plant, but an insect blight prevents the plant from growing. Here the set of factors mentioned remains, in Aquinas's opinion, a sufficient cause, even though it does not always necessarily result in plant growth. The impediment is an accidental and extraneous condition; it is no part of the total cause of plant growth. Hence, it can be said that a sufficient cause (or a set of causes that is sufficient to produce a particular effect) necessarily produces that effect in the absence of extraneous and accidental conditions that would operate to prevent it from doing so, but it cannot be said that a sufficient cause always operates with necessity.

Aquinas summarizes this argument by saying that natural causes do not always produce their effects by necessity, although they do so for the most part, the exceptions being the few times when they are impeded. This means that, in the realm of natural phenomena, there are many effects that necessarily result from the operation of causes, but there are also some effects that are contingent, in the sense of being the result of an accidental conjunction of natural causes without impeding conditions.

This argument is also advanced by Bishop Bramhall in his dispute with Hobbes in the seventeenth century. But Hobbes dismisses it, as he doubtless would have dismissed the same argument by Aquinas, on the grounds that the argument violates the meaning of sufficient cause. "A sufficient cause," he reiterates, is "that cause to which nothing is wanting needful to the producing of the effect." [49] If something is wanting, then the causal factors that are present do not constitute a sufficient cause; since they are not what Hobbes calls the "entire cause" of the given effect, but only part of it, they cannot be its sufficient cause. When all the conditions "needful to the producing of the effect" are present and operative, the effect cannot fail to occur.

The dispute between Hobbes, on the one hand, and Aquinas and Bramhall, on the other, turns on the definition of a sufficient cause. Hobbes applies his definition not only to natural phenomena but also to voluntary actions. Among the things needful to produce the effect, in the case of voluntary acts, Hobbes includes the will to do it, along with all the other causes that dispose the will to this particular decision. And he dismisses as nonsense the supposition that, all the other causes being present, the will retains the power not to will this particular decision, or to will some other. Referring to statements by Bramhall, he says:

> *These words, "the will hath the power to forbear willing what it doth will"; and these, "the will hath a dominion over its own acts"; and these, "the power to will is present* in actu primo, *determinable by ourselves"; are as wild as ever were any spoken within the walls of Bedlam: and if science, conscience, reason, and religion teach us to speak thus, they make us mad.*[50]

263

However, from the point of view of Aquinas and Bramhall, the acceptance of Hobbes's definition of a sufficient cause does not foreclose all further questions about liberty and necessity. Even if they were to concede that, in the action of all things other than man, every effect is necessitated by its causes and nothing ever happens contingently or by chance, they would still maintain that the human will is one outstanding exception to the reign of causal necessity. What they assert is that the will is a free rather than a necessary cause, and that its freedom consists in two respects in which it can operate with causal indeterminacy. (1) Confronted in this life with any object to be willed, a man is able either to will it or not will it. This "freedom of choice," as it is called, means that the action or inaction of the will is never necessitated. (2) Confronted by alternative objects, between which a choice is to be made, a man, if he wills at all, is able to will either one; or, to put it another way, if under the given conditions he chooses this one, then, under the same conditions, he could have chosen the other. This "freedom of specification," as it is called, means that no particular choice that is willed is ever necessitated.

Assertion is one thing, argument another. The argument is provided by Aquinas, if not by Bramhall. It is to be found compactly stated in the main body of the article in his *De Malo* to which is attached Aquinas's reply to the objection based on the definition of a sufficient cause, which the objector draws from Avicenna and which is the same one that Hobbes later employs. In the last sentence of his reply, Aquinas turns from talking about other causes to the consideration of the causes of volitions. He writes:

> *A cause, therefore, which makes the will will anything need not do this by necessity; because through the will itself an impediment can be set up, either by removing such consideration as leads to its willing, or by considering the opposite, namely, that which is proposed as good is not good in a certain respect.*[51]

This sentence refers to the point already made about impediments to sufficient causes. But it also refers to points made in the main body of the article, where the argument for the will's causal indeterminacy is stated quite apart from any comment on the operation of sufficient causes, with or without impediment. There, the will's exemption from causal necessity is not attributed to the contingency of accidental conditions but to an indeterminacy that is inherent in the very nature of the will as a cause. It is this indeterminacy that makes the will more, not less, than a sufficient cause.

According to Aquinas, the indeterminacy of the will—its power to act or not act, and, when acting, to choose this or that—lies in two things. The first is that the will, as an active power, moves itself so far as its exercise is concerned. The will is the efficient cause of its own action.

But when a man wills this or that, the objects to which he voluntarily directs himself are apprehended not by the will but by the intellect or reason. Here, so far as the object specifying its act is concerned, the will is moved not by itself but by the reason, but in the manner of a formal, not an efficient cause. The question, therefore, is whether the object apprehended by reason, functioning as the formal cause of what the will wills, necessarily determines what it wills. Is the will disposed by its very nature as an intellectual or rational appetite to will whatever the reason apprehends as an object to be willed?

Aquinas's answer to this question brings us to the second of the two things on which, in his view, the indeterminacy of the will depends. It is the fact that the will, by its very nature, is necessitated by one object and one alone—the complete or perfect good. Nothing less than that which is completely good—good in all respects and lacking in none—can, according to Aquinas, completely satisfy our appetite for the good insofar as that appetite is rooted in the intellect's power to apprehend the good in general; that is, the good universally considered, not just this or that particular good. That alone which can completely satisfy us is the end we naturally seek; and so it is the complete or perfect good that functions as the final cause in every act of willing. When that which we will is something good only in some particular aspect (a partial or imperfect good), we will it as a means to the end. It is in willing the means, not the end, that Aquinas places our power of free choice, precisely because the means, unlike the end, are always fragments of the good, not the whole good.

"If anything is apprehended as good and suitable in all respects," he writes, "it will move the will by necessity." It is in this way, he explains, that man wills the happiness that he conceives as consisting in "the perfect state of all goods together," and therefore as the complete good and the ultimate end to be sought. "But if there is a good such that it is not thought to be good in all respects which can be considered, it will not move the will by necessity"; for in this case, it is possible "to will the opposite . . . because it is good and suitable in some other respect which may be considered." [52]

Elsewhere, Aquinas sums up this argument as follows:

> *Man does not choose of necessity. And this is because that which is possible not to be, is not of necessity. Now the reason why it is possible not to choose, or to choose, may be gathered from a two-fold power in man. For man can will and not will, act and not act; and again, he can will this or that, and do this or that. The reason of this is seated in the very power of the reason. For the will can tend to whatever the reason can apprehend as good. Now the reason can apprehend as good not only this, viz., to will or to act, but also this, viz., not to will or not to act. Again, in all*

> *particular goods, the reason can consider an aspect of some good, and the lack of some good, which has the aspect of evil: and in this respect, it can apprehend any single one of such goods as to be chosen or to be avoided. The perfect good alone, which is Happiness, cannot be apprehended by the reason as an evil, or as lacking in any way. Consequently man wills Happiness of necessity, nor can he will not to be happy, or to be unhappy. Now since choice is not of the end, but of the means, as we stated above; it is not of the perfect good, which is Happiness, but of other particular goods. Therefore man chooses not of necessity, but freely.*[53]

Only the supreme good, which can completely satisfy our desire, attracts us irresistibly. To say that when we consider the supreme good, we cannot avoid willing it, is to say that when this object is among the causes of the will's action, its action is causally necessitated, so far as what is willed is concerned. The irresistible attraction that the supreme good exercises over the will is not only the source of the causal necessity to which the will is subject; it is also the source of the causal indeterminacy that the will possesses with respect to all other objects. Being less than the supreme good, none of these is attractive in a way that necessitates the will's action with respect to it. When such objects are among the causes of the will's action, any one of several alternative volitions may result from the same set of causes, which includes the will as efficient cause, the supreme good as final cause, and some particular good (as apprehended by the reason) as formal cause. It is not that this set of causes fails to necessitate because it is insufficient to produce any effect whatsoever. It fails to necessitate because it is more than sufficient to produce whatever effect it in fact produces, for it could have equally well produced some other.

The followers of Aquinas repeat this argument, emphasizing what they call the active or dominating indifference of the will to particular goods. They are aware that this theory of the causal indeterminacy of the will not only involves a conception of the nature of the will as a rational appetite that their opponents do not share but also involves an analysis of causation and distinctions among different types of causes, not acknowledged by determinists. They, for their part, do not reject the view that causal necessity obtains in the physical world, but they deny that it obtains universally even there, and, in addition, they insist that the action of such immaterial powers as reason and will involves a type of causality not to be found in the world of bodies.

Other writers, who do not subscribe to the Thomistic explanation of the causal indeterminacy of the will in its acts of choice, also argue against the universality of causal necessity on the ground that the actions of the mind, reason, or will involve a type of causality radically different from that to be found in the physical world. It is in this way that Price argues against Priestley, and Mansel against Mill, as we have already indicated.

Often, their argument makes use of what they charge is a begging of the question on the part of their opponents, the determinists. The determinists, by equating sufficient with necessary causes, demand that a statement of the causes for an effect be equivalent to a rational explanation of that effect. They regard as a rational explanation one that shows that the effect follows from its causes necessarily as a conclusion follows necessarily from premises that provide its rational ground. To say what its causes are is thus to give the reasons why the effect must occur. If a free choice is a caused effect and not a matter of chance, it should be possible, according to the determinists, to give the reason why this particular choice was made rather than that.

The defenders of free choice here interpret their opponents as confronting them with the following dilemma: either tell us the reasons why an individual makes the choices he does, or, if you admit that in the very nature of the case such causes cannot be found, then cease to claim that the causal indeterminacy of free choice is distinct from the indeterminacy of chance.

But, admitting that no rational explanation can ever be given for any choice that is freely made, Yves Simon, for one, rejects this dilemma as begging the question whether or not all causes necessitate their effects. He points out that the demand to know why this rather than that particular choice was made is legitimate on one meaning of the word *why*, and begs the question on another. If the "why" asks for causes without excluding the possibility of causes that do not necessitate, then it can be answered by an account of how the choice was caused without at the same time eliminating the freedom of the choice. But if the "why" requires the giving of causes that necessitate the choice, and afford a rational explanation of it, then it is always assumed, by the sense of the question, that the choice either is determined and not free or is a matter of chance.[54] Bergson also points out that every attempt to give a rational explanation for free choice is self-defeating, for the effort assumes a determinism that is incompatible with freedom.[55]

Bergson offers another argument as well. He does not deny all meaning to the words *cause* and *effect* when they are applied to the static relation between phenomena that are subject to the laws of mechanics. But he does insist that the notion of cause must have a radically different meaning in the inner world of conscious states, where duration is real and everything is in process of change. "If the causal relation still holds good in the realm of inner states," he writes, "it cannot resemble in any way what we call causality in nature. For the physicist the same cause always produces the same effect: for a psychologist who does not let himself be misled by merely apparent analogies, a deep-seated inner cause produces its effect once for all and will never reproduce it. . . . the principle of universal determination loses every shred of meaning in the inner world of conscious states." [56]

### *The dispute about indeterminacy and predictability*

Let us now consider another aspect of the discussion of this issue. For certain authors, causal determinism is inseparably connected with the theoretical or intrinsic predictability of all future events. By "theoretical" or "intrinsic" predictability is meant the predictability of future events with certitude, given adequate knowledge of the causes that determine or necessitate these events as to their effects. The lack of such knowledge, or even the unattainability of it, in a particular case or even in every case, does not alter the proposition that, were such knowledge possessed, future effects could be predicted with certitude.

In this dispute, the determinists sometimes argue that scientific inquiry and knowledge presuppose the truth of causal determinism and, with it, the uniformity of nature and the theoretical predictability of future events. Hence, to deny theoretical predictability in general is to undermine the scientific enterprise as a whole; and to insist, as some libertarians do, that certain natural phenomena, such as the voluntary acts of man, are not theoretically predictable is to preclude the attainment of scientific knowledge in the field of human behavior, or to say that the behavioral sciences will never be able to achieve the results obtained in other fields of scientific inquiry. As this form of the argument runs, the acknowledged achievements of science constitute evidence that causal indeterminacy does not obtain in nature. If, by extrapolation, it is held that science can extend its achievements to include human behavior, it is then argued that the possibility of these future developments of science means that causal determinism is universal and causal indeterminacy is nonexistent.

Those who take this position sometimes argue that the predictability of future events is an unquestionable fact, connected, of course, with the fact that scientific inquiry has succeeded in obtaining the knowledge from which such predictions can be made. This argument is often extended to include the predictability of human behavior, either as a matter of fact and as a result of accomplished scientific knowledge or as a genuine possibility to be realized by further developments in the behavioral sciences. The asserted predictability of future events, attained or attainable, then becomes the premise for the denial of causal indeterminacy, which is thought to be incompatible with it.

Before turning to the arguments on the other side of this question about the predictability of future events, we should note two points. One is that the determinists are explicit in asserting that human behavior does not constitute an exception—a field of phenomena in which science cannot hope to achieve what it has achieved elsewhere. The other is that these arguments are formulated, for the most part, without reference to the comparatively recent problem of the significance of indeterminacy in quantum mechanics or subatomic physics. The question here is whether this unpredictability and the indeterminacy that goes along with it in the world of subatomic particles have significance for the issue about free choice on man's part and for the causal indeterminacy that it involves.*

On the other side of the dispute, those who defend causal indeterminacy, either in general or in the particular case of human free choice, argue in one of the following ways. (1) They maintain, as a matter of fact, that no particular future effect is theoretically predictable; and in so doing, they deny the premise from which their opponents argue against causal indeterminacy in general. (2) Or they maintain that, as a matter of fact, although human behavior is to a certain extent predictable with probability, it is never wholly predictable with certitude; and here again they deny the premise from which their opponents argue against causal indeterminacy in human behavior. (3) Or they point out that scientific inquiry and scientific knowledge do not require an unqualified acceptance of causal determinism and its corollaries—the complete uniformity of nature and theoretical predictability; and thus, arguing that science only presupposes a high degree of probability in prediction, they maintain that the achievements of science, present and promised, do not establish or require the universal reign of causal necessity. (4) Or they point out that the uniformity of nature is only a postulate, useful in science and limited to certain areas of scientific inquiry; and thus, arguing that the uniformity of nature is not an established truth, nor one of universal applicability, they maintain that the assertion of causal indeterminacy, especially if it is limited to the sphere of human behavior, does not conflict with the principles of science nor undermine scientific inquiry.

We may consider two sets of statements, one on each side of the dispute, as indicative of the positions taken. "What experience makes known," says John Stuart Mill,

> *is the fact of an invariable sequence between every event and some special combination of antecedent conditions, in such sort that wherever and whenever that union of antecedents exists, the event does not fail to occur.*

He notes, however, that "any *must* in the case, any necessity, other than the unconditional universality of the fact, we know nothing of."[57] And he goes on to apply this reasoning to the field of human volition as well. "A volition," he declares, "is a moral effect which follows the corresponding moral causes as certainly and invariably as physical effects follow their physical causes." To which he adds:

> *Whether it* must *do so, I acknowledge myself to be entirely ignorant, be the phaenomenon moral or physical; and I condemn, accordingly, the word Necessity as applied to either case. All I know is, that it always* does.[58]

---

* This possible significance is examined in *The Idea of Freedom,* Vol. 2, pp. 387–89.

Despite these qualifications, however, Mill is clearly a determinist.

William James is not. According to him,

> *the most that any argument can do for determinism is to make it a clear and seductive conception, which a man is foolish not to espouse, so long as he stands by the great scientific postulate that the world must be one unbroken fact, and that prediction of all things without exception must be ideally, even if not actually, possible.*

But over against this scientific postulate James sets what he calls the "moral postulate" that ought implies can, that is, that men are free to choose between duty and contrary desires. Confronted with the conflicting postulates of necessity and freedom, James writes:

> *When scientific and moral postulates war thus with each other and objective proof is not to be had, the only course is voluntary choice, for scepticism itself, if systematic, is also voluntary choice. If, meanwhile, the will be undetermined, it would seem only fitting that the belief in its indetermination should be voluntarily chosen from amongst other possible beliefs. Freedom's first deed should be to affirm itself.*[59]

James's position here is based on his contention—in which he follows the French philosopher Charles Renouvier—that freedom is not logically demonstrable, any more than necessity is. Instead, both the thesis of necessity and that of freedom are postulates; one takes one's choice as to which one will believe in.

In the controversy about free choice, as we have examined it so far, arguments against causal indeterminacy have been met by replies or counterarguments in its favor, and the defense of free choice by libertarians has been criticized and challenged by determinists. But there is at least one argument that is advanced by libertarians to which no reply can be found on the part of determinists.

The argument is advanced by a number of modern libertarians, among them Morris Ginsberg, Paul Weiss, and E. L. Mascall. According to Ginsberg, the very process of scientific inquiry would be undermined if every judgment of the mind were causally necessitated, as the determinists maintain. If it is held, Ginsberg says, "that a man's judgments are themselves completely determined, that he cannot help making the judgments he makes, the answer is that this would make nonsense of all knowledge." For, he explains,

> *if all judgments were causally necessitated, they would all be on the same level and it would be impossible to distinguish some as true and others as false. Sense and nonsense would all be equally necessitated. The whole notion of going by the evidence would*

> *lose all its meaning, if in forming a judgment we were completely unable to resist the violence of present desire, the effects of past habits, the persistence of ancient prejudices or the forces of the unconscious.*

Furthermore, Ginsberg points out, there could be nothing like a rational debate of this issue, for "there would be no sense in arguing about determinism or indeterminism if all our arguments were rigidly determined in advance." We should be determined by our character and antecedents to be either determinists or indeterminists, and all our arguments would be a pretense at rationalization rather than an offer of genuine reasons. But, he concludes, "if we admit that we can sometimes eliminate bias, that we can sometimes act on the basis of a judgment we form of the facts and of the relative value of the alternatives between which we have to choose, we have the minimum freedom required for moral accountability or responsibility." [60]

Weiss also maintains that determinism is self-defeating. The determinist who willingly asserts his own theory to be true by that very assertion acknowledges implicitly his own freedom. For if the determinist denies that he has freely considered his position, and adopted it responsibly, then he is really denying the validity of the position itself. He is merely making one noise among many noises, all of which add up to nothing.

Mascall sees the problem in much the same way. The determinist position is "self-stultifying" and self-destructive, he claims, in the sense that "the mere statement of the position deprives it of any claim for acceptance"; for the position asserts that "my conviction that an argument is valid is no evidence of its validity." If the theory of determinism is true, he continues, "then no arguments against it have any force. But then, if it is true, no arguments in its favour have any force either. It is pretty clear that no one in normal society in fact holds this position in its fullness, for its consistent adoption would lead to insanity." [61] In other words, the doctrine of determinism, if carried out with rigorous consistency, would not only deny free choice in the sphere of human action but also independent intellectual decisions in the sphere of human thought; and so it would result in so thoroughgoing a skepticism that it could not rationally argue the truth of its own position.

\* \* \* \* \*

Before going on to the next subject—the theological issue about self-determination—we wish to make one point about the discussion of the two issues treated above. Although we have emphasized the apparent meeting of minds among disputants on the several questions involved in the issues examined so far, there is a level at which the arguments do not really meet. This is a serious defect in the controversy.

271

For example, in the dispute about indeterminacy and causation, we found that one party advanced a theory of sufficient causes, or of causes in general, that entailed the truth of the proposition that if anything is caused at all, it is necessitated. Hence, indeterminacy, being the absence of necessity, must be one with causelessness or chance. A second party advanced a contrary theory of sufficient causes, or of causes in general, that entailed the truth of the proposition that while some causes necessitate their effects, others do not, but operate with causal indeterminacy, which is quite different from chance. And a third party advanced still another contrary theory of causation that supported the conclusion that no cause necessitates the effect it produces.

Each of the three parties to this dispute gave some indication of the reasons for the causal theory advanced. To this extent, the argument reached a fundamental level. But what, ideally at least, one would wish, in order to see this dispute carried to bedrock, would be some indication, on the part of each of the major adversaries, that he understood the causal theories of his opponents and, in the light of that understanding, could give clear reasons for rejecting them. With few and slight exceptions, however, such understanding and rational criticism are not found.

A thoroughly developed debate about the principles of causation would involve disputes about a number of fundamental matters that are integrally involved in any theory of causation—such things as substance, powers (both material and immaterial), events, time, the reality of the future, and so on. We can observe the dim presence of these disputed matters in the rival causal theories that are advanced in support or denial of causal indeterminacy or free choice, and in support or denial of causal initiative. But the argument, on one side or another, proceeds without ever really bringing these fundamentals to the forefront and making them the center of the dispute. They are central, and the merely peripheral argumentation, interesting and instructive as it undoubtedly is, therefore remains seriously inadequate.

## 11. The theological issue concerning man's freedom of self-determination

Like the issues treated in the last section, the issue with which we are here concerned is an existential one. Man's possession of a freedom of self-determination is denied by those who, affirming the existence of an omnipotent and omniscient deity, argue that that precludes the existence of free will on man's part. Those who argue in this fashion are opposed by others who, affirming the existence of God, also affirm the existence of human free will, arguing that self-determination on man's part is not thereby precluded.

On the negative side of this issue, we find mainly writers who not only deny that human self-determination is compatible with God's foreordination and foreknowledge but who also affirm the existence of an omnipotent and omniscient deity and who, therefore, deny the existence of free will in man. However, the incompatibility of human free will with God's providence is sometimes asserted by writers who do not commit themselves on the question of God's existence. They do so for the purpose of arguing in the following hypothetical fashion. If you believe that an omnipotent and omniscient God exists, they say to their opponents, you cannot also affirm that man has free will; that is precluded by God's foreordination and foreknowledge of everything that happens, including all the actions of man.

On the affirmative side of this issue, we naturally find writers who affirm the existence of an omnipotent and omniscient deity. Other writers, who do not commit themselves on the question of God's existence, could argue in hypothetical fashion that even if God exists, man can also have free will, because the one does not preclude the other. But there is little or no evidence of such argumentation in the literature of freedom.

In what follows we shall be concerned mainly with the dispute between authors who disagree about the existence of free will in man while agreeing about the existence of God. The issue is therefore properly called "theological," since it is argued categorically only by writers who dispute the existence of free will within a common framework of theological assertions, namely, that God exists, that nothing happens contrary to God's will or his decrees, and that nothing can happen that would render God's knowledge inadequate or erroneous. The common theological framework does not extend farther than this. As we shall see, the authors who take opposite sides of this issue do so in virtue of different views of the relation of God's will and knowledge to the actions of man. It is on the basis of such theological differences that some of them assert that freedom of choice on man's part is precluded by God's omnipotence and omniscience, while others assert that free choice is compatible with an all-powerful and all-knowing God.

As we shall also see, it is the causal indeterminacy of free choice, not the causal initiative of the will, that is the focus of theological dispute. Furthermore, it is the intrinsic unpredictability of the freely chosen act that appears to be irreconcilable with God's foreknowledge. That is why most of the authors on the negative side of the dispute appeal to God's omniscience as the ground for their denial of free choice. But many of them also rest their case on God's omnipotence—that nothing happens except it be willed or decreed by God and that what God wills or decrees must necessarily happen. In their view, this leaves no room for indeterminacy. A few writers, notably Luther and Calvin, employ the word *foreordination* to cover both God's willing and God's knowing all that is to take place.

It is also God's foreknowledge that most of the affirmative authors recognize as the nub of the issue. They recognize its *apparent* irreconcilability with free choice, in view of their own conception of the freely chosen act as intrinsically unpredictable even by a mind that possesses perfect knowledge of all relevant causes. However, here as in the case of the negative authors, the consideration of God's will and providence also enters into the picture. How certain human acts can be exempt from necessitation and yet, like everything else, be subject to God's will must be explained. But explanations are not, in fact, offered by all the affirmative authors, for some of them accept the apparent irreconcilability of man's free choice with God's omniscience and omnipotence as a mystery beyond human comprehension.

We therefore have a threefold division of authors: (1) writers such as Luther, Calvin, and Jonathan Edwards, who maintain that God's foreknowledge or foreordination necessitates all that happens; (2) writers such as Descartes, Sir William Hamilton, and Henry Mansel, who maintain that we must affirm free choice together with God's omnipotence and omniscience even if we cannot explain how they are reconcilable; and (3) writers such as Augustine, Boethius, Maimonides, Aquinas, William James, and Paul Tillich, who attempt to show that the irreconcilability is only apparent and who thus try to counter the arguments advanced by the opponents of free choice.

Accordingly, we will begin with the representatives of the negative position, proceeding then to those who take the affirmative side but do not reply to the arguments of their opponents, and finally coming to those on the affirmative side who attempt to defend that position.

### The negative position

Cicero is described by Augustine as holding the view that the freedom of the will is irreconcilable with God's complete foreknowledge of the future. Evodius, a character in Augustine's dialogue *The Problem of Free Choice,* also poses the problem when he states that "I do not see how these two, God's foreknowledge of our sins and our free will in sinning, do not contradict one another." [62] And Boethius also poses it in his *Consolation of Philosophy.* "There seems to be," he writes there, ". . . incompatibility between the existence of God's universal foreknowledge and that of any freedom of judgment. For if God foresees all things and cannot in anything be mistaken, that which His Providence sees will happen, must result. Wherefore if it knows beforehand not only men's deeds but even their designs and wishes, there will be no freedom of judgment." [63]

None of these writers is a supporter of the negative position, but the problem they pose is one that confronts all later theologians in the Judaeo-Christian tradition, as well as philosophers whose thought takes account of accepted religious beliefs.

The negative response to the problem as posed is perhaps given most explicitly and simply by Martin Luther. "If we believe it to be true," he writes,

*that God foreknows and foreordains all things; that He can not
be deceived or obstructed in His foreknowledge and predestination; and that nothing happens but at His will (which reason itself
is compelled to grant), then on reason's own testimony, there can
be no free will in man, or angel, or in any creature.*[64]

John Calvin's position differs from Luther's by reason of the emphasis
he places on God's foreordination. It is this, rather than God's foreknowledge, which precludes free choice on man's part. The salvation and
damnation of particular men, Calvin says, "are acts of God's will, rather
than of his foreknowledge. If God simply foresaw the fates of men, and
did not also dispose and fix them by his determination, there would be
room to agitate the question, whether his providence or foresight rendered
them at all necessary. But since he foresees future events only in consequence of his decree that they shall happen, it is useless to contend about
foreknowledge, while it is evident that all things come to pass rather by
ordination and decree." [65]

Calvin is aware that those who attempt to reconcile free choice with
divine omniscience make the point that nothing is future to God and so
his "foreknowledge" must be understood without any temporal reference.
But this, according to Calvin, does not alter the case, since it is "predestination, by which God adopts some to the hope of life, and adjudges
others to eternal death." To recognize this is to avoid the "many cavils"
of "those who make foreknowledge the cause of it." [66]

Jonathan Edwards argues in similar fashion; and he takes the position
a step further. To those who insist that God's prescience, as such, has no
influence on our actions, he replies:

*What is said about knowledge, its not having influence on the
thing known to make it necessary, is nothing to the purpose, nor
does it in the least affect the foregoing reasoning. Whether prescience be the thing that* makes *the event necessary or no, it alters
not the case. Infallible foreknowledge may* prove *the necessity of
the event foreknown, and yet not be the thing which* causes *the
necessity. If the foreknowledge be absolute, this* proves *the event
known to be necessary.*[67]

Other writers assert the incompatibility of free will and divine omniscience without entering into the argument. Erwin Schrödinger, the
physicist, is a particularly interesting case in that he sees the theological
problem as the analogue of the scientific problem concerning free will:
"The part of the Law of Nature," he writes, "is taken by the omniscient
and almighty God." [68] His further statement that the religious attitude
toward this problem is that "we are here confronted with a deep mystery
into which we cannot penetrate" does not, as we will see, apply to all the

authors on the affirmative side of the issue. But it does describe the position of the writers to whom we now turn.

## The affirmative position not defended

In his *Principles of Philosophy,* Descartes asks "how the freedom of the will may be reconciled with Divine pre-ordination" and frankly acknowledges that the answer to this question is beyond our comprehension. We must remember, he asserts, that "our thought is finite, and that the omnipotence of God, whereby He has not only known from all eternity that which is or can be, but also willed and pre-ordained it, is infinite." Thus we will recognize, he says, that

> we may have intelligence enough to come clearly and distinctly to know that this power is in God, but not enough to comprehend how He leaves the free action of man indeterminate; and, on the other hand, we are so conscious of the liberty and indifference which exist in us, that there is nothing that we comprehend more clearly and perfectly.

Hence, Descartes concludes, "it would be absurd to doubt that of which we inwardly experience and perceive as existing within ourselves, just because we do not comprehend a matter which from its nature we know to be incomprehensible." [69]

According to Sir William Hamilton, the failure to explain rationally how man's free will can be reconciled with God's foreknowledge and fore-ordination does not exempt a Christian from believing in both. The problem, he concedes, is difficult; but he insists that the conciliation is possible when the things to be reconciled are regarded as "things to be believed," but not when they are taken as things to be understood. [70]

In his defense of Hamilton's position on free will against the attack of J. S. Mill, Henry Mansel says that he has "purposely avoided touching on a subject alluded to by Mr. Mill, the compatibility of man's free-will with God's foreknowledge. This question," Mansel confesses, "is insoluble, because we have nothing but negative notions to apply to it. . . . In this, as in all other revelations of God's relation to man, we must be content to believe without aspiring to comprehend." [71] And others, too, assert that both doctrines, from the religious point of view, must be affirmed, even if, from the philosophical point of view, their compatibility cannot be understood.

## The affirmative position defended

Other writers do try to explain how the difficulty may be resolved. Augustine, for example, in an early work, *The Problem of Free Choice,* declares that it does not follow that because "God has foreknown my future will, [and] because nothing can happen contrary to His foreknowledge, [therefore] I must necessarily will what He has foreknown." To defend this position, Augustine first points out that "our will would not be a will, if it were not in our power. Moreover, since it is in our power, it is free." He then argues as follows:

> *Since He has foreknowledge of our will, that will must exist, of which He has foreknowledge. It will be a will, because He has foreknowledge of a will. Nor could it be a will, if it were not in our power. So He has foreknowledge also of our power over it. My power is not taken away by His foreknowledge, but I shall have it all the more certainly because He whose foreknowledge is not mistaken has foreknown that I shall have it.*[72]

Therefore, he concludes, there is no need to deny that God has foreknowledge of all future events simply because we freely will what we will.

This argument, in all of its essential respects, is repeated by Augustine in *The City of God*. There, criticizing Cicero's denial of divine foreknowledge in order to affirm freedom of choice for man, Augustine concludes that

> *it is not the case . . . that because God foreknew what would be in the power of our wills, there is for that reason nothing in the power of our wills. For He who foreknew this did not foreknow nothing. . . . Therefore we are by no means compelled, either, retaining the prescience of God, to take away the freedom of the will, or, retaining the freedom of the will, to deny that He is prescient of future things, which is impious.*[73]

Boethius not only repeats but also expands Augustine's argument. Like Augustine, he maintains a threefold division of causes: some things are necessitated by their causes; some happen by chance or by the coincidence of causes; and some result from the free judgments that men make. He then argues that if all things, as caused, do not happen by necessity, then the fact that God has foreknowledge of everything cannot be interpreted to mean that everything happens by necessity; for God, foreknowing, foresees that only some things will happen by necessity, whereas others will happen by chance, and still others will result from free choice on man's part. The way things happen depends upon the way in which they are caused, not upon God's foreknowledge, which, being knowledge of the way things are caused, comprehends things that happen by free choice and by chance as well as things that happen by necessity.

What Boethius adds to Augustine's argument—it is a famous point in the history of philosophy—is a clarification of the meaning of *foreknowledge* when that is attributed to God. For both God and man, foreknowledge refers to future events. But whereas future events for man are those things which are still to come to pass, they are all co-present to God's eternal vision. The things that we experience happening successively in time, God sees in the eternal present and sees each thing as occurring in accordance with its own nature or character whether as cause or effect. Boethius calls our attention to the fact that we also see certain things happening in our temporal present—for example, the sun rising in the heavens, and a man walking on earth—but this does not affect the way in which they happen. The fact that we see both things happening does not prevent one from happening by necessity and the other from happening by free choice. "In like manner," Boethius maintains, "the perception of God looks upon all things without disturbing at all their nature, though they are present to Him but future under the conditions of time." If among these things are some that happen by man's free choice, God both knows that such events are occurring and knows that they are not occurring of necessity.[74]

Hence, Boethius argues, when "God looks in His present upon those future things which come to pass through free will," they have a conditional necessity (that is, "they come to pass of necessity under the condition of divine knowledge"—they could not occur without God knowing); but these same things "viewed by themselves . . . do not lose the perfect freedom of their nature. Without doubt then," he concludes,

> *all things that God foreknows do come to pass, but some of them proceed from free will; and though they result by coming into existence, yet they do not lose their own nature, because before they came to pass they could also not have come to pass.*[75]

Most of the Jewish philosophers of the Middle Ages take the affirmative side on this issue. According to Maimonides, for instance, "the theory of man's perfectly free will is one of the fundamental principles of the Law of our Teacher Moses, and of those who follow the Law." [76] Since, in his view, God's providence goes no further than the universal laws of nature that were established once and for all at creation, God does not predetermine the particular events that happen in accordance with these laws. This is especially true in the case of man, whom God created with free will. Man's free actions are thus preordained to be free.

The perplexity that others face on this question, Maimonides says, results from their failure to recognize that God's knowledge is totally unlike human knowledge. His knowledge is identical with His essence. "We cannot comprehend God's knowledge," Maimonides writes; "our minds cannot grasp it at all, for He is His knowledge and His knowledge is He." [77] Since we cannot comprehend God's knowledge, it is not surprising that we cannot understand how God has foreknowledge of future contingencies, including the free acts of man.

For Aquinas, as for several other writers we have considered, the problem is twofold: it relates to God's omnipotence, on the one hand, and to God's omniscience, on the other.

With regard to God's omnipotence, Aquinas holds that divine Providence "moves all things in accordance with their conditions; so that from necessary causes through the Divine motion, effects follow of necessity; but from contingent causes, effects follow contingently. Since, therefore," he continues,

> *the will is an active principle, not determinate to one thing, but having an indifferent relation to many things, God so moves it, that He does not determine it of necessity to one thing, but its movement remains contingent and not necessary.*[78]

To the objection that, since "God cannot be resisted, because His power is infinite," it must therefore follow that "the will is moved of necessity by God," Aquinas replies that "it would be more repugnant to the Divine motion, for the will to be moved of necessity, which is not fitting to its nature; than for it to be moved freely, which is becoming to its nature." [79] And to the objection that since God's will is unchangeable, and nothing can be in discord with the divine will, and that therefore man's will cannot be variable in its choices, Aquinas replies that "with respect to the mode of willing it is not needful that the will of man conform to God's will, because God wills everything eternally and infinitely, but man does not." [80]

A number of writers in the seven centuries since Aquinas have resembled him in the general manner of his reconciliation of man's freedom with God's omnipotence. Still other writers offer divergent solutions of the theological problem. Of these, William James and Paul Tillich are especially notable. Posing the problem in terms of Providence, James maintains that "the belief in free-will is not in the least incompatible with the belief in Providence, provided you do not restrict the Providence to fulminating nothing but *fatal* decrees." He explains what he means thus:

> *If you allow him [i.e., Providence] to provide possibilities as well as actualities to the universe, and to carry on his own thinking in those two categories just as we do ours, chances may be there, uncontrolled even by him, and the course of the universe be really ambiguous; and yet the end of all things may be just what he intended it to be from all eternity.*
>
> *. . . Suppose him to say, I will lead things to a certain end, but I will not now decide on all the steps thereto. At various points, ambiguous possibilities shall be left open, either of which, at a given instant, may become actual. But whichever branch of these bifurcations become real, I know what I shall do at the next bifurcation to keep things from drifting away from the final result I intend.*[81]

On this view of the matter, "the creator's plan of the universe," James says, "would thus be left blank as to many of its actual details, but all possibilities would be marked down. . . . So the creator himself would not need to know *all* the details of actuality until they came; and at any time his own view of the world would be a view partly of facts and partly of possibilities, exactly as ours is now." [82]

Tillich offers a somewhat similar interpretation of Providence, and one that also allows for all the intrinsically unpredictable novelties that are produced by the creative freedom of God's creatures, especially by that of man. "Providence," Tillich writes,

> *is a permanent activity of God. He never is a spectator; he always directs everything toward its fulfilment. Yet God's directing creativity always creates through the freedom of man and through the spontaneity and structural wholeness of all creatures. Providence works through the polar elements of being. . . . Providence is not interference; it is creation. It uses all factors, both those given by freedom and those given by destiny, in creatively directing everything toward its fulfilment.*[83]

Of the three views documented in this section—the view that God's omnipotence and/or omniscience rules out man's freedom of self-determination; the view that they are reconcilable, although incomprehensibly by man's reason; and the view that the reconciliation can be argued for on rational grounds—none seems more cogent than the others, nor do we come to any conclusion as to how they can be resolved.

## 12. A possible conceptual issue concerning self-determination: chance, responsibility, and freedom

We turn now, finally, to the last of the issues that we shall treat regarding self-determination. We have more than once referred to this issue in the foregoing, characterizing it as especially interesting and especially crucial. It is crucial because unless it is resolved the entire discussion of self-determination, and by extension the entire discussion of the idea of freedom itself, lacks the firm underpinnings that the philosopher would prefer to see in the understanding of such an important idea in human life. It is interesting for that reason, and also because the issue has the special character of being one that is capable of dispute but also one that is not directly disputed in the literature. We shall try to make these points clear in what follows.*

In the general controversy about man's freedom of self-determination, there are two distinct disputes about such freedom in relation to moral

---

\* We will not be able to devote as much space to the problem as it probably deserves. We therefore refer the reader to the much more extensive treatment of the issue that is to be found in *The Idea of Freedom*, Vol. 2, chap. 9, sec. 4, pp. 302–16; chap. 10, sec. 5, pp. 418–46; and chap. 12, pp. 488–525.

responsibility. A schematic summary of the first of these disputes would look like this:

I. The dispute is initiated by the *proponents* of the freedom of self-determination.

    A. They assert that moral responsibility presupposes a freedom that involves causal initiative, or causal indeterminacy, or both.

    B. From this premise they argue to the conclusion that anyone who wishes to employ the notion of responsibility must affirm the existence of a freedom of self-determination.

    C. What this does is to present their opponents with a dilemma: either abandon the notion of moral responsibility or affirm the existence of self-determination.

II. This argument is met by the *opponents* of the freedom of self-determination in the following manner.

    A. The "hard determinists" *accept* the dilemma as stated and therefore abandon the notion of moral responsibility, since they deny the existence of self-determination.

    B. The "soft determinists" *reject* the dilemma as stated and therefore see no reason to abandon the notion of moral responsibility, even though the existence of self-determination is denied.

        1. They assert that responsibility is tenable in the total absence of self-determination, and that it can be given meaning by reference to man's circumstantial freedom of self-realization.

        2. They do not conclude from this that the nonexistence of self-determination is demonstrated but only that the argument advanced by its adherents fails: its existence need not be affirmed in order to attribute responsibility to men.*

The following schematic summary of the second dispute about self-determination and responsibility shows the way in which it differs from the one just outlined.

I. The dispute is initiated by the *opponents* of the freedom of self-determination.

    A. They assert that moral responsibility precludes a freedom that involves causal initiative, or causal indeterminacy, or both.

    B. To reach this conclusion, they argue from three premises:

        1. First, that causal initiative or causal indeterminacy makes the free act or the free choice equivalent to a chance event.

        2. Second, that what a man does by chance cannot be imputed to him as his own act or his own choice, since an act is com-

---

* Documentation of the complicated dispute here summarized will be found in *The Idea of Freedom*, Vol. 2, chaps. 9–10.

monly said to be imputable to a man only if it can be seen to proceed from him as its cause.

    3. Third, that if an act or choice cannot be imputed to a man, he cannot be held morally responsible for it.

  C. Hence, they present their opponents with the dilemma: either deny the existence of self-determination or abandon the notion of moral responsibility.

II. This argument is met by the *proponents* of the freedom of self-determination in the following manner.

  A. They reject the dilemma as stated and, with it, the conclusion that moral responsibility precludes a freedom that involves causal initiative or causal indeterminacy or both.

  B. They do so on the following basis:

    1. First, they assert that self-determination is the very opposite of chance and involves no element of chance.

    2. Second, they maintain that, far from precluding imputability, self-determination is the indispensable basis of it.

    3. Third, they conclude that since the free act or the free choice can be imputed to a man as its agent or cause, he can be held morally responsible for it.

The question that is pivotal in both of these issues is whether free will or free choice involves chance, conceived as causelessness. It is probably the most fundamental issue in the whole controversy about self-determination. Hence, it is of great importance to discover how certain authors can hold that free will either is nothing but chance or involves an element of chance, whereas other writers deny that any element of chance is involved in free will.

If it is ever possible to resolve, one way or the other, the issue about free will and chance, that would go a long way toward resolving the issues about the existence of causal initiative and of causal indeterminacy. Hence, if we can find the reasons why opposite sides are taken on this issue, we have the key to most, if not all, of the disputes about self-determination.

### The position that free will precludes responsibility

David Hume was almost certainly the first to propose the argument with which we are here concerned and which is many times repeated by writers who come after him. Furthermore, the original statement of the argument by Hume is so complete that, apart from variations in expression, little is added in the subsequent repetitions.*

Hume's first statement of the argument is in his early work, *A Trea-*

---

\* These repetitions, with slight variations, are documented in *The Idea of Freedom,* Vol. 2, pp. 499–505.

*tise of Human Nature.* It occurs in a section immediately following the one that concludes with the statement already quoted: "Liberty, by removing necessity, removes also causes and is the very same thing with chance." [84] The argument opens with the observation that causal necessity—and with it the whole determinist view that a man's character and motives determine his choices and actions—is required for both religion and morality. Hume writes:

> *This kind of necessity is so essential to religion and morality, that without it there must ensue an absolute subversion of both, and . . . every other supposition is entirely destructive to all laws both divine and human. 'Tis indeed certain, that as all human laws are founded on rewards and punishments, 'tis suppos'd as a fundamental principle, that these motives have an influence on the mind, and both produce the good and prevent the evil actions. We may give to this influence what name we please; but as 'tis usually conjoin'd with the action, common sense requires it should be esteem'd a cause, and be look'd upon as an instance of that necessity, which I wou'd establish.* [85]

The argument then goes on to point out that free will (which Hume thinks he has shown to be synonymous with chance) would, if it existed, render it impossible to impute to an individual his freely willed actions and, therefore, impossible to hold him responsible for them. Referring to the connection of a person's actions with his character and motives, Hume says:

> *. . . according to the doctrine of liberty or chance, this connexion is reduc'd to nothing, nor are men more accountable for those actions, which are design'd and premeditated, than for such as are the most casual and accidental. Actions are by their very nature temporary and perishing; and where they proceed not from some cause in the characters and disposition of the person, who perform'd them, they infix not themselves upon him, and can neither redound to his honour, if good, nor infamy, if evil. The action itself may be blameable; it may be contrary to all the rules of morality and religion: But the person is not responsible for it; and as it proceeded from nothing in him, that is durable or constant, and leaves nothing of that nature behind it, 'tis impossible he can, upon its account, become the object of punishment or vengeance. According to the hypothesis of liberty, therefore, a man is as pure and untainted after having committed the most horrid crimes, as at the first moment of his birth . . . 'Tis only upon the principles of necessity, that a person acquires any merit or demerit from his actions, however the common opinion may incline to the contrary.* [86]

It is important to note that, for Hume, the lack of causal connection between a person's character and his acts makes the latter not *his* acts at all but products of chance. To say that free will means that a person's decisions are not determined by his character and motives is to say that free will is reduced to chance; for to exclude character and motives as the causal determinants of the so-called free decision is to leave it totally without causal determination. This is true not only for Hume but also for his followers—such writers as Jonathan Edwards and Joseph Priestley in the eighteenth century, F. H. Bradley toward the end of the nineteenth century, and L. T. Hobhouse and Bertrand Russell in the twentieth. A statement of Russell's makes the point clear. He contends that "it is not determinism but free-will that has subversive consequences" for morality.[87] And in a later work he asserts that "praise and blame, rewards and punishments, and the whole apparatus of the criminal law, are rational on the deterministic hypothesis, but not on the hypothesis of free will." [88]

### The position that free will does not preclude responsibility

A relatively small number of authors explicitly defend self-determination against the charge that it provides no basis for imputability and, therefore, no ground for attributing responsibility to men. The number of authors who argue affirmatively that freedom of choice is required to make sense of moral responsibility is very much larger. Clearly, authors who hold that attribution of responsibility to man depends on his possession of free choice would also deny that free choice destroys responsibility. In fact, almost every proponent of self-determination can be construed as an opponent of Hume's thesis that free will is identical with chance. Since that thesis is an essential premise in Hume's argument, as well as in the reasoning of those who follow him, the fact that almost all supporters of self-determination reject it means that, if they were to consider Hume's whole argument, they would reject it also. Yet, except for a few authors, the supporters of self-determination do not engage in the dispute with Hume and his followers by explicitly criticizing the reasoning that leads them to the conclusion that self-determination precludes responsibility.

Joseph Rickaby and W. G. MacLagan may be mentioned as typical of those who do so argue.* Referring to Hume's thesis, Rickaby contends that it does not touch "one single defender of free will. We will allow," he explains,

> that character has a vast influence on conduct; we only deny that it
> has an absolutely determining influence upon every single point of
> premeditated action. . . . Character is more or less permanent; but
> there is something still more permanent than character: that is the
> "person, or creature endowed with thought and consciousness," a

---

* The reasoning of others is examined in *The Idea of Freedom,* Vol. 2, pp. 506–15.

> *definition which I thankfully take from Hume. Free will in act is*
> *eminently a personal act: it is the rational creature's outpouring of*
> *its own vitality.*[89]

Of all the attacks on libertarianism, "the unkindest cut, considering the grounds of the theory, is," in the opinion of MacLagan, "the suggestion that it actually makes nonsense of moral experience." He recognizes the reason for this destructive suggestion. Those who make it argue as follows: to say "that a man may just as well choose either of his alternatives amounts to saying that, whichever he does choose, his choice is [an] inexplicable freak"; hence "such indeterminism, even if admissible in the natural world, is impossible in moral action; freak or chance can carry no moral significance whatsoever." [90] As a solution of this difficulty, MacLagan points out that the libertarian is not forced to choose between the hard alternatives of "determinism or chance" because he is not able to answer the question "Why did you choose this, rather than that?" The failure to answer this question does not reduce choice to chance.

### Interpretation and construction

Let us suppose that the following statement is true or closely approximates the truth: that all authors who are opposed to self-determination explicitly hold or maintain by implication that free will involves chance; and that all the authors who defend self-determination either explicitly deny or deny by implication that there is any element of chance in free will or free choice. If that is the case, we find them arrayed on opposite sides of the most fundamental issue in the controversy about self-determination. If the issue about free will and chance could be resolved, it would be a critical, perhaps the decisive, step toward resolving the other issues.

On the one hand, if the opponents of self-determination are right in thinking that causal initiative and causal indeterminacy reduce to chance, and if they could show that this is so, then they should have little difficulty in getting the adherents of self-determination to yield on the existential and conceptual issues about it. Since the adherents of self-determination are as unqualified as the opponents of it in denying the existence of chance events, conceived as totally uncaused or without any causal determination, it follows that they should concede the nonexistence of self-determination if it involves chance. Furthermore, since the adherents of self-determination agree with the opponents of it that what happens by chance cannot properly be called free, according to the common understanding of freedom, they should also concede that self-determination does not conform to the generic idea of freedom.

On the other hand, if the adherents of self-determination are right in thinking that causal initiative and causal indeterminacy do not involve chance, and if they could show that this is so, then they, too, should have little difficulty in getting the opponents of self-determination to yield on the other issues. Since the most fundamental reason that the opponents advance for denying the existence of self-determination, conceived as involving causal initiative or causal indeterminacy, is that it violates the universal principle of causation (which is another way of saying that choice is reduced to chance conceived as causelessness), they should concede its existence, or at least be compelled to find other reasons for denying it, if it could be shown that it is not "contracausal" in the sense in which chance is. Similarly, if self-determination does not involve chance, the reason for thinking that it does not conform to the generic idea of freedom is removed; and so the opponents of self-determination should concede that it does so conform, or find some other reason for still denying it.

Of course, one further condition must be satisfied in order to assure us that the foregoing analysis of the situation is sound. The opponents of self-determination and the adherents of it must be in minimal topical agreement about the critical terms in the issue; that is, they must have enough common understanding of the terms *causal initiative, causal indeterminacy,* and *chance* to be in genuine disagreement of the question "Does self-determination also involve chance, conceived as causelessness?"

Let us assume—admittedly a large assumption—that this minimal topical agreement exists. Then we see that the root of the real disagreement about free will and chance lies in conflicting theories of causation. If the parties to all these issues shared the same theory of causation, their common understanding of causal initiative and causal indeterminacy would be such that they could not disagree (not rationally at least) about whether free will exists and about whether or not it is genuinely a form of freedom, for they could not disagree about whether or not it reduces to chance. Precisely because they hold quite disparate theories of causation, their understanding of causal initiative and causal indeterminacy is sufficiently different to explain their disagreement on all these issues, and yet not so different that their disagreement is merely apparent rather than real.

The conclusion we reach, therefore, is that the basic issues in the controversy about self-determination cannot be resolved unless the basic issues in another controversy can be resolved first—the issues arising from conflicting theories of causation. But until a dialectical clarification of the vast literature concerning causation is undertaken, we cannot be sure that those issues are really joined and rationally debated in such a way that their resolution lies within the bounds of possibility.

Chapter IV.    Conclusions

## 13.    Three freedoms—no more, no less

We have now completed our identification of the three basic forms of freedom, and our analysis of the issues about them.*

We have distinguished these three basic forms by the mode of their possession by human beings. One form of freedom is circumstantial, another is acquired, the third is natural. Are we certain, however, that there are only these three ways in which writers about freedom conceive it as being possessed—no more, and no less?

We are, indeed, certain, but the statement of our hypothesis on this point may raise two questions. First, how can we be sure that *circumstantial, acquired,* and *natural* exhaust the ways in which freedom is thought to be possessed? And second, what grounds do we have for thinking that these three are exclusive of one another, and so are irreducible in number?

With regard to the first question, our answer is based entirely on the evidence afforded by the literature on freedom. We are saying, in short, that we have found in the literature no theory that affirms a freedom that cannot be identified, as far as mode of possession goes, by reference to one of these three, or some combination of them. We have found no theory that even suggests the possibility of a fourth way in which freedom is possessed, distinct from these three.

This does not mean that in fact there is no other way in which freedom can be possessed. There may be a fourth way, and a fifth, and a sixth. But we have examined the literature of freedom perhaps more thoroughly than it has ever been examined before, and we know that no writer of any significance has ever suggested any other way. Thus, although our contention possesses something less than the intuitive certitude of a purely logical exhaustion, it does have the high probability afforded empirically by a thorough examination of evidence.

The second question concerns our grounds for thinking that the three modes of possession are distinct and exclusive of one another, and so are irreducible in number. Here, too, our grounds are empirical. They are

---

* Actually, there are five forms of freedom, as we indicated in Chapters 1 and 2. Political liberty is a variant of circumstantial freedom, but as far as its mode of possession goes, this is the same as that of circumstantial freedom. Similarly, collective freedom is a variant of acquired freedom.

drawn from the evidence examined rather than developed from any purely logical insight.

It should be pointed out that the question is not whether the authors themselves distinguish three kinds of freedom by reference to these three modes of possession. Nor is the question whether authors who either explicitly or implicitly refer to the way in which freedom is possessed affirm two distinct freedoms when they distinguish two modes of possession, or three when they distinguish three. Some authors have theories that include less than three distinctive conceptions of freedom, or that involve less than three distinct ways of conceiving man's possession of it. But the question we are considering here is not addressed to authors who are expounding their own theories of freedom. Instead, it is addressed to ourselves as analysts who are treating the theories they expound. What is the evidence for thinking that the three modes we have identified are quite distinct, and for thinking that no less than these three distinct modes will suffice for identifying the varying conceptions of freedom we have encountered in the literature?

The first part of that question has, in a sense, already been answered in the preceding chapters. There we have shown that the meanings we have given *circumstantial, acquired,* and *natural* as identifying terms do not overlap or merge in any way.

In addition we have seen that certain questions that are asked about a freedom that is circumstantial are never asked about a freedom that is acquired or natural; and the same holds for each of the other two. We have seen that certain differences of opinion that occur with respect to a freedom that is acquired do not occur with respect to a freedom that is natural, or to one that is circumstantial; and this also holds for each of the other two. In short, we have observed three separate and distinct patterns of discussion that are significantly related to the meanings of these three identifying terms.

Finally, when we examine the views of certain authors, especially those who assert the existence of only one conception of freedom, we find further evidence and support for our contention. Considering only authors included in *Great Books of the Western World,* we find that Hobbes, Hume, and J. S. Mill affirm only a freedom that is circumstantial; Plato, Epictetus, Marcus Aurelius, and Plotinus affirm only a freedom that is acquired; and Descartes, Berkeley, and William James affirm only a freedom that is natural. In view of the fact that here are three groups of authors, each of which consists of writers who affirm only one freedom, and one that in each case is different from the freedoms affirmed by the other two groups, it is clear that no less than three distinct terms will serve to identify, by reference to mode of possession, the different freedoms that these three groups of authors each conceives to be man's only freedom.

## 14.   The general understanding of freedom: its generic meaning

The above considerations will have raised in the mind of the careful reader a question of even greater importance than the one they are designed to answer. Let us assume that three distinct freedoms must be identified in order to handle the extensive literature of the subject. That further question then is: "Do these three distinct conceptions have anything in common?"

They might not. There are words in any language that, although sounding the same and though spelled identically, have nothing in common insofar as meaning goes. An example in English is the word *pen*. A pen is something in which one places sheep; a pen is something with which one writes. These two meanings of the word have nothing whatsoever in common.*

There are other words that, while sounding the same and being spelled identically, seem to denote completely different things but really do not. An example is the word *fall*, which denotes the descent of something and a season of the year. But there is an underlying common note in these two meanings, for fall is that season of the year in which leaves fall.

The question, then, is whether the word *freedom*, as it is used in the three conceptions—the circumstantial *freedom* of self-realization, the acquired *freedom* of self-perfection, and the natural *freedom* of self-determination—is like the word *pen* or like the word *fall*.

We think *freedom* is like *fall* rather than like *pen*—that is, we think there is an underlying note, or general understanding, or generic meaning of freedom as it is discussed in the literature. Our reasons are as follows.

We have used brief summary statements of the common understandings of the freedoms that have been identified as (A) circumstantial self-realization, (B) acquired self-perfection, and (C) natural self-determination.

> A. To be free is to be able, under favorable circumstances, to act as one wishes for one's individual good as one sees it.
>
> B. To be free is to be able, through acquired wisdom or virtue, to will or live as one ought in conformity to the moral law or an ideal befitting human nature.
>
> C. To be free is to be able, by a power inherent in human nature, to change one's own character creatively by deciding for oneself what one shall do or shall become.

---

* There is a view that no words are absolutely and completely equivocal if one wishes to stretch far enough; that is, it is always possible to find some underlying common note of meaning as between two apparently equivocal uses of a word. For example, in the case of *pen* it might be pointed out that in one sense of the word a pen holds sheep, in another a pen holds ink. But we will ignore such subtleties in this discussion.

Each of these statements expresses what is common to a whole family of conceptions of freedom. Each is determinate enough to distinguish that family from other families of conceptions. Yet each is also indeterminate enough to be further determinable, and thus each permits the divergent determinations that actual conceptions—as expressed in the theories of writers on freedom—make of the points it leaves determinable. We can therefore refer to A, B, and C as "determinables," and the actual conceptions relative to each (as found in the writings of authors) as its "determinations."

Now let X stand for a summary statement of the general understanding of freedom that is analogously common to such diverse understandings of freedom as are expressed in statements A, B, and C. Statement X must be determinate enough to be meaningful in itself, and yet indeterminate enough, relative to statements A, B, and C, not to exclude the positive content that each of them adds; that is, X must be a determinable of which A, B, and C are determinations.

The problem of identifying X—freedom in general—is therefore the problem of filling in the blank space in the following test formula:

*A man who is able*

>   (A) under favorable circumstances, to act as he wishes for his own individual good as he sees it
>
>                                   or
>
>   (B) through acquired wisdom or virtue, to will or live as he ought in conformity to the moral law or an ideal befitting human nature
>
>                                   or
>
>   (C) by a power inherent in human nature, to change his own character creatively by deciding for himself what he shall do or shall become

*is free in the sense that he*

>   (X)  . . . . . . . . . . . . . . . . . . . . . . . . . . . . . . . . . . . . . . . . . . . . . . . . . . . . . .

The solution of the problem that we propose is suggested by three things. By comparing statements A, B, and C we find (1) that they are similar in certain respects. These similarities, together with (2) other similarities that have been found in comparing these three freedoms, help us to see what is common to all three. And (3) some of the authors we have treated say certain things that can be interpreted as applying to freedom in general. These remarks also give us some hint of the solution. Let us pursue these three hints in the order indicated.

(1) The word *able* is found in statements A, B, and C. This is the most obvious point they have in common. It suggests that freedom, in any conception of it, involves an ability or power of some sort. Nothing more determinate need be understood here than what everyone understands himself to mean when he uses the word *can*. The individual who can do

something, whatever it is, has the ability or power to perform in a certain way.

Some conceptions of freedom place the emphasis upon the *ability* to act in a certain way; others, upon the *exercise* of such ability; and still others insist upon both. The one thing that is common to all is having the ability, even if, for certain conceptions, that by itself is not sufficient.

Ability as the common or generic element in all three statements is subject to different specifications in each. To cover all the more specific or determinate statements about the ability requisite for freedom, as they are found in the literature, a statement about freedom in general must remain indeterminate, both with respect to how the individual comes to have the ability and with respect to the kind of action he is thereby enabled to perform. It can say no more than this: that having an ability to act is requisite for freedom.

One other common element is to be found by comparing statements A, B, and C. In each case a certain result is said to be aimed at by exercising the ability requisite for freedom. But the result aimed at is differently specified in each of the summary statements. Therefore, in order to be indeterminate with respect to this result, a statement about freedom in general would seem to be confined to saying no more than that the ability requisite for freedom is exercised *for the sake of a desired result*. But this is too vague. It can be made more meaningful by considering one other point of similarity that we have observed in comparing what is involved in self-realization, self-perfection, and self-determination.

(2) The word *self* is, of course, the clue. In our efforts at clarification of circumstantial, acquired, and natural freedom we compared the role that *self* played in each. While the precise character of self was differently specified in each case, just as ability to act was differently specified, nevertheless the *self*, as contrasted with some *other* (that is, as contrasted with something that is opposed to self), was seen to be involved in all three. *Self* and *other* are basic common terms in the general understanding of freedom, although they are differently specified in the understanding of self-realization, self-perfection, and self-determination.

We see now that the ability or power to act in a certain way, which is present in all conceptions of freedom, is also that whereby the self is exempt from the power of another. Through the exercise of such ability or power, what a person does is his own act. It proceeds from his self, and the result it achieves is a property of his self—the realization of his self, the perfection of his self, the determination or creation of his self. It is not something that happens in him, not something that is imposed on him, not something that is done to him or for him.

Hence to say that the self is the principle of freedom is to say that the free human being is always actively the source of that which manifests his freedom—the acts that he has the power to perform. A person is not free whenever and to whatever extent he is passively affected, through being subject to an alien power, the power of another rather than his own.* His lack of freedom is manifested by everything he does and in everything that happens to him as a passive subject, dominated by the power of another. These things are not his own—neither his own acts nor the properties of his self.

This explains why the words *independence* and *autonomy* are so frequently used as synonyms for *liberty* or *freedom* in the discussion of the subject. We are now also prepared to see how certain remarks about freedom, which appear here and there in the literature, contain insight into freedom as it is generically understood.

(3) At the very beginning of the discussion, at least so far as the Western tradition is concerned, we find Plato and Aristotle speaking of the free man as one who is his own master or master of himself. The slave, in contrast, is spoken of as one who is not his own man, but another's.

This contrast runs all through the literature. We find it expressed by authors in the context of their own detailed conception of freedom—from the point of view of circumstantial self-realization, of acquired self-perfection, or of natural self-determination. Thus, for example, from the point of view of self-realization, Harold Laski writes:

> If [a man's] will is set by the will of others, he ceases to be master of himself. I cannot believe that a man no longer master of himself is in any meaning sense free.[91]

From the point of view of self-perfection, Spinoza speaks of the man who

> is his own master and only performs such actions, as he knows are of primary importance in life, and therefore chiefly desires; wherefore I call [him] . . . a free man.[92]

And from the point of view of self-determination, Aquinas refers to the free agent as one who has "mastery of his own acts." [93]

There are also passages in which self is seen as the principle of freedom —the beginning and the end of the mastery, independence, or autonomy in which freedom consists. Thus, for example, Cicero, asking "What is freedom?" replies that it is "the power to live as you will." But who "lives as he wills"? The man, Cicero says,

> whose enterprises and courses of conduct all take their start from himself and likewise have their end in himself.[94]

Or, to take another example, there is the passage in which F. H. Bradley, beginning with the question "Well, then, what is freedom?" translates this into the question "What, in short, *is* this self, the assertion of which

---

* Sometimes, as we pointed out in our analysis in Chapter 2 of the acquired freedom of self-perfection, the "other" is conceived as being within the person himself. But it is alien and other nevertheless.

is freedom?" and then translates that question in turn into the following questions: "*What* am I to be free to assert? *What* am I to be free from?" These questions, Bradley finally maintains, "are answered by the answer to one question—*What* is my true self?" [95]

If they are read as allowing for all the different specifications of the "true self" (that which is the self of self-realization, or of self-perfection, or of self-determination), the foregoing statements come very close to expressing a general understanding of freedom. By a slight reformation of what they say, we reach a statement that is determinate enough to be a significant statement about human freedom, and yet also indeterminate enough to be generic and allow for all the specifications introduced by statements A, B, and C. That statement is as follows: A man is free who has in himself the ability or power whereby he can make what he does his own action and what he achieves his own property.

To be free is to have an ability or power to act in a certain way and for a certain result. To be free is, through the exercise of such power, to have what one does proceed from oneself rather than from another. Again, through the exercise of such power, to be free is to achieve a result that is proper to oneself, and not just to another. To be free is, therefore, to be the active source of what one does or becomes, not a passive subject acted upon by another; and it is in consequence of this that what a free man does is his own act, that what he becomes is of his own making, and that what he achieves is proper to himself, that is, is his property, his own. Finally, to be unfree is either to lack the power whereby the self can make what it does and what it achieves its own, or to be overpowered by another so that what happens to one is the work of another, not one's own.

That, at any rate, is the hypothesis we advance in proposing a solution to the problem of identifying X, human freedom as that is generically understood. The hypothesis can be tested by filling in the blanks in our test formula.

*A man who is able*

    (A) under favorable circumstances, to act as he wishes for his own individual good as he sees it

or

    (B) through acquired wisdom or virtue, to will or live as he ought in conformity to the moral law or an ideal befitting human nature

or

    (C) by a power inherent in human nature, to change his own character creatively by deciding for himself what he shall do or shall become

*is free in the sense that he*

    (X) has in himself the ability or power whereby he can make what he does his own action and what he achieves his property.

The tension between self and other that is implicit in the statement we have just made about freedom generically understood signifies that it is human freedom of which we are thinking, or at least the freedom of a finite being. An infinite being—infinite in existence, power, and perfection—can have no *other* in any sense that involves independence. Only the freedom of an infinite being is said to be one of complete or absolute independence. When we use the word *independence* as a synonym for the freedom we attribute to a finite being, we must therefore mean a relative independence or independence in a certain respect, not in all respects or absolutely.

We have seen that there are deep differences of opinion about how limited or unlimited man's freedom is. We have seen how sharply this difference of opinion divides conceptions of man's acquired freedom of self-perfection, of his natural freedom of self-determination, and even of his circumstantial freedom of self-realization. In each case the difference consists in different ways of conceiving the self as exempt from dependence on the other, or the other as exerting some limitation on the self, and also in different ways of estimating their relative power or lack of power.

Far from challenging it, these differences tend to confirm our hypothesis that self and other are the root terms in the generic meaning of human freedom, as well as being involved in any understanding of the distinction between human and divine freedom—or between the freedom of a finite and of an infinite being.

## 15.  Freedom, law, and responsibility

Our hypothesis also throws light on two other things that enter into the discussion of freedom, no matter from what point of view the subject is treated. One is the notion of responsibility. The other is the significance attached to law, either as a source of or as an obstacle to freedom.

With regard to responsibility, it suffices to recall the conclusions reached at the end of Chapter 3. The generic meaning of responsibility has the same roots as the generic meaning of freedom. As a man is free only in doing that which is his own action or in achieving that which is proper to himself, so a man is responsible only for the actions or achievements that are his own or proper to him. He is not answerable or accountable for that which is done by another or belongs to another, nor can such things be imputed to him. Hence, no matter how man's freedom is conceived in detail, he will be conceived to be responsible in whatever way and to whatever extent he is conceived to be free.

With regard to law, we recall that in dealing with the different forms taken by certain freedoms we have identified, law—positive law, moral law, physical law—is a pivotal term in the discussion.

The fact that law is intimately connected with liberty becomes intelligible in the light of our generic understanding of freedom. If some tension between self and other is involved in any conception of freedom, then law plays one role when it represents a power alien to the self, and another when the self is able to make the law somehow its own or an expression of its power. In the first role, law is an obstacle to freedom; in the second, it is a source of freedom, or even part of its substance.

The character of the law, as well as the role it plays, varies with variations in the conception of freedom. It is mainly the civil or positive law, the law of the state, that is being considered in the discussion of self-realization; it is the moral law primarily, and only secondarily the positive law, that is being considered in the discussion of self-perfection. The positive law alone is involved in conceptions of political liberty. In conceptions of collective freedom it is the laws of nature discovered by natural scientists that play a beneficent role, as against the adverse role played by the moral or positive rules that men make and impose on other men. And it is also the laws of nature discovered by natural scientists that enter into the discussion of self-determination. Furthermore, in all these connections except the last, the relation of law to liberty is differently conceived according as the type of law in question is thought to be purely an expression of reason, purely an arbitrary or willful imposition, or a mixture of the rational and the arbitrary.

The above remarks suggest certain difficulties involved in the task of analyzing the idea of freedom that have not been overcome and that, in the nature of things, could not have been overcome. In other words, we are brought to the realization that the treatment of a subject like freedom cannot be fully accomplished without a similar treatment of other, intimately connected subjects, such as law or (as we saw at the end of Chapter 3) causation. Consider the question "How is law related to liberty?" It is intelligible in the meaning of its principal terms. It is intelligible enough to be taken as a question to which a wide variety of authors appear to give quite different answers. But if they give different answers because they hold different conceptions of freedom and of law, the different answers they give do not directly bring them into genuine disagreement.

Let us consider this from the freedom side, as it were. We know, for example, that there are (1) authors who maintain that freedom consists in exemption *from* legal regulations or restrictions and (2) authors who maintain that freedom consists in obedience *to* law. On the face of it, it seems that these two groups of authors are in disagreement. But when, in the case of the first group, we have identified the freedom *from* law they are talking about as a circumstantial freedom of self-realization, and when, in the case of the second, we have identified the freedom *under* law they are talking about as an acquired freedom of self-perfection, we recognize that they are not talking about the same freedom.

The question about the relation of liberty to law shifts its meaning when the law being referred to is neither the law of the state nor the moral law but the laws of nature discovered by physical scientists. The question may then be interpreted as asking whether freedom is compatible with the kind of causal necessity that such laws represent. We know that there are (3) authors who maintain that freedom is completely compatible with such necessity and (4) authors who maintain that it is not. Again, the two statements appear to be contradictory. But when the freedom that is said to be compatible with the necessity of physical laws is identified as a circumstantial freedom of self-realization, and when the freedom that is said to be incompatible with such necessity is identified as a natural freedom of self-determination through choice, we again recognize that these two groups of authors, like the first two, are not talking about the same freedom and, therefore, are not directly in disagreement.

But these clarifications are doubtless only partial, based as they are on the analysis of only one of the two principal terms in the question. Until a similar clarification of the idea of law (as well as of other ideas) is undertaken, we cannot be certain that our understanding of the idea of freedom is complete. Nevertheless, we have made a start.

## 16. Concluding observations

We wish, finally, to make some general observations about the discussion of freedom as a whole, and about the role that we have reason to hope this study of freedom, and other, similar, studies of other basic ideas can play in the future intellectual progress of the human race.

With regard to freedom, it is our melancholy conclusion that, if the idea of rational debate is appropriate to the philosophical enterprise (as we think it is), then it would be hard to gainsay the fact that what has been accomplished in twenty-five centuries of Western thought about freedom is a very poor performance, indeed.

Individual thinkers have presented us with elaborate theories and have told us, with clarity and cogency, the reasons for the conclusions they have reached about freedom. There has been no dearth of theoretical insights, no lack of originality or variety. Century after century, great intellectual resources have been lavished on the discussion of freedom. The signal contributions of individual genius have started new ways of thinking about the subject and enriched or deepened others. Yet the fact remains that the profound disagreements that have emerged from all this intellectual effort have not been well-disputed issues in a sustained and rationally conducted series of controversies about freedom.

One might ask, "Why should there be?" But that is to deny that philosophy is a rational process of inquiry competent to advance men's knowledge of fundamental truths. It is to assert that the diversity of philosophical systems, like the diversity of great poetical works or other works of the imagination, should not be treated like conflicting hypotheses or formulations in the empirical sciences.

We cannot accept that view, and in rejecting it propose, instead, a division of labor in the philosophical enterprise as a whole. Creative philosophical thought is one kind of work; it is quite another task to review the whole discussion of a particular subject in order to discover the basic issues that have arisen and the extent to which they have been disputed.

With the latter task completed, here and in the parent work, the two-volume *Idea of Freedom,* it is, we think, reasonable to expect the philosophers of subsequent generations to dispute the issues about this subject more explicitly and extensively than their predecessors have done. If the ideal of rational debate were, in consequence, more fully approximated in the various controversies about freedom, that might lead to the resolution of some age-old issues or at least enable us to see why they are irresolvable. In either case, an advance would have been made.

It is important to point out that the contribution that is made to the pursuit of philosophical truth by studies such as this lies solely in the clarification of a field of thought for the sake of progress in that field. The progress itself must be made by the philosophers, not merely by the creative effort to supply the arguments and counterarguments that are called for by the issues that exist, and that either have not been disputed at all or have been inadequately debated.

We hope that this work on the idea of freedom will serve as a first step toward greater progress in man's thinking about this subject. Whether or not it effectively serves the purpose for which it is intended can be fairly and accurately judged only by those who try to make use of it to advance human thought about freedom. Should they find it of substantial assistance to them in that task, our labors will have been duly rewarded. In addition, others may be encouraged to undertake similar labors in the field of other basic ideas.

---

1 *A Discourse on the Origin of Inequality,* in *The Social Contract and Discourses,* trans. G. D. H. Cole (New York: E. P. Dutton & Co., Everyman's Library, 1950), p. 208; *GBWW,* Vol. 38, p. 338.

2 *Being and Nothingness: An Essay on Phenomenological Ontology,* trans. Hazel E. Barnes (New York: Philosophical Library, 1956), p. 25.

3 *Existentialism,* trans. Bernard Frechtman (New York: Philosophical Library, 1947), p. 27.

4 *Being and Nothingness,* p. 25.

5 *Man's Freedom* (New Haven: Yale University Press, 1950), p. 28.

6 *Systematic Theology* (Chicago: University of Chicago Press, 1951), 1:185. Tillich amplifies this by saying that in all natural things the polarity of spontaneity and law is analogous to the polarity of freedom and destiny in man. *See also* p. 186.

7 *Truth*, vol. 1, trans. Robert W. Mulligan, S.J. vol. 2, trans. James V. McGlynn, S.J.; vol. 3, trans. Robert W. Schmidt, S.J. (Chicago: Henry Regnery Co., 1952–54), vol. 3, q. 24, a. 1, reply 1, p. 139.

8 *How We Think* (New York: D. C. Heath & Co., 1910), chap. 5, sec. 2, p. 65.

9 *Experience and Education* (New York: The Macmillan Co., 1950), chap. 5, p. 74.

10 Ibid., p. 69.

11 *Philosophy and Civilization* (New York: Minton, Balch & Co., 1931), p. 286.

12 *Freedom in the Modern World,* trans. R. O'Sullivan (New York: Charles Scribner's Sons, 1936), p. 34.

13 *On Grace and Free Will,* trans. P. Holmes, in *Basic Writings of St. Augustine,* ed. Whitney J. Oates (New York: Random House, 1948), chap. 31, p. 758.

14 *Truth*, vol. 3, q. 24, a. 14, p. 205.

15 *Meditation IV,* in *The Philosophical Works of Descartes,* ed. and trans. E. S. Haldane and G. R. T. Ross, 2 vols. (Cambridge: Cambridge University Press, 1931–34), 1:175.

16 *The English Works of Thomas Hobbes,* ed. W. Molesworth, 11 vols. (London: John Bohn, 1839–45), 5:372–73.

17 Ibid., p. 390.

18 *Freedom of the Will,* ed. Paul Ramsey (New Haven: Yale University Press, 1957), p. 175.

19 Ibid., p. 178.

20 Ibid., p. 226.

21 *Method and Results* (New York: D. Appleton & Co., 1898), p. 244.

22 *A Treatise of Human Nature,* ed. L. A. Selby-Bigge (Oxford: Clarendon Press, 1896), bk. 2, pt. 3, sec. 1, p. 407.

23 *The Questions concerning Liberty, Necessity, and Chance,* in *The English Works of Thomas Hobbes,* 5:373.

24 Ibid., p. 374.

25 Ibid., p. 395.

26 *Free Will and Four English Philosophers* (London: Burns & Oates, 1906), p. 177.

27 Ibid., p. 197.

28 *See* ibid., pp. 67ff; 148ff.

29 *The Doctrine of Philosophical Necessity Illustrated* (London, 1782), pp. 13, 23–24.

30 Ibid., p. 36.

31 Ibid., p. 38.

32 Ibid., pp. 55–56.

33 *The Principles of Psychology,* 2 vols. (New York: Henry Holt & Co., 1902), 2:561; *GBWW,* Vol. 53, p. 815.

34 Ibid., pp. 576–77; *GBWW,* Vol. 53, p. 825.

35 Ibid., 1:447–48, 453–54; *GBWW,* Vol. 53, pp. 291, 294–95.

36 *The Questions concerning Liberty, Necessity, and Chance,* p. 380.

37 *The Ethics,* in vol. 2 of *The Chief Works of Benedict de Spinoza,* trans. R. H. M. Elwes, vols. 1 and 2 bound as one (New York: Dover Publications, 1951), pt. 1, prop. 33, n. 1, p. 71; *GBWW,* Vol. 31, p. 367.

38 *The Correspondence of Spinoza,* trans. and ed. A. Wolf (London: George Allen & Unwin, 1928), letter 62, pp. 390–91.

39 *A Treatise of Human Nature,* bk. 2, pt. 3, sec. 1, p. 407.

40 *An Enquiry concerning Human Understanding,* in *Enquiries concerning the Human Understanding and concerning the Principles of Morals,* ed. L. A. Selby-Bigge (Oxford: Clarendon Press, 1951), sec. 8, pt. 1, div. 74, pp. 95–96; *GBWW,* Vol. 35, p. 484.

41 *The Doctrine of Philosophical Necessity,* p. 9.

42 "Free-Will and Fatalism," in *Complete Essays of Schopenhauer,* trans. T. Bailey Saunders (New York: Willey Book Co., 1942), p. 57.

43 *An Examination of Sir William Hamilton's Philosophy,* 5th ed. (London: Longmans, Green, Reader and Dyer, 1878), p. 583.

44 *The Will to Power,* trans. Anthony M. Ludovici, 2 vols., in *Complete Works of*

*Friedrich Nietzsche*, ed. Oscar Levy (London: T. N. Foulis, 1914), 15:55–59, 109–23.

45 *Beyond Good and Evil*, in *The Philosophy of Nietzsche*, trans. Helen Zimmern (New York: Random House, The Modern Library, 1927), p. 403.

46 *The Will to Power*, 2:117.

47 Ibid., 2:116.

48 *De Malo*, in *Quaestiones Disputatae et Quaestiones Duodecim Quodlibetales* (Turin-Rome: Marietti, 1931), vol. 2, q. 6, a. 1.

49 *The Questions concerning Liberty, Necessity, and Chance*, p. 382.

50 Ibid., p. 388.

51 *De Malo*, q. 6, a. 1, reply to objection 15.

52 Ibid.

53 *Summa Theologica*, trans. Fathers of the English Dominican Province, 3 vols. (New York: Benziger Brothers, 1947–48), pt. 1–2, q. 13, a. 6; *GBWW*, Vol. 19, pp. 676–77.

54 See *Traité du libre arbitre* (Liège: Sciences et Lettres, 1951), chap. 7, p. 111.

55 *Time and Free Will*, trans. F. L. Pogson (London: George Allen & Unwin, 1950), pp. 219–21.

56 Ibid., pp. 200–1.

57 *Examination of Sir William Hamilton's Philosophy*, p. 576.

58 Ibid., p. 578.

59 *The Principles of Psychology*, 2:573; *GBWW*, Vol. 53, p. 823.

60 *On the Diversity of Morals*, in vol. 1, *Essays in Sociology and Social Philosophy* (New York: The Macmillan Co., 1957), p. 82.

61 *Christian Theology and Natural Science* (New York: The Ronald Press Co., 1956), p. 214.

62 *The Problem of Free Choice*, trans. Dom Mark Pontifex, Ancient Christian Writers, no. 22 (Westminster, Md.: Newman Press, 1955), p. 149.

63 *The Consolation of Philosophy*, trans. W. V. Cooper (New York: Random House, Modern Library, 1943), p. 104.

64 *On the Bondage of the Will*, trans. Henry Cole (Grand Rapids, Mich.: Wm. B. Eerdmans Publishing Co., 1931). In vol. 2: *The Bondage of the Will*, a new translation of *De Servo Arbitrio* (1525) by J. I. Packer and O. R. Johnston (London: James Clarke & Co., 1953), p. 317.

65 *Institutes of the Christian Religion*, trans. and ed. John Allen, 2 vols. (Grand Rapids, Mich.: Wm. B. Eerdmans Publishing Co., 1949), vol. 2, bk. 3, chap. 23, pp. 206–7.

66 Ibid., bk. 3, chap. 21, p. 175.

67 *Freedom of the Will*, p. 263.

68 *Science and Humanism* (Cambridge: Cambridge University Press, 1951), pp. 59–60.

69 *The Principles of Philosophy*, in *The Philosophical Works of Descartes*, principle 41, p. 235.

70 *Discussions on Philosophy and Literature, Education and University Reform*, 2d ed. (London: Longman, Brown, Green & Longmans, 1853), pp. 626–27.

71 *Prolegomena Logica* (Oxford: William Graham, 1851), pp. 304–5. Mill's allusion to the problem, mentioned by Mansel, occurs in his *A System of Logic, Ratiocinative and Inductive, Being a Connected View of the Principles of Evidence, and the Methods of Scientific Investigation*, 2 vols., 4th ed. (London: John W. Parker and Son, 1856), bk. 6, chap. 2, sec. 2.

72 *The Problem of Free Choice*, pp. 148–49.

73 *The City of God*, trans. Marcus Dods, 2 vols. (Edinburgh: T & T Clark, 1891), vol. 1, bk. 5, chap. 10, p. 196; *GBWW*, Vol. 18, p. 216.

74 *The Consolation of Philosophy*, pp. 108–9, 115–18.

75 Ibid., p. 118.

76 *The Guide of the Perplexed*, trans. M. Friedlander (London: George Routledge & Sons, 1928), pt. 3, chap. 17, p. 285.

77 *The Eight Chapters of Maimonides on Ethics*, ed. and trans. Joseph I. Gorfinkle (New York: Columbia University Press, 1912), chap. 8, p. 101.

78 *Summa Theologica*, pt. 1–2, q. 10, a. 4; *GBWW*, Vol. 19, pp. 665–66.

79 Ibid., objection 1 and reply 1.

80 *De Malo*, q. 6, a. 1, objection 5 and reply 5.

[81] "The Dilemma of Determinism," in *The Will to Believe* (New York: Longmans, Green & Co., 1917), p. 180–82.

[82] Ibid., p. 182.

[83] *Systematic Theology* (Chicago: University of Chicago Press, 1951), 1:266–67.

[84] *A Treatise of Human Nature,* bk. 2, pt. 3, sec. 1, p. 407.

[85] Ibid., sec. 2, p. 410. This statement is later repeated almost verbatim in the *Enquiry concerning Human Understanding,* sec. 8, pt. 2, div. 76, pp. 97–98, in *Enquiries concerning the Human Understanding and concerning the Principles of Morals; GBWW,* Vol. 35, p. 485.

[86] *A Treatise of Human Nature,* bk. 2, pt. 3, sec. 2, p. 411. *See* ibid., pp. 411–12. These pages are also repeated almost verbatim in the *Enquiry,* on pp. 98–99; *GBWW,* Vol. 35, p. 485.

[87] "Determinism and Morals," in *The Hibbert Journal* 7, no. 1 (October 1908): 121.

[88] *Human Society in Ethics and Politics* (New York: Simon and Schuster, 1955), p. 79. *See also* ibid., p. 80.

[89] *Free Will and Four English Philosophers,* p. 157.

[90] "Symposium: The Freedom of the Will," in *The Proceedings of the Aristotelian Society,* supp. vol. 25, pp. 193–94 (1951).

[91] *Liberty in the Modern State* (Harmondsworth, Middlesex: Penguin Books, 1937), chap. 1, sec. 1, p. 62.

[92] *Ethics,* pt. 4, prop. 66, note, p. 232; *GBWW,* Vol. 31, p. 444.

[93] *(Commentary on the Sentences) Scriptum super Libros Sententiarum,* ed. P. Mandonnet, O.P., and M. F. Moos, O.P., 4 vols. (Paris: P. Lethielleux, 1929–47), bk. 2, d. 25, q. 1, a. 1, reply 3.

[94] *Paradoxa Stoicorum,* in *De Oratore,* 2 vols., bk. 3, together with *De Fato, Paradoxa Stoicorum, De Partitione Oratoria,* trans. H. Rackham (Cambridge, Mass.: Harvard University Press, Loeb Classical Library, 1948), 34:287.

[95] *Ethical Studies,* 2d ed. (Oxford: Clarendon Press, 1927), pp. 56–57.

NOTE TO THE READER

Much of this part of "The Idea of Freedom," as also of the part that appeared in *The Great Ideas Today 1972,* is based upon readings listed in Chapter 47 of the *Syntopicon,* LIBERTY, under Topic 1*c,* which deals with the relation between liberty and personal development; under Topic 1*e,* which is concerned with liberty and license; and under Topic 3*c,* where virtue is considered as the discipline of free choice. But see, in addition, the readings listed under NECESSITY AND CONTINGENCY 5*a*(3), which discuss human freedom as the acceptance of necessity, and those at WILL 5*a*(2), 5*b*(2), and 8*a,* which are concerned with relevant aspects of the freedom of the will.

In *GGB,* the *Enchiridion* of Epictetus, which appears in Vol. 10, pp. 234–54, gives the Stoic position on freedom. Further relevant readings are Emerson's essay *Self-Reliance,* also in Vol. 10, at pp. 525–45, and the various *Great Documents* of liberty and human rights that are reprinted in Vol. 6, pp. 407–56.

# Additions
# to the
# Great Books Library

# In Defense of Socrates

Xenophon

## Editor's Introduction

Xenophon the historian was born in Athens around 430 B.C., and died, probably in the same city, sometime after 355. He is best remembered as the author of the *Anabasis,* or March of the Ten Thousand—a work, once known to every schoolboy who ever studied Greek, that recounts the efforts of an expedition of Greek mercenaries, of which Xenophon was one, to extricate themselves from their involvement in the abortive rebellion of the younger Cyrus against his brother Artaxerxes II of Persia in about the year 400. But we know Xenophon too for other writings, among them the *Memorabilia,* or "Recollections of Socrates," which is the only other extended account we have of that philosopher besides the one provided by Plato's Dialogues.

It was once thought that the *Memorabilia* was based upon actual conversations that Xenophon had with Socrates, who was certainly known to him, and of whose discourse he was a witness in his younger days, but this is now held to be doubtful. Relations between the two men were apparently not very close; it has been suggested, perhaps unfairly, that much of Xenophon's "recollection" was derived from Plato's work rather than from his own encounters with their common teacher, whose talk he did not understand very well, or at any rate did not understand as Plato understood it. Xenophon was a plain, blunt soldier, orthodox and pious in his outlook, who took a moral interest in Socrates but not a philosophical one. In setting down what he remembered, or what he thought he knew, Xenophon appears to have had in mind various occasions (parts of the *Memorabilia* were written at different times), such as the need to educate his sons, or a desire to influence public opinion, when it could seem useful to recall Socrates as an example.

Such an occasion was provided by the publication, in about the year 393, of an attack on Socrates's memory by a well-known sophist named Polycrates. The attack took the form of an imaginary speech by one of Socrates's three prosecutors, Anytus, at his trial. In fact, there was and is no exact record of what Anytus or anyone else said on this occasion; Polycrates, who had attended the trial, was really attacking the version of it given by Plato in the *Apology.* Nor can we be sure of what Polycrates actually wrote, since his attack, which became known as the "Accusation of Socrates," has not survived. All we have are a couple of rejoinders that were made subsequently by different persons, of which Xenophon's was the earliest. His point by point reply to Polycrates, who is the real "accuser" of whom he speaks, begins on page 307. What comes before is Xenophon's general defense of Socrates against the indictment that was brought against him.

This earlier part of the defense, in particular, should be read alongside Plato's *Apology*. For what Xenophon says on Socrates's behalf is precisely what Socrates himself, in Plato's account, refused to say, though if he had said it he would probably have been acquitted, or at most would have been let off with a fine. Xenophon ignores—may not have perceived—the real point of the *Apology*, which is that Socrates is guilty as charged but that the charge is radically defective because his accusers do not understand what they are talking about. This essential irony is missing from Xenophon, who defends Socrates on terms that deny the intent and meaning of his career. It seems to be right—it is the defense most men would have been tempted to make, then or since—but in fact it is deeply wrong, as the *Apology* makes clear, and would have betrayed Socrates if he had adopted it.

The portion of the *Memorabilia* that follows consists of Book I and a portion of Book II. The remainder of Book II contains examples, probably written at another time, of Socrates's teachings—examples that may well have been taken from Plato and other sources. Book III consists of miscellaneous dialogues strung together, and Book IV, written still later, apparently, contains more of the same, though it ends with a peroration in which the virtues of Socrates are summed up. This peroration appears in *Gateway to the Great Books,* Vol. 6, pp. 193–226, along with a portion of the *Anabasis.*

# In Defense of Socrates

I have often wondered by what arguments those who drew up the indictment against Socrates could persuade the Athenians that his life was forfeit to the state. The indictment against him was to this effect: *Socrates is guilty of rejecting the gods acknowledged by the state and of bringing in strange deities: he is also guilty of corrupting the youth.*

First then, that he rejected the gods acknowledged by the state—what evidence did they produce of that? He offered sacrifices constantly, and made no secret of it, now in his home, now at the altars of the state temples, and he made use of divination with as little secrecy. Indeed it had become notorious that Socrates claimed to be guided by "the deity" [1]: it was out of this claim, I think, that the charge of bringing in strange deities arose. He was no more bringing in anything strange than are other believers in divination, who rely on augury, oracles, coincidences and sacrifices. For these men's belief is not that the birds or the folk met by accident know what profits the inquirer, but that they are the instruments by which the gods make this known; and that was Socrates' belief too. Only, whereas most men say that the birds or the folk they meet dissuade or encourage them, Socrates said what he meant: for he said that the deity gave him a sign. Many of his companions were counselled by him to do this or not to do that in accordance with the warnings of the deity: and those who followed his advice prospered, and those who rejected it had

cause for regret. And yet who would not admit that he wished to appear neither a knave nor a fool to his companions? but he would have been thought both, had he proved to be mistaken when he alleged that his counsel was in accordance with divine revelation. Obviously, then, he would not have given the counsel if he had not been confident that what he said would come true. And who could have inspired him with that confidence but a god? And since he had confidence in the gods, how can he have disbelieved in the existence of the gods? Another way he had of dealing with intimate friends was this: if there was no room for doubt, he advised them to act as they thought best; but if the consequences could not be foreseen, he sent them to the oracle to inquire whether the thing ought to be done. Those who intended to control a house or a city, he said, needed the help of divination. For the craft of carpenter, smith, farmer or ruler, and the theory of such crafts, and arithmetic and economics and generalship might be learned and mastered by the application of human powers; but the deepest secrets of these matters the gods reserved to themselves; they were dark to men. You may plant a field well; but you know not who shall gather the fruits: you may build a house well; but you know not who shall dwell in it: able to command, you

---

[1] That immanent "divine something," as Cicero terms it, which Socrates claimed as his peculiar possession.

305

cannot know whether it is profitable to command: versed in statecraft, you know not whether it is profitable to guide the state: though, for your delight, you marry a pretty woman, you cannot tell whether she will bring you sorrow: though you form a party among men mighty in the state, you know not whether they will cause you to be driven from the state. If any man thinks that these matters are wholly within the grasp of the human mind and nothing in them is beyond our reason, that man, he said, is irrational. But it is no less irrational to seek the guidance of heaven in matters which men are permitted by the gods to decide for themselves by study: to ask, for instance, Is it better to get an experienced coachman to drive my carriage or a man without experience? Is it better to get an experienced seaman to steer my ship or a man without experience? So too with what we may know by reckoning, measurement or weighing. To put such questions to the gods seemed to his mind profane. In short, what the gods have granted us to do by help of learning, we must learn; what is hidden from mortals we should try to find out from the gods by divination: for to him that is in their grace the gods grant a sign.

Moreover, Socrates lived ever in the open; for early in the morning he went to the public promenades and training-grounds; in the forenoon he was seen in the market; and the rest of the day he passed just where most people were to be met: he was generally talking, and anyone might listen. Yet none ever knew him to offend against piety and religion in deed or word. He did not even discuss that topic so favoured by other talkers, "the Nature of the Universe": and avoided speculation on the so-called "Cosmos" of the Professors, how it works, and on the laws that govern the phenomena of the heavens: indeed he would argue that to trouble one's mind with such problems is sheer folly. In the first place, he would inquire, did these thinkers suppose that their knowledge of human

affairs was so complete that they must seek these new fields for the exercise of their brains; or that it was their duty to neglect human affairs and consider only things divine? Moreover, he marvelled at their blindness in not seeing that man cannot solve these riddles; since even the most conceited talkers on these problems did not agree in their theories, but behaved to one another like madmen. As some madmen have no fear of danger and others are afraid where there is nothing to be afraid of, as some will do or say anything in a crowd with no sense of shame, while others shrink even from going abroad among men, some respect neither temple nor altar nor any other sacred thing, others worship stocks and stones and beasts, so is it, he held, with those who worry with "Universal Nature." Some hold that *What is* is one, others that it is infinite in number: some that all things are in perpetual motion, others that nothing can ever be moved at any time: some that all life is birth and decay, others that nothing can ever be born or ever die. Nor were those the only questions he asked about such theorists. Students of human nature, he said, think that they will apply their knowledge in due course for the good of themselves and any others they choose. Do those who pry into heavenly phenomena imagine that, once they have discovered the laws by which these are produced, they will create at their will winds, waters, seasons and such things to their need? Or have they no such expectation, and are they satisfied with knowing the causes of these various phenomena?

Such, then, was his criticism of those who meddle with these matters. His own conversation was ever of human things. The problems he discussed were, What is godly, what is ungodly; what is beautiful, what is ugly; what is just, what is unjust; what is prudence, what is madness; what is courage, what is cowardice; what is a state, what is a statesman; what is government, and what is a governor—these and others like them, of which the knowledge made a "gentle-man," in his estimation, while ignorance should involve the reproach of "slavish-ness."

So, in pronouncing on opinions of his that were unknown to them it is not surpris-ing that the jury erred: but is it not aston-ishing that they should have ignored matters of common knowledge? For instance, when he was on the Council and had taken the counsellor's oath by which he bound him-self to give counsel in accordance with the laws, it fell to his lot to preside in the Assembly when the people wanted to con-demn Thrasyllus and Erasinides and their colleagues to death by a single vote. That was illegal, and he refused the motion in spite of popular rancour and the threats of many powerful persons. It was more to him that he should keep his oath than that he should humour the people in an unjust demand and shield himself from threats. For, like most men, indeed, he believed that the gods are heedful of mankind, but with an important difference; for whereas they do not believe in the omniscience of the gods, Socrates thought that they know all things, our words and deeds and secret pur-poses; that they are present everywhere, and grant signs to men of all that concerns man.

I wonder, then, how the Athenians can have been persuaded that Socrates was a freethinker, when he never said or did any-thing contrary to sound religion, and his utterances about the gods and his behaviour towards them were the words and actions of a man who is truly religious and deserves to be thought so.

No less wonderful is it to me that some believed the charge brought against Soc-rates of corrupting the youth. In the first place, apart from what I have said, in con-trol of his own passions and appetites he was the strictest of men; further, in endur-ance of cold and heat and every kind of toil he was most resolute; and besides, his needs were so schooled to moderation that having very little he was yet very content.

Such was his own character: how then can he have led others into impiety, crime, gluttony, lust, or sloth? On the contrary, he cured these vices in many, by putting into them a desire for goodness, and by giving them confidence that self-discipline would make them gentlemen. To be sure he never professed to teach this; but, by letting his own light shine, he led his disciples to hope that they through imitation of him would attain to such excellence. Furthermore, he himself never neglected the body, and re-proved such neglect in others. Thus over-eating followed by over-exertion he disap-proved. But he approved of taking as much hard exercise as is agreeable to the soul; for the habit not only insured good health, but did not hamper the care of the soul. On the other hand, he disliked foppery and preten-tiousness in the fashion of clothes or shoes or in behaviour. Nor, again, did he encour-age love of money in his companions. For while he checked their other desires, he would not make money himself out of their desire for his companionship. He held that this self-denying ordinance insured his liberty. Those who charged a fee for their society he denounced for selling themselves into bondage; since they were bound to con-verse with all from whom they took the fee. He marvelled that anyone should make money by the profession of virtue, and should not reflect that his highest reward would be the gain of a good friend; as though he who became a true gentleman could fail to feel deep gratitude for a benefit so great. Socrates indeed never promised any such boon to anyone; but he was con-fident that those of his companions who adopted his principles of conduct would throughout life be good friends to him and to one another. How, then, should such a man "corrupt the youth"? Unless, per-chance, it be corruption to foster virtue.

But, said his accuser, he taught his com-panions to despise the established laws by insisting on the folly of appointing public officials by lot, when none would choose a pilot or builder or flautist by lot, nor any other craftsman for work in which mistakes are far less disastrous than mistakes in statecraft. Such sayings, he argued, led the young to despise the established constitution and made them violent. But I hold that they who cultivate wisdom and think they will be able to guide the people in prudent policy never lapse into violence: they know that enmities and dangers are inseparable from violence, but persuasion produces the same results safely and amicably. For violence, by making its victims sensible of loss, rouses their hatred: but persuasion, by seeming to confer a favour, wins goodwill. It is not, then, cultivation of wisdom that leads to violent methods, but the possession of power without prudence. Besides, many supporters are necessary to him who ventures to use force: but he who can persuade needs no confederate, having confidence in his own unaided power of persuasion. And such a man has no occasion to shed blood; for who would rather take a man's life than have a live and willing follower?

But his accuser argued thus. Among the associates of Socrates were Critias and Alcibiades; and none wrought so many evils to the state. For Critias in the days of the oligarchy bore the palm for greed and violence: Alcibiades, for his part, exceeded all in licentiousness and insolence under the democracy. Now I have no intention of excusing the wrong these two men wrought the state; but I will explain how they came to be with Socrates. Ambition was the very life-blood of both: no Athenian was ever like them. They were eager to get control of everything and to outstrip every rival in notoriety. They knew that Socrates was living on very little, and yet was wholly independent; that he was strictly moderate in all his pleasures; and that in argument he could do what he liked with any disputant. Sharing this knowledge and the principles I have indicated, is it to be supposed that these two men wanted to adopt the simple life of Socrates, and with this object in view sought his society? Did they not rather think

that by associating with him they would attain the utmost proficiency in speech and action? For my part I believe that, had heaven granted them the choice between the life they saw Socrates leading and death, they would have chosen rather to die. Their conduct betrayed their purpose; for as soon as they thought themselves superior to their fellow-disciples they sprang away from Socrates and took to politics; it was for political ends that they had wanted Socrates.

But it may be answered: Socrates should have taught his companions prudence before politics. I do not deny it; but I find that all teachers show their disciples how they themselves practise what they teach, and lead them on by argument. And I know that it was so with Socrates: he showed his companions that he was a gentleman himself, and talked most excellently of goodness and of all things that concern man. I know further that even those two were prudent so long as they were with Socrates, not from fear of fine or blow, but because at that time they really believed in prudent conduct.

But many self-styled lovers of wisdom may reply: A just man can never become unjust; a prudent man can never become wanton; in fact no one having learned any kind of knowledge can become ignorant of it. I do not hold with this view. I notice that as those who do not train the body cannot perform the functions proper to the body, so those who do not train the soul cannot perform the functions of the soul: for they cannot do what they ought to do nor avoid what they ought not to do. For this cause fathers try to keep their sons, even if they are prudent lads, out of bad company: for the society of honest men is a training in virtue, but the society of the bad is virtue's undoing. As one of the poets says:

*"From the good shalt thou learn good things; but if thou minglest with the bad thou shalt lose even what thou hast of wisdom."* [2]

And another says:

*"Ah, but a good man is at one time noble, at another base."* 3

My testimony agrees with theirs; for I see that, just as poetry is forgotten unless it is often repeated, so instruction, when no longer heeded, fades from the mind. To forget good counsel is to forget the experiences that prompted the soul to desire prudence: and when those are forgotten, it is not surprising that prudence itself is forgotten. I see also that men who take to drink or get involved in love intrigues lose the power of caring about right conduct and avoiding evil. For many who are careful with their money no sooner fall in love than they begin to waste it: and when they have spent it all, they no longer shrink from making more by methods which they formerly avoided because they thought them disgraceful. How then can it be impossible for one who was prudent to lose his prudence, for one who was capable of just action to become incapable? To me indeed it seems that whatever is honourable, whatever is good in conduct is the result of training, and that this is especially true of prudence. For in the same body along with the soul are planted the pleasures which call to her: "Abandon prudence, and make haste to gratify us and the body."

And indeed it was thus with Critias and Alcibiades. So long as they were with Socrates, they found in him an ally who gave them strength to conquer their evil passions. But when they parted from him, Critias fled to Thessaly, and got among men who put lawlessness before justice; while Alcibiades, on account of his beauty, was hunted by many great ladies, and because of his influence at Athens and among her allies he was spoilt by many powerful men: and as athletes who gain an easy victory in the games are apt to neglect their training, so the honour in which he was held, the cheap triumph he won with the people, led him to neglect himself. Such was their

fortune: and when to pride of birth, confidence in wealth, vainglory and much yielding to temptation were added corruption and long separation from Socrates, what wonder if they grew overbearing? For their wrongdoing, then, is Socrates to be called to account by his accuser? And does he deserve no word of praise for having controlled them in the days of their youth, when they would naturally be most reckless and licentious? Other cases, at least, are not so judged. For what teacher of flute, lyre, or anything else, after making his pupils proficient, is held to blame if they leave him for another master, and then turn out incompetent? What father, whose son bears a good character so long as he is with one master, but goes wrong after he has attached himself to another, throws the blame on the earlier teacher? Is it not true that the worse the boy turns out with the second, the higher is his father's praise of the first? Nay, fathers themselves, living with their sons, are not held responsible for their boys' wrongdoing if they are themselves prudent men. This is the test which should have been applied to Socrates too. If there was anything base in his own life, he might fairly have been thought vicious. But, if his own conduct was always prudent, how can he be fairly held to blame for the evil that was not in him?

Nevertheless, although he was himself free from vice, if he saw and approved of base conduct in them, he would be open to censure. Well, when he found that Critias loved Euthydemus and wanted to lead him astray, he tried to restrain him by saying that it was mean and unbecoming in a gentleman to sue like a beggar to the object of his affection, whose good opinion he coveted, stooping to ask a favour that it was wrong to grant. As Critias paid no heed whatever to this protest, Socrates, it is said, exclaimed in the presence of Euthydemus and many others, "Critias seems to have the

---

2 Theognis.
3 Author unknown.

feelings of a pig: he can no more keep away from Euthydemus than pigs can help rubbing themselves against stones." Now Critias bore a grudge against Socrates for this; and when he was one of the Thirty and was drafting laws with Charicles, he bore it in mind. He inserted a clause which made it illegal "to teach the art of words." It was a calculated insult to Socrates, whom he saw no means of attacking, except by imputing to him the practice constantly attributed to philosophers,[4] and so making him unpopular. For I myself never heard Socrates indulge in the practice, nor knew of anyone who professed to have heard him do so. The truth came out. When the Thirty were putting to death many citizens of the highest respectability and were encouraging many in crime, Socrates had remarked: "It seems strange enough to me that a herdsman who lets his cattle decrease and go to the bad should not admit that he is a poor cowherd; but stranger still that a statesman when he causes the citizens to decrease and go to the bad, should feel no shame nor think himself a poor statesman." This remark was reported to Critias and Charicles, who sent for Socrates, showed him the law and forbade him to hold conversation with the young.

"May I question you," asked Socrates, "in case I do not understand any point in your orders?"

"You may," said they.

"Well now," said he, "I am ready to obey the laws. But lest I unwittingly transgress through ignorance, I want clear directions from you. Do you think that the art of words from which you bid me abstain is associated with sound or unsound reasoning? For if with sound, then clearly I must abstain from sound reasoning: but if with unsound, clearly I must try to reason soundly."

"Since you are ignorant, Socrates," said Charicles in an angry tone, "we put our order into language easier to understand. You may not hold any converse whatever with the young."

"Well then," said Socrates, "that there may be no question raised about my obedience, please fix the age limit below which a man is to be accounted young."

"So long," replied Charicles, "as he is not permitted to sit in the Council, because as yet he lacks wisdom. You shall not converse with anyone who is under thirty."

"Suppose I want to buy something, am I not even then to ask the price if the seller is under thirty?"

"Oh yes," answered Charicles, "you may in such cases. But the fact is, Socrates, you are in the habit of asking questions to which you know the answer: so that is what you are not to do."

"Am I to give no answer, then, if a young man asks me something that I know?—for instance, 'Where does Charicles live?' or 'Where is Critias?'"

"Oh yes," answered Charicles, "you may, in such cases."

"But you see, Socrates," explained Critias, "you will have to avoid your favourite topic —the cobblers, builders and metal workers; for it is already worn to rags by you in my opinion."

"Then must I keep off the subjects of which these supply illustrations, Justice, Holiness, and so forth?"

"Indeed yes," said Charicles, "and cowherds too: else *you* may find the cattle decrease."

Thus the truth was out: the remark about the cattle had been repeated to them: and it was this that made them angry with him.

So much, then, for the connexion of Critias with Socrates and their relation to each other. I venture to lay it down that learners get nothing from a teacher with whom they are out of sympathy. Now, all the time that Critias and Alcibiades associ-

---

[4] I.e., the practice of "making the worse appear the better argument." In Plato's *Apology* (*GBWW*, Vol. 7, p. 201), Socrates makes Aristophanes (*Clouds*) author of this charge against him. Aristotle in the *Rhetoric* (*GBWW*, Vol. 9, p. 651) associates the practice with the name of Protagoras.

ated with Socrates they were out of sympathy with him, but from the very first their ambition was political advancement. For while they were still with him, they tried to converse, whenever possible, with prominent politicians. Indeed, there is a story told of Alcibiades, that, when he was less than twenty years old, he had a talk about laws with Pericles, his guardian, the first citizen in the State.

"Tell me, Pericles," he said, "can you teach me what a law is?"

"Certainly," he replied.

"Then pray teach me. For whenever I hear men praised for keeping the laws, it occurs to me that no one can really deserve that praise who does not know what a law is."

"Well, Alcibiades, there is no great difficulty about what you desire. You wish to know what a law is. Laws are all the rules approved and enacted by the majority in assembly, whereby they declare what ought and what ought not to be done."

"Do they suppose it is right to do good or evil?"

"Good, of course, young man—not evil."

"But if, as happens under an oligarchy, not the majority, but a minority meet and enact rules of conduct, what are these?"

"Whatsoever the sovereign power in the State, after deliberation, enacts and directs to be done is known as a law."

"If, then, a despot, being the sovereign power, enacts what the citizens are to do, are his orders also a law?"

"Yes, whatever a despot as ruler enacts is also known as a law."

"But force, the negation of law, what is that, Pericles? Is it not the action of the stronger when he constrains the weaker to do whatever he chooses, not by persuasion, but by force?"

"That is my opinion."

"Then whatever a despot by enactment constrains the citizens to do without persuasion, is the negation of law?"

"I think so: and I withdraw my answer that whatever a despot enacts without per-

suasion is a law."

"And when the minority passes enactments, not by persuading the majority, but through using its power, are we to call that force or not?"

"Everything, I think, that men constrain others to do 'without persuasion,' whether by enactment or not, is not law, but force."

"It follows then, that whatever the assembled majority, through using its power over the owners of property, enacts without persuasion is not law, but force?"

"Alcibiades," said Pericles, "at your age, I may tell you, we, too, were very clever at this sort of thing. For the puzzles we thought about and exercised our wits on were just such as you seem to think about now."

"Ah, Pericles," cried Alcibiades, "if only I had known you intimately when you were at your cleverest in these things!"

So soon, then, as they presumed themselves to be the superiors of the politicians, they no longer came near Socrates. For apart from their general want of sympathy with him, they resented being cross-examined about their errors when they came. Politics had brought them to Socrates, and for politics they left him. But Criton was a true associate of Socrates, as were Chaerophon, Chaerecrates, Hermogenes, Simmias, Cebes, Phaedondas, and others who consorted with him not that they might shine in the courts or the assembly, but that they might become gentlemen, and be able to do their duty by house and household, and relatives and friends, and city and citizens. Of these not one, in his youth or old age, did evil or incurred censure.

"But," said his accuser, "Socrates taught sons to treat their fathers with contempt: he persuaded them that he made his companions wiser than their fathers: he said that the law allowed a son to put his father in prison if he convinced a jury that he was insane; and this was a proof that it was lawful for the wiser to keep the more ignorant in gaol." In reality Socrates held that, if you clap fetters on a man for his ignorance, you deserve to be kept in gaol yourself by those whose knowledge is greater than your own: and such reasoning led him frequently to consider the difference between Madness and Ignorance. That madmen should be kept in prison was expedient, he thought, both for themselves and for their friends: but those who are ignorant of what they ought to know deserve to learn from those who know it.

"But," said his accuser, "Socrates caused his companions to dishonour not only their fathers, but their other relations as well, by saying that invalids and litigants get benefit not from their relations, but from their doctor or their counsel. Of friends too he said that their goodwill was worthless, unless they could combine with it some power to help one: only those deserved honour who knew what was the right thing to do, and could explain it. Thus by leading the young to think that he excelled in wisdom and in ability to make others wise, he had such an effect on his companions that no one counted for anything in their estimation in comparison with him." Now I know that he did use this language about fathers, relations and friends. And, what is more, he would say that so soon as the soul, the only seat of intelligence, is gone out of a man, even though he be our nearest and dearest, we carry out his body and hide it in the tomb. Moreover, a man's dearest friend is himself: yet, even in his lifetime he removes or lets another remove from his body whatever is useless and unprofitable. He removes his own nails, hair, corns: he lets the surgeon cut and cauterize him, and, aches and pains notwithstanding, feels bound to thank and fee him for it. He spits out the saliva from his mouth as far away as he can, because to retain it doesn't help him, but harms him rather.

Now in saying all this, he was not giving a lesson on "the duty of burying one's father alive, or making mincemeat of one's body": he meant to show that unreason is unworth, and was urging the necessity of cultivating sound sense and usefulness, in order that he

who would fain be valued by father or by brother or by anyone else may not rely on the bond of familiarity and neglect him, but may try to be useful to all those by whom he would be valued.

Again, his accuser alleged that he selected from the most famous poets the most immoral passages, and used them as evidence in teaching his companions to be tyrants and malefactors: for example, Hesiod's line:

*"No work is a disgrace, but idleness is a disgrace."* [5]

He was charged with explaining this line as an injunction to refrain from no work, dishonest or disgraceful, but to do anything for gain. Now, though Socrates would fully agree that it is a benefit and a blessing to a man to be a worker, and a disadvantage and an evil to be an idler—that work, in fact, is a blessing, idleness an evil—"working," "being a worker," meant to him doing good work; but gambling and any occupation that is immoral and leads to loss he called idling. When thus interpreted there is nothing amiss with the line:

*"No work is a disgrace, but idleness is a disgrace."*

Again, his accuser said that he often quoted the passage from Homer, showing how Odysseus:

"Whenever he found one that was a captain and a man of mark, stood by his side, and restrained him with gentle words: 'Good sir, it is not seemly to affright thee like a coward, but do thou sit thyself and make all thy folk sit down. . . .' But whatever man of the people he saw and found him shouting, him he drove with his sceptre and chid him with loud words: 'Good sir, sit still and hearken to the words of others that are thy betters: but thou art no warrior and a weakling, never reckoned whether in

---

[5] *Works and Days* 309.

battle or in council.' " [6]

This passage, it was said, he explained to mean that the poet approved of chastising common and poor folk. But Socrates never said that: indeed, on that view he would have thought himself worthy of chastisement. But what he did say was that those who render no service either by word or deed, who cannot help army or city or the people itself in time of need, ought to be stopped, even if they have riches in abundance, above all if they are insolent as well as inefficient. But Socrates, at least, was just the opposite of all that: he showed himself to be one of the people and a friend of mankind. For although he had many eager disciples among citizens and strangers, yet he never exacted a fee for his society from one of them, but of his abundance he gave without stint to all. Some indeed, after getting from him a few trifles for nothing, became vendors of them at a great price to others, and showed none of his sympathy with the people, refusing to talk with those who had no money to give them.[7] But Socrates did far more to win respect for the State in the world at large than Lichas, whose services to Sparta have made his name immortal. For Lichas used to entertain the strangers staying at Sparta during the Feast of the Dancing Boys;[8] but Socrates spent his life in lavishing his gifts and rendering the greatest services to all who cared to receive them. For he always made his associates better men before he parted with them.

Such was the character of Socrates. To me he seemed to deserve honour rather than death at the hands of the State. And a consideration of his case in its legal aspect will confirm my opinion. Under the laws, death is the penalty inflicted on persons proved to be thieves, highwaymen, cutpurses, kidnappers, robbers of temples; and from such criminals no man was so widely separated as he. Moreover, to the State he was never the cause of disaster in war, or strife or treason or any evil whatever. Again, in private life no man by him was ever deprived of good or involved in ill. None of these crimes was ever so much as imputed to him. How then could he be guilty of the charges? For so far was he from "rejecting the gods," as charged in the indictment, that no man was more conspicuous for his devotion to the service of the gods: so far from "corrupting the youth," as his accuser actually charged against him, that if any among his companions had evil desires, he openly tried to reform them and exhorted them to desire the fairest and noblest virtue, by which men prosper in public life and in their homes. By this conduct did he not deserve high honour from the State?

---

[6] *Iliad* 2. 188; Walter Leaf's translation. Cf. *GBWW*, Vol. 4, p. 12.

[7] Aristippus especially is meant.

[8] According to Eusebius this festival, which was held in the summer, was instituted in honour of the Spartans who fell fighting against the Argives for the possession of Thyrea.

# The Song of Roland

The Silent Slain

*We too, we too, descending once again*
*The hills of our own land, we too have heard*
*Far off—Ah, que ce cor a longue haleine—*
*The horn of Roland in the passages of Spain,*
*The first, the second blast, the failing third,*
*And with the third turned back and climbed once more*
*The steep road southward, and heard faint the sound*
*Of swords, of horses, the disastrous war,*
*And crossed the dark defile at last, and found*
*At Roncevaux upon the darkening plain*
*The dead against the dead and on the silent ground*
*The silent slain—*

Archibald MacLeish

## Editor's Introduction

*The Song of Roland* is the finest of the medieval *chansons de geste*—literally, songs of action or deed; in effect, epic poems—that have come down to us. It tells how in the latter part of the eighth century, through the treachery of one Ganelon, certain knights in the army of Charles the Great of France under the command of Roland, Charles's nephew, were set upon by Saracens in the mountains between France and Spain, and how at a place called Roncevaux (or Roncesvalles), in a famous battle, all the French knights including Roland, Oliver, Archbishop Turpin, and the Twelve Peers were killed, notwithstanding their great bravery, because Roland would not blow his ivory horn to summon help as long as he could fight. Whether this actually happened, as a matter of history, or if it did happen, whether it happened in this way, is open to question. It does not matter. The elements of the poem—its simplicity, its swift, disastrous course, the courage of the knights, their prodigious feats in a losing cause, their love of one another and loyalty to their king, above all the pride and courage of Roland himself and the pathos of his death before a rescue that comes too late—these combine to make it one of the best stories in the world. Long ago it became a symbol of the heroic virtue that shines even in defeat. On the other hand it has been invoked

314

more recently, in the lines by Archibald MacLeish which are quoted above, to suggest, in the bitter aftermath of the first World War, the futility of heroic action, the isolation of heroic pride.

So far as history goes, a number of contemporary chronicles testify that some such battle indeed was fought in—to be exact—the year 778, though it appears that Charles's army, returning home after an abortive attempt to occupy Saragossa, then in possession of the Moors, was actually ambushed by Gascons, or perhaps Basques, who inflicted heavy casualties upon it and plundered its baggage train before escaping. There is evidence also that a Rodlandus or Rotholandus was of Charles's entourage. But the only indication that he was among those killed in this engagement is that provided by Charles's biographer, Einhard (or Eginhard), whose life of the king, composed around 820, mentions the battle and states, in a doubtful passage, that among those slain were "Eggihard, the king's steward; Anselm, Count Palatine; and Roland, governor of the March of Brittany [*Hruodlandus Britannici limitis praefectus*]."

How this event, supposing it occurred as Einhard says, got transformed into the *Song of Roland* can only be conjectured. It is not the first time that legend has changed what apparently was a humiliating defeat into a magnificent heroic stand, and has allowed even that to be avenged, as Roland's death is avenged in the poem, by a glorious victory—a victory, too, which is won not over any band of Gascon guerrillas but over the Saracens themselves, the great enemy of the French in those days. The oldest surviving manuscript of the *Song* is from the first half of the twelfth century (ca. 1130–40?), and the metamorphosis had been accomplished by then. Probably it had been worked out at least a century before, when an earlier *Song* is thought to have existed. This may have been the version known by the minstrel Taillefer, to whom William granted the honor of the first blow at the battle of Hastings, during the Norman Conquest, and who "rode before the Duke on a swift horse," as we learn from Wace, the Norman chronicler, "singing of Roland and Charlemagne, of Oliver and the knights who died at Roncevaux." The twelfth-century manuscript presents itself as the work of a certain Turold, evidently a Norman, who for all that he may have had such an earlier poem at hand, and who undoubtedly knew the story as any man of his time would have done, may fairly be considered the author of the poem as we have it. His text consists of approximately 4,000 lines in Old French, written in the plainest of styles, without visible literary contrivance beyond the assonance with which the lines end and the formulaic repetitions that occur in the course of the narrative it tells—devices appropriate to a work that was intended to be sung rather than read.

Many versions later than this are recorded in medieval France. By the fifteenth century the *Song* in one form or another had spread all over Europe. As early as the twelfth century, Germany had a "Rolandslied," translated from Turold's manuscript, or one exactly like it, by the priest Conrad. The same version appeared as part of the Icelandic *Karlamagnus Saga* in the thirteenth century. Both Chaucer and Dante were obviously familiar with the story. Chaucer speaks of a traitor as "a very Ganelon," and it is of Roland's horn that Dante thinks when in the ninth circle of Hell he hears a trumpet "so loud it turned all thunder faint." Even Saint Francis, in the fourteenth-century *Mirror of Perfection,* is reported to have rebuked a novice who liked to study better than to work with his hands by recalling the example of Roland and Oliver, how they, "pursuing the paynims [pagans] with sore sweat and travail even unto the death, did achieve a victory over them worthy of all remembrance, and at the last did themselves die in battle holy martyrs for the faith of Christ." And of course there are many representations of the story in medieval carvings, mosaics, and inscriptions—at Verona, at Brindisi, even at Chartres, where in the red glass of one of the cathedral windows Roland may be seen still blowing his horn, still smiting with Durendal upon the rock. No wonder that, to Dante, Charlemagne and Roland seemed to be among those heroes who "on earth were of so great fame that through them every Muse was made rich." It is true, during the Renaissance, when the stories of Greece and Rome drove out those of medieval France, the *Song* was forgotten, and it was not revived until the nineteenth century, when a new interest in all things medieval brought the twelfth-century manuscript to light for the attention of modern scholarship. Since then, however, it has been regarded as a classic, and has been reprinted in numerous editions.

The *Song* has had many noted English translators. Among recent ones have been C. K. Scott Moncrieff, Dorothy L. Sayers, and W. S. Merwin. The translation that follows, by Isabel Butler, is in prose and dates from 1904. It includes a glossary of antique and unusual words that appears with some added illustrations at the end.

# The Song of Roland

## Part I
## Ganelon's treachery

Charles the King, our great Emperor, has been for seven long years in Spain; he has conquered all the high land down to the sea; not a castle holds out against him, not a wall or city is left unshattered, save Saragossa, which stands high on a mountain. King Marsila holds it, who loves not God, but serves Mahound, and worships Apollon; ill hap must in sooth befall him.

King Marsila abides in Saragossa. And on a day he passes into the shade of his orchard; there he sits on a terrace of blue marble, and around him his men are gathered to the number of twenty thousand. He speaks to his dukes and his counts, saying: "Hear, lords, what evil overwhelms us; Charles the Emperor of fair France has come into this land to confound us. I have no host to do battle against him, nor any folk to discomfort his. Counsel me, lords, as wise men and save me from death and shame." But not a man has any word in answer, save Blancandrin of the castle of Val-Fonde.

Blancandrin was among the wisest of the paynims, a good knight of much prowess, discreet and valiant in the service of his lord. He saith to the King: "Be not out of all comfort. Send to Charles the proud, the terrible, proffer of faithful service and goodly friendship; give him bears and lions and dogs, seven hundred camels and a thousand falcons past the moulting time, four hundred mules laden with gold and silver, that he may send before him fifty full wains.

And therewith shall he richly reward his followers. Long has he waged war in this land, it is meet he return again to Aix in France. And do thou pledge thy word to follow him at the feast of Saint Michael, to receive the faith of the Christians, and to become his man in all honour and loyalty. If he would have hostages, send them to him, or ten or twenty, to make good the compact. We will send him the sons of our wives; yea, though it be to death, I will send mine own. Better it were that they lose their lives than that we be spoiled of lands and lordship, and be brought to beg our bread."

"By this my right hand," saith Blancandrin, "and by the beard that the wind blows about my breast, ye shall see the Frankish host straightway scatter abroad, and the Franks return again to their land of France. When each is in his own home, and Charles is in his chapel at Aix, he will hold high festival on the day of Saint Michael. The day will come, and the term appointed will pass, but of us he will have no word nor tidings. The King is proud and cruel of heart, he will let smite off the heads of our hostages, but better it is that they lose their lives than that we be spoiled of bright Spain, the fair, or suffer so great dole and sorrow." And the paynims cry: "Let it be as he saith."

So King Marsila hath ended his council; he then called Clarin de Balaguer, Estramarin, and Endropin, his fellow, and Priamon, and Garlan the Bearded, Machiner, and Maheu his uncle, Joïmer, and Malbien from oversea, and Blancandrin; ten of the fiercest he hath called, to make known his will unto them. "Lords, barons," he saith, "go ye to Charlemagne, who is at the siege of the city of Cordova, bearing olive branches in your hands in token of peace and submission. If by your wit ye can make me a covenant with Charles, I will give you great store of gold and silver, and lands and fiefs as much as ye may desire." "Nay," say the paynims, "of these things we have and to spare."

King Marsila has ended his council. And again he saith to his men: "Go ye forth, lords, and bear in your hands branches of olive; bid Charles the King that he have mercy on me for the love of his God; say before this first month ends, I will follow him with a thousand of my true liege people, to receive the Christian faith and become his man in all love and truth. If he would have hostages, they shall be given him." Then said Blancandrin: "We will make thee a fair covenant."

And King Marsila let bring the ten white mules the which had been sent him by the King of Suatilie; their bridles are of gold and their saddles wrought of silver. They who are to do the King's message set forth, bearing in their hands branches of olive. Anon thereafter they come before Charles, who holds France as his domain; alack, he cannot but be beguiled by them.

The Emperor is joyous and glad at heart; he has taken Cordova and overthrown its walls; and with his mangonels he has beaten down its towers. Great was the plunder which fell to his knights in gold and silver and goodly armour. Not a heathen is left in the city; all are either slain or brought to Christianity. The Emperor is in a wide orchard, and with him are Roland, and Oliver, Samson the Duke, and Anseïs the Proud, Geoffrey of Anjou, the King's standard bearer, and thereto are Gerin, and Gerier, and with them is many another man of France to the number of fifteen thousand. Upon the grass are spread cloths of white silk whereon the knights may sit; and some of these play at tables for their delight, but the old and wise play at chess, and the young lords practise the sword-play. Under a pine, beside an eglantine, stands a throne made all of beaten gold; there sits the King who rules sweet France; white is his beard and his head is hoary, his body is well fashioned and his countenance noble; those who seek him have no need to ask which is the King. And the messengers lighted down from their mules and saluted him in all love and friendship.

Blancandrin was the first to speak, and said to the King: "Greeting in the name of God the Glorious whom ye adore. Thus saith to you King Marsila the valiant: much has he enquired into the faith which brings salvation; and now he would fain give you good store of his substance, bears and lions, and greyhounds in leash, seven hundred camels and a thousand falcons past the moulting time, four hundred mules laden with gold and silver, that ye may carry away fifty full wains of treasure; so many bezants of fine gold shall there be that well may ye reward your men of arms therewith. Long have you tarried in this land, it is meet that ye return again to Aix in France; there my lord will follow you, he gives you his word, (and will receive the faith that you hold; with joined hands he will become your man, and will hold from you the kingdom of Spain)." At these words the Emperor stretches his two hands towards heaven, and then bows his head and begins to think.

The Emperor sat with bowed head, for he was in no wise hasty of his words, but was ever wont to speak at his leisure. When again he raised his head, proud was his face, and he said to the messengers: "Fairly have ye spoken. Yet King Marsila is much mine enemy. By what token may I set my trust in the words that ye have said?" "By hostages," the Saracen made answer, "of which you shall have or ten or fifteen or twenty. Though it be to death I will send mine own son, and you shall have others, methinks, of yet gentler birth. When you are in your kingly palace at the high feast of Saint Michael of the Peril, my lord will come to you, he gives you his word, and there in the springs that God made flow for you, he would be baptized a Christian." "Yea, even yet he may be saved," Charles made answer.

Fair was the evening and bright the sun. Charles has let stable the ten mules, and in a wide orchard has let pitch a tent wherein the ten messengers are lodged. Ten sergeants make them right good cheer; and there they abide the night through, till the clear dawn. The Emperor has risen early, and heard mass and matins; and now he sits under a pine tree, and calls his barons into council, for he would act in all matters by the advice of those of France.

The Emperor sits under the pine tree and summons his barons to council. Thither came Ogier, and Archbishop Turpin, Richard the Old, with Henry his nephew, and the brave Count Acelin of Gascony, Tedbalt of Rheims and Milon his cousin, and thereto Gerin and Gerier, and with them came Count Roland, and Oliver the brave, the gentle; of the Franks of France there are more than a thousand, and with the rest came Ganelon who did the treason. And now begins the council that wrought so great woe.

"Lords, barons," then saith Charles the Emperor, "King Marsila has sent me messengers: he would give me great store of his havings, bears and lions and leashed greyhounds, seven hundred camels and a thousand moulted falcons, four hundred mules laden with gold of Arabia, more than enough to fill fifty wains; but thereto he charges me that I go back to France, giving his word to come to me at my abiding place at Aix, and there to receive our most holy faith, and to hold his marches of me; but I know not what may be in his heart." "We must bethink ourselves," say the Franks in answer.

Now when the Emperor had ceased from speaking, Count Roland, who is in no wise in accord with his words, stands forth and nay-says him. He saith to the King: "It

were ill done to set thy trust in Marsila. It is seven full years since we came into Spain, and for you I have conquered Noples and Commibles, and I have taken Valtierra and the land of Pina, and Balaguer and Tudela and Sezilie. Now King Marsila was ever a traitor; aforetime he sent fifteen of his paynims, each bearing an olive branch, and they came unto you with a like tale. Then ye advised with your Franks, who counselled you folly; and you sent two of your counts, Basan and Basil, unto the paynims, and thereafter, below Haltilie, their heads were smitten off. Wherefore I counsel carry on the war even as ye have begun it, lead your assembled host unto Saragossa, lay siege to it, even though it be for all the days of your life, and revenge us for those whom the felons slew aforetime."

The Emperor sat with bent head, he stroked his beard and tugged at his moustache, nor answered he his nephew for either good or ill. The Franks are silent, all save Ganelon, he rises and comes before Charles, and speaks right haughtily, saying to the King: "It were ill done to hearken to a braggart—either me or any other—save that his counsel be to thine own profit. When King Marsila lets tell thee he will do homage to thee as thy vassal, and will hold all Spain in fief of thee, and thereafter will receive the faith that we hold, he who counsels thee that thou reject this proffer, recks little, lord, of what death we die. The counsel of pride should not prevail, let us leave folly and hold with the wise."

Thereafter Naymes stood forth—no better vassal was there in all the court—and thus bespoke the King: "Thou hast heard the answer of Ganelon the Count, and wise it is, and it be but heeded. King Marsila is spent with war, thou hast taken his castles, and with thy mangonels hast beaten down his walls, thou hast burned his cities and vanquished his men; when now that he entreats thy mercy, it were sin to press him further, the more that he would give thee surety by hostages. (Now send thou one of thy barons to him.) This great war should have an end." "The Duke hath spoken wisely," cry the Franks.

"Lords, barons, what messenger shall we send to King Marsila at Saragossa?" And Duke Naymes made answer: "By thy leave I will go; give me now the glove and the staff." But the King answered him: "Nay, thou art a man of good counsel, and thou shalt not at this time go thus far from me. Sit thou again in thy place since none hath summoned thee.

"Lords, barons, what messenger shall we send to the Saracen that holds Saragossa?" And Roland made answer: "Right glad were I to go." "Nay certes, not you," saith Count Oliver, "for you are fierce and haughty of temper and I fear lest you embroil yourself; I will myself go, if the King so wills it." "Peace," the King answered, "nor you nor he shall go thither; and by my beard which thou seest whiten, not one of the Twelve Peers shall be chosen." The Franks answer not, and lo, all are silent.

Turpin of Rheims then stood forth from the rest and bespoke the King, saying: "Let be thy Franks. Seven years hast thou been in this land, and much travail and woe hath been theirs. Give me, lord, the staff and the glove, and I will go to the Saracen of Spain, and learn what manner of man he is." But wrathfully the King made answer: "Sit thou again in thy place upon the white silk and speak not, save as I command thee."

"Ye knights of France," then said Charles the Emperor, "now choose me a baron of my marches who shall do my message to King Marsila." Then saith Roland: "Let it be Ganelon my stepfather." "Yea," say the Franks, "well will he do your errand; if ye pass him by ye will send none so wise."

Then said the King: "Ganelon, come thou hither, and receive the glove and the staff. Thou hast heard thou art chosen of the Franks." "Sir," Ganelon answered him, "it is Roland who has done this thing; never again shall I hold him in my love all the days of my life, nor yet Oliver in that he is his comrade, nor the Twelve Peers in

that they hold him dear, and here in thy sight, lord, I defy them." "Thy wrath is over great," then saith the King, "and certes, go thou must in that I command thee." "Go I may, but without surety, none was there for Basil and Basan his brother.

"Well I know I needs must go unto Saragossa, but for him who goes thither there is no return. And more than that, thy sister is my wife, and I have a son, never was there a fairer, and if he lives he will be a man of good prowess. To him I leave my lands and honours; guard him well, for never again shall I see him with these eyes." "Thou art too tender of heart," Charles answered him, "since I command thee, needs must thou go."

And Count Ganelon was in sore wrath thereat; he lets slip from about his neck his great cloak of sables, and stands forth in his tunic of silk. Gray blue are his eyes, and proud his face, well fashioned is he of body, and broad of chest. So comely he is, all his peers turn to look upon him. And he speaks to Roland, saying: "Thou fool, why art thou in so great wrath? It is known of all that I am thy stepfather, and thou hast named me to go unto Marsila. If God grants me to return again I shall bring woe upon thee so great it shall endure all the days of thy life." "Thou speakest pride and folly," Roland answered him, "and all men know I reck naught of threats. But a man of counsel should bear this message, and if the King wills it, I am ready to go in thy stead."

"Nay," Ganelon made answer, "in my stead thou shalt not go. Thou art not my man, nor am I thy over-lord. Charles has commanded me that I do his errand, and I will go unto Marsila in Saragossa. But mayhap I shall do there some folly to ease me of my great wrath." At these words Roland falls a-laughing.

When Ganelon sees that Roland bemocks him, so great anger is his he is near to bursting with wrath, and he wellnigh goes out of his senses. He saith to the Count:

"Little love have I for thee in that thou hast brought false judgment upon me. O just King, lo, I stand before thee, ready to do thy commandment."

The Emperor holds out to him his right glove, but fain had Count Ganelon been elsewhere, and when he should have taken it, he lets it fall to earth. And the Franks cry: "God, what may this betide? Great woe shall come upon us from this embassage." "Lords," saith Ganelon, "ye shall have tidings thereof.

"And O King," he said again, "I pray thy leave; since go I must, I would not delay." "Go in Jesus' name and in mine," the King made answer. With his right hand he shrove and blessed him, and then he gave him the staff and the letter.

Now Ganelon the Count gets him to his lodging and begins to don his armour, the goodliest he can find; he has fastened spurs of gold upon his feet, and at his side he has girt Murglais his sword; and when he mounted Tachebrun his steed, Guinemer his uncle it was, held his stirrup. Many a knight ye may see weep, and they say to him: "Woe worth the day, baron! Long hast thou been in the King's court; and ever hast thou been accounted a man of worship. He who judged thee to go will be nowise shielded or saved by Charles; Count Roland ought never to have had the thought, *for ye twain are near of kin.*" And they say further: "Lord, we pray thee take us with thee." But Ganelon answers: "No, so help me God! Better it were that I die alone than that so many good knights take their end. Ye will return again into sweet France, lords; greet ye my wife for me, and likewise Pinabel my friend and peer, and aid ye Baldwin my son, whom ye know, and make him your over-lord." Therewith he set forth and rode on his way.

As Ganelon fares forth under the high olives he overtakes the Saracen messengers. (They hold on their way and he follows behind), but anon Blancandrin falls back to ride beside him. Cunningly they speak one to another. "A marvel of a man is this Charles," saith Blancandrin, "he has conquered Apulia and all Calabria; he has crossed the salt sea into England and has won tribute therefrom for the profit of Saint Peter; but what would he of us in our marches?" Quoth Ganelon: "Such is his will; and no man avails to withstand him."

"The Franks are goodly men," then saith Blancandrin, "but your dukes and counts do much hurt to their liege lord in so advising him; they will bring loss and discomfiture to him and to others." But Ganelon answers him saying: "In sooth, I know no man save only Roland who shall be brought to shame thereby. On a day, as the Emperor was seated under the shade of the trees, his nephew came to him, clad in his hauberk—for he was come from the taking of spoils below Carcassonne—and in his hand he held a scarlet apple: 'Take it, fair sir,' saith Roland to his uncle, 'for even so I give over to thee the crowns of all the kings of the earth.' Of a surety, his great pride must undo him, for each day he runs in hazard of death; and if he be but slain we shall have quiet on the earth."

Then saith Blancandrin: "Fell and cruel is this Roland who would make all peoples yield them, and claim all lands for his. But by means of what folk does he think to win thus much?" "By the folk of France," Ganelon answers, "for he is so beloved by them that they will never fail him; many a gift he gives them of gold and silver, mules and war horses, silk and armour. And the Emperor likewise has all his desire; for him Roland will conquer all the lands from here even unto the East."

So Ganelon and Blancandrin rode on till each had pledged other to do what he might to compass the death of Roland. So they rode by highways and bypaths till they alighted under a yew tree in Saragossa. Hard by, under the shade of a pine tree, stood a throne covered over with silk of Alexandria; there sat the King who held all Spain, and around him were his Saracens to the number of twenty thousand;

yet not one opened his lips or spoke a word, so eager were they for tidings; and now behold you, Blancandrin and Ganelon.

So Blancandrin came before Marsila; he held Count Ganelon by the hand, and he spoke to the King, saying: "Greeting in the name of Mahound and Apollon whose blessed law we hold. We did thy message to Charles, who lifted up both his hands towards heaven, and praised his God, nor made he other answer. But here he sends thee one of his barons, who is of France, and a mighty man, and from him thou shalt hear if thou art to have peace or war." Saith Marsila: "Now speak, for we listen."

Count Ganelon had well bethought himself, and begins to speak with much cunning, as one who is skilful in words, saying to the King: "Greeting in the name of God the Glorious whom we should adore. Thus saith to thee Charles the mighty: if thou wilt receive Christianity he will give thee the half of Spain in fee; (the second half he will give unto Roland, in whom thou shalt find a haughty compeer). If thou wilt not accept this covenant (he will lay siege to Saragossa), and thou shalt be taken and bound by force, and brought unto the King's seat at Aix, and thou shalt be adjudged to end thy days, and there thou shalt die a vile and shameful death." At these words King Marsila was sore troubled; in his hand he held a javelin tipped with gold, and with it he would have struck Ganelon had his men not withheld him.

King Marsila hath waxed red with wrath, and hath shaken the shaft of his javelin. When Ganelon saw this, he laid a hand on his sword, and drew it forth from the sheath the length of two fingers, and spoke to it, saying: "Most fair and bright thou art; so long as I wear thee at this King's court, the Emperor of France will never say I should die here alone in a strange land, before the bravest have paid thee dear." But the paynims cry: "Let us stay this quarrel."

And the best of the Saracens so besought him, that Marsila again took his place on the throne. Saith the Caliph: "Thou hast done ill towards us in thy desire to smite the Frank. Thou shouldst give ear and listen to him." "Sir," then saith Ganelon, "I must endure it. But not for all the gold that God has made, nor for all the treasure of this land will I forego the word, so I be given leisure to say it, that Charles the great King has sent by me to his worst foe." Ganelon wore a mantle of sables covered over with silk from Alexandria, but now he lets it fall to the earth, and Blancandrin gathers it up; but from his sword he will not part, he holds it in his right hand by the golden pommel. And the paynims say one to another: "Here is a goodly baron."

Ganelon hath drawn near to the King, and saith: "Thou art wrong to be wroth; Charles who rules all France lets thee know that if thou wilt receive the faith of the Christians, he will give thee half of Spain in fee; the other half shall go to Roland, his nephew, in whom thou wilt have a haughty compeer. If thou wilt not do according to this covenant, the King will lay siege to thee in Saragossa; by force thou shalt be taken and bound, and conveyed anon to Aix, the King's seat; neither war horse nor palfrey shalt thou have for the journey, nor yet a she-mule or he-mule mayst thou ride, but thou shalt be cast upon a wretched sumpter; and by a judgment at Aix thy head shall be smitten off. Our Emperor sends thee this letter," and therewith Ganelon gave it into the right hand of the paynim.

Marsila has grown red with wrath; he breaks the seal and casts away the wax, he looks at the letter and sees the sum of it. "Charles who holds France in his power bids me bethink me of his sorrow and wrath: that is to say of Basan, and Basil, his brother, whose heads I did let smite off in the hills below Haltilie. If I would ransom the life of my body I must send him the Caliph my uncle, otherwise he will not hold me in his love." Thereafter spoke Marsila's son, and said to the King: "Ganelon hath uttered folly. Such words hath he said to thee it is unmeet that he live; give him over to me, and I will do justice upon him." When Ganelon hears him he brandishes his sword, and sets his back against the trunk of a pine tree.

Now for council the King hath past into his orchard, and gathered his chief men about him; thither came Blancandrin the hoary-headed, and Jurfaleu, his son and heir, and the Caliph, Marsila's uncle and faithful liegeman. Then saith Blancandrin: "Call hither the Frank, he has pledged me his faith to our welfare." "Do thou bring him," saith the King. And Blancandrin took Ganelon by the right hand, and brought him into the orchard before the King. And there they plotted the foul treason.

"Fair Sir Ganelon," saith the King, "I was guilty of some folly toward thee when I would have struck thee in my wrath. I give thee *as a pledge* these skins of sable, the border whereof is worth more than five hundred pounds. Before tomorrow at evening a fair amend shall be thine." "I will not refuse it," Ganelon answered him, "and may it please God give thee good thanks."

Then quoth Marsila: "Ganelon, in good faith I have it in my heart to love thee well. Tell me now of Charlemagne. Methinks, he is of great age and has outlived his time, for I deem him more than two hundred years old. Through many lands has he journeyed, and many a blow has he taken on his embossed shield, and many a mighty king has he brought low; when will he yield him in the strife?" "Nay, not such is Charles," Ganelon answered him: "Whosoever looks on the Emperor, or knows him, must account him a man of much prowess. I know not how to praise and glorify him to the full sum of his honour and bounty. Who can reckon his worth? and God has gifted him with such valour that rather had he die than give up his lordship."

Quoth the paynim: "Much I marvel at this Charles who is old and hoary; two hundred years and more he is, methinks.

Through many lands has he travelled, and has taken many a thrust of lance and spear, and many a mighty king has be brought low; when will he yield him in the strife?" "That will never be," saith Ganelon, "so long as his nephew is a living man, he hath not his fellow for courage under the cope of heaven; and Oliver his comrade is of good prowess, and likewise the Twelve Peers whom Charles holds right dear; they, together with twenty thousand knights, make up the vanguard; and Charles is safe and unafraid."

Saith the paynim: "Greatly I marvel at this Charles who is white-headed and hoary, methinks he is two hundred years and more. Through many lands has he ridden a conqueror, many a blow has he taken from good spears and sharp; when will he yield him in the strife?" "That will never be," quoth Ganelon, "so long as Roland is a living man, he hath not his like in courage from here even unto the East; and Oliver, his comrade, is right valiant, and the Twelve Peers whom Charles holds so dear, they, together with twenty thousand Franks, make up the vanguard. Secure is Charles and fearful of no man living."

"Fair Sir Ganelon," thus saith King Marsila, "a fairer folk than mine ye shall not see; I have upon four hundred thousand knights, with them I may well do battle against Charles and his Franks." "Nay, not at this time," Ganelon answers him, "or great will be the slaughter of thy paynims. Leave thou folly and seek after wisdom; give such store of thy substance unto the Emperor that there will be no Frank that does not marvel thereat; send him thereto twenty hostages, and the King will return again into fair France; but his rearguard he will leave behind him, and in it, of a surety, will be Count Roland, his nephew, and Oliver the valiant, the courteous: and both counts shall be slain, if thou wilt put thy trust in me. And the great pride of Charles shall come to its fall, and thenceforth he will have no desire to wage more war upon thee."

"Fair Sir Ganelon," then saith King Marsila, "how may I slay this Roland?" Quoth Ganelon: "Even that will I tell thee. The King will be at the main pass of Cizre, and he will have set his rearguard behind him; in it will be the mighty Count Roland, his nephew, and Oliver, in whom he sets his trust, and in their company will be twenty thousand Franks. But do thou send against them one hundred thousand of thy paynims, and do them battle a first time, that the men of France may be smitten and sore hurt. Now mayhap, in this first stour, thine own may be slain with great slaughter, but do thou set upon the Franks a second time, with like array, that Roland may in no wise escape. And for thy part thou wilt have done a noble deed of arms, and thou shalt be untroubled by war all the days of thy life.

"Whosoever may compass the death of Roland in that place will thereby smite off the right arm of Charles; his great armies will have an end, never again shall he call together such hosts, and the Great Land shall have peace." When Marsila heard this saying he kissed Ganelon upon the neck; then he began to open his treasures.

Quoth Marsila: "What need of more words? No counsel is good in which a man may not set his trust. Now do thou therefore swear me straight the treason (that I shall find Roland in the rearguard)." "Let it be as thou wilt," said Ganelon: and he swore the treason upon the relics in his sword Murglais, and therewith became a traitor.

Hard by, was a throne wrought of ivory, and to it Marsila let bring a book wherein was writ the law of Mahound and Tervagant, and upon it the Saracen of Spain swore that if he found Roland in the rearguard, he would set upon him with all his folk, and if that he might, forthwith slay him. "Blessed be our covenant," quoth Ganelon.

Thereupon came thither a paynim called Valdabrun, who aforetime had stood godfather to King Marsila; fair and laughing, he said to Ganelon: "Take thou my sword, no man weareth a better, and between the guards thereof are more than a thousand mangons. I give it thee, fair sir, in all friendship, but do thou aid us against Roland the baron, and take heed that we find him in the rearguard." "So shall it be," quoth Count Ganelon; and each kissed other on the cheek and the chin.

Thereafter came thither a paynim hight Climborin, frank and free, he said to Ganelon: "Take thou my helm, a better was never seen, but do thou help us against Roland Lord of the Marches, in such wise that we may bring him to shame." "Even so will I do," saith Ganelon; and each kissed other on the cheek and the mouth.

Then thither came Bramimonde the Queen, and saith to the Count: "Sir, thou art right dear to me, in that thou art beloved of my lord and all his men. To thy wife I would send these two bracelets, well seen are they with jacinth and gold and amethysts, and they are of a greater price than all the riches of Rome, thy Emperor hath none so goodly." And Ganelon takes the bracelets and bestows them in his boot.

Then the King calls Malduit his treasurer, saying: "Hast thou made ready the gifts for Charles?" "Yea, lord," he answers, "all is ready—seven hundred camels laden with gold and silver, and twenty hostages, the noblest under heaven."

Marsila lays a hand on Ganelon's shoulder and speaks to him, saying: "A goodly baron and wise thou art, but by that faith thou deemest most holy, have a heed that thou turn not thy heart from us; and I will give thee great store of my substance, ten mules laden with the finest gold of Arabia; and each year thou shalt have a like gift. Now take thou the keys of this great city, and convey thou to Charles the rich gifts, (and give over to him from me the twenty hostages): but thereafter have a care the rearguard be adjudged to Roland. And so be it I may come upon him in pass or defile, I will do him battle to the death." "Methinks I tarry too long," saith

Ganelon in answer; and therewith he mounts his horse and rides on his way.

Meantime the Emperor has turned back towards his own land, and has come to the city of Valtierra, which aforetime Count Roland had taken, and so destroyed that thenceforward for the space of a hundred years it was waste and desolate. There the King awaits tidings of Ganelon, and the tribute of the great land of Spain. And now on a morning, at dawn, with the first light, comes Ganelon into the camp.

The Emperor had risen early and heard mass and matins; and now he is on the green grass before his tent, and with him is Roland, and Oliver the valiant, Naymes the Duke and many another. Thither comes Ganelon, the felon, the traitor, and with cunning and falsehood speaks to the King, saying: "Blessed be thou of God! I bring thee hereby the keys of Saragossa, and great store of gifts, and twenty hostages—guard thou them well. But King Marsila bids thee blame him not that the Caliph be not among them; with mine own eyes I saw him and four hundred men of arms, clad in hauberks, with helms on head, and girt with swords whose hilts were inlaid with gold, embark together upon the sea. They were fleeing from Christianity which they would not receive or hold. But before they had sailed four leagues, storm and tempest fell upon them, and even there they were drowned, never shall ye see them more. Had the Caliph been alive I had brought him hither. As for the paynim King, in very truth, lord, this month shall not pass but he will come to thee in thy kingdom of France, and will receive the faith that thou holdest, and will join his hands in thine and become thy man, and will hold of thee his kingdom of Spain." Then saith the King: "Thanks be to God therefor. Well hast thou done, and great shall be thy reward." Thereafter he let sound a thousand trumpets throughout the host, and the Franks break up their camp, and load their sumpters, and set forth together towards fair France.

Charles the Great has laid waste all Spain, he has taken its castles and sacked its cities. But now the war is ended, so saith the King, and he rides on towards fair France. (The day passes and evening falls); Count Roland has set the King's standard on the crest of a hill against the sky; and the Franks pitch their tents in all the country round about. Meantime the paynims ride on through the valleys, clad in their hauberks and two-fold harness, helms on head, and girt with their swords, shields on shoulder, and lances in hand. They made stay in a wood, on the top of the mountains, and there four hundred thousand await the dawn. God, what sorrow the Franks know it not.

The day fades and night darkens; and Charles, the great Emperor, sleeps. He dreamed that he was come to the great pass of Cizre, and it seemed to him that he held the oaken shaft of his lance in his hand, but Ganelon the Count snatched it from him, brandished and broke it, that its pieces flew towards heaven. But still Charles sleeps and does not waken.

Thereafter he dreamed another dream; that he was before his chapel at Aix and a bear bit him in his arm right cruelly; and anon, from towards Ardennes, he saw come a leopard which fiercely assaulted him; but even then, from within the hall, a greyhound sprang out, and ran leaping to Charles; first he snapped off the right ear of the bear, then wrathfully he set upon the leopard; and the Franks cried that it was a great battle. Yet none knew which of the twain should conquer. But Charles still sleeps and doth not waken.

Night passes and the clear dawn shines forth, proudly the Emperor gets to horse, and lets sound the trumpets aloud throughout the host. "Lords, barons," then saith Charles, "nigh at hand is the pass and the strait defiles, now choose ye who shall be in the rearguard." And Ganelon answered: "Let it be Roland, my stepson, thou hast no baron so brave as he." Now when the King hears him, he looks at him haughtily, saying: "Thou art a very devil; and a mortal anger has entered into thee. And who shall go before me in the vanguard?" And Ganelon answered: "Let it be Ogier of Denmark, no baron hast thou more apt thereto."

When Count Roland hears that he is chosen, he speaks out in knightly wise, saying: "Sir kinsman, I should hold thee right dear in that thou hast adjudged the rearguard to me; and by my faith, Charles the King shall lose naught thereby, neither palfrey nor war-horse, nor any he-mule or she-mule whereon man may ride, nay, not so much as a pack-horse or sumpter, an it be not first well paid for by the sword." "Yea, thou speakest truly," said Ganelon, "that I know well."

—When Count Roland hears that he is to be in the rearguard, wrathfully he turns to his stepfather, saying: "Ha, coward and ill son of an ill race, thinkest thou that the glove shall fall from my hand even as did the staff from thine before Charles?"—

(And Count Roland turns to Charles, saying:) "Give me now the bow that you bear in your hand; verily, you shall have no need to chide me that I let it fall, as did Ganelon your right glove when you gave him the herald's staff." But still the Emperor sits with bent head; he plucks at his beard and strokes his moustache, and he may not help but weep.

Thereafter Naymes came before him, a better vassal was not in all the court, and he spoke to the King, saying: "Well hast thou heard, Count Roland is all in wrath; but the rearguard is adjudged to him, and thou hast no baron who would dare supplant him therein. Give him therefore the bow that you hold, and take heed that he hath good aid." The King holds out the bow and Roland receives it.

And the Emperor speaks to Roland, saying: "Fair sir nephew, know for sooth that I will give over unto thee the half of my army, keep them with thee that they may be thy safeguard." "Nay, not so will I,"

saith the Count. "May God confound me if I belie my house. I will keep with me twenty thousand Franks of good valour; and do thou cross the mountains in all surety, for so long as I live thou needst fear no man."

Count Roland has mounted his horse; and Oliver his comrade came to stand over against him, and thither came Gerier, and Oton, and Berengier, and thereto came Samson, and Anseïs (the Proud, Ivon and Ivory whom the King holds full dear); and after them came Gerard the Old of Roussillon, and thereto Engelier the Gascon. Then said the Archbishop: "By my head, I too will go." "And I with thee," quoth Count Gualter, "I am Roland's man and to follow him is my devoir." Then among them they choose out twenty thousand knights.

Thereafter Count Roland calls Gualter del Hum, saying: "Take thou one thousand Franks of our land of France, and hold the hills and defiles that the Emperor may lose none of his own." "It is my part to do this for thee," saith Gualter. And with a thousand Franks of France he ranges through the hills and passes, nor will he leave the heights for any ill tidings before seven hundred swords have been drawn. Now the same day King Almaris of the kingdom of Belferne shall do him and his men fierce battle.

High are the hills and dark the valleys, brown are the rocks and dread the defiles. That same day the main host of the Franks pass with toil and travail, and fifteen leagues away men might hear the noise of their march. But when that they draw near to the Great Land, and see Gascony, their lord's domain, they call to mind their own fiefs and havings, their young maidens and gentle wives, till there is not one that does not weep for pity. More than all the rest is Charles heavy of heart, in that he has left his nephew in the passes of Spain; pity takes him, and he cannot help but weep.

The Twelve Peers abide in Spain, and in

their fellowship are twenty thousand Franks who know not fear or any dread of death. But the Emperor as he draws near to France, hides his face in his mantle. Beside him rides Duke Naymes and he speaks to the King, saying: "Why makest thou such sorrow?" "Ye do ill to ask it," Charles answers him; "such grief is mine I cannot help but make lament. I fear lest through Ganelon France shall be destroyed. This past night, by means of an angel, a dream came to me, and it seemed to me that Ganelon shattered to bits the lance I held in my hand; and he it was who adjudged the rearguard to Roland. And now him I have left behind in a strange land. God, if I lose him never shall I find his fellow."

Charles the Great cannot help but weep; and a hundred thousand Franks are full of pity for him, and a marvellous fear for Roland. Ganelon the felon has done this treason; and rich are the gifts he has received therefor from the paynim king, gold and silver, silks and ciclatons, mules and horses, and camels and lions. Meantime King Marsila calls together the barons of Spain, counts, and viscounts, dukes, and almaçurs, and emirs, and sons of counts; four hundred thousand has he gathered together in three days. He lets sound his tabours throughout Saragossa; and on the topmost tower the paynims raise an image of Mahound, and there is not a man but offers prayers to it and worships it. Thereafter they ride through the land of Cerdagne, over hill and through dale, each seeking to outdo other, till they see the gonfanons of the men of France, the rearguard of the Twelve Peers; they will not fail to do them battle.

Among the foremost comes the nephew of Marsila, riding a mule the which he urges on with a staff; frank and free he saith to his uncle: "Fair Sir King, well have I served thee and much travail and hardship has been mine thereby; for thee have I done battle many a time and for thee have I conquered, and now in return I

would fain have a gift—the death blow of Roland. Slay him I will with the point of my lance, an Mahound will help me; and thereby will I set free all the parts of Spain, from the passes of Aspre even unto Durestant. Charles will grow weary, and his Franks will yield them; and thou shalt have peace all the days of thy life." And in answer King Marsila gives him his glove.

Holding the glove in his hand, the nephew of Marsila speaks to his uncle right proudly, saying: "Fair Sir King, this is a goodly gift thou hast given me. Now choose for me eleven of thy barons, that I may do battle with the Twelve Peers." The first to answer him was Falsaron, the brother of King Marsila: "Fair sir nephew, I will go with thee; together, in good sooth, we will do this battle; and for the rearguard of the great army of Charles, certes, we shall slay them."

Then forth stands King Corsablis, he is of Barbary and a man of wiles; and now he speaks out like a knight of good courage, for not for all God's gold would he do cowardly. And behold Malprimis de Brigal comes hasting up, swifter than horse can gallop he speeds on foot, and before Marsila he cries in a loud voice: "I will go into Roncevals, and if I find Roland I will slay him with my own hand."

An Emir there is of Balaguer, well fashioned is he of body, and fair and proud of face; and mounted on his horse he rejoices in the bearing of arms; well famed is he for his courage, and had he but Christianity he were a goodly baron. He now comes before Marsila and cries: "I would go into Roncevals, and if I find Roland he shall die the death, and thereto shall Oliver and all the Twelve Peers, and the Franks shall die in dolour and shame. Charles the Great is old and in his dotage, he will weary of waging strong war upon us, and Spain shall rest in peace." And therefor King Marsila gives him good thanks.

Among the paynims is an Almaçur of Moriane, there is none more fell in all the land of Spain. He likewise has made his boast before Marsila: "Into Roncevals I will lead my men, to the number of twenty thousand, all armed with shields and lances. And if I find Roland I pledge me to slay him, never will the day dawn when Charles shall not lament him."

Then stands forth Turgis of Tortosa, Count he is, and lord of the aforesaid city, and he would slay the Christians with a great slaughter. Beside the others he takes his place before Marsila, saying to the King: "Be not afraid. Mahound is mightier than Saint Peter of Rome, serve ye him and ye shall have victory in the field; at Roncevals I will seek out Roland, and no man shall save him from death. Lo, here is my sword, long it is and goodly, and I will measure it against Durendal, and ye shall hear which of the twain avails most in the fight. The Franks shall die or yield them to us, and thereby shall Charles the Old be brought to dolour and shame; nevermore shall he wear crown on head."

Hard by is Escremis of Valtierra, a Saracen is he, and lord of that land; and now from amid the press about Marsila he cries: "I will go into Roncevals and bring to naught the proud; if I find Roland he shall not bear thence his head, nor shall Oliver the captain; and for the Twelve Peers, they are doomed; the Franks shall perish, and France shall be made desolate, and of goodly vassals Charles shall be despoiled."

Hard by is a paynim hight Esturgant, and with him is Estramaris, his comrade, felons both and misbelieving traitors. Them Marsila called, saying: "Come hither, lords, I would that ye twain go into the passes of Roncevals, and there help to array my folk." And they make him answer, saying: "Lord, even as thou commandest so will we do. And we will set upon Roland and Oliver, and the Twelve Peers shall have no surety from death, for our swords are sharp and goodly, and we will smite till they be all red with the warm blood. The Franks shall die, and Charles shall be sore

stricken. And as a gift we will give thee the Great Land; come thither, lord, and thou shalt see these things in very sooth; yea, and the Emperor himself we will give over unto thee."

Now thither comes hasting Margaris of Sibilie, he who holds all the land down to the sea. Well loved is he of ladies by reason of his fairness, and no woman can set eyes upon him but her face brightens, and will she, nill she, she must laugh for very joy of him. And of his prowess he has no fellow among the paynims. He now presses through the throng, crying above all the rest to the King: "Be ye no whit adread. I will go into Roncevals and there slay Roland, nor shall Oliver go thence a living man, and the Twelve Peers abide there but for their death. Lo, here is my sword hilted with gold; the Amiral of Primes it was gave it me, and I pledge my faith it shall seek and find the red blood. The Franks shall perish and France be brought to shame. Never shall the day dawn when Charles the Old of the white beard shall not suffer dolour and wrath thereby. Within the year we shall have taken France, and thou mayst lie in the burg of Saint Denis." And at his words the paynim King bows low.

Hard by is Chernuble of the Black Valley. His long hair falls even unto the ground; and in jest, for his disport, he can bear a greater burden than can be laid upon seven mules. The land (wherein he dwells filleth men with fear); there the sun doth not shine nor can the corn ripen, no rain falls, neither does the dew gather upon the earth; all black are the rocks of that land, and some say it is the abode of devils. And now Chernuble speaks, saying: "I have girt on my good sword, and at Roncevals I will dye it red; if on my path I meet with Roland the valiant, never believe me more if I do not set upon him in battle, and with my own sword I will conquer Durendal. The Franks shall perish, and France shall be destroyed." And when he had spoken the Twelve Peers gathered together, and with them went a hundred thousand Saracens; keen and eager for battle were they all, and in a fir wood, hard by, they did on their harness.

The paynims arm themselves with Saracen hauberks, of which the more part are of three-fold thickness; they lace on helms of right good Saracen work, and gird on swords of Viennese steel, fair are their shields, and their lances are of Valencia, tipped with gonfanons white and blue and scarlet. They leave behind them the mules and palfries, and mounting their war-horses, ride forth in close ranks. Fair was the day and bright the sun, and all their harness glistens in the light. And for the more joy they let sound a thousand trumpets; so great is the noise thereof that the Franks hear it. Then saith Oliver: "Sir comrade, methinks we shall have ado with the Saracens." "Now God grant it be as thou sayest," Roland answers him, "for to make stand here for our King is to do as good men ought to do. Verily for his liege a man well ought to suffer pain and woe, and endure both great heat and great cold, and should hold him ready to lose both hide and hair in his lord's service. Now let each have a care that he strikes good blows and great, that no man may mis-say us in his songs. These misbelieving men are in the wrong, and right is with the Christians, and for my part I will give ye no ill example."

## Part II
## The battle at Roncevals

Then Oliver goes up into a high mountain, and looks away to the right, all down a grassy valley, and sees the host of the heathen coming on, and he called to Roland, his comrade, saying: "From the side of Spain I see a great light coming, thousands of white hauberks and thousands of gleaming helms. They will fall upon our Franks with great wrath. Ganelon the felon has done this treason, and he it was adjudged us to the rearguard, before the Emperor." "Peace Oliver," saith Count

Roland, "he is my mother's husband, speak thou no ill of him."

Oliver has fared up the mountain, and from the summit thereof he sees all the kingdom of Spain and the great host of the Saracens. Wondrous is the shine of helmets studded with gold, of shields and broidered hauberks, of lances and gonfanons. The battles are without number, and no man may give count thereof, so great is the multitude. Oliver was all astonied at the sight; he got him down the hill as best he might, and came to the Franks, and gave them his tidings.

"I have seen the paynims," said Oliver; "never was so great a multitude seen of living men. Those of the vanguard are upon a hundred thousand, all armed with shields and helmets, and clad in white hauberks; right straight are the shafts of their lances, and bright the points thereof. Such a battle we shall have as was never before seen of man. Ye lords of France, may God give you might! and stand ye firm that we be not overcome." "Foul fall him who flees!" then say the Franks, "for no peril of death will we fail thee."

"Great is the host of the heathen," saith Oliver, "and few is our fellowship. Roland, fair comrade, I pray thee sound thy horn of ivory that Charles may hear it and return again with all his host." "That were but folly," quoth Roland, "and thereby would I lose all fame in sweet France. Rather will I strike good blows and great with Durendal, that the blade thereof shall be blooded even unto the hilt. Woe worth the paynims that they came into the passes! I pledge thee my faith short life shall be theirs."

"Roland, comrade, blow now thy horn of ivory, and Charles shall hear it, and bring hither his army again, and the King and his barons shall succour us." But Roland answers him, saying: "Now God forfend that through me my kinsman be brought to shame, or aught of dishonour with Durendal, the good sword that is befall fair France. But first I will lay on girded here at my side, and thou shalt see the blade thereof all reddened. Woe worth the paynims when they gathered their hosts! I pledge me they shall all be given over to death."

"Roland, comrade, blow thy horn of ivory, that Charles may hear it as he passes the mountains, and I pledge me the Franks will return hither again." But Roland saith: "Now God forfend it be said of any living man that I sounded my horn for dread of paynims. Nay, that reproach shall never fall upon my kindred. But when I am in the stour I will smite seven hundred blows, or mayhap a thousand, and thou shalt see the blade of Durendal all crimson. The Franks are goodly men, and they will lay on right valiantly, nor shall those of Spain have any surety from death."

Saith Oliver, "I see no shame herein. I have seen the Saracens of Spain, they cover the hills and the valleys, the heaths and the plains. Great are the hosts of this hostile folk, and ours is but a little fellowship." And Roland makes answer: "My desire is the greater thereby. May God and His most holy angels forfend that France should lose aught of worship through me. Liefer had I die than bring dishonour upon me. The Emperor loves us for dealing stout blows."

Roland is brave, and Oliver is wise, and both are good men of their hands; once armed and a-horseback, rather would they die than flee the battle. Hardy are the Counts and high their speech. The felon paynims ride on in great wrath. Saith Oliver: "Roland, prithee look. They are close upon us, but Charles is afar off. Thou wouldst not deign to sound thy horn of ivory; but were the King here we should suffer no hurt. Look up towards the passes of Aspre and thou shalt see the woeful rearguard; they who are of it will do no more service henceforth." But Roland answers him: "Speak not so cowardly. Cursed be the heart that turns coward in the breast! Hold we the field, and ours be the buffets and the slaughter."

When Roland sees that the battle is close upon them he waxes fiercer than lion or leopard. He calls to the Franks, and he saith to Oliver: "Comrade, friend, say not so. When the Emperor left us his Franks he set apart such a twenty thousand of men that, certes, among them is no coward. For his liege lord a man ought to suffer all hardship, and endure great heat and great cold, and give both his blood and his body. Lay on with thy lance, and I will smite with Durendal, my good sword that the King gave me. If I die here, may he to whom it shall fall, say, 'This was the sword of goodly vassal.'"

Nigh at hand is Archbishop Turpin; he now spurs his horse to the crest of a knoll, and speaks to the Franks, and this is his sermon: "Lords, barons, Charles left us here, and it is a man's devoir to die for his King. Now help ye to uphold Christianity. Certes, ye shall have a battle, for here before you are the Saracens. Confess your sins and pray God's mercy, and that your souls may be saved I will absolve you. If ye are slain ye will be holy martyrs, and ye shall have seats in the higher Paradise." The Franks light off their horses and kneel down, and the Archbishop blesses them, and for a penance bids them that they lay on with their swords.

The Franks get upon their feet, freed and absolved from sin; and the Archbishop blesses them in the name of God. Then they mounted their swift horses, and armed themselves after the manner of knights, and made them ready for battle. Count Roland calls to Oliver, saying: "Sir comrade, rightly thou saidst Ganelon hath betrayed us all, and hath received gold and silver and goods therefor; but the Emperor will well revenge us. King Marsila hath bought and sold us, but he shall pay for it with the sword."

Roland rides through the passes of Spain on Veillantif, his good horse and swift. He is clad in his harness, right well it becomes him, and as he rides he brandishes his spear, turning its point towards heaven; and to its top is bound a gonfanon of pure white, whereof the golden fringes fall down even unto his hands. Well fashioned in his body, and his face hair and laughing; close behind him rides his comrade; and all the Franks claim him as their champion. Full haughtily he looks on the Saracens, but gently and mildly on the Franks, and he speaks to them courteously, saying: "Lords, barons, ride on softly. The paynims come seeking destruction, and this day we shall have plunder so goodly and great that no King of France hath ever taken any of so great price." At these words the two hosts come together.

Saith Oliver: "I have no mind for more words. Thou wouldst not deign to sound thy horn of ivory, and no help shalt thou get from Charles, naught he knows of our case, nor is the wrong his, the baron. They who are beyond the mountains are no wise to blame. Now ride on with what might ye may. Lords, barons, hold ye the field! And in God's name I pray you bethink you both how to deal good blows and how to take them. And let us not forget the device of our King." At these words all the Franks cried out together, and whosoever may have heard that cry of Montjoy must call to mind valour and worth. Then they rode forward, God! how proudly, spurring their horses for the more speed, and fell a-smiting—how else should they do? But no whit adread were the Saracens. And lo you, Franks and paynims come together in battle.

The nephew of Marsila, who was called Ælroth, rides before all his host, and foul are his words to our Franks: "Ye Frankish felons, today ye shall do battle with us. He who should have been your surety has betrayed you; mad is the King who left you behind in the passes. Today shall fair France lose her fame, and the right arm of Charles shall be smitten off from his body." When Roland hears this, God! how great is his wrath. He spurs as fast as his horse may run, and with all the might he hath he smites Ælroth, and breaks his shield, and rends apart his hauberk, that he cleaves his

breast and breaks the bone, and severs the spine from his back; with his lance he drives out the soul from the body, for so fierce is the blow Ælroth wavers, and with all the force of his lance Roland hurls him from his horse dead, his neck broken in two parts. Yet Roland still chides him, saying: "Out coward! Charles is not mad, nor loves he treason. He did well and knightly to leave us in the passes. Today shall France lose naught of her fame. Franks, lay on! Ours is the first blow. Right is with us, and these swine are in the wrong."

Among the paynims is a Duke, Falsaron by name, who was brother to King Marsila, and held the land of Dathan and Abiram; there is no more shameless felon on all the earth; so wide is his forehead that the space between his eyes measures a full half foot. When he sees his nephew slain, he is full of dole, and he drives through the press as swift as he may, and cries aloud the paynim war-cry. Great is his hatred of the Franks. "Today shall fair France lose her fame!" Oliver hears him and is passing wroth; with his golden spurs he pricks on his horse and rides upon him like a true baron; he breaks the shield, tears asunder the hauberk, and drives his lance into the body up to the flaps of his pennon, and with the might of his blow hurls him dead from the saddle. He looks to earth where lies the felon, and speaks him haughtily: "Coward, naught care I for thy threats. Lay on Franks, certes, we shall overcome them." And he cries out Montjoy, the war-cry of Charles.

A King there is. Corsablis by name; he is of Barbary, a far-off land, and he spoke to the Saracens, saying: "We shall win a fair day on these Franks for few is their fellowship. And such as be here shall prove themselves of small avail, nor shall one be saved alive for Charles; the day has come whereon they must die." Archbishop Turpin hears him right well, and to no man under heaven has he ever borne such hate; with his spurs of fine gold he pricks on his horse, and rides upon the King with great might, cleaves his shield and rends his hauberk, and thrusts his great lance into his body, and so drives home the blow that sorely the King wavers, and with all the force of his lance Turpin hurls him dead into the path. He looks on the ground where he sees the glutton lie, nor doth he withhold him from speech, but saith: "Coward and heathen, thou hast lied! Charles, my liege lord, is ever our surety, and our Franks have no mind to flee; and we shall have a care that thy comrades go not far hence; yea, and a second death must ye suffer. Lay on ye Franks, let no man forget himself! This first blow is ours, thanks be to God." And he cries out Montjoy, to hold the field.

And Gerin smites Malprimis de Brigal, that his good shield no whit avails him, he shatters the jewelled boss thereof, and half of it falls to earth, he pierces the hauberk to the flesh, and drives his good lance into the body; the paynim falls down in a heap, and his soul is carried away by Satan.

And Gerier, the comrade of Gerin, smites the Emir, and shatters his shield and unmails his hauberk, and thrusts his good lance into his heart; so great is the blow his lance drives through the body, and with all the force of his shaft he throws him to the ground dead. "Ours is a goodly battle," quoth Oliver.

Samson the Duke rides upon the Almaçur, and breaks his shield all flowered and set with gold, nor doth his good hauberk give him any surety, but Samson pierces him through heart and liver and lungs, and fells him dead, whether any one grieves for him or no. Saith the Archbishop: "That was knightly stricken."

And Anseïs urges on his horse and encounters with Turgis of Tortosa, cleaves his shield below the golden boss, rends asunder his twofold hauberk, and sets the point of his good lance in his body, and thrusts so well that the iron passes sheer through him, that the might of the blow hurls him to the ground dead. "That was the buffet of a man of good prowess," saith Roland.

And Engelier, the Gascon of Bordeaux, spurs his horse, slackens his rein, and encounters with Escremis of Valtierra, breaks and carves the shield from his shoulder, rends apart the ventail of his hauberk, and smites him in his breast between his two collar bones, and with the might of the blow hurls him from the saddle, saying: "Ye are all given over to destruction."

And Oton smites the paynim Esturgant upon the leathern front of his shield, marring all the blue and white thereof, breaks through the sides of his hauberk, and drives his good spear and sharp into his body, and casts him from his swift horse, dead. "Naught may save thee," saith Oliver thereat.

And Berengier rides on Estramaris, shatters his shield, rends asunder his hauberk, and drives his stout lance into his body, and smites him dead amid a thousand Saracens. Of the Twelve Peers ten are now slain and but two are still living men, to wit, Chernuble and Count Margaris.

Margaris is a right valiant knight, strong and goodly, swift and keen; he spurs his horse and rides on Oliver, breaks his shield below the boss of pure gold, that the lance past along his side, but by God's help, it did not pierce the body; the shaft grazes him but doth not overthrow him, and Margaris drives on, in that he has no hindrance, and sounds his horn to call his men about him.

Now the battle waxes passing great on both parties. Count Roland spares himself no whit, but smites with his lance as long as the shaft holds, but by fifteen blows it is broken and lost; thereupon he draws out Durendal his good sword, all naked, spurs his horse and rides on Chernuble, breaks his helm whereon the carbuncles blaze, cleaves his mail-coif and the hair of his head that the sword cuts through eyes and face, and the white hauberk of fine mail and all the body to the fork of the legs sheer into the saddle of beaten gold, nor did the sword stint till it had entered the horse and cleft the backbone, never staying for joint, that man and horse fell dead upon the thick grass. Thereupon Roland cried: "Coward, woe worth the day thou camest hither! no help shalt thou get from Mahound; nor by such swine as thou shall today's battle be achieved."

Count Roland rides through the press; in his hand he hath Durendal, right good for hacking and hewing, and doth great damage upon the Saracens. Lo, how he hurls one dead upon another, and the bright blood flows out on the field. All reddened are his hauberk and his arms, and the neck and shoulders of his good horse. Nor doth Oliver hold back from the battle; the Twelve Peers do not shame themselves, and all the Franks smite and slay, that the paynims perish or fall swooning. Then saith the Archbishop, "Our barons do passing well," and he cries out Montjoy, the war-cry of Charles.

Oliver drives through the stour; his lance is broken and naught is left him but the truncheon; yet he smites the paynim Malsaron that his shield patterned with gold and flowers is broken, and his two eyes fly out from his head, and his brains fall at his feet; among seven hundred of his fellows Oliver smites him dead. Then he slew Turgin and Esturgus, and thereby broke his lance that it splintered even unto the pommel. Thereat Roland saith: "Comrade what dost thou? I have no mind for a staff in so great battle, rather a man hath need of iron and steel. Where is thy sword Halteclere?" "I may not draw it," Oliver answered him. "So keen am I to smite."

But now the lord Oliver hath drawn his good sword, even as his comrade had besought him, and hath shown it to him in knightly wise; and therewith he smites the paynim Justin de Val Ferrée that he severs his head in twain, cuts through his broidered hauberk and his body, through his good saddle set with gold, and severs the backbone of his steed, that man and horse fall dead on the field before him. Then said Roland: "Now I hold you as my brother, and 'tis for such buffets the Em-

peror loves us." And on all sides they cry out Montjoy.

Count Gerin rides his horse Sorel, and Gerier, his comrade, rides Passecerf; both slacken rein, and spurring mightily set upon the paynim Timosel; one smites him on the shield, and the other on the hauberk, that both their lances break in his body; and he falls dead in the field. I wot not, nor have I ever heard man say, which of the twain was the more swift. Then Esperveris, son of Borel, died at the hand of Engelier of Bordeaux. And the Archbishop slew Siglorel, that enchanter who of old had passed down into hell, led thither by the spells of Jupiter. "Of him we are well rid," quoth Turpin. And Roland answered him: "Yea, the coward is overthrown. Oliver, my brother, such buffets please me right well."

Meantime the battle waxes passing hard; and both Franks and paynims deal such blows that it is wonder to see; here they smite, and there make what defence they may; and many a lance is broken and reddened, and there is great rending of pennons and ensigns. Many a good Frank loses his youth, and will never again see wife or mother, or the men of France who await him in the passes. Charles the Great weeps for them, and makes great sorrow; but what avails it? no help shall they get therefrom. An ill turn Ganelon did them the day he sold his own kindred in Saragossa. Thereafter he lost both life and limb therefor; in the council at Aix, he was condemned to hang, and with him upon thirty of his kindred to whom death left no hope.

Dread and sore is the battle. Roland and Oliver lay on valiantly, and the Archbishop deals more than a thousand buffets, nor are the Twelve Peers backward, and all the Franks smite as a man. The paynims are slain by hundreds and thousands, whosoever does not flee has no surety from death, but will he, nill he, must take his end. But the Franks lose their goodliest arms; [lances adorned with gold, and trenchant spears, and gonfanons red and white and blue, and

the blades of their good swords are broken, and thereto they lose many a valiant knight]. Never again shall they see father or kindred, or Charles their liege lord who abides for them in the passes.

Meantime, in France, a wondrous tempest broke forth, a mighty storm of wind and lightning, with rain and hail out of all measure, and bolts of thunder that fell ever and again; and verily therewith came a quaking of the earth that ran through all the land from Saint Michael of the Peril, even unto *Xanten*, and from Besançon to the port of Guitsand; and there was not a dwelling whose walls were not rent asunder. And at noon fell a shadow of great darkness, nor was there any light save as the heavens opened. They that saw these things were sore afraid, and many a one said: "This is the day of judgment and the end of the world is at hand." But they were deceived, and knew not whereof they spoke; it was the great mourning for the death of Roland.

Meantime the Franks smote manfully and with good courage, and the paynims were slain by thousands and by multitudes; of a hundred thousand not two may survive. Then said the Archbishop: "Our Franks are of good prowess, no man under heaven hath better, it is written in the annals of France that valiant they are for our Emperor." And the Franks fare through the field seeking their fellows, and weeping from dole and pity for their kin, in all love and kindness. But even now King Marsila is upon them with his great host.

[Count Roland is a knight of much worship, so likewise are Oliver and the Twelve Peers, and all the Franks are good warriors. By their great might they have made such slaughter of paynims that of a hundred thousand, only one hath escaped, Margaris to wit. Blame him not that he fled, for in his body he bore the wounds of four lances. Back he fared in haste towards Spain, and came to Marsila and gave him tidings. . . .

And in a loud voice he cried: "Good King of Spain, now ride on with all speed, the Franks are weary and spent with the smiting and slaying of our Saracens; they have lost their lances and spears, and a good half of their men, and those who yet live are weakened, and the more part of them maimed and bleeding, nor have they more arms wherewith to help themselves.]

Marsila comes on down the valley with the mighty host that he has assembled; full twenty battles the King has arrayed. There is a great shining of helmets, set with gold and precious stones, and of shields and of broidered hauberks. Trumpets to the number of seven thousand sound the onset, and the din thereof runs far and wide. Then saith Roland: "Oliver, comrade and brother, Ganelon the felon has sworn our death. The treason is manifest, and great vengeance shall the Emperor take therefor. The battle will be sore and great, such a one as was never before fought of man. I will smite with Durendal my sword, and do thou, comrade, lay on with Halteclere. Through many lands have we carried them, and with them have we conquered many a battle, no ill song must be sung of them."

When the Franks see how great is the multitude of the paynims, that on all sides they cover the field, they call upon Roland, and Oliver, and the Twelve Peers, that they be their defence. Then the Archbishop tells them his mind, saying: "Lords, barons, put from you all cowardly thoughts; and in God's name I pray you give not back. Better it were that we die in battle than that men of worship should speak foully of us in their songs. Certain it is we shall straightway take our end, nor shall we from today be living men; yet there is a thing I can promise ye, blessed paradise shall be opened to you, and ye shall take your place among the innocent." At his words, the Franks take heart, and every man cries out Montjoy.

[Wily and cunning is King Marsila, and he saith to the paynims: "Now set you trust in me; this Roland is of wondrous might, and he who would overcome him must strive his uttermost; in two encounters he will not be vanquished methinks, and if not, we will give him three. Then Charles the King shall lose his glory, and shall see France fall into dishonour. Ten battles shall abide here with me, and the remaining ten shall set upon the Franks." Then to Grandonie he gave a broidered banner that it might be a sign unto the rest, and gave over to him the commandment.

King Marsila abides on the mountain, and Grandonie comes on down the valley. By three golden nails he has made fast his gonfanon; and he cries aloud: "Now ride on, ye barons!" And for the more goodly noise he bids them sound a thousand trumpets. Say the Franks: "God our Father, what shall we do? Woe worth the day we saw Count Ganelon! he hath sold us by foul treason. Now help us, ye Twelve Peers!" But the first to answer them is the Archbishop, saying: "Good knights, this day great honour shall be yours, for God will give you crowns and flowers in Paradise among the glorious; but therein the coward shall not enter." And the Franks make answer: "We will lay on as one man, and though we die we will not betray him." Then they spur on with their golden spurs to smite the miscreant felons.]

Among the paynims is a Saracen of Saragossa, lord he is of half the city, and Climborin, he hight; never will he flee from any living man. He it was who swore fellowship with Count Ganelon, kissed him in all friendship upon the lips, and gave him his helm and his carbuncle. And he hath sworn to bring the Great Land to shame, and to strip the Emperor of his crown. He rides his horse whom he calls Barbamusche, that is swifter than falcon or swallow; and slackening his rein, he spurs mightily, and rides upon Engelier of Gascony that neither shield nor byrnie may save him, but he drives the head of his lance into his body, thrusting so manfully that the point thereof passes through to the other side, and with all the might of his lance hurls him in the field dead. Thereafter he cries: "These folk are good to slay!" But the Franks say: "Alack, that so good a knight should take his end."

And Count Roland speaks to Oliver, saying: "Sir comrade, now is Engelier slain, nor have we any knight of more valour." And the Count answers him, saying: "Now God grant me to avenge him." He pricks on his horse with spurs of pure gold, and he grasps Halteclere—already is the blade thereof reddened—and with all his strength he smites the paynim; he drives the blow home that the Saracen falls; and the devils carry away his soul. Then Oliver slew Duke Alphaïen, and cut off the head of Escababi, and unhorsed seven Arabs—never again shall they do battle. Then said Roland: "Wroth is my comrade, and now at my side he wins great worship; for such blows Charles holds us the more dear." And he cried aloud: "To battle, knights, to battle!"

Hard by is the paynim Valdabrun, that had stood godfather to King Marsila; on the sea he is lord of four hundred dromonds, and well honoured of all shipmen. He it was who aforetime took Jerusalem by treason, violated the temple of Solomon, and slew the patriarch before the baptismal fonts. And he had sworn fellowship with Ganelon, and had given him a sword and a thousand mangons. He rides a horse called Gramimond, swifter than any falcon; he spurs him well with his sharp spurs, and rides upon Samson the mighty Duke, breaks his shield, and rends his hauberk, and drives the flaps of his gonfanon into his body, and with all the force of his lance hurls him from the saddle dead. "Lay on, paynims, for hardily we shall overthrow them!" But the Franks cry: "God, woe worth the good baron!"

When Roland sees that Samson is dead, ye may guess he is sore stricken, he spurs his horse and lets him run as fast as he may, in his hand he holds Durendal, of greater worth than is pure gold, and with all the might he hath, he smites the paynim on the helm set with gold and gems, and cuts through head and hauberk and body, and through the good saddle set with gold and jewels, deep into the back of the horse, and slays both him and his rider, whosoever has dole or joy thereof. Cry the paynims: "That was a woeful blow for us." Then quoth Roland: "No love have I for any one of ye, for yours is the pride and the iniquity."

Among the paynims is an African, Malquiant, son of King Malcud; his armour is all of the beaten gold, and brighter than all the rest it shines to heaven. His horse, which he calls Salt-Perdut, is so swift that he has not his fellow in any four-footed beast. And now Malquiant rode on Anseïs, and smote him full on the shield that its scarlet and blue were hewn away, and he rent the sides of his hauberk, and drave his lance into his body, both point and shaft. Dead is the Count and done are his life days. Thereat cry the Franks: "Alack for thee, good baron!"

Through the press rides Turpin the Archbishop—never did another priest say mass who did with his own strength so great deeds of arms—and he saith to the paynim: "Now may God bring all evil upon thee! for thou hast slain one for whom my heart is sore stricken." Then he set his good horse at a gallop, and smote Malquiant on his shield of Toledo, that he fell dead upon the green grass.

Hard by is the paynim Grandonie, son of Capuel, King of Cappadocia; he rides a horse called Marmorie, swifter than any bird that flies; he now slackens rein, and spurring well, thrusts mightily upon Gerin, breaks his crimson shield that it falls from his shoulder, and rends all asunder his hauberk, and thereafter drives all his blue gonfanon into his body that he falls dead beside a great rock. Then he slays Gerier, Gerin's comrade, and Berengier, and Guyon of Saint-Antonie; and thereafter he smote Austor, the mighty Duke that held

Valence and the land along the Rhône, and felled him dead that the paynims had great joy thereof. But the Franks cry: "How many of ours are stricken."

Roland holds his ruddied sword in his hand; he has heard the Franks make lament, and so great is his sorrow that his heart is nigh to bursting, and he saith to the paynims: "Now may God bring all evil upon thee! Methinks thou shalt pay me dear for him thou hast slain." And he spurs his horse, which springs forward eagerly; and let whoso will pay the price, the two knights join battle.

Grandonie was a man of good prowess, of much valour and hardiness, and amid the way he encounters with Roland, and albeit before that time he had never set eyes upon him, he none the less knew him of a certainty by his look and countenance; and he could not but be sore adread at the sight, and fain would he have fled, but he could not. The Count smites him mightily that he rends all his helm down to the nasal, cleaves through nose and mouth and teeth, through the hauberk of fine mail, and all the body, splits the silver sides from off the golden saddle, and cuts deep into the back of the horse, that both he and his rider are slain beyond help. Thereat those of Spain make great lament, but the Franks cry: "That was well stricken of our captain."

Wondrous and fierce is the battle; the Franks lay on in their wrath and their might, that hands and sides and bones fall to earth, and garments are rent off to the very flesh, and the blood runs down to the green grass. (The paynims cry: "We may not longer endure.") May the curse of Mahound fall upon the Great Land, for its folk have not their fellows for hardiness." And there was not a man but cried out: "Marsila! haste, O King, for we are in sore need of thy help."

Wondrous and great is the battle. And still the Franks smite with their burnished lances. There is great dolour of folk, and many a man is slain and maimed and bleeding, and one lies on another, or on his back, or face down. The Saracens may not longer endure, but howsoever unwillingly they must give back. And eagerly the Franks pursue after them.

Marsila sees the slaughter of his people, and lets sound his horns and bussynes, and gets to horse with all his vassal host. In the foremost front rides the Saracen Abisme, the falsest knight of his fellowship, all compact of evil and villainy. He believes not in God the son of Mary; and he is black as melted pitch. Dearer than all the gold of Galicia he loves treachery and murder, nor did any man ever see him laugh or take disport. But he is a good man of arms, and bold to rashness, wherefor he is well beloved of the felon King Marsila, and to him it is given to bear the Dragon, around which the paynims gather. The Archbishop hath small love for Abisme, and so soon as he sees him he is all desirous to smite him, and quietly, within himself, he saith: "This Saracen seems a misbelieving felon, I had liefer die than not set upon him to slay him; never shall I love coward or cowardice."

Whereupon the Archbishop begins the battle. He rides the horse that he won from Grossaille, a King whom he slew in Denmark; the good steed is swift and keen, featly fashioned of foot, and flat of leg; short in the thigh and large of croupe, long of flank and high of back; his tail is white and yellow his mane, his head is the colour of the fawn, and small are his ears; of all four-footed beasts none may outstrip him. The Archbishop spurs mightily, and will not fail to meet with Abisme and smite him on his shield, a very marvel, set with gems —topaz and amethysts, and precious crystals, and blazing carbuncles; the gift it was of Galafré the Amiral, who had received it of a devil in Val-Metas. Now Turpin smites it and spares it not, that after his buffet it has not the worth of a doit. And he pierces Abisme through the body, and hurls him dead in the open field. And the Franks say: "That was a good deed of arms; in the hands of our Archbishop safe is the crosier."

And Count Roland speaks to Oliver, saying: "Sir comrade, what say ye, is not the Archbishop a right good knight, that there is no better under heaven? for well he knows how to smite with lance and spear." "Now let us aid him," the Count makes answer. And at these words the Franks go into battle again; great are the blows and grievous the slaughter, and great is the dolour of the Christians.

[The Franks have lost much of their arms, yet still there are a good four hundred of naked swords with which they smite and hew on shining helmets. God, how many a head is cleft in twain; and there is great rending of hauberks and unmailing of byrnies; and they smite off feet and hands and heads. The paynims cry: "These Franks sore mishandle us, whoso doth not defend himself hath no care for his life." (King Marsila hears them make lament, and saith in his wrath): "Terra Major, now may Mahound destroy thee, for thy folk hath discomfited mine, and hath destroyed and spoiled me of many cities which Charles of the white beard now holds; he hath conquered Rome and Apulia and Calabria, Constantinople, and Saxony the wide, liefer had I die than flee before him. Paynims, now lay on that the Franks may have no surety. If Roland dies, Charles loses the life of his body; if he lives, we shall all take our end."

The felon paynims again smite with their lances upon shields and bright helmets; so great is the shock of iron and steel that the flame springs out toward heaven; and lo, how the blood and the brains run down! Great is the dolour and grief of Roland when he sees so many good knights take their end; he calls to remembrance the land of France, and his uncle, Charlemagne the good King, and he cannot help but be heavy.

Yet still he thrust through the press and did not leave from smiting. In his hand he held Durendal, his good sword, and rent hauberks, and broke helmets, and pierced hands and heads and trunks that he threw a hundred paynims to ground, they who had held themselves for good men of arms.

And on his side the lord Oliver drave forward, smiting great blows; in his hand he held Halteclere, his good and trusty sword that had not its fellow under heaven, save only Durendal, and with it he fought valorously; all stained he was with blood even to his arms. "God," saith Roland, "that is a goodly baron. O gentle Count, all courage and all loyalty, this day our friendship must have an end, for today through great woe we twain must part. Never again shall we see the Emperor; never again shall there be such lamentation in fair France. The Frankish folk will pray for us, and in holy churches orisons will be offered; certes, our souls will come into Paradise." Oliver slackens rein and spurs his horse, and in the thick of press comes nigh unto Roland, and one saith unto other: "Comrade, keep near me; so long as death spares me I will not fail thee."]

Would ye had seen Roland and Oliver hack and hew with their swords, and the Archbishop smite with his lance. We can reckon those that fell by their hands for the number thereof is written in charter and record; the Geste says more than four thousand. In four encounters all went well with the Franks, but the fifth was sore and grievous to them, for in this all their knights were slain save only sixty, spared by God's mercy. Before they die they will sell their lives dear.

When Count Roland is ware of the great slaughter of his men, he turns to Oliver, saying: "Sir comrade, as God may save thee, see how many a good man of arms lies on the ground; we may well have pity on sweet France, the fair, that must now be desolate of such barons. Ah, King and friend, would thou were here! Oliver, my brother, what shall we do? How shall we send him tidings?" "Nay, I know not how to seek him," saith Oliver; "but liefer had I die than bring dishonour upon me."

Then saith Roland: "I will sound my horn of ivory, and Charles, as he passes the mountains, will hear it; and I pledge thee my faith the Franks will return again." Then saith Oliver: "Therein would be great shame for thee, and dishonour for all thy kindred, a reproach that would last all the days of their life. Thou wouldst not sound it when I bid thee, and now thou shalt not by my counsel. And if thou dost sound it, it will not be hardily, for now both thy arms are stained with blood." "Yea," the Count answers him, "I have dealt some goodly blows."

Then saith Roland: "Sore is our battle, I will blow a blast, and Charles the King will hear it." "That would not be knightly," saith Oliver; "when I bid thee, comrade, thou didst disdain it. Had the King been here, we had not suffered this damage; but they who are afar off are free from all reproach. By this my beard, an I see again my sister, Aude the Fair, never shalt thou lie in her arms."

Then saith Roland: "Wherefore art thou wroth with me?" And Oliver answers him, saying: "Comrade, thou thyself art to blame. Wise courage is not madness, and measure is better than rashness. Through thy folly these Franks have come to their death; nevermore shall Charles the King have service at our hands. Hadst thou taken my counsel, my liege lord had been here, and this battle had been ended, and King Marsila had been or taken or slain. Woe worth thy prowess, Roland! Henceforth Charles shall get no help of thee; never till God's Judgment Day shall there be such another man; but thou must die, and France shall be shamed thereby. And this day our loyal fellowship shall have an end; before this evening grievously shall we be parted."

The Archbishop, hearing them dispute together, spurs his horse with his spurs of pure gold, and comes unto them, and rebukes them, saying: "Sir Roland, and thou, Sir Oliver, in God's name I pray ye, let be this strife. Little help shall we now have of thy horn; and yet it were better to sound it; if the King come, he will revenge us, and the paynims shall not go hence rejoicing. Our Franks will light off their horses, and find us dead and maimed, and they will lay us on biers, on the backs of sumpters, and will weep for us with dole and pity; and they will bury us in the courts of churches, that our bones may not be eaten by wolves and swine and dogs." "Sir, thou speakest well and truly," quoth Roland.

And therewith he sets his ivory horn to his lips, grasps it well and blows it with all the might he hath. High are the hills, and the sound echoes far, and for thirty full leagues they hear it resound. Charles and all his host hear it, and the King saith: "Our men are at battle." But Count Ganelon denies it, saying: "Had any other said so, we had deemed it great falsehood."

With dolour and pain, and in sore torment, Count Roland blows his horn of ivory, that the bright blood springs out of his mouth, and the temples of his brain are broken. Mighty is the blast of the horn, and Charles, passing the mountains, hears it, and Naymes hears it, and all the Franks listen and hear. Then saith the King: "I hear the horn of Roland; never would he sound it, an he were not at battle." But Ganelon answers him saying: "Battle is there none; thou art old and white and hoary, and thy words are those of a child. Well thou knowest the great pride of Roland—a marvel it is that God hath suffered it thus long. Aforetime he took Noples against thy commandment, and when the Saracens came out of the city and set upon Roland the good knight, (he slew them with Durendal his sword); thereafter with water he washed away the blood which stained the meadow, that none might know of what he had done. And for a single hare he will blow his horn all day long; and now he but boasts among his fellows, for there is no folk on earth would dare do him battle. I prithee ride on. Why tarry we? The Great Land still lies far before us."

Count Roland's mouth has burst out a-bleeding, and the temples of his brain are broken. In dolour and pain he sounds his horn of ivory; but Charles hears it and the Franks hear it. Saith the King: "Long drawn is the blast of that horn." "Yea," Naymes answers, "for in sore need is the baron who blows it. Certes, our men are at battle; and he who now dissembles hath betrayed Roland. Take your arms and cry your war-cry, and succour the men of your house. Dost thou not hear Roland's call?"

The Emperor has commanded that his trumpets be sounded, and now the Franks light down from their horses and arm themselves with hauberks and helms and swords adorned with gold; fair are their shields, and goodly and great their lances, and their gonfanons are scarlet and white and blue. Then all the barons of the host get them to horse, and spur through the passes; and each saith to other: "An we may but see Roland a living man, we will strike good blows at his side." But what avails it? for they have abode too long.

Clear is the evening as was the day, and all their armour glistens in the sun, and there is great shining of hauberks, and helms, and shields painted with flowers, and lances, and gilded gonfanons. The Emperor rides on in wrath, and the Franks are full of care and foreboding; and not a man but weeps full sore and hath great fear for Roland. Then the King let take Count Ganelon, and gave him over to the cooks of his household; and he called Besgon their chief, saying: "Guard him well, as beseems a felon who hath betrayed my house." Besgon took him, and set a watch about him of a hundred of his fellows of the kitchen, both best and worst. They plucked out the hairs of Ganelon's beard and moustache, and each one dealt him four blows with his fist, and hardily they beat him with rods and staves; then they put about his neck a chain, and bound him even as they would a bear, and in derision they set him upon a sumpter. So they guard him till they return him unto Charles.

341

High are the hills and great and dark, deep the valleys, and swift the waters. To answer Roland's horn all the trumpets are sounded, both rear and van. The Emperor rides on in wrath, and the Franks are full of care and foreboding; there is not a man but weepeth and maketh sore lament, praying to God that he spare Roland until they come unto the field, that at his side they may deal good blows. But what avails it? They have tarried too long, and may not come in time.

Charles the King rides on in great wrath, and over his hauberk is spread his white beard. And all the barons of France spur mightily, not one but is full of wrath and grief that he is not with Roland the captain who is at battle with the Saracens of Spain. If he be wounded, what hope that one soul be left alive? God, what a sixty he still hath in his fellowship; no king or captain ever had better.

Roland looks abroad over hill and heath and sees the great multitude of the Frankish dead, and he weeps for them as beseems a gentle knight, saying: "Lords and barons now may God have mercy upon you, and grant Paradise to all your souls, that ye may rest among the blessed flowers. Man never saw better men of arms than ye were. Long and well, year in and year out, have ye served me, and many wide lands have ye won for the glory of Charles. Was it to such an end that he nourished you? O France, fair land, today art thou made desolate by rude slaughter. Ye Frankish barons, I see ye die through me, yet can I do naught to save or defend you. May God, who knows no lie, aid you! Oliver, brother, I must not fail thee; yet I shall die of grief, an I be not slain by the sword. Sir comrade, let us get us into battle."

So Count Roland falls a-smiting again. He holds Durendal in his hand, and lays on right valiantly, that he cleaves in twain Faldron de Pui, and slays four and twenty of the most worshipful of the paynims. Never shall ye see man more desirous to revenge himself. And even as the hart flies before the hounds, so flee the heathen from before Roland. "Thou dost rightly," then said the Archbishop; "such valour well beseems a knight who bears arms and sits a good horse; in battle such a one should be fell and mighty, or he is not worth four deniers, and it behooves him to turn monk and get him into a monastery to pray the livelong day for our sins." And Roland answered him, saying: "Smite and spare not." And at these words the Franks go into battle again; but great is the slaughter of the Christians.

That man who knows he shall get no mercy defends him savagely in battle. Wherefore the Franks are fierce as lions. Marsila like a true baron sits his horse Gaignon; he spurs him well and rides on Bevon—lord he was of Beaune and Dijon —and breaks his shield, and rends his hauberk, that without other hurt he smites him dead to ground. And thereafter he slew Ivon and Ivory, and with them Gerard the Old of Roussillon. Now nigh at hand is Count Roland, and he saith to the paynim: "May the Lord God bring thee to mishap! And because thou hast wrongfully slain my comrades thou shalt thyself get a buffet before we twain dispart, and this day thou shalt learn the name of my sword." And therewith he rides upon him like a true baron, and smites off his right hand, and thereafter he takes off the head of Jurfaleu the Fair, the son of King Marsila. Thereat the paynims cry: "Now help us, Mahound! O ye, our gods, revenge us upon Charles! He has sent out against us into our marches men so fierce that though they die they will not give back." And one saith to another: "Let us fly." At these words a hundred thousand turn and flee, and let whosoever will, call them, they will not return again.

[King Marsila has lost his right hand; and now he throws his shield to earth, and pricks on his horse with his sharp spurs, and with slackened rein, flees away towards Spain. Upon twenty thousand Saracens follow after him, nor is there one among them who is not maimed or hurt of body, and they say one to another: "The nephew of Charles has won the field."]

But alack, what avails it? for though Marsila be fled his uncle the Caliph yet abides, he who ruled Aferne, Carthage, Garmalie, and Ethiopia, a cursed land; under his lordship he has the black folk, great are their noses and large their ears, and they are with him to the number of fifty thousand. And now they come up in pride and wrath, and cry aloud the war-cry of the paynims. Then saith Roland: "Now must we needs be slain, and well I know we have but a little space to live; but cursed be he who doth not sell himself right dear. Lay on, lords, with your burnished swords, and debate both life and death; let not sweet France be brought to shame through us. When Charles, my liege lord, shall come into this field, he will see such slaughter of the Saracens, that he shall find fifteen of them dead over against each man of ours, and he will not fail to bless us."

When Roland sees the cursed folk whose skin is blacker than any ink, and who have naught of white about them save their teeth, he saith: "Now I know in very sooth that we shall die this day. Lay on, lords, and yet again I bid thee, smite." "Now foul fall him who lags behind," quoth Oliver. And at this word the Franks haste into the fray.

Now when the paynims see how few are the Franks, they have great pride and joy thereof; and one saith to another: "Certes, the Emperor is in the wrong." The Caliph bestrides a sorrel horse, he pricks him on with his spurs of gold, and smites Oliver from behind, amid the back, that he drives the mails of his white hauberk into his body, and his lance passes out through his breast: "Now hast thou got a good buffet," quoth the Caliph. "On an ill day Charles the Great left thee in the passes; much wrong hath he done us, yet he shall not boast thereof, for on thee alone have I well revenged us."

Oliver feels that he is wounded unto death; in his hand he holds Halteclere,

bright was its blade, and with it he smites the Caliph on his golden pointed helmet, that its flowers and gems fall to earth, and he cleaves the head even unto the teeth, and with the force of the blow smote him dead to earth, and said: "Foul fall thee, paynim! *Say not that I am come to my death through Charles;* and neither to thy wife, nor any other dame, shalt thou ever boast in the land from which thou art come, that thou hast taken from me so much as one farthing's worth, or hast done any hurt to me or to others." And thereafter he called to Roland for succour.

Oliver feels that he is wounded unto death; never will he have his fill of vengeance. In the thick of the press he smites valiantly, cleaving lances and embossed shields, and feet and hands and flanks and shoulders. Whosoever saw him thus dismember the Saracens, and hurl one dead upon another, must call to mind true valiance; nor did he forget the war-cry of Charles, but loud and clear he cries out Montjoy! And he calls to Roland, his friend and peer: "Sir comrade, come stand thou beside me. In great dolour shall we twain soon be disparted."

Roland looks Oliver in the face, pale it is and livid and all discoloured; the bright blood flows down from amid his body and falls in streams to the ground. "God," saith the Count, "now I know not what to do. Sir comrade, woe worth thy valour! Never shall the world see again a man of thy might. Alas, fair France, today art thou stripped of goodly vassals, and fallen and undone. The Emperor will suffer great loss thereby." And so speaking he swoons upon his horse.

Lo, Roland has swooned as he sits his horse, and Oliver is wounded unto death, so much has he bled that his sight is darkened, and he can no longer distinguish any living man whether far off or near at hand; and now, as he meets his comrade, he smites him upon the helm set with gold and gems, and cleaves it down to the nasal, but does not come unto the head. At the blow

Roland looks up at him, and asks him full softly and gently: "Comrade, dost thou this wittingly? I am Roland who so loves thee. Never yet hast thou mistrusted me." Then saith Oliver: "Now I hear thee speak, but I cannot see thee; may the Lord God guard thee. I have struck thee, but I pray thy pardon." "Thou hast done me no hurt," Roland answers him; "I pardon thee before God, as here and now." So speaking each leans forward towards other, and lo, in such friendship they are disparted.

Oliver feels the anguish of death come upon him; his two eyes turn in his head; and his hearing goes from him, and all sight. He lights down from his horse and lies upon the ground, and again and again he confesses his sins; he holds out his clasped hands toward heaven and prays God that he grant him Paradise, and he blesses Charles and sweet France, and Roland, his comrade, above all men. Then his heart fails him, and his head sinks upon his breast, and he lies stretched at all his length upon the ground. Dead is the Count and gone from hence. Roland weeps for him and is sore troubled; never on the earth shall ye see a man so sorrowful.

When Count Roland sees his friend lie prone and dead, facing the East, gently he begins to lament him: "Sir comrade, woe worth thy hardiness! We twain have held together for years and days, never didst thou me wrong or I thee. Since thou art dead, alack that I yet live." So speaking, the Count swoons as he sits Veillantif his horse, but his golden spurs hold him firm, and let him go where he will, he cannot fall.

So soon as Roland comes to his senses, and is restored from his swoon, he is ware of the great slaughter about him. Slain are the Franks, he has lost them all save only Gualter del Hum and the Archbishop. Gualter has come down from the mountains where he fought hardily with those of Spain; the paynims conquered, and his men are slain, and howsoever unwillingly, he must perforce flee down into the valley and call upon Roland for succour. "O gentle Count, brave captain, where art thou? for where thou art I have no fear. It is I, Gualter, who conquered Maëlgut, I the nephew of Droön the old, the hoary, I whom thou wert wont to love for my hardihood. Now my shield is pierced, and the shaft of my lance is broken, and my hauberk rent and unmailed; I have the wounds of eight lances in my body, and I must die, but dear have I sold myself." So he saith, and Roland hears him, and spurs his horse and rides towards him.

["Sir Gualter," then saith Roland, "thou hast, as I know, done battle with the paynims, and thou art a hardy and valiant warrior. A thousand good knights thou didst take with thee, my men they were, and now I would ask them of thee again; give them over to me, for sore is my need." But Gualter makes answer: "Never again shall ye see one of them alive. I left them on the dolourous field. We encountered a great host of Saracens, Turks and Armenians, Persians, and men of Canaan and of Lude, warriors of the best, mounted on swift Arabian horses. And we fought a battle so fierce that never a paynim shall boast thereof, sixty thousand lie dead and bleeding; and we, on our part, lost all our Franks, but vengeance we took therefor with our swords of steel. Rent and torn is my hauberk, and deadly wounds I have in side and flank, and from all my body flows out the bright blood, and takes from me my strength; certes, my time is nigh spent. Thy man am I, and I look to thee as protector. Blame me not, that I fled." "Nay, blame thee no whit," quoth Count Roland. "But now do thou aid me, so long as thou art a living man."]

Full sorrowful is Roland and of great wrath; he falls a-smiting in the thick of the press, and of those of Spain he cast twenty to the ground dead, and Gualter slew six, and the Archbishop five. Then say the paynims: "Fierce and fell are these men. Take ye heed, lords, that they go not hence alive. He who doth not set upon them is traitor,

and recreant he who lets them go hence."
Then the hue and cry begins again, and
from all sides they close about the three
Franks.

Count Roland is a full noble warrior,
and a right good knight is Gualter del
Hum, the Archbishop is of good valour and
well tried; not one would leave aught to his
fellows, and together, in the thick of the
press, they smite the paynims. A thousand
Saracens get them to foot, and there are
still forty thousand on horseback, yet in
sooth they dare not come nigh unto the
three, but they hurl upon them lances and
spears, arrows and darts and sharp javelins.
In the first storm they slew Gualter, and
sundered the shield of Turpin of Rheims,
broke his helmet and wounded him in his
head, and rent and tore his hauberk that
he was pierced in the body by four spears;
and his horse was slain under him. The
Archbishop falls; great is the pity thereof.

But so soon as Turpin of Rheims finds
himself beaten down to earth with the
wounds of four lances in his body, he right
speedily gets him' afoot again; he looks
toward Roland, and hastes to him, and
saith: "I am nowise vanquished; no good
vassal yields him so long as he is a living
man." And he draws Almace, his sword of
brown steel, and in the thick of the press
he deals well more than a thousand buffets.
Afterwards Charles bore witness that Turpin spared himself no whit, for around him
they found four hundred dead, some
wounded, some cut in twain amid the body,
and some whose heads had been smitten
off; so saith the Geste and he who was on
the field, the valiant Saint Gilles, for whom
God wrought miracles; he it was who wrote
the annals of the monastery of Laon. And
he who knows not this, knows naught of
the matter.

Count Roland fights right nobly, but all
his body is a-sweat and burning hot, and in
his head he hath great pain and torment,
for when he sounded his horn he rent his
temples. But he would fain know that
Charles were coming, and he takes his horn

of ivory, and feebly he sounds it. The
Emperor stops to listen: "Lords," he saith,
"now has great woe come upon us, this day
shall we lose Roland my nephew, I wot
from the blast of his horn that he is nigh
to death. Let him who would reach the
field ride fast. Now sound ye all the trumpets of the host." Then they blew sixty
thousand, so loud that the mountains resound and the valleys give answer. The
paynims hear them and have no will to
laugh, but one saith to another: "We shall
have ado with Charles anon."

Say the paynims: "The Emperor is returning, we hear the trumpets of France;
if Charles come hither, we shall suffer sore
loss. Yet if Roland live, our war will begin
again, and we shall lose Spain our land."
Then four hundred armed in their helmets,
and of the best of those on the field, gather
together, and on Roland they make onset
fierce and sore. Now is the Count hard
bestead.

When Count Roland sees them draw
near he waxes hardy and fierce and terrible;
never will he yield as long as he is a living
man. He sits his horse Veillantiff, and spurs
him well with his spurs of fine gold, and
rides into the stour upon them all; and at
his side is Archbishop Turpin. And the
Saracens say one to another: "Now save
yourselves, friends. We have heard the
trumpets of France; Charles the mighty
King is returning."

Count Roland never loved the cowardly,
or the proud, or the wicked, or any knight
who was not a good vassal, and now he
calls to Archbishop Turpin saying: "Lord,
thou art on foot and I am a-horseback, for
thy love I would make halt, and together
we will take the good and the ill; I will not
leave thee for any living man; the blows
of Almace and of Durendal shall give back
this assault to the paynims." Then saith the
Archbishop: "A traitor is he who doth not
smite; Charles is returning, and well will
he revenge us."

"In an evil hour," say the paynims, "were
we born; woeful is the day that has dawned

for us! We have lost our lords and our peers. Charles the valiant cometh hither again with his great host, we hear the clear trumpets of those of France, and great is the noise of their cry of Montjoy. Count Roland is of such might he cannot be vanquished by any mortal man. Let us hurl our missiles upon him, and then leave him." Even so they did; and cast upon him many a dart and javelin, and spears and lances and feathered arrows. They broke and rent the shield of Roland, tore open and unmailed his hauberk, but did not pierce his body: but Veillantif was wounded in thirty places, and fell from under the Count, dead. Then the paynims flee, and leave him; Count Roland is left alone and on foot.

The paynims flee in anger and wrath, and in all haste they fare toward Spain. Count Roland did not pursue after them, for he has lost his horse Veillantif, and whether he will or no, is left on foot. He went to the help of Archbishop Turpin, and unlaced his golden helm from his head, and took off his white hauberk of fine mail, and he tore his tunic into strips and with the pieces bound his great wounds. Then he gathers him in his arms, and lays him down full softly upon the green grass, and gently he beseeches him: "O gracious baron, I pray thy leave. Our comrades whom we so loved are slain, and it is not meet to leave them thus. I would go seek and find them, and range them before thee." "Go and return again," quoth the Archbishop. "Thank God, this field is thine and mine."

Roland turns away and fares on alone through the field, he searches the valleys and the hills; (and there he found Ivon and Ivory), and Gerin, and Gerier his comrade, (and he found Engelier the Gascon), and Berengier, and Oton, and he found Anseïs and Samson, and Gerard the Old of Roussillon. One by one he hath taken up the barons, and hath come with them unto the Archbishop, and places them

in rank before him. The Archbishop cannot help but weep; he raises his hand and gives them benediction, and thereafter saith: "Alas for ye, lords! May God the Glorious receive your souls, and bring them into Paradise among the blessed flowers. And now my own death torments me sore; never again shall I see the great Emperor."

Again Roland turned away to search the field; and when he found Oliver his comrade, he gathered him close against his breast, and as best he might returned again unto the Archbishop, and laid his comrade upon a shield beside the others; and the Archbishop absolved and blessed him. Then their sorrow and pity broke forth again, and Roland saith: "Oliver, fair comrade, thou wert son of the great Duke Reinier, who held the Marches of Rivier and Genoa; for the breaking of lances or the piercing of shields; for vanquishing and affrighting the proud, for upholding and counselling the good, never in any land was there a better knight."

When Roland sees the peers, and Oliver whom he so loved, lying dead, pity takes him and he begins to weep and his face is all discoloured; so great is his grief he cannot stand upright, but will he, nill he, falls to the ground in a swoon. Saith the Archbishop: "Alack for thee, good baron."

When the Archbishop sees Roland swoon, he has such dole as he has never known before. He stretches out his hand and takes the horn of ivory, for in Roncevals there is a swift streamlet, and he would go to it to bring of its water to Roland. Slowly and falteringly he sets forth, but so weak he is he cannot walk, his strength has gone from him, too much blood has he lost, and before a man might cross an acre his heart faileth, and he falls forward upon his face, and the anguish of death comes upon him.

When Count Roland recovers from his swoon he gets upon his feet with great torment; he looks up and he looks down, and beyond his comrades, on the green grass, he sees that goodly baron, the Archbishop, appointed of God in His stead. Turpin saith his *mea culpa,* and looks up, and stretches out his two hands towards heaven, and prays God that He grant him Paradise. And so he dies, the warrior of Charles. Long had he waged strong war against the paynims, both by his mighty battling and his goodly sermons. May God grant him His holy benison.

Count Roland sees the Archbishop upon the ground; his bowels have fallen out of his body, and his brains are oozing out of his forehead; Roland takes his fair, white hands and crosses them upon his breast between his two collar bones; and lifting up his voice, he mourns for him, after the manner of his people: "Ah gentle man, knight of high parentage, now I commend thee to the heavenly Glory; never will there be a man who shall serve Him more willingly; never since the days of the apostles hath there been such a prophet to uphold the law, and win the hearts of men; may thy soul suffer no dole or torment, but may the doors of Paradise be opened to thee."

Now Roland feels that death is near him, and his brains flow out at his ears; he prays to the Lord God for his peers that He will receive them, and he prays to the Angel Gabriel for himself. That he may be free from all reproach, he takes his horn of ivory in the one hand, and Durendal, his sword, in the other, and farther than a cross-bow can cast an arrow, through a cornfield he goeth on towards Spain. At the crest of a hill, beneath two fair trees, are four stairs of marble; there he falls down on the green grass in a swoon, for death is close upon him.

High are the hills and very tall are the trees; the four stones are of shining marble; and there Count Roland swoons upon the green grass. Meantime a Saracen is watching him; he has stained his face and body with blood, and feigning death, he lies still among his fellows; but now he springs to his feet and hastens forward. Fair he was, and

strong, and of good courage; and in his pride he breaks out into mighty wrath, and seizes upon Roland, both him and his arms, and he cries: "Now is the nephew of Charles overthrown. This his sword will I carry into Arabia." But at his touch the Count recovered his senses.

Roland feels that his sword hath been taken from him, he opens his eyes, and saith: "Certes, thou art not one of our men." He holds his horn of ivory which he never lets out of his grasp, and he smites the Saracen upon the helm which was studded with gold and gems, and he breaks steel and head and bones that his two eyes start out, and he falls down dead at his feet. Then saith Roland: "Coward, what made thee so bold to lay hands upon me, whether right or wrong? No man shall hear it but shall hold thee a fool. Now is my horn of ivory broken in the bell, and its gold and its crystals have fallen."

Now Roland feels that his sight is gone from him. With much striving he gets upon his feet; the colour has gone from his face; before him lies a brown stone, and in his sorrow and wrath he smites ten blows upon it. The sword grates upon the rock, but neither breaks nor splinters; and the Count saith: "Holy Mary, help me now! Ah Durendal, alas for your goodness! *Now am I near to death, and have no more need of you.* Many a fight in the field have I won with you, many a wide land have I conquered with you, lands now ruled by Charles with the white beard. May the man who would flee before another, never possess you. For many a day have you been held by a right good lord, never will there be such another in France the free."

Roland smote upon the block of *hard stone,* and the steel grates, but neither breaks nor splinters. And when he sees that he can in nowise break it, he laments, saying: "O Durendal, how fair and bright thou art, in the sunlight how thou flashest and shinest! Charles was once in the valley of Moriane, when God commanded him by one of his angels that he should give thee to a chieftain Count; then the great and noble King girded thee upon me; and with thee I won for him Anjou and Bretagne, and I conquered Poitou and Maine for him, and for him I conquered Normandy the free, and Provence, and Acquitaine; and Lombardy, and all of Romagna; and I conquered for him Bavaria, and Flanders, and Bulgaria, and all of Poland; Constantinople which now pays him fealty, and Saxony, where he may work his will. And I conquered for him Wales, and Scotland, and Ireland, and England which he holds as his demesne. Many lands and countries have I won with thee, lands which Charles of the white beard rules. And now am I heavy of heart because of this my sword; rather would I die than that it should fall into the hands of the paynims. Lord God our Father, let not this shame fall upon France."

And again Roland smote upon the brown stone and beyond all telling shattered it; the sword grates, but springs back again into the air and is neither dinted nor broken. And when the Count sees he may in nowise break it, he laments, saying: "O Durendal, how fair and holy a thing thou art! In thy golden hilt is many a relic—a tooth of Saint Peter, and some of the blood of Saint Basil, and hairs from the head of my lord, Saint Denis, and a bit of the raiment of the Virgin Mary. It is not meet that thou fall into the hands of the paynims, only Christians should wield thee. May no coward ever possess thee! Many wide lands have I conquered with thee, lands which Charles of the white beard rules; and thereby is the Emperor great and mighty."

Now Roland feels that death has come upon him, and that it creeps down from his head to his heart. In all haste he fares under a pine tree, and hath cast himself down upon his face on the green grass. Under him he laid his sword and his horn of ivory; and he turned his face towards the paynim folk, for he would that Charles and all his

men should say that the gentle Count had died a conqueror. Speedily and full often he confesses his sins, and in atonement he offers his glove to God.

Roland lies on a high peak looking towards Spain; he feels that his time is spent, and with one hand he beats upon his breast: "O God, I have sinned; forgive me through thy might the wrongs, both great and small, which I have done from the day I was born even to this day on which I was smitten." With his right hand he holds out his glove to God; and lo, the angels of heaven come down to him.

Count Roland lay under the pine tree; he has turned his face towards Spain, and he begins to call many things to remembrance—all the lands he had won by his valour, and sweet France, and the men of his lineage, and Charles, his liege lord, who had brought him up in his household; and he cannot help but weep. But he would not wholly forget himself, and again he confesses his sins and begs forgiveness of God: "Our Father, who art truth, who raised up Lazarus from the dead, and who defended Daniel from the lions, save thou my soul from the perils to which it is brought through the sins I wrought in my life days." With his right hand he offers his glove to God, and Saint Gabriel has taken it from his hand. Then his head sinks on his arm, and with clasped hands he hath gone to his end. And God sent him His cherubim, and Saint Michael of the Seas, and with them went Saint Gabriel, and they carried the soul of the Count into Paradise.

## Part III
## The vengeance of Charles

Dead is Roland, God in heaven has his soul.

The Emperor has come into Roncevals. There is no road, nor path, nor open space of land, though it be but the width of an ell or the breadth of a foot, that is not strewn with Franks or paynims. And Charles cries out: "Where art thou, fair nephew? Where is Count Oliver, and where the Archbishop? Where is Gerin, and Gerier his comrade? Where is Oton the Duke, and Count Berengier, and Ivon and Ivory whom I hold so dear? What has befallen Engelier the Gascon, Samson the Duke, and Anseïs the Proud? Where is Gerard the Old of Roussillon? Where are the Twelve Peers that I left behind me?" But what avails his call since no one gives answer? "O God," saith the King, "much it weighs on me that I was not here to begin the onset." And he plucks at his beard even as a man in wrath. His knights and barons weep, and twenty thousand fall swooning to the ground; great is the sorrow of Naymes the Duke.

[Mighty is the woe at Roncevals.] There is no knight or baron but weeps right sore for pity. They weep for their sons and brothers and nephews, and for their friends, and for their liege lords; many a one falls swooning to the ground. But Duke Naymes bears him like a man of valour, he is the first to bespeak the Emperor, saying: "Look two leagues before us, where on the dusty highroad fares the throng of the paynim folk. I prithee ride on and revenge this woe." "Ah God," saith Charles, "already are they far from us. Now grant me justice and honour. They have taken from me the flower of sweet France."

Then the King commands Gebuin and Odo, Tedbalt of Rheims and Count Milon, saying: "Guard ye this field, the valleys and the mountains; let the dead lie even as they are, let not the lions or any wild beast come nigh them, neither the sergeants nor the varlets, let not any man lay hands on them, until God grants us to return to this field." And they answered him gently in their love: "Just Emperor, dear lord, even so will we do." And they keep with them a thousand of their knights.

The Emperor bids the trumpets be sounded, and then he rides on with his great host. They have found the traces of those of Spain, and they pursue after them, and all are of one mind. And when the King sees the night coming on, he dismounts in a meadow of green grass, and casts himself upon the ground, and prays to the Lord God that He make the sun to stand still for him, the darkness to delay and the light to abide. And an angel that was wont to speak with him straightway commanded him, saying: "Charles, mount thy horse, and the light shall not fail thee. Thou hast lost the flower of France, and this God knows; it is granted thee to revenge thyself upon this guilty folk." At these words the Emperor gets him to horse.

For Charles God has wrought a great wonder; and the sun is stayed in the heavens. The heathen flee, and fiercely the Franks pursue them; in Val Tenebres they come upon them; and with their swords they drive them towards Saragossa, and slay them as they go with great slaughter; and they cut them off from the roads and the footways. The stream of the Ebro is before them, deep it is, and swift and terrible, and there is neither ferry nor barge nor dromond. The paynims call upon their god Tervagant; then they leap into the stream, but find no safety. The armed knights are the heaviest, and some among them sink to the bottom, others are swept along by the current, and even those who fare best drink deep of the water; all alike are miserably drowned. And the Franks cry to them, saying: "Woe worth the day ye saw Roland!"

When Charles sees that all the paynims are dead, some slain by the sword, and the more part drowned—great was the booty his knights had of them—the gentle King dismounts, and casts himself upon the ground and gives thanks to God. When he again gets upon his feet the sun is set. "Time it is to make encampment," he saith; "too late it is to return again to Roncevals. Our horses are weary and spent; take off their saddles and bridles, and let them graze in the meadows." "Lord, thou sayest well and truly," the Franks make answer.

The Emperor has made stay for the night. The Franks dismount beside the Ebro; they unsaddle their horses and take the golden bridles from off their heads, and they turn them into meadows of fresh grass; no other cheer can they make them. Those who are weary sleep upon the ground; that night no guard was set.

The Emperor lies him down in the meadow; at his head he puts his great lance; this night he will not disarm himself, but dons his white hauberk, laces his gold-adorned helmet, and girds on Joyeuse—never was there its like, thirty times a day it changes its light. Much we might tell you of the spear with which Our Lord was pierced upon the cross; Charles has the point thereof, thanks be to God, and has encased it in the golden hilt of his sword; for this honour and excellence it has been called Joyeuse. The barons of France should hold this in mind, for from this, they took their cry of Montjoy; and thus it is that no folk can withstand them.

Clear is the night and fair the moon. Charles lies upon the ground, but is full of dole for Roland, and right heavy of heart because of Oliver, and the Twelve Peers, and the Frankish folk that he has left at Roncevals dead and stained with blood; he cannot help but weep and make lament, and he prays God that He save their souls. Weary is the King, for his woe is very great, and he sleeps, he cannot help but sleep. Now throughout all the fields the Franks lie at rest; nor is there a horse with strength to stand upon his feet, if any wishes grass he takes it as he lies. Much has he learned who knows sorrow.

Charles sleeps like a man spent with toil and grief. God sent Saint Gabriel to him, and bid him guard the Emperor. All night the angel watched by his pillow, and in a vision he made known to him a battle which is to be levied against him and the grave import thereof. Charles looks up into the heavens, and sees thunder and cold and whirlwinds, storms and mighty tempests, and fire and flame are kindled there; and all these straightway fall upon his people. The fire burns their lances of oak and apple wood, and their shields even to the bosses of pure gold; the shafts of their sharp lances

are shattered, and their hauberks and helmets of steel are destroyed. Sore bestead are his knights, lions and leopards are ready to devour them, serpents and vipers, dragons, and devils; and of griffons there are more than thirty thousand; and all these fall upon the Franks. They cry: "Help us, Charles!" The King is full of grief and pity for their sake, and would fain go to them, but he is withheld; for from without the wood comes a great lion proud and mighty and fierce, he sets upon the King's self, and each clasps other in the struggle; but who conquers and who falls is not made plain. Still the Emperor does not waken.

Thereafter came another vision to him, and it seemed to him that he was at Aix in France on a terrace, and was holding a bear in a double chain, when he saw coming from Ardennes thirty more bears, who spoke to him as they had been men, saying: "Give him to us again, lord, it is not just that ye withhold him from us; it is our part to rescue our kinsman." But even then from without the palace ran a deerhound and set upon the greatest of the bears, a little apart from his fellows on the green grass. Then saw the King a wondrous battle, but he knew not which won or which failed therein. These things God's angel made manifest to the baron. And Charles slept even to bright day.

King Marsila has fled away to Saragossa, and lights down from his horse under the shade of an olive, he takes off sword and helmet and byrnie, and casts himself all woe-begone upon the green grass. He has lost his right hand and swoons from pain and loss of blood. Beside him Bramimonde, his wife, weeps and makes lament, bitterly she bemoans herself; and with her are more than thirty thousand men who all curse Charles and fair France.

They haste to their god Apollon in a grotto hard by, and upbraid him, and lay rude hands upon him, saying: "O cruel god, why hast thou brought this shame upon us? why hast thou let our King be vanquished?

An ill reward thou givest him who has served thee well." Then they took away his sceptre and his crown, (and dragged him down from the column with their hands), and trod him to earth under their feet; with great staves they beat him and brake him to bits. And they robbed Tervagant of his carbuncle; and they cast Mahound into a ditch, for the dogs and the pigs to worry and gnaw.

Marsila has recovered from his swoon, and they have brought him into his vaulted chamber, painted and inscribed with many colours. And Bramimonde the Queen weeps for him, tears her hair, and makes great moan. Then she lifts up her voice and cries aloud: "O Saragossa, now art thou made desolate of the gentle King who held thee in fee. Traitors to him were the gods who failed him this day in battle. The Amiral will do cowardly, an he does not set upon this bold people, who are so proud they have no care for life or death. The Emperor of the hoary beard is valiant and of good courage; if there be a battle he will not flee the field. Woe it is there is none to slay him."

The Emperor by his might has abode for seven long years in Spain; he has taken its castles and many a city. King Marsila has striven against him; and in the first year he let seal letters, and sent them to Baligant in Babylon—he is the old Amiral of antiquity who has outlived Homer and Virgil —that he come with succour to Saragossa; if he comes not, Marsila swears he will forsake his gods and all the idols he was wont to worship, and will receive the Christian faith, and will make peace with Charles. But the Amiral is afar off and has tarried long. From forty kingdoms he has summoned his people; he has had his great dromonds made ready, his boats and barges and galleys and ships; all his fleet he has gathered together at his port of Alexandria. It is in May, on the first day of summer, that all his armies embark on the sea.

Great is the host of this hostile folk, and swiftly they steer with sail and oar. On the yards and topmasts are hung many a lantern and carbuncle, and from on high they shed forth such a brightness that by night the sea is yet more fair. And as they draw near to the land of Spain all the countryside is lighted thereby and illumed; and the news thereof comes to Marsila.

The paynim folk would make no stay, they leave the sea and come into fresh water; they leave behind them Marbrise and Marbruse, and pass with all their ships up the Ebro. They have lanterns and carbuncles without number, which give them light all the night through. And with the day they come to Saragossa.

Fair is the day and bright the sun. The Amiral has left his ship; at his right hand walks Espanelis and seventeen kings follow after him, and counts and dukes I know not how many. Under a laurel tree, amid an open field, they spread a cloth of white silk upon the green grass, and by it they placed a throne of ivory whereon sits the paynim Baligant, and all the rest stand about him. Their lord was the first to speak: "Now hearken brave knights and free: Charles, the Emperor of the Franks, must eat no more, unless I so command it. He has waged strong war upon me throughout all Spain; and now I would seek him in fair France, nor will I rest my life long until he be slain, or yields him alive." And with his glove he smites his right knee.

So said he, and maintains that for all the gold under heaven he will not fail to go unto Aix, where Charles is wont to hold his court. And his men gave him counsel and praised him. Then he called two of his knights, Clarien and Clarifan, saying: "Ye are sons of King Maltraïen who was ever a ready messenger; and now I command you that you go unto Saragossa, and say to Marsila that I am come to aid him against the Franks, if I come upon their host, great will be the battle. Give him now this glove embroidered with gold, give it into his right hand, and take to him this baton of pure gold, and let him come to me to do me homage. And thereafter I will go into France to war upon Charles; if he doth not fall at my feet and cry my mercy and doth not forsake the faith of the Christians, I will strip the crown from off his head." "Well said, lord," the paynims make answer.

"Now fare ye forth, barons," saith Baligant; "let one carry the glove, the other the staff." "Even so will we do, dear lord," they make answer. So they rode forth till they came unto Saragossa. They pass ten gates and cross four bridges, and fare through the streets where dwell the burgesses. As they draw nigh to the upper city they hear a mighty noise from about the palace, where a great throng of the paynims are weeping and making great dole; and they cry out upon their gods Tervagant and Mahound and Apollon, who have no whit availed them. And one saith to another: "Woe is me, what will become of us? Now are we undone, for we have lost King Marsila, yesterday Roland smote off his right hand; and Jurfaleu the Fair hath been taken from us; and now all Spain will fall into the hands of the Franks." Meantime the two messengers dismount at the stairway.

They have left their horses under an olive tree; two Saracens took the bridles, and the messengers, each holding the other's mantle, mounted to the highest palace. As they enter the vaulted chamber they give greeting to Marsila in all friendship: "May Mahound who hath us in his power, and our lord Apollon, and Tervagant save the King and keep the Queen." "Ye speak folly," then saith Bramimonde, "for these our gods have proved recreant; little virtue they showed at Roncevals; they let our knights be slain, and failed my lord in battle, he has lost his right hand, smitten off it was by Roland the mighty Count. Anon Charles will have all Spain in his power. What will become of me, caitiff and wretched? Ah me, if some man of ye would but slay me!"

"Dame," saith Clarien, "be not so full of words. Messengers are we from the paynim

Baligant; he will save Marsila, he saith, and sends him his glove and staff. In the Ebro he hath four thousand shallops, boats, and barges, and swift galleys; and dromonds he hath without number. The Amiral is strong and mighty, he will go into France to seek out Charles, and he thinks to either slay him or make him yield him." "No need to go so far," quoth Bramimonde, "nigh at hand will you find the Franks. The Emperor hath been seven full years in this land; he is a valiant and great warrior, rather would he die than fly the field; no King under heaven is there whom he doth not hold as a child. Charles fears no man living."

"Nay, let be," saith King Marsila. And he turns to the messengers: "Speak ye to me, lords. Ye see that I am hurt to death; and I have neither son nor daughter nor heir— one I had who was slain yesterday at eventide. Say ye to my liege lord that he come hither to me. He has rights upon this land of Spain, and I will give it over to him, if he would have it so; then let him defend it against the Franks. Concerning Charles I will give him good counsel, and mayhap by this day month he will have conquered him. Take to him the keys of Saragossa, and bid him go not far from hence, an he would take my counsel." "Lord thou speakest well and truly," they make answer.

Quoth Marsila: "Charles the Emperor hath slain my men, and laid waste my land, sacked and despoiled my cities; (and now his men are assembled on the banks of the Ebro), not more than seven leagues from here, as I deem it. Tell the Amiral to bring up his hosts and do him battle, so charge him from me." Then Marsila gave over to them the keys of Saragossa; and both messengers bow before him, and take their leave and go thence.

The two messengers have mounted their horses, swiftly they ride forth from the city, and come to the Amiral, sore troubled; and they give over to him the keys of Saragossa: "What news have ye?" saith Baligant.

"Where is Marsila whom I summoned?"
"He is hurt unto death," Clarien makes answer. "Yesterday Charles set forth through the passes, for he thought to return again to fair France. For his honour he set behind him a rearguard, and with it staid Count Roland, his nephew, and Oliver, and all the Twelve Peers, together with twenty thousand armed knights of France. King Marsila did them battle like a true baron, and in the field he and Roland fought together man to man, and Roland gave him so mighty a blow with Durendal that his right hand was smitten from off his body; and his son whom he so loved was slain, and likewise the barons he had in his company. He fled, for he could no longer make stand, and the Emperor pursued him full hotly. The King bids you come to his succour, and gives over into your hands the kingdom of Spain." And Baligant falls a-thinking; so great dole he has thereof that he wellnigh goes out of his senses.

"My lord Amiral," then saith Clarien, "yesterday a battle was fought at Roncevals. Dead are Roland and Count Oliver, and the Twelve Peers whom Charles held so dear, together with twenty thousand of the knights of France. There King Marsila lost his right hand, and fiercely did Charles pursue after him; and no knights are left alive in this land, all are either slain or drowned in the Ebro. On its banks the Franks have now their camp, so near have they come to us in our marches, but if you so will it, their retreat shall be sore." And now Baligant is proud of look, and is glad and joyous of heart; he rises from his great chair, and cries aloud: "Barons, tarry not; leave the ships, mount and ride! If Charles the Old flee not before us King Marsila shall be revenged upon him; in return for his right hand I will bring him a head."

The paynims of Arabia have come forth from their ships, they have mounted their horses and mules, and thereafter they rode forward—how else should they do? When he had set them on the march, the Amiral called Gemalfin, his dear friend, saying: "Lead thou all my host, I command thee." Then he mounted his brown war horse, and bid four dukes follow him, and together they rode on till they came unto Saragossa. By the marble stairway he has lighted down from his horse, and four counts hold his stirrup. As he mounts the stair of the palace, Bramimonde runs forth to meet him, and saith: "Woe worth the day on which I was born, for now in shameful wise have I lost my lord!" She falls at the feet of the Amiral, but he raises her up, and sorrowfully they went up into the chamber.

When King Marsila saw Baligant he called to him two Saracens of Spain, saying: "Put your arms about me that I may sit up." Then he took one of his gloves in his left hand, and said: "My lord and Amiral, I hereby give over all my land unto you, both Saragossa and all its dependencies. I have lost both my life and my folk." And the Amiral answered him: "For this am I right sorry. But I may not stay now for more words with thee, for full well I know Charles will not stay for us; yet none the less I will accept thy glove of thee." And for pity he weeps as he turns away. Then he hastes down the stair of the palace, mounts his horse and spurs as fast as he may back to his own folk. So fast he rode that he comes up with the foremost; and ever and again he cries aloud: "Haste ye, paynims, for even now the Franks flee before us."

In the morning, when the first dawn brightens, Charles the Emperor awakes. Saint Gabriel, who by God's command has guarded him, stretches out his hand and makes the sign of the cross upon him. The King has risen, and laid aside his armour, and all the men of the host likewise disarm themselves. Then they mount, and ride right speedily by long paths and wide ways, for they go to see the dread carnage at Roncevals where was the battle.

Charles is come into Roncevals. He begins to weep because of the dead he finds there, and he saith to the Franks: "Barons, ride softly, for I would go on before, to seek my nephew, whom I myself would find. Once at Aix, *at the feast of Christmas,* when my good knights were boasting of great battles and of fierce onsets, I heard Roland speak his mind, saying, that if he should hap to die in a strange land, it would be at the head of his men and his peers, and his face would be turned to the land of his foes, and he would die as a conqueror, the baron." And farther than a man may throw a staff, before all the rest Charles rides on up the mountain.

As the Emperor went seeking his nephew, he found the grass and the flowers of the field bright red with the blood of his barons. Great pity he has thereof, and he may not help but weep. He has come up the hill to the two trees, full well he knew Roland's blows on the three stairs, and he sees his nephew lying stretched on the green grass. No wonder is it that Charles is full of wrath. He lights down from his horse, and runs to Roland and gathers him in his arms; and he swoons over him so great is his grief.

The Emperor has recovered from his swoon; and Naymes the Duke and Count Acelin, Geoffrey of Anjou, and his brother Thierry take the King and help him to sit up under a pine tree. He looks to the ground and sees his nephew lying there, and begins softly to lament him: "Dear Roland, may God have mercy upon thee! For the arraying and winning of great battles, never has the world seen thy like. My glory is near to its setting." And Charles cannot help but swoon again.

Charles the King has recovered from his swoon, four of his barons hold him in their arms; he looks to the ground and sees his nephew lying dead, still strong and gallant of seeming, but his colour is gone, and his eyes, which have turned upwards, are darkened. Charles makes lament for him in all faith and love: "Dear Roland, may God bring thy soul among the flowers of Paradise, amid the glorious. Woe worth the day

thou camest into Spain, baron! Never shall the day dawn whereon I shall not grieve for thee. Now my pride and my power will pass; for who henceforth will uphold my kingdom? In all the world I do not think to have a single friend; though I have other kindred none are valiant as thou wert." With both his hands he plucks the hair of his head; and so great is the dole of the Franks, that of a hundred thousand men there is not one that doth not weep.

"Dear Roland, I shall go back into France, and when I am come to Laon, to my great hall there, strange men will come to me from many lands, and they will ask of me where is the Count, the great chieftain, and I shall say to them that he lies dead in Spain. Thenceforth in sorrow shall I maintain my kingdom; never shall the day dawn whereon I shall not mourn for thee.

"Dear Roland, brave captain, fair youth, when I am come to Aix, to my chapel there, men will come to me asking news, and I shall tell them marvellous and heavy news: 'My nephew, who has conquered many lands for me, is dead.' Then the Saxons will rise up against me, and the Hungarians and the Bulgarians, and many hostile people, the Romans and the Apulians, and all those of Palermo, and those of Africa and those of Califerne; then my woes and troubles will increase; for who will lead my armies against such a host when he is dead who was ever our champion? Ah fair France, how art thou made desolate! So great is my sorrow that gladly would I lay down my life." With both hands the King plucks his white beard and the hairs of his head. And a hundred thousand Franks fall swooning to the ground.

"Dear Roland, woe worth thy life days! May thy soul be brought into Paradise. He who slew thee wrought shame to sweet France. Now is my grief so great that I would not outlive those of my household who lie dead for my sake. May God, the son of Mary, grant that before I am come to the pass of Cizre, my soul may part from my body, and follow their souls, and that my body may be laid in the earth beside their bodies." And the King weeps and plucks his white beard. "Now great is the wrath of Charles," quoth Naymes the Duke.

"My lord and Emperor," then saith Geoffrey of Anjou, "make ye not such great dole; rather let the field be searched and our dead, whom those of Spain have slain in battle, be brought together in a common grave." "Now blow thy horn," the King makes answer.

Geoffrey of Anjou has sounded his horn; and the Franks light down from their horses, so Charles hath bidden it. And all their comrades which they find dead they straightway bring to the fosse. Many a bishop and abbot is there, and monks and canons and tonsured priests, and they have absolved the dead, and blessed them in God's name. And they kindled myrrh and sweet spices, and richly they perfumed them with incense, and buried them with great honour; and then they left them—how else should they do?

But the Emperor had Roland and Oliver and Archbishop Turpin laid apart from the rest, and he ordered their bodies to be opened in his presence, and had their hearts wrapped in silken cloths, and placed in caskets of white marble. Then they took the bodies of the three barons, and when they had washed them well with wine and spices, they wrapped them in hide of the deer. And the King commanded Tedbalt and Gebuin, Count Milon, and Odo the Marquis, saying: "Carry ye them upon the march in three wains." Richly were they covered over with silk of Galaza.

And now, even as Charles would set forth, the vanguard of the paynims is upon him. From the foremost ranks ride forth two messengers, and in the name of the Amiral announce the battle: "Haughty King, flight now were cowardly. Lo, Baligant is upon thee, and great are the hosts he brings with him out of Arabia; this day we shall try thy valiance." The King plucks at his beard, and calls to mind his grief and his great loss; proudly he looks on his men, and lifting up his voice, which is great and mighty, he calls to them, saying: "Ye barons of France, now arm yourselves and get ye to horseback!"

The Emperor is the first to take arms; speedily has he donned his hauberk and laced his helmet, and girded on Joyeuse whose light outshines the sun, and now about his neck he hangs a shield of Gironde, and takes his lance which was fashioned at Blandonne, and then he mounts Tencendur, his good horse that he won at the ford below Marsonne, when he struck down and slew Malpalin of Narbonne; he slackens rein, and he spurs his horse that he springs and curvets before the eyes of a hundred thousand men. And he cries upon God and the Apostle of Rome.

Throughout the field the Franks light down from their horses, and more than a hundred thousand don their armour; harness they have which well becomes them, and swift horses and goodly arms. As men well skilled they sprang to the saddle; if they meet with the paynim host, hardily will they do them battle. And their gonfanons sweep down to their helmets. Now when Charles sees their goodly bearing, he bespeaks Jozeran of Provence, Naymes the Duke and Antelme of Maïence, saying: "In such vassals a man may well set his trust, with them at his side it were folly to be dismayed. If the Arabs do not repent them of the battle, Roland's death shall cost them dear." "Now may God grant it to be as thou sayest," Naymes makes answer.

Then Charles calls Rabel and Guineman, saying: "Lords, I would have you be to me in the stead of Roland and Oliver; let one of you bear the sword, the other the horn of ivory, and do ye lead the host, taking with you fifteen thousand Franks, young men and of our most valiant. After these shall be as many more whom Gebuin and Lorent shall lead." Naymes the Duke and Count Jozeran array these battles; if they come upon the paynims, great will be the slaughter.

These first divisions are of men of France, but after these two a third is arrayed of the vassals of Bavaria, their knights they reckon at twenty thousand, and never will battle be shunned by them; there is no folk in all the world whom Charles holds so dear, save those of France who have conquered the kingdoms of the earth. Count Ogier the Dane, the great warrior, will lead them, for they are a haughty fellowship.

Thus Charles has already three companies. Then Naymes the Duke establishes a fourth of right valiant barons; Germans are they, the bravest of their folk, and they are reckoned at twenty thousand; well provided are they with horses and arms; never for fear of death would they flee the battle. Their leader is Herman Duke of Thrace; rather would he die than do cowardly.

Naymes the Duke and Count Jozeran have made up the fifth division of Normans; they number twenty thousand, so say the Franks; goodly are their arms and swift their horses; never for fear of death will they prove recreant; there is no folk under heaven more valiant in battle. Richard the Old will lead them to the field, and there will he deal good blows with his sharp spear.

The sixth battle is of Bretons, and forty thousand knights they number; straight are their lances and well fixed their gonfanons. Eudes is their over-lord, and he commands Count Nivelon, Tedbalt of Rheims and Odo the Marquis, saying: "Lead ye my folk, I give them into your hands."

Thus the Emperor has six battles arrayed. Thereafter Naymes the Duke establishes the seventh of Poitevins and barons of Auvergne; they number upon forty thousand knights, good are their horses and fair their arms. They stand apart, in a valley, under a hillock, and Charles stretches out his right hand to them and blesses them. Their leaders are Jozeran and Godselme.

And now Naymes establishes the eighth battle of Flemings and of barons of Friesland; more than forty thousand knights they number, and never will they flee the field. "Well will they serve me," saith the King; "and Rembald and Hamon de Galice shall lead them in all knightliness."

Together Naymes and Count Jozeran array the ninth battle of brave warriors, men of Lorraine and Burgundy, knights to the number of fifty thousand; they have laced on their helmets and donned their byrnies, stout are their lances and short of shaft. If the Arabs hold not back from the encounter, these men will give them good blows; and Thierry the Duke of Argonne will lead them.

The tenth battle is of barons of France, a hundred thousand of our noblest knights, hardy of body and proud of bearing, hoary of head and white of beard, clad in hauberks and two-fold byrnies, girt with swords of France or Spain, and bearing shields with divers devices. They mount their horses and clamour for battle, crying out Montjoy. With them is Charles. Geoffrey of Anjou bears the oriflamme. Saint Peter's ensign it was, and thence had been called Romaine, but this day its name was changed to Montjoy.

The Emperor lights down from his horse, and throws himself upon the green grass, he turns his face to the rising sun and calls upon God with all his soul: "O our true Father, defend me this day, thou who saved Jonah from the whale in whose belly he was, and spared the King of Nineveh, and rescued Daniel from the dread torment of the lions' den, and preserved the three children in the fiery furnace. Let thy love be with me this day; and grant me in thy mercy, if it be thy will, that I may revenge Roland my nephew." And when he had prayed, he rose up, and upon his forehead made the sign which has so great power. Then the King mounts his swift horse—Naymes and Jozeran held his stirrup for him—and he takes his shield and sharp lance. He is full noble of person, comely and strong, clear of face and goodly of bearing. Then he rides forward right firmly. In rear and van the trumpets are sounded, and clear above the rest resounds the horn of ivory. And the Franks weep in pity for Roland.

The Emperor rides forward right nobly; he has spread out his beard over his hauberk, and for love of him the rest have done likewise, and thereby the hundred thousand Franks are known to all. They pass rocky cliffs and heights, deep valleys and dread defiles, and at last come beyond the passes and the waste lands, into the marches of Spain, and there on a space of level ground, they make halt. Meantime Baligant's advance-guard returns to him, and a Syrian among them tells his message: "We have seen Charles the haughty King, proud are his men, no mind have they to fail him. Arm yourselves, anon we shall have battle." Then saith Baligant: "Ye bring brave tidings. Sound your trumpets, that my paynims may know thereof."

Throughout all the host tabours are sounded, bussynes and clear trumpets. The paynims dismount and arm themselves. The Amiral would have no delay; he dons his hauberk, the skirt whereof is broidered and fringed, laces on his helmet adorned with gold; then he girds his sword at his left side, in his pride he has found a name for it, because of the sword of Charles whereof he has heard, (and his he now calls Precieuse); and he has made it his war-cry in the field, and has bidden his knights to cry it. And about his neck he hangs his shield which is wide and great, the boss thereof is gold and the border of precious stones, and its guige is of goodly silk patterned with roses. He grasps his lance which he calls Maltet, its shaft was as thick and great as a club, and the iron point thereof was as much as a mule might carry. Marcule from over-sea holds the stirrup as Baligant mounts his charger. Wide is the fork of the baron's legs, thin his flanks and great his sides; deep of chest he is, and well made of body, broad are his shoulders, and clear is his forehead, proud is his look and his hair right curly; and white he is as is the flower in summer time. Many a time has his prowess been proved. God, he were a goodly vassal, an he had but Christianity. He spurs his horse that the bright blood flows out, he sets him at a gallop and leaps a ditch which measures a good fifty feet. And the paynims cry: "Well he will defend our marches. The Frank who encounters with him, will he, nill he, must take his end. Charles is mad in that he has not fled."

The Amiral looks a goodly baron; white is his beard even as is the flower. And wise he is according to his law, and in battle he is fierce and mighty. His son Malpramis is full knightly, tall he is and strong and like to the men of his line. He saith to his father: "Lord, let us ride forward! much I doubt me if we see aught of Charles." "Yea, for he is a man of prowess," Baligant makes answer. "Great honour is done him in many a story; but now that he is bereft of Roland, his nephew, he will not have the might to withstand us."

"Malpramis, fair son," saith Baligant again, "yesterday was slain Roland the good knight, and Oliver the wise, the valiant, and the Twelve Peers whom Charles held so dear, and with them twenty thousand warriors of France. Those that are left I rate at less than my glove. Yet sooth it is that the Emperor has returned hither again, so the Syrian, my messenger tells me, and that he has arrayed ten great battles. Right valiant is he who sounds the horn of ivory; with a clear trumpet his comrade answers him again, and together they ride at the head of the host; and with them are fifteen thousand Franks, young warriors whom Charles calls his children. And after these come as many more, and they will lay on right fiercely." Then saith Malpramis: "Lord, let the first blow be mine."

"Malpramis, fair son," answers Baligant, "I grant thee thy boon. Go, and fall anon upon the Franks, and take with thee Torleu the King of Persia, and Dapamort the King of Leutis. If thou canst mate the great pride of the Franks I will give thee a part of my kingdom from Cheriont even to Val-Marchis." "Lord, I thank thee," Malpramis made answer, and stood forth to receive the gift—the land it was which aforetime King Flurit held—but never from that day was Malpramis to see it, never was he to be vested therein and installed.

And now the Amiral rides through the host, and his son, who is tall of stature, follows him with the two Kings, Torleu and Dapamort. Quickly they array thirty great companies, and so great is the multitude of his knights that the least of these numbers thirty thousand men. The first is arrayed of men of Botentrot, and the second of Milciani—they have huge heads, and along the spine of their backs grow bristles like those of a wild boar. The third is of Blos and of Nubians; the fourth of Slavs and Russians; the fifth is of the Sorbi; the sixth of Moors and Armenians; the seventh of men of Jericho; the eighth of Blacks and the ninth of Gros; and the tenth is made up of men of Balide-la-Forte, a folk that loves evil. Then the Amiral swears a great oath by the might and the body of Mahound: "Mad is Charles of France to ride forward; a battle there will be, if he doth not give back; and nevermore shall he wear golden crown on head."

Thereafter they array another ten battles; the first is of the men of Canelieu—they have come across from Val-Fuit, and full hideous are they to look upon; the second is of Turks; and of Persians the third; the fourth is made up of fierce Pincenati; the fifth of Soltras and Avars; and the sixth of Ormaleus and Uglici; the seventh is arrayed of the people of Samuel; the eighth is of the men of Prussia; the ninth of Slavs; and the tenth of warriors of the desert of Occiant—a folk they are who do no service to the Lord God, never shall you hear of men more evil; and their skins are hard like iron, wherefore they have no

need of hauberks or helms; and in battle they are fell and cruel.

Now the Amiral arrays another ten battles. The first is of the Giants of Malpruse; the second of Huns, and the third of Hungarians; in the fourth ride the folk of Baldise-la-Longue, and in the fifth those of the Dread Valley; the sixth is made up of men of Joi and of Maruse; the seventh of Lechs and Astrimunies; the eighth is of warriors of Arguille; the ninth of those of Clarbonne; and in the tenth ride the bearded folk of Val Fronde—they are a people who have no love of God. So in the chronicle of France are named the thirty columns. Great are the hosts, and many a trumpet is sounded. The paynims ride on like goodly warriors.

Great and mighty is the Amiral; before him he lets bear the Dragon, and the standard of Tervagant and Mahound, and an image of Apollon the felon. Enclosing these ride ten men of Canelieu, and with a loud voice they cry: "Let those who would have the protection of our gods pray to them and serve them in all contrition!" And the paynims bow their heads, and bend full low their bright helmets. But the Franks cry: "Now die, ye swine! May ye be brought to confusion this day. And thou, our God, be Charles's shield, and let the battle be adjudged in his name."

Crafty and wise is the Amiral; he calls his son and the two Kings, saying: "Barons ride on before, and lead all my host; but three companies, and of the best, I keep with me, that of the Turks, and that of the Ormalies, and for the third, the Giants of Malpruse. And the men of Occiant shall abide with me, and they shall set upon Charles and his Franks. If the Emperor will do battle with me his head shall be severed from his body, let him be assured thereof, for such is his deserving."

Great are the two hosts and goodly the columns. Between them is neither hill nor height nor valley, neither holt nor forest, no hiding can there be, for each is clear to other in the open plain. Then saith Baligant: "Ride on, my paynims, and seek the battle!" Amboire d'Oluferne bears the standard; and the paynims lift up their voices, and cry aloud "Precieuse!" But the Franks make answer: "This day shall ye be given over to destruction!" And again and again they raise the cry of Montjoy. The Emperor bids his trumpets be sounded, and clear above them all rings out the horn of ivory. "Goodly is Charles's host," say the paynims; "great and sore will be the battle."

Vast is the plain and wide the fields. There is great shining of helmets adorned with gold, of shields and broidered hauberks, of lances and gonfanons. Trumpets blow, right clear are their blasts, and high is the swell of the ivory horn. The Amiral calls to his brother, Canabeu, the King of Floredée, who held all the land even to Val Sevrée, and showed him the ten companies of Charles: "See the glory of France, the far-famed; proudly rides the Emperor, he is behind among the bearded folk; they have spread out their beards over their hauberks, white they are as is snow on ice. These men will deal good blows with lance and sword, great and terrible will be the battle, such a one as was never before seen of men." Then farther than a man can throw a peeled wand, Baligant rode out before his army, and bespoke them, saying: "Follow, for I lead, O paynims!" And he hath shaken the shaft of his lance, and turned its point towards Charles.

When Charles the Great saw the Amiral, his Dragon and ensign and standard, and the great host of the Arabs, how that they covered all the plain save that part which the Emperor himself held, he cried out with a loud voice: "Barons of France, good vassals are ye, and many are the battles ye have fought in the field; see now the paynims before you, felons they are and cowards, and their faith avails them no whit; so though their number be great, what care ye, lords? Let him who would fain ride forward follow me." Then he spurred his horse, and Tencendur sprang

four times into the air. And the Franks say: "Valiant is our King. Ride on, lord, not one of us shall fail you."

Fair was the day and bright the sun; goodly the hosts and mighty the columns. And now the foremost ranks join battle. Count Rabel and Count Guineman slacken rein, and spur on their swift horses; and all the Franks drive forward, and fall a-smiting with their sharp spears.

Count Rabel is a knight of good hardihood, he pricks on his horse with his spurs of fine gold and rides on Torleu the Persian King; neither shield nor hauberk can withstand the blow, and he thrust his golden lance into the King's body, and hurled him dead among the brambles. Thereat the Franks cry: "May the Lord God aid us! Charles has the right, and we must not fail him."

And Guineman sets upon the King of Leutis and shatters his targe adorned with flowers, and thereafter rent asunder his byrnie, and drave all his gonfanon into his body that he fell dead, let whoso will laugh or weep therefor. At this buffet the Franks cry: "Lay on barons, hold not back! Charles has the right against the paynim folk; and the true judgment of God is with us."

Malpramis, on his white charger, drives into the press of the Franks, ever and again striking great blows, that ofttimes he hurls one dead upon another. Baligant speaks first, saying: "Barons, ye whom I have so long nourished, see now my son who goes seeking Charles, and challenging many a baron to the combat; a better vassal I could not wish for. To his rescue now with your lances!" At his words the paynims haste forward, dealing goodly blows that great is the slaughter. Wondrous hard is the battle; never before or after was one so great.

Vast are the hosts and noble the columns; and now all the companies are at battle. The paynims lay on that it is wonder to see. God! but the shaft of many a lance is broken, and shields are shattered, and hauberks unmailed. (Thick lie the maimed and the dead); lo, the ground is so encumbered with them that the fair grass of the fields which had been green, (is now all reddened with blood). Yet again the Amiral calls to his followers, saying: "Smite, smite the Christian folk, ye barons." Sore and dread is the battle, that never before or after was one so fierce and so great. Death alone will end it.

The Amiral calls to his folk: "Smite, O paynims, for that and nought else have ye come. I will give you women fair and comely, and fiefs and honours and lands." And the paynims make answer: "Yea, it behooves us so to do." And so fierce are their blows that they may not recover their lances, and more than a hundred thousand swords are drawn. Great and dolourous is the slaughter. What a battle saw the men who were there.

The Emperor calls to his Franks, saying: "Lords and barons, ye are full dear to me, and in you I set my trust; many a battle have you won for me, many lands have you conquered, and many a King dethroned. Right well I know the guerdon I owe you with my lands and my gold and my body. Revenge now your brothers and sons and heirs who yesterday were slain at Roncevals. Well ye know the right is mine against these paynims." And the Franks make answer: "Lord, thou sayest truly." Twenty thousand men Charles has with him, and with one voice they pledge him their faith that they will not fail him for any torment or death. There is not one among them but lays on with his lance, and fiercely they smite with their swords. Wondrous hard is the battle.

Malpramis, the baron, rides through the press doing great slaughter to those of France. But now Naymes the Duke looks haughtily upon him, and encounters with him like a man of good hardiness, rends the leather of his shield, hews off two cantles of his broidered hauberk, and drives his yellow gonfanon into his body,

and hurls him dead to ground among seven hundred of his comrades.

King Canabeu, the Amiral's brother, spurs on his horse, and draws his sword, the hilt whereof is set with precious stones, and smites Naymes on his princely helmet, cleaves it in two halves, and with his steel blade cuts through five of its latchets; his steel cap naught avails the Duke, his coif is cut through even to the flesh, and a piece of it falls to the ground. Mighty was the blow, and so astonied thereby is the Duke that he had straightway fallen, an God had not aided him; he clutched the neck of his horse, and if the paynim had dealt him another blow, the noble vassal had been slain straightway. But now Charles of France comes to his succour.

Naymes the Duke is in sore torment, and hastily the paynim makes him ready to strike again. But Charles cries to him: "Coward, thy stroke shall cost thee dear!" And he deals him a buffet with all his strength, shatters his shield and breaks it upon his heart, rends asunder the ventail of his hauberk, and hurls him down dead; and his saddle goes empty.

Great is the sorrow of Charles the King when he sees Duke Naymes wounded before him, and his blood flowing out on the green grass. The Emperor saith to him, speaking low: "Fair Sir Naymes, now ride with me. Dead is the felon who brought thee to this strait; once only I set my lance in his body." And the Duke makes answer: "Lord, I believe thee; if I live great honour shall be thine thereby." Then lovingly and loyally they joined company. With them are twenty thousand Franks, and there is not one among them but deals good blows and fights hardily.

The Amiral rides through the press and thrusts upon Count Guineman, breaks his white shield above his heart, rends the sides of his hauberk, and hews off two of his ribs, that he falls dead from his swift horse. Thereafter the Amiral slew Gebuin, and Lorant, and Richard the Old, the liege lord of the Normans; and the paynims cry: "Doughty is Precieuse! Lay on, barons, we have good surety."

Would ye might see the knights of Arabia, and those of Occiant and Arguille and Bascle! Well they smite with their lances, dealing stout blows; yet the Franks have no mind to give back, and on both sides many a man is slain. Until evening full sore is the battle, great is the slaughter among the barons of France, and yet more woe will there be or ever the two hosts are disparted.

Both Franks and Arabs deal great blows that lances are shivered, both shafts and bright points. He who saw so many a shield dishonoured, and heard the ring of the bright hauberks and the clash of shield on helm, and saw so many brave knights go down, and heard men cry out as they lay dying upon the ground, must call to mind dolour sore and great. That battle was hard to endure. The Amiral calls upon Apollon, Tervagant and Mahound: "My lords and gods, well have I served you; and I will make you images of fine gold (an ye will succour me against Charles)." But now Gemalfin, one of those he holds dear, comes before him with ill tidings, saying: "Baligant, lord, misfortune hath come upon you this day; you have lost Malpramis your son, and Canabeu your brother is slain. The victory fell to two of the Franks; of the twain one is the Emperor, methinks, large is he of limb, and looks a mighty lord, and his beard is white as is the flower in April." At the news the Amiral bowed his head, and thereafter hid his face; so great was his grief he thought to die straightway. And he called to him Jangleu of over-sea.

"Come hither, Jangleu," saith the Amiral, "thou art valiant and wise; many a time have I followed thy counsel. What sayest thou now of the Franks and the Arabs, will the victory be with us?" And Jangleu makes answer: "Thou art doomed, Baligant. Thy gods will not save thee.

Charles is proud, and his men valiant; never have I seen so warlike a folk. But call ye in the barons of Occiant, the Turks and Enfruns, Arabs and Giants. Do what it behooves you to do and delay not."

The Amiral has spread out his beard over his hauberk, white it is as is flower on thorn. Come what may he will not skulk from it. He puts a clear trumpet to his lips, and clearly he sounds it that all the paynims hear it, and throughout the field his followers rally. The men of Occiant bray out and neigh, and the men of Arguille yelp like dogs, and they fall upon the Franks with such fury that the stoutest ranks break and give way, and seven thousand fall dead at the one onset.

Count Ogier knew not cowardice, a better warrior never donned hauberk. When he saw the Frankish companies give way, he called Thierry the Duke of Argonne, Geoffrey of Anjou, and Jozeran the Count, and bespoke Charles right proudly: "See now the paynims, how they slay your men! May it please God that ye never more wear crown, an ye do not fight hardily to revenge your shame." No man spoke any word in answer, but they spur on, giving their horses free rein, and smiting the paynims wheresoever they meet them.

Charles the King deals great blows, so likewise do Naymes the Duke, Ogier the Dane, and Geoffrey of Anjou, he who bore the King's standard. Ogier the Dane is full valiant, he pricks on his horse to a gallop, and smites him who holds the Dragon so fiercely that he bears down both the Dragon and the King's ensign. Baligant sees his gonfanon fall and the ensign of Mahound left unguarded, and begins to know that he is in the wrong and the right is with Charles. And the paynims of Arabia begin to weary. The Emperor calls to his Franks: "Tell me now, barons, in God's name, will you aid me?" "Thou dost ill to ask it," the Franks make answer: "Base would he be who did not strike hardily."

The day passes and turns towards

evening. The Franks and paynims still lay on with their swords. They who arrayed these two hosts were mighty men of battle; and still neither side forgets its war-cry, the Amiral calls aloud Precieuse, and Charles the famous cry Montjoy. Each knows other by his strong voice and clear, and amid the press they met and hurtled together, each dealing great blows with his lance upon the flowered shield of the other, till the spears shiver against the broad bucklers; and they rent apart one another's hauberk, but they did not come at the flesh. Their girths are broken, their saddles thrown back that the two Kings are brought to ground, but swiftly they sprang to their feet, and valiantly they have drawn their swords. This combat cannot be stayed, nor ended save by one man's death.

Valiant is Charles of fair France, yet the Amiral is neither adread nor dismayed. Both have their bare swords in hand, and each deals other great blows on his shield; they cut through the leather and twofold wood that the nails fall out and the bosses are shattered, then without let or hindrance they strike on their hauberks, and the light springs out from their bright helmets. This combat cannot be staid till one or other cries him in the wrong.

"Bethink thyself, Charles," saith the Amiral, "take counsel and repent thee of thy wrong towards me. Thou hast, as I know, slain my son, and wrongfully hast thou harried my land of Spain; become my man and I will grant it to thee in fee, come and serve me both here and in the East." But Charles makes answer: "That, methinks, were great villainy; I may give neither peace nor love to a paynim. Receive the law which God has made manifest to us, accept Christianity and I will love thee straightway; then believe in the King that wields the world and serve Him." "Nay," saith Baligant, "I like not thy sermon." Then they set to again with the swords with which they are girded.

Strong and mighty is the Amiral, he smites Charles upon the helmet of brown steel, breaks and shatters it upon his head, and with his sword carves through the thick hair, and hews off a palm's breadth and more of the flesh, that the bone is left bare. Charles reels and is nigh to falling, but it is not God's will that he be either slain or vanquished; Saint Gabriel hath come to him again, and speaks to him, saying: "What wouldst thou do, great King?"

When Charles heard the blessed voice of the angel he lost all fear and dread of death, and his wit and his strength returned to him. He smites the Amiral with the sword of France, shatters the helmet which shines with precious stones, carves through the skull that the brain runs out, and through all the face even to the white beard, that the Amiral falls dead beyond all help. And Charles cries out Montjoy to summon his men. At his call Duke Naymes comes to him, and seizing Tencendur, helps the King to mount him. The paynims flee; it is not God's will that they abide; and now the prayer of the Franks is granted.

The paynims flee, so the Lord God wills it, and Franks and Emperor pursue after them. Saith the King: "Lords, revenge now your woe. Ease your hearts and your longing, for this morning I saw you weep." And the Franks make answer: "Sire, even so will we do." And every man strikes as many good blows as he may, that few of the paynims escape.

Great is the heat and the dust rises thick; the paynims flee and the Franks press them hard, that the chase lasts even to Saragossa. Bramimonde has mounted her tower; with her are clerks and canons of the false faith never loved of God, unordained they are, and their heads are untonsured. When the Queen saw the rout of the Arabs she cried aloud: "Help us, O Mahound! Ah gentle King, now are our men vanquished, and the Amiral shamefully slain!" When Marsila heard, he turned him to the wall, and weeping, hid his face. Even so he dies of sorrow; and as he was burdened with sin, eager devils seize upon his soul.

The paynims are slain save some few who flee, and Charles hath won the battle. He has beaten down the gate of Saragossa, well he knows it is no longer defended. He has taken the city and enters therein with his army, and in triumph they lie there that night. Mighty is the King of the hoary beard, and Bramimonde has given over to him the towers, whereof ten are great, and fifty of less size. Well he labours whom the Lord God aids.

The day passes and night darkens, clear is the moon and bright the stars. The Emperor hath taken Saragossa. He commands a thousand Franks that they search the city, the synagogues and the mosques; with axes and mallets of iron they shatter the walls and the idols, till naught is left of their sorcery and their lies. The King believes in God and would do His service; and now the bishops bless the waters, and the paynims are brought to baptism. And if any among them gainsay Charles, he must hang or burn or perish by the sword. More than a hundred thousand are baptized and become true Christians, all save only the Queen; she will be brought a captive to fair France, and it is by love the King would have her converted.

The night passes and the clear day dawns. Charles has stuffed the towers of Saragossa with troops, leaving there a thousand stout knights, who keep the city in the name of the Emperor. The King gets to horse with all his men, and Bramimonde whom he takes with him as a captive; naught but good would he do her. And now in all joy and mirth they turn homewards; in their strength and their might they past Narbonne, and came to the proud city of Bordeaux; and there Charles left the horn of ivory filled with gold and mangons upon the altar of Saint Sevérin the baron, where it may still be seen of pilgrims. Thereafter Charles crossed the Gironde on great ships which he had there, and unto Blaye he bore his nephew, and Oliver, Roland's gentle comrade, and the Archbishop who was both wise and brave; he has the three lords laid in tombs of white marble, in Saint Romain, and there the barons lie even unto this day. The Franks commend them to God and his angels, and Charles rides on over hill and dale; he will make no stay until he comes to Aix, but hastens on till he reaches the entrance stair. And when he is come into his high palace, by messenger he summons his judges, Bavarians and Saxons, men of Lorraine and Friesland, Germans and Burgundians, Poitevins, Normans and Bretons, and the wisest of those of France. And then begins the trial of Ganelon.

The Emperor has returned from Spain, and come again to Aix, the fairest seat in France; he has gone up into his palace and has passed into the hall. To him comes Aude, that fair damsel, and saith to the King: "Where is Roland, the captain, who pledged him to take me as his wife?" Thereat Charles is filled with dolour and grief, he weeps and plucks his white beard, saying: "Sister, sweet friend, thou askest me of one who is dead. But I will make good thy loss to thee, and will give thee Louis—a better I cannot name—my son he is, and will hold my marches." "Lord, thy words are strange to me," Aude makes answer. "May it not please God or His saints or His angels that after Roland's death I should yet live." She loses her colour and falls at the feet of Charles, and lo, she is dead. God have mercy upon her soul. The barons of France weep and lament her.

Aude the Fair has gone to her end. But the King thinks her in a swoon, he is full of pity for her, and he weeps; he takes her by the hands and raises her up, but her head falls back upon her shoulders. When Charles sees that she is dead, he straightway calls four countesses; Aude is borne to a convent of nuns hard by, and they watch by her the night through till dawn. Richly and fairly they bury her beside an altar, and the King does her great honour.

The Emperor is come again to Aix. And Ganelon the felon, in chains of iron, is in the city, before the palace; servingmen bound him to a stake, and made fast his hands with strips of deer's hide; well they beat him with staves and leathern thongs, for he hath deserved no other bounty. Thus in sore torment he awaits his trial.

It is written in the ancient Geste that Charles did summon men from many lands, and assemble them in the chapel at Aix. Proud is the day and high the festival, that of Saint Silvestre the baron, some men say. And now begins the trial, and ye shall hear of Ganelon who did the treason. The Emperor has commanded that he be brought before him.

"Lords and barons," then said Charles the King, "now judge me the right concerning Ganelon. He went among my host into Spain with me, and he reft me of twenty thousand of my Franks, and of my nephew whom ye shall see no more, and of Oliver, the courteous, the valiant; and the Twelve Peers likewise he betrayed for money." Then quoth Ganelon: "I were a felon should I deny it. Roland spoiled me of money and goods, for this I sought his death and destruction. But that it was treason I deny." "Now let us take counsel," say the Franks in answer.

So Ganelon stood before the King; he is strong of body and his face is fresh of hue, if he were true hearted he were a goodly baron. He looks on the men of France, and all the judges and on his own kin, thirty of whom are with him, and he cries with a loud voice: "For the love of God now hear me, ye barons! Yea, I was in the host with the Emperor, and I did him service in all faith and love. Then Roland, his nephew, conceived a hatred against me, and condemned me to dolour and death. Messenger I was to King Marsila, and if I returned unhurt it was by mine own wit.

And I defied Roland the chieftain, and Oliver, and all their comrades, and this was heard of Charles and his barons. Revenged me I have, but in that is no treason." "Let us go into council," the Franks make answer.

Now that Ganelon sees that his trial is opened, he calls about him thirty of his kinsmen. One there is among them to whom all the rest give ear, and he is Pinabel of the castle of Sorence. Ready of speech he is, and he can plead full well, and if it be a question of arms he is a goodly warrior. Then saith Ganelon: "In you I set my trust; save me now from calumny and death." "Thou shalt be saved, and that speedily," saith Pinabel. "If any Frank condemn thee to hang I will give him the lie with the point of my sword wheresoever the Emperor shall summon us to do battle man to man." And Ganelon the Count throws himself at his kinsman's feet.

Bavarians and Saxons have gone into council, Poitevins and Normans and Franks, and with them is many a German and Teuton. The men of Auvergne were the most inclined to grace, and the most friendly towards Pinabel. They said one to another: "Best let be. Let us leave the trial, and pray the King that he pardon Ganelon for this time, if he will henceforth serve him in all faith and love. Dead is Roland, ye shall see him no more, nor can ye bring him back with gold or goods; folly it were to hold trial by combat." And there was none who did not agree to this and yea-say it, save only Thierry, the brother of Lord Geoffrey.

The barons return to Charles, and say to the King: "Lord, we beseech you that you pardon Count Ganelon, that henceforth he may serve you in all faith and love. Let him live, for he is of gentle birth. (Roland is dead, never shall ye see him more), nor will any price restore him to you." "Faithless ye are to me," saith the King in answer.

When Charles sees that they have all

failed him, his face and his countenance darken, and "Woe is me!" he cried in his grief. But before him is a good knight, Thierry, brother to the Angevin Duke, Geoffrey. Lean he is of body, nimble and slender; black-haired, and brown of face he is, not tall, and yet not overshort. Courteously he bespeaks the Emperor: "Fair Sir King, make not such sorrow; thou knowest that I have served thee well, and by my lineage I have a right to a share in this trial. Howsoever Roland may have wronged Ganelon thy service should have been his protection; Ganelon is a felon in that he betrayed him, for thereby he has broken his oath to thee and transgressed. And for this I condemn him to hanging and death, and that his body be cast out to the dogs as that of a traitor, since he did traitorously. If he hath any kinsman who will give me the lie, I will uphold my judgment by the sword I have girded here at my side." "That is well said," the Franks make answer.

Then came Pinabel before the King; tall he is, and strong and hardy and swift; short is the term of the man who gets a stroke at his hands. And he saith to the King: "Lord, thine is the quarrel; I pray thee put an end to this clamour. Lo, Thierry has pronounced his judgment, I give him the lie and would do him battle." And he gives him his right glove made of skin of the deer. Saith the Emperor: "I must have good hostages." Thereupon the thirty kinsmen of Ganelon offer themselves as surety. Then saith the King: "I likewise will give thee pledges; and let these be guarded till the right be made manifest."

When Thierry saw that the battle was toward, he gave Charles his right glove; and the Emperor on his part gave hostages. Then he commanded that four benches be brought into the great square, and thereon they who were to do battle took their places. By the rest the combat was pronounced lawful; and Ogier of Denmark declared the terms. Then the combatants call for their horses and arms.

In that they are near to battle they confess their sins, and are shriven and blessed; they hear mass and receive the communion, and rich offerings they make to the churches. Then the twain come again before Charles. They have fastened on their spurs, and donned their shining hauberks which are both strong and light, made fast upon their heads their bright helmets, and girt on their swords hilted with pure gold, hung their quartered shields about their necks, and now in their right hands they grip their sharp spears, and mount their swift coursers. Thereupon a hundred thousand knights fell a-weeping, for they had pity upon Thierry for Roland's sake. But God knows what the end will be.

Below Aix is a wide meadow, and there the two barons are to do battle. They are men of good prowess and valour, and their horses are swift and keen. The two knights slacken rein, and spurring hard, ride each at other with all the might they have, that their shields are cleft and shattered, their hauberks rent, and thereto their girths are broken that their *saddles turn and fall to earth.* And the hundred thousand men who watch them weep.

Both knights are on the ground, but lightly they spring to their feet. Pinabel is strong and swift and nimble; and each runs upon other, for both now are unhorsed, and with their swords, whereof the pommels are all of gold, they hack and hew their helms of steel; and strong are the blows for the breaking of helms. The Frankish knights make great sorrow; and "O God, make clear the right," cried Charles.

Then saith Pinabel: "Now yield thee, Thierry, and I will be thy man in all love and faith, and of my havings I will give thee whatsoever thou wilt; but do thou make Ganelon's peace with the King." "Nay, that will I not do," quoth Thierry; "I were a very traitor an I should agree. May God judge between thee and me this day."

Quoth Thierry: "Pinabel, thou art a

good man of thy hands, tall thou art, and strong, and well fashioned of body, and thy peers account well of thy valour; now let be this battle, and I will make thy peace with Charles, but to Ganelon such justice shall be done that men shall not stint talking of it till the world's end." "No, so God help me!" quoth Pinabel. "I will hold by my kin, nor will I ever yield me to any man living, rather would I die than bring that shame upon me." Thereupon they began again to strike great blows on their helmets studded with gold and gems, that the fire sprang out towards heaven. By no power may they now be disparted, nor may the combat be ended save by death.

Right valiant is Pinabel of Sorence; he smites Thierry on his helm of Provence, that the fire sprang out therefrom and kindled the grass; he thrusts at him with the point of his sword, cleaves his helmet above his forehead, that the stroke carries to the middle of the face, and the right cheek bursts out a-bleeding; his hauberk is rent down to his belly, but God so guards him that he is not slain.

Thierry sees that he is wounded in the face, and the bright blood flows down upon the grass of the field; he smites Pinabel upon his helm of brown steel, rends it asunder even to the nasal that the brains run out; and he drives the blow home that Pinabel falls dead. So with this stroke the battle is won. And the Franks cry: "God has made manifest His might. It is meet that Ganelon be hung, and likewise his kinsmen, who answered for him."

When that Thierry had won the battle, Charles the Emperor came to him with four of his barons, Naymes the Duke, Ogier of Denmark, Geoffrey of Anjou and William of Blaye. The King hath taken Thierry in his arms, and dried his face with his great cloak of marten skin, then he throws it down and another is wrapped about him. Thereafter they full gently disarmed the knight, and mounted him upon an Arabian mule; and so he returns again

joyously and nobly. They come to Aix and alight in the great square. And now begins the slaying of Ganelon and his kin.

Charles calls his dukes and his counts, saying: "What counsel ye me concerning those I have in my prison, they who came to the trial to uphold Ganelon, and gave themselves as hostages for Pinabel." And the Franks make answer: "It were ill done an one were let to live." Then the King commands one of his wardens, Basbrun, saying: "Go thou and hang them all to yon blasted tree; by this my beard whereof the hairs are hoary, and if thou let one escape, thou shalt be given over to death and destruction." And Basbrun answered him: "How else should I do?" And by the help of a hundred sergeants he led them away by force; and they were all hung to the number of thirty. For the traitor brings death to both himself and to others.

Thereafter the Bavarians and Germans returned home again, and thereto the Poitevins and Bretons and Normans. Above all the rest the Franks agreed that Ganelon should die by great torture. They let bring four chargers, and then they bind the traitor hand and foot; wild and fleet are the horses, and four sergeants urge them on towards a meadow wherein is a mare. So Ganelon is come to sore punishment, all his sinews are put to the rack, and all his limbs are torn out from his body, and the bright blood flows out on the green grass. Thus Ganelon dies the death of a felon. It is not meet that he who betrays others should boast thereof.

When that the Emperor had done vengeance, he called to him the bishops of France, together with those of Bavaria and Germany, and saith to them: "In my court is a captive, a lady of high parentry, who, having heard many sermons and examples would believe in God, and entreats Christianity. Baptize her that God may receive her soul." And they answer him, saying: "Now for godmothers let there be called four noble dames of good lineage."

At the baths of Aix is a great assembly; there they baptize the Queen of Spain, and call her by the name of Juliana. By full knowledge has she become a Christian.

So the Emperor has done justice and appeased his great wrath; and he has brought Bramimonde to Christianity. The day passes and night darkens, and as the King lies in his vaulted chamber, Saint Gabriel comes to him from God, saying: "Charles, now call together the hosts of thy empire, and go in thy might into the land of Bire, and give succour to King Vivien at Imph, for the paynims have laid a siege about his city, and the Christians cry out to thee and entreat thee." Little will had the Emperor to go. "Ah God," he saith, "how is my life oppressed with burdens." And he weeps and plucks his white beard.

Here ends the Geste which Turoldus tells.

NOTE TO THE READER

The reader who wishes to follow up on courage, honor, and certain other ideas that appear in *The Song of Roland* might begin by consulting the *Syntopicon* references that will be found, in the present volume of *The Great Ideas Today,* at the beginning of the essay on "Heroism and the Heroic Ideal in Great Books of the Western World." This essay discusses many of those references.

In addition, see under Chapter 13, COURAGE, the readings about the nature of courage which are listed at Topic 1; those about cowardice and foolhardiness which come at Topic 2; and those dealing with the motives of courage, such as fame, honor, and religious faith, which may be found at Topic 5. See also Chapter 35, HONOR, especially 2c, which is concerned with honor as pride; 2e, which deals with honor as the pledge of friendship; and 5a, where honor as the motive of heroism is discussed.

Relevant too is the discussion of the fear of death and the attitude toward death of the hero in Topic 8c of Chapter 48, LIFE AND DEATH. And so is Topic 2b of Chapter 98, WAR AND PEACE, which deals with religious wars and the propagation of religious faith.

Going still a bit further, readers who own GGB might be interested in two very different stories about men in life and death situations that are to be found in GGB, Vol. 2: Victor Hugo's "The Battle with the Cannon," from *Ninety-three* (pp. 146–54) , and "The Killers," by Ernest Hemingway (pp. 169–77). The subject of heroism is considered also in two plays that appear in GGB, Vol. 4: George Bernard Shaw's *The Man of Destiny* (pp. 300–338) and Eugene O'Neill's *The Emperor Jones* (pp. 357–82).

# List of words not in common use

*almaçur:* a title of dignity among the Saracens.

*amiral* (the old spelling of admiral): a prince among the Saracens; an emir.

*astonied:* (1) confounded, terrified; (2) stunned, as by a blow.

*battle:* a division of an army. "The French are bravely in their battles set." (*Henry V,* act 4, sc. 3; *GBWW,* Vol. 26, p. 556.)

*beseen:* furnished with, provided with.

*bezant:* a gold coin of variable value issued by the Eastern emperors, and commonly used throughout Western Europe in the Middle Ages.

*boss:* an ornamental projection in the center of a shield. It was usually of metal, sometimes round in shape, sometimes sharply pointed, and in the *Roland* is often set with precious stones.

*bussyne* (Old French buisine): a kind of trumpet.

*byrnie* (Old French brunie): sometimes, apparently, used in the *Roland* synonymously with hauberk to indicate the coat of chain mail; but properly the byrnie was a garment of leather or heavy woven stuff upon which were sewn rings or plates of metal.

*caitiff:* wretched, miserable.

*cantle:* a piece, a fragment.

*carbuncle:* a deep red gem formerly supposed to give light of itself. *See* page 351, where carbuncles help to light Baligant's fleet.

*ciclaton:* a rich fabric much used in the Middle Ages for garments and hangings. It was a kind of silk or brocade, but was sometimes woven with gold. Chaucer's Sir Thopas wore a robe "of ciclatoun/That coste many a jane." (*Canterbury Tales; GBWW,* Vol. 22, p. 396.)

*coif:* a close-fitting hood of chain mail, attached to the hauberk, and which so covered the head and face that only the eyes, nose, and mouth were left exposed.

*dole:* sorrow.

*dolour:* (1) grief; (2) pain.

*dromond:* a light war vessel.

*embossed* (of a shield): provided with a boss or ornamental projection.

The shield, at the end of the eleventh century, was usually kite-shaped. It was made of wood covered with leather, painted, gilded, and edged with metal. It was slightly convex. In the center was the boss, and from this bands of iron radiated to the outer edge. The shields carried by the Normans at the time of the conquest of England were about four feet long, and at the top, where they were broadest, some twenty inches wide. The shields were painted in bright colors, sometimes in simple flat tints, sometimes with geometric patterns, scrolls, flowers, and strange beasts; hence "the shields of many devices" of the *Roland;* but armorial bearings proper were not introduced till toward the end of the twelfth century. On the march the shield was hung about the neck by means of a strap, called the guige; when used for defense in battle it was carried on the forearm, and had for this purpose at its back, behind the boss, two short straps, called the *enarmes,* through which the knight thrust his arm to support the shield.

*fee:* a feud; land, that is, held of a superior lord in return for certain services.

GONFANONS

SHIELDS

guige

boss

enarmes

SWORD

from the Bayeux Tapestry

HAUBERK

chain
mail
(detail)

COIF

HELMS

nasal

*geste:* a history. The word first meant exploit, but afterward came to be used for the chronicle or story in which the exploits were narrated.

*gonfanon:* a pennon attached to the shaft of a lance just below the point.

*guige:* the strap or band by which the shield was hung about the wearer's neck.

*hauberk:* a coat of chain mail reaching to the knee, and provided with a hood or coif for covering the head. It sometimes had a border or fringe, formed by weaving gilded wire into the links of the mail; hence the "broidered hauberks" mentioned in the *Roland.* The "two-fold hauberks" may mean either a hauberk made with double links or one that has an inner lining of leather or heavy stuff under the mail.

*helm:* a cone-shaped casque, or high steel cap, for protecting the head. It was worn over the mail coif, to which it was fastened by means of laces. From the front, downward over the face, extended a projection called the nasal, which covered the nose. For decoration the helm had around its base a circlet that was either carved or set with precious stones. From this there sometimes ran up the height of the cone either two or four bands, also set with jewels. The top was sometimes finished with a ball or knob of metal, but crests did not come into use till later.

*hight:* is called, or named.

*hurtle:* to dash against, to meet in encounter.

*law:* faith.

*mangon:* a coin of either gold or silver, the precise value of which is unknown.

*mangonel:* an engine of war, used for casting heavy stones.

*mate:* to defeat utterly, to confound.

*nasal* (of a helmet): the face-guard, or projection that covers the nose.

*paynim* (Old French paien): a pagan, a heathen.

*peer:* the Twelve Peers, the twelve equals or companions, that is. The list varies in the later *chansons de geste;* in the *Roland* they are: Roland, Oliver, Ivon, Ivory, Oton, Berengier, Samson, Anseïs, Gerin, Gerier, Engelier, and Gerard de Roussillon.

*quartered* (of a shield): divided into four or more parts by the transversal bands that form the framework of the shield.

*stour:* tumult, conflict, press of battle.

*valiance:* bravery, valor.

*ventail* (of a hauberk): that part of the hood of mail that protected the lower part of the face.

*worshipful:* worthy of honor. *Cf.* "a man of worship."

# Religio Medici

Sir Thomas Browne

## Editor's Introduction

Sir Thomas Browne (1605–82), who holds an eminent place among the great writers of English prose, was also a distinguished if eccentric figure in the intellectual history of his time—and for something like the same reason. Both in the elaborate style for which he is famous and in the exotic subjects which, in three or four of the most unusual books ever written, he undertook to discuss, he brought discordant elements together, achieving harmonies of expression and thought that were at once peculiar and profound. In his writing we can alternately hear the notes of Milton and the notes of Dryden—magnificent organ music varied by the pithiest of plain talk. In the play of his mind we observe a delight in fancy balanced by concern for fact. It was fitting that his life should have nearly spanned the interval between the appearance of *Hamlet* and the publication of Newton's *Principia*. His was the sort of intelligence that can regard with equal interest the law of gravity and the likelihood of ghosts.

Browne was a doctor by profession. Born in London, he took two degrees at Oxford, traveled widely abroad, and then settled in Norwich, at that time the largest of English provincial towns. There he lived for nearly half a century, practicing medicine, raising a large family, and pursuing the study of curious, sometimes forgotten lore, out of which he produced at intervals the several volumes of reflections by which he has ever since been known.

*Religio Medici,* or "The Religion of a Doctor," was written about 1635, when he was just short of thirty. He had lately returned from medical studies on the continent, where he had been obliged to worship with people of different faiths. The book was undertaken, Browne said, as "a private exercise directed to myself," from a desire on his part to clarify his beliefs. It was not intended for publication, but was circulated in manuscript among his friends. In 1642, however, it was printed in London without his permission, and so had to be acknowledged. An authorized and corrected version appeared in 1643.

By "religion" Browne did not mean simply "creed," but doctrinal and dogmatic tenets, ceremonies and public observances, and questions of ecclesiastical organization. Whether these things could be accepted by a man of science without compromising his rational principles was what Browne undertook to consider, well aware, as he admitted in the first sentence of the book, that it might be generally assumed, "as the general scandal of my Profession," that he had no religion at all. Of course he did have one, as the book famously proclaims, and could respect the different religions of other men—no common trait in that intolerant age. And although he acknowledged that his faith was in logic opposed to reason, yet he considered that faith and reason were one symbolically, united by what he called God's Wisdom, which created the world to be "studied and contemplated by Man: 'tis the Debt of our Reason we owe unto God, and the homage we pay for not being Beasts."

In a subsequent book known as *Pseudodoxia Epidemica* (1646), Browne paid his debt to what he called philosophy, by which he meant what we call science, and which he was as concerned to preserve from magic and superstition (things he was far from rejecting in what he conceived to be their place) as he had earlier been to maintain the high mysteries and incalculable marvels that are the stuff of faith. The *Pseudodoxia* is an encyclopedia of the errors and delusions about the natural world which Browne had come across in his omnivorous reading, and which he undertook with many entertaining digressions to refute.

Still later, in 1658, Browne published two more strange and striking works. One of these, called *Hydriotaphia* (*Urn-Burial*), is a meditation upon life, death, and the human condition occasioned by the discovery near Norwich of some prehistoric urns containing human bones; the fifth chapter of this little book contains some of the most dazzling and best-known passages Browne ever wrote. The other work, called *The Garden of Cyrus,* undertakes to trace the history of horticulture from the Garden of Eden to the Persian gardens of the time of Cyrus, but before it proceeds very far it becomes a discussion, with almost innumerable examples, of the quincunx or five-spot pattern, familiar to us in dominoes or dice, which Browne sees repeated in a staggering variety of natural things. "But the Quincunx of Heaven runs low," begins the paragraph, also widely known, that introduces the concluding portion of this extraordinary treatise,

> and 'tis time to close the five ports of knowledge; we are unwilling to spin out our waking thoughts into the phantasms of sleep, which often continueth precogitations; making Cables of Cobwebs, and Wildernesses of handsome Groves. Besides Hippocrates hath spoke so little, and the Oneirocritical Masters have left such frigid Interpretations from plants, that there is little encouragement to dream of Paradise itself. Nor will the sweetest delight of Gardens afford much comfort in sleep; wherein the dullness of that sense shakes hands with delectable odours; and though in the Bed of Cleopatra, one can hardly with any delight raise up the ghost of a Rose.

The text of *Religio Medici* here reprinted is taken from *The Works of Sir Thomas Browne,* edited by Charles Sayle (3 vols., 1904–07). It is based upon an edition of 1682, the year of Browne's death.

# Religio Medici

## The First Part

### I

For my Religion, though there be several Circumstances that might perswade the World I have none at all, as the general scandal of my Profession, the natural course of my Studies, the indifferency of my Behaviour and Discourse in matters of Religion, neither violently Defending one, nor with that common ardour and contention Opposing another; yet, in despight hereof, I dare, without usurpation, assume the honourable Stile of a Christian. Not that I meerly owe this Title to the Font, my Education, or Clime wherein I was born, as being bred up either to confirm those Principles my parents instilled into my Understanding, or by a general consent proceed in the Religion of my Country: But having in my riper years and confirmed Judgment, seen and examined all, I find my self obliged by the Principles of Grace, and the Law of mine own Reason, to embrace no other name but this: Neither doth herein my zeal so far make me forget the general Charity I owe unto Humanity, as rather to hate than pity *Turks, Infidels,* and (what is worse) *Jews;* rather contenting my self to enjoy that happy Stile, than maligning those who refuse so glorious a Title.

### II

But because the Name of a Christian is become too general to express our Faith, there being a Geography of Religion as well as Lands, and every Clime distinguished not only by their Laws and Limits, but circumscribed by their Doctrines and Rules of Faith; to be particular, I am of that Reformed new-cast Religion, wherein I dislike nothing but the Name; of the same belief our Saviour taught, the Apostles disseminated, the Fathers authorized, and the Martyrs confirmed, but by the sinister ends of Princes, the ambition and avarice of Prelates, and the fatal corruption of times, so decayed, impaired, and fallen from its native Beauty, that it required the careful and charitable hands of these times to restore it to its primitive Integrity. Now the accidental occasion whereupon, the slender means whereby the low and abject condition of the Person by whom so good a work was set on foot, which in our Adversaries beget contempt and scorn, fills me with wonder, and is the very same Objection the insolent Pagans first cast at Christ and his Disciples.

### III

Yet have I not so shaken hands with those desperate Resolutions, who had rather venture at large their decayed bottom, than bring her in to be new trimm'd in the Dock; who had rather promiscuously retain all, than abridge any, and obstinately be what they are, than what they have been, as to stand in Diameter and Swords point with them: We have reformed from them, not against them; for omitting those Impropriations and Terms of Scurrility betwixt us, which only difference our Affections, and not our Cause, there is between us one common Name and Appellation, one Faith and necessary body of Principles common to us both; and therefore I am not scrupulous to converse and live with them, to enter their Churches in defect of ours, and either pray with them, or for them. I could never perceive any rational Consequence from those many Texts which prohibit the Children of *Israel* to pollute themselves with the Temples of the Heathens; we being all Christians, and not divided by such detested impieties as might prophane our Prayers, or the place wherein we make them; or that a resolved Conscience may not adore her Creator any where, especially in places devoted to his Service; where, if their Devotions offend him, mine may please him; if theirs prophane it, mine may hallow it. Holy-water and Crucifix (dangerous to the common people) deceive not my judgment, nor abuse my devotion at all: I am, I confess, naturally inclined to that which misguided Zeal terms Superstition: my common conversation I do acknowledge austere, my behaviour full of rigour, sometimes not without morosity; yet at my Devotion I love to use the civility of my knee, my hat, and hand, with all those outward and sensible motions which may express or promote my invisible Devotion. I should violate my own arm rather than a Church; nor willingly deface the name of Saint or Martyr. At the sight of a Cross or Crucifix I can dispense with my hat, but scarce with the thought or memory of my Saviour: I cannot laugh at, but rather pity, the fruitless journeys of Pilgrims, or contemn the miserable condition of Fryars; for though misplaced in Circumstances there is something in it of Devotion. I could never hear the *Ave-Mary* Bell[1] without an elevation, or think it a sufficient warrant, because they erred in one circumstance, for me to err in all, that is, in silence and dumb contempt; whilst therefore they directed their Devotions to Her, I offered mine to God, and rectifie the Errors of their Prayers by rightly ordering mine own: At a solemn Procession I have wept abundantly, while my consorts blind with opposition and prejudice, have fallen into an excess of scorn and laughter:

There are questionless both in *Greek, Roman,* and *African* Churches, Solemnities and Ceremonies, whereof the wiser Zeals do make a Christian use, and stand condemned by us, not as evil in themselves, but as allurements and baits of superstition to those vulgar heads that look asquint on the face of Truth, and those unstable Judgments that cannot resist in the narrow point and centre of Virtue without a reel or stagger to the Circumference.

### IV

As there were many Reformers, so likewise many Reformations; every Country proceeding in a particular way and method, according as their national Interest, together with their Constitution and Clime, inclined them; some angrily, and with extremity; others calmly, and with mediocrity; not rending, but easily dividing the community, and leaving an honest possibility of a reconciliation; which though peaceable Spirits do desire, and may conceive that revolution of time and the mercies of God may effect, yet that judgment that shall continue the present antipathies between the two extreams, their contrarieties in condition, affection, and opinion, may with the same hopes expect an union in the Poles of Heaven.

### V

But to difference my self nearer, and draw into a lesser Circle, There is no Church, whose every part so squares unto my Conscience; whose Articles, Constitutions, and Customs, seem so consonant unto reason, and as it were framed to my particular Devotion, as this whereof I hold my Belief, the Church of *England,* to whose Faith I am a sworn Subject; and therefore in a

---

[1] A Church Bell that tolls every day at six and twelve of the clock; at the hearing whereof, every one in what place soever, either of House or Street, betakes himself to his prayer which is commonly directed to the Virgin.

double Obligation subscribe unto her Articles, and endeavour to observe her Constitutions; whatsoever is beyond, as points indifferent, I observe according to the rules of my private reason, or the humour and fashion of my Devotion; neither believing this, because *Luther* affirmed it, or disproving that, because *Calvin* hath disavouched it. I condemn not all things in the Council of *Trent,* nor approve all in the Synod of *Dort.* In brief, where the Scripture is silent, the Church is my Text; where that speaks, 'tis but my comment: where there is a joynt silence of both, I borrow not the rules of my Religion from *Rome* or *Geneva,* but the dictates of my own reason. It is an unjust scandal of our adversaries, and a gross errour in our selves, to compute the Nativity of our Religion from *Henry* the Eighth, who, though he rejected the Pope, refus'd not the faith of *Rome,* and effected no more than what his own Predecessors desired and assayed in Ages past, and was conceived the State of *Venice* would have attempted in our days. It is as uncharitable a point in us to fall upon those popular scurrilities and opprobrious scoffs of the Bishop of *Rome,* to whom as a temporal Prince, we owe the duty of good language: I confess there is cause of passion between us; by his sentence I stand excommunicated, Heretick is the best language he affords me; yet can no ear witness I ever returned him the name of Antichrist, Man of Sin, or Whore of *Babylon.* It is the method of Charity to suffer without reaction: Those usual Satyrs and invectives of the Pulpit may perchance produce a good effect on the vulgar, whose ears are opener to Rhetorick than Logick; yet do they in no wise confirm the faith of wiser Believers, who know that a good cause needs not to be pardon'd by passion, but can sustain it self upon a temperate dispute.

## VI

I could never divide my self from any man upon the difference of an opinion, or be angry with his judgment for not agreeing with me in that from which perhaps within a few days I should dissent my self. I have no Genius to disputes in Religion, and have often thought it wisdom to decline them, especially upon a disadvantage, or when the cause of truth might suffer in the weakness of my patronage: Where we desire to be informed, 'tis good to contest with men about our selves; but to confirm and establish our opinions, 'tis best to argue with judgments below our own, that the frequent spoils and Victories over their reasons may settle in ourselves an esteem and confirmed Opinion of our own. Every man is not a proper Champion for Truth, nor fit to take up the Gauntlet in the cause of Verity: Many, from the ignorance of these Maximes, and an inconsiderate Zeal unto Truth, have too rashly charged the Troops of Error, and remain as Trophies unto the enemies of Truth: A man may be in as just possession of Truth as of a City, and yet be forced to surrender; 'tis therefore far better to enjoy her with peace, than to hazzard her on a battle: if therefore there rise any doubts in my way, I do forget them, or at least defer them till my better setled judgement and more manly reason be able to resolve them; for I perceive every man's own reason is his best *Œdipus,* and will upon a reasonable truce, find a way to loose those bonds wherewith the subtleties of error have enchained our more flexible and tender judgements. In Philosophy, where Truth seems double-fac'd, there is no man more Paradoxical than my self: but in Divinity I love to keep the Road; and, though not in an implicite, yet an humble faith, follow the great wheel of the Church, by which I move, not reserving any proper Poles or motion from the Epicycle of my own brain; by this means I leave no gap for Heresie, Schismes, or Errors, of which at present I hope I shall not injure Truth to say I have no taint or tincture: I must confess my greener studies have been polluted with two or three, not any begotten in the latter Centuries, but old and obsolete, such as could never have been revived, but by such extravagant and irregular heads as mine: for indeed Heresies perish not with their Authors, but, like the river *Arethusa,* though they lose their currents in one place, they rise up again in another: One General Council is not able to extirpate one single Heresie; it may be cancell'd for the present; but revolution of time, and the like aspects from Heaven, will restore it, when it will flourish till it be condemned again. For as though there were a *Metempsuchosis,* and the soul of one man passed into another; Opinions do find, after certain Revolutions, men and minds like those that first begat them. To see ourselves again, we need not look for Plato's year:[2] every man is not only himself; there hath been many *Diogenes,* and as many *Timons,* though but few of that name; men are liv'd over again, the world is now as it was in Ages past; there was none then, but there hath been some one since that Parallels him, and is, as it were, his revived self.

## VII

Now the first of mine was that of the *Arabians,* That the Souls of men perished with their Bodies, but should yet be raised again at the last day: not that I did absolutely conceive a mortality of the Soul; but if that were, which Faith, not Philosophy hath yet thoroughly disproved, and that both entred the grave together, yet I held the same conceit thereof that we all do of the body, that it should rise again. Surely it is but the merits of our unworthy Natures, if we sleep in darkness until the last Alarm. A serious reflex upon my own unworthiness did make me backward from challenging this prerogative of my Soul; so that I might enjoy my Saviour at the last, I could with patience be nothing almost unto Eternity. The second was that of *Origen,* That God would not persist in his vengeance for ever, but after a definite time of his wrath, he would release the damned Souls from torture:

which error I fell into upon a serious contemplation of the great Attribute of God, his Mercy; and did a little cherish it in my self, because I found therein no malice, and a ready weight to sway me from the other extream of despair, whereunto Melancholy and Contemplative Natures are too easily disposed. A third there is which I did never positively maintain or practise, but have often wished it had been consonant to Truth, and not offensive to my Religion, and that is the Prayer for the dead; where unto I was inclin'd from some charitable inducements, whereby I could scarce contain my Prayers for a friend at the ringing of a Bell, or behold his Corps without an Orison for his Soul: 'Twas a good way, methought, to be remembered by posterity, and far more noble than an History. These opinions I never maintained with pertinacy, or endeavoured to inveagle any mans belief unto mine, nor so much as ever revealed or disputed them with my dearest friends; by which means I neither propagated them in others, nor confirmed them in my self; but suffering them to flame upon their own substance, without addition of new fuel, they went out insensibly of themselves: therefore these Opinions, though condemned by lawful Councels, were not Heresies in me, but bare Errors, and single Lapses of my understanding, without a joynt depravity of my will: Those have not onely depraved understandings, but diseased affections, which cannot enjoy a singularity without an Heresie, or be the Author of an Opinion without they be of a Sect also; this was the villany of the first Schism of *Lucifer,* who was not content to err alone, but drew into his Faction many Legions; and upon this experience he tempted only *Eve,* as well understanding the Communicable nature of Sin, and that to deceive but one, was

---

[2] A revolution of certain thousand years, when all things should return unto their former estate, and he be teaching again in his School as when he delivered this Opinion.

tacitely and upon consequence to delude them both.

## VIII

That Heresies should arise, we have the Prophesie of Christ; but that old ones should be abolished, we hold no prediction. That there must be Heresies, is true, not only in our Church, but also in any other: even in doctrines heretical, there will be super-heresies; and Arians not only divided from their Church, but also among themselves: for heads that are disposed unto Schism and complexionally propense to innovation, are naturally disposed for a community; nor will be ever confined unto the order or œconomy of one body; and therefore when they separate from others, they knit but loosely among themselves, nor contented with a general breach or dichotomy with their Church, do subdivide and mince themselves almost into Atoms. 'Tis true, that men of singular parts and humours have not been free from singular opinions and conceits in all Ages; retaining something, not only beside the opinion of his own Church or any other, but also any particular Author; which notwithstanding a sober Judgment may do without offence or heresie; for there is yet, after all the Decrees of Councils and the niceties of Schools, many things untouch'd, unimagin'd, wherein the liberty of an honest reason may play and expatiate with security, and far without the circle of an Heresie.

## IX

As for those wingy Mysteries in Divinity, and airy subtleties in Religion, which have unhing'd the brains of better heads, they never stretched the *Pia Mater* of mine. Methinks there be not impossibilities enough in Religion for an active faith; the deepest Mysteries ours contains have not only been illustrated, but maintained, by Syllogism and the rule of Reason. I love to lose my self in a mystery, to pursue my Reason to an *O altitudo!* 'Tis my solitary recreation to pose my apprehension with those involved Ænigma's and riddles of the Trinity, with Incarnation, and Resurrection. I can answer all the Objections of Satan and my rebellious reason with that odd resolution I learned of *Tertullian, Certum est quia impossibile est.*\* I desire to exercise my faith in the difficultest point; for to credit ordinary and visible objects is not faith, but perswasion. Some believe the better for seeing Christ's Sepulchre; and when they have seen the Red Sea, doubt not of the Miracle. Now contrarily, I bless my self and am thankful that I lived not in the days of Miracles, that I never saw Christ nor His Disciples; I would not have been one of those *Israelites* that pass'd the Red Sea, nor one of Christ's patients on whom he wrought his wonders; then had my faith been thrust upon me, nor should I enjoy that greater blessing pronounced to all that believe and saw not. 'Tis an easie and necessary belief, to credit what our eye and sense hath examined: I believe he was dead, and buried, and rose again; and desire to see him in his glory, rather than to contemplate him in his Cenotaphe or Sepulchre. Nor is this much to believe; as we have reason, we owe this faith unto History: they only had the advantage of a bold and noble Faith, who lived before his coming, who upon obscure prophesies and mystical Types could raise a belief, and expect apparent impossibilities.

## X

'Tis true, there is an edge in all firm belief, and with an easie Metaphor we may say, the Sword of Faith; but in these obscurities I rather use it in the adjunct the Apostle gives it, a Buckler; under which I conceive a wary combatant may lye invulnerable. Since I was of understanding to know we knew nothing, my reason hath been more pliable to the will of Faith; I am now

---

\* It is true, because it is impossible.

content to understand a mystery without a rigid definition, in an easie and Platonick description. That allegorical description of *Hermes*,[3] pleaseth me beyond all the Metaphysical definitions of Divines: where I cannot satisfie my reason, I love to humour my fancy: I had as live you tell me that *anima est angelus hominis, est Corpus Dei* [the soul is man's angel, God's body], as [that it is] *Entelechia; Lux est umbra Dei* [Light is God's shadow], as [that it is] *actus perspicui* [the active force of the clear]; where there is an obscurity too deep for our Reason, 'tis good to sit down with a description, periphrasis, or adumbration; for by acquainting our Reason how unable it is to display the visible and obvious effects of nature, it becomes more humble and submissive unto the subtleties of Faith; and thus I teach my haggard and unreclaimed reason to stoop unto the lure of Faith. I believe there was already a tree whose fruit our unhappy Parents tasted, though, in the same Chapter when God forbids it, 'tis positively said, the plants of the field were not yet grown, for God had not caus'd it to rain upon the earth. I believe that the Serpent (if we shall literally understand it) from his proper form and figure, made his motion on his belly before the curse. I find the tryal of the Pucellage and virginity of Women, which God ordained the *Jews*, is very fallible. Experience and History informs me, that not onely many particular Women, but likewise whole Nations have escaped the curse of Childbirth, which God seems to pronounce upon the whole Sex; yet do I believe that all this is true, which indeed my Reason would perswade me to be false; and this I think is no vulgar part of Faith, to believe a thing not only above, but contrary to Reason, and against the Arguments of our proper Senses.

## XI

In my solitary and retired imagination (*Neque enim cum porticus, aut me lectulus accepit, desum mihi*) * I remember I am not alone, and therefore forget not to contemplate him and his Attributes who is ever with me, especially those two mighty ones, his Wisdom and Eternity; with the one I recreate, with the other I confound my understanding: for who can speak of Eternity without a solœcism, or think thereof without an Extasie? Time we may comprehend; 'tis but five days elder than our selves, and hath the same Horoscope with the World; but to retire so far back as to apprehend a beginning, to give such an infinite start forwards as to conceive an end in an essence that we affirm hath neither the one nor the other, it puts my Reason to *St. Paul's* Sanctuary: my Philosophy dares not say the Angels can do it; God hath not made a Creature that can comprehend him; 'tis a privilege of His own nature. *I am that I am,* was his own definition unto *Moses;* and 'twas a short one, to confound mortality, that durst question God, or ask him what he was; indeed he only is; all others have and shall be; but in Eternity there is no distinction of Tenses; and therefore that terrible term *Predestination,* which hath troubled so many weak heads to conceive, and the wisest to explain, is in respect to God no prescious determination of our Estates to come, but a definitive blast of his Will already fulfilled, and at the instant that he first decreed it; for to his Eternity which is indivisible and all together, the last Trump is already sounded, the reprobates in the flame, and the blessed in *Abraham's* bosome. *St. Peter* speaks modestly, when he saith, a thousand years to God are but as one day: for to speak like

---

3 *Sphæra cujus centrum ubique, circumferentia nullibi* [God is a sphere whose center is everywhere and circumference nowhere]. This description is traditionally attributed to Hermes Trismegistos, personification of the Egyptian god Thoth, to whom is ascribed a body of writings on theology and the occult.

* For when porch or bed has received me, I do not lose myself.

a Philosopher, those continued instances of time which flow into a thousand years, make not to Him one moment; what to us is to come, to his Eternity is present, his whole duration being but one permanent point, without Succession, Parts, Flux, or Division.

## XII

There is no Attribute that adds more difficulty to the mystery of the Trinity, where, though in a relative way of Father and Son, we must deny a priority. I wonder how *Aristotle* could conceive the World eternal, or how he could make good two Eternities: his similitude of a Triangle, comprehended in a square, doth somewhat illustrate the Trinity of our Souls, and that the Triple Unity of God; for there is in us not three, but a Trinity of Souls, because there is in us, if not three distinct Souls, yet differing faculties, that can and do subsist apart in different Subjects, and yet in us are thus united as to make but one Soul and substance: if one Soul were so perfect as to inform three distinct Bodies, that were a pretty Trinity: conceive, the distinct number of three, not divided nor separated by the Intellect, but actually comprehended in its Unity, and that is a perfect Trinity. I have often admired the mystical way of *Pythagoras*, and the secret Magick of numbers. Beware of Philosophy, is a precept not to be received in too large a sense; for in this Mass of Nature there is a set of things that carry in their Front, though not in Capital Letters, yet in Stenography and short Characters, something of Divinity, which to wiser Reasons serve as Luminaries in the Abyss of Knowledge, and to judicious beliefs as Scales and Roundles to mount the Pinacles and highest pieces of Divinity. The severe Schools shall never laugh me out of the Philosophy of *Hermes*, that this visible World is but a Picture of the invisible, wherein as in a Pourtraict, things are not truely, but in equivocal shapes, and as they counterfeit

some more real substance in that invisible Fabrick.

## XIII

That other Attribute wherewith I recreate my devotion, is his Wisdom, in which I am happy; and for the contemplation of this only, do not repent me that I was bred in the way of Study: The advantage I have of the vulgar, with the content and happiness I conceive therein, is an ample recompence for all my endeavours, in what part of knowledge soever. Wisdom is his most beauteous Attribute, no man can attain unto it, yet *Solomon* pleased God when he desired it. He is wise, because he knows all things; and he knoweth all things, because he made them all: but his greatest knowledge is in comprehending that he made not, that is, himself. And this is also the greatest knowledge in man. For this do I honour my own profession, and embrace the Counsel even of the Devil himself: had he read such a Lecture in Paradise as he did at *Delphos*,[4] we had better known our selves; nor had we stood in fear to know him. I know he is wise in all, wonderful in what we conceive, but far more in what we comprehend not; for we behold him but asquint, upon reflex or shadow; our understanding is dimmer than *Moses* Eye; we are ignorant of the back-parts or lower side of his Divinity, therefore to prie into the maze of his Counsels is not only folly in man, but presumption even in Angels; like us, they are his Servants, not his Senators; he holds no Counsel, but that mystical one of the Trinity, wherein though there be three Persons, there is but one mind that decrees without Contradiction: nor needs he any; his actions are not begot with deliberation, his Wisdom naturally knows what's best; his intellect stands ready fraught with the superlative and purest *Idea's* of goodness;

---

4 Know thyself [Greek: γνῶθι σεαυτόν; Latin: *nosce teipsum*]; admonition of the oracle of Apollo at Delphi, Greece.

consultation and election, which are two motions in us, make but one in him; his actions springing from his power at the first touch of his will. These are Contemplations Metaphysical: my humble speculations have another Method, and are content to trace and discover those expressions he hath left in his Creatures, and the obvious effects of Nature; there is no danger to profound these mysteries, no *sanctum sanctorum* in Philosophy: the World was made to be inhabited by Beasts, but studied and contemplated by Man: 'tis the Debt of our Reason we owe unto God, and the homage we pay for not being Beasts; without this, the World is still as though it had not been, or as it was before the sixth day, when as yet there was not a Creature that could conceive, or say there was a World. The wisdom of God receives small honour from those vulgar Heads that rudely stare about, and with a gross rusticity admire his works; those highly magnifie him, whose judicious inquiry into His Acts, and deliberate research into His Creatures, return the duty of a devout and learned admiration. Therefore,

*Search while thou wilt, and let thy reason go,*
*To ransome truth, even to th' Abyss below;*
*Rally the scattered Causes; and that line*
*Which Nature twists, be able to untwine:*
*It is thy Makers will, for unto none,*
*But unto reason can he e'er be known.*
*The Devils do know Thee, but those damn'd Meteors*
*Build not thy Glory, but confound thy Creatures,*
*Teach my indeavours so thy works to read,*
*That learning them in thee, I may proceed.*
*Give thou my reason that instructive flight,*
*Whose weary wings may on thy hands still light.*
*Teach me to soar aloft, yet ever so,*
*When neer the Sun, to stoop again below.*

*Thus shall my humble Feathers safely hover,*
*And, though near Earth, more than the Heavens discover.*
*And then at last, when homeward I shall drive,*
*Rich with the Spoils of nature to my hive,*
*There will I sit like that industrious Flie,*
*Buzzing thy praises, which shall never die,*
*Till death abrupts them, and succeeding Glory*
*Bid me go on in a more lasting story.*

And this is almost all wherein an humble Creature may endeavour to requite and some way to retribute unto his Creator: for if not he that saith, *Lord, Lord,* but *he that doth the will of his Father, shall be saved;* certainly our wills must be our performances, and our intents make out our Actions; otherwise our pious labours shall find anxiety in our Graves, and our best endeavours not hope, but fear a resurrection.

## XIV

There is but one first cause, and four second causes of all things; some are without efficient, as God; others without matter, as Angels; some without form, as the first matter: but every Essence created or uncreated, hath its final cause, and some positive end both of its Essence and Operation; this is the cause I grope after in the works of Nature; on this hangs the providence of God: to raise so beauteous a structure as the World and the Creatures thereof, was but his Art; but their sundry and divided operations, with their predestinated ends, are from the Treasure of his wisdom. In the causes, nature, and affections of the Eclipses of the Sun and Moon, there is most excellent speculation; but to profound farther, and to contemplate a reason why his providence hath so disposed and ordered their motions in that vast circle as to conjoyn and obscure each other, is a sweeter piece of Reason, and a diviner point of Philosophy; therefore sometimes, and in some things, there appears to me as much Divinity in *Galen* his books *De Usu Partium,* as in *Suarez* Metaphysicks: Had *Aristotle* been as curious in the enquiry of this cause as he was of the other, he had not left behind him an imperfect piece of Philosophy, but an absolute tract of Divinity.

## XV

*Natura nihil aget frustra,** is the only indisputed Axiome in Philosophy; there are no *Grotesques* in nature; not any thing framed to fill up empty Cantons, and unnecessary spaces: in the most imperfect Creatures, and such as were not preserved in the Ark, but having their Seeds and Principles in the womb of Nature, are every where, where the power of the Sun is; in these is the Wisdom of his hand discovered. Out of this rank *Solomon* chose the object of his admiration; indeed what reason may not go to School to the wisdom of Bees, Ants, and Spiders? what wise hand teacheth them to do what reason cannot teach us? ruder heads stand amazed at those prodigious pieces of Nature, Whales, Elephants, Dromidaries and Camels; these, I confess, are the Colossus and Majestick pieces of her hand: but in these narrow Engines there is more curious Mathematicks; and the civility of these little Citizens, more neatly sets forth the Wisdom of their Maker. Who admires not *Regio-Montanus* his Fly beyond his Eagle, or wonders not more at the operation of two Souls in those little Bodies, than but one in the Trunk of a Cedar? I could never content my contemplation with those general pieces of wonder, the Flux and Reflux of the Sea, the increase of *Nile,* the conversion of the Needle to the North; and have studied to match and parallel those in the more obvious and neglected pieces of Nature, which without further trouble I can do in the Cosmography of my self; we carry with us the wonders we seek without

us: There is all *Africa* and her prodigies in us; we are that bold and adventurous piece of nature, which he that studies wisely learns in a *compendium* what others labour at in a divided piece and endless volume.

## XVI

Thus there are two Books from which I collect my Divinity; besides that written one of God, another of his servant Nature, that universal and publick Manuscript, that lies expans'd unto the Eyes of all, those that never saw him in the one, have discovered him in the other: this was the Scripture and Theology of the Heathens: the natural motion of the Sun made them more admire him, than its supernatural station did the Children of *Israel;* the ordinary effects of nature wrought more admiration in them than in the other all his Miracles; surely the Heathens knew better how to joyn and read these mystical Letters than we Christians, who cast a more careless Eye on these common Hieroglyphicks, and disdain to suck Divinity from the flowers of Nature. Nor do I so forget God as to adore the name of Nature; which I define not with the Schools, to be the principle of motion and rest, but that streight and regular line, that settled and constant course the Wisdom of God hath ordained the actions of His creatures, according to their several kinds. To make a revolution every day, is the Nature of the Sun, because of that necessary course which God hath ordained it, from which it cannot swerve but by a faculty from that voice which first did give it motion. Now this course of Nature God seldome alters or perverts, but like an excellent Artist hath so contrived his work, that with the self same instrument, without a new creation, he may effect his obscurest designs. Thus he sweetneth the Water with a Word, preserveth the Creatures in the Ark, which the blast

---

* Nature does nothing in vain.

of his mouth might have as easily created; for God is like a skilful Geometrician, who when more easily and with one stroak of his Compass he might describe or divide a right line, had yet rather do this in a circle or longer way; according to the constituted and fore-laid principles of his Art: yet this rule of his he doth sometimes pervert, to acquaint the World with his Prerogative, lest the arrogancy of our reason should question his power, and conclude he could not; and thus I call the effects of Nature the works of God, whose hand and instrument she only is; and therefore to ascribe his actions unto her, is to devolve the honour of the principal agent upon the instrument; which if with reason we may do, then let our hammers rise up and boast they have built our houses, and our pens receive the honour of our writings. I hold there is a general beauty in the works of God, and therefore no deformity in any kind or species of creature whatsoever: I cannot tell by what Logick we call a *Toad,* a *Bear,* or an *Elephant* ugly, they being created in those outward shapes and figures which best express the actions of their inward forms. And having past that general Visitation of God, who saw that all that he had made was good, that is, conformable to his Will, which abhors deformity, that is the rule of order and beauty; there is no deformity but in Monstrosity; wherein, notwithstanding, there is a kind of Beauty. Nature so ingeniously contriving the irregular parts, as they become sometimes more remarkable than the principal Fabrick. To speak yet more narrowly, there was never any thing ugly or mis-shapen, but the Chaos; wherein, notwithstanding, to speak strictly, there was no deformity, because no form; nor was it yet impregnant by the voice of God; now Nature was not at variance with Art, nor Art with Nature, they being both servants of his providence: Art is the perfection of Nature: were the World now as it was the sixth day, there were yet a Chaos: Nature hath made one World, and Art another. In brief, all things are artificial; for Nature is the Art of God.

## XVII

This is the ordinary and open way of his providence, which Art and Industry have in a good part discovered, whose effects we may foretel without an Oracle: to foreshew these, is not Prophesie, but Prognostication. There is another way, full of Meanders and Labyrinths, whereof the Devil and Spirits have no exact Ephemerides, and that is a more particular and obscure method of his providence, directing the operations of individuals and single Essences: this we call Fortune, that serpentine and crooked line, whereby he draws those actions his wisdom intends, in a more unknown and secret way: This cryptick and involved method of his providence have I ever admired, nor can I relate the History of my life, the occurrences of my days, the escapes of dangers, and hits of chance, with a *Bezo las Manos* to Fortune, or a bare Gramercy to my good Stars: *Abraham* might have thought the *Ram* in the thicket came thither by accident; humane reason would have said, that meer chance conveyed *Moses* in the Ark to the sight of *Pharoh's* daughter: what a Labyrinth is there in the story of *Joseph,* able to convert a Stoick? Surely there are in every man's Life certain rubs, doublings, and wrenches, which pass a while under the effects of chance, but at the last well examined, prove the meer hand of God. 'Twas not dumb chance, that to discover the Fougade or Powder-plot,* contrived a miscarriage in the Letter. I like the victory of 88† the better for that one occurrence, which our enemies imputed to our dishonour and the partiality of Fortune, to wit, the tempests and contrariety of Winds. King *Philip* did not detract from the Nation, when he said, he sent his Armado to fight with men, and not to combate with

---

* Gunpowder Plot, 1605.
† Defeat of the Spanish Armada, 1588.

the Winds. Where there is a manifest disproportion between the powers and forces of two several agents, upon a Maxime of reason we may promise the Victory to the Superiour; but when unexpected accidents slip in, and unthought of occurences intervene, these must proceed from a power that owes no obedience to those Axioms; where, as in the writing upon the wall, we may behold the hand, but see not the spring that moves it. The success of that petty province of *Holland* (of which the Grand *Seignour* proudly said, if they should trouble him as they did the *Spaniard,* he would send his men with shovels and pick-axes, and throw it into the Sea,) I cannot altogether ascribe to the ingenuity and industry of the people, but the mercy of God, that hath disposed them to such a thriving Genius; and to the will of his Providence, that disposeth her favour to each Country in their pre-ordinate season. All cannot be happy at once; for, because the glory of one State depends upon the ruine of another, there is a revolution and vicissitude of their greatness, and must obey the swing of that wheel, not moved by Intelligences, but by the hand of God, whereby all Estates arise to their *Zenith* and Vertical points according to their predestinated periods. For the lives, not only of men, but of Commonwealths, and the whole World, run not upon an Helix that still enlargeth; but on a Circle, where arriving to their Meridian, they decline in obscurity, and fall under the Horizon again.

## XVIII

These must not therefore be named the effects of Fortune, but in a relative way, and as we term the works of Nature: it was the ignorance of mans reason that begat this very name, and by a careless term miscalled the Providence of God: for there is no liberty for causes to operate in a loose and stragling way; nor any effect whatsoever, but hath its warrant from some universal or superiour Cause. 'Tis not a ridiculous devotion to say a pray before a game at Tables; for even in *sortilegies* and matters of greatest uncertainty, there is a settled and preordered course of effects. It is we that are blind, not Fortune: because our Eye is too dim to discover the mystery of her effects, we foolishly paint her blind, and hoodwink the Providence of the Almighty. I cannot justifie that contemptible Proverb, *That fools only are Fortunate;* or that insolent Paradox, *That a wise man is out of the reach of Fortune;* much less those opprobrious epithets of Poets, *Whore, Bawd,* and *Strumpet.* 'Tis, I confess, the common fate of men of singular gifts of mind to be destitute of those of Fortune, which doth not any way deject the Spirit of wiser judgments, who throughly understand the justice of this proceeding; and being inrich'd with higher donatives, cast a more careless eye on these vulgar parts of felicity. It is a most unjust ambition to desire to engross the mercies of the Almighty, not to be content with the goods of mind, without a possession of those of body or Fortune: and it is an error worse than heresie, to adore these complemental and circumstantial pieces of felicity, and undervalue those perfections and essential points of happiness wherein we resemble our Maker. To wiser desires it is satisfaction enough to deserve, though not to enjoy the favours of Fortune; let Providence provide for Fools: 'tis not partiality, but equity in God, who deals with us but as our natural Parents; those that are able of Body and Mind, he leaves to their deserts; to those of weaker merits he imparts a larger portion, and pieces out the defect of one, by the access of the other. Thus have we no just quarrel with Nature, for leaving us naked; or to envy the Horns, Hoofs, Skins, and Furs of other Creatures, being provided with Reason, that can supply them all. We need not labour with so many Arguments to confute Judicial Astrology; for if there be a truth therein, it doth not injure Divinity: if to be born under *Mer-*

*cury* disposeth us to be witty, under *Jupiter* to be wealthy; I do not owe a Knee unto those, but unto that merciful Hand that hath ordered my indifferent and uncertain nativity unto such benevolous Aspects. Those that hold that all things are governed by Fortune, had not erred, had they not persisted there: The *Romans* that erected a temple to Fortune, acknowledged therein, though in a blinder way, somewhat of Divinity; for in a wise supputation all things begin and end in the Almighty. There is a nearer way to Heaven than *Homer's* Chain;* an easy Logick may conjoin heaven and Earth, in one Argument, and with less than a *Sorites* resolve all things unto God. For though we christen effects by their most sensible and nearest Causes, yet is God the true and infallible Cause of all, whose concourse though it be general, yet doth it subdivide it self into the particular Actions of every thing, and is that Spirit, by which each singular Essence not only subsists, but performs its operation.

### XIX

The bad construction, and perverse comment on these pair of second Causes, or visible hands of God, have perverted the Devotion of many unto Atheism; who, forgetting the honest Advisoes of Faith, have listened unto the conspiracy of Passion and Reason. I have therefore always endeavoured to compose those Feuds and angry Dissensions between Affection, Faith and Reason: For there is in our Soul a kind of Triumvirate, or triple Government of three Competitors, which distracts the Peace of this our Common-wealth, not less than did that other the State of *Rome*.

As Reason is a Rebel unto Faith, so Passion unto Reason: As the Propositions of Faith seem absurd unto Reason, so the Theorems of Reason unto Passion, and both unto Reason; yet a moderate and peaceable discretion may so state and order the matter, that they may be all Kings, and yet make but one Monarchy, every one

exercising his Soveraignty and Prerogative in a due time and place, according to the restraint and limit of circumstance. There is, as in Philosophy, so in Divinity, sturdy doubts and boisterous Objections, wherewith the unhappiness of our knowledge too nearly acquainteth us. More of these no man hath known than my self, which I confess I conquered, not in a martial posture, but on my Knees. For our endeavours are not only to combat with doubts, but always to dispute with the Devil: the villany of that Spirit takes a hint of Infidelity from our Studies, and by demonstrating a naturality in one way, makes us mistrust a miracle in another. Thus having perused the *Archidoxes* and read the secret Sympathies of things, he would disswade my belief from the miracle of the Brazen Serpent, make me conceit that Image worked by Sympathy, and was but an *Ægyptian* trick to cure their Diseases without a miracle. Again, having seen some experiments of *Bitumen,* and having read far more of *Naphtha,* he whispered to my curiosity the fire of the Altar might be natural; and bid me mistrust a miracle in *Elias,* when he entrenched the Altar round with Water: for that inflamable substance yields not easily unto Water, but flames in the Arms of its Antagonist. And thus would he inveagle my belief to think the combustion of *Sodom* might be natural, and that there was an Asphaltick and Bituminous nature in that Lake before the Fire of *Gomorrah.* I know that *Manna* is now plentifully gathered in *Calabria;* and *Josephus* tells me, in his days it was as plentiful in *Arabia;* the Devil therefore made the *quære,* Where was then the miracle in the days of *Moses:* the *Israelite* saw but that in his time, the Natives of those Countries behold in ours. Thus the Devil played at Chess with me, and yielding a Pawn, thought to gain a Queen of me, taking advantage of my honest endeavours; and whilst I laboured to raise

* *Iliad* 8; *GBWW,* Vol. 4, p. 51.

the structure of my Reason, he strived to undermine the edifice of my Faith.

## XX

Neither had these or any other ever such advantage of me, as to incline me to any point of Infidelity or desperate positions of Atheism; for I have been these many years of opinion there was never any. Those that held Religion was the difference of Man from Beasts, have spoken probably, and proceed upon a principle as inductive as the other. That doctrine of *Epicurus,* that denied the Providence of God, was no Atheism, but a magnificent and high strained conceit of his Majesty, which he deemed too sublime to mind the trivial Actions of those inferiour Creatures. That fatal Necessity of the Stoicks, is nothing but the immutable Law of his will. Those that heretofore denied the Divinity of the Holy Ghost, have been condemned, but as Hereticks; and those that now deny our Saviour (thought more than Hereticks) are not so much as Atheists: for though they deny two persons in the Trinity, they hold as we do, there is but one God.

That Villain and Secretary of Hell, that composed that miscreant piece of the Three Impostors, though divided from all Religions, and was neither Jew, Turk, nor Christian, was not a positive Atheist. I confess every country hath its *Machiavel,* every Age its *Lucian,* whereof common Heads must not hear, nor more advanced Judgments too rashly venture on: It is the Rhetorick of Satan, and may pervert a loose or prejudicate belief.

## XXI

I confess I have perused them all, and can discover nothing that may startle a discreet belief; yet are there heads carried off with the Wind and breath of such motives. I remember a Doctor in Physick of *Italy,* who could not perfectly believe the immortality of the Soul, because *Galen* seemed to make a doubt thereof. With another I was familiarly acquainted in *France,* a Divine,

and a man of singular parts, that on the same point was so plunged and gravelled with three lines of *Seneca,*[5] that all our Antidotes, drawn from both Scripture and Philosophy, could not expel the poyson of his errour. There are a set of Heads, that can credit the relations of Mariners, yet question the Testimonies of St. *Paul;* and peremptorily maintain the traditions of *Ælian* or *Pliny,* yet in Histories of Scripture raise Queries and Objections, believing no more than they can parallel in humane Authors. I confess there are in Scripture Stories that do exceed the Fables of Poets, and to a captious Reader sound like *Garagantua* or *Bevis:* Search all the Legends of times past, and the fabulous conceits of these present, and 'twill be hard to find one that deserves to carry the Buckler unto *Sampson;* yet is all this of an easie possibility, if we conceive a divine concourse, or an influence but from the little Finger of the Almighty. It is impossible that either in the discourse of man, or in the infallible Voice of God, to the weakness of our apprehensions, there should not appear irregularities, contradictions, and antinomies: my self could shew a Catalogue of doubts, never yet imagined nor questioned, as I know, which are not resolved at the first hearing; not fantastick Queries or Objections of Air; for I cannot hear of Atoms in Divinity. I can read the History of the Pigeon that was sent out of the Ark, and returned no more, yet not question how she found out her Mate that was left behind: That *Lazarus* was raised from the dead, yet not demand where in the interim his Soul awaited; or raise a Law-case, whether his Heir might lawfully detain his inheritance bequeathed unto him

---

5 *Post Mortem nihil est, ipsaque Mors nihil. Mors individua est, noxia corpori, nec patiens anima.... Toti morimur, nullaque pars manet nostri* [There is nothing after death; death itself is nothing. Death is indivisible: fatal to the body and does not spare the soul. . . . We die wholly, and no part of us remains], from *The Trojan Women.*

by his death, and he, though restored to life, have no Plea or Title unto his former possessions. Whether *Eve* was framed out of the left side of *Adam,* I dispute not; because I stand not yet assured which is the right side of a man, or whether there be any such distinction in Nature: that she was edified out of the Rib of *Adam,* I believe, yet raise no question who shall arise with that Rib at the Resurrection. Whether *Adam* was an Hermaphrodite, as the Rabbins contend upon the Letter of the Text, because it is contrary to reason, there should be an Hermaphrodite before there was a Woman; or a composition of two Natures before there was a second composed. Likewise, whether the World was created in Autumn, Summer, or the Spring, because it was created in them all; for whatsoever Sign the Sun possesseth, those four Seasons are actually existent: It is the Nature of this Luminary to distinguish the several Seasons of the year, all which it makes at one time in the whole Earth, and successive in any part thereof. There are a bundle of curiosities, not only in Philosophy, but in Divinity, proposed and discussed by men of most supposed abilities, which indeed are not worthy our vacant hours, much less our serious Studies. Pieces only fit to be placed in *Pantagruel's* Library, or bound up with Tartaretus, *De modo Cacandi.**

## XXII

These are niceties that become not those that peruse so seriously a Mystery: There are others more generally questioned and called to the Bar, yet methinks of an easie and possible truth.

'Tis ridiculous to put off, or down the general Flood of *Noah* in that particular inundation of *Deucalion:* that there was a Deluge once, seems not to me so great a Miracle, as that there is not one always. How all the kinds of Creatures, not only in their own bulks, but with a competency of food and sustenance, might be preserved in one Ark, and within the extent of three hundred Cubits, to a reason that rightly examines it, will appear very feasible. There is another secret not contained in the Scripture, which is more hard to comprehend, and put the honest Father to the refuge of a Miracle: and that is, not only how the distinct pieces of the World, and divided Islands should be first planted by men, but inhabited by Tigers, Panthers, and Bears. How *America* abounded with Beasts of prey, and noxious Animals, yet contained not in it that necessary Creature, a Horse, is very strange. By what passage those, not only Birds, but dangerous and unwelcome Beasts, came over: How there be Creatures there (which are not found in this Triple Continent); all which must needs be strange unto us, that hold but one Ark, and that the Creatures began their progress from the Mountains of *Ararat:* They who to salve this would make the Deluge particular, proceed upon a principle that I can no way grant; not only upon the negative of holy Scriptures, but of mine own Reason, whereby I can make it probable, that the World was as well peopled in the time of *Noah,* as in ours; and fifteen hundred years to people the World, as full a time for them, as four thousand years since have been to us. There are other assertions and common Tenents drawn from Scripture, and generally believed as Scripture, whereunto notwithstanding, I would never betray the liberty of my Reason. 'Tis a Paradox to me, that *Methusalem* was the longest liv'd of all the Children of *Adam:* and no man will be able to prove it; when from the process of the Text, I can manifest it may be otherwise. That *Judas* perished by hanging himself, there is no certainty in Scripture: though in one place it seems to affirm it, and by a doubtful word hath given occasion to translate it; yet in another place, in a more punctual description, it makes it improbable, and seems to overthrow it.

---

* An imaginary book in the list in Rabelais's *Pantagruel.*

That our Fathers, after the Flood, erected the Tower of *Babel* to preserve themselves against a second Deluge, is generally opinioned and believed, yet is there another intention of theirs expressed in Scripture: Besides, it is improbable from the circumstance of the place, that is, a plain in the Land of *Shinar:* These are no points of Faith, and therefore may admit a free dispute. There are yet others, and those familiarly concluded from the Text, wherein (under favour) I see no consequence: the Church of *Rome,* confidently proves the opinion of Tutelary Angels, from that Answer when *Peter* knockt at the Door; *'Tis not he, but his Angel;* that is, might some say, his Messenger, or some body from him; for so the Original signifies, and is as likely to be the doubtful Families meaning. This exposition I once suggested to a young Divine, that answered upon this point; to which I remember the *Franciscan* Opponent replyed no more, but That it was a new, and no authentick interpretation.

## XXIII

These are but the conclusions and fallible discourses of man upon the Word of God, for such I do believe the holy Scriptures: yet were it of man, I could not chuse but say, it was the singularest and superlative piece that hath been extant since the Creation: were I a Pagan, I should not refrain the Lecture of it; and cannot but commend the judgment of *Ptolomy,* that thought not his Library compleat without it. The Alcoran of the *Turks* (I speak without prejudice) is an ill composed Piece, containing in it vain and ridiculous Errors in Philosophy, impossibilities, fictions, and vanities beyond laughter, maintained by evident and open Sophisms, the Policy of Ignorance, deposition of Universities, and banishment of Learning, that hath gotten Foot by Arms and violence: This without a blow, hath disseminated it self through the whole Earth. It is not unremarkable what *Philo* first observed, That the Law of *Moses* continued two thousand years without the least alteration; whereas, we see, the Laws of other Common-weals do alter with occasions; and even those, that pretended their Original from some Divinity, to have vanished without trace or memory. I believe besides *Zoroaster,* there were divers that writ before *Moses,* who, notwithstanding, have suffered the common fate of time. Mens Works have an age like themselves; and though they out-live their Authors, yet have they a stint and period to their duration: This only is a work too hard for the teeth of time, and cannot perish but in the general Flames, when all things shall confess their Ashes.

## XXIV

I have heard some with deep sighs lament the lost lines of *Cicero;* others with as many groans deplore the combustion of the Library of *Alexandria:* for my own part, I think there be too many in the World, and could with patience behold the urn and ashes of the *Vatican,* could I, with a few others, recover the perished leaves of *Solomon.* I would not omit a Copy of *Enoch's* Pillars, had they many nearer Authors than *Josephus,* or did not relish somewhat of the Fable. Some men have written more than others have spoken; *Pineda*[6] quotes more Authors in one work, than are necessary in a whole World. Of those three great inventions in *Germany,* there are two which are not without their incommodities, and 'tis disputable whether they exceed not their use and commodities. 'Tis not a melancholy *Utinam* of my own, but the desires of better heads, that there were a general Synod; not to unite the incompatible difference of Religion, but for the benefit of learning, to reduce it as it lay at first, in a few, and solid Authors; and to condemn to the fire those swarms & millions of *Rhapsodies* begotten only to distract and abuse the weaker judgements of

---

6 [Juan de] *Pineda* in his *Monarchica Ecclesiastica* [1588] quotes one thousand and forty Authors.

Scholars, and *to maintain the trade and mystery of Typographers.*

## XXV

I cannot but wonder with what exception the *Samaritans* could confine their belief to the *Pentateuch,* or five Books of *Moses.* I am ashamed at the Rabbinical Interpretation of the Jews, upon the Old Testament, as much as their defection from the New. And truly it is beyond wonder, how that contemptible and degenerate issue of *Jacob,* once so devoted to Ethnick Superstition, and so easily seduced to the Idolatry of their Neighbours, should now in such an obstinate and peremptory belief adhere unto their own Doctrine, expect impossibilities, and, in the face and eye of the Church, persist without the least hope of Conversion. This is a vice in them, that were a vertue in us; for obstinacy in a bad Cause is but constancy in a good. And herein I must accuse those of my own Religion; for there is not any of such a fugitive Faith, such an unstable belief, as a Christian; none that do so oft transform themselves, not unto several shapes of Christianity and of the same Species, but unto more unnatural and contrary Forms, of Jew and Mahometan; that, from the name of Saviour, can condescend to the bare term of Prophet; and from an old belief that he is come, fall to a new expectation of his coming. It is the promise of Christ to make us all one Flock; but how and when this Union shall be, is as obscure to me as the last day. Of those four Members of Religion we hold a slender proportion; there are, I confess, some new additions, yet small to those which accrew to our Adversaries, and those only drawn from the revolt of Pagans, men but of negative Impieties, and such as deny Christ, but because they never heard of him: but the Religion of the Jew is expressly against the Christian, and the Mahometan against both. For the Turk, in the bulk he now stands, is beyond all hope of conversion; if he fall asunder, there may be conceived hopes, but not without strong improbabilities. The Jew is obstinate in all fortunes; the persecution of fifteen hundred years hath but confirmed them in their Errour: they have already endured whatsoever may be inflicted, and have suffered, in a bad cause, even to the condemnation of their enemies. Persecution is a bad and indirect way to plant Religion: It hath been the unhappy method of angry Devotions, not only to confirm honest Religion, but wicked Heresies, and extravagant Opinions. It was the first stone and Basis of our Faith; none can more justly boast of Persecutions, and glory in the number and valour of Martyrs; for, to speak properly, those are true and almost only examples of fortitude: Those that are fetch'd from the field, or drawn from the actions of the Camp, are not ofttimes so truely precedents of valour as audacity, and at the best attain but to some bastard piece of fortitude: If we shall strictly examine the circumstances and requisites which *Aristotle* requires to true and perfect valour, we shall find the name only in his Master *Alexander,* and as little in that Roman Worthy, *Julius Cæsar;* and if any, in that easie and active way have done so nobly as to deserve that name, yet in the passive and more terrible piece these have surpassed, and in a more heroical way may claim the honour of that Title. 'Tis not in the power of every honest Faith to proceed thus far, or pass to Heaven through the flames; every one hath it not in that full measure, nor in so audacious and resolute a temper, as to endure those terrible tests and trials; who notwithstanding, in a peaceable way do truely adore their Saviour, and have (no doubt) a Faith acceptable in the eyes of God.

## XXVI

Now as all that dye in the War are not termed Souldiers; so neither can I properly term all those that suffer in matters of Religion, Martyrs. The Council of *Constance* condemns *John Huss* for an Heretick; the Stories of his own Party stile him a Martyr: He must needs offend the Divinity of both, that says he was neither the one nor the other: There are many (questionless) canonised on earth, that shall never be Saints in Heaven; and have their names in Histories and Martyrologies, who in the eyes of God are not so perfect Martyrs, as was that wise Heathen *Socrates,* that suffered on a fundamental point of Religion, the Unity of God. I have often pitied the miserable Bishop that suffered in the cause of *Antipodes,* yet cannot chuse but accuse him of as much madness, for exposing his living on such a trifle; as those of ignorance and folly, that condemned him. I think my conscience will not give me the lye, if I say there are not many extant that in a noble way fear the face of death less than myself; yet, from the moral duty I owe to the Commandment of God, and the natural respects that I tender unto the conservation of my essence and being, I would not perish upon a Ceremony, Politick points, or indifferency: nor is my belief of that untractible temper, as not to bow at their obstacles, or connive at matters wherein there are not manifest impieties: The leaven therefore and ferment of all, not only Civil, but Religious actions, is Wisdom; without which, to commit our selves to the flames is Homicide, and (I fear) but to pass through one fire into another.

## XXVII

That Miracles are ceased, I can neither prove, nor absolutely deny, much less define the time and period of their cessation: that they survived Christ, is manifest upon the Record of Scripture: that they out-lived the Apostles also, and were revived at the Conversion of Nations, many years after, we cannot deny, if we shall not question those Writers whose testimonies we do not controvert in points that make for our own opinions; therefore that may have some truth in it that is reported by the Jesuites of their Miracles in the *Indies;* I could wish it were true, or had any other testimony than their own Pens. They may easily believe those Miracles abroad, who daily conceive a greater at home, the transmutation of those visible elements into the Body and Blood of our Saviour: for the conversion of Water into Wine, which he wrought in *Cana,* or what the Devil would have had him done in the Wilderness, of Stones into Bread, compared to this, will scarce deserve the name of a Miracle. Though indeed to speak properly, there is not one Miracle greater than another, they being the extraordinary effects of the Hand of God, to which all things are of an equal facility; and to create the World as easie as one single Creature. For this is also a Miracle, not onely to produce effects against, or above Nature, but before Nature; and to create Nature as great a Miracle as to contradict or transcend her. We do too narrowly define the Power of God, restraining it to our capacities. I hold that God can do all things; how he should work contradictions, I do not understand, yet dare not therefore deny. I cannot see why the Angel of God should question *Esdras* to recal the time past, if it were beyond his own power; or that God should pose mortality in that, which he was not able to perform himself. I will not say God cannot, but he will not perform many things, which we plainly affirm he cannot: this I am sure is the mannerliest proposition, wherein, notwithstanding, I hold no Paradox. For strictly his power is the same with his will, and they both with all the rest do make but one God.

## XXVIII

Therefore that Miracles have been, I do believe; that they may yet be wrought by the living, I do not deny: but have no confidence in those which are fathered on the dead; and this hath ever made me suspect the efficacy of reliques, to examine the bones, question the habits and appurtenances of Saints, and even of Christ himself. I cannot conceive why the Cross that *Helena* found, and whereon Christ himself dyed, should have power to restore others unto life: I excuse not *Constantine* from a fall off his Horse, or a mischief from his enemies, upon the wearing those nails on his bridle, which our Saviour bore upon the Cross in his hands. I compute among *Piæ fraudes,* nor many degrees before consecrated Swords and Roses, that which *Baldwyn,* King of *Jerusalem,* return'd the *Genovese* for their cost and pains in his War, to wit, the ashes of *John* the Baptist. Those that hold the sanctity of their Souls doth leave behind a tincture and sacred faculty on their bodies, speak naturally of Miracles, and do not salve the doubt. Now one reason I tender so little Devotion unto Reliques, is, I think, the slender and doubtful respect I have always held unto Antiquities: for that indeed which I admire, is far before Antiquity, that is, Eternity; and that is, God himself; who, though he be styled the ancient of days, cannot receive the adjunct of Antiquity, who was before the World, and shall be after it, yet is not older than it; for in his years there is no Climacter; his duration is Eternity, and far more venerable than Antiquity.

### XXIX

But above all things I wonder how the curiosity of wiser heads could pass that great and indisputable Miracle, the cessation of Oracles; and in what swoun their Reasons lay, to content themselves, and sit down with such a far-fetch'd and ridiculous reason as *Plutarch* alleadgeth for it. The Jews, that can believe the supernatural Solstice of the Sun in the days of *Joshua,* have yet the impudence to deny the Eclipse, which every Pagan confessed, at his death: but for this, it is evident beyond all contradiction, the Devil himself confessed it.[7] Certainly it is not a warrantable curiosity, to examine the verity of Scripture by the concordance of humane history, or seek to confirm the Chronicle of *Hester* or *Daniel* by the authority of *Megasthenes* or *Herodotus.* I confess, I have had an unhappy curiosity this way, till I laughed my self out

of it with a piece of *Justine,* where he delivers that the Children of *Israel* for being scabbed were banished out of *Egypt.* And truely since I have understood the occurrences of the World, and know in what counterfeit shapes, and deceitful vizards times present represent on the stage things past; I do believe them little more then things to come. Some have been of my opinion, and endeavoured to write the History of their own lives; wherein *Moses* hath outgone them all, and left not onely the story of his life, but as some will have it, of his death also.

### XXX

It is a riddle to me, how this story of Oracles hath not worm'd out of the World that doubtful conceit of Spirits and Witches; how so many learned heads should so far forget their Metaphysicks, and destroy the ladder and scale of creatures, as to question the existence of Spirits: for my part, I have ever believed, and do now know, that there are Witches: they that doubt of these, do not onely deny them, but spirits; and are obliquely and upon consequence a sort not of Infidels, but Atheists. Those that to confute their incredulity desire to see apparitions, shall questionless never behold any, nor have the power to be so much as Witches; the Devil hath them already in a heresie as capital as Witchcraft; and to appear to them, were but to convert them. Of all the delusions wherewith he deceives mortality, there is not any that puzleth me more than the Legerdemain of *Changelings;* I do not credit those transformations of reasonable creatures into beasts, or that the Devil hath a power to transpeciate a man into a Horse, who tempted Christ (as a trial of his Divinity) to convert but stones into bread. I could believe that Spirits use with man the act of carnality, and that in both sexes; I conceive they may assume, steal, or contrive a body, wherein there

---

[7] In his Oracle to *Augustus.*

may be action enough to content decrepit lust, or passion to satisfie more active veneries; yet in both, without a possibility of generation: and therefore that opinion that Antichrist should be born of the Tribe of *Dan,* by conjunction with the Devil, is ridiculous, and a conceit fitter for a Rabbin than a Christian. I hold that the Devil doth really possess some men, the spirit of Melancholly others, the spirit of Delusion others; that as the Devil is concealed and denyed by some, so God and good Angels are pretended by others whereof the late defection of the Maid of *Germany* hath left a pregnant example.

## XXXI

Again, I believe that all that use sorceries, incantations, and spells, are not Witches, or, as we term them, Magicians; I conceive there is a traditional Magick, not learned immediately from the Devil, but at second hand from his Scholars, who having once the secret betrayed, are able, and do emperically practise without his advice, they both proceeding upon the principles of Nature; where actives, aptly conjoyned to disposed passives, will under any Master produce their effects. Thus I think at first a great part of Philosophy was Witchcraft, which being afterward derived to one another, proved but Philosophy, and was indeed no more but the honest effects of Nature: What invented by us is Philosophy, learned from him is Magick. We do surely owe the discovery of many secrets to the discovery of good and bad Angels. I could never pass that sentence of *Paracelsus,\** without an asterisk, or annotation; *Ascendens constellatum multa revelat, quærentibus magnalia naturæ,†* i.e. *opera Dei.*[8] I do think that many mysteries ascribed to our own inventions, have been the courteous revelations of Spirits; for those noble essences in Heaven bear a friendly regard unto their fellow Natures on Earth; and therefore believe that those many prodigies and ominous prognosticks, which fore-run the ruines of States, Princes, and private persons, are the charitable premonitions of good Angels, which more careless enquiries term but the effects of chance and nature.

## XXXII

Now, besides these particular and divided Spirits, there may be (for ought I know) an universal and common Spirit to the whole World. It was the opinion of *Plato,* and it is yet of the *Hermetical* Philosophers: if there be a common nature that unites and tyes the scattered and divided individuals into one species, why may there not be one that unites them all? However, I am sure there is a common Spirit that plays within us, yet makes no part of us; and that is the Spirit of God, the fire and scintillation of that noble and mighty Essence, which is the life and radical heat of Spirits, and those essences that know not the vertue of the Sun, a fire quite contrary to the fire of Hell: This is that gentle heat that broodeth on the waters, and in six days hatched the World; this is that irradiation that dispels the mists of Hell, the clouds of horrour, fear, sorrow, despair; and preserves the region of the mind in serenity: Whatsoever feels not the warm gale and gentle ventilation of this Spirit, (though I feel his pulse) I dare not say he lives; for truely without this, to me there is no heat under the Tropick; nor any light, though I dwelt in the body of the Sun.

*As when the labouring Sun hath wrought*
*his track*
*Up to the top of lofty* Cancers *back,*
*The ycie Ocean cracks, the frozen pole*
*Thaws with the heat of the Celestial coale;*
*So when thy absent beams begin t'impart*
*Again a Solstice on my frozen heart,*
*My winter's ov'r; my drooping spirits sing,*

---

\* 1493–1541; Swiss physician, chemist, and alchemist.

† The ascending constellation reveals to inquirers many of nature's great things.

[8] Thereby is meant our good Angel appointed us from our Nativity.

*And every part revives into a Spring.*
*But if thy quickening beams a while*
*    decline,*
*And with their light bless not this Orb of*
*    mine,*
*A chilly frost supriseth every member,*
*And in the midst of* June *I feel* December.
*O how this earthly temper doth debase*
*The noble Soul in this her humble place.*
*Whose wingy nature ever doth aspire*
*To reach that place whence first it took its*
*    fire.*
*These flames I feel, which in my heart do*
*    dwell,*
*Are not thy beams but take their fire from*
*    Hell.*
*O quench them all and let thy light divine*
*Be as the Sun to this poor Orb of mine;*
*And to thy sacred Spirit convert those*
*    fires,*
*Whose earthly fumes choak my devout*
*    aspires.*

## XXXIII

Therefore for Spirits, I am so far from denying their existence, that I could easily believe, that not onely whole Countries, but particular persons, have their Tutelary and Guardian Angels: It is not a new opinion of the Church of *Rome,* but an old one of *Pythagoras* and *Plato;* there is no heresie in it; and if not manifestly defin'd in Scripture, yet is it an opinion of a good and wholesome use in the course and actions of a mans life, and would serve as an *Hypothesis* to salve many doubts, whereof common Philosophy affordeth no solution. Now if you demand my opinion and Metaphysicks of their natures, I confess them very shallow, most of them in a negative way, like that of God; or in a comparative, between our selves and fellow-creatures; for there is in this Universe a Stair, or manifest Scale of creatures, rising not disorderly, or in confusion, but with a comely method and proportion. Between creatures of meer existence and things of life, there is a large disproportion of nature; between plants and animals or creatures of sense, a wider difference; between them and man, a far greater: and if the proportion hold one, between Man and Angels there should be yet a greater. We do not comprehend their natures, who retain the first definition of *Porphyry,* and distinguish them from our selves by immortality; for before his Fall, 'tis thought, Man also was Immortal; yet must we needs affirm that he had a different essence from the Angels; having therefore no certain knowledge of their Natures, 'tis no bad method of the Schools, whatsoever perfection we find obscurely in our selves, in a more compleat and absolute way to ascribe unto them. I believe they have an extemporary knowledge, and upon the first motion of their reason do what we cannot without study or deliberation; that they know things by their forms, and define by specifical difference what we describe by accidents and properties; and therefore probabilities to us may be demonstrations unto them: that they have knowledge not onely of the specifical, but numerical forms of individuals, and understand by what reserved difference each single *Hypostasis* (besides the relation to its species) becomes its numerical self. That as the Soul hath a power to move the body it informs, so there's a faculty to move any, though inform none; ours upon restraint of time, place, and distance; but that invisible hand that conveyed *Habakkuk* to the Lyons Den, or *Philip* to *Azotus,* infringeth this rule, and hath a secret conveyance, wherewith mortality is not acquainted: if they have that intuitive knowledge, whereby as in reflexion they behold the thoughts of one another, I cannot peremptorily deny but they know a great part of ours. They that to refute the Invocation of Saints, have denied that they have any knowledge of our affairs below, have proceeded too far, and must pardon my opinion, till I can thoroughly answer that piece of Scripture, *At the conversion of a sinner the Angels in Heaven rejoyce.* I cannot with those in that great Father securely interpret the work of the first day, *Fiat lux,* to the creation of Angels, though I confess there is not any creature that hath so neer a glympse of their nature, as light in the Sun and Elements. We stile it a bare accident, but where it subsists alone, 'tis a spiritual Substance, and may be an Angel: in brief, conceive light invisible, and that is a Spirit.

## XXXIV

These are certainly the Magisterial and master-pieces of the Creator, the Flower, or (as we may say) the best part of nothing, actually existing, what we are but in hopes and probability; we are onely that amphibious piece between a corporal and spiritual Essence, that middle form that links those two together, and makes good the Method of God and Nature, that jumps not from extreams, but unites the incompatible distances by some middle and participating natures: that we are the breath and similitude of God it is indisputable, and upon record of holy Scripture; but to call ourselves a Microcosm, or little World, I thought it only a pleasant trope of Rhetorick, till my neer judgement and second thoughts told me there was a real truth therein: for first we are a rude mass, and in the rank of creatures, which onely are, and have a dull kind of being, not yet privileged with life, or preferred to sense or reason; next we live the life of Plants, the life of Animals, the life of Men, and at last the life of Spirits, running on in one mysterious nature those five kinds of existences, which comprehend the creatures not onely of the World, but of the Universe; thus is man that great and true *Amphibium,* whose nature is disposed to live not onely like other creatures in divers elements, but in divided and distinguished worlds: for though there be but one to sense, there are two to reason, the one visible, the other invisible, whereof *Moses* seems to have left description, and of the other so obscurely, that some parts thereof are yet in controversie. And truely for the first chapters of *Genesis,* I must confess a great deal of obscurity; though Divines have to the power of humane reason endeavoured to make all go in a literal meaning, yet those allegorical interpretations are also probable and perhaps the mystical method of *Moses* bred up in the Hieroglyphical Schools of the Egyptians.

## XXXV

Now for that immaterial world, methinks we need not wander so far as beyond the first moveable; for even in this material Fabrick the spirits walk as freely exempt from the affection of time, place, and motion, as beyond the extreamest circumference: do but extract from the corpulency of bodies, or resolve things beyond their first matter, and you discover the habitation of Angels, which if I call the ubiquitary and omnipresent essence of God, I hope I shall not offend Divinity: for before the Creation of the World God was really all things. For the Angels he created no new World, or determinate mansion, and therefore they are everywhere where is his Essence, and do live at a distance even in himself. That God made all things for man, is in some sense true, yet not so far as to subordinate the Creation of those purer Creatures unto ours, though as ministring Spirits they do, and are willing to fulfil the will of God in these lower and sublunary affairs of man: God made all things for himself, and it is impossible he should make them for any other end than his own Glory; it is all he can receive, and all that is without himself: for honour being an external adjunct, and in the honourer rather than in the person honoured, it was necessary to make a Creature, from whom he might receive this homage; and that is in the other world Angels, in this, Man; which when we neglect we forget the very end of our Creation, and may justly provoke God, not onely to repent that he hath made the World, but that he hath sworn he would not destroy it. That there is but one World, is a conclusion of Faith. *Aristotle* with all his Philosophy hath not been able to prove it, and as weakly that the world was eternal; that dispute much troubled the Pen of the Philosophers, but *Moses* decided that question, and all is salved with the new term of a Creation, that is, a production of something out of nothing; and what is that? Whatsoever is opposite to something; or more exactly, that which is truely contrary unto God; for he onely is, all others have an existence with dependency, and are something but by a distinction; and herein is Divinity conformant unto Philosophy, and generation not onely founded on contrarieties, but also creation; God being all things, is contrary unto nothing, out of which were made all things, and so nothing became something, and *Omneity* informed *Nullity* into an Essence.

## XXXVI

The whole Creation is a Mystery, and particularly that of Man; at the blast of his mouth were the rest of the Creatures made, and at his bare word they started out of nothing: but in the frame of Man (as the Text describes it) he played the sensible operator, and seemed not so much to create, as make him; when he had separated the materials of other creatures, there consequently resulted a form and soul; but having raised the walls of man, he has driven to a second and harder creation of a substance like himself, an incorruptible and immortal Soul. For these two affections we have the Philosophy and opinion of the Heathens, the flat affirmative of *Plato,* and not a negative from *Aristotle:* there is another scruple cast in by Divinity (concerning its production) much disputed in the *Germane* auditories, and with that indifferency and equality of arguments, as leave the controversie undetermined. I am not of *Paracelsus* mind, that boldly delivers a receipt to make a man without conjunction; yet cannot but wonder at the multi-

tude of heads that do deny traduction, having no other argument to confirm their belief, then that Rhetorical sentence, and *Antimetathesis* of *Augustine, Creando infunditur, infundendo creatur:** either opinion will consist well enough with Religion; yet I should rather incline to this, did not one objection haunt me, not wrung from speculations and subtilties, but from common sense and observation; not pickt from the leaves of any Author, but bred amongst the weeds and tares of mine own brain: And this is a conclusion from the equivocal and monstrous productions in the copulation of Man with Beast: for if the Soul of man be not transmitted, and transfused in the seed of the Parents, why are not those productions meerly beasts, but have also an impression and tincture of reason in as high a measure, as it can evidence it self in those improper Organs? Nor truely can I peremptorily deny, that the Soul in this her sublunary estate, is wholly, and in all acceptions inorganical, but that for the performance of her ordinary actions, there is required not onely a symmetry and proper disposition of Organs, but a Crasis and temper correspondent to its operations. Yet is not this mass of flesh and visible structure the instrument and proper corps of the Soul, but rather of Sense, and that the hand of Reason. In our study of Anatomy there is a mass of mysterious Philosophy, and such as reduced the very Heathens to Divinity: yet amongst all those rare discourses, and curious pieces I find in the Fabrick of man, I do not so much content my self, as in that I find not, there is no Organ or Instrument for the rational soul: for in the brain, which we term the seat of reason, there is not any thing of moment more than I can discover in the crany of a beast: and this is a sensible and no inconsiderable argument of the inorganity of the Soul, at least in that sense we usually so

---

* By creating it is poured in, by pouring in it is created.

conceive it. Thus we are men, and we know not how; there is something in us that can be without us, and will be after us, though it is strange that it hath no history, what it was before us, nor cannot tell how it entred in us.

## XXXVII

Now for these walls of flesh, wherein the Soul doth seem to be immured, before the Resurrection, it is nothing but an elemental composition, and a Fabrick that must fall to ashes. *All flesh is grass,* is not onely metaphorically, but litterally, true; for all those creatures we behold, are but the herbs of the field, digested into flesh in them, or more remotely carnified in our selves. Nay further, we are what we all abhor, *Anthropophagi* and Cannibals, devourers not onely of men, but of our selves; and that not in an allegory, but a positive truth: for all this mass of flesh which we behold, came in at our mouths; this frame we look upon, hath been upon our trenchers; in brief, we have devour'd our selves. I cannot believe the wisdom of *Pythagoras* did ever positively, and in a literal sense, affirm his *Metempsychosis,* or impossible transmigration of the Souls of men into beasts: of all Metamorphoses, or transmigrations, I believe only one, that is of *Lots* wife; for that of *Nebuchodonosor* proceeded not so far; in all others I conceive there is no further verity than is contained in their implicite sense and morality. I believe that the whole frame of a beast doth perish, and is left in the same state after death as before it was materialled unto life; that the souls of men know neither contrary nor corruption; that they subsist beyond the body, and outlive death by the priviledge of their proper natures, and without a Miracle; that the Souls of the faithful, as they leave Earth, take possession of Heaven: that those apparitions and ghosts of departed persons are not the wandring souls of men, but the unquiet walks of Devils, prompting and suggesting us unto mischief, blood, and villany; instilling and stealing into our hearts that the blessed spirits are not at rest in their graves, but wander sollicitous of the affairs of the World; but that those phantasms appear often, and do frequent Cœmeteries, Charnel-houses, and Churches, it is because those are the dormitories of the dead, where the Devil like an insolent Champion beholds with pride the spoils and Trophies of his Victory over *Adam*.

## XXXVIII

This is that dismal conquest we all deplore, that makes us so often cry *(O) Adam, quid fecisti?* * I thank God I have not those strait ligaments, or narrow obligations to the World, as to dote on life, or be convulst and tremble at the name of death: Not that I am insensible of the dread and horrour thereof, or by raking into the bowels of the deceased, continual sight of Anatomies, Skeletons, or Cadaverous reliques, like Vespilloes, or Gravemakers, I am become stupid, or have forgot the apprehension of Mortality; but that marshalling all the horrours, and contemplating the extremities thereof, I find not any thing therein able to daunt the courage of a man, much less a well-resolved Christian: And therefore am not angry at the errour of our first Parents, or unwilling to bear a part of this common fate, and like the best of them to dye, that is, to cease to breathe, to take a farewel of the elements, to be a kind of nothing for a moment, to be within one instant of a spirit. When I take a full view and circle of my self, without this reasonable moderator, and equal piece of Justice, Death, I do conceive my self the miserablest person extant; were there not another life that I hope for, all the vanities of this World should not intreat a moment's breath from me: could the Devil work my belief to imagine I could never dye, I would not outlive that very thought; I have so abject a

---

* O Adam, what hast thou done?

conceit of this common way of existence, this retaining to the Sun and Elements, I cannot think this is to be a man, or to live according to the dignity of humanity: in exspectation of a better, I can with patience embrace this life, yet in my best meditations do often defie death: I honour any man that contemns it, nor can I highly love any that is afraid of it: this makes me naturally love a Souldier, and honour those tattered and contemptible Regiments, that will dye at the command of a Sergeant. For a Pagan there may be some motives to be in love with life; but for a Christian to be amazed at death, I see not how he can escape this Dilemma, that he is too sensible of this life, or hopeless of the life to come.

## XXXIX

Some Divines count Adam 30 years old at his creation, because they suppose him created in the perfect age and stature of man. And surely we are all out of the computation of our age, and every man is some months elder than he bethinks him; for we live, move, have a being, and are subject to the actions of the elements, and the malice of diseases, in that other world, the truest Microcosm, the Womb of our Mother. For besides that general and common existence we are conceived to hold in our Chaos, and whilst we sleep within the bosome of our causes, we enjoy a being and life in three distinct worlds, wherein we receive most manifest graduations: In that obscure World and womb of our mother, our time is short, computed by the Moon; yet longer then the days of many creatures that behold the Sun, our selves being not yet without life, sense, and reason; though for the manifestation of its actions, it awaits the opportunity of objects, and seems to live there but in its root and soul of vegetation; entring afterwards upon the scene of the World, we arise up and become another creature, performing the reasonable actions of man, and obscurely manifesting that part of Divinity in us, but not in complement and perfection, till we have once more cast our secondine, that is, this slough of flesh, and are delivered into the last world, that is, that ineffable place of *Paul,* that proper *ubi* of spirits. The smattering I have of the Philosophers Stone (which is something more then the perfect exaltation of Gold) hath taught me a great deal of Divinity, and instructed my belief, how that immortal spirit and incorruptible substance of my Soul may lye obscure, and sleep a while within this house of flesh. Those strange and mystical transmigrations that I have observed in Silk-worms, turned my Philosophy into Divinity. There is in these works of nature, which seem to puzzle reason, something Divine, and hath more in it then the eye of a common spectator doth discover.

## XL

I am naturally bashful, nor hath conversation, age or travel, been able to effront, or enharden me; yet I have one part of modesty which I have seldom discovered in another, that is, (to speak truely) I am not so much afraid of death, as ashamed thereof; 'tis the very disgrace and ignominy of our natures, that in a moment can so disfigure us, that our nearest friends, Wife, and Children stand afraid and start at us. The Birds and Beasts of the field, that before in a natural fear obeyed us, forgetting all allegiance, begin to prey upon us. This very conceit hath in a tempest disposed and left me willing to be swallowed up in the abyss of waters; wherein I had perished unseen, unpityed, without wondering eyes, tears of pity, Lectures of mortality, and none had said, *Quantum mutatus ab illo!\** Not that I am ashamed of the Anatomy of my parts, or can accuse Nature for playing the bungler in any part of me, or my own vitious life for contracting any shameful disease upon me, whereby I might not call

---

\* How changed from that man!

my self as wholesome a morsel for the worms as any.

## XLI

Some upon the courage of a fruitful issue, wherein, as in the truest Chronicle, they seem to outlive themselves, can with greater patience away with death. This conceit and counterfeit subsisting in our progenies, seems to me a meer fallacy, unworthy the desires of a man, that can but conceive a thought of the next World; who, in a nobler ambition, should desire to live in his substance in Heaven, rather than his name and shadow in the earth. And therefore at my death I mean to take a total adieu of the world, not caring for a Monument, History, or Epitaph, not so much as the memory of my name to be found any where, but in the universal Register of God. I am not yet so Cynical, as to approve the Testament of *Diogenes,*[9] nor do I altogether allow that *Rodomontado of Lucan;*

—— *Cælo tegitur, qui non habet urnam.*

*He that unburied lies wants not his Herse,*
*For unto him a Tomb's the Universe.*

But commend in my calmer judgement, those ingenuous intentions that desire to sleep by the urns of their Fathers, and strive to go the neatest way unto corruption. I do not envy the temper of Crows and Daws, nor the numerous and weary days of our Fathers before the Flood. If there be any truth in Astrology, I may outlive a Jubilee; as yet I have not seen one revolution of Saturn, nor hath my pulse beat thirty years; and yet excepting one, have seen the Ashes, & left under ground all the Kings of *Europe;* have been contemporary to three Emperours, four Grand Signiours, and as many Popes: methinks I have outlived my self, and begin to be weary of the Sun; I have shaken hands with delight: in my warm blood and Canicular days, I perceive I do anticipate the vices of age; the World

to me is but a dream or mock-show, and we all therein but Pantalones and Anticks, to my severer contemplations.

## XLII

It is not, I confess, an unlawful prayer to desire to surpass the days of our Saviour, or wish to outlive that age wherein he thought fittest to dye; yet if (as Divinity affirms) there shall be no gray hairs in Heaven, but all shall rise in the perfect state of men, we do but outlive those perfections in this World, to be recalled unto them by a greater Miracle in the next, and run on here but to be retrograde hereafter. Were there any hopes to outlive vice, or a point to be super-annuated from sin, it were worthy our knees to implore the days of *Methuselah.* But age doth not rectifie, but incurvate our natures, turning bad dispositions into worser habits, and (like diseases) brings on incurable vices; for every day as we grow weaker in age, we grow stronger in sin; and the number of our days doth make but our sins innumerable. The same vice committed at sixteen, is not the same, though it agree in all other circumstances, at forty, but swells and doubles from the circumstance of our ages, wherein, besides the constant and inexcusable habit of transgressing, the maturity of our judgement cuts off pretence unto excuse or pardon: every sin the oftner it is committed, the more it acquireth in the quality of evil; as it succeeds in time, so it proceeds in degrees of badness; for as they proceed they ever multiply, and like figures in Arithmetick, the last stands for more than all that went before it. And though I think no man can live well once, but he that could live twice, yet for my own part I would not live over my hours past, or begin again the thred of my days: not upon *Cicero's* ground, because I have lived them

----

[9] Who willed his friend not to bury him, but hang him up with a staff in his hand to fright away the crows.

well, but for fear I should live them worse: I find my growing Judgment daily instruct me how to be better, but my untamed affections and confirmed vitiosity makes me daily do worse; I find in my confirmed age the same sins I discovered in my youth; I committed many then because I was a Child, and because I commit them still, I am yet an infant. Therefore I perceive a man may be twice a Child before the days of dotage; and stands in need of *Æsons* Bath before threescore.

## XLIII

And truely there goes a great deal of providence to produce a mans life unto threescore: there is more required than an able temper for those years; though the radical humour contain in it sufficient oyl for seventy, yet I perceive in some it gives no light past thirty: men assign not all the causes of long life, that write whole Books thereof. They that found themselves on the radical balsome, or vital sulphur of the parts, determine not why *Abel* lived not so long as *Adam*. There is therefore a secret glome or bottome of our days: 'twas his wisdom to determine them, but his perpetual and waking providence that fulfils and accomplisheth them; wherein the spirits, our selves, and all the creatures of God in a secret and disputed way do execute his will. Let them not therefore complain of immaturity that die about thirty; they fall but like the whole World, whose solid and well-composed substance must not expect the duration and period of its constitution: when all things are compleated in it, its age is accomplished; and the last and general fever may as naturally destroy it before six thousand, as me before forty; there is therefore some other hand that twines the thread of life than that of Nature: we are not onely ignorant in Antipathies and occult qualities; our ends are as obscure as our beginnings; the line of our days is drawn by night, and the various effects therein by a pensil that is invisible; wherein though we confess our ignorance, I

am sure we do not err if we say it is the hand of God.

## XLIV

I am much taken with two verses of *Lucan,* since I have been able not onely as we do at School, to construe, but understand.

*Victurosque Dei celant ut vivere durent,*
*Felix esse mori.\**

*We're all deluded, vainly searching ways*
*To make us happy by the length of days;*
*For cunningly to make's protract this*
*    breath,*
*The Gods conceal the happiness of Death.*

There be many excellent strains in that Poet, wherewith his Stoical Genius hath liberally supplied him; and truely there are singular pieces in the Philosophy of *Zeno,* and doctrine of the Stoicks, which I perceive, delivered in a Pulpit, pass for current Divinity: yet herein are they in extreams, that can allow a man to be his own *Assassine,* and so highly extol the end and suicide of *Cato;* this is indeed not to fear death, but yet to be afraid of life. It is a brave act of valour to contemn death; but where life is more terrible than death, it is then the truest valour to dare to live; and herein Religion hath taught us a noble example: For all the valiant acts of *Curtius, Scevola,* or *Codrus,* do not parallel or match that one of *Job;* and sure there is no torture to the rack of a disease, nor any Ponyards in death it self like those in the way or prologue to it. *Emori nolo, sed me esse mortuum nihil curo;* I would not die, but care not to be dead. Were I of *Cæsar*'s Religion, I should be of his desires, and wish rather to go off at one blow, then to be sawed in pieces by the grating torture of a disease. Men that look no farther than their outsides, think health an appurtenance unto life, and quarrel with their constitutions for being sick; but I, that have examined the

---

\* *Pharsalia* 4. 510.

parts of man, and know upon what tender filaments that Fabrick hangs, do wonder that we are not always so; and considering the thousand doors that lead to death, do thank my God that we can die but once. 'Tis not onely the mischief of diseases, and villany of poysons, that make an end of us; we vainly accuse the fury of Guns, and the new inventions of death; it is in the power of every hand to destroy us, and we are beholding unto every one we meet, he doth not kill us. There is therefore but one comfort left, that, though it be in the power of the weakest arm to take away life, it is not in the strongest to deprive us of death: God would not exempt himself from that, the misery of immortality in the flesh; he undertook not that was immortal. Certainly there is no happiness within this circle of flesh, nor is it in the Opticks of these eyes to behold felicity; the first day of our Jubilee is Death; the Devil hath therefore failed of his desires; we are happier with death than we should have been without it: there is no misery but in himself, where there is no end of misery; and so indeed in his own sense the Stoick is in the right. He forgets that he can dye who complains of misery; we are in the power of no calamity while death is in our own.

## XLV

Now besides the literal and positive kind of death, there are others whereof Divines make mention, and those I think, not meerly Metaphorical, as mortification, dying unto sin and the World; therefore, I say, every man hath a double Horoscope, one of his humanity, his birth; another of his Christianity, his baptism, and from this do I compute or calculate my Nativity; not reckoning those *Horæ combustæ* and odd days, or esteeming my self any thing, before I was my Saviours, and inrolled in the Register of Christ: Whosoever enjoys not this life, I count him but an apparition, though he wear about him the sensible affections of flesh. In these moral acceptions, the way to be immortal is to dye

daily; nor can I think I have the true Theory of death, when I contemplate a skull, or behold a Skeleton with those vulgar imaginations it casts upon us; I have therefore enlarged that common *Memento mori*, into a more Christian memorandum, *Memento quatuor Novissima*,* those four inevitable points of us all, Death, Judgement, Heaven, and Hell. Neither did the contemplations of the Heathens rest in their graves, without further thought of Rhadamanth or some judicial proceeding after death, though in another way, and upon suggestion of their natural reasons. I cannot but marvail from what *Sibyl* or Oracle they stole the Prophesie of the worlds destruction by fire, or whence *Lucan* learned to say,

*Communis mundo superest rogus, ossibus astra Misturus.*†

*There yet remains to th' World one common Fire,*
*Wherein our bones with stars shall make one Pyre.*

I believe the World grows near its end, yet is neither old nor decayed, nor shall ever perish upon the ruines of its own Principles. As the work of Creation was above nature, so its adversary annihilation; without which the World hath not its end, but its mutation. Now what force should be able to consume it thus far, without the breath of God, which is the truest consuming flame, my Philosophy cannot inform me. Some believe there went not a minute to the Worlds creation, nor shall there go to its destruction; those six days, so punctually described, make not to them one moment, but rather seem to manifest the method and Idea of the great work of the intellect of God, than the manner how he proceeded in its operation. I cannot dream that there should be at the last day any such Judicial proceeding, or calling to the Bar, as indeed

---

* Remember the four last things.
† *Pharsalia* 7. 814.

the Scripture seems to imply, and the literal Commentators do conceive: for unspeakable mysteries in the Scriptures are often delivered in a vulgar and illustrative way; and being written unto man, are delivered, not as they truely are, but as they may be understood; wherein notwithstanding the different interpretations according to different capacities may stand firm with our devotion, nor be any way prejudicial to each single edification.

### XLVI

Now to determine the day and year of this inevitable time, is not onely convincible and statute-madness, but also manifest impiety: How shall we interpret *Elias* 6000 years,* or imagine the secret communicated to a Rabbi, which God hath denyed unto his Angels? It had been an excellent Quære to have posed the Devil of *Delphos,* and must needs have forced him to some strange amphibology; it hath not onely mocked the predictions of sundry Astrologers in Ages past, but the prophesies of many melancholy heads in these present, who neither understanding reasonably things past or present, pretend a knowledge of things to come; heads ordained onely to manifest the incredible effects of melancholy, and to fulfil old prophecies rather than be the authors of new. In those days there shall come Wars and rumours of Wars, to me seems no prophecy, but a constant truth, in all times verified since it was pronounced: There shall be signs in the Moon and Stars; how comes he then like a Thief in the night, when he gives an item of his coming? That common sign drawn from the revelation of Antichrist, is as obscure as any: in our common compute he hath been come these many years; but for my own part to speak freely, I am half of opinion that Antichrist is the Philosophers stone in Divinity; for the discovery and invention thereof, though there be prescribed rules and probable inductions, yet hath hardly any man attained the perfect discovery thereof. That general

opinion that the World grows neer its end, hath possessed all ages past as neerly as ours; I am afraid that the Souls that now depart, cannot escape that lingring expostulation of the Saints under the Altar, *Quousque, Domine? How long, O Lord?* and groan in the expectation of that great Jubilee.

### XLVII

This is the day that must make good that great attribute of God, his Justice; that must reconcile those unanswerable doubts that torment the wisest understandings, and reduce those seeming inequalities, and respective distributions in this world, to an equality and recompensive Justice in the next. This is that one day, that shall include and comprehend all that went before it; wherein, as in the last scene, all the Actors must enter, to compleat and make up the Catastrophe of this great piece. This is the day whose memory hath only power to make us honest in the dark, and to be vertuous without a witness. *Ipsa sui pretium virtus sibi,* that Vertue is her own reward, is but a cold principle, and not able to maintain our variable resolutions in a constant and setled way of goodness. I have practised that honest artifice of *Seneca,* and in my retired and solitary imaginations, to detain me from the foulness of vice, have fancied to my self the presence of my dear and worthiest friends, before whom I should lose my head, rather than be vitious: yet herein I found that there was nought but moral honesty, and this was not to be vertuous for his sake who must reward us at the last. I have tryed if I could reach that great resolution of his, to be honest without a thought of Heaven or Hell; and indeed I found, upon a natural inclination, and inher without a livery; yet not in that resolved bred loyalty unto virtue, that I could serve

---

* The age of the world according to a tradition attributed to the school of Elijah in the Talmud.

and venerable way, but that the frailty of my nature, upon [any] easie temptation, might be induced to forget her. The life therefore and spirit of all our actions, is the resurrection, and a stable apprehension that our ashes shall enjoy the fruit of our pious endeavours: without this, all Religion is a fallacy, and those impieties of *Lucian, Euripides,* and *Julian,* are no blasphemies, but subtle verities, and Atheists have been the onely Philosophers.

## XLVIII

How shall the dead arise, is no question of my Faith; to believe only possibilities, is not Faith, but meer Philosophy. Many things are true in Divinity, which are neither inducible by reason, nor confirmable by sense; and many things in Philosophy confirmable by sense, yet not inducible by reason. Thus it is impossible by any solid or demonstrative reasons to perswade a man to believe the conversion of the Needle to the North; though this be possible and true, and easily credible, upon a single experiment unto the sense. I believe that our estranged and divided ashes shall unite again; that our separated dust after so many Pilgrimages and transformations into the parts of Minerals, Plants, Animals, Elements, shall at the Voice of God return into their primitive shapes, and joyn again to make up their primary and predestinate forms. As at the Creation there was a separation of that confused mass into its pieces; so at the destruction thereof there shall be a separation into its distinct individuals. As at the Creation of the World, all the distinct species that we behold lay involved in one mass, till the fruitful Voice of God separated this united multitude into its several species: so at the last day, when those corrupted reliques shall be scattered in the Wilderness of forms, and seem to have forgot their proper habits, God by a powerful Voice shall command them back into their proper shapes, and call them out by their single individuals: Then shall appear the fertility of *Adam,*

and the magick of that sperm that hath dilated into so many millions. I have often beheld as a miracle, that artificial resurrection and revivification of *Mercury,* how being mortified into a thousand shapes, it assumes again its own, and returns into its numerical self. Let us speak naturally, and like Philosophers, the forms of alterable bodies in these sensible corruptions perish not; nor as we imagine, wholly quit their mansions, but retire and contract themselves into their secret and unaccessible parts, where they may best protect themselves from the action of their Antagonist. A plant or vegetable consumed to ashes, by a contemplative and school-Philosopher seems utterly destroyed, and the form to have taken his leave for ever: But to a sensible Artist the forms are not perished, but withdrawn into their incombustible part, where they lie secure from the action of that devouring element. This is made good by experience, which can from the Ashes of a Plant revive the plant, and from its cinders recal it into its stalk and leaves again. What the Art of man can do in these inferiour pieces, what blasphemy is it to affirm the finger of God cannot do in these more perfect and sensible structures? This is that mystical Philosophy, from whence no true Scholar becomes an Atheist, but from the visible effects of nature grows up a real Divine, and beholds not in a dream, as *Ezekiel,* but in an ocular and visible object the types of his resurrection.

## XLIX

Now, the necessary Mansions of our restored selves, are those two contrary and incompatible places we call Heaven and Hell; to define them, or strictly to determine what and where these are, surpasseth my Divinity. That elegant Apostle* which seemed to have a glimpse of Heaven, hath left but a negative description thereof; *which neither eye hath seen, nor ear hath heard, nor can*

---

* Saint Paul.

*enter into the heart of man:* he was translated out of himself to behold it; but being returned into himself, could not express it. St. *John's* description by Emerals, Chrysolites, and precious Stones, is too weak to express the material Heaven we behold. Briefly therefore, where the Soul hath the full measure and complement of happiness; where the boundless appetite of that spirit remains compleatly satisfied, that it can neither desire addition nor alteration; that I think is truly Heaven: and this can onely be in the injoyment of that essence, whose infinite goodness is able to terminate the desires of it self, and the unsatiable wishes of ours; wherever God will thus manifest himself, there is Heaven though within the circle of this sensible world. Thus the Soul of man may be in Heaven any where, even within the limits of his own proper body; and when it ceaseth to live in the body, it may remain in its own soul, that is, its Creator: and thus we may say that St. *Paul,* whether in the body, or out of the body, was yet in Heaven. To place it in the Empyreal, or beyond the tenth sphear, is to forget the world's destruction; for when this sensible world shall be destroyed, all shall then be here as it is now there, an Empyreal Heaven, a *quasi* vacuity; when to ask where Heaven is, is to demand where the Presence of God is, or where we have the glory of that happy vision. *Moses* that was bred up in all the learning of the *Egyptians,* committed a gross absurdity in Philosophy, when with these eyes of flesh he desired to see God, and petitioned his Maker, that is, truth it self, to a contradiction. Those that imagine Heaven and Hell neighbours, and conceive a vicinity between those two extreams, upon consequence of the Parable, where *Dives* discoursed with *Lazarus* in *Abraham's* bosome, do too grosly conceive of those glorified creatures, whose eyes shall easily out-see the Sun, and behold without a perspective the extreamest distances: for if there shall be in our glorified eyes, the faculty of sight and reception of objects, I could think the visible species there to be

in as unlimitable a way as now the intellectual. I grant that two bodies placed beyond the tenth sphear, or in a vacuity, according to *Aristotle's* Philosophy, could not behold each other, because there wants a body or Medium to hand and transport the visible rays of the object unto the sense; but when there shall be a general defect of either Medium to convey, or light to prepare and dispose that Medium, and yet a perfect vision, we must suspend the rules of our Philosophy, and make all good by a more absolute piece of opticks.

## L

I cannot tell how to say that fire is the essence of Hell: I know not what to make of Purgatory, or conceive a flame that can either prey upon, or purifie the substance of a Soul: those flames of sulphur mention'd in the Scriptures, I take not to be understood of this present Hell, but of that to come, where fire shall make up the complement of our tortures, and have a body or subject wherein to manifest its tyranny. Some who have had the honour to be textuary in Divinity, are of opinion it shall be the same specifical fire with ours. This is hard to conceive, yet can I make good how even that may prey upon our bodies, and yet not consume us: for in this material World there are bodies that persist invincible in the powerfullest flames; and though by the action of fire they fall into ignition and liquation, yet will they never suffer a destruction. I would gladly know how *Moses* with an actual fire calcin'd, or burnt the Golden Calf into powder: for that mystical metal of Gold, whose solary and celestial nature I admire, exposed unto the violence of fire, grows onely hot, and liquifies, but consumeth not; so when the consumable and volatile pieces of our bodies shall be refined into a more impregnable and fixed temper, like Gold, though they suffer from the action of flames, they shall never perish, but lye immortal in the arms of fire. And surely if this frame must suffer onely by the action of this element, there will many bodies escape, and not onely Heaven, but Earth will not be at an end, but rather a beginning. For at present it is not earth, but a composition of fire, water, earth, and air; but at that time, spoiled of these ingredients, it shall appear in a substance more like it self, its ashes. Philosophers that opinioned the worlds destruction by fire, did never dream of annihilation, which is beyond the power of sublunary causes; for the last [and proper] action of that element is but vitrification, or a reduction of a body into glass; and therefore some of our Chymicks facetiously affirm, that at the last fire all shall be christallized and reverberated into glass, which is the utmost action of that element. Nor need we fear this term annihilation, or wonder that God will destroy the works of his Creation: for man subsisting, who is, and will then truely appear, a Microcosm, the world cannot be said to be destroyed. For the eyes of God, and perhaps also of our glorified selves, shall as really behold and contemplate the World in its Epitome or contracted essence, as now it doth at large and in its dilated substance. In the seed of a Plant to the eyes of God, and to the understanding of man, there exists, though in an invisible way, the perfect leaves, flowers, and fruit thereof: (for things that are in *posse* to the sense, are actually existent to the understanding). Thus God beholds all things, who contemplates as fully his works in their Epitome, as in their full volume; and beheld as amply the whole world in that little compendium of the sixth day, as in the scattered and dilated pieces of those five before.

## LI

Men commonly set forth the torments of Hell by fire, and the extremity of corporal afflictions, and describe Hell in the same method that *Mahomet* doth Heaven. This indeed makes a noise, and drums in popular ears; but if this be the terrible piece thereof, it is not worthy to stand in diameter with Heaven, whose happiness consists in that part that is best able to comprehend it, that immortal essence, that translated divinity and colony of God, the Soul. Surely though we place Hell under Earth, the Devil's walk and purlue is about it: men speak too popularly who place it in those flaming mountains, which to grosser apprehensions represent Hell. The heart of man is the place the Devils dwell in; I feel sometimes a Hell within my self; *Lucifer* keeps his Court in my breast; *Legion* is revived in me. There are as many Hells, as *Anaxagoras* conceived worlds; there was more than one Hell in *Magdalene,* when there were seven Devils; for every Devil is an Hell unto himself; he holds enough of torture in his own *ubi,* and needs not the misery of circumference to afflict him. And thus a distracted Conscience here, is a shadow or introduction unto Hell hereafter. Who can but pity the merciful intention of those hands that do destroy themselves? the Devil, were it in his power, would do the like; which being impossible, his miseries are endless, and he suffers most in that attribute wherein he is impassible, his immortality.

## LII

I thank God that with joy I mention it, I was never afraid of Hell, nor never grew pale at the description of that place; I have so fixed my contemplations on Heaven, that I have almost forgot the Idea of Hell, and am afraid rather to lose the Joys of the one, than endure the misery of the other: to be deprived of them is a perfect Hell, and needs methinks no addition to compleat our afflictions; that terrible term hath never detained me from sin, nor do I owe any good action to the name thereof; I fear God, yet am not afraid of him; his mercies make me ashamed of my sins, before his Judgements afraid thereof: these are the forced and secondary method of his wisdom, which he useth but as the last remedy, and upon provocation; a course rather to deter the wicked, than incite the virtuous to his worship. I can hardly think there was ever any scared into Heaven; they go the fairest way to Heaven that would serve God without a Hell; other Mercenaries, that crouch into him in fear of Hell, though they term themselves the servants, are indeed but the slaves of the Almighty.

## LIII

And to be true, and speak my soul, when I survey the occurrences of my life, and call into account the Finger of God, I can perceive nothing but an abyss and mass of mercies, either in general to mankind, or in particular to my self: and whether out of the prejudice of my affection, or an inverting and partial conceit of his mercies, I know not; but those which others term crosses, afflictions, judgements, misfortunes, to me who inquire farther into them then their visible effects, they both appear, and in event have ever proved, the secret and dissembled favours of his affection. It is a singular piece of Wisdom to apprehend truly, and without passion, the Works of God, and so well to distinguish his Justice from his Mercy, as not miscall those noble Attributes: yet it is likewise an honest piece of Logick, so to dispute and argue the proceedings of God, as to distinguish even his judgments into mercies. For God is merciful unto all, because better to the worst, than the best deserve; and to say he punisheth none in this world, though it be a Paradox, is no absurdity. To one that hath committed Murther, if the Judge should only ordain a Fine, it were a madness to call this a punishment, and to repine at the sentence, rather than admire the clemency of the Judge. Thus our offences being mortal, and deserving not onely Death, but Damnation; if the goodness of God be content to traverse and pass them over with a loss, misfortune, or disease; what frensie were it to term this a punishment, rather than an extremity of mercy; and to groan under the rod of his Judgements, rather than admire the Scepter of his Mercies? Therefore to adore, honour, and admire him, is a debt of gratitude due from the obligation of our nature, states, and conditions; and with these thoughts, he that knows them best, will not deny that I adore him. That I obtain Heaven, and the bliss thereof, is accidental, and not the intended work of my devotion; it being a felicity I can neither think to deserve, nor scarce in modesty to expect. For these two ends of us all, either as rewards or punishments, are mercifully ordained and disproportionably disposed unto our actions; the one being so far beyond our deserts, the other so infinitely below our demerits.

## LIV

There is no Salvation to those that believe not in *Christ*, that is, say some, since his Nativity, and as Divinity affirmeth, before also; which makes me much apprehend the ends of those honest Worthies and Philosophers which dyed before his Incarnation. It is hard to place those Souls in Hell, whose worthy lives do teach us Virtue on Earth: methinks amongst those many subdivisions of Hell, there might have been one Limbo left for these. What a strange vision will it be to see their Poetical fictions converted into Verities, and their imagined and fancied Furies into real Devils? how strange to them will sound the History of *Adam,* when they shall suffer for him they never heard of? when they who derive their genealogy from the Gods, shall know they are the unhappy issue of sinful man? It is an insolent part of reason, to controvert the Works of God, or question the Justice of his proceedings. Could Humility teach others, as it hath instructed me, to contemplate the infinite and incomprehensible distance betwixt the Creator and the Creature; or did we seriously perpend that one simile of St. *Paul, Shall the Vessel say to the Potter, Why hast thou made me thus?* it would prevent these arrogant disputes of reason, nor would we argue the definitive sentence of God, either to Heaven or Hell. Men that live according to the right rule and law of reason, live but in their own kind, as beasts do in theirs; who justly obey the prescript of their natures, and therefore cannot reasonably demand a reward of their actions, as onely obeying the natural dictates of their reason. It will therefore, and must at last appear, that all salvation is through *Christ;* which verity I fear these great examples of virtue must confirm, and make it good, how the perfectest actions of earth have no title or claim unto Heaven.

## LV

Nor truely do I think the lives of these or of any other, were ever correspondent, or in all points conformable unto their doctrines. It is evident that *Aristotle* transgressed the rule of his own Ethicks; the Stoicks that condemn passion, and command a man to laugh in *Phalaris* his Bull, could not endure without a groan a fit of the Stone or Colick. The *Scepticks* that affirmed they knew nothing, even in that opinion confute themselves, and thought they knew more than all the World beside. *Diogenes* I hold to be the most vain-glorious man of his time, and more ambitious in refusing all Honours, than *Alexander* in rejecting none. Vice and the Devil put a Fallacy upon our Reasons, and provoking us too hastily to run from it, entangle and profound us deeper in it. The Duke of *Venice,* that weds himself unto the Sea by a Ring of Gold, I will not argue of prodigality, because it is a solemnity of good use and consequence in the State: but the Philosopher that threw his money into the Sea to avoid Avarice, was a notorious prodigal. There is no road or ready way to virtue; it is not an easie point of art to disentangle our selves from this riddle, or web of Sin: To perfect virtue, as to Religion, there is required a *Panoplia,* or compleat armour; that whilst we lye at close ward against one Vice, we lye not open to the venny of another. And indeed wiser discretions that have the thred of reason to conduct them, offend without pardon; whereas, under-heads may stumble without dishonour. There go so many circumstances to piece up one good action, that it is a lesson to be good, and we are forced to be virtuous by the book. Again, the Practice of men holds not an equal pace, yea, and often runs counter to their Theory; we naturally know what is good, but naturally pursue what is evil: the Rhetorick wherewith I perswade another, cannot perswade my self: there is a depraved appetite in us, that will with patience hear the learned instructions of Reason, but yet perform no farther than agrees to its own irregular humour. In brief, we all are monsters, that is, a composition of Man and Beast; wherein we must endeavour to be as the Poets fancy that wise man *Chiron,* that is, to have the region of Man above that of Beast, and Sense to sit but at the feet of Reason. Lastly, I do desire with God that all, but yet affirm with men, that few shall know Salvation; that the bridge is narrow, the passage strait unto life: yet those who do confine the Church of God, either to particular Nations, Churches or Families, have made it far narrower then our Saviour ever meant it.

## LVI

The vulgarity of those judgements that wrap the Church of God in *Strabo's* cloak, and restrain it unto *Europe,* seem to me as bad Geographers as *Alexander,* who thought he had Conquer'd all the World, when he had not subdued the half of any part thereof. For we cannot deny the Church of God both in *Asia* and *Africa,* if we do not forget the Peregrinations of the Apostles, the deaths of the Martyrs, the Sessions of many, and, even in our reformed judgement, lawful Councils, held in those parts in the minority and nonage of ours. Nor must a few differences, more remarkable in the eyes of man than perhaps in the judgement of God, excommunicate from Heaven one another, much less those Christians who are in a manner all Martyrs, maintaining their Faith, in the noble way of persecution, and serving God in the Fire, whereas we honour him in the Sunshine. 'Tis true, we all hold there is a number of Elect, and many to be saved; yet take our Opinions together, and from the confusion thereof there will be no such thing as salvation, nor shall any one be saved. For first, the Church of *Rome* condemneth us, we likewise them; the Sub-reformists and Sectaries sentence the Doctrine of our Church as damnable; the Atomist, or Familist, reprobates all these; and all these, them again. Thus whilst the Mercies of God do promise us Heaven, our conceits and opinions exclude us from that place. There must be, therefore, more than one St. *Peter:* particular Churches and Sects usurp the gates of Heaven, and turn the key against each other: and thus we go to Heaven against each others wills, conceits and opinions; and with as much uncharity as ignorance, do err I fear in points not only of our own, but one anothers salvation.

## LVII

I believe many are saved, who to man seem reprobated; and many are reprobated, who in the opinion and sentence of man, stand elected: there will appear at the Last day, strange and unexpected examples both of his Justice and his Mercy; and therefore to define either, is folly in man, and insolency even in the Devils: those acute and subtil spirits in all their sagacity, can hardly divine who shall be saved; which if they could Prognostick, their labour were at an end; nor need they compass the earth seeking whom they may devour. Those who upon a rigid application of the Law, sentence *Solomon* unto damnation, condemn not onely him, but themselves, and the whole World: for by the Letter and written Word of God, we are without exception in the state of Death; but there is a prerogative of God, and an arbitrary pleasure above the Letter of his own Law, by which alone we can pretend unto Salvation, and through which *Solomon* might be as easily saved as those who condemn him.

## LVIII

The number of those who pretend unto Salvation, and those infinite swarms who think to pass through the eye of this Needle,

have much amazed me. That name and compellation of *little Flock,* doth not comfort, but deject my Devotion; especially when I reflect upon mine own unworthiness, wherein, according to my humble apprehensions, I am below them all. I believe there shall never be an Anarchy in Heaven, but as there are Hierarchies amongst the Angels, so shall there be degrees of priority amongst the Saints. Yet is it (I protest) beyond my ambition to aspire unto the first ranks; my desires onely are, and I shall be happy therein, to be but the last man, and bring up the Rere in Heaven.

## LIX

Again, I am confident and fully perswaded, yet dare not take my oath, of my Salvation: I am as it were sure, and do believe without all doubt, that there is such a City as *Constantinople;* yet for me to take my Oath thereon were a kind of Perjury, because I hold no infallible warrant from my own sense to confirm me in the certainty thereof: And truly, though many pretend an absolute certainty of their Salvation, yet when an humble Soul shall contemplate our own unworthiness, she shall meet with many doubts, and suddenly find how little we stand in need of the Precept of St. *Paul, Work out your salvation with fear and trembling.* That which is the cause of my Election, I hold to be the cause of my Salvation, which was the mercy and beneplacit of God, before I was, or the foundation of the World. *Before Abraham was, I am,* is the saying of Christ; yet is it true in some sense, if I say it of myself; for I was not onely before myself, but *Adam,* that is, in the Idea of God, and the decree of that Synod held from all Eternity. And in this sense, I say, the World was before the Creation, and at an end before it had a beginning; and thus was I dead before I was alive: though my grave be *England,* my dying place was Paradise; and *Eve* miscarried of me, before she conceiv'd of Cain.

## LX

Insolent zeals that do decry good Works, and rely onely upon Faith, take not away merit: for depending upon the efficacy of their Faith, they enforce the condition of God, and in a more sophistical way do seem to challenge Heaven. It was decreed by God, that only those that lapt in the water like Dogs, should have the honour to destroy the *Midianites;* yet could none of those justly challenge, or imagine he deserved that honour thereupon. I do not deny, but that true Faith, and such as God requires, is not onely a mark or token, but also a means of our Salvation; but where to find this, is as obscure to me, as my last end. And if our Saviour could object unto his own Disciples and Favourites, a Faith, that, to the quantity of a grain of Mustard-seed, is able to remove Mountains; surely that which we boast of, is not any thing, or at the most, but a remove from nothing. This is the Tenor of my belief; wherein, though there be many things singular, and to the humour of my irregular self; yet if they square not with maturer Judgements I disclaim them, and do no further favour them, than the learned and best judgements shall authorize them.

## The Second Part

### I

Now for that other Virtue of Charity, without which Faith is a meer notion, and of no existence, I have ever endeavoured to nourish the merciful disposition and humane inclination I borrowed from my Parents, and regulate it to the written and prescribed Laws of Charity; and if I hold the true Anatomy of my self, I am delineated and naturally framed to such a piece of virtue. For I am of a constitution so general, that it comforts and sympathizeth with all things; I have no antipathy, or rather Idio-syncrasie, in dyet, humour, air, any thing: I wonder not at the *French* for their dishes of Frogs, Snails, and Toadstools, nor at the Jews for Locusts and Grasshoppers; but being amongst them, make them my common Viands, and I find they agree with my Stomach as well as theirs. I could digest a Sallad gathered in a Churchyard, as well as in a Garden. I cannot start at the presence of a Serpent, Scorpion, Lizard, or Salamander: at the sight of a Toad or Viper, I find in me no desire to take up a stone to destroy them. I feel not in my self those common Antipathies that I can discover in others: Those National repugnances do not touch me, nor do I behold with prejudice the *French, Italian, Spaniard,* or *Dutch;* but where I find their actions in balance with my Country-men's, I honour, love, and embrace them in the same degree. I was born in the eighth Climate, but seem for to be framed and constellated unto all: I am no Plant that will not prosper out of a Garden: All places, all airs make unto me one Countrey; I am in *England,* every where, and under any Meridian. I have been shipwrackt, yet am not enemy with the Sea or Winds; I can study, play, or sleep in a Tempest. In brief, I am averse from nothing; my Conscience would give me the lye if I should absolutely detest or hate any essence but the Devil; or so at least abhor any thing, but that we might come to composition. If there be any among those common objects of hatred I do contemn and laugh at, it is that great enemy of Reason, Virtue and Religion, the Multitude; that numerous piece of monstrosity, which taken asunder seem men, and the reasonable creatures of God; but confused together, make but one great beast, and a monstrosity more prodigious than Hydra: it is no breach of Charity to call these Fools;

409

it is the style all holy Writers have afforded them, set down by *Solomon* in Canonical Scripture, and a point of our Faith to believe so. Neither in the name of Multitude do I only include the base and minor sort of people; there is a rabble even amongst the Gentry, a sort of Plebeian heads, whose fancy moves with the same wheel as these; men in the same Level with Mechanicks, though their fortunes do somewhat guild their infirmities, and their purses compound for their follies. But as in casting account, three or four men together come short in account of one man placed by himself below them: So neither are a troop of these ignorant Doradoes, of that true esteem and value, as many a forlorn person, whose condition doth place him below their feet. Let us speak like Politicians, there is a Nobility without Heraldry, a natural dignity, whereby one man is ranked with another; another filed before him, according to the quality of his Desert, and preheminence of his good parts: Though the corruption of these times, and the bias of present practice wheel another way. Thus it was in the first and primitive Commonwealths, and is yet in the integrity and Cradle of well-order'd Polities, till corruption getteth ground, ruder desires labouring after that which wiser considerations contemn; every one having a liberty to amass and heap up riches, and they a licence or faculty to do or purchase any thing.

## II

This general and indifferent temper of mine doth more neerly dispose me to this noble virtue. It is a happiness to be born and framed unto virtue, and to grow up from the seeds of nature, rather than the inoculation and forced graffs of education: yet if we are directed only by our particular Natures, and regulate our inclinations by no higher rule than that of our reasons, we are but Moralists; Divinity will still call us Heathens. Therefore this great work of charity must have other motives, ends, and impulsions: I give no alms only to satisfie the hunger of my Brother, but to fulfil and accomplish the Will and Command of my God: I draw not my purse for his sake that demands it, but his that enjoyned it; I relieve no man upon the Rhetorick of his miseries, nor to content mine own commiserating disposition: for this is still but moral charity, and an act that oweth more to passion than reason. He that relieves another upon the bare suggestion and bowels of pity, doth not this so much for his sake, as for his own; for by compassion we make others misery our own, and so by relieving them, we relieve our selves also. It is as erroneous a conceit to redress other Mens misfortunes upon the common considerations of merciful natures, that it may be one day our own case; for this is a sinister and politick kind of charity, whereby we seem to bespeak the pities of men in the like occasions: and truly I have observed that those professed Eleemosynaries, though in a croud or multitude, do yet direct and place their petitions on a few and selected persons: there is surely a Physiognomy, which those experienced and Master Mendicants observe; whereby they instantly discover a merciful aspect, and will single out a face, wherein they spy the signatures and marks of Mercy: for there are mystically in our faces certain Characters which carry in them the motto of our Souls, wherein he that can read *A.B.C.* may read our natures. I hold moreover that there is a Phytognomy, or Physiognomy, not only of Men but of Plants and Vegetables; and in every one of them, some outward figures which hang as signs or bushes of their inward forms. The Finger of God hath left an Inscription upon all his works, not graphical, or composed of Letters, but of their several forms, constitutions, parts, and operations; which aptly joyned together do make one word that doth express their natures. By these Letters God calls the Stars by their names; and by this Alphabet *Adam* assigned to every creature a name peculiar to its nature. Now there are, besides these Characters in our Faces, certain mystical figures in our Hands, which I dare not call meer dashes, strokes *a la volee,* or at random, because delineated by a Pencil that never works in vain; and hereof I take more particular notice, because I carry that in mine own hand, which I could never read of, nor discover in another. *Aristotle* I confess, in his acute and singular Book of Physiognomy, hath made no mention of Chiromancy; yet I believe the *Egyptians,* who were neerer addicted to those abstruse and mystical sciences, had a knowledge therein; to which those vagabond and counterfeit *Egyptians* did after pretend, and perhaps retained a few corrupted principles, which sometimes might verifie their prognosticks.

It is the common wonder of all men, how among so many millions of faces, there should be none alike: Now contrary, I wonder as much how there should be any. He that shall consider how many thousand several words have been carelessly and without study composed out of 24 Letters; withal, how many hundred lines there are to be drawn in the Fabrick of one Man; shall easily find that this variety is necessary: And it will be very hard that they shall so concur, as to make one portract like another. Let a Painter carelessly limb out a million of Faces, and you shall find them all different; yea let him have his Copy before him, yet after all his art there will remain a sensible distinction; for the pattern or example of every thing is the perfectest in that kind, whereof we still come short, though we transcend or go beyond it, because herein it is wide, and agrees not in all points unto the Copy. Nor doth the similitude of Creatures disparage the variety of Nature, nor any way confound the Works of God. For even in things alike there is diversity; and those that do seem to accord, do manifestly disagree. And thus is man like God; for in the same things that we resemble him, we are utterly different from him. There was never any thing so like another, as in all points to concur; there will ever some reserved difference slip in, to prevent the identity, without which, two several things would not be alike, but the same, which is impossible.

## III

But to return from Philosophy to Charity: I hold not so narrow a conceit of this virtue, as to conceive that to give Alms is onely to be Charitable, or think a piece of Liberality can comprehend the Total of Charity. Divinity hath wisely divided the act thereof into many branches, and hath taught us in this narrow way, many paths unto goodness: as many ways as we may do good, so many ways we may be charitable: there are infirmities, not onely of Body, but of Soul, and Fortunes, which do require the merciful hand of our abilities. I cannot contemn a man for ignorance, but behold him with as much pity as I do *Lazarus.* It is no greater Charity to cloath his body, than apparel the nakedness of his Soul. It is an honourable object to see the reasons of other men wear our Liveries, and their borrowed understandings do homage to the bounty of ours: It is the cheapest way of beneficence, and like the natural charity of the Sun, illuminates another without obscuring it self. To be reserved and caitiff in this part of goodness, is the sordidest piece of covetousness, and more contemptible than pecuniary Avarice. To this (as calling my self a Scholar) I am obliged by the duty of my condition: I make not therefore my head a grave, but a treasure of knowledge; I intend no Monopoly, but a community in learning; I study not for my own sake only, but for theirs that study not for themselves. I envy no man that knows more than my self, but pity them that know less. I instruct no man as an exercise of my knowledge, or with an intent rather to nourish and keep it alive in mine own head, then beget and propagate it in his; and in the midst of all my endeavours, there is but one thought that dejects me, that my acquired parts must perish with my self, nor can be Legacied among my honoured Friends. I cannot fall out, or contemn a man for an errour, or conceive why a difference in Opinion should divide an affection: For Controversies, Disputes, and Argumentations, both in Philosophy and in Divinity, if they meet with discreet and peaceable natures, do not infringe the Laws of Charity: in all disputes, so much as there is of passion, so much there is of nothing to the purpose; for then Reason, like a bad Hound, spends upon a false Scent, and forsakes the question first started. And this is one reason why Controversies are never determined; for though they be amply proposed, they are scarce at all handled, they do so swell with unnecessary Digressions; and the Parenthesis on the party, is often as large as the main discourse upon the subject. The Foundations of Religion are already established, and the Principles of Salvation subscribed unto by all: there remains not many controversies worth a Passion, and yet never any disputed without, not only in Divinity, but inferiour Arts: What a βατραχομυομαχία* and hot skirmish is betwixt S. and T. in *Lucian:*† How do Grammarians hack and slash for the Genitive case in *Jupiter?* How do they break their own pates to salve that of *Priscian! Si foret in terris, rideret Democritus.*‡ Yea, even amongst wiser militants, how many wounds have been given, and credits slain, for the poor victory of an opinion, or beggerly conquest of a distinction? Scholars are men of Peace, they bear no Arms, but their tongues are sharper than Actus his razor; their Pens carry farther, and give a lowder report than Thunder: I had rather stand the shock of a Basilisco, than the fury of a merciless Pen. It is not meer Zeal to Learning, or Devotion to the Muses, that wiser Princes Patron the Arts, and carry an indulgent aspect unto Scholars; but a desire to have their names eternized by the memory of their writings, and a fear of the revengeful Pen of succeeding ages: for these are the men, that when they have played their parts, and had their *exits,* must step out and give the moral of their Scenes, and deliver unto Posterity an Inventory of their Virtues and Vices. And surely there goes a great deal of Conscience to the compiling of an History: there is no reproach to the scandal of a Story; it is such an authentick kind of falsehood, that with authority belies our good names to all Nations and Posterity.

## IV

There is another offence unto Charity, which no Author hath ever written of, and few take notice of; and that's the reproach, not of whole professions, mysteries and conditions, but of whole Nations; wherein by opprobrious Epithets we miscal each other, and by an uncharitable Logick, from a disposition in a few, conclude a habit in all.

*Le mutin Anglois, & le bravache Escossois;*
*Le bougre Italian, & le fol François;*
*Le poultron Romain, le larron de Gascongne,*
*L'Espagnol superbe, & l'Aleman yvrongne.*§

St. *Paul,* that calls the *Cretians* lyars, doth it but indirectly, and upon quotation of their own Poet. It is as bloody a thought in one way, as *Nero's* was in another. For by a word we wound a thousand, and at one blow assassine the honour of a Nation. It is as compleat a piece of madness to miscal and rave against the times, or think to recal men to reason, by a fit of passion: *Democritus,* that thought to laugh the times into goodness, seems to me as deeply Hypochondriack, as *Heraclitus* that bewailed them. It

---

\* Battle of the frogs and mice.

† *Judicium Vocalium (Trial before the Vowels).* The letter S accuses T of interfering with the other consonants.

‡ If he were on earth, Democritus would laugh.

§ The stubborn Englishman, the swaggering Scot, the blackguard Italian, the foolish Frenchman, the cowardly Roman, the Gascon thief, the proud Spaniard, and the drunken German.

moves not my spleen to behold the multitude in their proper humours, that is, in their fits of folly and madness, as well understanding that wisdom is not prophan'd unto the World, and 'tis the priviledge of a few to be Vertuous. They that endeavour to abolish Vice, destroy also Virtue; for contraries, though they destroy one another, are yet in life of one another. Thus Virtue (abolish vice) is an Idea; again, the community of sin doth not disparage goodness; for when Vice gains upon the major part, Virtue, in whom it remains, becomes more excellent; and being lost in some, multiplies its goodness in others, which remain untouched, and persist intire in the general inundation. I can therefore behold Vice without a Satyr, content only with an admonition, or instructive reprehension, for Noble Natures, and such as are capable of goodness, are railed into vice, that might as easily be admonished into virtue; and we should be all so far the Orators of goodness, as to protract her from the power of Vice, and maintain the cause of injured truth. No man can justly censure or condemn another, because indeed no man truly knows another. This I perceive in my self; for I am in the dark to all the world, and my nearest friends behold me but in a cloud: those that know me but superficially, think less of me than I do of my self; those of my neer acquaintance think more; God, who truly knows me, knows that I am nothing; for he only beholds me and all the world; who looks not on us through a derived ray, or a trajection of a sensible species, but beholds the substance without the helps of accidents, and the forms of things, as we their operations. Further, no man can judge another, because no man knows himself; for we censure others but as they disagree from that humour which we fancy laudible in our selves, and commend others but for that wherein they seem to quadrate and consent with us. So that in conclusion, all is but that we all condemn, Self-love. 'Tis the general complaint of these times, and perhaps of those past, that charity grows cold; which I perceive most verified in those which most do manifest the fires and flames of zeal; for it is a virtue that best agrees with coldest natures, and such as are complexioned for humility. But how shall we expect Charity towards others, when we are uncharitable to our selves? Charity begins at home, is the voice of the World; yet is every man his greatest enemy, and as it were, his own Executioner. *Non occides,* is the Commandment of God, yet scarce observed by any man; for I perceive every man his own *Atropos,* and lends a hand to cut the thred of his own days. *Cain* was not therefore the first Murtherer, but *Adam,* who brought in death; whereof he beheld the practice and example in his own son *Abel,* and saw that verified in the experience of another, which faith could not perswade him in the Theory of himself.

## V

There is, I think, no man that apprehends his own miseries less than my self, and no man that so neerly apprehends anothers. I could lose an arm without a tear, and with few groans, methinks, be quartered into pieces; yet can I weep most seriously at a Play, and receive with true passion, the counterfeit grief of those known and professed Impostures. It is a barbarous part of inhumanity to add unto any afflicted parties misery, or indeavour to multiply in any man, a passion, whose single nature is already above his patience: this was the greatest affliction of *Job;* and those oblique expostulations of his Friends, a deeper injury than the down-right blows of the Devil. It is not the tears of our own eyes only, but of our friends also, that do exhaust the current of our sorrows; which falling into many streams, runs more peaceably, and is contented with a narrower channel. It is an act within the power of charity, to translate a passion out of one brest into another, and to divide a sorrow almost out of it self; for an affliction, like a dimension, may be so divided, as if not indivisible, at least to become insensible. Now with my friend I desire not to share or participate, but to engross, his sorrows; that by making them mine own, I may more easily discuss them; for in mine own reason, and within my self, I can command that, which I cannot intreat without my self, and within the circle of another. I have often thought those noble pairs and examples of friendship not so truly Histories of what had been, as fictions of what should be; but I now perceive nothing in them but possibilities, nor any thing in the Heroick examples of *Damon* and *Pythias*, *Achilles* and *Patroclus*, which methinks upon some grounds I could not perform within the narrow compass of my self. That a man should lay down his life for his Friend, seems strange to vulgar affections, and such as confine themselves within that Worldly principle, Charity begins at home. For mine own part I could never remember the relations that I held unto my self, nor the respect that I owe unto my own nature, in the cause of God, my Country, and my Friends. Next to these three I do embrace my self: I confess I do not observe that order that the Schools ordain our affections, to love our Parents, Wives, Children, and then our Friends; for excepting the injunctions of Religion, I do not find in my self such a necessary and indissoluble Sympathy to all those of my blood. I hope I do not break the fifth Commandment, if I conceive I may love my friend before the nearest of my blood, even those to whom I owe the principles of life: I never yet cast a true affection on a woman, but I have loved my friend as I do virtue, my soul, my God. From hence me thinks I do conceive how God loves man, what happiness there is in the love of God. Omitting all other, there are three most mystical unions, two natures in one person; three persons in one nature; one soul in two bodies. For though indeed they be really divided, yet are they so united, as they seem but one, and make rather a duality than two distinct souls.

## VI

There are wonders in true affection; it is a body of *Enigma's*, mysteries, and riddles; wherein two so become one, as they both become two: I love my friend before my self, and yet methinks I do not love him enough: some few months hence, my multiplied affection will make me believe I have not loved him at all: when I am from him, I am dead till I be with him; when I am with him, I am not satisfied, but would still be nearer him. United souls are not satisfied with imbraces, but desire to be truly each other; which being impossible, their desires are infinite, and must proceed without a possibility of satisfaction. Another misery there is in affection, that whom we truly love like our own, we forget their looks, nor can our memory retain the Idea of their faces; and it is no wonder, for they are our selves, and our affection makes their looks our own. This noble affection falls not on vulgar and common constitutions, but on such as are mark'd for virtue: he that can love his friend with this noble ardour, will in a competent degree affect all. Now if we can bring our affections to look beyond the body, and cast an eye upon the soul, we have found out the true object, not only of friendship, but Charity; and the greatest happiness that we can bequeath the soul, is that wherein we all do place our last felicity, Salvation; which though it be not in our power to bestow, it is in our charity and pious invocations to desire, if not procure and further. I cannot contentedly frame a prayer for my self in particular, without a catalogue for my friends; nor request a happiness wherein my sociable disposition doth not desire the fellowship of my neighbour. I never hear the Toll of a passing Bell, though in my mirth, without my prayers and best wishes for the departing spirit: I cannot go to cure the body of my patient, but I forget my profession, and call unto God for his soul: I cannot see one say his prayers, but in stead of imitating him, I fall into a supplication for him, whe perhaps is no more to me than a common nature: and if God hath vouchsafed an ear to my supplications, there are surely many happy that never saw me, and enjoy the blessing of mine unknown devotions. To pray for Enemies, that is, for their salvation, is no harsh precept, but the practice of our daily and ordinary devotions. I cannot believe the story of the Italian:* our bad wishes and uncharitable desires proceed no further than this life; it is the Devil, and the uncharitable votes of Hell, that desire our misery in the World to come.

## VII

To do no injury, nor take none, was a principle, which to my former years, and impatient affections, seemed to contain enough of Morality; but my more setled years, and Christian constitution, have fallen upon severer resolutions. I can hold there is no such thing as injury; that if there be, there is no such injury as revenge, and no such revenge as the contempt of an injury: that to hate another, is to malign himself; that the truest way to love another, is to despise our selves. I were unjust unto mine own Conscience, if I should say I am at variance with any thing like my self. I find there are many pieces in this one fabrick of man; this frame is raised upon a mass of Antipathies: I am one methinks, but as the World; wherein notwithstanding there are a swarm of distinct essences, and in them another World of contrarieties; we carry private and domestick enemies within, publick and more hostile adversaries without. The Devil, that did but buffet St. *Paul*, plays methinks at sharp with me. Let me be nothing, if within the compass of my self I do not find the battail of *Lepanto*, Passion against Reason, Reason against Faith, Faith against the Devil, and my Conscience against all. There is another man within me, that's angry with me, rebukes, commands, and dastards me. I have no Conscience of Marble, to resist the hammer of more heavy offences; nor yet too soft and waxen, as to take the im-

pression of each single peccadillo or scape of infirmity: I am of a strange belief, that it is as easie to be forgiven some sins, as to commit some others. For my Original sin, I hold it to be washed away in my Baptism, for my actual transgressions, I compute and reckon with God, but from my last repentance, Sacrament, or general absolution; and therefore am not terrified with the sins or madness of my youth. I thank the goodness of God, I have no sins that want a name; I am not singular in offences; my transgressions are Epidemical, and from the common breath of our corruption. For there are certain tempers of body, which matcht with an humorous depravity of mind, do hatch and produce vitiosities, whose newness and monstrosity of nature admits no name; this was the temper of that Lecher that carnal'd with a Statua, and constitution of *Nero* in his Spintrian recreations. For the Heavens are not only fruitful in new and unheard-of stars, the Earth in plants and animals; but mens minds also in villany and vices: now the dulness of my reason, and the vulgarity of my disposition, never prompted my invention, nor sollicited my affection unto any of those; yet even those common and quotidian infirmities that so necessarily attend me, and do seem to be my very nature, have so dejected me, so broken the estimation that I should have otherwise of my self, that I repute my self the most abjectest piece of mortality. Divines prescribe a fit of sorrow to repentance; there goes indignation, anger, sorrow, hatred, into mine; passions of a contrary nature, which neither seem to sute with this action, nor my proper constitution. It is no breach of charity to our selves, to be at variance with our Vices; nor to abhor that part of us, which is an enemy to the ground of charity our God; wherein we do but imitate our great selves the world, whose divided Antipathies and contrary faces do

---

* A man who killed his enemy after inducing him to blaspheme, so that he would go to hell.

yet carry a charitable regard unto the whole by their particular discords, preserving the common harmony, and keeping in fetters those powers, whose rebellions once Masters, might be the ruine of all.

## VIII

I thank God, amongst those millions of Vices I do inherit and hold from *Adam*, I have escaped one, and that a mortal enemy to Charity, the first and fa[r]ther-sin, not onely of man, but of the devil, Pride; a vice whose name is comprehended in a Monosyllable, but in its nature not circumscribed with a World. I have escaped it in a condition that can hardly avoid it. Those petty acquisitions and reputed perfections that advance and elevate the conceits of other men, add no feathers unto mine. I have seen a Grammarian towr and plume himself over a single line in *Horace,* and shew more pride in the construction of one Ode, than the Author in the composure of the whole book. For my own part, besides the *Jargon* and *Patois* of several Provinces, I understand no less than six Languages; yet I protest I have no higher conceit of my self, than had our Fathers before the confusion of *Babel,* when there was but one Language in the World, and none to boast himself either Linguist or Critick. I have not onely seen several Countries, beheld the nature of their Climes, the Chorography of their Provinces, Topography of their Cities, but understood their several Laws, Customs, and Policies; yet cannot all this perswade the dulness of my spirit unto such an opinion of my self, as I behold in nimbler and conceited heads, that never looked a degree beyond their Nests. I know the names, and somewhat more, of all the constellations in my Horizon; yet I have seen a prating Mariner, that could only name the pointers and the North Star, out-talk me, and conceit himself a whole Sphere above me. I know most of the Plants of my

Countrey, and of those about me; yet methinks I do not know so many as when I did but know a hundred, and had scarcely ever Simpled further than *Cheapside.* For indeed, heads of capacity, and such as are not full with a handful, or easie measure of knowledge, think they know nothing, till they know all; which being impossible, they fall upon the opinion of *Socrates,* and only know they know not any thing. I cannot think that *Homer* pin'd away upon the riddle of the fishermen; or that *Aristotle,* who understood the uncertainty of knowledge, and confessed so often the reason of man too weak for the works of nature, did ever drown himself upon the flux and reflux of *Euripus.* We do but learn to-day, what our better advanced judgements will unteach tomorrow; and *Aristotle* doth but instruct us, as *Plato* did him; that is, to confute himself. I have run through all sorts, yet find no rest in any: though our first studies and *junior* endeavours may style us Peripateticks, Stoicks, or Academicks, yet I perceive the wisest heads prove, at last, almost all Scepticks, and stand like *Janus* in the field of knowledge. I have therefore one common and authentick Philosophy I learned in the Schools, whereby I discourse and satisfie the reason of other men; another more reserved, and drawn from experience, whereby I content mine own. *Solomon,* that complained of ignorance in the height of knowledge, hath not only humbled my conceits, but discouraged my endeavours. There is yet another conceit that hath sometimes made me shut my books, which tells me it is a vanity to waste our days in the blind pursuit of knowledge; it is but attending a little longer, and we shall enjoy that by instinct and infusion which we endeavour at here by labour and inquisition. It is better to sit down in a modest ignorance, and rest contented with the natural blessing of our own reasons, than buy the uncertain knowledge of this life, with sweat and vexation, which Death gives every fool *gratis,* and is an accessary of our glorification.

## IX

I was never yet once, and commend their resolutions who never marry twice: not that I disallow of second marriage; as neither in all cases, of Polygamy, which considering some times, and the unequal number of both sexes, may be also necessary. The whole World was made for man, but the twelfth part of man for woman: Man is the whole World, and the Breath of God; Woman the Rib and crooked piece of man. I could be content that we might procreate like trees, without conjunction, or that there were any way to perpetuate the World without this trivial and vulgar way of coition; it is the foolishest act a wise man commits in all his life; nor is there any thing that will more deject his cool'd imagination, when he shall consider what an odd and unworthy piece of folly he hath committed. I speak not in prejudice, nor am averse from that sweet Sex, but naturally amorous of all that is beautiful; I can look a whole day with delight upon a handsome Picture, though it be but of an Horse. It is my temper, and I like it the better, to affect all harmony; and sure there is musick even in the beauty, and the silent note which *Cupid* strikes, far sweeter than the sound of an instrument. For there is a musick where ever there is a harmony, order or proportion; and thus far we may maintain the musick of the Sphears: for those well-ordered motions, and regular paces, though they give no sound unto the ear, yet to the understanding they strike a note most full of harmony. Whosoever is harmonically composed, delights in harmony; which makes me much distrust the symmetry of those heads which declaim against all Church-Musick. For my self, not only from my obedience, but my particular Genius, I do embrace it: for even that vulgar and

Tavern-Musick, which makes one man merry, another mad, strikes in me a deep fit of devotion, and a profound contemplation of the first Composer. There is something in it of Divinity more than the ear discovers: it is an Hieroglyphical and shadowed lesson of the whole World, and creatures of God; such a melody to the ear, as the whole World well understood, would afford the understanding. In brief, it is a sensible fit of that harmony, which intellectually sounds in the ears of God. I will not say with *Plato,* the soul is an harmony, but harmonical, and hath its nearest sympathy unto Musick: thus some whose temper of body agrees, and humours the constitution of their souls, are born Poets, though indeed all are naturally inclined unto Rhythme. This made *Tacitus* in the very first line of his Story,[10] fall upon a verse, and *Cicero* the worst of Poets, but declaiming for a Poet, falls in the very first sentence upon a perfect Hexameter.[11] I feel not in me those sordid and unchristian desires of my profession; I do not secretly implore and wish for Plagues, rejoyce at Famines, revolve Ephemerides and Almanacks, in expectation of malignant Aspects, fatal Conjunctions, and Eclipses: I rejoyce not at unwholesome Springs, nor unseasonable Winters; my Prayer goes with the Husbandman's; I desire every thing in its proper season, that neither men nor the times be put out of temper. Let me be sick my self, if sometimes the malady of my patient be not a disease unto me; I desire rather to cure his infirmities than my own necessities: where I do him no good, methinks it is scarce honest gain; though I confess 'tis but the worthy salary of our

---

10 *Urbem Romam in principio Reges Habuere* [Rome at the beginning was ruled by kings]. *The Annals* 1; *GBWW,* Vol. 15, p. 1.

11 *In qua me non inficior mediocriter esse* [I do not deny that I have had more than usual practice (in the oratorical art)], from *Pro Archia Poeta.*

well-intended endeavours. I am not only ashamed, but heartily sorry, that besides death, there are diseases incurable; yet not for my own sake, or that they be beyond my Art, but for the general cause and sake of humanity, whose common cause I apprehend as mine own. And to speak more generally, those three Noble Professions which all civil Commonwealths do honour, are raised upon the fall of *Adam,* and are not exempt from their infirmities; there are not only diseases incurable in Physick, but cases indissolvable in Laws, Vices incorrigible in Divinity: if general Councils may err, I do not see why particular Courts should be infallible; their perfectest rules are raised upon the erroneous reasons of Man; and the Laws of one, do but condemn the rules of another; as *Aristotle* ofttimes the opinions of his Predecessours, because, though agreeable to reason, yet were not consonant to his own rules, and Logick of his proper Principles. Again, to speak nothing of the Sin against the Holy Ghost, whose cure not onely, but whose nature is unknown; I can cure the Gout or Stone in some, sooner than Divinity Pride or Avarice in others. I can cure Vices by Physick, when they remain incurable by Divinity; and shall obey my Pills, when they contemn their precepts. I boast nothing, but plainly say, we all labour against our own cure; for death is the cure of all diseases. There is no Catholicon or universal remedy I know but this, which, though nauseous to queasie stomachs, yet to prepared appetites is Nectar, and a pleasant potion of immortality.

## X

For my Conversation, it is like the Sun's with all men, and with a friendly aspect to good and bad. Methinks there is no man bad, and the worst, best; that is, while they are kept within the circle of those qualities, wherein they are good; there is no man's mind of such discordant and jarring a temper, to which a tunable dis-

position may not strike a harmony. *Magnæ virtutes, nec minora vitia;** it is the posie of the best natures, and may be inverted on the worst; there are in the most depraved and venemous dispositions, certain pieces that remain untoucht, which by an *Antiperistasis* become more excellent, or by the excellency of their antipathies are able to preserve themselves from the contagion of their enemy vices, and persist intire beyond the general corruption. For it is also thus in nature. The greatest Balsomes do lie enveloped in the bodies of most powerful Corrosives; I say moreover, and I ground upon experience, that poisons contain within themselves their own Antidote, and that which preserves them from the venome of themselves, without which they were not deleterious to others onely, but to themselves also. But it is the corruption that I fear within me, not the contagion of commerce without me. 'Tis that unruly regiment within me, that will destroy me; 'tis I that do infect my self; the man without a Navel yet lives in me; I feel that original canker corrode and devour me; and therefore *Defenda me* Dios *de me,* Lord deliver me from my self, is a part of my Letany, and the first voice of my retired imaginations. There is no man alone, because every man is a *Microcosm,* and carries the whole World about him; *Nunquam minus solus quam cum solus,†* though it be the Apothegme of a wise man, is yet true in the mouth of a fool; indeed, though in a Wilderness, a man is never alone, not only because he is with himself and his own thoughts, but because he is with the Devil, who ever consorts with our solitude, and is that unruly rebel that musters up those disordered motions which accompany our sequestred imaginations. And to speak more narrowly, there is no such thing as solitude, nor any thing that can be said to be alone and by itself, but God, who is his

---

* Great virtues, nor less vices.

† Never less alone than when alone.

own circle, and can subsist by himself; all others, besides their dissimilary and Heterogeneous parts, which in a manner multiply their natures, cannot subsist without the concourse of God, and the society of that hand which doth uphold their natures. In brief, there can be nothing truly alone and by it self, which is not truly one; and such is only God: All others do transcend an unity, and so by consequence are many.

## XI

Now for my life, it is a miracle of thirty years, which to relate, were not a History, but a piece of Poetry, and would sound to common ears like a Fable; for the World, I count it not an Inn, but an Hospital; and a place not to live, but to dye in. The world that I regard is my self; it is the Microcosm of my own frame that I cast mine eye on; for the other, I use it but like my Globe, and turn it round sometimes for my recreation. Men that look upon my outside, perusing only my condition and Fortunes, do err in my Altitude, for I am above *Atlas* his shoulders. The earth is a point not only in respect of the Heavens above us, but of that heavenly and celestial part within us: that mass of Flesh that circumscribes me, limits not my mind: that surface that tells the Heavens it hath an end, cannot persuade me I have any: I take my circle to be above three hundred and sixty; though the number of the Ark do measure my body, it comprehendeth not my mind: whilst I study to find how I am a Microcosm, or little World, I find my self something more than the great. There is surely a piece of Divinity in us, something that was before the Elements, and owes no homage unto the Sun. Nature tells me I am the Image of God, as well as Scripture: he that understands not thus much, hath not his introduction or first lesson, and is yet to begin the Alphabet of man. Let me not injure the felicity of others, if I say I am as happy as any: *Ruat cælum, Fiat voluntas tua,** 

salveth all; so that whatsoever happens, it is but what our daily prayers desire. In brief, I am content, and what should providence add more? Surely this is it we call Happiness, and this do I enjoy; with this I am happy in a dream, and as content to enjoy a happiness in a fancy, as others in a more apparent truth and realty. There is surely a neerer apprehension of any thing that delights us in our dreams, than in our waked senses; without this I were unhappy: for my awaked judgment discontents me, ever whispering unto me, that I am from my friend; but my friendly dreams in night requite me, and make me think I am within his arms. I thank God for my happy dreams, as I do for my good rest, for there is a satisfaction in them unto reasonable desires, and such as can be content with a fit of happiness. And surely it is not a melancholy conceit to think we are all asleep in this World, and that the conceits of this life are as meer dreams to those of the next, as the Phantasms of the night, to the conceits of the day. There is an equal delusion in both, and the one doth but seem to be the embleme or picture of the other; we are somewhat more than our selves in our sleeps, and the slumber of the body seems to be but the waking of the soul. It is the ligation of sense, but the liberty of reason, and our waking conceptions do not match the Fancies of our sleeps. At my Nativity, my Ascendant was the watery sign of *Scorpius;* I was born in the Planetary hour of *Saturn,* and I think I have a piece of that Leaden Planet in me. I am no way facetious, nor disposed for the mirth and galliardize of company; yet in one dream I can compose a whole Comedy, behold the action, apprehend the jests, and laugh my self awake at the conceits thereof: were my memory as faithful as my reason is then fruitful, I would never study but in my dreams; and this time also would

---

* Let thy will be done, though the heavens fall.

I chuse for my devotions: but our grosser memories have then so little hold of our abstracted understandings, that they forget the story, and can only relate to our awaked souls, a confused and broken tale of that that hath passed. *Aristotle,* who hath written a singular Tract of Sleep, hath not methinks throughly defined it; nor yet *Galen,* though he seem to have corrected it; for those *Noctambuloes* and night-walkers, though in their sleep, do yet injoy the action of their senses: we must therefore say that there is something in us that is not in the jurisdiction of *Morpheus;* and that those abstracted and ecstatick souls do walk about in their own corps, as spirits with the bodies they assume; wherein they seem to hear, and feel, though indeed the Organs are destitute of sense, and their natures of those faculties that should inform them. Thus it is observed, that men sometimes upon the hour of their departure, do speak and reason above themselves; for then the soul beginning to be freed from the ligaments of the body, begins to reason like her self, and to discourse in a strain above mortality.

## XII

We term sleep a death, and yet it is waking that kills us, and destroys those spirits that are the house of life. 'Tis indeed a part of life that best expresseth death; for every man truely lives, so long as he acts his nature, or some way makes good the faculties of himself: *Themistocles* therefore that slew his Soldier in his sleep, was a merciful Executioner: 'tis a kind of punishment the mildness of no laws hath invented; I wonder the fancy of *Lucan* and *Seneca* did not discover it. It is that death by which we may be literally said to dye daily; a death which *Adam* dyed before his mortality; a death whereby we live a middle and moderating point between life and death; in fine, so like death, I dare not trust it without my prayers, and an half adieu unto the World, and take my farewell in a Colloquy with God.

*The night is come, like to the day;*
*Depart not thou great God away.*
*Let not my sins, black as the night,*
*Eclipse the lustre of thy light.*
*Keep still in my Horizon; for to me*
*The Sun makes not the day, but thee.*
*Thou whose nature cannot sleep,*
*On my temples centry keep;*
*Guard me 'gainst those watchful foes,*
*Whose eyes are open while mine close.*
*Let no dreams my head infest,*
*But such as* Jacob's *temples blest.*
*While I do rest, my Soul advance;*
*Make my sleep a holy trance.*
*That I may, my rest being wrought,*
*Awake into some holy thought;*
*And with as active vigour run*
*My course, as doth the nimble Sun.*
*Sleep is a death; O make me try,*
*By sleeping, what it is to die:*
*And as gently lay my head*
*On my grave, as now my bed.*
*Howere I rest, great God, let me*
*Awake again at last with thee.*
*And thus assur'd, behold I lie*
*Securely, or to awake or die.*
*These are my drowsie days; in vain*
*I do now wake to sleep again:*
*O come that hour, when I shall never*
*Sleep again, but wake for ever.*

This is the Dormative I take to bedward; I need no other *Laudanum* than this to make me sleep; after which, I close mine eyes in security, content to take my leave of the Sun, and sleep unto the resurrection.

## XIII

The method I should use in distributive Justice, I often observe in commutative; and keep a Geometrical proportion in both; whereby becoming equable to others, I become unjust to my self, and supererogate in that common principle, *Do unto others as thou wouldst be done unto thy self.* I was not born unto riches, neither is it I think my Star to be wealthy; or if it were, the freedom of my mind, and frankness of my disposition, were able to contradict and cross my fates. For to me avarice seems not so much a vice, as a deplorable piece of madness; to conceive ourselves Urinals, or be perswaded that we are dead, is not so ridiculous, nor so many degrees beyond the power of Hellebore, as this. The opinion of Theory, and positions of men, are not so void of reason as their practised conclusions: some have held that Snow is black, that the earth moves, that the Soul is air, fire, water; but all this is Philosophy, and there is no *delirium,* if we do but speculate the folly and indisputable dotage of avarice, to that subterraneous Idol, and God of the Earth. I do confess I am an Atheist; I cannot perswade myself to honour that the World adores; whatsoever virtue its prepared substance may have within my body, it hath no influence nor operation without: I would not entertain a base design, or an action that should call me villain, for the Indies; and for this only do I love and honour my own soul, and have methinks two arms too few to embrace myself. *Aristotle* is too severe, that will not allow us to be truely liberal without wealth, and the bountiful hand of Fortune; if this be true, I must confess I am charitable only in my liberal intentions, and bountiful well-wishes. But if the example of the Mite be not only an act of wonder, but an example of the noblest Charity, surely poor men may also build Hospitals, and the rich alone have not erected Cathedrals. I have a private method which others observe not; I take the opportunity of my self to do good; I borrow occasion of Charity from mine own necessities, and supply the wants of others, when I am in most need my self; for it is an honest stratagem to make advantage of our selves, and so to husband the acts of vertue, that where they were defective in one circumstance, they may repay their want, and multiply their goodness in another. I have not *Peru* in my desires, but a competence, and ability to perform those good works to which he hath

inclined my nature. He is rich, who hath enough to be charitable; and it is hard to be so poor, that a noble mind may not find a way to this piece of goodness. *He that giveth to the poor, lendeth to the Lord;* there is more Rhetorick in that one sentence, than in a Library of Sermons; and indeed if those Sentences were understood by the Reader, with the same Emphasis as they are delivered by the Author, we needed not those Volumes of instructions, but might be honest by an Epitome. Upon this motive only I cannot behold a Beggar without relieving his Necessities with my Purse, or his Soul with my Prayers; these scenical and accidental differences between us, cannot make me forget that common and untoucht part of us both; there is under these *Cantoes* and miserable outsides, these mutilate and semi-bodies, a soul of the same alloy with our own, whose Genealogy is God as well as ours, and in as fair a way to Salvation as our selves. Statists that labour to contrive a Common-wealth without our poverty, take away the object of charity, not understanding only the Common-wealth of a Christian, but forgetting the prophecie of Christ.

## XIV

Now there is another part of charity, which is the Basis and Pillar of this, and that is the love of God, for whom we love our neighbour; for this I think charity, to love God for himself, and our neighbour for God. All that is truly amiable is God, or as it were a divided piece of him, that retains a reflex or shadow of himself. Nor is it strange that we should place affection on that which is invisible; all that we truly love is thus; what we adore under affection of our senses, deserves not the honour of so pure a title. Thus we adore virtue, though to the eyes of sense she be invisible: thus that part of our noble friends that we love, is not that part that we imbrace, but that insensible part that our arms cannot embrace. God being all goodness, can love nothing but himself, and the traduction of his holy Spirit. Let us call to assize the loves of our parents, the affection of our wives and children, and they are all dumb shows and dreams, without reality, truth or constancy: for first, there is a strong bond of affection between us and our Parents; yet how easily dissolved? We betake our selves to a woman, forget our mother in a wife, and the womb that bare us, in that that shall bear our Image: this woman blessing us with children, our affection leaves the level it held before, and sinks from our bed unto our issue and picture of Posterity, where affection holds no steady mansion. They, growing up in years, desire our ends; or applying themselves to a woman, take a lawful way to love another better than our selves. Thus I perceive a man may be buried alive, and behold his grave in his own issue.

## XV

I conclude therefore and say, there is no happiness under (or as *Copernicus* will have it, above) the Sun, nor any Crambe in that repeated verity and burthen of all the wisdom of *Solomon, All is vanity and vexation of Spirit.* There is no felicity in that the World adores: *Aristotle* whilst he labours to refute the Idea's of *Plato*, falls upon one himself: for his *summum bonum* is a *Chimæra*, and there is no such thing as his Felicity. That wherein God himself is happy, the holy Angels are happy, in whose defect the Devils are unhappy; that dare I call happiness: whatsoever conduceth unto this, may with an easy Metaphor deserve that name: whatsoever else the World terms Happiness, is to me a story out of *Pliny*, a tale of *Boccace* or *Malizspini;* an apparition or neat delusion, wherein there is no more of Happiness, than the name. Bless me in this life with but peace of my Conscience, command of my affections, the love of thy self and my dearest friends, and I shall be happy enough to pity *Cæsar*. These are, O Lord, the humble desires of my most reasonable ambition, and all I dare call happiness on earth; wherein I set no rule or limit to thy Hand or Providence; dispose of me according to the wisdom of thy pleasure. Thy will be done, though in my own undoing.

*Finis*

### NOTE TO THE READER

Browne ranges so far, in his discussion of the sort of religion he possesses, that any reader who wishes to follow him completely may well find himself obliged to go through the larger part of the *GBWW* readings that are listed in the *Syntopicon* under Chapter 29, GOD, Chapter 55, MEDICINE, and Chapter 79, RELIGION. For those who are less ambitious, it may be enough to consider some of the references under GOD 2*b,* concerning the evidences and proofs of God's existence; GOD 3*e,* which deals with the worship of God in various forms and ceremonies; and GOD 6*b* and 6*c,* where there are discussions of the kinds of knowledge men can have of God through metaphorical and symbolic representations and from the evidence of nature. In addition, see RELIGION 1*a,* for readings on the nature, the causes, and the conditions of faith; RELIGION 1*b,* for discussions of the sources of religious belief; and RELIGION 6*g,* where references are given to works in which the relation between sacred doctrine and secular learning is considered, and where the conflict between science and religion is addressed.

A chapter from Browne's *Hydriotaphia (Urn-Burial)* appears in *GGB,* Vol. 10, pp. 575–80. Browne's style, which appears there in nearly its richest and most elaborate development, may be contrasted with that of Sir Francis Bacon, some of whose essays are reprinted in the same volume of *GGB* (pp. 346–60). This volume, incidentally, also contains William James's essay "The Will to Believe" (pp. 39–57), which as the work of a scientist of a much later age offers a substantive contrast to *Religio Medici* as well as a stylistic one.

Browne is often referred to as a skeptic. To many people this is likely to mean that he was a man who believed in nothing, whereas it should rather be understood to mean that he could believe in everything. For a discussion of that kind of skepticism, see Emerson's essay on Montaigne, which appears in *GGB,* Vol. 10, pp. 546–62.

# She Stoops to Conquer

Oliver  Goldsmith

## Editor's Introduction

If one were to cast about among writers of enduring works for a contrast to Sir Thomas Browne, whose *Religio Medici,* or "The Religion of a Doctor," appears elsewhere in this volume, it would be unnecessary to look beyond Oliver Goldsmith (ca. 1730–74). Two men could hardly have been more different in their circumstances, their characters, and the writings they produced. Browne's family background was comfortable, his education and upbringing as good as anything his times afforded. Goldsmith was the son of an impoverished Irish curate who was able to send him only on inferior terms to Trinity College, Dublin, where he was unfortunate in his tutors and indifferent to his studies. Like Browne, Goldsmith went on to become a doctor (or to profess that he was a doctor; in fact his training was obscure, his skill dubious, and his attempts at practice unsuccessful), and he likewise traveled extensively abroad (he made the Grand Tour on foot, without a penny in his pocket, carrying only a flute which he played for his supper). Unlike Browne, however, who afterward settled quietly into the provincial atmosphere of Norwich, Goldsmith, whose life until he was thirty had been largely one of vagabondage, gravitated to London. There he managed, uncouth and unlearned as he was, and perpetually improvident, to make a living with his pen. Moreover, by virtue of his wit and his charm, and on the strength of the writings he turned out, beginning about 1760, he was taken into the society of intellectuals and aristocrats, among them Boswell, Dr. Johnson, Edmund Burke, David Garrick, and Sir Joshua Reynolds, who became his friends. For ten years or so he was the most popular and perhaps the best paid of English literary figures. When he died at the early age of forty-four, nevertheless deeply in debt and otherwise, too, unchanged in his feckless ways, he was more famous than anybody except Johnson himself, who composed a fine and heartfelt epitaph for him in Westminster Abbey, where, much loved and greatly mourned, he was given a place in the Poets' Corner.

Of the three works, one of them a poem, another a novel, and the third a play, for which Goldsmith is best known—*The Deserted Village, The Vicar of Wakefield,* and *She Stoops to Conquer*—none would have been conceivable in Browne's century, or indeed at any time before the rise of a middle class and the development of a sentimental consciousness. But even if they had been, it is not conceivable that Browne could have

425

written them. His style—that rich, elaborate, baroque way he had of talking—was utterly unsuited to the task Goldsmith undertook, which was to depict human existence not in its religious or philosophical aspects but in social and familiar terms. For this a very different style was required, as Goldsmith himself observed in an early essay that urged his contemporaries, "instead of writing finely," to "try to write naturally." Such was the way he wrote himself, both in prose and in verse, sounding a clear, even tone that never strains for effects, that seems hardly aware of itself. The result is something famous in its own right, as indicating a regard for everything simple, human, and affecting, a scorn of all pretense and sham.

Possibly there are limits to what can be said in a voice as good-natured, as temperate, as Goldsmith's seems to be, and it is true that he has never been regarded as a profound writer. Indeed, he is generally thought to have had only conventional ideas—perhaps to have had, aside from his literary principles, no ideas at all. Of course there is a sense in which writers who endeavor to imitate or recreate human life in stories, as Goldsmith did—even the greatest writers of the greatest of such works— never have any ideas, if by these are meant something apart from the stories themselves. On the other hand, it could be argued that as a matter of fact Goldsmith did have certain convictions, from particular views of a social nature, such as appear in *The Deserted Village,* to more general notions of human existence, as that its manners and customs are defensible only when they are based upon good sense, which is implied in *She Stoops to Conquer.* But it cannot be claimed that he is either a philosophical poet or a didactic playwright, as such expressions are commonly understood. All that can be said is that in the humor and the irony and the compassion of his best work there is a good deal of what may be called human insight, which is not the less acute for the fact that Goldsmith himself seldom chose to make anything of it. *She Stoops to Conquer* is, among other things, about a young man who cannot sustain any normal, human relationship with a woman—who is, as one might say, socially impotent— except when the woman is a servingmaid or when he mistakenly believes she is one. Goldsmith does not indicate what he thought about this situation, or if he gave it any thought whatever. But it would be presumptuous to conclude that he was less perceptive about it than we may think we are, as it would be wrong to fault him because, having seen the social implications of his story, as we should suppose he was perfectly capable of doing, he did not stop there, but let the fun go on.

*She Stoops to Conquer,* one of the most successful comedies ever to appear on the English stage, was first produced in 1773. Its appearance in this issue of *The Great Ideas Today* thus marks its two-hundredth anniversary.

# She Stoops to Conquer

### or

# The Mistakes of a Night

To SAMUEL JOHNSON, L.L.D.

Dear Sir,

By inscribing this slight performance to you, I do not mean so much to compliment you as myself. It may do me some honour to inform the public, that I have lived many years in intimacy with you. It may serve the interests of man-kind also to inform them, that the greatest wit may be found in a character, without impairing the most unaffected piety.

I have, particularly, reason to thank you for your partiality to this perfor-mance. The undertaking a comedy, not merely sentimental, was very dangerous; and Mr. Colman, who saw this piece in its various stages, always thought it so. However, I ventured to trust it to the public; and though it was necessarily delayed till late in the season, I have every reason to be grateful.

I am, Dear Sir,

Your most sincere friend,

And admirer,

Oliver Goldsmith

### PROLOGUE

#### By David Garrick, Esq.

*Enter* MR. WOODWARD, *Dressed in Black, and holding a Handkerchief to his Eyes.*

*Excuse me, Sirs, I pray—I can't yet speak—*
*I'm crying now—and have been all the week!*
*'Tis not alone this mourning suit, good masters;*
*I've that within—for which there are no plaisters!*
*Pray wou'd you know the reason why I'm crying?*
*The Comic muse, long sick, is now a dying!*
*And if she goes, my tears will never stop;*
*For as a play'r, I can't squeeze out one drop:*
*I am undone, that's all—shall lose my bread—*
*I'd rather, but that's nothing—lose my head.*
*When the sweet maid is laid upon the bier,*
*Shuter and I shall be chief mourners here.*

*To* her *a mawkish drab of spurious breed,*
*Who deals in* sentimentals *will succeed!*
*Poor Ned and I are dead to all intents,*
*We can as soon speak Greek as* sentiments!
*Both nervous grown, to keep our spirits up,*
*We now and then take down a hearty cup.*
*What shall we do?—If Comedy foresake us!*
They'll turn us out, and no one else will take us;
*But why can't I be moral?—Let me try—*
*My heart thus pressing—fix'd my face and eye—*
*With a sententious look, that nothing means,*
*(Faces are blocks, in sentimental scenes)*
*Thus I begin—*All is not gold that glitters,
Pleasure seems sweet, but proves a glass of bitters,
When ign'rance enters, folly is at hand;
Learning is better far than house and land.
Let not your virtue trip, who trips may stumble,
And virtue is not virtue, if she tumble.
   *I give it up—morals won't do for me;*
*To make you laugh I must play tragedy.*
*One hope remains—hearing the maid was ill,*
*A* doctor *comes this night to shew his skill.*
*To cheer her heart, and give your muscles motion,*
*He in* five draughts *prepar'd, presents a potion:*
*A kind of magic charm—for be assur'd*
*If you will* swallow *it, the maid is cur'd:*
*But desp'rate the Doctor, and her case is,*
*If you reject the dose, and make wry faces!*
*This truth he boasts, will boast it while he lives,*
*No* pois'nous drugs *are mix'd in what he gives;*
*Should he succeed, you'll give him his degree;*
*If not, within he will receive no fee!*
*The college* you, *must his pretensions back,*
*Pronounce him* regular, *or dub him* quack.


## DRAMATIS PERSONÆ

### Men

SIR CHARLES MARLOW
YOUNG MARLOW *(his Son)*
HARDCASTLE
HASTINGS
TONY LUMPKIN
DIGGORY

### Women

MRS. HARDCASTLE
MISS HARDCASTLE
MISS NEVILLE
MAID

LANDLORD, SERVANTS, ETC., ETC.

# ACT I

*Scene—A Chamber in an old-fashioned House.*

*Enter* MRS. HARDCASTLE *and* MR. HARDCASTLE.

MRS. HARDCASTLE: I vow, Mr. Hardcastle, you're very particular. Is there a creature in the whole country, but ourselves, that does not take a trip to town now and then, to rub off the rust a little? There's the two Miss Hoggs, and our neighbour, Mrs. Grigsby, go to take a month's polishing every winter.

HARDCASTLE: Ay, and bring back vanity and affectation to last them the whole year. I wonder why London cannot keep its own fools at home. In my time, the follies of the town crept slowly among us, but now they travel faster than a stage-coach. Its fopperies come down, not only as inside passengers, but in the very basket.

MRS. HARDCASTLE: Ay, *your* times were fine times, indeed; you have been telling us of *them* for many a long year. Here we live in an old rumbling mansion, that looks for all the world like an inn, but that we never see company. Our best visitors are old Mrs. Oddfish, the curate's wife, and little Cripplegate, the lame dancing-master: And all our entertainment your old stories of Prince Eugene and the Duke of Marlborough. I hate such old-fashioned trumpery.

HARDCASTLE: And I love it. I love every thing that's old: old friends, old times, old manners, old books, old wine; and, I believe, Dorothy [*taking her hand*], you'll own I have been pretty fond of an old wife.

MRS. HARDCASTLE: Lord, Mr. Hardcastle, you're for ever at your Dorothy's and your old wife's. You may be a Darby, but I'll be no Joan, I promise you. I'm not so old as you'd make me, by more than one good year. Add twenty to twenty, and make money of that.

HARDCASTLE: Let me see; twenty added to twenty, makes just fifty and seven.

MRS. HARDCASTLE: It's false, Mr. Hardcastle: I was but twenty when I was brought to bed of Tony, that I had by Mr. Lumpkin, my first husband; and he's not come to years of discretion yet.

HARDCASTLE: Nor ever will, I dare answer for him. Ay, you have taught *him* finely!

MRS. HARDCASTLE: No matter, Tony Lumpkin has a good fortune. My son is not to live by his learning. I don't think a boy wants much learning to spend fifteen hundred a year.

HARDCASTLE: Learning, quotha! A mere composition of tricks and mischief.

MRS. HARDCASTLE: Humour, my dear: nothing but humour. Come, Mr. Hardcastle, you must allow the boy a little humour.

HARDCASTLE: I'd sooner allow him an horse-pond. If burning the footmen's shoes, frighting the maids, and worrying the kittens, be humour, he has it. It was but yesterday he fastened my wig to the back of my chair, and when I went to make a bow, I popt my bald head in Mrs. Frizzle's face.

MRS. HARDCASTLE: And am I to blame? The poor boy was always too sickly to do any good. A school would be his death. When he comes to be a little stronger, who knows what a year or two's Latin may do for him?

HARDCASTLE: Latin for him! A cat and fiddle. No, no, the ale-house and the stable are the only schools he'll ever go to.

MRS. HARDCASTLE: Well, we must not snub the poor boy now, for I believe we shan't have him long among us. Any body that looks in his face may see he's consumptive.

HARDCASTLE: Ay, if growing too fat be one of the symptoms.

MRS. HARDCASTLE: He coughs sometimes.

HARDCASTLE: Yes, when his liquor goes the wrong way.

MRS. HARDCASTLE: I'm actually afraid of his lungs.

HARDCASTLE: And truly, so am I; for he sometimes whoops like a speaking trumpet—[TONY *hallooing behind the Scenes*]—O, there he goes—A very consumptive figure, truly.

*Enter* TONY, *crossing the Stage.*

MRS. HARDCASTLE: Tony, where are you going, my charmer? Won't you give papa and I a little of your company, lovee?

TONY: I'm in haste, mother, I cannot stay.

MRS. HARDCASTLE: You shan't venture out this raw evening, my dear: You look most shockingly.

TONY: I can't stay, I tell you. *The Three Pigeons* expects me down every moment. There's some fun going forward.

HARDCASTLE: Ay; the ale-house, the old place: I thought so.

MRS. HARDCASTLE: A low, paltry set of fellows.

TONY: Not so low neither. There's Dick Muggins the excise-man, Jack Slang the horse doctor, Little Aminadab that grinds the music box, and Tom Twist that spins the pewter platter.

MRS. HARDCASTLE: Pray, my dear, disappoint them for one night at least.

TONY: As for disappointing *them,* I should not so much mind; but I can't abide to disappoint *myself.*

MRS. HARDCASTLE [*detaining him*]: You shan't go.

TONY: I will, I tell you.

MRS. HARDCASTLE: I say you shan't.

TONY: We'll see which is strongest, you or I. [*Exit hawling her out.*

HARDCASTLE, *solus.*

HARDCASTLE: Ay, there goes a pair that only spoil each other. But is not the whole age in a combination to drive sense and discretion out of doors? There's my pretty darling, Kate; the fashions of the times have almost infected her too. By living a year or two in town, she is as fond of gauze, and French frippery, as the best of them.

*Enter* MISS HARDCASTLE.

HARDCASTLE: Blessings on my pretty innocence! Drest out as usual, my Kate. Goodness! What a quantity of superfluous silk hast thou got about thee, girl! I could never teach the fools of this age, that the indigent world could be cloathed out of the trimmings of the vain.

MISS HARDCASTLE: You know our agreement, Sir. You allow me the morning to receive and pay visits, and to dress in my own manner; and in the evening, I put on my housewife's dress to please you.

HARDCASTLE: Well, remember, I insist on the terms of our agreement; and, by the bye, I believe I shall have occasion to try your obedience this very evening.

MISS HARDCASTLE: I protest, Sir, I don't comprehend your meaning.

HARDCASTLE: Then, to be plain with you, Kate, I expect the young gentleman I have chosen to be your husband from town this very day. I have his father's letter, in which he informs me his son is set out, and that he intends to follow himself shortly after.

MISS HARDCASTLE: Indeed! I wish I had known something of this before. Bless me, how shall I behave? It's a thousand to one I shan't like him; our meeting will be so formal, and so like a thing of business, that I shall find no room for friendship or esteem.

HARDCASTLE: Depend upon it, child, I'll never controul your choice; but Mr. Marlow, whom I have pitched upon, is the son of my old friend, Sir Charles Marlow, of whom you have heard me talk so often. The young gentleman has been bred a scholar, and is designed for an employment in the service of his country. I am told he's a man of an excellent understanding.

MISS HARDCASTLE: Is he?

HARDCASTLE: Very generous.

MISS HARDCASTLE: I believe I shall like him.

HARDCASTLE: Young and brave.

MISS HARDCASTLE: I'm sure I shall like him.

HARDCASTLE: And very handsome.

MISS HARDCASTLE: My dear papa, say no more [*kissing his hand*], he's mine, I'll have him.

HARDCASTLE: And to crown all, Kate, he's one of the most bashful and reserved young fellows in all the world.

MISS HARDCASTLE: Eh! you have frozen me to death again. That word *reserved* has undone all the rest of his accomplishments. A reserved lover, it is said, always makes a suspicious husband.

HARDCASTLE: On the contrary, modesty seldom resides in a breast that is not enriched with nobler virtues. It was the very feature in his character that first struck me.

MISS HARDCASTLE: He must have more striking features to catch me, I promise you. However, if he be so young, so handsome, and so every thing, as you mention, I believe he'll do still. I think I'll have him.

HARDCASTLE: Ay, Kate, but there is still an obstacle. It's more than an even wager, he may not have *you*.

MISS HARDCASTLE: My dear Papa, why will you mortify one so?—Well, if he refuses, instead of breaking my heart at his indifference, I'll only break my glass for its flattery. Set my cap to some newer fashion, and look out for some less difficult admirer.

HARDCASTLE: Bravely resolved! In the mean time I'll go prepare the servants for his reception; as we seldom see company, they want as much training as a company of recruits, the first day's muster. [*Exit.*

MISS HARDCASTLE, *sola.*

MISS HARDCASTLE: Lud, this news of Papa's, puts me all in a flutter. Young, handsome; these he put last; but I put them foremost. Sensible, good-natured; I like all that. But then reserved, and sheepish, that's much against him. Yet, can't he be cured of his timidity, by being taught to be proud of his wife? Yes, and can't I—But I vow I'm disposing of the husband, before I have secured the lover.

*Enter* MISS NEVILLE.

MISS HARDCASTLE: I'm glad you're come, Neville, my dear. Tell me, Constance, how do I look this evening? Is there any thing whimsical about me? Is it one of my well looking days, child? Am I in face to day?

MISS NEVILLE: Perfectly, my dear. Yet now I look again—bless me!—sure no accident has happened among the canary birds or the gold-fishes. Has your brother or the cat been meddling? Or has the last novel been too moving?

MISS HARDCASTLE: No; nothing of all this. I have been threatened—I can scarce get it out—I have been threatened with a lover.

MISS NEVILLE: And his name—

MISS HARDCASTLE: Is Marlow.

MISS NEVILLE: Indeed!

MISS HARDCASTLE: The son of Sir Charles Marlow.

MISS NEVILLE: As I live, the most intimate friend of Mr. Hastings, *my* admirer. They are never asunder. I believe you must have seen him when we lived in town.

MISS HARDCASTLE: Never.

MISS NEVILLE: He's a very singular character, I assure you. Among women of reputation and virtue, he is the modestest man alive; but his acquaintance give him a very different character among creatures of another stamp: you understand me.

MISS HARDCASTLE: An odd character, indeed. I shall never be able to manage him. What shall I do? Pshaw, think no more of him, but trust to occurrences for success. But how goes on your own affair, my dear? has my mother been courting you for my brother Tony, as usual?

MISS NEVILLE: I have just come from one of our agreeable *tête-à--têtes*. She has been saying a hundred tender things, and setting off her pretty monster as the very pink of perfection.

MISS HARDCASTLE: And her partiality is such, that she actually thinks him so. A fortune like your's is no small temptation. Besides, as she has the sole management of it, I'm not surprized to see her unwilling to let it go out of the family.

MISS NEVILLE: A fortune like mine, which chiefly consists in jewels, is no such mighty temptation. But at any rate, if my dear Hastings be but constant, I make no doubt to be too hard for her at last. However, I let her suppose that I am in love with her son, and she never once dreams that my affections are fixed upon another.

MISS HARDCASTLE: My good brother holds out stoutly. I could almost love him for hating you so.

MISS NEVILLE: It is a good natured creature at bottom, and I'm sure would wish to see me married to any body but himself. But my aunt's bell rings for our afternoon's walk round the improvements. *Allons*. Courage is necessary, as our affairs are critical.

MISS HARDCASTLE: Would it were bed time and all were well.     [*Exeunt.*

*Scene—An Ale-house Room. Several shabby fellows, with Punch and Tobacco.* TONY *at the head of the Table, a little higher than the rest: A mallet in his hand.*

OMNES: Hurrea, hurrea, hurrea, bravo!

FIRST FELLOW: Now, gentlemen, silence for a song. The 'Squire is going to knock himself down for a song.

OMNES: Ay, a song, a song.

TONY: Then I'll sing you, gentlemen, a song I made upon this ale-house, *The Three Pigeons*.

### SONG

*Let school-masters puzzle their brain,*
*With grammar, and nonsense, and learning;*
*Good liquor, I stoutly maintain,*
*Gives genus a better discerning.*
*Let them brag of their Heathenish Gods,*
*Their Lethes, their Styxes, and Stygians;*
*Their Quis, and their Quæs, and their Quods,*
*They're all but a parcel of Pigeons.*
*Toroddle, toroddle, toroll!*

*When Methodist preachers come down,*
*A preaching that drinking is sinful,*
*I'll wager the rascals a crown,*
*They always preach best with a skinful.*
*But when you come down with your pence,*
*For a slice of their scurvy religion,*
*I'll leave it to all men of sense,*
*But you, my good friend, are the pigeon.*
*Toroddle, toroddle, toroll!*

*Then come, put the jorum about,*
*And let us be merry and clever,*
*Our hearts and our liquors are stout,*
*Here's the Three Jolly Pigeons for ever.*
*Let some cry up woodcock or hare,*
*Your bustards, your ducks, and your widgeons;*
*But of all the birds in the air,*
*Here's a health to the Three Jolly Pigeons.*
*Toroddle, toroddle, toroll!*

OMNES: Bravo, bravo.

FIRST FELLOW: The 'Squire has got spunk in him.

SECOND FELLOW: I loves to hear him sing, bekeays he never gives us nothing that's *low*.

THIRD FELLOW: O damn any thing that's *low*, I cannot bear it.

FOURTH FELLOW: The genteel thing is the genteel thing at any time. If so be that a gentleman bees in a concatenation accordingly.

THIRD FELLOW: I like the maxum of it, Master Muggins. What, tho' I am obligated to dance a bear, a man may be a gentleman for all that. May this be my poison if my bear ever dances but to the very genteelest of tunes. *Water*

433

*Parted,* or the minuet in *Ariadne.*

SECOND FELLOW: What a pity it is the 'Squire is not come to his own. It would be well for all the publicans within ten miles round of him.

TONY: Ecod, and so it would, Master Slang. I'd then shew what it was to keep choice of company.

SECOND FELLOW: O, he takes after his own father for that. To be sure old 'Squire Lumpkin was the finest gentleman I ever set my eyes on. For winding the streight horn, or beating a thicket for a hare, or a wench, he never had his fellow. It was a saying in the place, that he kept the best horses, dogs and girls in the whole county.

TONY: Ecod, and when I'm of age I'll be no bastard, I promise you. I have been thinking of Bet Bouncer and the miller's grey mare to begin with. But come, my boys, drink about and be merry, for you pay no reckoning. Well, Stingo, what's the matter?

*Enter* LANDLORD.

LANDLORD: There be two gentlemen in a post-chaise at the door. They have lost their way upo' the forest; and they are talking something about Mr. Hardcastle.

TONY: As sure as can be, one of them must be the gentleman that's coming down to court my sister. Do they seem to be Londoners?

LANDLORD: I believe they may. They look woundily like Frenchmen.

TONY: Then desire them to step this way, and I'll set them right in a twinkling. [*Exit* LANDLORD.] Gentlemen, as they mayn't be good enough company for you, step down for a moment, and I'll be with you in the squeezing of a lemon.

[*Exeunt* MOB.

TONY, *solus.*

TONY: Father-in-law has been calling me whelp, and hound, this half year. Now if I pleased, I could be so revenged upon the old grumbletonian. But then I'm afraid—afraid of what? I shall soon be worth fifteen hundred a year, and let him frighten me out of that if he can.

*Enter* LANDLORD, *conducting* MARLOW *and* HASTINGS.

MARLOW: What a tedious, uncomfortable day have we had of it! We were told it was but forty miles across the country, and we have come above threescore.

HASTINGS: And all, Marlow, from that unaccountable reserve of yours, that would not let us enquire more frequently on the way.

MARLOW: I own, Hastings, I am unwilling to lay myself under an obligation to every one I meet; and often, stand the chance of an unmannerly answer.

HASTINGS: At present, however, we are not likely to receive any answer.

TONY: No offence, gentlemen. But I'm told you have been enquiring for one Mr. Hardcastle, in these parts. Do you know what part of the country you are in?

HASTINGS: Not in the least, Sir, but should thank you for information.

TONY: Nor the way you came?

HASTINGS: No, Sir; but if you can inform us—

TONY: Why, gentlemen, if you know neither the road you are going, nor where you are, nor the road you came, the first thing I have to inform you is, that— You have lost your way.

MARLOW: We wanted no ghost to tell us that.

TONY: Pray, gentlemen, may I be so bold as to ask the place from whence you came?

MARLOW: That's not necessary towards directing us where we are to go.

TONY: No offence; but question for question is all fair, you know. Pray, gentlemen, is not this same Hardcastle a cross-grain'd, old-fashion'd, whimsical fellow, with an ugly face, a daughter, and a pretty son?

HASTINGS: We have not seen the gentleman, but he has the family you mention.

TONY: The daughter, a tall trapesing, trolloping, talkative maypole—The son, a pretty, well-bred, agreeable youth, that every body is fond of.

MARLOW: Our information differs in this. The daughter is said to be well-bred and beautiful; the son, an awkward booby, reared up, and spoiled at his mother's apron-string.

TONY: He-he-hem—Then, gentlemen, all I have to tell you is, that you won't reach Mr. Hardcastle's house this night, I believe.

HASTINGS: Unfortunate!

TONY: It's a damn'd long, dark, boggy, dirty, dangerous way. Stingo, tell the gentlemen the way to Mr. Hardcastle's [*winking upon the* LANDLORD]; Mr. Hardcastle's, of Quagmire Marsh, you understand me.

LANDLORD: Master Hardcastle's! Lock-a-daisy, my masters, you're come a deadly deal wrong! When you came to the bottom of the hill, you should have cross'd down Squash-lane.

MARLOW: Cross down Squash-lane!

LANDLORD: Then you were to keep streight forward, 'till you came to four roads.

MARLOW: Come to where four roads meet!

TONY: Ay, but you must be sure to take only one of them.

MARLOW: O, Sir, you're facetious.

TONY: Then keeping to the right, you are to go side-ways till you come upon Crack-skull Common: there you must look sharp for the track of the wheel, and go forward, 'till you come to farmer Murrain's barn. Coming to the farmer's barn, you are to turn to the right, and then to the left, and then to the right about again, till you find out the old mill—

MARLOW: Zounds, man! we could as soon find out the longitude!

HASTINGS: What's to be done, Marlow?

MARLOW: This house promises but a poor reception; though perhaps the Landlord can accommodate us.

LANDLORD: Alack, master, we have but one spare bed in the whole house.

TONY: And to my knowledge, that's taken up by three lodgers already. [*after a pause, in which the rest seem disconcerted*] I have hit it. Don't you think, Stingo, our landlady could accommodate the gentlemen by the fire-side, with—three chairs and a bolster?

HASTINGS: I hate sleeping by the fire-side.

MARLOW: And I detest your three chairs and a bolster.

TONY: You do, do you?—then let me see—what—if you go on a mile further to the Buck's Head; the old Buck's Head on the hill, one of the best inns in the whole county?

HASTINGS: O ho! so we have escaped an adventure for this night, however.

LANDLORD [*apart to* TONY]: Sure, you ben't sending them to your father's as an

435

inn, be you?

TONY: Mum, you fool you. Let *them* find that out. [*to them*] You have only to keep on streight forward, till you come to a large old house by the road side. You'll see a pair of large horns over the door. That's the sign. Drive up the yard, and call stoutly about you.

HASTINGS: Sir, we are obliged to you. The servants can't miss the way?

TONY: No, no: But I tell you though, the landlord is rich, and going to leave off business; so he wants to be thought a Gentleman, saving your presence, he! he! he! He'll be for giving you his company, and, ecod, if you mind him, he'll persuade you that his mother was an alderman, and his aunt a justice of peace.

LANDLORD: A troublesome old blade, to be sure; but a keeps as good wines and beds as any in the whole country.

MARLOW: Well, if he supplies us with these, we shall want no further connexion. We are to turn to the right, did you say?

TONY: No, no; streight forward. I'll just step myself, and shew you a piece of the way. [*to the* LANDLORD] Mum.

LANDLORD: Ah, bless your heart, for a sweet, pleasant—damn'd mischievous son of a whore.                                    [*Exeunt.*

*End of the First Act*

## ACT II

*Scene—An old-fashioned House.*

*Enter* HARDCASTLE, *followed by three or four awkward* SERVANTS.

HARDCASTLE: Well, I hope you're perfect in the table exercise I have been teaching you these three days. You all know your posts and your places, and can shew that you have been used to good company, without ever stirring from home.

OMNES: Ay, ay.

HARDCASTLE: When company comes, you are not to pop out and stare, and then run in again, like frighted rabbits in a warren.

OMNES: No, no.

HARDCASTLE: You, Diggory, whom I have taken from the barn, are to make a shew at the side-table; and you, Roger, whom I have advanced from the plough, are to place yourself behind *my* chair. But you're not to stand so, with your hands in your pockets. Take your hands from your pockets, Roger; and from your head, you blockhead you. See how Diggory carries his hands. They're a little too stiff indeed, but that's no great matter.

DIGGORY: Ay, mind how I hold them. I learned to hold my hands this way, when I was upon drill for the militia. And so being upon drill—

HARDCASTLE: You must not be so talkative, Diggory. You must be all attention to the guests. You must hear us talk, and not think of talking; you must see us drink, and not think of drinking; you must see us eat, and not think of eating.

DIGGORY: By the laws, your worship, that's perfectly unpossible. Whenever Diggory sees yeating going forward, ecod, he's always wishing for a mouthful himself.

HARDCASTLE: Blockhead! Is not a belly-full in the kitchen as good as a belly-full in the parlour? Stay your stomach with that reflection.

DIGGORY: Ecod, I thank your worship, I'll make a shift to stay my stomach with a slice of cold beef in the pantry.

HARDCASTLE: Diggory, you are too talkative. Then, if I happen to say a good thing, or tell a good story at table, you must not all burst out a-laughing, as if you made part of the company.

DIGGORY: Then, ecod, your worship must not tell the story of Ould Grouse in the gun-room: I can't help laughing at that—he! he he!—for the soul of me. We have laughed at that these twenty years—ha! ha! ha!

HARDCASTLE: Ha! ha! ha! The story is a good one. Well, honest Diggory, you may laugh at that—but still remember to be attentive. Suppose one of the company should call for a glass of wine, how will you behave? A glass of wine, Sir, if you please. [*to* DIGGORY]—Eh, why don't you move?

DIGGORY: Ecod, your worship, I never have courage till I see the eatables and drinkables brought upo' the table, and then I'm as bauld as a lion.

HARDCASTLE: What, will no body move?

FIRST SERVANT: I'm not to leave this pleace.

SECOND SERVANT: I'm sure it's no pleace of mine.

THIRD SERVANT: Nor mine, for sartain.

DIGGORY: Wauns, and I'm sure it canna be mine.

HARDCASTLE: You numbskulls! and so while, like your betters, you are quarrelling for places, the guests must be starved. O you dunces! I find I must begin all over again.—But don't I hear a coach drive into the yard? To your posts, you blockheads. I'll go in the mean time and give my old friend's son a hearty reception at the gate. [*Exit* HARDCASTLE.

DIGGORY: By the elevens, my pleace is gone quite out of my head.

ROGER: I know that my pleace is to be every where.

FIRST SERVANT: Where the devil is mine?

SECOND SERVANT: My pleace is to be no where at all; and so I'ze go about my business. [*Exeunt* SERVANTS, *running about as if frighted, different ways.*

*Enter* SERVANT *with Candles, shewing in* MARLOW *and* HASTINGS.

SERVANT: Welcome, gentlemen, very welcome. This way.

HASTINGS: After the disappointments of the day, welcome once more, Charles, to the comforts of a clean room and a good fire. Upon my word, a very well-looking house; antique, but creditable.

MARLOW: The usual fate of a large mansion. Having first ruined the master by good housekeeping, it at last comes to levy contributions as an inn.

HASTINGS: As you say, we passengers are to be taxed to pay all these fineries. I have often seen a good sideboard, or a marble chimney-piece, tho' not actually put in the bill, enflame a reckoning confoundedly.

MARLOW: Travellers, George, must pay in all places. The only difference is, that in good inns, you pay dearly for luxuries; in bad inns, you are fleeced and starved.

HASTINGS: You have lived pretty much among them. In truth, I have been often surprized, that you who have seen so much of the world, with your natural good sense, and your many opportunities could never yet acquire a requisite share of assurance.

MARLOW: The Englishman's malady. But tell me, George, where could I have learned that assurance you talk of? My life has been chiefly spent in a college, or an inn, in seclusion from that lovely part of the creation that chiefly teach men confidence. I don't know that I was ever familiarly acquainted with a single modest woman—except my mother—But among females of another class you know—

HASTINGS: Ay, among them you are impudent enough of all conscience.

MARLOW: They are of *us,* you know.

HASTINGS: But in the company of women of reputation I never saw such an ideot, such a trembler; you look for all the world as if you wanted an opportunity of stealing out of the room.

MARLOW: Why, man, that's because I *do* want to steal out of the room. Faith, I have often formed a resolution to break the ice, and rattle away at any rate. But I don't know how, a single glance from a pair of fine eyes has totally overset my resolution. An impudent fellow may counterfeit modesty, but I'll be hanged if a modest man can ever counterfeit impudence.

HASTINGS: If you could but say half the fine things to them that I have heard you lavish upon the bar-maid of an inn, or even a college bed maker—

MARLOW: Why, George, I can't say fine things to them, They freeze, they petrify me. They may talk of a comet, or a burning mountain, or some such bagatelle. But to me, a modest woman, drest out in all her finery, is the most tremendous object of the whole creation.

HASTINGS: Ha! ha! ha! At this rate, man, how can you ever expect to marry!

MARLOW: Never, unless, as among kings and princes, my bride were to be courted by proxy. If, indeed, like an Eastern bridegroom, one were to be introduced to a wife he never saw before, it might be endured. But to go through all the terrors of a formal courtship, together with the episode of aunts, grandmothers and cousins, and at last to blurt out the broad staring question of, madam, will you marry me? No, no, that's a strain much above me, I assure you.

HASTINGS: I pity you. But how do you intend behaving to the lady you are come down to visit at the request of your father?

MARLOW: As I behave to all other ladies. Bow very low. Answer yes, or no, to all her demands—But for the rest, I don't think I shall venture to look in her face, till I see my father's again.

HASTINGS: I'm surprised that one who is so warm a friend can be so cool a lover.

MARLOW: To be explicit, my dear Hastings, my chief inducement down was to be instrumental in forwarding your happiness, not my own. Miss Neville loves you, the family don't know you, as my friend you are sure of a reception, and let honour do the rest.

HASTINGS: My dear Marlow! But I'll suppress the emotion. Were I a wretch, meanly seeking to carry off a fortune, you should be the last man in the world I would apply to for assistance. But Miss Neville's person is all I ask, and that is mine, both from her deceased father's consent, and her own inclination.

MARLOW: Happy man! You have talents and art to captivate any woman. I'm doom'd to adore the sex, and yet to converse with the only part of it I despise. This stammer in my address, and this aukward prepossessing visage of mine, can never permit me to soar above the reach of a milliner's 'prentice, or one of the dutchesses of Drury-lane. Pshaw! this fellow here to interrupt us.

*Enter* HARDCASTLE.

HARDCASTLE: Gentlemen, once more you are heartily welcome. Which is Mr. Marlow? Sir, you're heartily welcome. It's not my way, you see, to receive my friends with my back to the fire. I like to give them a hearty reception in the old stile, at my gate. I like to see their horses and trunks taken care of.

MARLOW [*aside*]: He has got our names from the servants already. [*to him*] We approve your caution and hospitality, Sir. [*to* HASTINGS] I have been thinking, George, of changing our travelling dresses in the morning. I am grown confoundedly ashamed of mine.

HARDCASTLE: I beg, Mr. Marlow, you'll use no ceremony in this house.

HASTINGS: I fancy, George, you're right: the first blow is half the battle. I intend opening the campaign with the white and gold.

MR. HARDCASTLE: Mr. Marlow—Mr. Hastings—gentlemen—pray be under no constraint in this house. This is Liberty-hall, gentlemen. You may do just as you please here.

MARLOW: Yet, George, if we open the campaign too fiercely at first, we may want ammunition before it is over. I think to reserve the embroidery to secure a retreat.

HARDCASTLE: Your talking of a retreat, Mr. Marlow, puts me in mind of the Duke of Marlborough, when we went to besiege Denain. He first summoned the garrison—

MARLOW: Don't you think the *ventre dor* waistcoat will do with the plain brown?

HARDCASTLE: He first summoned the garrison, which might consist of about five thousand men—

HASTINGS: I think not: brown and yellow mix but very poorly.

HARDCASTLE: I say, gentlemen, as I was telling you, he summoned the garrison, which might consist of about five thousand men—

MARLOW: The girls like finery.

HARDCASTLE: Which might consist of about five thousand men, well appointed with stores, ammunition, and other implements of war. "Now," says the Duke of Marlborough, to George Brooks, that stood next to him—You must have heard of George Brooks; "I'll pawn my Dukedom," says he, "but I take that garrison without spilling a drop of blood." So—

MARLOW: What, my good friend, if you gave us a glass of punch in the mean time; it would help us to carry on the siege with vigour.

HARDCASTLE: Punch, Sir! [*aside*] This is the most unaccountable kind of modesty I ever met with.

MARLOW: Yes, Sir, Punch. A glass of warm punch, after our journey, will be comfortable. This is Liberty-hall, you know.

HARDCASTLE: Here's Cup, Sir.

MARLOW [*aside*]: So this fellow, in his Liberty-hall, will only let us have just what he pleases.

HARDCASTLE [*taking the Cup*]: I hope you'll find it to your mind. I have prepared it with my own hands, and I believe you'll own the ingredients are tolerable. Will you be so good as to pledge me, Sir? Here, Mr. Marlow, here is to our better acquaintance. [*Drinks.*

MARLOW [*aside*]: A very impudent fellow this! but he's a character, and I'll humour him a little. Sir, my service to you. [*Drinks.*

HASTINGS [*aside*]: I see this fellow wants to give us his company, and forgets he's an innkeeper, before he has learned to be a gentleman.

MARLOW: From the excellence of your cup, my old friend, I suppose you have a good deal of business in this part of the country. Warm work, now and then, at elections, I suppose?

HARDCASTLE: No, Sir, I have long given that work over. Since our betters have hit upon the expedient of electing each other, there's no business *for us that sell ale.*

HASTINGS: So, then you have no turn for politics, I find.

HARDCASTLE: Not in the least. There was a time, indeed, I fretted myself about the mistakes of government, like other people; but finding myself every day grow more angry, and the government growing no better, I left it to mend itself. Since that, I no more trouble my head about Heyder Ally, or Ally Cawn, than about Ally Croaker. Sir, my service to you.

HASTINGS: So that with eating above stairs, and drinking below, with receiving your friends within, and amusing them without, you lead a good, pleasant, bustling life of it.

HARDCASTLE: I do stir about a great deal, that's certain. Half the differences of the parish are adjusted in this very parlour.

MARLOW [*after drinking*]: And you have an argument in your cup, old gentleman, better than any in Westminster-hall.

HARDCASTLE: Ay, young gentleman, that, and a little philosophy.

MARLOW [*aside*]: Well, this is the first time I ever heard of an innkeeper's philosophy.

HASTINGS: So then, like an experienced general, you attack them on every quarter. If you find their reason manageable, you attack it with your philosophy; if you find they have no reason, you attack them with this. Here's your health, my philosopher. [*Drinks.*

HARDCASTLE: Good, very good, thank you; ha! ha! Your Generalship puts me in mind of Prince Eugene, when he fought the Turks at the battle of Belgrade. You shall hear—

MARLOW: Instead of the battle of Belgrade, I believe it's almost time to talk about supper. What has your philosophy got in the house for supper?

HARDCASTLE: For Supper, Sir! [*aside*] Was ever such a request to a man in his own house!

MARLOW: Yes, Sir, supper, Sir; I begin to feel an appetite. I shall make devilish work to-night in the larder, I promise you.

HARDCASTLE [*aside*]: Such a brazen dog sure never my eyes beheld. [*to him*] Why really, Sir, as for supper I can't well tell. My Dorothy, and the cook maid, settle these things between them. I leave these kind of things entirely to them.

MARLOW: You do, do you?

HARDCASTLE: Entirely. By-the-bye, I believe they are in actual consultation upon what's for supper this moment in the kitchen.

MARLOW: Then I beg they'll admit *me* as one of their privy council. It's a way I have got. When I travel, I always chuse to regulate my own supper. Let the cook be called. No offence, I hope, Sir.

HARDCASTLE: O, no, Sir, none in the least; yet I don't know how: our Bridget, the cook maid, is not very communicative upon these occasions. Should we send for her, she might scold us all out of the house.

HASTINGS: Let's see your list of the larder then. I ask it as a favour. I always match my appetite to my bill of fare.

MARLOW [to HARDCASTLE, *who looks at them with surprize*]: Sir, he's very right, and it's my way too.

HARDCASTLE: Sir, you have a right to command here. Here, Roger, bring us the bill of fare for to night's supper. I believe it's drawn out. Your manner, Mr. Hastings, puts me in mind of my uncle, Colonel Wallop. It was a saying of his, that no man was sure of his supper till he had eaten it.

HASTINGS [*aside*]: All upon the high ropes! His uncle a Colonel! We shall soon hear of his mother being a justice of peace. But let's hear the bill of fare.

MARLOW [*perusing*]: What's here? For the first course; for the second course; for the desert. The devil, Sir, do you think we have brought down the whole Joiners Company, or the Corporation of Bedford, to eat up such a supper? Two or three little things, clean and comfortable, will do.

HASTINGS: But, let's hear it.

MARLOW [*reading*]: For the first course, at the top, a pig, and pruin sauce.

HASTINGS: Damn your pig, I say.

MARLOW: And damn your pruin sauce, say I.

HARDCASTLE: And yet, gentlemen, to men that are hungry, pig, with pruin sauce, is very good eating.

MARLOW: At the bottom, a calve's tongue and brains.

HASTINGS: Let your brains be knock'd out, my good Sir; I don't like them.

MARLOW: Or you may clap them on a plate by themselves. I do.

HARDCASTLE [*aside*]: Their impudence confounds me. [*to them*] Gentlemen, you are my guests, make what alterations you please. Is there any thing else you wish to retrench or alter, gentlemen?

MARLOW: Item: A pork pie, a boiled rabbet and sausages, a florentine, a shaking pudding, and a dish of tiff—taff—taffety cream!

HASTINGS: Confound your made dishes, I shall be as much at a loss in this house as at a green and yellow dinner at the French Ambassador's table. I'm for plain eating.

HARDCASTLE: I'm sorry, gentlemen, that I have nothing you like, but if there be any thing you have a particular fancy to—

MARLOW: Why, really, Sir, your bill of fare is so exquisite, that any one part of it is full as good as another. Send us what you please. So much for supper. And now to see that our beds are air'd, and properly taken care of.

HARDCASTLE: I entreat you'll leave all that to me. You shall not stir a step.

MARLOW: Leave that to you! I protest, Sir, you must excuse me, I always look to these things myself.

HARDCASTLE: I must insist, Sir, you'll make yourself easy on that head.

MARLOW: You see I'm resolved on it. [*aside*] A very troublesome fellow this, as ever I met with.

HARDCASTLE: Well, Sir, I'm resolved at least to attend you. [*aside*] This may be modern modesty, but I never saw any thing look so like old-fashioned impudence.                    [*Exeunt* MARLOW *and* HARDCASTLE.

HASTINGS, *solus.*

HASTINGS: So I find this fellow's civilities begin to grow troublesome. But who can be angry at those assiduities which are meant to please him? Ha! what do I see? Miss Neville, by all that's happy!

*Enter* MISS NEVILLE.

MISS NEVILLE: My dear Hastings! To what unexpected good fortune, to what accident am I to ascribe this happy meeting?

HASTINGS: Rather let me ask the same question, as I could never have hoped to meet my dearest Constance at an inn.

MISS NEVILLE: An inn! sure you mistake! my aunt, my guardian, lives here. What could induce you to think this house an inn?

HASTINGS: My friend Mr. Marlow, with whom I came down, and I, have been sent here as to an inn, I assure you. A young fellow whom we accidentally met at a house hard by directed us hither.

MISS NEVILLE: Certainly it must be one of my hopeful cousin's tricks, of whom you have heard me talk so often, ha! ha! ha! ha!.

HASTINGS: He whom your aunt intends for you? He of whom I have such just apprehensions?

MISS NEVILLE: You have nothing to fear from him, I assure you. You'd adore him if you knew how heartily he despises me. My aunt knows it too, and has undertaken to court me for him, and actually begins to think she has made a conquest.

HASTINGS: Thou dear dissembler! You must know, my Constance, I have just seized this happy opportunity of my friend's visit here to get admittance into the family. The horses that carried us down are now fatigued with their journey, but they'll soon be refreshed; and then, if my dearest girl will trust in her faithful Hastings, we shall soon be landed in France, where even among slaves the laws of marriage are respected.

MISS NEVILLE: I have often told you, that though ready to obey you, I yet should leave my little fortune behind with reluctance. The greatest part of it was left me by my uncle, the India Director, and chiefly consists in jewels. I have been for some time persuading my aunt to let me wear them. I fancy I'm very near succeeding. The instant they are put into my possession you shall find me ready to make them and myself yours.

HASTINGS: Perish the baubles! Your person is all I desire. In the meantime, my friend Marlow must not be let into his mistake. I know the strange reserve of his temper is such, that if abruptly informed of it, he would instantly quit the house before our plan was ripe for execution.

MISS NEVILLE: But how shall we keep him in the deception? Miss Hardcastle is just returned from walking; what if we still continue to deceive him?—This, this way— *[They confer.*

*Enter* MARLOW.

MARLOW: The assiduities of these good people teize me beyond bearing. My host seems to think it ill manners to leave me alone, and so he claps not only himself but his old-fashioned wife on my back. They talk of coming to sup with us too; and then, I suppose, we are to run the gauntlet thro' all the rest of the family.—What have we got here!—

HASTINGS: My dear Charles! Let me congratulate you!—The most fortunate accident!—Who do you think is just alighted?

MARLOW: Cannot guess.

HASTINGS: Our mistresses, boy, Miss Hardcastle and Miss Neville. Give me leave to introduce Miss Constance Neville to your acquaintance. Happening to dine in the neighbourhood, they called, on their return, to take fresh horses, here. Miss Hardcastle has just stept into the next room, and will be back in an instant. Wasn't it lucky? eh!

MARLOW [*aside*]: I have just been mortified enough of all conscience, and here comes something to complete my embarrassment.

HASTINGS: Well! but wasn't it the most fortunate thing in the world?

MARLOW: Oh! yes. Very fortunate—a most joyful encounter—But our dresses, George, you know, are in disorder—What if we should postpone the happiness 'till to-morrow?—To-morrow at her own house—It will be every bit as convenient —And rather more respectful—To-morrow let it be.                    [*Offering to go.*

MISS NEVILLE: By no means, Sir. Your ceremony will displease her. The disorder of your dress will shew the ardour of your impatience. Besides, she knows you are in the house, and will permit you to see her.

MARLOW: O! the devil! how shall I support it? Hem! hem! Hastings, you must not go. You are to assist me, you know. I shall be confoundedly ridiculous. Yet, hang it! I'll take courage. Hem!

HASTINGS: Pshaw, man! it's but the first plunge, and all's over. She's but a woman, you know.

MARLOW: And of all women, she that I dread most to encounter!

*Enter* MISS HARDCASTLE *as returned from walking, a Bonnet, etc.*

HASTINGS [*introducing him*]: Miss Hardcastle, Mr. Marlow; I'm proud of bringing two persons of such merit together, that only want to know, to esteem each other.

MISS HARDCASTLE [*aside*]: Now, for meeting my modest gentleman with a demure face, and quite in his own manner. [*after a pause, in which he appears very uneasy and disconcerted*] I'm glad of your safe arrival, Sir—I'm told you had some accidents by the way.

MARLOW: Only a few, madam. Yes, we had some. Yes, Madam, a good many accidents, but should be sorry—Madam—or rather glad of any accidents—that are so agreeably concluded. Hem!

HASTINGS [*to him*]: You never spoke better in your whole life. Keep it up, and I'll insure you the victory.

MISS HARDCASTLE: I'm afraid you flatter, Sir. You that have seen so much of the finest company can find little entertainment in an obscure corner of the country.

MARLOW [*gathering courage*]: I have lived, indeed, in the world, Madam; but I have kept very little company. I have been but an observer upon life, Madam, while others were enjoying it.

MISS NEVILLE: But that, I am told, is the way to enjoy it at last.

HASTINGS [*to him*]: Cicero never spoke better. Once more, and you are confirm'd in assurance for ever.

MARLOW [*to him*]: Hem! Stand by me then, and when I'm down, throw in a word or two to set me up again.

MISS HARDCASTLE: An observer, like you, upon life, were, I fear, disagreeably employed, since you must have had much more to censure than to approve.

MARLOW: Pardon me, Madam. I was always willing to be amused. The folly of most people is rather an object of mirth than uneasiness.

HASTINGS [*to him*]: Bravo, bravo. Never spoke so well in your whole life. Well! Miss Hardcastle, I see that you and Mr. Marlow are going to be very good company. I believe our being here will but embarrass the interview.

MARLOW: Not in the least, Mr. Hastings. We like your company of all things. [*to him*] Zounds! George, sure you won't go? How can you leave us?

HASTINGS: Our presence will but spoil conversation, so we'll retire to the next room. [*to him*] You don't consider, man, that we are to manage a little tête-à-tête of our own. [*Exeunt.*

MISS HARDCASTLE [*after a pause*]: But you have not been wholly an observer, I presume, Sir: The ladies I should hope have employed some part of your addresses.

MARLOW [*relapsing into timidity*]: Pardon, me Madam, I—I—I—as yet have studied—only—to—deserve them.

MISS HARDCASTLE: And that, some say, is the very worst way to obtain them.

MARLOW: Perhaps so, madam. But I love to converse only with the more grave and sensible part of the sex.—But I'm afraid I grow tiresome.

MISS HARDCASTLE: Not at all, Sir; there is nothing I like so much as grave conversation myself; I could hear it for ever. Indeed I have often been surprized how a man of *sentiment* could ever admire those light, airy pleasures, where nothing reaches the heart.

MARLOW: It's—a disease—of the mind, Madam. In the variety of tastes there must be some who, wanting a relish—for—um—a—um.

MISS HARDCASTLE: I understand you, Sir. There must be some, who, wanting a relish for refined pleasures, pretend to despise what they are incapable of tasting.

MARLOW: My meaning, Madam, but infinitely better expressed. And I can't help observing—a—

MISS HARDCASTLE [*aside*]: Who could ever suppose this fellow impudent upon some occasions. [*to him*] You were going to observe, Sir—

MARLOW: I was observing, Madam—I protest, Madam, I forget what I was going to observe.

MISS HARDCASTLE [*aside*]: I vow and so do I. [*to him*] You were observing, Sir, that in this age of hypocrisy—something about hypocrisy, Sir.

MARLOW: Yes, Madam. In this age of hypocrisy there are few who upon strict enquiry do not—a—a—a—

MISS HARDCASTLE: I understand you perfectly, Sir.

MARLOW [*aside*]: Egad! and that's more than I do myself.

MISS HARDCASTLE: You mean that in this hypocritical age there are few that do not condemn in public what they practise in private, and think they pay every debt to virtue when they praise it.

MARLOW: True, Madam; those who have most virtue in their mouths, have least of it in their bosoms. But I'm sure I tire you, Madam.

MISS HARDCASTLE: Not in the least, Sir; there's something so agreeable and spirited in your manner, such life and force—pray, Sir, go on.

MARLOW: Yes, Madam. I was saying—that there are some occasions—when a total want of courage, Madam, destroys all the—and puts us—upon a—a—a—

MISS HARDCASTLE: I agree with you entirely: a want of courage upon some occasions assumes the appearance of ignorance, and betrays us when we most want to excel. I beg you'll proceed.

MARLOW: Yes, Madam. Morally speaking, Madam—But I see Miss Neville expecting us in the next room. I would not intrude for the world.

MISS HARDCASTLE: I protest, Sir, I never was more agreeably entertained in all my life. Pray go on.

MARLOW: Yes, Madam. I was—But she beckons us to join her. Madam, shall I do myself the honour to attend you?

MISS HARDCASTLE: Well then, I'll follow.

MARLOW [*aside*]: This pretty smooth dialogue has done for me.          [*Exit.*

MISS HARDCASTLE, *sola.*

MISS HARDCASTLE: Ha! ha! ha! Was there ever such a sober, sentimental interview? I'm certain he scarce look'd in my face the whole time. Yet the fellow, but for his unaccountable bashfulness, is pretty well too. He has good sense, but then so buried in his fears, that it fatigues one more than ignorance. If I could teach him a little confidence, it would be doing somebody that I know of a piece of service. But who is that somebody?—that, faith, is a question I can scarce answer.          [*Exit.*

*Enter* TONY *and* MISS NEVILLE, *followed by* MRS. HARDCASTLE *and* HASTINGS.

TONY: What do you follow me for, Cousin Con? I wonder you're not ashamed to be so very engaging.

MISS NEVILLE: I hope, Cousin, one may speak to one's own relations, and not be to blame.

TONY: Ay, but I know what sort of a relation you want to make me though; but it won't do. I tell you, Cousin Con, it won't do, so I beg you'll keep your distance. I want no nearer relationship.

[*She follows coqueting him to the back scene.*

MRS. HARDCASTLE: Well! I vow, Mr. Hastings, you are very entertaining. There's nothing in the world I love to talk of so much as London, and the fashions, though I was never there myself.

HASTINGS: Never there! You amaze me! From your air and manner, I concluded you had been bred all your life either at Ranelagh, St. James's, or Tower Wharf.

MRS. HARDCASTLE: O! Sir, you're only pleased to say so. We Country persons can have no manner at all. I'm in love with the town, and that serves to raise me above some of our neighbouring rustics; but who can have a manner, that has never seen the Pantheon, the Grotto Gardens, the Borough, and such places where the Nobility chiefly resort? All I can do, is to enjoy London at second-hand. I take care to know every tête-à-tête from the *Scandalous Magazine,* and have all the fashions, as they come out, in a letter from the two Miss Rickets of Crooked-lane. Pray how do you like this head, Mr. Hastings?

HASTINGS: Extremely elegant and *degagée,* upon my word, Madam. Your Friseur is a Frenchman, I suppose?

MRS. HARDCASTLE: I protest, I dressed it myself from a print in the *Ladies Memorandum book* for the last year.

HASTINGS: Indeed. Such a head in a side-box, at the Play-house, would draw as many gazers as my Lady May'ress at a City Ball.

MRS. HARDCASTLE: I vow, since inoculation began, there is no such thing to be seen as a plain woman; so one must dress a little particular or one may escape in the crowd.

HASTINGS: But that can never be your case Madam, in any dress.     [*Bowing.*

MRS. HARDCASTLE: Yet, what signifies *my* dressing when I have such a piece of antiquity by my side as Mr. Hardcastle: all I can say will never argue down a single button from his cloaths. I have often wanted him to throw off his great flaxen wig, and where he was bald, to plaister it over like my Lord Pately, with powder.

HASTINGS: You are right, Madam; for, as among the ladies, there are none ugly, so among the men there are none old.

MRS. HARDCASTLE: But what do you think his answer was? Why, with his usual Gothic vivacity, he said I only wanted him to throw off his wig to convert it into a tête for my own wearing.

HASTINGS: Intolerable! At your age you may wear what you please, and it must become you.

MRS. HARDCASTLE: Pray, Mr. Hastings, what do you take to be the most fashionable age about town?

HASTINGS: Some time ago, forty was all the mode; but I'm told the ladies intend to bring up fifty for the ensuing winter.

MRS. HARDCASTLE: Seriously? Then I shall be too young for the fashion.

HASTINGS: No lady begins now to put on jewels 'till she's past forty. For instance, Miss there, in a polite circle, would be considered as a child, as a mere maker of samplers.

MRS. HARDCASTLE: And yet Mrs. Niece thinks herself as much a woman, and is as fond of jewels as the oldest of us all.

HASTINGS: Your niece, is she? And that young gentleman—a brother of yours, I should presume?

MRS. HARDCASTLE: My son, Sir. They are contracted to each other. Observe their little sports. They fall in and out ten times a day, as if they were man and wife already. [*to them*] Well, Tony, child, what soft things are you saying to your Cousin Constance this evening?

TONY: I have been saying no soft things; but that it's very hard to be followed about so. Ecod! I've not a place in the house now that's left to myself but the stable.

MRS. HARDCASTLE: Never mind him, Con, my dear. He's in another story behind your back.

MISS NEVILLE: There's something generous in my cousin's manner. He falls out before faces to be forgiven in private.

TONY: That's a damned confounded—crack.

MRS. HARDCASTLE: Ah! he's a sly one. Don't you think they're like each other about the mouth, Mr. Hastings? The Blenkinsop mouth to a T. They're of a size too. Back to back, my pretties, that Mr. Hastings may see you. Come Tony.

TONY: You had as good not make me, I tell you.     [*Measuring.*

MISS NEVILLE: O lud! he has almost cracked my head.

MRS. HARDCASTLE: O the monster! For shame, Tony. You a man, and behave so!

TONY: If I'm a man, let me have my fortin. Ecod! I'll not be made a fool of no longer.

MRS. HARDCASTLE: Is this, ungrateful boy, all that I'm to get for the pains I have taken in your education? I that have rock'd you in your cradle, and fed that pretty mouth with a spoon! Did not I work that waistcoat to make you genteel?

Did not I prescribe for you every day, and weep while the receipt was operating?

TONY: Ecod! you had reason to weep, for you have been dosing me ever since I was born. I have gone through every receipt in the complete huswife ten times over; and you have thoughts of coursing me through *Quincy* next spring. But, Ecod! I tell you, I'll not be made a fool of no longer.

MRS. HARDCASTLE: Wasn't it all for your good, viper? Wasn't it all for your good?

TONY: I wish you'd let me and my good alone then. Snubbing this way when I'm in spirits. If I'm to have any good, let it come of itself; not to keep dinging it, dinging it into one so.

MRS. HARDCASTLE: That's false; I never see you when you're in spirits. No, Tony, you then go to the alehouse or kennel. I'm never to be delighted with your agreeable, wild notes, unfeeling monster!

TONY: Ecod! Mamma, your own notes are the wildest of the two.

MRS. HARDCASTLE: Was ever the like? But I see he wants to break my heart, I see he does.

HASTINGS: Dear Madam, permit me to lecture the young gentleman a little. I'm certain I can persuade him to his duty.

MRS. HARDCASTLE: Well! I must retire. Come, Constance, my love. You see, Mr. Hastings, the wretchedness of my situation: Was ever poor woman so plagued with a dear, sweet, pretty, provoking, undutiful boy.

[*Exeunt* MRS. HARDCASTLE *and* MISS NEVILLE.

HASTINGS, TONY.

TONY [*singing*]: *There was a young man riding by, and fain would have his will. Rang do didlo dee.* Don't mind her. Let her cry. It's the comfort of her heart. I have seen her and sister cry over a book for an hour together, and they said, they liked the book the better the more it made them cry.

HASTINGS: Then you're no friend to the ladies, I find, my pretty young gentleman?

TONY: That's as I find 'um.

HASTINGS: Not to her of your mother's chusing, I dare answer? And yet she appears to me a pretty, well-tempered girl.

TONY: That's because you don't know her as well as I. Ecod! I know every inch about her; and there's not a more bitter, cantanckerous toad in all Christendom.

HASTINGS [*aside*]: Pretty encouragement this for a lover!

TONY: I have seen her since the height of that. She has as many tricks as a hare in a thicket, or a colt the first day's breaking.

HASTINGS: To me she appears sensible and silent!

TONY: Ay, before company. But when she's with her playmates, she's as loud as a hog in a gate.

HASTINGS: But there is a meek modesty about her that charms me.

TONY: Yes, but curb her never so little, she kicks up, and you're flung in a ditch.

HASTINGS: Well, but you must allow her a little beauty.—Yes, you must allow her some beauty.

TONY: Bandbox! She's all a made up thing, mun. Ah! could you but see Bet Bouncer of these parts, you might then talk of beauty. Ecod, she has two eyes as black as sloes, and cheeks as broad and red as a pulpit cushion. She'd make two of she.

HASTINGS: Well, what say you to a friend that would take this bitter bargain off your hands?

TONY: Anon.

HASTINGS: Would you thank him that would take Miss Neville and leave you to happiness and your dear Betsy?

TONY: Ay; but where is there such a friend, for who would take *her?*

HASTINGS: I am he. If you but assist me, I'll engage to whip her off to France, and you shall never hear more of her.

TONY: Assist you! Ecod, I will, to the last drop of my blood. I'll clap a pair of horses to your chaise that shall trundle you off in a twinkling, and may be get you a part of her fortin beside, in jewels, that you little dream of.

HASTINGS: My dear 'Squire, this looks like a lad of spirit.

TONY: Come along then, and you shall see more of my spirit before you have done with me. [*Singing.*

> *We are the boys*
> *That fears no noise*
> *Where the thundering cannons roar.* [*Exeunt.*

*End of the Second Act*

## ACT III

*Enter* HARDCASTLE, *solus.*

HARDCASTLE: What could my old friend Sir Charles mean by recommending his son as the modestest young man in town? To me he appears the most impudent piece of brass that ever spoke with a tongue. He has taken possession of the easy chair by the fire-side already. He took off his boots in the parlour, and desired me to see them taken care of. I'm desirous to know how his impudence affects my daughter.—She will certainly be shocked at it.

*Enter* MISS HARDCASTLE, *plainly dress'd.*

HARDCASTLE: Well, my Kate, I see you have changed your dress as I bid you; and yet, I believe, there was no great occasion.

MISS HARDCASTLE: I find such a pleasure, Sir, in obeying your commands, that I take care to observe them without ever debating their propriety.

HARDCASTLE: And yet, Kate, I sometimes give you some cause, particularly when I recommended my *modest* gentleman to you as a lover to-day.

MISS HARDCASTLE: You taught me to expect something extraordinary, and I find the original exceeds the description.

HARDCASTLE: I was never so surprized in my life! He has quite confounded all my faculties!

MISS HARDCASTLE: I never saw any thing like it: And a man of the world too!

HARDCASTLE: Ay, he learned it all abroad—what a fool was I, to think a young man could learn modesty by travelling. He might as soon learn wit at a masquerade.

MISS HARDCASTLE: It seems all natural to him.

HARDCASTLE: A good deal assisted by bad company and a French dancing-master.

MISS HARDCASTLE: Sure, you mistake, papa! a French dancing-master could never have taught him that timid look—that aukward address—that bashful manner—

HARDCASTLE: Whose look? whose manner? child!

MISS HARDCASTLE: Mr. Marlow's: his *mauvaise honte,* his timidity struck me at the first sight.

HARDCASTLE: Then your first sight deceived you; for I think him one of the most brazen first sights that ever astonished my senses.

MISS HARDCASTLE: Sure, Sir, you rally! I never saw any one so modest.

HARDCASTLE: And can you be serious! I never saw such a bouncing, swaggering puppy since I was born. Bully Dawson was but a fool to him.

MISS HARDCASTLE: Surprizing! He met me with a respectful bow, a stammering voice, and a look fixed on the ground.

HARDCASTLE: He met me with a loud voice, a lordly air, and a familiarity that made my blood freeze again.

MISS HARDCASTLE: He treated me with diffidence and respect; censured the manners of the age; admired the prudence of girls that never laughed; tired me with apologies for being tiresome; then left the room with a bow, and, "madam, I would not for the world detain you."

HARDCASTLE: He spoke to me as if he knew me all his life before. Asked twenty questions, and never waited for an answer. Interrupted my best remarks with some silly pun, and when I was in my best story of the Duke of Marlborough and Prince Eugene, he asked if I had not a good hand at making punch. Yes, Kate, he ask'd your father if he was a maker of punch!

MISS HARDCASTLE: One of us must certainly be mistaken.

HARDCASTLE: If he be what he has shewn himself, I'm determined he shall never have my consent.

MISS HARDCASTLE: And if he be the sullen thing I take him, he shall never have mine.

HARDCASTLE: In one thing then we are agreed—to reject him.

MISS HARDCASTLE: Yes. But upon conditions. For if you should find him less impudent, and I more presuming; if you find him more respectful, and I more importunate—I don't know—the fellow is well enough for a man—Certainly we don't meet many such at a horse race in the country.

HARDCASTLE: If we should find him so—But that's impossible. The first appearance has done my business. I'm seldom deceived in that.

MISS HARDCASTLE: And yet there may be many good qualities under that first appearance.

HARDCASTLE: Ay, when a girl finds a fellow's outside to her taste, she then sets about guessing the rest of his furniture. With her, a smooth face stands for good sense, and a genteel figure for every virtue.

MISS HARDCASTLE: I hope, Sir, a conversation begun with a compliment to my good sense won't end with a sneer at my understanding?

HARDCASTLE: Pardon me, Kate. But if young Mr. Brazen can find the art of reconciling contradictions, he may please us both, perhaps.

MISS HARDCASTLE: And as one of us must be mistaken, what if we go to make further discoveries?

HARDCASTLE: Agreed. But depend on't I'm in the right.

449

MISS HARDCASTLE: And depend on't I'm not much in the wrong.　　　[*Exeunt.*

*Enter* TONY, *running in with a Casket.*

TONY: Ecod! I have got them. Here they are. My Cousin Con's necklaces, bobs and all. My mother shan't cheat the poor souls out of their fortin neither. O! my genus, is that you?

*Enter* HASTINGS.

HASTINGS: My dear friend, how have you managed with your mother? I hope you have amused her with pretending love for your cousin, and that you are willing to be reconciled at last? Our horses will be refreshed in a short time, and we shall soon be ready to set off.

TONY: And here's something to bear your charges by the way. [*giving the casket*] Your sweetheart's jewels. Keep them, and hang those, I say, that would rob you of one of them.

HASTINGS: But how have you procured them from your mother?

TONY: Ask me no questions, and I'll tell you no fibs. I procured them by the rule of thumb. If I had not a key to every drawer in mother's bureau, how could I go to the alehouse so often as I do? An honest man may rob himself of his own at any time.

HASTINGS: Thousands do it every day. But to be plain with you; Miss Neville is endeavouring to procure them from her aunt this very instant. If she succeeds, it will be the most delicate way at least of obtaining them.

TONY: Well, keep them, till you know how it will be. But I know how it will be well enough; she'd as soon part with the only sound tooth in her head.

HASTINGS: But I dread the effects of her resentment, when she finds she has lost them.

TONY: Never you mind her resentment, leave *me* to manage that. I don't value her resentment the bounce of a cracker. Zounds! here they are. Morrice, Prance.

　　　[*Exit* HASTINGS.

TONY, MRS. HARDCASTLE, MISS NEVILLE.

MRS. HARDCASTLE: Indeed, Constance, you amaze me. Such a girl as you want jewels? It will be time enough for jewels, my dear, twenty years hence, when your beauty begins to want repairs.

MISS NEVILLE: But what will repair beauty at forty, will certainly improve it at twenty, Madam.

MRS. HARDCASTLE: Yours, my dear, can admit of none. That natural blush is beyond a thousand ornaments. Besides, child, jewels are quite out at present. Don't you see half the ladies of our acquaintance, my Lady Kill-day-light, and Mrs. Crump, and the rest of them, carry their jewels to town, and bring nothing but Paste and Marcasites back?

MISS NEVILLE: But who knows, Madam, but somebody that shall be nameless would like me best with all my little finery about me?

MRS. HARDCASTLE: Consult your glass, my dear, and then see, if with such a pair of eyes, you want any better sparklers. What do you think, Tony, my dear, does your Cousin Con want any jewels, in your eyes, to set off her beauty?

TONY: That's as thereafter may be.

MISS NEVILLE: My dear aunt, if you knew how it would oblige me.

MRS. HARDCASTLE: A parcel of old-fashioned rose and table-cut things. They would make you look like the court of King Solomon at a puppet-shew. Besides, I believe I can't readily come at them. They may be missing, for aught I know to the contrary.

TONY [*apart to* MRS. HARDCASTLE]: Then why don't you tell her so at once, as she's so longing for them. Tell her they're lost. It's the only way to quiet her. Say they're lost, and call me to bear witness.

MRS. HARDCASTLE [*apart to* TONY]: You know, my dear, I'm only keeping them for you. So if I say they're gone, you'll bear me witness, will you? He! he! he!

TONY: Never fear me. Ecod! I'll say I saw them taken out with my own eyes.

MISS NEVILLE: I desire them but for a day, Madam. Just to be permitted to shew them as relicks, and then they may be lock'd up again.

MRS. HARDCASTLE: To be plain with you, my dear Constance, if I could find them, you should have them. They're missing, I assure you. Lost, for aught I know; but we must have patience wherever they are.

MISS NEVILLE: I'll not believe it; this is but a shallow pretence to deny me. I know they're too valuable to be so slightly kept, and as you are to answer for the loss.

MRS. HARDCASTLE: Don't be alarm'd, Constance. If they be lost, I must restore an equivalent. But my son knows they are missing, and not to be found.

TONY: That I can bear witness to. They are missing, and not to be found, I'll take my oath on't.

MRS. HARDCASTLE: You must learn resignation, my dear; for tho' we lose our fortune, yet we should not lose our patience. See me, how calm I am.

MISS NEVILLE: Ay, people are generally calm at the misfortunes of others.

MRS. HARDCASTLE: Now, I wonder a girl of your good sense should waste a thought upon such trumpery. We shall soon find them; and, in the mean time, you shall make use of my garnets till your jewels be found.

MISS NEVILLE: I detest garnets.

MRS. HARDCASTLE: The most becoming things in the world to set off a clear complexion. You have often seen how well they look upon me. You *shall* have them.                                                                                                       [*Exit.*

MISS NEVILLE: I dislike them of all things. You shan't stir.—Was ever any thing so provoking—to mislay my own jewels, and force me to wear her trumpery.

TONY: Don't be a fool. If she gives you the garnets, take what you can get. The jewels are your own already. I have stolen them out of her bureau, and she does not know it. Fly to your spark, he'll tell you more of the matter. Leave me to manage *her.*

MISS NEVILLE: My dear cousin.

TONY: Vanish. She's here, and has missed them already. [*Exit* MISS NEVILLE.] Zounds! how she fidgets and spits about like a Catharine wheel.

*Enter* MRS. HARDCASTLE.

MRS. HARDCASTLE: Confusion! thieves! robbers! We are cheated, plundered, broke open, undone.

TONY: What's the matter, what's the matter, mamma? I hope nothing has happened to any of the good family!

MRS. HARDCASTLE: We are robbed. My bureau has been broke open, the jewels taken out, and I'm undone.

TONY: Oh! is that all? Ha! ha! ha! By the laws, I never saw it better acted in my life. Ecod, I thought you was ruin'd in earnest, ha, ha, ha.

MRS. HARDCASTLE: Why, boy, I *am* ruin'd in earnest. My bureau has been broke open, and all taken away.

TONY: Stick to that; ha, ha, ha! stick to that. I'll bear witness, you know, call me to bear witness.

MRS. HARDCASTLE: I tell you, Tony, by all that's precious, the jewels are gone, and I shall be ruin'd for ever.

TONY: Sure I know they're gone, and I am to say so.

MRS. HARDCASTLE: My dearest Tony, but hear me. They're gone, I say.

TONY: By the laws, mamma, you make me for to laugh, ha! ha! I know who took them well enough, ha! ha! ha!

MRS. HARDCASTLE: Was there ever such a blockhead, that can't tell the difference between jest and earnest. I tell you I'm not in jest, booby.

TONY: That's right, that's right: You must be in a bitter passion, and then nobody will suspect either of us. I'll bear witness that they are gone.

MRS. HARDCASTLE: Was there ever such a cross-grain'd brute, that won't hear me! Can you bear witness that you're no better than a fool? Was ever poor woman so beset with fools on one hand, and thieves on the other?

TONY: I can bear witness to that.

MRS. HARDCASTLE: Bear witness again, you blockhead you, and I'll turn you out of the room directly. My poor niece, what will become of *her*! Do you laugh, you unfeeling brute, as if you enjoyed my distress?

TONY: I can bear witness to that.

MRS. HARDCASTLE: Do you insult me, monster? I'll teach you to vex your mother, I will.

TONY: I can bear witness to that.         *[He runs off, she follows him.*

*Enter* MISS HARDCASTLE *and* MAID.

MISS HARDCASTLE: What an unaccountable creature is that brother of mine, to send them to the house as an inn, ha! ha! I don't wonder at his impudence.

MAID: But what is more, Madam, the young gentleman as you passed by in your present dress, ask'd me if you were the bar-maid. He mistook you for the bar-maid, Madam.

MISS HARDCASTLE: Did he? Then as I live, I'm resolved to keep up the delusion. Tell me, Pimple, how do you like my present dress? Don't you think I look something like *Cherry* in the *Beaux' Stratagem?*

MAID: It's the dress, Madam, that every lady wears in the country, but when she visits, or receives company.

MISS HARDCASTLE: And are you sure he does not remember my face or person?

MAID: Certain of it.

MISS HARDCASTLE: I vow, I thought so; for though we spoke for some time together, yet his fears were such, that he never once looked up during the interview. Indeed, if he had, my bonnet would have kept him from seeing me.

MAID: But what do you hope from keeping him in his mistake?

MISS HARDCASTLE: In the first place, I shall be *seen*, and that is no small advantage to a girl who brings her face to market. Then I shall perhaps make an acquaintance, and that's no small victory gained over one who never addresses any but the wildest of her sex. But my chief aim is to take my gentleman off his guard, and, like an invisible champion of romance, examine the giant's force before I offer to combat.

MAID: But are you sure you can act your part, and disguise your voice, so that he may mistake that, as he has already mistaken your person?

MISS HARDCASTLE: Never fear me. I think I have got the true bar-cant.—Did your honour call?—Attend the Lion there.—Pipes and tobacco for the Angel. —The Lamb has been outrageous this half hour.

MAID: It will do, Madam. But he's here.                              [*Exit* MAID.

*Enter* MARLOW.

MARLOW: What a bawling in every part of the house. I have scarce a moment's repose. If I go to the best room, there I find my host and his story. If I fly to the gallery, there we have my hostess with her curtesy down to the ground. I have at last got a moment to myself, and now for recollection.          [*Walks and muses.*

MISS HARDCASTLE: Did you call, Sir? Did your honour call?

MARLOW [*musing*]: As for Miss Hardcastle, she's too grave and sentimental for me.

MISS HARDCASTLE: Did your honour call?

                    [*She still places herself before him, he turning away.*

MARLOW: No child. [*musing*] Besides, from the glimpse I had of her, I think she squints.

MISS HARDCASTLE: I'm sure, Sir, I heard the bell ring.

MARLOW: No, no. [*musing*] I have pleased my father, however, by coming down, and I'll to-morrow please myself by returning.

                    [*Taking out his tablets, and perusing.*

MISS HARDCASTLE: Perhaps the other gentleman called, Sir?

MARLOW: I tell you, no.

MISS HARDCASTLE: I should be glad to know, Sir. We have such a parcel of servants.

MARLOW: No, no, I tell you. [*looks full in her face*] Yes, child, I think I did call. I wanted—I wanted—I vow, child, you are vastly handsome.

MISS HARDCASTLE: O la, Sir, you'll make one asham'd.

MARLOW: Never saw a more sprightly, malicious eye. Yes, yes, my dear, I did call. Have you got any of your—a—what d'ye call it in the house?

MISS HARDCASTLE: No, Sir, we have been out of that these ten days.

MARLOW: One may call in this house, I find, to very little purpose. Suppose I should call for a taste, just by way of trial, of the nectar of your lips; perhaps I might be disappointed in that too.

MISS HARDCASTLE: Nectar! nectar! That's a liquor there's no call for in these parts. French, I suppose. We keep no French wines here, Sir.

MARLOW: Of true English growth, I assure you.

MISS HARDCASTLE: Then it's odd I should not know it. We brew all sorts of wines in this house, and I have lived here these eighteen years.

MARLOW: Eighteen years! Why one would think, child, you kept the bar before you were born. How old are you?

MISS HARDCASTLE: O! Sir, I must not tell my age. They say women and music should never be dated.

MARLOW: To guess at this distance, you can't be much above forty. [*approaching*] Yet nearer, I don't think so much. [*approaching*] By coming close to some women, they look younger still; but when we come very close indeed—

[*Attempting to kiss her.*

MISS HARDCASTLE: Pray, Sir, keep your distance. One would think you wanted to know one's age as they do horses, by mark of mouth.

MARLOW: I protest, child, you use me extremely ill. If you keep me at this distance, how is it possible you and I can be ever acquainted?

MISS HARDCASTLE: And who wants to be acquainted with you? I want no such acquaintance, not I. I'm sure you did not treat Miss Hardcastle that was here awhile ago in this obstropalous manner. I'll warrant me, before her you look'd dash'd, and kept bowing to the ground, and talk'd, for all the world, as if you was before a justice of peace.

MARLOW [*aside*]: Egad! she has hit it, sure enough. [*to her*] In awe of her, child? Ha! ha! ha! A mere, aukward, squinting thing, no, no! I find you don't know me. I laugh'd, and rallied her a little; but I was unwilling to be too severe. No, I could not be too severe, curse me!

MISS HARDCASTLE: O! then, Sir, you are a favourite, I find, among the ladies?

MARLOW: Yes, my dear, a great favourite. And yet, hang me, I don't see what they find in me to follow. At the Ladies Club in town, I'm called their agreeable Rattle. Rattle, child, is not my real name, but one I'm known by. My name is Solomons. Mr. Solomons, my dear, at your service.          [*Offering to salute her.*

MISS HARDCASTLE: Hold, Sir; you are introducing me to your club, not to yourself. And you're so great a favourite there, you say?

MARLOW: Yes, my dear. There's Mrs. Mantrap, Lady Betty Blackleg, the Countess of Sligo, Mrs. Langhorns, old Miss Biddy Buckskin, and your humble servant, to keep up the spirit of the place.

MISS HARDCASTLE: Then it's a very merry place, I suppose?

MARLOW: Yes, as merry as cards, suppers, wine, and old women can make us.

MISS HARDCASTLE: And their agreeable Rattle, ha! ha! ha!

MARLOW [*aside*]: Egad! I don't quite like this chit. She looks knowing, methinks. You laugh, child!

MISS HARDCASTLE: I can't but laugh to think what time they all have for minding their work or their family.

MARLOW [*aside*]: All's well; she don't laugh at me. [*to her*] Do *you* ever work, child?

MISS HARDCASTLE: Ay, sure. There's not a screen or a quilt in the whole house but what can bear witness to that.

MARLOW: Odso! Then you must shew me your embroidery. I embroider and draw patterns myself a little. If you want a judge of your work you must apply to me.                              [*Seizing her hand.*

MISS HARDCASTLE: Ay, but the colours don't look well by candle-light. You shall see all in the morning.                              [*Struggling.*

MARLOW: And why not now, my angel? Such beauty fires beyond the power of resistance.—Pshaw! the father here! My old luck: I never nick'd seven that I did not throw ames ace three times following.          [*Exit* MARLOW.

*Enter* HARDCASTLE, *who stands in surprize.*

HARDCASTLE: So, Madam. So I find *this* is your *modest* lover. This is your humble admirer that kept his eyes fixed on the ground, and only ador'd at humble distance. Kate, Kate, art thou not asham'd to deceive your father so?

MISS HARDCASTLE: Never trust me, dear papa, but he's still the modest man I first took him for; you'll be convinced of it as well as I.

HARDCASTLE: By the hand of my body, I believe his impudence is infectious! Didn't I see him seize your hand? Didn't I see him hawl you about like a milk-maid? and now you talk of his respect and his modesty, forsooth!

MISS HARDCASTLE: But if I shortly convince you of his modesty, that he has only the faults that will pass off with time, and the virtues that will improve with age, I hope you'll forgive him.

HARDCASTLE: The girl would actually make one run mad! I tell you I'll not be convinced. I am convinced. He has scarcely been three hours in the house, and he has already encroached on all my prerogatives. You may like his impudence, and call it modesty. But my son-in-law, madam, must have very different qualifications.

MISS HARDCASTLE: Sir, I ask but this night to convince you.

HARDCASTLE: You shall not have half the time, for I have thoughts of turning him out this very hour.

MISS HARDCASTLE: Give me that hour then, and I hope to satisfy you.

HARDCASTLE: Well, an hour let it be then. But I'll have no trifling with your father. All fair and open, do you mind me.

MISS HARDCASTLE: I hope, Sir, you have ever found that I considered your commands as my pride; for your kindness is such, that my duty as yet has been inclination. [*Exeunt.*

*End of the Third Act*

## ACT IV

*Enter* HASTINGS *and* MISS NEVILLE.

HASTINGS: You surprize me! Sir Charles Marlow expected here this night? Where have you had your information?

MISS NEVILLE: You may depend upon it. I just saw his letter to Mr. Hardcastle, in which he tells him he intends setting out a few hours after his son.

HASTINGS: Then, my Constance, all must be completed before he arrives. He knows me; and should he find me here, would discover my name, and perhaps my designs, to the rest of the family.

MISS NEVILLE: The jewels, I hope, are safe.

HASTINGS: Yes, yes. I have sent them to Marlow, who keeps the keys of our baggage. In the meantime, I'll go to prepare matters for our elopement. I have had the Squire's promise of a fresh pair of horses; and, if I should not see him again, will write him further directions. [*Exit.*

MISS NEVILLE: Well! success attend you. In the meantime, I'll go amuse my aunt with the old pretence of a violent passion for my cousin. [*Exit.*

*Enter* MARLOW, *followed by a* SERVANT.

MARLOW: I wonder what Hastings could mean by sending me so valuable a thing as a casket to keep for him, when he knows the only place I have is the seat of a post-coach at an Inn-door. Have you deposited the casket with the landlady, as I ordered you? Have you put it into her own hands?

SERVANT: Yes, your honour.

MARLOW: She said she'd keep it safe, did she?

SERVANT: Yes, she said she'd keep it safe enough; she ask'd me how I came by it? and she said she had a great mind to make me give an account of myself.

[*Exit* SERVANT.

MARLOW: Ha! ha! ha! They're safe, however. What an unaccountable set of beings have we got amongst! This little bar-maid, though, runs in my head most strangely, and drives out the absurdities of all the rest of the family. She's mine, she must be mine, or I'm greatly mistaken.

*Enter* HASTINGS.

HASTINGS: Bless me! I quite forgot to tell her that I intended to prepare at the bottom of the garden. Marlow here, and in spirits too!

MARLOW: Give me joy, George! Crown me, shadow me with laurels! Well, George, after all, we modest fellows don't want for success among the women.

HASTINGS: Some women you mean. But what success has your honour's modesty been crowned with now, that it grows so insolent upon us?

MARLOW: Didn't you see the tempting, brisk, lovely little thing that runs about the house with a bunch of keys to its girdle?

HASTINGS: Well! and what then?

MARLOW: She's mine, you rogue you. Such fire, such motion, such eyes, such lips—but, egad! she would not let me kiss them though.

HASTINGS: But are you so sure, so very sure of her?

MARLOW: Why man, she talk'd of shewing me her work above stairs, and I am to improve the pattern.

HASTINGS: But how can *you*, Charles, go about to rob a woman of her honour?

MARLOW: Pshaw! pshaw! we all know the honour of the bar-maid of an inn. I don't intend to *rob* her, take my word for it; there's nothing in this house, I shan't honestly *pay* for.

HASTINGS: I believe the girl has virtue.

MARLOW: And if she has, I should be the last man in the world that would attempt to corrupt it.

HASTINGS: You have taken care, I hope, of the casket I sent you to lock up? It's in safety?

MARLOW: Yes, yes. It's safe enough. I have taken care of it. But how could you think the seat of a post-coach at an Inn-door a place of safety? Ah! numbskull! I have taken better precautions for you than you did for yourself.—I have—

HASTINGS: What!

MARLOW: I have sent it to the landlady to keep for you.

HASTINGS: To the landlady!

MARLOW: The landlady.

HASTINGS: You did!

MARLOW: I did. She's to be answerable for its forth-coming, you know.

HASTINGS: Yes, she'll bring it forth, with a witness.

MARLOW: Wasn't I right? I believe you'll allow that I acted prudently upon this occasion?

HASTINGS [*aside*]: He must not see my uneasiness.

MARLOW: You seem a little disconcerted though, methinks. Sure nothing has happened?

HASTINGS: No, nothing. Never was in better spirits in all my life. And so you left it with the landlady, who, no doubt, very readily undertook the charge?

MARLOW: Rather too readily. For she not only kept the casket; but, thro' her great precaution, was going to keep the messenger too. Ha! ha! ha!

HASTINGS: He! he! he! They're safe, however.

MARLOW: As a guinea in a miser's purse.

HASTINGS [*aside*]: So now all hopes of fortune are at an end, and we must set off without it. [*to him*] Well, Charles, I'll leave you to your meditations on the pretty bar-maid, and, he! he! he! may you be as successful for yourself as you have been for me. [*Exit.*

MARLOW: Thank ye, George! I ask no more. Ha! ha! ha!

*Enter* HARDCASTLE.

HARDCASTLE: I no longer know my own house. It's turned all topsey-turvey. His servants have got drunk already. I'll bear it no longer, and yet, from my respect for his father, I'll be calm. [*to him*] Mr. Marlow, your servant. I'm your very humble servant. [*Bowing low.*

MARLOW: Sir, your humble servant. [*aside*] What's to be the wonder now?

HARDCASTLE: I believe, Sir, you must be sensible, Sir, that no man alive ought to be more welcome than your father's son, Sir. I hope you think so?

MARLOW: I do from my soul, Sir. I don't want much intreaty. I generally make my father's son welcome wherever he goes.

HARDCASTLE: I believe you do, from my soul, Sir. But tho' I say nothing to your own conduct, that of your servants is insufferable. Their manner of drinking is setting a very bad example in this house, I assure you.

MARLOW: I protest, my very good Sir, that's no fault of mine. If they don't drink as they ought, *they* are to blame. I ordered them not to spare the cellar. I did, I assure you. [*to the side scene*] Here, let one of my servants come up. [*to him*] My positive directions were, that as I did not drink myself, they should make up for my deficiencies below.

HARDCASTLE: Then they had your orders for what they do! I'm satisfied!

MARLOW: They had, I assure you. You shall hear from one of themselves.

*Enter* SERVANT *drunk.*

MARLOW: You, Jeremy! Come forward, Sirrah! What were my orders? Were you not told to drink freely, and call for what you thought fit, for the good of the house?

HARDCASTLE [*aside*]: I begin to lose my patience.

JEREMY: Please your honour, liberty and Fleet-street for ever! Tho' I'm but a servant, I'm as good as another man. I'll drink for no man before supper, Sir, dammy! Good liquor will sit upon a good supper, but a good supper will not sit upon—*hiccup*—upon my conscience, Sir. [*Exit* JEREMY.

MARLOW: You see, my old friend, the fellow is as drunk as he can possibly be. I don't know what you'd have more, unless you'd have the poor devil soused in a beer-barrel.

HARDCASTLE: Zounds! He'll drive me distracted if I contain myself any longer.

Mr. Marlow. Sir; I have submitted to your insolence for more than four hours, and I see no likelihood of its coming to an end. I'm now resolved to be master here, Sir, and I desire that you and your drunken pack may leave my house directly.

MARLOW: Leave your house!—Sure you jest, my good friend! What, when I'm doing what I can to please you!

HARDCASTLE: I tell you, Sir, you don't please me; so I desire you'll leave my house.

MARLOW: Sure you cannot be serious? At this time o'night, and such a night. You only mean to banter me?

HARDCASTLE: I tell you, Sir, I'm serious; and, now that my passions are rouzed, I say this house is mine, Sir; this house is mine, and I command you to leave it directly.

MARLOW: Ha! ha! ha! A puddle in a storm. I shan't stir a step, I assure you. [*in a serious tone*] This, your house, fellow! It's my house. This is my house. Mine, while I chuse to stay. What right have you to bid me leave this house, Sir? I never met with such impudence, curse me, never in my whole life before.

HARDCASTLE: Nor I, confound me if ever I did. To come to my house, to call for what he likes, to turn me out of my own chair, to insult the family, to order his servants to get drunk, and then to tell me *This house is mine, Sir*. By all that's impudent, it makes me laugh. Ha! ha! ha! Pray, Sir [*bantering*], as you take the house, what think you of taking the rest of the furniture? There's a pair of silver candlesticks, and there's a fire-screen, and here's a pair of brazen nosed bellows, perhaps you may take a fancy to them?

MARLOW: Bring me your bill, Sir, bring me your bill, and let's make no more words about it.

HARDCASTLE: There are a set of prints too. What think you of the *Rake's Progress* for your own apartment?

MARLOW: Bring me your bill, I say; and I'll leave you and your infernal house directly.

HARDCASTLE: Then there's a mahogany table, that you may see your own face in.

MARLOW: My bill, I say.

HARDCASTLE: I had forgot the great chair, for your own particular slumbers, after a hearty meal.

MARLOW: Zounds! bring me my bill, I say, and let's hear no more on't.

HARDCASTLE: Young man, young man, from your father's letter to me, I was taught to expect a well-bred, modest man, as a visitor here, but now I find him no better than a coxcomb and a bully; but he will be down here presently, and shall hear more of it. [*Exit.*

MARLOW: How's this! Sure I have not mistaken the house? Every thing looks like an inn. The servants cry, Coming. The attendance is aukward; the bar-maid, too, to attend us. But she's here, and will further inform me. Whither so fast, child? A word with you.

*Enter* MISS HARDCASTLE.

MISS HARDCASTLE: Let it be short then. I'm in a hurry. [*aside*] I believe he begins to find out his mistake, but it's too soon quite to undeceive him.

MARLOW: Pray, child, answer me one question. What are you, and what may your business in this house be?

MISS HARDCASTLE: A relation of the family, Sir.

MARLOW: What! A poor relation?

MISS HARDCASTLE: Yes, Sir. A poor relation appointed to keep the keys, and to see that the guests want nothing in my power to give them.

MARLOW: That is, you act as the bar-maid of this inn.

MISS HARDCASTLE: Inn. O Law—What brought that in your head? One of the best families in the county keep an inn! Ha, ha, ha, old Mr. Hardcastle's house an inn?

MARLOW: Mr. Hardcastle's house? Is this house Mr. Hardcastle's house, child?

MISS HARDCASTLE: Ay, sure. Whose else should it be?

MARLOW: So then all's out, and I have been damnably imposed on. O, confound my stupid head, I shall be laugh'd at over the whole town. I shall be stuck up in caricatura in all the print-shops. The Dullissimo Maccaroni. To mistake this house of all others for an inn, and my father's old friend for an inn-keeper. What a swaggering puppy must he take me for. What a silly puppy do I find myself. There again, may I be hang'd, my dear, but I mistook you for the bar-maid.

MISS HARDCASTLE: Dear me! dear me! I'm sure there's nothing in my *behaviour* to put me upon a level with one of that stamp.

MARLOW: Nothing, my dear, nothing. But I was in for a list of blunders, and could not help making you a subscriber. My stupidity saw every thing the wrong way. I mistook your assiduity for assurance, and your simplicity for allurement. But its over—This house I no more shew *my* face in.

MISS HARDCASTLE: I hope, Sir, I have done nothing to disoblige you. I'm sure I should be sorry to affront any gentleman who has been so polite, and said so many civil things to me. I'm sure I should be sorry [*pretending to cry*] if he left the family upon my account. I'm sure I should be sorry, people said any thing amiss, since I have no fortune but my character.

MARLOW [*aside*]: By heaven, she weeps. This is the first mark of tenderness I ever had from a modest woman, and it touches me. [*to her*] Excuse me, my lovely girl, you are the only part of the family I leave with reluctance. But to be plain with you, the difference of our birth, fortune and education, make an honourable connexion impossible; and I can never harbour a thought of seducing simplicity that trusted in my honour, or bringing ruin upon one, whose only fault was being too lovely.

MISS HARDCASTLE [*aside*]: Generous man! I now begin to admire him. [*to him*] But I'm sure my family is as good as Miss Hardcastle's, and though I'm poor, that's no great misfortune to a contented mind, and, until this moment, I never thought that it was bad to want fortune.

MARLOW: And why now, my pretty simplicity?

MISS HARDCASTLE: Because it puts me at a distance from one, that if I had a thousand pound I would give it all to.

MARLOW [*aside*]: This simplicity bewitches me, so that if I stay I'm undone. I must make one bold effort, and leave her. [*to her*] Your partiality in my favour, my dear, touches me most sensibly, and were I to live for myself alone, I could easily fix my choice. But I owe too much to the opinion of the world, too much to the authority of a father, so that—I can scarcely speak it—it affects me. Farewell.                                                                                        [*Exit.*

MISS HARDCASTLE: I never knew half his merit till now. He shall not go, if I have power or art to detain him. I'll still preserve the character in which I stoop'd to conquer, but will undeceive my papa, who, perhaps may laugh him out of his resolution.                                                              [*Exit.*

*Enter* TONY, MISS NEVILLE.

TONY: Ay, you may steal for yourselves the next time. I have done my duty. She has got the jewels again, that's a sure thing; but she believes it was all a mistake of the servants.

MISS NEVILLE: But, my dear cousin, sure you won't forsake us in this distress. If she in the least suspects that I am going off, I shall certainly be locked up, or sent to my Aunt Pedigree's, which is ten times worse.

TONY: To be sure, aunts of all kinds are damn'd bad things. But what can I do? I have got you a pair of horses that will fly like Whistlejacket, and I'm sure you can't say but I have courted you nicely before her face. Here she comes; we must court a bit or two more, for fear she should suspect us.

[*They retire, and seem to fondle.*

*Enter* MRS. HARDCASTLE.

MRS. HARDCASTLE: Well, I was greatly fluttered, to be sure. But my son tells me it was all a mistake of the servants. I shan't be easy, however, till they are fairly married, and then let her keep her own fortune. But what do I see! Fondling together, as I'm alive. I never saw Tony so sprightly before. Ah! have I caught you, my pretty doves? What, billing, exchanging stolen glances, and broken murmurs. Ah!

TONY: As for murmurs, mother, we grumble a little now and then, to be sure. But there's no love lost between us.

MRS. HARDCASTLE: A mere sprinkling, Tony, upon the flame only to make it burn brighter.

MISS NEVILLE: Cousin Tony promises to give us more of his company at home. Indeed, he shan't leave us any more. It won't leave us, Cousin Tony, will it?

TONY: O! it's a pretty creature. No, I'd sooner leave my horse in a pound, than leave you when you smile upon one so. Your laugh makes you so becoming.

MISS NEVILLE: Agreeable cousin! Who can help admiring that natural humour, that pleasant, broad, red, thoughtless [*patting his cheek*], ah! it's a bold face.

MRS. HARDCASTLE: Pretty innocence!

TONY: I'm sure I always lov'd Cousin Con's hazle eyes, and her pretty long fingers, that she twists this way and that, over the haspicholls, like a parcel of bobbins.

MRS. HARDCASTLE: Ah, he would charm the bird from the tree. I was never so happy before. My boy takes after his father, poor Mr. Lumpkin, exactly. The jewels, my dear Con, shall be your's incontinently. You shall have them. Isn't he a sweet boy, my dear? You shall be married to-morrow, and we'll put off the rest of his education, like Dr. Drowsy's sermons, to a fitter opportunity.

*Enter* DIGGORY.

DIGGORY: Where's the 'Squire? I have got a letter for your worship.

TONY: Give it to my mamma. She reads all my letters first.

DIGGORY: I had orders to deliver it into your own hands.

TONY: Who does it come from?

DIGGORY: Your worship mun ask that o' the letter itself.    *[Exit* DIGGORY.

TONY: I could wish to know, tho'.    *[Turning the letter, and gazing on it.*

MISS NEVILLE *[aside]*: Undone, undone. A letter to him from Hastings. I know the hand. If my aunt sees it, we are ruined for ever. I'll keep her employ'd a little if I can. *[to* MRS. HARDCASTLE*]* But I have not told you, Madam, of my cousin's smart answer just now to Mr. Marlow. We so laugh'd—You must know, Madam—this way a little, for he must not hear us.    *[They confer.*

TONY *[still gazing]*: A damn'd cramp piece of penmanship, as ever I saw in my life. I can read your print-hand very well. But here there are such handles, and shanks, and dashes, that one can scarce tell the head from the tail. *To Anthony Lumpkin, Esquire.* It's very odd, I can read the outside of my letters, where my own name is, well enough. But when I come to open it, it's all—buzz. That's hard, very hard; for the inside of the letter is always the cream of the correspondence.

MRS. HARDCASTLE: Ha! ha! ha! Very well, very well. And so my son was too hard for the philosopher.

MISS NEVILLE: Yes, Madam; but you must hear the rest, Madam. A little more this way, or he may hear us. You'll hear how he puzzled him again.

MRS. HARDCASTLE: He seems strangely puzzled now himself, methinks.

TONY *[still gazing]*: A damn'd up and down hand, as if it was disguised in liquor. *[reading] Dear Sir.* Ay, that's that. Then there's an *M*, and a *T*, and an *S*, but whether the next be an izzard or an *R*, confound me, I cannot tell.

MRS. HARDCASTLE: What's that, my dear? Can I give you any assistance?

MISS NEVILLE: Pray, aunt, let me read it. No body reads a cramp hand better than I. *[twitching the letter from her]* Do you know who it is from?

TONY: Can't tell, except from Dick Ginger the feeder.

MISS NEVILLE: Ay, so it is. *[pretending to read]* Dear 'Squire, Hoping that you're in health, as I am at this present. The gentlemen of the Shake-bag club has cut the gentlemen of Goose-green quite out of feather. The odds—um—odd battle—um—long fighting—um, here, here, it's all about cocks, and fighting; it's of no consequence; here, put it up, put it up.

   *[Thrusting the crumpled letter upon him.*

TONY: But I tell you, Miss, it's of all the consequence in the world. I would not lose the rest of it for a guinea. Here, mother, do you make it out. Of no consequence!    *[Giving* MRS. HARDCASTLE *the letter.*

MRS. HARDCASTLE: How's this! *[reads]* "Dear 'Squire, I'm now waiting for Miss Neville, with a post-chaise and pair, at the bottom of the garden, but I find my horses yet unable to perform the journey. I expect you'll assist us with a pair of fresh horses, as you promised. Dispatch is necessary, as the *hag*, (ay, the hag) your mother, will otherwise suspect us. Your's, Hastings." Grant me patience. I shall run distracted. My rage choaks me.

MISS NEVILLE: I hope, Madam, you'll suspend your resentment for a few moments, and not impute to me any impertinence, or sinister design that belongs to another.

MRS. HARDCASTLE *[curtesying very low]*: Fine spoken, Madam; you are most miraculously polite and engaging, and quite the very pink of curtesy and circumspection, Madam. [*changing her tone*] And you, you great ill-fashioned oaf, with scarce sense enough to keep your mouth shut. Were you too join'd against me? But I'll defeat all your plots in a moment. As for you, Madam, since you have got a pair of fresh horses ready, it would be cruel to disappoint them. So, if you please, instead of running away with your spark, prepare, this very moment, to run off with *me*. Your old Aunt Pedigree will keep you secure, I'll warrant me. You too, Sir, may mount your horse, and guard us upon the way. Here, Thomas, Roger, Diggory! I'll shew you, that I wish you better than you do yourselves.

[*Exit.*

MISS NEVILLE: So now I'm completely ruined.

TONY: Ay, that's a sure thing.

MISS NEVILLE: What better could be expected from being connected with such a stupid fool, and after all the nods and signs I made him.

TONY: By the laws, Miss, it was your own cleverness, and not my stupidity, that did your business. You were so nice and so busy with your Shake-bags and Goose-greens, that I thought you could never be making believe.

### Enter HASTINGS.

HASTINGS: So, Sir, I find by my servant, that you have shewn my letter, and betray'd us. Was this well done, young gentleman?

TONY: Here's another. Ask Miss there who betray'd you. Ecod, it was her doing, not mine.

### Enter MARLOW.

MARLOW: So I have been finely used here among you. Rendered contemptible, driven into ill manners, despised, insulted, laugh'd at.

TONY: Here's another. We shall have old Bedlam broke loose presently.

MISS NEVILLE: And there, Sir, is the gentleman to whom we all owe every obligation.

MARLOW: What can I say to him, a mere boy, an ideot, whose ignorance and age are a protection.

HASTINGS: A poor contemptible booby, that would but disgrace correction.

MISS NEVILLE: Yet with cunning and malice enough to make himself merry with all our embarrassments.

HASTINGS: An insensible cub.

MARLOW: Replete with tricks and mischief.

TONY: Baw! damme, but I'll fight you both one after the other—with baskets.

MARLOW: As for him, he's below resentment. But your conduct, Mr. Hastings, requires an explanation. You knew of my mistakes, yet would not undeceive me.

HASTINGS: Tortured as I am with my own disappointments, is this a time for explanations? It is not friendly, Mr. Marlow.

MARLOW: But, Sir—

MISS NEVILLE: Mr. Marlow, we never kept on your mistake, till it was too late to undeceive you. Be pacified.

### Enter SERVANT.

SERVANT: My mistress desires you'll get ready immediately, Madam. The horses are putting to. Your hat and things are in the next room. We are to go thirty miles before morning. [*Exit* SERVANT.

MISS NEVILLE: Well, well; I'll come presently.

MARLOW [to HASTINGS]: Was it well done, Sir, to assist in rendering me ridiculous? To hang me out for the scorn of all my acquaintance? Depend upon it, Sir, I shall expect an explanation.

HASTINGS: Was it well done, Sir, if you're upon that subject, to deliver what I entrusted to yourself, to the care of another, Sir?

MISS NEVILLE: Mr. Hastings. Mr. Marlow. Why will you increase my distress by this groundless dispute? I implore, I intreat you—

*Enter* SERVANT.

SERVANT: Your cloak, Madam. My mistress is impatient.

MISS NEVILLE: I come. [*Exit* SERVANT.] Pray be pacified. If I leave you thus, I shall die with apprehension.

*Enter* SERVANT.

SERVANT: Your fan, muff, and gloves, Madam. The horses are waiting.

MISS NEVILLE: O, Mr. Marlow! if you knew what a scene of constraint and ill-nature lies before me, I'm sure it would convert your resentment into pity.

MARLOW: I'm so distracted with a variety of passions, that I don't know what I do. Forgive me, Madam. George, forgive me. You know my hasty temper, and should not exasperate it.

HASTINGS: The torture of my situation is my only excuse.

MISS NEVILLE: Well, my dear Hastings, if you have that esteem for me that I think, that I am sure you have, your constancy for three years will but encrease the happiness of our future connexion. If—

MRS. HARDCASTLE [*within*]: Miss Neville. Constance, why Constance, I say.

MISS NEVILLE: I'm coming. Well, constancy. Remember, constancy is the word.
[*Exit.*

HASTINGS: My heart! How can I support this. To be so near happiness, and such happiness.

MARLOW [*to* TONY]: You see now, young gentleman, the effects of your folly. What might be amusement to you, is here disappointment, and even distress.

TONY [*from a reverie*]: Ecod, I have hit it. It's here. Your hands. Yours and yours, my poor Sulky. My boots there, ho! Meet me two hours hence at the bottom of the garden; and if you don't find Tony Lumpkin a more good-natur'd fellow than you thought for, I'll give you leave to take my best horse, and Bet Bouncer into the bargain. Come along. My boots, ho!          [*Exeunt.*

*End of the Fourth Act*


ACT V


*Scene—Continues.*


*Enter* HASTINGS *and* SERVANT.

HASTINGS: You saw the Old Lady and Miss Neville drive off, you say?

SERVANT: Yes, your honour. They went off in a post coach, and the young

'Squire went on horseback. They're thirty miles off by this time.

HASTINGS: Then all my hopes are over.

SERVANT: Yes, Sir. Old Sir Charles is arrived. He and the Old Gentleman of the house have been laughing at Mr. Marlow's mistake this half hour. They are coming this way.

HASTINGS: Then I must not be seen. So now to my fruitless appointment at the bottom of the garden. This is about the time.                              [*Exit.*

*Enter* SIR CHARLES *and* HARDCASTLE.

HARDCASTLE: Ha! ha! ha: The peremptory tone in which he sent forth his sublime commands.

SIR CHARLES: And the reserve with which I suppose he treated all your advances.

HARDCASTLE: And yet he might have seen something in me above a common inn-keeper, too.

SIR CHARLES: Yes, Dick, but he mistook you for an uncommon inn-keeper, ha! ha! ha!

HARDCASTLE: Well, I'm in too good spirits to think of any thing but joy. Yes, my dear friend, this union of our families will make our personal friendships hereditary; and tho' my daughter's fortune is but small—

SIR CHARLES: Why, Dick, will you talk of fortune to *me*. My son is possessed of more than a competence already, and I can want nothing but a good and virtuous girl to share his happiness and encrease it. If they like each other as you say they do—

HARDCASTLE: *If,* man. I tell you they *do* like each other. My daughter as good as told me so.

SIR CHARLES: But girls are apt to flatter themselves, you know.

HARDCASTLE: I saw him grasp her hand in the warmest manner myself; and here he comes to put you out of your *ifs,* I warrant him.

*Enter* MARLOW.

MARLOW: I come Sir, once more, to ask pardon for my strange conduct. I can scarce reflect on my insolence without confusion.

HARDCASTLE: Tut, boy, a trifle. You take it too gravely. An hour or two's laughing with my daughter will set all to rights again. She'll never like you the worse for it.

MARLOW: Sir, I shall be always proud of her approbation.

HARDCASTLE: Approbation is but a cold word, Mr. Marlow; if I am not deceived, you have something more than approbation thereabouts. You take me.

MARLOW: Really, Sir, I have not that happiness.

HARDCASTLE: Come, boy, I'm an old fellow, and know what's what, as well as you that are younger. I know what has past between you; but mum.

MARLOW: Sure, Sir, nothing has past between us but the most profound respect on my side, and the most distant reserve on hers. You don't think, Sir, that my impudence has been past upon all the rest of the family?

HARDCASTLE: Impudence! No, I don't say that—Not quite impudence— Though girls like to be play'd with, and rumpled a little, too, sometimes. But she has told no tales, I assure you.

MARLOW: I never gave her the slightest cause.

HARDCASTLE: Well, well, I like modesty in its place well enough. But this is over-acting, young gentleman. You may be open. Your father and I will like you the better for it.

MARLOW: May I die, Sir, if I ever—

HARDCASTLE: I tell you, she don't dislike you; and as I'm sure you like her—

MARLOW: Dear Sir—I protest, Sir—

HARDCASTLE: I see no reason why you should not be joined as fast as the parson can tie you.

MARLOW: But hear me, Sir—

HARDCASTLE: Your father approves the match, I admire it, every moment's delay will be doing mischief, so—

MARLOW: But why won't you hear me? By all that's just and true, I never gave Miss Hardcastle the slightest mark of my attachment, or even the most distant hint to suspect me of affection. We had but one interview, and that was formal, modest and uninteresting.

HARDCASTLE [*aside*]: This fellow's formal, modest impudence is beyond bearing.

SIR CHARLES: And you never grasp'd her hand, or made any protestations!

MARLOW: As heaven is my witness, I came down in obedience to your commands. I saw the lady without emotion, and parted without reluctance. I hope you'll exact no further proofs of my duty, nor prevent me from leaving a house in which I suffer so many mortifications. [*Exit.*

SIR CHARLES: I'm astonish'd at the air of sincerity with which he parted.

HARDCASTLE: And I'm astonish'd at the deliberate intrepidity of his assurance.

SIR CHARLES: I dare pledge my life and honour upon his truth.

HARDCASTLE: Here comes my daughter, and I would stake my happiness upon her veracity.

*Enter* MISS HARDCASTLE.

HARDCASTLE: Kate, come hither, child. Answer us sincerely, and without reserve; has Mr. Marlow made you any professions of love and affection?

MISS HARDCASTLE: The question is very abrupt, Sir! But since you require unreserved sincerity, I think he has.

HARDCASTLE [*to* SIR CHARLES]: You see.

SIR CHARLES: And pray, Madam, have you and my son had more than one interview?

MISS HARDCASTLE: Yes, Sir, several.

HARDCASTLE [*to* SIR CHARLES]: You see.

SIR CHARLES: But did he profess any attachment?

MISS HARDCASTLE: A lasting one.

SIR CHARLES: Did he talk of love?

MISS HARDCASTLE: Much, Sir.

SIR CHARLES: Amazing! And all this formally?

MISS HARDCASTLE: Formally.

HARDCASTLE: Now, my friend, I hope you are satisfied.

SIR CHARLES: And how did he behave, Madam?

MISS HARDCASTLE: As most profest admirers do. Said some civil things to my face, talked much of his want of merit, and the greatness of mine; mentioned his heart, gave a short tragedy speech, and ended with pretended rapture.

SIR CHARLES: Now I'm perfectly convinced, indeed. I know his conversation among women to be modest and submissive. This forward, canting, ranting manner by no means describes him, and I am confident, he never sate for the picture.

MISS HARDCASTLE: Then what, Sir, if I should convince you to your face of my sincerity? If you and my papa, in about half an hour, will place yourselves behind that screen, you shall hear him declare his passion to me in person.

SIR CHARLES: Agreed. And if I find him what you describe, all my happiness in him must have an end.                                              [*Exit.*

MISS HARDCASTLE: And if you don't find what I describe—I fear my happiness must never have a beginning.                                    [*Exeunt.*

*Scene—Changes to the Back of the Garden.*

*Enter* HASTINGS.

HASTINGS: What an ideot am I, to wait here for a fellow, who probably takes delight in mortifying me. He never intended to be punctual, and I'll wait no longer. What do I see! It is he, and perhaps with news of my Constance.

*Enter* TONY, *booted and spattered.*

HASTINGS: My honest 'Squire! I now find you a man of your word. This looks like friendship.

TONY: Ay, I'm your friend, and the best friend you have in the world, if you knew but all. This riding by night, by the bye, is cursedly tiresome. It has shook me worse than the basket of a stage-coach.

HASTINGS: But how? Where did you leave your fellow travellers? Are they in safety? Are they housed?

TONY: Five and twenty miles in two hours and a half is no such bad driving. The poor beasts have smoaked for it: Rabbet me, but I'd rather ride forty miles after a fox, than ten with such *varment.*

HASTINGS: Well, but where have you left the ladies? I die with impatience.

TONY: Left them? Why, where should I leave them, but where I found them?

HASTINGS: This is a riddle.

TONY: Riddle me this then. What's that goes round the house, and round the house, and never touches the house?

HASTINGS: I'm still astray.

TONY: Why that's it, mon. I have led them astray. By jingo, there's not a pond or slough within five miles of this place but they can tell the taste of.

HASTINGS: Ha, ha, ha, I understand; you took them in a round, while they supposed themselves going forward. And so you have at last brought them home again.

TONY: You shall hear. I first took them down Feather-bed-lane, where we stuck fast in the mud. I then rattled them crack over the stones of Up-and-down Hill— I then introduc'd them to the gibbet on Heavy-tree Heath, and from that, with a circumbendibus, I fairly lodged them in the horse-pond at the bottom of the garden.

HASTINGS: But no accident, I hope.

TONY: No, no. Only mother is confoundedly frightened. She thinks herself forty miles off. She's sick of the journey, and the cattle can scarce crawl. So if your own horses be ready, you may whip off with Cousin, and I'll be bound that no soul here can budge a foot to follow you.

HASTINGS: My dear friend, how can I be grateful?

TONY: Ay, now its dear friend, noble 'Squire. Just now, it was all ideot, cub, and run me through the guts. Damn *your* way of fighting, I say. After we take a knock in this part of the country, we kiss and be friends. But if you had run me through the guts, then I should be dead, and you might go kiss the hangman.

HASTINGS: The rebuke is just. But I must hasten to relieve Miss Neville; if you keep the old lady employed, I promise to take care of the young one.

[*Exit* HASTINGS.

TONY: Never fear me. Here she comes. Vanish. She's got from the pond, and draggled up to the waist like a mermaid.

*Enter* MRS. HARDCASTLE.

MRS. HARDCASTLE: Oh, Tony, I'm killed. Shook. Battered to death. I shall never survive it. That last jolt that laid us against the quickset hedge has done my business.

TONY: Alack, mama, it was all your own fault. You would be for running away by night, without knowing one inch of the way.

MRS. HARDCASTLE: I wish we were at home again. I never met so many accidents in so short a journey. Drench'd in the mud, overturn'd in a ditch, stuck fast in a slough, jolted to a jelly, and at last to lose our way. Whereabouts do you think we are, Tony?

TONY: By my guess we should be upon Crackskull Common, about forty miles from home.

MRS. HARDCASTLE: O lud! O lud! the most notorious spot in all the country. We only want a robbery to make a complete night on't.

TONY: Don't be afraid, mama, don't be afraid. Two of the five that kept here are hanged, and the other three may not find us. Don't be afraid. Is that a man that's galloping behind us? No; it's only a tree. Don't be afraid.

MRS. HARDCASTLE: The fright will certainly kill me.

TONY: Do you see any thing like a black hat moving behind the thicket?

MRS. HARDCASTLE: O death!

TONY: No, it's only a cow. Don't be afraid, mama; don't be afraid.

MRS. HARDCASTLE: As I'm alive, Tony, I see a man coming towards us. Ah! I'm sure on't. If he perceives us, we are undone.

TONY [*aside*]: Father-in-law, by all that's unlucky, come to take one of his night walks. [*to her*] Ah, it's a highwayman, with pistils as long as my arm. A damn'd ill-looking fellow.

MRS. HARDCASTLE: Good heaven defend us! He approaches.

TONY: Do you hide yourself in that thicket, and leave me to manage him. If there be any danger, I'll cough, and cry hem. When I cough be sure to keep close.             [MRS. HARDCASTLE *hides behind a tree in the back scene.*

*Enter* HARDCASTLE.

HARDCASTLE: I'm mistaken, or I heard voices of people in want of help. Oh, Tony, is that you? I did not expect you so soon back. Are your mother and her charge in safety?

TONY: Very safe, Sir, at my Aunt Pedigree's. Hem.

MRS. HARDCASTLE [*from behind*]: Ah death! I find there's danger.

HARDCASTLE: Forty miles in three hours; sure, that's too much, my youngster.

TONY: Stout horses and willing minds make short journies, as they say. Hem.

MRS. HARDCASTLE [*from behind*]: Sure he'll do the dear boy no harm.

HARDCASTLE: But I heard a voice here; I should be glad to know from whence it came?

TONY: It was I, Sir, talking to myself, Sir. I was saying that forty miles in four hours was very good going. Hem. As to be sure it was. Hem. I have got a sort of cold by being out in the air. We'll go in, if you please. Hem.

HARDCASTLE: But if you talk'd to yourself, you did not answer yourself. I am certain I heard two voices, and am resolved [*raising his voice*] to find the other out.

MRS. HARDCASTLE [*from behind*]: Oh! he's coming to find me out. Oh!

TONY: What need you go, Sir, if I tell you? Hem. I'll lay down my life for the truth—hem—I'll tell you all, Sir. [*Detaining him.*

HARDCASTLE: I tell you, I will not be detained. I insist on seeing. It's in vain to expect I'll believe you.

MRS. HARDCASTLE [*running forward from behind*]: O lud, he'll murder my poor boy, my darling. Here, good gentleman, whet your rage upon me. Take my money, my life, but spare that young gentleman, spare my child, if you have any mercy!

HARDCASTLE: My wife! as I'm a Christian. From whence can she come, or what does she mean?

MRS. HARDCASTLE [*kneeling*]: Take compassion on us, good Mr. Highwayman. Take our money, our watches, all we have, but spare our lives. We will never bring you to justice, indeed we won't, good Mr. Highwayman.

HARDCASTLE: I believe the woman's out of her senses. What, Dorothy, don't you know *me?*

MRS. HARDCASTLE: Mr. Hardcastle, as I'm alive! My fears blinded me. But who, my dear, could have expected to meet you here, in this frightful place, so far from home. What has brought you to follow us?

HARDCASTLE: Sure, Dorothy, you have not lost your wits. So far from home, when you are within forty yards of your own door. [*to him*] This is one of your old tricks, you graceless rogue you. [*to her*] Don't you know the gate, and the mulberry-tree; and don't you remember the horse-pond, my dear?

MRS. HARDCASTLE: Yes, I shall remember the horse-pond as long as I live; I have caught my death in it. [*to TONY*] And is it to you, you graceless varlet, I owe all this? I'll teach you to abuse your mother, I will.

TONY: Ecod, mother, all the parish says you have spoil'd me, and so you may take the fruits on't.

MRS. HARDCASTLE: I'll spoil you, I will. [*Follows him off the stage. Exit.*

HARDCASTLE: There's morality, however, in his reply. [*Exit.*

*Enter* HASTINGS *and* MISS NEVILLE.

HASTINGS: My dear Constance, why will you deliberate thus? If we delay a moment, all is lost for ever. Pluck up a little resolution, and we shall soon be out of the reach of her malignity.

MISS NEVILLE: I find it impossible. My spirits are so sunk with the agitations I have suffered, that I am unable to face any new danger. Two or three years patience will at last crown us with happiness.

HASTINGS: Such a tedious delay is worse than inconstancy. Let us fly, my charmer. Let us date our happiness from this very moment. Perish fortune. Love and content will encrease what we possess beyond a monarch's revenue. Let me prevail.

MISS NEVILLE: No, Mr. Hastings; no. Prudence once more comes to my relief, and I will obey its dictates. In the moment of passion, fortune may be despised, but it ever produces a lasting repentance. I'm resolved to apply to Mr. Hardcastle's compassion and justice for redress.

HASTINGS: But tho' he had the will, he has not the power to relieve you.

MISS NEVILLE: But he has influence, and upon that I am resolved to rely.

HASTINGS: I have no hopes. But since you persist, I must reluctantly obey you.

[*Exeunt.*

*Scene—Changes.*

*Enter* SIR CHARLES *and* MISS HARDCASTLE.

SIR CHARLES: What a situation am I in. If what you say appears, I shall then find a guilty son. If what he says be true, I shall then lose one that, of all others, I most wish'd for a daughter.

MISS HARDCASTLE: I am proud of your approbation, and to shew I merit it, if you place yourselves as I directed, you shall hear his explicit declaration. But he comes.

SIR CHARLES: I'll to your father, and keep him to the appointment.

[*Exit* SIR CHARLES.

*Enter* MARLOW.

MARLOW: Tho' prepar'd for setting out, I come once more to take leave, nor did I, till this moment, know the pain I feel in the separation.

MISS HARDCASTLE [*in her own natural manner*]: I believe these sufferings cannot be very great, Sir, which you can so easily remove. A day or two longer, perhaps, might lessen your uneasiness, by shewing the little value of what you now think proper to regret.

MARLOW [*aside*]: This girl every moment improves upon me. [*to her*] It must not be, Madam. I have already trifled too long with my heart. My very pride begins to submit to my passion. The disparity of education and fortune, the anger of a parent, and the contempt of my equals, begin to lose their weight; and nothing can restore me to myself, but this painful effort of resolution.

MISS HARDCASTLE: Then go, Sir. I'll urge nothing more to detain you. Tho' my family be as good as her's you came down to visit, and my education, I hope, not inferior, what are these advantages without equal affluence? I must remain contented with the slight approbation of imputed merit; I must have only the mockery of your addresses, while all your serious aims are fix'd on fortune.

*Enter* HARDCASTLE *and* SIR CHARLES *from behind.*

SIR CHARLES: Here, behind this screen.

HARDCASTLE: Ay, ay, make no noise. I'll engage my Kate covers him with confusion at last.

MARLOW: By heavens, Madam, fortune was ever my smallest consideration.

Your beauty at first caught my eye; for who could see that without emotion? But every moment that I converse with you steals in some new grace, heightens the picture, and gives it stronger expression. What at first seem'd rustic plainness, now appears refin'd simplicity. What seem'd forward assurance, now strikes me as the result of courageous innocence, and conscious virtue.

SIR CHARLES: What can it mean! He amazes me!

HARDCASTLE: I told you how it would be. Hush!

MARLOW: I am now determined to stay, Madam, and I have too good an opinion of my father's discernment, when he sees you, to doubt his approbation.

MISS HARDCASTLE: No, Mr. Marlow, I will not, cannot detain you. Do you think I could suffer a connexion, in which there is the smallest room for repentance? Do you think I would take the mean advantage of a transient passion, to load you with confusion? Do you think I could ever relish that happiness, which was acquired by lessening your's?

MARLOW: By all that's good, I can have no happiness but what's in your power to grant me. Nor shall I ever feel repentance, but in not having seen your merits before. I will stay, even contrary to your wishes; and tho' you should persist to shun me, I will make my respectful assiduities atone for the levity of my past conduct.

MISS HARDCASTLE: Sir, I must entreat you'll desist. As our acquaintance began, so let it end, in indifference. I might have given an hour or two to levity; but seriously, Mr. Marlow, do you think I could ever submit to a connexion, where *I* must appear mercenary, and *you* imprudent? Do you think I could ever catch at the confident addresses of a secure admirer?

MARLOW [*kneeling*]: Does this look like security? Does this look like confidence? No, Madam, every moment that shews me your merit, only serves to encrease my diffidence and confusion. Here let me continue—

SIR CHARLES: I can hold it no longer. Charles, Charles, how hast thou deceived me! Is this your indifference, your uninteresting conversation!

HARDCASTLE: Your cold contempt; your formal interview! What have you to say now?

MARLOW: That I'm all amazement! What can it mean!

HARDCASTLE: It means that you can say and unsay things at pleasure. That you can address a lady in private, and deny it in public; that you have one story for us, and another for my daughter.

MARLOW: Daughter!—this lady your daughter!

HARDCASTLE: Yes, Sir, my only daughter. My Kate, whose else should she be?

MARLOW: Oh, the devil!

MISS HARDCASTLE: Yes, Sir, that very identical tall, squinting lady you were pleased to take me for. [*curtesying*] She that you addressed as the mild, modest, sentimental man of gravity, and the bold, forward, agreeable Rattle of the Ladies Club; ha, ha, ha.

MARLOW: Zounds, there's no bearing this; it's worse than death.

MISS HARDCASTLE: In which of your characters, Sir, will you give us leave to address you? As the faultering gentleman, with looks on the ground, that speaks just to be heard, and hates hypocrisy; or the loud, confident creature, that keeps it up with Mrs. Mantrap, and old Miss Biddy Buckskin, till three in the morning; ha, ha, ha!

MARLOW: O, curse on my noisy head. I never attempted to be impudent yet, that I was not taken down. I must be gone.

HARDCASTLE: By the hand of my body, but you shall not. I see it was all a mistake, and I am rejoiced to find it. You shall not, Sir, I tell you. I know she'll forgive you. Won't you forgive him, Kate? We'll all forgive you. Take courage, man.                                         [*They retire, she tormenting him, to the back Scene.*

*Enter* MRS. HARDCASTLE, TONY.

MRS. HARDCASTLE: So, so, they're gone off. Let them go, I care not.

HARDCASTLE: Who gone?

MRS. HARDCASTLE: My dutiful niece and her gentleman, Mr. Hastings, from Town. He who came down with our modest visitor here.

SIR CHARLES: Who, my honest George Hastings? As worthy a fellow as lives, and the girl could not have made a more prudent choice.

HARDCASTLE: Then, by the hand of my body, I'm proud of the connexion.

MRS. HARDCASTLE: Well, if he has taken away the lady, he has not taken her fortune; that remains in this family to console us for her loss.

HARDCASTLE: Sure, Dorothy, you would not be so mercenary?

MRS. HARDCASTLE: Ay, that's my affair, not your's. But you know if your son, when of age, refuses to marry his cousin, her whole fortune is then at her own disposal.

HARDCASTLE: Ay, but he's not of age, and she has not thought proper to wait for his refusal.

*Enter* HASTINGS *and* MISS NEVILLE.

MRS. HARDCASTLE [*aside*]: What! returned so soon? I begin not to like it.

HASTINGS [*to* HARDCASTLE]: For my late attempt to fly off with your niece, let my present confusion be my punishment. We are now come back, to appeal from your justice to your humanity. By her father's consent, I first paid her my addresses, and our passions were first founded in duty.

MISS NEVILLE: Since his death, I have been obliged to stoop to dissimulation to avoid oppression. In an hour of levity, I was ready even to give up my fortune to secure my choice. But I'm now recover'd from the delusion, and hope from your tenderness what is denied me from a nearer connexion.

MRS. HARDCASTLE: Pshaw, pshaw, this is all but the whining end of a modern novel.

HARDCASTLE: Be it what it will, I'm glad they're come back to reclaim their due. Come hither, Tony boy. Do you refuse this lady's hand whom I now offer you?

TONY: What signifies my refusing? You know I can't refuse her till I'm of age, father.

HARDCASTLE: While I thought concealing your age, boy, was likely to conduce to your improvement, I concurred with your mother's desire to keep it secret. But since I find she turns it to a wrong use, I must now declare, you have been of age these three months.

TONY: Of age! Am I of age, father?

HARDCASTLE: Above three months.

TONY: Then you'll see the first use I'll make of my liberty. [*taking* MISS

471

NEVILLE's *hand*] Witness all men by these presents, that I, Anthony Lumpkin, Esquire, of Blank place, refuse you, Constantia Neville, spinster, of no place at all, for my true and lawful wife. So Constance Neville may marry whom she pleases, and Tony Lumpkin is his own man again!

SIR CHARLES: O brave 'Squire!

HASTINGS: My worthy friend!

MRS. HARDCASTLE: My undutiful offspring!

MARLOW: Joy, my dear George, I give you joy sincerely. And could I prevail upon my little tyrant here to be less arbitrary, I should be the happiest man alive, if you would return me the favour.

HASTINGS [*to* MISS HARDCASTLE]: Come, Madam, you are now driven to the very last scene of all your contrivances. I know you like him, I'm sure he loves you, and you must and shall have him.

HARDCASTLE [*joining their hands*]: And I say so too..And Mr. Marlow, if she makes as good a wife as she has a daughter, I don't believe you'll ever repent your bargain. So now to supper; to-morrow we shall gather all the poor of the parish about us, and the Mistakes of the Night shall be crowned with a merry morning; so boy, take her; and as you have been mistaken in the mistress, my wish is, that you may never be mistaken in the wife.

*Finis*


## EPILOGUE

### By Dr. Goldsmith

> *Well, having stoop'd to conquer with success,*
> *And gain'd a husband without aid from dress,*
> *Still as a Bar-maid, I could wish it too,*
> *As I have conquer'd him to conquer you:*
> *And let me say, for all your resolution,*
> *That pretty Bar-maids have done execution.*
> *Our life is all a play, compos'd to please,*
> *"We have our exits and our entrances."*
> *The first act shews the simple country maid,*
> *Harmless and young, of ev'rything afraid;*
> *Blushes when hir'd, and with unmeaning action,*
> *I hopes as how to give you satisfaction.*
> *Her second act displays a livelier scene—*
> *Th'unblushing Bar-maid of a country inn,*
> *Who whisks about the house, at market caters,*
> *Talks loud, coquets the guests, and scolds the waiters.*
> *Next the scene shifts to town, and there she soars,*
> *The chop-house toast of ogling connoissieurs.*
> *On 'Squires and Cits she there displays her arts,*
> *And on the gridiron broils her lovers' hearts—*
> *And as she smiles, her triumphs to compleat,*
> *Even Common Councilmen forget to eat.*

*The fourth act shews her wedded to the 'Squire,*
*And Madam now begins to hold it higher;*
*Pretends to taste, at Operas cries* caro,
*And quits her Nancy Dawson, for* Che Faro.
*Doats upon dancing, and in all her pride,*
*Swims round the room, the* Heinel *of Cheapside:*
*Ogles and leers with artificial skill,*
*Till having lost in age the power to kill,*
*She sits all night at cards, and ogles at spadille.*
*Such, thro' our lives, the eventful history—*
*The fifth and last act still remains for me.*
*The Bar-maid now for your protection prays,*
*Turns Female Barrister, and pleads for Bayes.*


## EPILOGUE

### To be spoken in the character of TONY LUMPKIN[1]

### By J. Craddock, Esq.

*Well—now all's ended—and my comrades gone,*
*Pray what becomes of* mother's *nonly son?*
*A hopeful blade!—in town I'll fix my station,*
*And try to make a bluster in the nation.*
*As for my cousin Neville, I renounce her,*
*Off—in a crack—I'll carry big Bet Bouncer.*
  *Why should not I in the great world appear?*
*I soon shall have a thousand pounds a year;*
*No matter what a man may here inherit,*
*In London—'gad, they've some regard to spirit.*
*I see the horses prancing up the streets,*
*And big Bet Bouncer bobs to all she meets;*
*Then hoikes to jiggs and pastimes ev'ry night—*
*Not to the plays—they say it a'n't polite,*
*To Sadler's-Wells perhaps, or Operas go,*
*And once, by chance, to the roratorio.*
*Thus here and there, for ever up and down,*
*We'll set the fashions, too, to half the town;*
*And then at auctions—money ne'er regard,*
*Buy pictures like the great, ten pounds a yard;*
*Zounds, we shall make these London gentry say,*
*We know what's damn'd genteel, as well as they.*

---

[1] This came too late to be spoken.

# PICTURE CREDITS

—**FRONTISPIECE** Peter Lloyd  —**10** * Vatican Museum, Rome  —**11** Philip Jones Griffiths/Magnum  —**15** (t.) Alinari/SCALA  —**15** (b.) Stern/Black Star  —**18** (l.) Culver Pictures Inc.  —**18** (r.) UPI/Compix  —**19** (t.) * Louvre/Giraudon  —**22** Photo Archives Pierre et Marie Curie/UNESCO Courier  —**23** * The Metropolitan Museum of Art, Wolfe Fund, 1931  —**26** (l.) In the Church of St. Peter in Vincoli, Rome/Alinari  —**26** (r.)  * Louvre/Alinari  —**27** (l.) Camera Press Ltd./Pictorial Parade  —**27** (r.) * "China Pictorial"  —**30** Philip Jones Griffiths/Magnum  —**31** (t.) Kenneth Murray/Nancy Palmer Agency  —**31** (b.) Tom Picton/Black Star  —**37** Lee Cain  —**63** * New York University  —**70** * Knopf/Jill Krementz  —**78** * Pomona College  —**130** (r.) William Mares  —**161** * Charles Eames  —**163** from the collection of M. S. and R. B. Honeyman/ * Charles Eames  —**167, 173** * Charles Eames  —**180** * Lakeville Journal/Richard Hayward  —**188–89** * Trustees of the British Museum/J. R. Freeman  —**193–225** * The Huntington Library, San Marino, Calif.  —**302** Culver Pictures Inc.  —**334–35** illustration by Will Gallagher  —**369** illustration by Don Meighan  —**372, 424** * National Portrait Gallery, London

# Authors

*in Great Books of the Western World*

Homer

Aeschylus

Sophocles

Herodotus

Euripides

Thucydides

Hippocrates

Aristophanes

Plato

Aristotle

Euclid

Archimedes

Apollonius

Lucretius

Virgil

Plutarch

Tacitus

Epictetus

Nicomachus

Ptolemy

Marcus Aurelius

Galen

Plotinus

Augustine

Thomas Aquinas

Dante

Chaucer

Machiavelli

Copernicus

Rabelais

Montaigne

Gilbert

Cervantes

Francis Bacon

Galileo

Shakespeare

Kepler